A New Insurgency

A New Insurgency

The *Port Huron Statement* and Its Times

Edited by Howard Brick and Gregory Parker

In memory of John Owen King III (1943–2001)
  —H.B.
To Connie, Henry, Vivian
  —G.P.

Acknowledgments

The editors hope that this book indicates the University of Michigan's (UM) acknowledgment of the *Port Huron Statement* as part of this institution's best traditions of critical thought and social responsibility. Nearly forty distinct departments, programs, institutes, and offices at UM sponsored the 2012 conference on which this book is based, and we are grateful for the funding they provided. Especially generous were Terrence J. McDonald, then dean of the College of Literature, Science, and the Arts, and Geoff Eley of the History Department. Special thanks go to the Department of History and the Eisenberg Institute for Historical Studies for additional aid in preparing this volume and to Aaron Bekemeyer and Grace Goudiss for research assistance. We are indebted to Tom Hayden for providing three historic documents—early memos forecasting themes of the *Statement*—that are published in their entirety here for the first time. Thanks to University of Michigan Press for welcoming this volume as one of the first editions of Maize Books—and above all to the dozens of participants at the 2012 conference and the many faculty and students who helped organize it.

(The full list of conference sponsors, organizers, and original participants can be found at the conference website, which has been maintained as an archive, http://www.lsa.umich.edu/phs.)

Contents

Introduction

Cover, November 1963 *Liberation;* illustration by Vera Williams. *Liberation,* founded by radical pacifists in 1956, called for "a new left" in its founding statement. University of Michigan Library (Special Collections Library)

A New Insurgency and the *Port Huron Statement*
by Howard Brick

Well-behaved students—to paraphrase historian Laurel Thatcher Ulrich—
seldom make history, and according to quite a few observers of American
life after World War II, that was precisely the problem with the "silent
generation" of young people in the 1950s.[1] In June 1962, however, a group
of University of Michigan students and their comrades from elsewhere in
the country (and the world) made history by breaking the silence: they
convened a lakeside meeting of a small, national organization, Students
for a Democratic Society (SDS), and drafted a declaration, the *Port Huron
Statement*, that became the best-known US expression of left-wing dissent
in the unexpectedly turbulent sixties. Above all, the *Statement*'s vision of
"participatory democracy" sought to revitalize political life and radical
commitment in Cold War America.

A conference held at the University of Michigan (UM) to mark the
fiftieth anniversary of that meeting, A New Insurgency: The *Port Huron
Statement* in Its Time and Ours (October 31–November 2, 2012), provides
the basis for this volume. Featuring a dozen veterans of the Port Huron
SDS convention of 1962, approximately thirty visiting scholars from Europe and the United States, a dozen participating UM faculty, and as many
contemporary student activists, the New Insurgency conference attracted
overflow crowds, over two full days and evenings, to reflect on the experience of social-justice protest movements past and present. Comprising
the greater part of those proceedings, this book attempts not only to en-
rich the history of SDS in its early years but also to provide a portrait of the
broad and deep context of left-wing dissent, in the United States and globally, that first shaped the perspectives and ambitions of Port Huron
conferees—and then reflected, in part, the vision they helped sketch there.

It was hardly surprising that UM should host a monster conference
commemorating the *Port Huron Statement*. Ann Arbor was home to the

core group of young activists and intellectuals who created SDS in 1960 as the reincarnation of the old Student League for Industrial Democracy (SLID), which had enjoyed its height as part of the US left in the 1930s. SLID, in turn, had descended from the Intercollegiate Socialist Society that flourished alongside Eugene V. Debs's Socialist Party of America during the 1910s. In other words, SDS derived from a long left-wing tradition, but it became, in the United States, the organization most commonly associated with the "*New* Left" of the 1960s—that is, with the rejuvenation and reinvention of older movements that had previously gone into eclipse.

The meeting at Port Huron was held in the cabins of the Franklin D. Roosevelt Camp, maintained as a retreat and conference center by the Detroit-based United Automobile Workers (UAW); among the SDS organizers, Sharon Jeffrey was the daughter of longtime UAW organizer Millie Jeffrey, one of the links that led from UM to the shore of Lake Huron, a few hours' drive away. Ann Arbor and the UM chapter of SDS, furthermore, was home to almost all the early presidents of SDS: Al Haber (1960–62), Tom Hayden (1962–63), Todd Gitlin (1963–64), Paul Potter (1964–65), and Carl Oglesby (1965–66). Ann Arbor was also the site of the first teach-in, then a creative new form of campus-based protest, on the Vietnam War (March 24–25, 1965); a center for organizing the first major protest rally against the war in Washington, DC, renowned for Paul Potter's stirring address there (April 17, 1965); *and* likely the location of the first antiwar draft-board sit-in in the country (October 15, 1965). It continued to be a magnet for radical intellectuals and organizers through the rest of the 1960s.

The heart of prior left-wing movements lay elsewhere—usually with a social base in the labor movement and organizational headquarters in places like Chicago or New York. What now made Ann Arbor such a radical center, considering it had long been a small, Republican Party–dominated town and the university a distinguished but usually quiet, academic retreat? To be sure, Detroit, some forty miles away, had its own labor and left-wing movement in the industrializing period around the turn of the twentieth century. In the Depression years, youth and student wings of all the major leftist organizations had representation at UM. Members of the Student Socialist Club started a local alliance of housing cooperatives in 1932 that became one of the largest in the country and survives today; the Communist Party–led National Student League and the socialist-aligned SLID were both active on campus by the mid-1930s, merging into the American Student Union that persisted until it was barred from campus by the UM administration in 1940. University administrations typically wielded the tools of censorship and dismissal against student protesters and were, for the most part, able to withstand criticism for doing so. Yet Michigan was far from the most active campus in the 1930s, when student activism was considerably stronger in the New York area and at the big California schools. A number of left-wing UM students went on to some sort of notoriety or distinction (such as the playwright Arthur Miller), but in most such cases, political engagement took them away from rather than toward Ann Arbor.

Nonetheless, the Old Left at its height helped focus radical energies in this region after World War II. The auto industry and its demand for labor helped make Detroit the nation's fourth largest city at midcentury, when it was, labor historian Nelson Lichtenstein writes, the "workshop of the world."[2] UAW victories before and during World War II made that union both a bellwether of the new Congress of Industrial Organizations and a focus of radical politics, as assorted Socialist and Communist factions vied for union leadership. Detroit also became, amid racial tensions stirred by the war, home of the largest National Association for the Advancement of Colored People (NAACP) chapter in the country, a mass-membership, activist chapter flush with adherents among the newly unionized black labor force in the auto industry. In the late 1940s, radical visionaries of many persuasions relocated to Detroit as the hub of potentially revolutionary prospects, and that included the brilliant Trinidad-born Marxist writer C. L. R. James and his collaborators in black-worker agitation Grace Lee and James Boggs, whose prominence on Detroit's left was growing in the time of Port Huron.

Union power excited as well a potent anticommunism, and repeated Red Scare inquisitions were visited on the state—on Detroit's black labor left in 1952 and then, in 1954, on the university, when UM president Harlan Hatcher bowed to pressure in dismissing two faculty members (and suspending a third) who had been "uncooperative witnesses" before a House Committee on Un-American Activities hearing into Communist influence in higher education. Despite the apparent "silence" of the fifties, several hundred Michigan students gathered at the campus's center (the "Diag") to debate the suspensions, one thousand signed a petition in defense of the targeted professors, and the *Michigan Daily* letters page was dominated by protests in their favor.[3] It was a small group of such dissenters that first drew future SDS organizer Al Haber into activism and an effort to promote a "new" left that began bearing fruit within about five years. That same five-year period saw prodigious growth in college enrollments, which renewed their climb after stagnating in the early 1950s and thus commenced the making of a genuinely mass university (nearing forty thousand students by 1965). That demographic pressure did much to undermine the capacity of college officials to act in loco parentis as moral monitors of students' lives, but other forces lay behind the appearance of a more restless and critical disposition on campus, here and elsewhere: a growing number of working-class and lower-middle-class students in higher education; the cultural latitude encouraged by flush times that provided youth with some money on hand and helped generalize among them "bohemian" principles of self-expression and personal experimentation; and the gradual wearing off of the most intense Cold War fears, which had reached their height in the early 1950s.

It is also clear, then, that it was not only Ann Arbor that fostered such a new left-wing departure and that it was not really a *sudden* event in the early 1960s that sparked it. Much larger, contextual forces—operating locally, nationally, globally—helped pose the questions, present the examples, and arouse the energies that would turn the characteristic restlessness of youth into channels of radical dissent, criticism, agitation, and organization that took on historically distinctive social, cultural, and political causes. Roughly in the mid-1950s, things everywhere began to shift. In 1955, the Montgomery, Alabama, bus boycott began (a thirteen-month-long, successful movement by black city-dwellers to undo decades of abusive racial segregation in public transit), while a world away, the Afro-Asian Conference in Bandung, Indonesia, marked a first coming-of-age of new countries emerging from European colonial domination. In early 1957, after the Montgomery victory, its spokesman, Martin Luther King Jr., traveled to celebrate the independence of Ghana in West Africa, while peace agitators seized the moment to turn the bus boycott example of resolute social action into protest against the mounting US nuclear arsenal. Nor did it hurt that the Communist Party USA—shocked by Soviet premier Nikita Khrushchev's admission of a record of state terror under Joseph Stalin—fell into a near-terminal crisis, which had the unanticipated consequence, at least in part, of encouraging the disenchanted to seek a new start, a return to the socialist movement's original democratic principles in order to rouse fresh energy on the left. If there was to be "a new left," its essential ingredients were already there in the few years following 1955: a set of conditions and range of issues that old and new radical activists would build on—peace, anticolonialism, antiracism, democracy, and youth's desire for self-fulfillment.

The decade from 1955 to 1965 marks the period in which the "New Left" emerged. The *mood* of a new left was echoed in one place and another, across national boundaries and ocean divides. In Britain, activists started talking about a "new left" after hearing the French do so (the term *nouvelle gauche* had been coined in the early 1950s); their motivation for radical innovation followed the conjunction in fall 1956 of the Suez affair—a coordinated attack by France, Britain, and Israel on Egypt—and the bloody Soviet suppression of a Hungarian worker and student revolt, arousing both outrage against Western imperialism and disgust with Soviet terror. As at Bandung, the emergence of some kind of "third" force in the world to challenge both Cold War powers was a keynote of the "new." This quest had been linked with the original French notion of a *nouvelle gauche*; such a left took practical form in France also during the late 1950s, as young radicals showed their solidarity with the Algerian struggle for independence, while an older left, the substantial Communist Party in France, failed to take a clear stand.

The desire for a new beginning in Britain also grew, as in the United States, from concern for racial equality (after West Indian Londoners were attacked by white mobs in the Notting Hill riots of 1958) and protest against nuclear arsenals, as the Campaign for Nuclear Disarmament (CND) organized stirring marches, annually in the spring, from 1958 on. The intellectual tenor of UK dissent was set by a sequence of three books of collected essays: *Declaration* (1957), a combination of cultural disaffection and a lone call by novelist and former Communist Doris Lessing to maintain radical political commitment in writing; *Conviction* (1958), most of whose contributors identified with a vision of socialism pinned on a "true community life," where work-life could be transformed "from something senseless which forms no real part of the personality . . . into something creative and significant"; and finally *Out of Apathy* (1960), led by historian E. P. Thompson's call to fuse the egalitarianism of the traditional labor movement with the moral fervor of the CND.[4] The tone had shifted remarkably in just a few years: in *Declaration*, most essays shared the languid plaint of the protagonist in John Osborne's famous 1956 play, *Look Back in Anger*: "There aren't any good, brave causes left." In 1960, Thompson instead called on the nascent New Left to chart its path "out of apathy" as an act of will and imagination.

Thus the "New Left" was born of transnational connections. They are clear in Tom Hayden's "Manifesto Notes," which quotes Iris Murdoch's call in *Conviction* to build a "house of theory" that would capture the ethical vision of socialism and in the recollections of Michael Vester, a young German socialist then living as an exchange student in the United States and advising his SDS friends on how to respond politically to the Cold

War division of Europe. The links were live and the sentiments analogous, transnationally. The radical American sociologist C. Wright Mills lectured in England and charmed the intellectuals around the journal *New Left Review* (*NLR*), founded in 1960, with his critique of concentrated power in Cold War America. Charmed in turn by the warm welcome he received there, Mills started writing a review of *Out of Apathy*, which ended up as his "Letter to the New Left" in the fifth issue of *NLR*. When Mills's essay was reprinted in the United States, it introduced the term to the American scene. And while Mills's earlier work had decried the loss of vital political argument in the 1950s due to the concentration of power in a narrow elite so distant from everyday public life, it was Thompson's urging to move *out of* apathy that gave a keynote to the *Port Huron Statement*. When Tom Hayden and friends walked away from the cabins of Port Huron after hammering out the basic contours of their manifesto, Hayden reportedly told his co-organizer, Dick Flacks, "The British guys [though he must have meant Murdoch as well] are going to like what we did."[5]

Nonetheless, particular and local incitements could be definitive. In the United States, the mood of the British New Left might have had no impact on someone like Hayden if it were not for the more proximate and more directly influential struggle mounted by the Student Nonviolent Co-ordinating Committee (SNCC), the militant youth in the southern civil rights struggle. SNCC's boldness in challenging white segregationists directly and at great personal risk made the idea of moral commitment in action palpable, and its method of self-effacing organizing among the poor small-town residents of the Black Belt provided a democratic ethos— egalitarian and participatory—that rang out in the slogan both SNCC and SDS embraced: "Let the People Decide!"

There was, in other words, no Ann Arbor SDS without the deep context set by a legacy of the old labor movement, a just-past and very mixed heritage of socialist and communist activism, a sudden surge in the mid-fifties of civil rights and pacifist energies already nurtured by long-term movements, an intellectual/moral sensibility widely shared in pursuit of "commitment" and personal "truth," even hints of women's emancipation not entirely stamped out by conservative family norms of the 1950s, and a world scene in which decolonization provided a setting for Cold War antagonism (in Cuba, Vietnam, and also Africa) but perhaps also (just maybe, as in the call for a nonaligned force for peace at Bandung) an alternative to it.

The New Insurgency conference was, then, devoted to exploring the multiple dimensions of radical activism in recent history. It was guided in part by a historian's sense of comparison, hopscotching between then and now for the sake of gaining perspective; conference participants considered similarities—particularly the theme of "democracy" that figured so prominently in the protests and upheavals of 2011 as it had for the drafters of Port Huron—but also differences across time as well as differences *within* the broad milieu of the left. This collection seeks to address the multiplicity of the left-wing scene by going beyond a simple identification of the New Left with SDS or the "sixties" and adding other dimensions to those most familiar. Northern civil rights agitation coexisted with the more legendary southern civil rights movement; incipient Black Power ideology could be found in Detroit while the ideal of desegregation seemed regnant among reformers; "Old Left" political groups persisted in the 1960s alongside the self-consciously "New."

A New Insurgency addresses this plurality in terms of both *connections* and *comparisons*. It was indeed a watchword of New Left thought and activism to "draw the connections" between disparate problems: so SDS president Paul Potter said, when he urged antiwar protesters in 1965 to "name the system" that "disenfranchises people in the South, leaves millions upon millions of people throughout the country impoverished . . . that creates faceless and terrible bureaucracies . . . consistently puts material values before human values—and still persists in calling itself free and . . . fit to police the world."[6] At times, however, connections can be misleading; comparisons (and contrasts) may be more apt: the same period, roughly speaking, roused activism seeking equality for African Americans, Asian Americans, and American Indians, but as Ramón Gutiérrez points out, it was a fiction of the time that made the Pentecostal preacher and defender of Hispano land grants in New Mexico, Reies López Tijerina, into the legendary progenitor of a "nationalist" Chicano "revolution" directly analogous to Black Power.

Then, too, the coincidence of distinct struggles and campaigns yielded contrasts and conflicts, as in the tensions between a rising women's liberation movement and the rest of the New Left or between black and white activists within both SNCC and the Northern Student Movement—as Frank Joyce recounts. Likeness and difference ran through the ensemble of movements that ranged across the world, as Caribbean activists (see Paul Hébert's chapter) saw their struggle as anticolonial (like that of peoples in Africa and Asia) and antiracist (like that of African Americans) and yet requiring a consciousness of difference that highlighted the peculiar circumstances and dispositions of the West Indies as the means of achieving autonomy.

The connective and the comparative have become watchwords as well of the distinctive "global" approaches to writing history that have arisen recently. Here, Louise Walker shows that a student left arose in Mexico facing some of the same questions that North American radicals broached—namely, *who* (what social "agent of change") had the resources to really transform society radically—though the political system and the nature of class differentiation in Mexico was very much its own. Leslie Pincus draws a fascinating portrait of a Japanese activist couple whose career traversed, in a fashion akin to the historical fluidity Christopher Phelps finds in the United States, the Old Left and New Left—terms that were meaningful but also somewhat artificial.

For the most part, however, *A New Insurgency* keeps the focus on the emergence of New Lefts over a span of time more or less centered on the Port Huron moment. The year 1965 figures roughly as the limit of our survey, but not because we subscribe to the well-worn tendency to distinguish a "good sixties" from a "bad sixties"—that is, the stereotypical contrast between the morally exalted "beloved community" sought by Martin Luther King Jr.'s nonviolent convictions from the social disruption stirred by student strikes, Black Power rhetoric, and radical terrorists of the late 1960s. Rather, we accept a dividing line at 1965 simply in recognition of the fact that the escalation of the US war in Vietnam and the sudden accompanying rise of a mass antiwar movement established a new kind of center to New Left activism (though still historically stamped by the specific confluence of causes first charted in the late 1950s). The war was the "revealing event" of the time, as a French radical put it—or, in the same vein, "the razor, the terrifying sharp cutting edge that has finally severed the last vestiges of our illusion that morality and democracy are the guiding principles of American foreign policy," as Paul Potter put it in his April 17, 1965, speech.[7] The first campus antiwar teach-in, convened at UM the prior month, also makes 1965 at least a turning point—teach-ins thereafter became a new and widespread technique of protest and a model of the "engaged campus." The double-edged question raised in the *Port Huron Statement* about the nature of the contemporary research university—tied to "centers of power" in potentially corrupting ways while also possibly a center in itself of critical thinking and radical challenge to the surrounding society—only became more urgent and pressing as campus-based antiwar organizing accelerated toward the student strikes of 1968–70. In the story of New Lefts, our chosen historical boundary leaves us only in midstream, pending the more self-consciously "revolutionary" commitments of those who came to identify themselves as "68ers." Our middecade boundary was inevitably a porous one, and a number of chapters in this volume cross it.

Social movements rarely end full stop but usually have lingering effects of all sorts, and New Left–inspired social protest and grassroots organizing continued through the 1970s and 1980s, in feminist, gay and lesbian, environmentalist, antinuclear, peace, antiracist, and international solidarity campaigns. Only in the early 1990s did there appear a genuine lull in radical protest and organizing, though even then upstart movements were incubating under the surface, to burst forth in the Seattle demonstrations of November–December 1999 against free-trade "globalization" and in pursuit of "global social justice," which was for the most part cut short by the Bush administration's fervent War on Terror following the terrorist attacks of September 11, 2001.

Planning for the fiftieth anniversary of the *Port Huron Statement*, however, coincided with the rise of yet new protest movements to expand democratic practices around the world, from the overthrow of dictatorships in Tunisia and Egypt in 2011 to the "Occupy" movement in the United States during fall 2011 and a range of "antiausterity" mobilizations abroad in that same year. By fall 2012, when the conference took place, it seemed that the *Statement*'s fiftieth anniversary coincided with the revival of urgent concerns about how to build genuinely egalitarian and participatory democracies. Consequently, the final conference session reflected on the movements of 2011–12 and their results and prospects. Radicalism in recent decades has been episodic, rising in great flares of mass mobilization and enthusiasm and then dying down quickly, sometimes to be followed (as in Syria or Egypt) by disaster or apparent reversal. Still, street demonstrations of 2013 in Turkey, Greece, Germany, Spain, Brazil, and more showed persistent dissent in our time against autocratic government policies and policies of economic austerity since 2008 that have worsened social, economic, and political inequality. The history of new insurgencies is always unfinished.

Prologue

Cover, *Revolution in Mississippi*; illustration by Isaac Trompetter, 1961. University of Michigan Library (Special Collections Library)

Before Port Huron

by Tom Hayden

In all the writings about the *Port Huron Statement*, three 1962 documents have never been published until now. Historians and activists should find them interesting as "windows" into the internal and improvised thinking that finally resulted in the twenty-five-thousand-word finished product in June 1962. The memos ramble, wander, speculate, embarrass, and frustrate the reader. But they reveal an honest searching—not packaged talking points—meant to stimulate the coming days of discussion at Port Huron that resulted in the *Statement*. Convention Documents #1 and #2, both dated March 19, 1962, along with an undated third memo, were sent to Students for a Democratic Society (SDS) delegates on April 25.

The mailing looked duller than any publication I remember from the sixties. The twenty-page, single-spaced, mimeographed "Convention Bulletin/number one" of SDS was mailed from a cluttered New York office on April 25, 1962, announcing that a national convention would take place in mid-June, the location still to be announced, but "somewhere toward the East," perhaps a mid-Atlantic state, or maybe Michigan.

It was an inauspicious, unattractive invitation to participate in the writing of the *Port Huron Statement* two months later. No graphics, no charts, no color, only typing in black and white.

"It's necessary to establish some order," according to the bulletin. Our one-dollar dues weren't being paid. Membership wasn't clearly defined, and voting at the upcoming convention, when the place was located, would be limited strictly to members. Six weeks later, about sixty-three certified members would participate at Port Huron.

The component parts of the future SDS were being assembled. Membership would escalate from sixty-three to more than one hundred thousand within five years. Two weeks before the first "Convention Bulletin" was issued, SDS was a cosponsor of the first national conference of independent student political parties at Oberlin College, in Ohio, coordinated by Oberlin student Rennie Davis, who would go on to play a leading role in the Vietnam antiwar movement five years later. According to the "Convention Bulletin," the SDS line was that "the university as an agent of social change, rather than the transmitter of culture-as-we-know-it, should be our goal," to be achieved by students working for reform. In those days it was heretical to claim that students and young intellectuals—as opposed to factory workers, peasants, or "adult" intellectuals—could be an agency of radical change in our own right. This was the idealistic seed of what became known as the "new working class" in the emerging "knowledge economy," an attempt to pour new wine into old bottles.

How did the Oberlin conference come to pass? When I became editor of the *Michigan Daily* in spring 1960, I hitchhiked that summer to California, writing short stories "on the road," following my curiosity toward two beacons of change. First, I planned to hang out in Berkeley for a few weeks, trying to understand and write for the *Daily* about the spirit of student activism in the air. Then I would visit the Democratic convention in Los Angeles, where I unexpectedly met Martin Luther King Jr. on a picket line while writing about the New Frontier for the *Daily*.

In that summer of 1960, my life floated between a Berkeley crash pad and the Los Angeles convention booth of the *Detroit News*, whose editor quartered me as a Michigan favor. In Berkeley, a little activist circle gladly put me up in an apartment where intense political discussions went on 24-7. An idealistic student editor from Ann Arbor was a find, a potential recruit to their grand revolutionary design. These were the founders of SLATE, the earliest student party fighting the university over the right of students to take stands on "off-campus" issues. Already in 1960, SLATE had made an issue of free-speech rights at the campus's traditional rallying point, Sather Gate, several years before the massive Free Speech Movement (FSM) electrified Berkeley and the world. What was at stake for FSM was the right to leaflet undergraduates to join the burgeoning civil disobedience campaign against Jim Crow. My new friends pushed me to advocate and form a similar campus party when I returned to Ann Arbor. This I did by making a public speech that fall calling on students to speak out, which led to VOICE, the first chapter of SDS. Meanwhile, my lengthy *Daily* dispatches from summer 1960, and afterward, about the student movement caused extreme anxiety among University of Michigan administrators, who worried that a picket line would escalate into full-blown revolution. At the time I was just learning the difference between a picket line and a picket fence, but I could see something arising from beneath the surface of apathy, which they either wanted to deny or suffocate.

In October 1960, Senator John Kennedy made a historic campaign stop in Ann Arbor where I took notes and accompanied him up a Michigan Union elevator. Just before his speech, a small activist group succeeded in handing him a letter with my signature at the top, calling on Kennedy to push for disarmament; one of our lesser utopian demands was to create a peaceful alternative to military conscription. Kennedy read the letter on the spot, told us he would refer to it in his impromptu remarks, stepped out into the October rain, and endorsed the Peace Corps.

These two experiences, at Berkeley's Sather Gate and on the steps of the Michigan Union, are marked by historic plaques today. I had the prophetic sense that there could be a rich intertwining of the new student movement and the New Frontier. SDS and the Student Nonviolent Coordinating Committee (SNCC) were perfectly positioned to exploit the historic moment. We needed the president to reverse the nuclear arms race and protect civil rights workers in the South. He needed a new generation of student activism.

After Kennedy barely won the election, 1961 was filled with ups and downs, including the shocking Bay of Pigs invasion. I took more trips to the southern frontlines, and in May a university scandal erupted that brought home the crises of race and student rights. The *Daily* exposed how the dean of women spied on white co-eds seen in the company of any black men. Before that scandal, I never heard of "investigative journalism" except in occasional references to "muckrakers" long before our time. The university was driven by in loco parentis doctrine to treat undergraduates as some sort of preadults, which clashed with our activist impulses. The mass university felt like a paternalistic plantation. We didn't face the violence endured by southern blacks, but we had no voice, no vote; we could be expelled from school or fired without cause and, in the case of young men, drafted into "twilight" wars we knew or cared little about.

Experiences such as these, on campus and in the South, shaped my evolving thought process. Witnessing black sharecroppers claiming their rights taught me that democracy still required battle and sacrifice. It would not be given but only wrested from the powers that be. It required a faith in the potential of people whose very color and dispossession made them "unqualified" to participate in decisions affecting their lives. I discovered that the limits of my elite education in Ann Arbor could be overcome only by direct experience among people who couldn't themselves be admitted. The eye-opening experience of participatory democracy made possible the thought.

Nineteen sixty-one was the pivotal year when most SDS leaders graduated from college and were "looking uncomfortably to the world we inherit."[1] That December in Ann Arbor, a small planning meeting assigned me to draft a vision statement for the first SDS convention the next summer. Actually, we didn't use today's organizational planning term, "vision statement"; the SDS preconvention planners described it in more left-wing language as a "manifesto," and, in the end, it became "the Statement," "a living document open to change with our times and experiences."[2]

I left the South to closet myself in a dingy New York railroad apartment buried amid hundreds of books and articles, searching for the concepts and language that might give voice to a student movement that did not even exist in the minds of any mainstream Americans or journalists. Unfortunately, John Dewey, the theorist of learning by doing, had passed a decade before. In Ann Arbor we had some supportive faculty friends like Kenneth and Elise Boulding, Ted Newcomb, and Arnold Kaufman, who first used the phrase "participatory democracy" in 1960. Among the media there was the *New York Times* correspondent Claude Sitton, who had taken notice of SNCC on the southern frontlines. The iconic Albert Camus died in 1960, Frantz Fanon in 1961, and C. Wright Mills just one month before the "Convention Bulletin" was mailed out. Some like myself had read the Beats and had grown up absurd, in the phrase of Paul Goodman, but didn't believe madness was the only proper response. I craved for a political "Howl." I empathized with James Joyce's yearning to express "the uncreated conscience" of our generation.

If creating campus chapters were the first blocks in building SDS, anchoring ourselves in an alliance with SNCC was equally important as far as I was concerned. SNCC leaders recognized me as a useful writer and speaker to carry their message north. Charles McDew and Julian Bond believed that if a white Tom Hayden was beaten up in the Black Belt, that would help end the blackout of mainstream news coverage, draw the Justice Department's attention, and perhaps deter violent attacks on black people trying to vote. They were proven right when an Associated Press photo of me being kicked and beaten in McComb, Mississippi, in October 1961, along with future SDS president Paul Potter, went global. I did speak to Burke Marshall, Robert Kennedy's civil rights deputy in the Justice Department, and my January 1962 report, *Revolution in Mississippi*, was published by SDS and widely circulated on campuses everywhere.

SNCC decided then they would send delegates to attend the SDS convention, wherever it would be. That meant we had secured an interracial alliance with the most important force in the student and civil rights movements. SNCC sought to use SDS for outreach and recruitment, but as young intellectuals they too were drawn to participatory democracy. For them, gaining democracy was a life-or-death matter, and "participation" meant putting one's body on the line as a necessary step toward voting rights. Many had studied Thoreau's "Civil Disobedience," especially the passage about voting with "one's whole life," not only with "a mere strip of paper."

On May 4–6, 1962, one month before Port Huron, we organized a workshop of SDS and SNCC organizers on "race and politics in the South," in Chapel Hill, North Carolina. There we laid plans for pushing the racist Dixiecrat bloc out of their dominance in national politics, a power based entirely on suppressing blacks' right to vote. The meeting solidified an understanding that SNCC workers were the shock troops, or vanguard, in a struggle toward a wider political goal: by enfranchising black people in the South, the racist Dixiecrat order could be overthrown. But a frontline struggle wasn't enough. A mobilization of political conscience was needed among constituencies across the country, especially among northern Democrats and labor who would gain from expelling the Dixiecrats. Students would be the catalysts, but the effort required a coalition of labor, clergy, and rank-and-file Democrats. That was the plan as we left Chapel Hill. The SDS manifesto would focus on that political goal.

This strategy, however, contained an underlying tension within SDS—between those from liberal-left backgrounds who saw realignment as a political end in itself and those who sought more radical goals that could not be achieved through a realignment of the two political parties. Beyond a more representative democracy, for example, lay the quest for a participatory democracy sought in the workplace and family life. Realignment alone could not express the emerging cultural revolution among young poets, musicians, and Beats. These differences foreshadowed, in a way, the division several years later between the more ideological New Left, on the one hand, and a "movement politics" based on changing morality, culture, and spirituality, on the other. Both would be needed for a time. The *Statement* would have to blend the differences.

We all came to Port Huron as seekers. We were young, the age of soldiers. Many of our friends had seen battle and shed blood in the South. Our lives were altered, our career paths deflected. Beyond voting rights, a war on poverty, a reversal of the Cold War—all wildly ambitious in scope—there were even more fundamental questions to be settled at Port Huron. To what values, what hopes, were we committing the rest of our lives? We already had formed parts of the whole—chapters, legal defense, newsletters, political campaigns, and so on—but what was the larger cause, the connecting vision that let us call ourselves "brothers and sisters" and speak of a "blessed community"? These were existential questions.

The three preparatory memos published in this book give an insight into these deeper concerns and how some of us prepared for them. They are not notes toward a political platform so much as a philosophical and moral one. They are worth reading today if only to sense our struggle to become articulate. Since they are very wordy, here is a brief guide to their content.

"Convention Document #1" proposes that we attempt to build "a house of theory," a phrase borrowed by the British writer Iris Murdoch. Beginning with a complaint that we were living in "a barren period in the development of human values," the memo paraphrases Murdoch as commenting that "our liberal and socialist ancestors were plagued by vision without program while our generation is plagued by program without vision." Our generation lacked "authentic prophets." We sought an intellectual and political practice that would not result in compromise and selling out, and a "house of theory" might meet that need. Given our experience, we went beyond the notion of an overly intellectual "house" by insisting that its foundation should be built "right out in public, in the middle of the neighborhood."

The very lengthy "Convention Document #2," called "Problems of Democracy," is like a university thesis going through the many intellectual objections to participatory democracy (that it rests on a utopian view of human nature, which is selfish; that it requires too much complex information for masses of people to absorb; that it leads to "the sovereignty of the unqualified" or to mass totalitarian movements; that students cannot be equals with the experienced faculties instructing us, etc.). Twenty-five books and papers are cited in the bibliography, with Erich Fromm the most extensively quoted. The purpose of this document was to fortify us against the pervasive belief, internalized among us, that the general public wasn't qualified to participate in the decisions affecting their lives. In contrast to this elite view, the paper quotes Fromm approvingly where he wrote that democracy was only possible in an economic system that works for the vast majority of the population, including "democracy in the work situation." In its summary, the document speaks of participatory democracy as liberating the potential of the individual and the overall quality of life (a theme emphasized by Arnold Kaufman).

The third set of notes, titled "RE: Manifesto," is written "in the best tradition of groping" but definitely advances toward the final arguments of the *Port Huron Statement*. The overarching issues are stated briefly and with frank confusion about where SDS should stand. The Cold War/nuclear arms race is identified first, with a question about whether advocating unilateral disarmament would "cut one off totally." Instead, "I think we might talk about the Bomb as something that's been with us nearly all our life . . . and the brutalizing effect it has had on our sense of values." The other big issue identified was "the anti-colonial revolution," including not only our civil rights movement but the question of the Cuban Revolution, where the liberals are slapped for excluding Cuba from the Organization of American States (OAS).

These big topics aside, the rest of the long manifesto is about a moral awakening to the democratic value of direct action and participation. "I think we want to say something about ourselves before we dash off our political perspective," the document begins, a foreshadowing of the Port Huron conference decision to begin the *Statement* with the "Values" section coming first. "Normative theories of creativity ought not to go unattached to the advocacy of 'realignment,'" it goes on, in response to the SDS faction bent on political realignment as their program. Later, the memo extols the spontaneous activism of the emerging New Left and cautions against imposing a preexisting program. The SNCC activists should be respected for the courage to stand up ("whose courage is their own courage") and for wishing to be "creators instead of simply creatures." Let this new spirit "remain ambiguous for a while; don't kill it by immediately imposing formulas for 'realignment.' We have to grow and expand, and let moral values get a bit realigned."

What are we to make of this? The *Port Huron Statement* was an intentional blend of contending visions at the time, held together by a binding sense that we were giving birth to something new and unique. Given the fact that a whole section of the *Statement* on spirituality was left on the floor when the sleepless delegates staggered away, it is fair to say that the original draft was a blend of the spiritual and political with the overriding goal of declaring ourselves as the first major American student movement. For a creative time, the blending worked well—the drive toward the 1965 Voting Rights Act, which fulfilled the quest for political realignment; President Kennedy's 1963 nuclear arms treaty and speech against the Cold War; and the 1964 Berkeley Free Speech Movement, which fully expressed and built on the ideals of the *Port Huron Statement*.

After those victories, the process withered. The goal of "expelling the Dixiecrats" mentioned in the 1962 documents faltered when the Democrats in 1964 rejected the Mississippi Freedom Democratic Party, a perfect model of participatory democracy. The Vietnam escalation in 1965, which we could not anticipate in 1962, turned our early hopes into ashes. The murders of King and the Kennedy brothers finished what might have been.

Among the original SDS factions, the more spiritually driven ones evolved toward the counterculture, liberation theology, or environmental movements. The politicos among us saw their realignment come to pass in the Carter and Clinton-Gore eras, including Jesse Jackson's campaigns. Their Democratic Party splintered over Iraq and hastened corporate globalization. We named the One Percent in the *Port Huron Statement* but never stopped them.

Theorists from Kenneth Keniston to Richard Flacks have struggled for years to understand why, in that particular time, so many young Americans took up the paths that led to the sixties revolution. I myself have never been certain. One common trait was that many of us tended to be young leaders—student body presidents, student editors—who felt deeply thwarted and so rechanneled their energy toward rebellion. For young blacks or Latinos, the obstacles were clear. Their parents were forced to settle for lives of blocked opportunity. The young leadership of SNCC refused to accept the sentence of second-class citizenship imposed on their elders. All young women began to feel the same thwarting of their futures (we were awakening with Doris Lessing's *The Golden Notebook*, while *The Feminine Mystique* came one year after Port Huron). Some of our radical "best and brightest"—Jack Kerouac, Allen Ginsberg, James Baldwin, Ken Kesey—were forsaking mainstream careers in favor of a wild side. One parallel with many other social revolutions might be that an emerging leadership generation was frustrated at the prospect of whole lifetimes of disenfranchisement and blockage. Making it outrageous was the shared perception that the "adults"—those in the ruling establishment—were self-satisfied idiots. C. Wright Mills called the architects of nuclear war "crackpot realists." The skulls of racist governors and sheriffs were bloated with preposterous nonsense. The intelligence of our professors was too often wasted on explaining the virtues of gradualism. When President Eisenhower warned in 1961 of the military-industrial complex, he was far to the left of our intellectuals.

These tensions were sharpened to a breaking point, I believe, by forces outside the common explanations of a "generation gap" as the psychosocial cause of the sixties "unrest." Externally, the Cold War and the rise of a Non-Aligned Movement, including the Cuban Revolution, propelled the sense that another world was possible, to borrow a phrase from the 1990s antiglobalization movement. We didn't notice it at the time, but the rising movements of black sharecroppers, Mexican farmworkers, and other displaced immigrants (Filipinos, Puerto Ricans, etc.), along with their nationalist intellectual allies, were all signs of the Third World Within, what Juan Gonzales describes as "the harvest of empire."[3]

There was a similar generation more than a century before, the Transcendentalists, who called their time "the Newness." Our SDS forerunners, such as Thoreau, rejected the elitism of higher education, adopted a voluntary simplicity, responded to the challenges of Frederick Douglass and John Brown, and opposed the wars against native people and the imperial war against Mexico. They too searched for a whole that was greater than the sum of its parts, a whole that was transcendent.

So did we. In our time, let no one forget, a mass movement of American students never had occurred, much less a student-led movement in American society. In those early times, both left and right defined students as a privileged handful, not the creative base for radical change. The reason some called us the New Left was that the left itself was dead effectively, done in by FBI and McCarthy's repression, absorption into the mainstream New Deal, or sectarian self-destruction. In short, we were given no reason to believe that students as students could build a movement, and the left's historical models were yellow blinkers warning not to go there.

On some level, history was working through us in those days leading to Port Huron. Others—the SNCC people and the numerous spiritual seekers who were at Port Huron—would more likely say that the Spirit did it, or that it was "a holy time."[4] As a main channeler of this "history" or "spirit," all I can add in retrospect is that it felt like the *Port Huron Statement* wrote us, not the other way around.

Editor's note: Aside from the correction of obvious errors of typing and punctuation, this document appears exactly as it was typed, mimeographed, and sent to Students for a Democratic Society (SDS) members in 1962. Historical annotations were added by the editors.

Students for a Democratic Society

<u>Convention Document #1</u>
<u>March 19, 1962</u>
Manifesto Notes: A Beginning Draft (Hayden)

We are the inheritors and the victims of a barren period in the development of human values. The conventional moral terms of the age—"free enterprise," "free world," "our way of life," "people's democracy," "shareholder's democracy," "the national interest," "atheistic materialism"—are the manipulated myths of ruling parties whose essential but masked "values" seem to be little more than power, security, and economic aggrandizement; absent are principles which freely shape and are shaped freely by the life of society.

We cannot stomach the politician morality. In the place of clarity we hear, with William Faulkner: "a cacophony of terror and conciliation and compromise, babbling only the mouth sounds, the loud and empty words—'freedom, democracy, patriotism'—from which we have emasculated all meaning whatever."[1] Marx, Freud, Darwin and others challenge and even embarrass our efforts to root ethics in a fixed order of things, in a natural law of the universe that gives security and loses the capacity for firm action. Doubt, nihilism, and despair abscess the conscience which demands justification for truth, for justice, for beauty, for living itself. The advance of science and technology, the sudden clear relevance of every nation's action to every other's fate, the new crisis caused by mounting population, the flux of power among and within nations, changing the bond of man to work and to community: these and other complexities aggravate our moral uncertainty, and force us to be more urgent than patient in the search for values.

We seem too far sunk within our social niche to obtain that breadth of view which might integrate our scattered thoughts and hunches. We are too tightly confined to specialized roles to understand and take up the citizen's role which might integrate us as participants in society's total preservation. We are instead as spectators; no—not even that—we are as strangers, living in the caverns of the community of man, sometimes overhearing, but never fully understanding what the other fellow is doing. The closer and more crowded the world becomes, the more remote from its momentous activities we seem. "Things are in the saddle and ride mankind"—men feel their large institutions to be operated by an alien "them," or as a group of British socialists has written: "as individuals we have our various moralities . . . but somehow all these attitudes are not effective socially. Our public life is more and more seen as a moral vacuum, a realm of accident shaped only by the chance collisions of individuals and groups in the chase to get ahead."[2]

Strangely, we are in the universities but gain little enlightenment there—the old promise that knowledge and increased rationality would liberate society seems hollow, if not a lie. Our most educated men, the professors and administrators, sacrifice controversy to public relations; their curriculums change more slowly than the living events of the world; their skills and silence are purchased by the makers of war; passion is thought unscholarly; the intellectuals are consumed more and more in the quest for evidence that is "value free." The questions a man wants raised—what is really important? Can we live better than this? How should we be as people?—are "not questions of an empirical, fruitful nature" (We do not know how to answer them; questions that can't be answered should not be asked if a man is to be productive; there is no foundation money to support superfluity—and the rest of it).

But the default of the politicians and the professors, we might indeed say, is to be expected. The real question is whether or not society contains <u>any</u> prophets who can speak in language and concept that is authentic for us, that can make luminous the inner self that burns for understanding—if only for the understanding that, ultimately, there might be no final understanding.

One of the problems facing youth today is that there are too few, if any, of these prophets. Unlike youth in other countries, we are used to moral leadership being exercised and the moral dimension of life being clarified by our elders—for the left movement, the elders have been connected with trade unions, or early socialism, or the broad fields of literature and scholarship. But today, while the supply of elders is undiminished, their moral statements seem to prove that pouring old wine in new bottles is as futile as the converse dictum preached by Christ. That is, the statements of the past do not fit the form of the present. Consider: Capitalism Cannot Reform Itself, Unite Against Fascism, General Strike, All Out on May Day. Or, more recently: No

Cooperation with Commies and Fellow Travellers, Political Ideologies Are Exhausted, Bipartisanship, Peace With Freedom, Shackle the Utopians, The National Interest Demands Liberating the Negro and Helping the Revolution of Rising Expectations. These are petty, irrelevant, and worst of all, incomplete.

Iris Murdoch makes the interesting comment that our liberal and socialist ancestors were plagued by vision without program while our generation is plagued by program without vision.[3] There is today astute grasp of method, technique, and program—the committee, the commission, the ad hoc group, the lobbyists, the hard and soft sell, the make, the image projected—but, if pressed critically, such expertise yields only a "brief and denuded" explanation of its underlying ideals. This is understandable: the criterion in judging program is "success," that of value is deeper and more readily dismissed. When a moral principle is enunciated, e.g., I am for human dignity (the inscription on a recent button), it is hurriedly stated, introduced and completed by the old apology, "You know generally what I'm getting at," then really defined by "concrete examples"—such as one's position on medical care for the aged. This is an unreflective and shocking manner of clarifying values. But usually the listener does not press the advocate (of medical care, or whatever) for his root interest; instead, it is fashionable to nod "of course" when values are buried in the rubbish of "it's decent to do" or "it seems humane" and "progressive." Values are controlled more extremely than children: not only are they not heard, they are not seen. In some cases they are no longer even experienced, but the young have not been around long enough for the moral appetite to be rendered arid, and so the young are disaffected. The questions we think existentially important receive deferential treatment, if any treatment at all, for the men whose minds and imaginations are respected by society. The asking of serious questions is discouraged, the answering is never attempted. The grade, the seniority, the mental prostitution is the thing. Soon we stop raising the questions, and find it easier to "get by." This is called growing up absurd.

Iris Murdoch again: "There is a Tory contention that theorizing leads to violence, and there is a liberal contention that theories are obscurantist and blinding. Now, on the contrary, it is the absence of theory which renders us blind and enables bureaucracy, in all its sense, to keep us mystified; and as for violence, the absence of civilized theorizing can also lead in that direction. It is dangerous to starve the moral imagination of the young. We require a social analysis which is both detailed and frank in its moral orientation. A more ambitious conceptual picture, thought out anew in the light of modern critical philosophy and our improved knowledge of the world, of the moral centre and moral direction of socialism would enable those of us who are not experts to pick up the facts of the situation in a reflective, organized, and argumentative way: would give us what Shelley called the power to imagine what we know. Socialist thought is hampered, and the appeal of Socialism is restricted, because our technical concepts are highly esoteric and our moral concepts are excessively simple and there is nothing in between. We need, and the Left should provide, some refuge from the cold, open field of Benthamite empiricism, a framework, a house of theory."[4]

The "house of theory" of which Iris Murdoch speaks, is not a private one, not a monastery. In its planning, in its construction and occasional reconstruction, it must be relevant to the public order, else our vision is wastefully or selfishly spent. C. Wright Mills says it cogently: "Every time intellectuals have the chance to speak yet do not speak, they join the forces that train men not to be able to think and imagine and feel in morally and politically adequate ways. When they do not speak, when they do not demand, when they do not think and feel and act as intellectuals—and so as public men—they too contribute to the moral paralysis, the intellectual rigidity, that now grip leaders and men around the world."[5]

I am proposing that we cease in our use of the slogans, the slams, the "tyranny of categories." I am proposing that we stop filching our values by copying what stand is taken by the man we admire. I am proposing that the world is not too complex, our knowledge not too limited, our time not so short, as to prevent the orderly building of a house of theory, or at least its foundation, right out in public, in the middle of the neighborhood. I am proposing that the inner dialogue of man can be regenerated and so also can the appreciative communication between man and man. I am proposing that man must integrate, or try to integrate, his confused sentiments and discrete notions, to become a creator and self-maker rather than a pitiless and buffeted thing unable to reach the forces that control.

Students for a Democratic Society

<u>Convention Document #2</u>
<u>March 19, 1962</u>
Manifesto Notes: Problems of Democracy (Hayden)

One of our central problems is: what does it mean, in theory and practice, to be "for a democratic society"? I don't hope to answer such a question fully, nor even exhaust the approaches to an answer, in these pages. I begin, however, with the insistence that our traditional democratic images are the subject of genuinely serious criticism, and if we are to view ourselves as responsible members of a community of discourse, then we better work out defenses, accommodations, or other capitulations to the critics, else we surrender by default.

This paper intends to (1) offer a definition of "participatory democracy," (2) enumerate several of the problems posed by its critics or by persons who, though sympathetic, cannot share democratic faith any longer.

<u>The Participatory Democracy</u>

In this Society, man is seen as both creator and creature; that is, while in a sense, her personality is no more than the buffeted consequence of all the social, physical, and historical forces which have shaped him, he is also an individual with felt identity, a sense of purpose, and independence. "Human nature" is not an evil or corrosive substance to be feared or contained; rather, it represents a potential for material and spiritual development which, no matter how lengthily or rapidly unfolded, can never be dissipated. The liberation of this individual potential is the just end of society; the directing of the same potential, through voluntary participation, to the benefit of society, is the just end of the individual. For a participatory democracy, freedom is present since man needs the opportunity to become. But freedom is more than the absence of arbitrary restrictions on personal development. For the democratic man, freedom must be a condition of the inner self as well, achieved by reflection confronting dogma, and humility overcoming pride. "Participation" means both <u>personal initiative</u>—that men feel obliged to help resolve social problems—and <u>social opportunity</u>—that society feel obliged to maximize the possibility for personal initiative to find creative outlets.

In the democracy of participation, government and politics are not negative phenomena isolated from the highest experiences of life, nor are they mere tools with which man prevents himself from destroying his fellows, nor are they monstrosities that inexorably come to dominate and subvert the individual capacity for initiative. On the contrary, government and politics represent a desirable, necessary (though not sufficient) part of the experience through which man discovers and develops himself; they are among the instruments by which man becomes the measure and maker of all things. The institutional form of this process involves the organizing of representative political parties or other associations to advance or change public policies, to link the individual to the state decisions-making structure, to channel private problems to public issue and make public issues relevant to private problems, to guarantee peaceful transitions, and to clarify at all times the meaning of the issues.

Like the political experience, the economic one is of decisive and positive character for the individual. It is a means by which man comes to understand his capacities, unleash his creative potential in a useful manner, and gain influence over the direction of his life. Therefore the individual should not be isolated from the control and ownership of his work, and the society should not be divided into economic groups who own and are owned, or who manage and are managed. The individual should have responsibility for his own occupational development, and the society should be organized in a way that allows the greatest opportunity for the exercise of this responsibility.

Participation is especially needed in a large, fragmented society, since it can integrate the many sentiments and roles of the individual into the function of "citizenship," whereby identity is found in relation to the general society, not to a limited, isolated or fragmented part.
Participation in the full life of society is the process by which man comes to a consciousness of his dignity and a respect for the same fundamental quality in his striving fellows. Participation animates the abstract ideas of freedom and responsibility, and ensures that morality has meaning in the practical life of men.

Accept, if you can, the above as an adequate etching of the ideal that democrats seek to realize in society. If it is inadequate as ideal, then continue to etch until contours become acceptable. This done, I think our task is to examine, or better, find a way to examine in some detail the real meaning of these seductive moral statements: what values remain implicit and unexplored, what parts of the ideal are less clear than others, what values should be exported from or imported into the structure, etc. etc. As this examination proceeds, we will naturally be drawn into empirical findings in political behavior, in comparative political and cultural systems, and so on.

Some of the quite relevant problems, presumably, are the following (these obviously do not exhaust the list):

1) Some arguments against democracy rest on a view of "human nature" that precludes participation of the kind suggested. One such view holds that democracy depends on the "rationality" of man: his ability to comprehend his true self-interest, and devise methods of obtaining that interest. However, man is seen as decidedly not rational: he is a package of confusion, irrationality and anxiety not competent to consistently, if at all, judge the "best course." From this judgment usually follows a statement of the need for a rational elite that will look on the inferior majority with compassion, and necessarily an elite which submits itself to examination via checks-and-balances, rigorous constitutionalism and periodic elections.

It is usually added as a reinforcing point that man by nature is selfish, or aggressive, or power-lusting, or cursed by original sin, or combinations of these. Or it is insisted that all men really do not desire freedom (Mencken: "The average man does not want to be free; he wants to be safe").[1] Again, the next step is the construction of an elite principle of some kind.

In all of this it is clear that the aim of political organization, as Sheldon Wolin wrote of the early American political theorists, is "not to educate men, but to deploy them; not to alter their moral character, but to arrange institutions in such a manner that human drives would cancel each other or, without conscious intent, be deflected toward the common good."[2] A similar distrust of men leads writers to concur with Andrew Scott, author of a contemporary political theory anthology, in this curious form of hopefulness: "The existence of a dark side of man's nature does not vitiate a belief in democracy. If man is irrational, he has been that way a long time; yet democratic regimes have persisted through it all. Man is not always rational, but he is sufficiently so for democratic government to work passably well."[3]

In this view, it seems, the idea of a fully participatory democracy is not only impossible to achieve, but misguided—since it is based on a false estimate of man's "nature."

2) Other thinkers have remained agnostic toward the issue of "human nature" and, instead, claimed that the problem of popular democracy derives from a mistaken idea of human "capacity" or "ability" for public participation—in other words, all metaphysical questions about "nature" aside, the facts of history demonstrate conclusively that people never have—and therefore can't—govern themselves. People, it is insisted, are never "informed" enough to permit their full participation in the major events of history. Not only are they mal-informed, they are apathetic as well. Furthermore, they have not the proper training to inherit central positions in real government. The traditional glorification of the "sovereign public" is nonsense propounded by utopian liberals, or worse, it is myth-making by the manipulative men of power.

In this formulation is included a statement about the growing complexity of modern society: complexity of information, of administration in the large and organized society, of the more general trends expressed in science, industrialization, geographic and demographic change and interconnected institutions of the other fields of knowledge.

In this confused situation, modern man is in need of leadership—an elite, preferably, of experts equipped with the training, knowledge and maturity to make proper decisions about public matters. Special guidance becomes increasingly required as the functions of life undergo division and subdivision. Man is "incapable" in the sense that he is without the time, the breadth of understanding, the preparation, and the interest to undertake the direction of society. Democracy is now conceived not as the free participation of people in their common affairs but as the free competition of elites for the periodic consent of electors (whose business is finished after voting). The criterion is not: Does the individual have the opportunity to develop his consciousness and potential? but rather: Is there a way to guarantee equality of opportunity for anyone who wants to seek political office? The realization of the second statement is not seen as conditional on acceptance of the first; that is, there can be a free competition and circulation of elites without participation by the mass of men.

The needs for technical expertise and specialized skill are usually seen in conjunction with such social phenomena as apathy, reliance on habit, enforced remoteness of the individual from the centers of power, the psychological urge for authority, and so on; the final vision is for permanent although perhaps beneficent, oligarchy or oligarchies. When Robert Michels said sadly that socialists might win, but socialism never, he was predicting the impossibility of dismantling the structure of oligarchy and the tendencies that sustain it.[4] Once an incoming leadership stabilizes itself, no matter how revolutionary its goals when it sought power, it creates new interests in conflict with those of the movement it originally represented. A "tragicomic" process is set off, in which "the masses are content to devote all their energies to effecting a change of masters." Social change is simply a progression of elites, each promising to its followers a dream that is tarnished by the first brush with power. True or false?

3) How much democracy does an organized, rational bureaucratic society need? Curiously, as Wolin points out, it seems "that there still exists in the West an impressive capacity for political participation and interest which is not, however, being diverted towards the traditional forms of political life."[5] This kind of "participation," he indicates, is diverted towards institutions commonly thought "private" at one time: chief among these is the large corporation, which is probably the most important institution in contemporary society. The goal of the corporation, or any similarly imposing institution, is not <u>simply</u> profit or other forms of aggrandizement. The goals now prominently include providing a sense of personal warmth and fraternity for the worker. In the language of A. A. Berle, the corporation is "the collective soul" and "conscience carrier" of modern life.[6] What does all this mean for a theory which gives the decisive place in public decision-making to government and the political, but not such to economic institutions? Is there a way to understand the corporation as a "public" institution subject to the control of the political representatives of the people? And is organizational "togetherness" the perversion or perfection of "participation"?

4) The idea (or ideas) of "mass society" is obviously related to the problem of participatory democracy.

"When the normal inhibitions enforced by tradition and social structure are loosened . . . the <u>undifferentiated mass</u> emerges," writes Philip Selznick.[7] While men are forced into greater and more complicated interdependence, they also are estranged from each other radically, in the absence of unifying values. Their tastes are shaped by institutions geared to the lowest common human denominator. Their activity is divided into a number of roles, often without coherent or even anticipated pattern. Herbert Blumer analogizes mass society to the audience at a movie theatre, each person "separate, detached, and anonymous," with "no social organization, no organized group of sentiments, no structure of status roles and no established leadership."[8] Liberals and conservatives alike seem uneasy, and often terrified, of the "mass"—it invokes images of anarchy, the mob, violence, corruption. This apparent consensus among writers of different political affiliations is a happening worth consideration, since traditionally the "left" has hallowed the masses (the popular will, the proletariat, the brotherhood of man, etc.) while the "right" has reviled them as the most dangerous of threats to civilization. Today the conservative has not changed his mind about the mass, but the liberal has done so more and more—is this a sign of disenchantment among men whose expectations were never realized? Should younger radicals heed it?

From the generally accepted notion of the mass, participatory democracy is criticized thoroughly. It opens the possibility for mass-man to dominate society, bringing about the feared "sovereignty of the unqualified."[9] If the masses imprint their concerns everywhere in society, then incompetence permeates the decisive institutions, and the potential of great men is constrained for the benefit of the sluggish progress of lesser men. Perhaps even revolution will result, since the masses are susceptible to charisma, new symbols, and sudden outlets. The democrats, it is claimed, don't recognize the importance of a creative elitist minority which nurtures and preserves the essence of culture, the values of civilization, the stability of traditional institutions. As Selznick outlines the aristocratic view, the democrat wants "a leveling process in education, literature, and politics (which) substitutes the standardless appetites of the mass market for the canons of refinement and social restraint."[10] The democrat advocates implicitly the breakup of standards and moral direction for society since his form of democracy: 1) expands the number of elite groups so greatly that none can decisively influence the whole society, 2) ends the insulation of elites from the mundane burdens of life, thus making it more difficult for them to pursue their role of renewing and preserving culture.

5) What is involved in an ideal "totalitarian" form of participation? How is it different from "democratic participation"? Surely there is considerable evidence that dictatorships exist not only through total control of the means of violence or through the enforcement of whatever conditions make rebellion impossible, but also often through sincerely

expressed popular support. People in such a society can be mobilized by a sense of mission, an identity with some transcendent cause that appears to be attainable. For this goal they will sacrifice their freedom willingly, and continue to make the sacrifice so long as their movement seems to be progressing. Such people might find genuine pleasure in their work, be it on a collective farm or in a factory, in a bureaucratic political post or in a university professorship. They sense a solidarity with their fellows. They are swept up not only in a vision of their goal but also usually in a reinforcing image of their enemies. They are happy, integrated into a group, purposeful, dedicated, sacrificing. Yet they truly are separated from the means of decision-making. They are manipulated from "above" by an open, controlling elite. They have only tangential influence over the tactics and direction of their group and their society. They are not "free" in any liberal or democratic sense.

Numerous questions immediately come to mind. What are the moral issues involved in claiming that an exuberant, creative man is not living "the good life"? Is there anything innate in man that yearns for attachment to a consuming cause or a transcendent form of being? If so, how does the non-totalitarian society deal with that human yearning? Can a non-totalitarian society generate the same élan, mission, purposefulness? If totalitarianism involves an attack on privacy, what place do we give to privacy in our participatory society? And if privacy really has no place, if the really democratic political order is universal, how is it different from totalitarianism?

6) How are we to apply the idea of participation to a country engaged in the colonial revolution? Where industrialization is just beginning, where educated and competent leadership is scarce and poverty, illiteracy and disease are prevalent? Where tribal patterns are as important as Cold War politicking? Where counter-revolution and complete anarchy are twin menaces? Are our democratic notions applicable only to the industrialized nations? If not, by what values do we judge the development of these new nations?

In evaluating a form of development, is centralized economic planning our primary concern, or the establishment of democratic institutions, or the existence of political parties or the form of national government, or cold war policies? These questions indicate the real inadequacy of our ideal theory and demand that we develop at least two instruments: 1) a theory of social change, 2) a scale of greater and lesser values. The former will allow us to grasp what is absolutely necessary for a country's development, what is peripheral, what is flexible and what is not: the prerequisites of evaluation, in other words. The latter will give us a formula for judging the quality of various institutions or nations. For example, Erich Fromm in May Man Prevail? seems to argue that non-corrupt government, economic planning, individual hope, technical skill and capital are needed before democracy can exist. And explicitly, he asks that we "look at the problem of democracy in several dimensions," then lists the four "most important" qualities of democracy as: 1) Political democracy in the Western sense: a multiparty system and free elections (provided they are real, and not a sham); 2) "An atmosphere of personal freedom" in which the individual can "feel free to voice any opinion (including one critical of the government), without fear of any reprisals"; 3) "If one wants to judge the role of the individual in any given country, one cannot do so without examining for whose benefit the economic system works. If a system works mainly for the benefit of a small upper class, what is the use of free elections for the majority? Or rather, how can there be any authentically free election in a country which has such an economic system? Democracy is only possible in an economic system that works for the vast majority of the population"; 4) "... there is a social criterion of democracy, namely the role of the individual in his work situation, and in the concrete decisions of his daily life. Does a system tend to turn people into conforming automatons, or does it tend to increase their individual activity and responsibility"?[11] Fromm's criteria are perhaps inadequate, but his style of evaluating democracies is perhaps the kind that must be developed in relation especially to underdeveloped nations.

A special consideration for SDS, of course, is that of importing democratic ideas into the university experience. Briefly, it might be said that our primary interest must be: what are the decisive elements in the structure and activity of the university, and who regulates them? These surely include: content of curriculum; academic requirements, opportunity for free inquiry, non-academic living and working conditions. Generally these decisions are governed undemocratically: by authoritarian fiat of administration, and occasionally with faculty participation. The various rationalizations for this procedure are similar to the attitude toward democracy already mentioned: "Students are not capable of exercising rights responsibly," "the university is too delicate an enterprise to risk student influence," "even if students were capable, they are apathetic," "if you give rights away indiscriminately, you are inviting license, perhaps of a catastrophic kind," "why not hire trained specialists to do the complicated work of governing?" Supplementing these are several new themes: "Educational institutions are like business establishments, not societies," "Parents expect us to keep a fatherly eye on their kids, especially those who are away from home the first time," "students are transient, the administration staff is permanent," etc.

How are we to respond to these theses? Presumably the answer itself might carry the thinker into the more general problems of the democratic social structure and pattern of life.

(It would be desirable to continue, or to return to earlier sections in need of elaboration, but these notes already grow too long, and I hope they establish some basis for thought and correspondence about the meaning of "Students for a Democratic Society." Short notes or longer treatises can be stenciled and periodically sent out so that discussion goes on among all SDS associates.)

Editor's note: Aside from the correction of obvious errors of typing and punctuation, this document appears exactly as it was typed, mimeographed, and sent to Students for a Democratic Society (SDS) members in 1962. Historical annotations were added by the editors.

TO: SDS executive committee, others
FROM: Hayden
RE: manifesto

This is one of several letters going out about the "manifesto" that is to be drafted at the June Convention. I very much want your responses to this, and to the other two I've written (one on "values," the other on "democracy"). When I receive enough responses I'll try to get them on mimeo and circulate them for purposes of dialogue and cross-fertilization. This will be hard as hell since I'm not a good typist or mimeographer, but we'll get along somehow—if you write back, however briefly.

Where does one begin thinking about manifestoes? These are some of my sketchy notions, offered not as definite statements but in the best tradition of groping.

I think we want to say something about ourselves before we dash off our political perspective. We are, like it or not, young intellectuals in an anti-intellectual society. Even society's politics are not intellectual, though intellectuals manipulate the politics. That is the state of knowledge: unexalted. As for the state of power, very little of it is distributed to men of knowledge. And as for the place of youth, we are relevant only peripherally.

Objectively we are "out" politically. We do not have access to the circles of men and institutions making final and decisive decisions. As youth passes, the possibility of being "in" becomes objectively greater. But being really "in" will be impossible until we give up intellectual independence.

Furthermore, we will be "out" if we are explicitly socialists, or if we espouse any minority political views honestly (we can be further "in" if we are willing to call socialism liberalism, or if we are willing to say "the free world" instead of the "capitalist bloc"; but these, again, amount to sacrificing intellectual independence).

These enormous objective political disadvantages make a certain kind of politics especially desirable, I think. We should be pursuing a politics of vision and relevance. This means:

1. A moral aspiration for social equality, unaccompanied by a political and economic view of society, is at best wistful (I think I mimic Harrington[1]) and, at worst, politically irresponsible. But an economic and political analysis, without an active, open moral pulse, dwindles to uninspired and uninspiring myopia. We need to be concerned with weltanschaung and strategy, with vision and program. Normative theories of creativity ought not to go unattached to the advocacy of political "realignment."[2]

2. We want to be involved enough within the structural mainstream to be influential, but detached enough from it to maintain personal intellectual independence and perspective. We want to be active in the civil rights movement, but not among its bureaucrats. We want to be Young Democrats, but the independent left-wing bloc of the Young Democrats. Etcetera.

3. We want to reach well into the liberal campus community and radicalize it. We want not only to expand the consciousness of specific individuals, we also want to bring them into social action [so] the abstract commitments of consciousness (new born) can be forged to permanence.

4. Where honesty and short-range effectiveness are in conflict, we should be reluctant to forsake honesty. This is partly because nobody is expressing convictions with clarity, partly because we rarely have the opportunity to be genuinely effective, partly because so much "effective action" today is what Mills called "crackpot realism,"[3] and finally because there are certain serious social problems that ought to be discussed and can't be discussed now by "effective" people (the future of capitalism, democratic potential in the Soviet Union, perhaps the need for last-ditch actions against war).

Our basic unit of organization is the University. The university as an agent of social change, rather than the transmitter of culture-as-we-know-it, should be our goal. By "agent of social change" I have in mind:

a. a place of terrific controversy, within and without the classroom;
b. a place where current events are fought about;
c. where leftist intellectuals have time to engage in writing and practical politics;
d. where direct influence can be generated against men in power.

Surely the manifesto must say something about higher education; should it not also talk about the university as our place of operation?

Leadership. I have the impression that we have been our own leadership to a far greater degree than most "student radicals" of the past. More directly, the point is that we are mostly critical (not always with precision; more emotionally) of the nominal leadership of the American "left." Nominal leadership includes politicians, labor, civil rights and other agency people, and intellectuals. Democratic party liberals are seen as people we are supposed to help, not as people who will lead us chillun home. The socialist parties are in shambles; often their vision is clouded by sectarianism or queer jargon; as for relevance, they have little, except as they infiltrate non-socialist ranks (Fromm, for example[4]). The civil rights leadership is more militant than most, but they confine their movement to a single issue out of some intellectual default but more out of a concern for financial support. Organized labor, the working class etc., is just not the missionary force we can count on; again, labor is more a group we do things for than a group whose banner we rally 'round. The intellectuals, after Mills' tragic death,[5] are few and disorganized (they were before he died, but it didn't seem to show so much). In addition, all these groupings share certain features which make getting along with them extremely difficult: a conservative temperament, modest hope, pride in the achievement of the Welfare State, bureaucratic mental structures, end-of-ideology paranoia ("causes are no good; they indicate psychic disorder, not a sense of justice; popular movements have always led to wars; the Populists rallied behind Father Coughlin;[6] besides the issues are too complex for summary in any moral or ideological construct; have a cigar," and all the rest . . .). Too, there is a curious fear of things Left: socialism is thought ineffective; leftists who are not on record with adamant anti-communist utterances are distrusted; the "democratic left" concept takes on more the qualities of fetish than of phrase; "communists" are dismissed with about the same finesse and sensitivity that Dean Rusk[7] displays. Reinforcing these tendencies are other intellectual doctrines which are increasingly respectable. The neo-orthodox Protestants, especially Niebuhr[8] (a left-wing socialist twenty years ago) are fond of contemplating the inherent faults of man which prevent social change and progress. As life has become more complex and high hopes broken, I think there has been an upsurge in this "nature of things" explanation, along with a widespread criticism (distorted always) of Enlightenment hopefulness, especially that of Condorcet.[9]

Perhaps the manifesto should comment on this leadership of youth.

The Issues. I think it is unrealistic to try to incorporate policy statements on every important problem. On some we might never get consensus (economics, nonviolence). On many we may have little contributive to say (SEATO?).[10] If it were a responsible statement it would be too long for the convention to handle. And we have an out: the NEC[11] or convention can mandate groups to carry on program in certain areas not necessarily mentioned in the general manifesto (like seeing the Young Demos about an anti-Dixiecrat effort at the '64 convention). Given these qualifications, what are the issues that should be mentioned?

A. <u>Thermonuclear War</u>. I'm really perplexed on this. I would never advocate U.S. engagement in any such war. At this point, however, urging unilateral disarmament cuts one off quite totally.[12] It is perhaps not necessary to advocate it anyway; for now, I think it is reasonable to advocate some kind of phased disarmament retaining an equal proportion of deterrent strength all the way down to the destruction of the weapons and means of production. (For me, this is advocacy of a lie, unfortunately, since I would never use the deterrent except as a threat.) I say this about myself to indicate the confusion I'm in regarding the manifesto. I think we might talk about the Bomb as something that's been with us nearly all our life, that has shaped much of our past, present, and surely our future, the brutalizing effect it has had on our sense of values, the fears that are manifest in our discussion of what we'll do on the Last Day, or of our children, etc etc. Take the war issue out of the political context, that is. Then put it back in the political context, and advocate disarmament, criticizing the lack of credibility in the American position, etc.

B. <u>The Cold War</u>. Again, I think our statements should be more than just political here. We grew up in the Cold War. We commonly share a great hate of it, I'm sure, and this is not a political hate so much as it is a plain human hate of the way our future has been constructed for us, the way our private lives are twisted by worries about war, the way our minds are conditioned to react with distrust when somebody says something which sounds politically unusual, the whole way in which we seem to be constrained—from getting on with Human Business because of the infernal "East-West" conflict. We should talk about growing up in the Cold War world, how when we were seven years old Churchill was announcing our destiny from Fulton, Missouri.[13] In addition to all this, perhaps we want to make policy recommendations. These might include a suggestion that we look at the world in a special way. Not like the Chinese who look at it in terms of class conflicts slicing across national boundaries. Not like the Americans who look at it in terms of free peoples and slave peoples, western and Eastern "worlds." Not like the people in America, Russia and the UN who see all these phenomena <u>plus</u> the momentum of nation-states. I think we should be encouraging people to also divide men and nations into war-oriented and peace-oriented camps, and attempt to strengthen the position of the latter. This will mean some fine distinctions between the camps; surely they melt together somewhere in the arms control circles, and surely, too, we'll have to establish criteria not directly related to positions on disarmament, arms control and deterrence (such as interest in economic development programs, kind of economic aids—private investment, credit, soft credit, outright grant—the group is willing to undertake concern for personal freedom, political democracy). With this perspective developing, we can talk more concretely about how to foment liberal breakthroughs or, conversely, check militarist breakthroughs in various regions. I have in mind the advocacy of international cooperative efforts (scientific exchanges, space explorations, communications satellites, Antarctica-type projects), any enterprises that benefit communication, development of soft credit international development authorities which create rotating funds for aid to emergent nations, a larger congressional appropriation for the Disarmament Agency,[14] national and local planning for economic conversion to peacetime production, a major effort against the Southern Democrats in 1964–1968, etc. etc. This latter suggestion (anti-Dixiecrats) leads into a host of general positions we might take against the war orientation. These would include less reliance on NATO and other military alliances, exposure and every other kind of criticism of military influence on policy making, the same type attack on corporate interests in military production, local efforts against rural political dominance (as with Tennessee presently), etc. etc.[15] We would probably have to advocate various limits on sovereignty, new avenues of international expression and order, etc. We would also warn of the pitfalls in the Common market:[16] its anti-socialist principles, neo-colonialist potential, and its rigidifying effect on the Cold War. And so on . . .

C. The anti-colonial revolution. I'm perplexed here, too. We could get into a complex but perhaps worthwhile analysis of the very decisive significance of these developments for the Cold War, the location of power in the world, the future of capitalism, etc. Or we could pay more attention to the exemplary way these peoples are breaking out from the crust of the old order into a new and highly experimental period of development, the way "participation" really does mean something in these countries, the way in which the individual, courage, conviction, and the mind are all at once relevant again, in a situation where there are imperative and immediate things to do. Though Daniel Bell will label this "romantic protest," I think I almost prefer to emphasize these latter, less mechanical, aspects of these revolutions.

Why this treatment? Because it fits most consistently with my feelings about the style, form and content of the American Way of life, and it is the American Way of Life which should be the central concern of this manifesto. I am primarily concerned about the complete absence of an active and creative set of publics, people working in union to conform the structures and direction of events to their interests. This is a central fatal fact about the United States. It is a republic, not a democracy, and nearly everyone wants to keep it that way.

Look at politics. Petty men, unconnected to a constituency except in manipulative or gross baby-kissing style, dominate the legislatures and the National Congress. They do not give a damn about the public, except for the public's public relation value (Senator Morse concluded his summary of the knifing of Cuba at Punta del Este[17] with several genuflections to the "informed public, who would see the rightness of JFK's position, if they weren't confused by the false Latin American journalists." His entire presentation was rooted in either deliberate or terrifyingly unconscious false interpretations of the OAS constitution, the American pressures on certain countries to vote with Rusk, etc.)

These men are, however, reflections of the democracy without publics. They are conventional, ratify lying as a necessary political evil, conform to a low denominator of taste, dance to the music of the rich and powerful, and generally act like the mentally inactive and intellectually unchallenged crackpots they are. Read the CR transcript of the current filibuster against the poll tax bill, including Dodd's remarks about the United Nations.[18] This will be called an extreme example, but it is not: it is the politician mentality so exposed that we can't believe it is real.

Among the population generally, rarely more than a fraction of the individual's total time is given to public affairs. The sphere of the political and collective life is minute; participation goes on through non-political institutions. Chief among these is the friendly corporation, with its wive's club, and family picnics and baseball teams.

Need I mention the mass-media which police this public vacuum by pumping out privately conceived trash and the Official Word? Need I mention automation which, instead of making meaningless work obsolete, makes work itself meaningless and men obsolete?[19]

We should be critical of the commodity-oriented economic system which encourages gross materialistic individualism by continuing to place "exchange value" before "use value." This is a system which is fundamentally opposed to the interests of a democratic community, in that it encourages private activity with public consequences, personal financial success over an equitable distribution of wealth, wasteful entrepreneurialism instead of controlled community planning. The dominance of this system over politics can be seen best in the "permanent war economy" which has a vastly more influential role over disarmament negotiations than does public opinion.[20] In fact public opinion has come to be something of a commodity itself, responding to pseudo-needs created by the agents of a chronically overproductive economic system.

Public apathy is further reinforced by the status of controversy in America: it is either absent or absurd. The political parties, which are supposed to enable and encourage men to deal with public life, are divided internally more than against each other (Joseph Clark and James Eastland are party colleagues; or, recall Senator Javits recently urging the GOP to take a "positive" stance against Kennedy by urging stronger civil rights legislation, federal aid to schools, housing programs etc.).[21] In addition, much of the party structure is either machine- or bureaucracy-dominated so that it hardly encourages mass participation. Various interest groups, especially the corporations and certain voluntary associations, carry on public controversy to be sure, but theirs is economically motivated propaganda, hardly directed at creating an alive and curious public. In this situation, given the intensification of the Cold War, it is easy to understand that controversy itself has fallen into ill repute. The truly sensitive issues are supposed to be handled in a "bipartisan" manner. Unpopular opinions are branded communist. Congressional committees investigating ideas are approved by the majority of the people (who have never thought an unpopular idea). The President is able to publicly ask the nation's editors to censor themselves when the interests of the Free World are at stake. The Communist Party is pilloried brutally and thrown beyond the perimeter of legitimate debate by the same powers who worry so deeply about the need to positively confront international communism. Official secrecy becomes so widespread that some scholars wonder if it is possible for any unclassified citizen to make meaningful statements about the conduct of domestic and foreign policy. The techniques of propaganda and the channels of communication become increasingly controlled by reactionary or status groupings. What we say is irrelevant, unheard much of the time.

Our own universities provide a close and terrifying glimpse of what happens (I've got a very long analysis of this in the NY office if you want to read it and compare notes). The extracurricular organization is founded on in loco parentis doctrine, on the "let's pretend" theory of participation by students, thus encouraging participation by students who want to pretend, discouraging it by students who have real, live concerns, and reinforcing among the rest the popular notion that politics is a farce. The academic organization operates on a teacher-student relationship analogous to the parent-child relationship, thus locking with the extracurricular organization to keep students in their place. It is also founded on a radical division of student from subject (the objectification of data, of reality), thus strengthening the separation of student from life which is the crucial feature of in loco parentis. The bureaucratic structure, which permeates both extracurricular and academic life, completes the impersonalizing of life that makes the student convinced of his powerlessness. The end result is a commodity again, not a citizen. This commodity wants to attract modest but comfortable offers on the employment market; it does not want to be the center of controversy; it gets along best in a private friendly world. The suburb is just right.

Even within the debased American community there are elements suffering a relatively greater degree of debasement. These are the minority groups and the 40 million people who are just plain poor by usual social standards. Various power cliques maintain themselves because of this extreme debasement; other groups don't care and often don't know much about it; few groups are fighting to rectify the extreme impoverishment of the minorities and poor. The existence of such widespread social and economic injustice will continue as long as an active public is absent, as long as those interested in the democracy without a public are in power. Especially this is true in the South, and in the nation's larger economic institutions.

Finally, there is the difficult-to-measure role of the permanent military, which influences society as an independent phenomenon (UMT[22] is something that started in our lifetimes), and also in various conjunctions with industrial and political institutions. The militarization of society means the pulverizing of democracy. When it goes on in concert with the growth of fantastic economic alliances and with a constantly diminishing area of serious political discussion, then perhaps all of democracy (save the comfort of the affluent myopic) is gone. Its forms remain, but are used more and more by people who want to pretend, while the truly serious decisions are made in private by a few paying lip service to the forms.

The revolutions in the new nations are important precisely here, because they are trying to defy the tendencies toward stultification by the hard assertion of individual personality and with the harsh legacy of voluntary denial and suffering. The same is true often in the Southern sit-in movement: it is a movement out of privacy, against an undemocratic order, by individuals who are their own leaders, whose courage is their own courage, whose human foibles are at least their own foibles, whose passion to be at last creators instead of simply creatures is authentic and truly self-constructed. Our immediate concern in the manifesto, perhaps, should be with making this an <u>exemplary</u> habit (instead of standing off, and criticizing the intellectual faults or the various "excesses" of the new movements), that is, the habit of personally willed participation, intervention in the movement of human affairs. Perhaps we should encourage a similar incentive among American youth, giving it outlets at local levels (for instance, against CD).[23] Let it remain ambiguous in direction for a while; don't kill it by immediately imposing formulas for "realignment." We have to grow and expand, and let moral values get a bit realigned. Then, when consciousness is at its proper stage, we might talk seriously and in an action-oriented way about solutions.

I'm not sure I see any other way. The role of the intellectuals and of the universities (and therefore, I think, SDS) is to enable people to actively enjoy the common life and feel some sense of genuine influence over their personal and collective affairs. As social existence greatly determines social consciousness, we must affect the real social existence, the life experience, of individuals with our message. Therefore a complex and extremely difficult organizational program has to be mounted, encompassing many kinds of issues, anticipating many levels of consciousness, fluctuating from moderation to radicalism, balancing direct action with scholarly investigation and social criticism, cemented by a concern for democracy which, as I said at the outset, can be neither romantically abstract nor programmatically concrete, but one that is at once visionary and relevant.

Write back. Peace.

Bob Ross speaks on the University of Michigan Diag. Courtesy of the *Michiganensian* yearbook (1963 edition)

I.

Experiences

Being There

A fair sampling of early Students for a Democratic Society (SDS) activists revisited Ann Arbor for the New Insurgency conference, many of them featured on panels devoted to their recollections. Most distinctive was a panel consisting entirely of women who were early SDS leaders—Casey Hayden, Maria Varela, Sharon Jeffrey Lehrer, Barbara Haber, Dorothy Dawson Burlage, Leni Wildflower, and Martha Prescod Noonan, another University of Michigan (UM) student of the early 1960s who helped link SDS with the path-breaking civil rights group of the South, the Student Nonviolent Coordinating Committee (SNCC).

The extended reflections included here provide a number of pointed insights about the personal and political experience of these activists. Dick Flacks (see Chapter 33) and Bob Ross both distinguish the Port Huron notion of "participatory democracy" from "consensus" models of decision making that have been widely influential in subsequent movements. Maria Varela illuminates one of the religious routes (Roman Catholic social thought and youth movements) contributing to 1960s radicalism. Kim Moody explains why and how the role of "labor"—working-class and union-based struggles—were far from irrelevant or absent from the early New Left experience.

Other insights emerge from these chapters. For early members like Bob Ross, Dick and Mickey Flacks, and others, who had been raised in families and communities tied to the old Communist Party USA (even though they had left that behind in favor of a new, determinedly democratic radicalism), the stringent anticommunism of SDS's parent group, the League for Industrial Democracy (LID), was personally threatening.

Anti-anticommunism was a political necessity if the young SDS was to hold together. Women in early SDS recognized the dominance of men in the leadership ranks of the group (memorably challenged, later, by Casey Hayden's pioneering essay, with Mary King, "Sex and Caste"), but also they rarely surrendered the sense they had of themselves as political actors in their own right.[1] The experience of race was no less complicated. Martha Prescod Noonan genuinely felt that Ann Arbor SDS was a zone free of white racism. As explained here by Frank Joyce, it was the non-SDS group known as the Northern Student Movement (and later People against Racism) that would become more multiracial in composition and in his view more focused on combating northern white supremacy.

While the term "counterculture" was, for all intents and purposes, coined at a later date (around 1968, to identify youth whose nonconformity and apparent search for "alternative" lifestyles and communities had a more "cultural" than "political" bent), the attitudes and life practices of the early Port Huron cohort showed a significant streak leaning in that direction. Alongside the organizing imperatives of the movement, a style sensitive to emotion and direct interpersonal exchange (or as Barbara Haber puts it, "relational" politics)—as well as desire for a wholesale moral renovation both in their everyday lives and in the country at large—guided a good number of these activists, anticipating their own countercultural leanings later on, as Casey Hayden, Sharon Jeffrey Lehrer, and Alan Haber all suggest in varying ways. Nonetheless, the *political* vision of early SDS activists was remarkably ambitious. As Martha Prescod Noonan says, "We were all dealing with really BIG ideas, envisioning really BIG roles for ourselves, as well as originating and connecting to the BIG social movements of our time." The audacity of dedicated activists, no older than twenty-five years, in imagining they could help spark a social movement to transform the nation might still elicit wonder.

—Howard Brick

1 | A Call, Again
by Alan Haber

This is a call to the "sds inclusive," to scholars for a democratic society and, of course, students for a democratic society; I call to us survivors who have gotten here this far, seniors for a democratic society and all strugglers and seekers for real democracy. I call on singers and sisters; siblings and sons; socialists, sociologists, socialites, scientists, and syndicalists; even sectarians and skeptics; slackers, sleepers—semites for a democratic society are especially close to my heart—a to z, anarchists to zealots; workers of all sorts; people of the spirit and faith; all of us, whoever for a democratic society, those willing: continuing from Port Huron, what we began did not end.

University of Michigan Library
(Special Collections Library)

Our last words then were these: "If we appear to seek the unattainable, we do so to avoid the unimaginable."[1] And now "the unimaginable" is increasingly upon us. The situation is far more dire than then. I needn't color in the detail of the picture; enough is clear for all to see, and what we don't yet know for sure seems even worse.

Hence, "the unattainable" is far more urgent to attain.

Fortunately, what in our rhetorical flourish we called then "unattainable" is now conceivably closer at hand than may seem. Dark as is the age and the foretelling of corporate rule, shadow government, endless war, and climate calamity, the fifty years from then to now have not been lost. Tremendous learning has advanced in the whole society. And in breadth and depth, the movement has grown, and many particulars of better ways and of winning plans have been field tested.

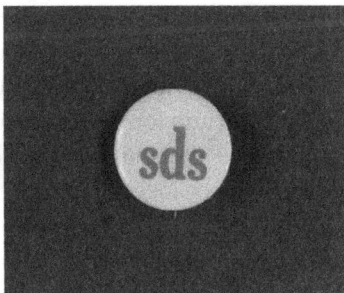

This call is that we more deeply re-member and re-animate the reality of "we." The "we" we knew are now some grown old, others gone, new generations come; we are fragmented and siloed, our we-ness near forgotten. We hardly know ourselves. Yet in all of us, I believe, "we" continues, latent, perched in the soul like a thing with feathers (as Emily Dickinson called our "hope"), singing the tune without the words and never stopping at all.

We are also now three and four generations—live, conscious, and caring and international, diverse in gender, class, and race and varied enough to reveal our common humanity. This call is that we turn our hearts to one another and to the "other," reaching across generations and divisions, seeing ourselves all in the same continuity of the freedom struggle. We are in a common predicament as the system of war and domination leads humanity and the life system itself to heartbreaking doom and bloody murder. The old bible wisdom says the sins of the fathers are unto the children, to the third and fourth generation. We need all of us, thinking together, to understand the situations we have inherited, what has happened, what needs to be changed, and how to do it.

We need to use the knowledges we have, to put what we have each learned in our diverse life courses to common tasks. In this we continue the ageless mission for humanity, making real the liberating vision of a freer life and wider justice for all.

Port Huron

What was most strong to me in the *Port Huron Statement* was its process as a whole. In its intention, its conception, its creation, its defense, and its promotion, Port Huron brought together an association of people who gave human reality to the high ideals and well-crafted words.

The *intention* was (and remains), as the membership card said, the better world that is possible, without war, exploitation, poverty, racism, "a democratic society where people at all levels have control of the decisions that affect them and the resources on which they are dependent," seeking change at the most basic level of economic, political, and social life.

The *conception* was to say the why, the what, and the way (our values, our vision, and our politics) in a "manifesto," a declaration of our selves.

The *creation* was by inviting everyone to participate, to model the participatory democracy that we put forward as a central idea.

The *defense* was the post–Port Huron struggle with the Old Left about anticommunism and union bureaucracy, when we declared our independence and our right to think our own thoughts.

The *promotion* was first in the multiplication: there was a "work democracy" in the office, teamwork for a change at 112 East 19th Street, New York City: physically typing stencils and printing thousands of copies—twenty-six sheets/two sides on a Gestetner mimeograph—and then collating and stapling. We were amplifying our statement with our energy. And then came the distribution: the mimeographed copies (and later the printed ones) went out the door, carried to chapters with organizers, sent to members, taken to meetings like the annual Congress of the National Student Association. We had made a physical thing, a karmic object to pass among us, and send outward. And then beyond the thing itself, the knowledge was created that this statement existed, speaking as "our generation" and putting many ideas together in accessible form. It helped conversation, both about the big picture and about the "we" declaring our intention to do something about it.

The *Port Huron Statement* came with a membership card of this intention. It was not an essay in a scholarly journal or academic anthology. It expressed a commitment to action.

To me, the community that followed from Port Huron became my family. My love, lovers, and heart developed in sds. I met my first wife, Barbara Jacobs, at Port Huron. My wife now, Odile Hugonot, was attracted to sds—before she met me—by an article she read in Amsterdam about the "Romanticism of the New Left in America." The recruits to sds back in the day were like my brothers and sisters, and I mourned specially the deaths of those whom I drew into the nexus.

Very many of us are still alive, and we collectively touched many people in our works, and they in turn touched many more. Our personal networks and our children and children's children reach everywhere.

The underemphasized aspect of the idea of participatory democracy was about "community." Deciding together creates recognition of other views and promotes understanding, growth, and innovation. Society improves as people participate. Participation is a way of human learning and development of cooperation and trust. These ideas, brought to Michigan by John Dewey, came to guide the elementary school, the high school, and the university I attended and were carried on by philosophy professor Arnold Kaufman in the 1950s, who taught a course on communism, socialism, and democracy and was the faculty advisor of the Political Issues Club and a friend from our beginning. Participatory democracy became the signature of the New Left in the 1960s. We made community among ourselves, a first principle of exemplary politics.

The ways of the lonely crowd in the 1950s were mostly apathy, alienation, anomie, abdication. But then came an awakening: engagement, empathy, empowerment, action.

As legend has it, the four from Greensboro said the night before their sit-in of February 1, 1960, "We've talked long enough, let's do something about it."

I believe everyone who joined "the movement" had their moment of decision before some willful action: Do I stay in ordinary reality or do I move? Do I cross over, thrusting myself into a maelstrom of many, the outcome of which I know not? From the sidewalk to the street? From the spectator to the actor? Then comes the instant of "yes," spontaneous or after long debate. And once one moves and is in the stream, a new reality prevails; new antecedents and expectations create a frame of transformation. One's perception of strength grows and is reinforced in the collective. The nonviolent movement touched the soul force in thousands and thousands of people, transmitted to thousands and thousands more. In the beloved community, every soul counted. Like being touched by an angel—one never forgets.

The reality, of course, over the years, was harder love than the first kiss, and we suffered from the patriarchy, racism, homophobia, classism, ageism, ignorance, and thoughtlessness endemic in our society and in growing up. We suffered also from the determined (illegal) campaign of the government to destroy what we and those like us were doing.

Life has moved on. Some have stayed obsessively engaged, like myself, others less so; everyone has focused and learned more about some part of the whole.

I believe there is a potency, a latent strength in American society, generations of people who have been touched by the freedom struggle, who remember, who never forgot, who are still doing it, or who are just beginning. People with ears to hear a reveille call. That's my belief. I find us everywhere.

Like that thing with feathers perched in the soul, there is an inner reserve, never having given up the big vision, what was once so palpable, that still pulsates when the music is right—an undercurrent of readiness for one more try or a first time. That is why people even bothered to have fifty-year conferences on the *Port Huron Statement*.

And what we did made history; and it is taught in the history books and has been incorporated in the revolutionary, radical democratic tradition in America.

That little blip of consciousness and commitment that we made at that time became, for half a decade at least and now still resonating, a fulcrum on which a lever can rest to move the world in these times.

Democracy remains a revolutionary idea; it is the voice and the means of the people to challenge the power of the system of the few and prevail.

Getting There

Someday I may write my story of doing it and how I came to the consciousness and commitment I did, but for here, it is enough to say I became a college student in 1954 at the University of Michigan.

My first moment of decision came early in my first semester one September day while I was on my happy way to morning class. I saw a group of people standing with signs at the other end of the wide stairway I was climbing into the Angell Hall classroom building. I had never seen a group of people with signs. I looked a minute. I saw it was a demonstration. Curious, I took a "deviation to the left," as it were, and walked across the stairway, south to north, to see what it was about. The protest signs were held by older students: it was about three professors the university had suspended for refusing to testify before the House Un-American Activities Committee. It was about McCarthyism, of which I had heard, a protest against a wrong action by the university, about academic freedom. Which side was I on? On that stairway, I joined the "freedom movement." I was enveloped in an energy field (mini, to be sure) of purpose and commitment that I knew in a feeling way to be true. I was welcomed and invited to meet the sign holders at lunch, after morning classes, and then began my political education.

Around an ongoing bridge game, in the basement cafe of the Michigan League, flowed fascinating conversations ranging from Wilhelm Reich, Orgone energy, and "The Mass Psychology of Fascism" to the university "censorship committee" that had to approve all "outside speakers" to folk music, Woody Guthrie and Pete Seeger, and the left.

Since there was no public discussion group on campus to consider such things that were controversial or banned from having outside speakers talk about, it seemed a good idea to start one. And since I was the only undergraduate around the table, I agreed to register a "Political Issues Club" as an official student organization. This allowed us to use university rooms and even have an office in the Student Activities Building, along with the Inter-Fraternity Council, the Pan-Hellenic (Sorority) Association, co-ops, Young Democrats, Young Republicans, Young Christians,

Sailing Club, and Student Government Council. There I began to learn the skill set of activism, about making meetings, publicity, typing stencils, running the mimeograph, posting leaflets, and so on.

We were an informal, changing group, generating programs every month or so, sometimes with speakers, sometimes not, with topics like school segregation, nuclear testing, the Hungarian uprising and its suppression, the war in Algeria, public housing, conscientious objection, national health care, the South African Freedom Charter, and so on. We even helped host Eleanor Roosevelt when she came to town, speaking on the Universal Declaration of Human Rights. We tried to get a place for Paul Robeson to sing at the university (denied) or anywhere in Ann Arbor (without success). I got a threatening letter from the German American Bund in Ann Arbor on Berlin Nazi Adolf Hitler stationery. We hosted Bayard Rustin when he was organizing marches on Washington for integrated schools, and we learned from him the history of nonviolence. May 17 was a date on the political calendar, the anniversary of the 1954 Supreme Court decision.

Some of the older ones among us had been connected, in pre-McCarthy times, with the then more vibrant Student League for Industrial Democracy (SLID), and they wrote to the New York office of the League for Industrial Democracy (LID) suggesting they send a recruiter to Ann Arbor, perhaps making me a member and the Political Issues Club into a SLID chapter.

André Schiffrin, of later publishing fame, came from the East to Ann Arbor in 1957 and told me about SLID. There was no talk I remember of changing SLID's name, though I said at the time "slid" was all too descriptive of the state of the organization as he described it, with but a few chapters, a shadow of the thousands of members it had once had. Our local group saw no persuasive reason then to affiliate, though national organization and international connections were seen as important.

I was invited to join SLID's executive committee in 1958, and I accepted, greatly influenced by the offer of a plane ticket to New York for the meeting. I had been to New York for my high school senior trip in 1954 and loved the jazz. I was introduced to adult political players in the social-democratic left and unions (remembering A. Philip Randolph, A. J. Muste, Norman Thomas, Jim Farmer) and the organizations of the student Cold War. I saw what a political office looked like, with years of files showing the continuities of commitment and "address-o-graph plates" for every member keeping up the communication network.

Back at school, my candle was burning at all ends: I was ever more excited about my studies in the history of science and the shifts from feudalism to capitalism (and the party scene was compelling as well), kept with the Political Issues Club, and joined the Student Government Council, first by appointment and then election. Through student government, I became part of the national student organization world. (I also worked, grinding mirrors and running an infrared spectrometer in the Physics Department.)

In August 1959, I was invited back for another (transportation-paid) meeting in New York, and this time I was asked to be vice president of SLID. Another moment of decision: I first hesitated, saying we had to change the name before I would get more involved; we needed to imagine how to reverse the slide of SLID. Perhaps that precipitated or renewed a simmering discussion in the old SLID. A number of names were ventured. The discussion of "Students for a Democratic Society" was concerned with differentiating us from the student group of the liberal Americans for Democratic Action—Students for Democratic Action. The "a" we put in made us sound different. Thus SDS came into being.

Once the name was changed, I was ready and eager to make the new organization. When asked to propose the next year's program, I suggested (presciently) a spring 1960 "National Conference on Human Rights in the North," to be hosted in Ann Arbor and organized, I hoped, by the Political Issues Club.

When I got back to Ann Arbor and the next school year began, something had changed—a different atmosphere—in my world. Nineteen fifty-nine was the fifth year I convened the fall meetings of the Political Issues Club, usually pretty thinly attended, low-key affairs. The new students who came in that year, though, were unlike any before, and unlike me too. Eager, bold, ready, activist, fresh: Sharon Jeffrey, Carol Cohen, Nancy Press, Bobbie Cohen, Bob Ross, Dickie Magidoff, Brian Glick, Ken McEldowney—and I omit or forget many names. These are the people who took on the job of organizing that first sds conference. Theirs was a loving, open, inviting energy; in my mind they were the true sds beginners.

The conference, "ACT NOW!," from April 28 to May 1, 1960, became in effect the founding meeting of sds. A great activist mix of several hundred people came, North and South, black and white, students, faculty, unions, and church, a liaison with the new SNCC, fraternal organizations and student governments, and journalists, including Tom Hayden, who was about to become editor of the *Michigan Daily* for the next year.

The LID staffer (Aryeh Neier, who later worked long for Human Rights Watch and George Soros's Open Society Foundation) liked the affair so much he offered me a job organizing sds nationally, to be paid as the student field secretary of the LID. I thought about it for a moment and accepted. I had already committed myself, job or no. I moved to New York in June 1960, also in time for the formal convention reorganizing SLID as sds. Dwight Macdonald spoke, and quite a few "members" from Ann Arbor, as well as New York residents who had been engaged by the "human rights" conference, attended. I met Gabriel Kolko there and others from the old SLID. The convention elected me president of sds, complementing my "staff" job as traveler for the LID.

I got sds more engaged in action and extended our connections, attending the National Student Congress in Minneapolis that summer and traveling to SNCC's steering committee meetings in Atlanta. LID got worried. Stalwart unionists and socialists (and Cold War warriors) on their board, doubting I had the astute judgment needed in the political world they knew, hesitated to risk their organization in my hands. They feared that I, and we, were too open and friendly, likely soft on "Stalinists," likely "Stalinoid" ourselves.

I was writing and gathering contributions for an intended fall 1960 movement newsletter. I had written an article in our magazine, *Venture*, titled "From Protest to Radicalism." The newsletter was intended as an educational and organizing tool to introduce sds to the thousands of activists whose names I had gathered—petition signers, conference attendees, people I'd met face to face. The newsletter would report on what we saw in the movement. It would offer a political, economic, historical analysis of racism and discrimination and a framework for the civil rights struggle that was going on and that people were joining all over the country.

I was opening the big tent. I was not being exclusive. I was too naive, according to the battle-scarred LID. And so they changed their minds, and around Thanksgiving they fired me from my job as student field secretary, expecting I would go back to Michigan. I was already there, on the road, when I received notice that they had suppressed the movement newsletter, the address list, and me. However, having been elected president by the membership in the June convention, I returned to occupy the office in New York, living on such dues as came in the mail slot, and I didn't go away. The old SLID people weren't interested in the new sds, and the LID eventually rehired me, reservations and all, because, ultimately, they needed a student organization to justify their funding from the labor movement.

When they rehired me, the one condition was that we not have an annual convention in 1961 but wait until 1962, hoping that people they knew better would return to the organization, and their fears would be allayed. That delay is why we wanted to make a big deal out of the 1962 meeting and were impatient to declare ourselves.

In December 1961 at our national "executive committee" meeting in Ann Arbor, we began planning the convention, eager for an early meeting in June. And we agreed we would focus the meeting on making a "manifesto" as well as selecting new officers and getting organized.

Why Manifesto?

Manifestoes were in the air, blowing in the wind, as it were. I think we set on a manifesto because there had come to be a bond connecting us that called out to be affirmed, even though it was wordless and without ideology or antecedent. The bond was "the movement," the self-liberating experience of joining in a collective shift and focusing of energy, being caught up in the dance, with my mind set on freedom.

It's so real we want to name it, we want to flesh it out, give it words.

Had we come from one or another of the left antecedents, the words would be given to us, from which we would begin. But we were a "new left." I called us indigenous radicals, tracing from Upton Sinclair, Jack London, and Clarence Darrow. Those agitators circuited the campuses decrying the "passionless pursuit of passionless knowledge," as Harvard president Charles W. Eliot sought to name the mission of the university. We, like them, were for shaking up the university, putting forward the urgencies of social justice, seeing the total community as our classroom, and "making history" our final exam.

When I say that "we" produced our manifesto, it is hard to say just who "we" were. My mode of organizing was to go to places, to meetings, and meet people and watch—and when the occasion presented itself, ask people or a person if they wanted to help make a movement organization, work together, be friends, be a member, have a card—for a better world.

I was not particularly pushing membership, though I always had cards; I was pushing eye-to-eye, simpatico. Rarely did I ask people who didn't want to say yes. And out of this open invitation, there came together an amazing steering committee of beautiful people, trusting enough in one another to try to make something happen together, at least to the next step, and then look again.

There was something among us, which some say I conveyed in my open way of inviting the individuals who made up the first generation of sds. I would say now that this something was the common striving, the life force, the chi in each of us that is incomplete without the all of us.

The people who came to the early sds came with activist passion. The ideologues mostly stayed elsewhere, with the Young Peoples Socialist League or Student Peace Union or journals of review and thought.

So when it came time for all of us to get together, it seemed altogether fitting and proper that we would think about what we would say to one another, about who we were. The intent was a matter not of detached analysis but of collective thinking and talking so that we could better act together and realize changes in the world that we sought.

Our manifesto was our talking, and actually the first thing we said is, let's keep talking. This was a "statement" to consider further, not a manifesto forever and all. The method we adopted in 1961 was to ask and to listen, to reflect back and ask again, listen further, put it all together, and reflect it back as a draft. And then to consider together, face to face.

Tom Hayden is the worker in the writing craft who put it all together. He had manifesto on the mind before we even began. We in the New York office put out a call to the "membership," everyone on any list that we had of people we connected with: "What should be in a manifesto?" People wrote back, and we typed up a newsletter of replies and mailed it back to people as a first reflection of our oneness, with these questions: What is left out? What is distorted? What more is needed? And again people wrote back and we reflected back again and then gave it all to Tom to shape into a draft.

We had an sds apartment on West 21st Street, in the Chelsea District, across Manhattan from the office. Parts of the draft were discussed there, before being carried over to the office to be retyped on stencils and mimeographed, collated, and so on. Some people, such as Michael Vester and Robb Burlage, were consulted further. Stanley Aronowitz was a regular. We barely got the draft together and stapled before leaving for Port Huron. And the convention itself broke it into parts, considered it again as a whole, and gave instructions for revisions to the styles committee.

The quality of the document and its capacity to speak to people in ways that can be heard reflects not only Tom's skill as a writer but also the many voices that helped give shape to what needed expression. E pluribus unum in fifty pages. It gave a multivoiced expression to the insurgency of the time.

The Port Huron initiative led us through a series of projects over the following five years, in retrospect a program of field research. The Political Education Project (PEP) focused on electoral action, voting and registration, and free and fair elections. We looked for a political realignment. We presumed at some time we would be in the electoral field. The Peace Research and Education Project (PREP) examined the university in the Cold War, the role of weapons research and money penetrating the university. We began the analysis of who rules in America and in the military-intellectual-industrial-congressional complex of the power structure. The Economic Research and Action Project (ERAP) took our work across class lines into the communities of the poor, expanded experience in models of community organization, and practiced door-to-door local organizing, recreating the commons in community where political questions can be talked about. The Radical Education Project (REP) concentrated on the connections of action and education and on writing so ordinary people have a knowledge base about action campaigns. The Freedom Schools in the Mississippi Summer were an inspiration, as were the teach-ins, the free university initiatives, and the continuing work of the Highlander Folk School in Tennessee.

For many of us there at Port Huron, the late-1960s Radicals in the Professions Project laid out a "long haul" perspective. How do students who graduate as radicals survive in the very conservative reality outside the campus? We described an extended community, "getting by with a little help from our friends," creating insurgencies and affinity groups in every profession and field where we found ourselves such as law, medicine, economics, social work, planning, and so on. And now in almost all professional fields there are the likes of Historians against the War, Union of Radical Political Economics, Humanist Sociologists, Health Policy Advisory Council, Midwest Academy Organizers School, and more.

End of sds

We tried to envision a "Movement for a Democratic Society" as an allied postcollege community into which sdsers could move, an organization that could be a factor in the overall political scene—multi-issue, coalition building, big tent, changing the system, in your face, keeping up the sds method.

Our efforts to project poststudent ongoingness were not successful. We imagined that political differences could be debated and resolved in our own internal democracy. Different views of the revolution split the New Left just as they had the Old. COINTELPRO didn't help. The violence of the war, repression, and assassinations made everyone a little crazy.

The hypermilitancy at the end of the 1960s and early 1970s was mostly symbolic. Yet the urgency to "imagine a revolution" created breaks among us. Those of us who thought a revolution might take longer than the day after yesterday came to seem "counterrevolutionary," or "in the way." And so, ironically, like Kennedy, whom I saw as the reasonable face of the government, sds, which was the reasonable face of the revolution, was finished by a symbolic assassination—our mailing lists dumped into the Hudson River, as a rebel of the time is said to have bragged, and later lamented.[2]

In my view, it would have been better if the continuity of the names and the networks had not been drowned like a puppy. It was a sad moment when dogmatism prevailed and inclusiveness failed. We had created a political commons where everyone, pretty much, was welcome and ideas could be hashed out, projects and actions reported, memory accumulated.

Or perhaps, indeed, it was revolutionary farsightedness that dissolved an organizational form that had ceased to serve and could no longer embrace the exponential growth and diversity of the movement. sds outgrew itself. It had by the midsixties essentially severed its ties with the LID, which had grown increasingly anticommunist in a paranoid way and prowar. Thus there was no friendly social-democratic progressive home to which we could return. An independent left did continue out of sds, expressing itself in the "Port Authority Statement" issued in 1967 by the revolutionary "Praxis Axis" group of New York and, more widely—later in the 1990s—in the Committees of Correspondence for Democracy and Socialism, as well as in a succession of annual gatherings, commie camps, Socialist Scholars Conferences, Left Forums, social forums, coalitions, march committees, and so on.[3]

Some took a direction into the working class as workers, union staff, or legal aid attorneys. And while far from successful, the reform movements and rank-and-file groups in the labor movement are alive and sometimes ascendant.

After sds

I view the "end of sds time" both as the completion (or exhaustion) of a political path and as a budding and blooming interlude, when every one of us went each our particular path. There was a lot of disruption. My life turned on its head. People explored ten thousand different beautiful ways, and some in ways less beautiful, but most pressing the bounds of freedom and liberation wherever oppression was felt. The personal became political and vice versa. In all directions, creativity was let loose. If we could only cooperate enough to reconnect and focus this diversity of learning, the world could be changed. That is the reason of this call.

Personally, I got the smell of wood. At that point in 1969, living in Berkeley, California, I was a freelance intellectual, an academic without walls, writing about poverty, the American underclass, and new careers for the poor and studying, in particular, how independent political groups could develop an economic base to sustain political education and organizing in the local community. I lived on grant money. After sds ceased to be a reference point and had no interest in my researches, I had to change my life. I became a woodworker.

I continued to act out the "do it," politics-by-example implicit in the *Port Huron Statement*.

I took the grant money I had at the time, bought machinery, and began a woodshop to teach myself and others a trade and make enough at it to live and participate. We called it our "Splinter Group," a collective working with wood. We learned there were thousands of collectives and worker cooperatives and a whole alternative economy of local self-reliance. I also learned the trade and the satisfaction of right livelihood.

The next stage on my "doing it" was beginning and, being in a commune, breaking out of the traditional family ways I had always assumed. Our commune was called "the Circus," from the E. E. Cummings line "damn everything but the circus." We became enmeshed in an urban-rural, low-income, mutual-aid, farm-to-family support network, a web of human connection of individual associations and households in our Bay Area bioregion. Similar webs appeared throughout the state and in every other bioregion; I could travel anywhere in the country, and I found us everywhere.

Beyond the communal household, what is a sustainable neighborhood? All over the country, people were beginning participatory planning, struggling against the onslaught of urban renewal/removal. In the old Ocean View neighborhood of Berkeley, environmentalists and craftspeople built an integral urban house and proposed an integral neighborhood, converting to a sustainable energy system and training people to rehabilitate their own homes and establish a business to do further rehab work in the city.

Changing the neighborhood engaged us in a contest with mainstream liberal Democrats and "developers" who dominated city politics, blocked significant innovation, and denied attention to the poor and not-so-rich who lived in Ocean View. The "we" of the time, an ad hoc assemblage of grass roots activists, of which I was one, recruited and persuaded a man new to town, a black radical activist, to run for mayor and champion a people's program of community self-reliance; renewable energy; a fiber-optic information utility; and manufacturing for local transportation, independent living, and other good ideas. A Community Memory project, before the Internet, was an early recognition that open-source information is essential for democratic politics.

In a six-month campaign, 1978–79, we went door to door in every precinct; we defeated the very good liberal person in the local Democratic Party organization, and then we were victorious in the general election and won for mayor. It was joyous to discover an election can be won. No celebrity name recognition or high oratory but a good interesting program and a grassroots, person-to-person, direct outreach.

After the mayor's election, which we ran from the Circus commune, our ad hoc coalition needed a base for the long haul. A lot of politics is around the kitchen table, but collective action and movement also need places outside the home where ideas get talked about, about what's happening and what to do. We established the "Long Haul" as a movement center based on a "land trust," in whose name our building was "owned," and we had a "lease in perpetuity, until victory." Offices, meeting spaces, kitchens, computer connectivity, libraries, and info shop sales also came to provide a base for the quarterly newspaper *The Slingshot* for free national and international distribution and a calendar, "Slingshot Organizer," that generates sufficient income to keep the center going—still strong after all these years, thirty-six now, since 1979. There are comparable activist and peace centers in many communities.

In this time, I ran an independent union presidential campaign, 1974–76, to see if it could be done (yes) and work on the steps in a winning plan. I also made a "peace table" projecting the meetings needed to shift from the war system to the peace system. And I connected with the "spiritual" and sacred side of politics and began to make Arks for the Torah.

The Commons

In all this evolution of learning and doing, one memory only implicit in the *Port Huron Statement* has emerged through critical scholarship for democratic society, a memory of "the commons" and a recognition of its centrality in the history of the freedom struggle around the world. For nearly everywhere, including now, there has been the class of takers, monopolizers, privatizers, kings, barons, dictators, corporations, and bankers trying to get exclusive use of lands and resources that were in the common wealth, that had belonged to all. The commons is essential to collective survival. The people's strength is in community: this was the unexamined part of participatory democracy. Democracy also requires space for people to interact and meet. Increasingly, it is knowledge that the powers-that-have-been would privatize; longer ago and still, it was the land and water they take, expropriating and exploiting. Protecting and reclaiming the commons—stopping the thieves—is now a common theme connecting struggles all over the world.

We hold together an intellectual commons. Fifty years ago, we put the *Port Huron Statement* into that commons, and in the years since we have added to our knowledge commons and our collective experience. My experience, local, state, national, and global, in the system and outside, is tiny compared to what we all know together and our collective creativity. I believe we know enough to change the world, and there are enough of us, here and worldwide, to attain the unattainable, forestall the unimaginable.

If only:
if we would re-member ourselves as a "we,"
if we would each bring the knowledge we have,
if we would think together, as before, what is "the Manifesto for Now,"
if we would carry the urgency through our personal networks and to
    our neighbors,
if we would open source our sources and the inspirations of "Radical
    Democracy,"
if we would make a "Freedom School" in every precinct where we live
    and be teachers for democracy,
if we would make a composite of people's programs and put
    alternatives before the voters in every place where there is a
    candidate and a chance for a free and fair election, including the
    next presidential contests,
if we would agree to cooperate, put ego aside, initiate an all-fronts
    offensive, promote new insurgencies wherever justice and human
    rights require.
If only we would be strong and of good courage and just do it!

As at Port Huron, my job is to urge people off the beach and into the workshops to the tasks at hand.

Please answer this call. Contact me at megiddo@umich.edu.

2 | Experiencing the Sixties at the Intersection of SDS and SNCC

by Martha Prescod Noonan

If I had a hammer, I'd hammer in the morning
I'd hammer in the evening, all over this land
I'd hammer out danger, I'd hammer out a warning
I'd hammer out love between my brothers and my sisters
All over this land.

If I had a bell, I'd ring it in the morning
I'd ring it in the evening, all over this land
I'd ring out danger, I'd ring out a warning
I'd ring out love between my brothers and my sisters
All over this land.

If I had a song, I'd sing it in the morning
I'd sing it in the evening, all over this land
I'd sing out danger, I'd sing out a warning
I'd sing out love between my brothers and my sisters
All over this land.[1]

I begin with this song, written by Pete Seeger and Lee Hays, that became a favorite of folks in Students for a Democratic Society (SDS) and of people in the Student Nonviolent Coordinating Committee (SNCC), including Mrs. Fannie Lou Hamer. The words symbolize what the sixties meant for me as an individual spending my college years connected to both SDS and SNCC. At the end of this chapter, I will discuss some of the lessons I learned as a result of my association with both groups. First I want to address what it was like to be a black person, a woman, and—to use a term that I will explain fully later—a "little person" within the SDS community. Looking back today with all our current understanding of past and present social discriminations and hierarchies, my association with SDS was not one of being or feeling "less than" but one that was enriching and empowering for me. How was this so?

The answer lies, I think, with my own personal background, the surrounding historical activism, and the openness and commitments within early SDS. Growing up in Providence, Rhode Island, I lived with what I would categorize as a face-to-face miniracism, which was part of my daily life even as a young child. Usually this kind of racism was manifested in petty meanness, a series of not-so-subtle exclusions and put-downs, like the public library finding an excuse not to award me a reading prize that I deserved, being excluded from a girls' glee club that held dances with boys' choruses, or my ninth-grade math teacher refusing to help me catch up after I'd been out for several weeks with the German measles. "You're too dumb to learn algebra," she told me. When I taught myself and did exceptionally well on our final exam, she said, "Well, I don't know how you did it. I know you didn't cheat, though, because I watched you through the entire exam."

Occasionally, it was dangerous or physically painful. When I was six, we moved from one all-white neighborhood to another. Initially, our new neighbors threw stones into our home and once tried to set the house on fire. The most frightening experience was when a white man, after imbibing at the neighborhood bar, entered our backyard waving a gun and threatening to kill my father and me if we did not leave at once.

I still remember how it felt when shortly after we moved in, one of the older boys in the neighborhood attacked me, repeatedly punching me in the stomach. Later, when I was in high school, my mother found and sent me to a University of Michigan dentist in Providence. After my first visit, he scheduled me on his lunch hour when there were no other patients in the office. He did not give me Novocain, I soon figured out, because he wanted to finish quickly before his afternoon patients arrived. Although my cavities were not especially deep and I stopped going to him after two or three visits, this process hurt enough that I was terrified of going to the dentist for years.

From a young age, I heard adults talking about their own challenges navigating through American racism. Many, like my mother, were never able to find employment close to the level of their education, training, or abilities. Among the various recollections she shared with me about her life as a black woman were her experiences here at the University of Michigan in the early twenties. In 1921, she graduated from high school in Ann Arbor at fourteen with a stellar record. Rather than being embraced by the university for her accomplishments, her initial attempt to attend was rebuffed by a university official telling her she was too young to be admitted and should go to work instead. Afterward, one of her best friends, Letty Wickliffe, also African American and already at Michigan, informed my mother of a university regulation that allowed any state high school graduate to attend summer school and then matriculate at the university if they maintained a B average. My mother got in through this back door.

She graduated in only three years at the age of seventeen while working to help support her mother and brother. Her father, a barber who had had a shop and family living quarters at 117 E. Ann Street, had died when she was nine years old. Next my mother went on to the university's law school. She explained to me that the law school had accepted her and a number of other black students, not realizing their race because they all had graduated from predominately white universities. To undo this situation, she believed, the law school unfairly flunked them all out.

Nevertheless, she was proud of her connection to the University of Michigan and was so determined that I attend that she found a job in Michigan at the beginning of my junior year in high school to be certain to qualify for in-state tuition. This meant she lived apart from my father and me until I graduated from high school. Then we moved to join her in Detroit. "You don't need college counseling," she told me, "You are going to the University of Michigan, unless you can't get in, and then you'll have to go to Michigan State." "The Victors," with all its flourishes and grandeur, was one of the few songs she could sit down at the piano and play from memory throughout her life and one of the first songs she taught me, along with "The House I Live In," an ode to democracy and diversity.

Still, neither my parents nor I thought that my years at the University of Michigan would be racially diverse. We knew I would be attending classes and living in a dorm with white students when I enrolled in fall 1961, but we expected that my social life would be spent exclusively in the company of other African American students. In addition to obtaining a first-rate education, my mother encouraged me to make lifelong friendships and connections among the other black students in college and, of course, as was common at that time, to look for a husband. "It's unlikely," she would remark, "that you will be in the company of so many bright and gifted young black folks, all in one place, ever again." After so many years of being the only black child in my neighborhood and the only black student or one of two at school, I was really looking forward to no longer being *the* black student and becoming a part of the larger group of the some three hundred black students then on campus.

Instead I ended up as the only black undergraduate in VOICE, the SDS chapter on campus. Once in my sophomore year, thinking my parents would feel better about my association with VOICE if they met the whole crew, I asked my mother and father to come to campus on an afternoon when everyone was gathered at Casey and Tom Hayden's house. (After all, my parents had been active in the Progressive Party.) My mom and dad walked through the Arch Street house in a circle, from the living room through the bedroom around to the kitchen and back out the front hall, engaging in polite conversation as they met everyone. By that time, my father, a former optometrist, had lost his sight. When we reached the sidewalk, he and my mother prepared to leave and go back to Detroit. His parting words, spoken with great disappointment, were, "Martha Susan, I may be blind, but I am certain that there was no one in that house that looks like you."

At the time, I just shrugged my shoulders and mumbled something about his being correct. I really had no explanation for him and couldn't have articulated why I was in VOICE other than to say it was where I felt I belonged on campus. I do know that in SDS/VOICE, I found an absence of the kinds of racism and racial stereotyping that had always been a part of my life. There was complete inclusiveness without the subtle put-downs, paternalism, and assumptions of ignorance that I have found in most other similar situations. There were no "put-ups," either—that is, the excessive adulation and praise that can be typical in some leftist groups. As I think about that little circle of Joan and Mark Chesler, Mickey (Miriam) and Dick Flacks, Barbara and Al Haber, Casey and Tom Hayden, Nancy and Andy Hawley, Sharon Jeffrey, Bob Ross, Dick Magidoff, Nancy Hollander, and others, in part, I believe it was because they were just good people. Also, from the little I know of their backgrounds, I suspect that most of these early VOICE members had already had interracial experiences and had already wrestled through quite a bit.

Most importantly, many SDSers had already had direct contact with the early stages of the Black Freedom Movement and understood that this movement had the potential to greatly liberalize—maybe even radicalize— American society and politics. For example, Casey Hayden was involved the early sit-ins in Austin, Texas; Tom was part of the 1961 Freedom Rides; and VOICE members had raised food and supplies for black residents of Haywood and Fayette Counties in Tennessee who lost their residences and jobs when they tried to register to vote in 1959 and 1960. Through this connection with black activism, SDSers had direct experience with black students and community members engaged in a heroic struggle, thus learning that there were indeed strengths in the black community and qualities worthy of admiration. They also saw firsthand the bravery and courage required to be black in America during the fifties and sixties.

Although both my political and social life centered around SDS/VOICE, I did pledge a predominately black sorority, Delta Sigma Theta. This was another legacy from my mother and her friend, Letty Wickliffe, whom I called Aunt Letty. Aunt Letty was a founding member of the chapter at the university, and my mother crossed shortly afterward. (I was a little amazed the sorority accepted me, given my activism and related dressing down.) One day I might be in the Fishbowl staffing a political table and the next, I might be dressed in sorority colors, holding a yellow cloth duck and marching in formation with the other pledges. I was comfortable with this duality, feeling at home in both places, though eventually my efforts to support the Southern Freedom Movement took up more of my time and the sorority less.

Just as with race, I did not feel any particular restrictions or put-downs as a woman in VOICE. Whenever I have spoken or written about what it was like to be a young woman while working for SNCC in the South or doing support work in the North, I have said that I had no real idea of what the men were thinking, I only know how I was treated, and I never had a sense of being held back or held down. I pretty much did whatever it was I could think up to do. It was the same for me as a member of VOICE. I felt free to initiate and direct activities rather than just follow the plans made within the organization. My first year on campus, I started fund-raising for SNCC and, in my sophomore year, began and headed a Friends of SNCC chapter there. Soon we had an office in the Student Activities Building, but the Friends of SNCC group was initially based in the women's Osterweil Co-op where I and several of the key members of the chapter—Helen Jacobson, Sue Wender, and Jill Hamberg—lived. We were all also VOICE members. Helen really served as Friends of SNCC cochair, and we ladies figured out what we were going to do.

We held one of the earliest concerts for the SNCC Freedom Singers in the country and quickly organized a citywide food drive after receiving a letter from Bob Moses, head of SNCC's Mississippi project, explaining that local Mississippians who tried to register to vote often lost their means of support and needed food. Our vanload of food was the first response to the national outreach Moses had made. The two Michigan State University students who drove the truck to Mississippi over the Christmas break were immediately arrested, and our support work turned to keeping them safe in jail, raising bond money, and campaigning to get their charges dropped. Our work for the Southern Freedom Movement not only enjoyed the full support of VOICE members but also benefitted from their sharing organizing tips with us.

Several times, we reformed our Friends of SNCC group as an ad hoc committee for other causes. Once, during the Cuban Missile Crisis, we young women played a significant role in organizing a national protest against the US blockade of the island. I spoke with Helen Jacobson recently, and those years were so active, we can't remember which other protests our little ad hoc committees worked on and which were more under VOICE's umbrella. Things were overlapping and mutually supported. I do recall that more than once, I called Quaker activists Fran and Johan Eliot, who had lent us their van to take the food we raised to Mississippi, to ask to use their van again to go to protest marches in Washington, DC. I also remember that we demonstrated locally against the visit of South Vietnamese president's wife Madame Nhu to the United States and on another occasion against the murder of Patrice Lumumba, carrying picket signs that read, "I don't want to live in Uncle Tshombe's cabin."

Both in SNCC and in SDS, the slightly older women were my role models. They were more important to me than what the men in both organizations thought and did. Many of these women were so exceptional that they set a standard I didn't expect to achieve, but I hoped I could just be a bit like them. Through civil rights activism, I met and sometimes worked with women like Rosa Parks, Ella Baker, Diane Nash, and Fannie Lou Hamer. Through SDS, I came to admire Elise Boulding (a sociologist and another Quaker activist), Millie Jeffrey (Sharon Jeffrey's mother), Mickey Flacks, and Casey Hayden. With the exception of Sharon's mother, who held high positions in the UAW and the national Democratic Party, none of these women held any powerful offices or positions, but they certainly modeled strength and independence. With women like these in view, men's opinions and actions faded into the background.

Of course, I grew up with women who also demonstrated these qualities in daily life. I think particularly of my mother—who became the major breadwinner in our family after my father's sight failed—and my Aunt Letty. A lifelong Republican, Aunt Letty became a major force in Ann Arbor community issues after she retired from teaching gifted and special needs children.

I suspect my relationship with SDS men was somewhat limited, since I did not expect to date within that group. Among my race-conscious parents' greatest fears regarding my SDS/VOICE affiliation was that I would bring home a white husband and as a result not remain an integral part of the black community. At the same time I felt I belonged in VOICE, I also felt as my parents did that my future life and work should and would be within the black community. We agreed that it was my responsibility to use whatever skills and talents I developed for the benefit of my community, and, further, it was my duty to strive to go as far as I was able educationally. For my parents, this meant earning a professional degree, specifically becoming a minister, doctor, or lawyer. My mother, in particular, wanted the satisfaction of seeing me graduate from the University of Michigan Law School.[2]

My main identity in SDS/VOICE was not so much as a black person or as a young woman but more as what some of us called ourselves then, "a little person." SDS "little persons," as I recall, were both male and female. We were the younger, first- and second-year students rather than upperclass and graduate students. We had no name recognition on campus, like Tom Hayden and Bob Ross, and we didn't say much at the Friday-night "Studies on the Left" sessions held in the Haydens' basement, partially because we didn't always do all the heavy reading. Our role was clear: we were the audience—there to listen and learn.

As "little persons," however, we were not diminished. I felt we were at the beginning of the same path the big people had already walked. We were right there going to all the events and meetings with all the other SDS folks. I had no sense that the "big people" were formally or informally doing things together that excluded us "little people." We were all dealing with really BIG ideas, envisioning really BIG roles for ourselves as well as originating and connecting to the BIG social movements of our time. We were all singing along with Joan Baez and Bob Dylan when they were performing in high school auditoriums in Ann Arbor. We were all listening to people like Michael Harrington and Mario Savio when they came to campus. It was so wonderful, exciting, and empowering.

I would use these same words to describe what is was like to live the sixties connected to both SDS and SNCC—wonderful, exciting, and empowering. It was a time of learning new lessons and grasping fresh ideas. Although we activists often talked about college as irrelevant, as unrelated to the real world we were seeing, I believe that our activities and discussions within SDS/VOICE heightened our interest in and understanding of certain college classes. The classes, in turn, sometimes offered insights into political activism and regularly strengthened the skills we needed for our SDS/VOICE work and discussions. (Of course, when I brought up this notion of the irrelevancy of school with my parents, it gave them something else to worry about, a position they couldn't even begin to fathom.) At the same time we talked about academic irrelevancy, we were still doing the college thing, some like me less wholeheartedly than others, reading Camus, taking Philosophy 101, and studying other world cultures as well as our own.

When I spent my junior year at Wayne State University, I took one of my most exciting and life-changing classes. It was about the history of Reconstruction. Because of my exposure in SDS and SNCC to social change, I understood quickly from our readings and the material presented in class that the Emancipation Proclamation did not actually free anyone. I saw that the actions of tens of thousands of slaves, who began freeing themselves and crossing into union lines, actually made the Proclamation imaginable. Additionally, the slaves' actions made slavery a central issue of a war that was supposed to be limited to preserving the union. I learned that thousands of slaves escaped the South and joined the Union army as requested in the Proclamation and so fought for their freedom two times over and helped Lincoln win the Civil War. What a concept—my slave ancestors, without outside guidance, acting in their own self-interest and thus determining a national policy that in turn was favorable to the slaves' interests. This was a huge personal and political lesson for me as a young person involved in social activism and one I don't think was shared by the other members of the class, who were all white and not connected to SDS or SNCC. At the same time I recognized how history can be distorted, with Lincoln remembered as the "Great Emancipator" and the slaves who did so much to gain their freedom remembered with the passive term "freedmen."

Before taking the class on Reconstruction, I had already learned several key lessons and new ideas related to social activism outside of the classroom. The fall semester of my first year on campus, Curtis Hayes, a young man from SNCC's McComb, Mississippi, project came to the Guild House ministry on campus to describe SNCC's work and philosophy as the organization moved into community organizing. Also that fall, I heard Bob Ross giving a speech out on the Diag. He included in his talk a description of how VOICE members had gotten the previous dean of women fired because of her racially discriminating actions. There it was, from Curtis and Bob, a huge lesson—people my age could come together and do something to fight against racism. Even though I had been following the southern student movement from afar since I was in high school and wanted to join it, this message was not solidified for me until I met activists around my age face to face.

The next semester, I learned more about the Southern Freedom Movement when Tom Hayden came to campus fresh from jail in Albany, Georgia, and then invited VOICE folks to a 1962 SDS/SNCC spring conference in Chapel Hill, North Carolina. SDS members Sharon Jeffrey and Mike Zweig, along with my dorm mate Kathy Inness, local activist Dick Sleet, and I, put in $5 each for gas, packed up oranges and sandwiches, and rode back and forth at night to attend this weekend conference. The sessions consisted of reports by SNCC field secretaries on the community organizing work they were doing and the demonstrations they were holding. Music began and punctuated every session. In between, we sat on the grass and talked with individual SNCC folk about what they hoped to accomplish.

There were less than one hundred people at this conference. Together they were the core of the predominately black student groups that ended segregation and won the vote in the South as well as the predominately white groups that spearheaded the antiwar protests that ended the war in Vietnam. As I watched history unfold in the sixties, I learned that in the right historical circumstances, just a small number of dedicated people could have a huge effect on events.

That same semester, I also learned more about the purposes and goals of SDS when I helped type Hayden's early memos that led to the *Port Huron Statement*. In those days multiple copies were made by first typing a stencil that would be run off on an ink-filled roller. My typing skills were fairly basic and my recollection is that we were sometimes working with handwritten notes, so I had to read everything I was typing word for word while continuing to check for typing errors.

Through these connections, I learned to think on a much broader and more concrete scale. When SNCC people talked about building a civil rights movement in Mississippi, they insisted that addressing the needs of black people in Mississippi would by definition take care of the needs of black people everywhere else in the country. When SNCC people talked about community organization, they talked about building a South-wide mass movement based in the people hardest hit by racism that would move the country as a whole in a more liberal—perhaps radical—direction.

SDSers were also talking and writing about racism and different methods of organizing. They were talking about making needed change in ever-widening circles from campus issues to issues in our home communities to national and global ones. The *Port Huron Statement* in particular set lofty goals like ending war, hatred, and hunger.

Within these discussions was a new basis for how we would live our lives. Rather than choosing a standard profession or job, our profession or lifetime job would be working to make a better world and fighting for social change. This was not the kind of charity work that people today seem to be following in the tradition of the sixties. (I get a little upset when I see the Martin Luther King Jr. holiday turned into clean-up, sweep-up activities.) It was not about "giving back" or "helping those less fortunate" or doing something for other people. It was about making social change with the understanding that we are all linked together on this earth. It was a "doing with"—not "doing for"—people who were not treated fairly.

I learned to organize on an open-door basis. Both organizations essentially took in whoever came, and they refused to redbait. While involved with both groups, I met people with various political philosophies, religious beliefs, and humanitarian concerns—all able to unite for larger, more encompassing goals. In the early sixties, I believe this was a key ingredient in the ability of both organizations to function and grow.

In both groups, I learned the power of song. In the South, the Movement tapped into the great musical and oratorical traditions as well as the cultural rituals of the southern black community. In Ann Arbor, SDS/ VOICE members tapped into traditional labor songs and contemporary folk music. We even had our own local African American folk singer, songwriter, and guitar player Bill McAdoo. Although he had graduated by the time I arrived, we still listened to and memorized his self-titled record of social protest songs about bringing peace to the world and social justice to the South.

Most important of all, both SNCC and SDS were involved in issues on the highest and most profound level. We organized and sang about freedom in the South, and SDS pledged to create a safer and more peaceful world. Today, it seems clear that my own early experiences with racism led me to seek ways to get rid of it and to believe that my generation could make things different for the next generation. That is exactly why I could belong in VOICE, because it was all about working for justice and peace. Being in SDS/VOICE and SNCC, I did learn that I had a hammer, a bell, and a song with which to push for a better world. I am so glad that I had the good fortune to experience the sixties connected to both organizations. I hope when we—both academics and veterans of the Movement— remember this historical period, we will start at its center. It was about young people, oppressed people, and people without any of the trappings of traditional power, like the slaves a hundred years earlier, knowing they could change their life circumstances. At heart it was about peace and justice, justice and peace, peace and justice, justice and peace. Sing with me:

> Well I got a hammer, and I got a bell
> And I got a song to sing, all over this land
> It's the hammer of Justice
> It's the bell of Freedom
> It's the song about love between my brothers and my sisters
> All over this land.

3 | Returning to Ann Arbor
by Casey Hayden

I lived in Ann Arbor briefly, in fall 1962 and through that winter, with my husband, Tom Hayden. We had the ground floor of a little house on Arch Street, a makeshift bathroom, and a Social Action Center in our basement. I couldn't manage the transition from southern white nonviolent revolutionary to graduate student's wife, or the bitter cold, and I left at the midterm, back to the South. When I was invited to speak at the 2012 New Insurgency conference, I resisted it as too loaded, suggesting other women from my era in Students for a Democratic Society (SDS) instead. We ended up as a panel together, a chance for the invisible women of early SDS to emerge. I had written autobiographically in two collections of women's memoirs (*Deep in Our Hearts: Nine White Women in the Freedom Movement* and *Hands on the Freedom Plow: Personal Accounts by Women in SNCC*) as well as in Tom Hayden's recent retrospective, *Inspiring Participatory Democracy*.[1] Thus I had the luxury of considering what I wanted to leave behind in this talk, a closing chapter of my SDS life.

I addressed the southern freedom movement first. It was so important, the primary root of all else that followed. I had given talks like this several times, a story of love and loss. I cried all the way through every time.

Second, I chose an obscure philosophical convergence and its implications. My politics originated in Christian existentialism and morphed into radical nonviolence. Both are usually eclipsed by Marx and materialism in the historiography of our beautiful politics, our participatory democracy.

And finally, the wild: the intelligence of nature and harmony with it are dear to me. Deep ecology is almost impossible for the left to address, trapped as we are in celebrating the changes commencing with the industrial revolution, notions of progress that this revolution has spun, our greed for a lifestyle based on imperialism and fast-fading resources, and a species myopia we call humanism.

We had very limited time, and these big topics were far too condensed, perhaps even opaque, but it seemed this was what I could uniquely offer, and I barreled through, in tears.

Reading from my essay "The Movement," published in the now-defunct journal *Witness*, edited into the preface for Mary King's book *Freedom Song* in the mid-1980s, I gave voice to the girl I was in the early 1960s:

The Movement was everything to me, home and family, food and work, love and a reason to live. When we were young and in the South, we were so beautiful and naive. It was partly our naiveté which allowed us to jump into this position of freedom, the freedom of absolute right action. I think we are the only Americans who will ever experience integration. We were the beloved community, harassed and happy, just like we'd died and gone to heaven and it was integrated there. We simply dropped race. This doesn't happen anymore. And in those little hot black rural churches, we went into the music, into the sound, and everyone was welcome in this perfect place.

We were revolutionists. We loved the untouchables. We believed the last should be first, and in fact were first, in our value system, and it was only the blindness of everyone else not to recognize this fact. They were first because they were redeemed already, purified by their suffering, and they could therefore take the lead in the redemption of us all. We wanted to turn everything not only upside down, but inside out. This is not mild stuff. It is not much in vogue now. We believed pre-Beatles, that love was the answer. Love, not power, was the answer.

And we did love each other so much. We were living in a community so true to itself that all we wanted was to organize everyone into it, make the whole world beloved with us, make the whole world our beloved, lead the whole world to the consciousness that it was our beloved, and please come in to the fire, come in here by the fire. This is where it is truly safe.

The Movement in its early days was a grandeur which feared no rebuke and assumed no false attitudes. It was a holy time.

For the Zen teacher body and mind are one. So for a brief time in history, in our very own lives, art, religion, and politics were one. Those of us with SNCC [Student Nonviolent Coordinating Committee] in the early days were political, it is true, but, more radically, we were observers, participants, and midwives to a great upheaval, uprising, outpouring of the human spirit. This was the spirit of the thousands and thousands of poor Southern blacks who were in fact the Movement. The style, the form, the very life of the Movement, was theirs. They were there when we got there, and there when we left. Many of them could not read or write, and they could barely speak the English language. They will never see this writing. They, and not we, were the heroes, the heroines. I was privileged to have been their servant for a while. To them, for all I learned from them, and all the beauty I witnessed, I offer my most sincere and humble thanks.[2]

It's said we placed values before analysis at Port Huron, that our analysis derived from our values.

I never quite understood the significance of that. It's true we stated some values there, but the meeting was, to my mind, mostly analytical, endless policy wonking. Lately, though, I've come to see that this values-before-analysis notion represents a primary concern, and outcome, for my college generation of the 1950s. We were the silent generation. I've written about my entry into freedom mode at that time in my essay for Tom's book, *Inspiring Participatory Democracy*.[3] Port Huron was also about freedom, now cast in a political format, out of an old stream of thought and into a new one.

The original stream was a European intellectual movement called "systematic philosophy." Hegel was the starter. He thought about thinking and believed that all meaning derived from thinking about thinking the right way, that he could do that, and that would be the end of philosophy. This school went on a long time. Kant was big. Marx was in it. He thought about thinking about social change and how to achieve it and, like Hegel, believed he could get it right. And that would issue in utopia, the final answer. They were mostly Germans.

But back in Hegel's time, at the beginning, there was this deviant, a Dane, Søren Kierkegaard. He said, no, meaning does not derive from systematic thinking by intellectuals. We each create ourselves and the meaning of our lives by enacting our values. He was an existentialist. This stream was resurrected mid-twentieth century by Christian theologians. They saw the authoritarian results of the social theories that sprang from systematic philosophy: fascism and communism. They brought out this little-known Danish churchman in response. The existentialists, especially Camus; the nonviolent social movement most clearly exemplified by Dr. King; and the sit-ins and early SNCC and SDS—all of them were of this K stream.

So that's what is meant when we said we put values first. We threw in with the K school. But SDS included Marxists. We all agreed to participatory democracy as our goal and our means, both as an egalitarian civic order and in our relations with each other. Michael Harrington warned us that, nevertheless, Reds couldn't be trusted, because they were committed to their analysis. They would act without regard to our pact regarding internal social relations, and they would act undemocratically, if necessary, to control our organizations, in order to enact their ideas, their analysis. I didn't understand the roots of the issue he was raising, which actually go very deep. Our choice of inclusion was made for good reasons, but it had unexpected consequences, and as time passed, SDS's core commitment to participatory democracy faded. Perhaps because our new politics were forged in the midst of a social uprising and therefore called into play before they had time to deepen and be absorbed, SDS did fragment along the lines Mike predicted.

In a similar vein, two major aspects of my own work in the movement—linking SDS and SNCC (white North and black South) and the papers on women that I coauthored—also had unexpected outcomes, like side effects. I wonder if the new insurgencies have learned from our experience and shaped themselves accordingly. It seems perhaps they have.

The fate of the earth and our part in that fate are the universal issues of our time. This is the greatest change I perceive from how it was when we met at Port Huron. While writing for this conference, I was reading Anita Desai's novel *The Inheritance of Loss*. In my mind's eye, I saw the wooden windmills that drew water for the small farms along the South Texas coast in my youth. They are part of our inheritance and legacy of loss, along with two hundred species a day, the health of the oceans and the land, forests and whole ecosystems, indigenous languages, and the last few tribes still living in reciprocity with nature. The remains of those dear dead dinosaurs will be depleted within generations, along with other readily available natural resources, including water.

I call the emotion that greets this information, when it is sincerely met, the genuine heart of sadness. This heart is what we need to access, and work through, if we want to be useful, to create a politics of reality today with regard for the days to come. That's what we tried for back then. Why we are not doing so now is worth the most serious discussion we can muster. It seems young people today seem more attuned to the realities of their times than we grayhairs, as we were in our flaming youth. May it be so.

* * *

Back in the day we sang, really meaning it, "This may be the last time." My gratitude to Howard Brick and the many others who put this event together, to Barbara Haber for recognizing my presentation as performance art, to all those with whom I sailed the turbulent seas of the sixties, and to the girl I was, for surviving.

4 | Many Inheritances . . . One Legacy
by Maria Varela

My path to Port Huron was cut by others whose shoulders I stood on. It began early in the twentieth century with Catholic "worker priests" who took jobs in factories and mines, organizing with workers to change oppressive conditions. These experiences expressed a turn-of-the-century social justice theology, where Pope Leo XIII called upon Catholics to "reconstruct society altogether, a task which would have to engage people at all levels of society."[1] Between World War I and the aftermath of World War II, thousands of young people created lay movements to apply this social gospel in efforts to change oppressive conditions in workplaces, schools, and communities. Organizations such as the Young Christian Workers (YCW), Young Christian Students (YCS), and the Christian Family Movement (CFM) were founded to train participants in the social inquiry method to "see, reflect and act." (This was also known in Europe as the Jocist—that is, the *Jeunesse Ouvrière Chrétienne*—method.) The intent of this method was to move Catholics out of their religious insularity to engage in the secular world to build a more just society.

I first encountered YCS in the mid-1950s at my Catholic high school on the South Side of Chicago. Extracurricular choices included joining a prayer club or the YCS. While I came from a rosary-praying, mass-going, traditional Mexican-Irish American family, I joined YCS as I wasn't particularly prayerful. During this formative time in my life, training in the social inquiry method grounded me in a lifetime engagement in community organizing. I went on to join YCS at Alverno College in Milwaukee and in 1961 was invited onto the YCS national staff to become a full-time organizer.

At that time, YCS was a worldwide student movement growing in strength and influence in the United States, Africa, and Latin America. While on the national staff, I developed friendships with students involved in the YCS of Latin America, *Juventud Estudiantil Cristiana* (JEC). Many JEC leaders were involved in resistance movements in the Americas. In Brazil, especially, several disappeared and/or were killed. I believe that the praxis of this movement in Latin America led to the formulation of *teología de la liberación*, or liberation theology.

These winds of change in the 1950s and 1960s opened a window on what we called the "Catholic ghetto." Similarly, young people on the left were also drawn to open a window on the enclave of the traditional left. At least that is what I understood, when in late 1961, Students for a Democratic Society (SDS) founders Al Haber and Tom Hayden invited me to participate in drafting a manifesto at the 1962 SDS convention. Looking for more diverse views, Hayden and Haber wanted to involve progressives and liberal religious groups in writing a manifesto that would criticize US social and foreign policy and lay out a vision for reconstructing US society through participatory democracy. This political ecumenism would serve to bring together a group whose diverse sociopolitical inheritances were the legacies of those who went before us in forming modern social justice movements.

Frankly, for most of the five days at Port Huron, I was at sea. The discussions and debates were intensely intellectual. I did not come from an intellectual background. The books in our home were either operations manuals for chemical plants or novels my mother ordered from the *Reader's Digest* Book Club. My father thought college was a waste as his five girls were destined to be wives and mothers. Then a close friend died and left a widow with few marketable skills to support four children. Dad changed his mind. My college education was administered within the "Catholic ghetto," which (except for YCS) eschewed critical theory. I had not read Marx or Mills. While on YCS staff, we read Dorothy Day, Peter Maurin, Emanuel Meunier, and Hans Küng. I was not fluent in the philosophies or rhetoric of the left. What helped me get my sea legs at Port Huron were evening debriefings by Tim Jenkins, a Yale Law School student who helped me understand the terms, discussions, and debates.

In a letter sent from Port Huron to a YCS colleague, I described the experience:

There is so much that is new here . . . so much to understand . . . so many new personalities to be encountered and understood. It's a tense kind of situation for me. . . . Word gets around quickly that "she's a Catholic representing a Catholic organization." [Another] problem is articulated thusly: "If we accept . . . if we encourage the Christian or religious based liberal, will we lose the respect of the secular liberal. Will we have to re-define the left?"

I have been impressed by much of the thinking going on: am waiting to see the kinds of [resulting] programming or action. I am to state to the convention tomorrow what YCS expects of SDS. The statement is shaping up to be a strong demand for action . . . [to achieve] effective social change. . . . Perhaps also a criticism of the left's [over]reaction . . . to religious based ideas, groups, and people. Perhaps a plea for re-examination. . . .

I'm a little afraid to criticize. I'm afraid I'd have a very hard time holding my own here. I'm beginning to see myself in that "activist with little intellectual theorizing by way of background" camp. I don't necessarily want to be in that camp, so have so much catching up to do by way of ideas.

Interestingly enough, we in YCS were outliers in the Catholic Church. I thought that activists for social justice, whether from other faiths or secular backgrounds, were more committed to accomplishing a just society than were Catholics. As a critic of the Catholic Church, I didn't quite know how to handle the distrust of organized religions—especially of the Catholic Church—that I found at Port Huron. But what did I expect? After all, how would most on the left know about the "outlier church" and its progressive theology? Much of my struggle during the convention was finding the language to make bridges. The walls of our mutual ghettos didn't magically come tumbling down, at least in the first few days of Port Huron.

Where I did feel more at home was in the discussions about values, especially the view that "human relationships should involve fraternity and honesty . . . [and] human brotherhood." Also, the discussions about participatory democracy resonated with my YCS experience. Our work had already honored the *Port Huron Statement*'s call to establish a participatory democracy where "the individual shares in those social decisions determining the quality and direction of his life."[2]

These same sentiments were reflected in the teachings of Pope John XXIII (1958–63). We in YCS were critical Catholics, outliers to the mainstream church. John, however, had gathered up these sentiments and reflected back to the official church many of the principles that we and other outliers valued, trained in, and worked for. These included democratic participation, active resistance to oppression, and building communities of love. The *Port Huron Statement* and John's encyclical *Mater et Magistra*

(May 1961) could, in many parts, stand side by side in calling for the just reconstruction of society.

Perhaps this is the moment, when speaking of that encyclical, to reexamine what has been said about my role at Port Huron. There was an intense discussion examining assumptions about good and evil in human nature and how that related to the belief that all people had the right to participate in decisions affecting their lives. Some versions describe me waving the encyclical in the air and quoting from it in order to reach a compromise between the political "realists" and "idealists" about their conflicting views of human nature. The narrative then culminates as follows: "Inspired by Pope John XXIII . . . [Varela] suggested that we follow the doctrine that humans have 'unfulfilled' rather than 'unlimited' capacities for good, and are 'infinitely precious' rather than 'infinitely perfectible.' The theological amendment drew no objections and was incorporated without citation."[3]

Anyone who remembers me in those days knows that I generally faded into the woodwork in order to watch—a favorite coping method of mine to understand new situations. That I would insert myself as a "quasi theologian" in this discussion and wave *anything* around does not ring true to my sense of who I was at that time. My vague remembrance is that there was a struggle over semantics and people took strong positions on either side. I had an insight, most likely drawn from Hans Küng, who served as a theological expert for Pope John during the Second Vatican Council. The thread of his assertion that "a human person is infinitely precious and must be unconditionally protected" runs throughout his writings.

What is true about this characterization of my role at Port Huron is this: we were able to settle on language that created a bridge between us. That I felt secure enough to share these insights was evidence that perhaps the ghetto walls were eroding. The discussions leading to the *Port Huron Statement* brought the secular and faith-based together, teaching us that we could work together in this place, at this historic event.

Another gift from Port Huron was meeting Casey Hayden, who in late 1962 asked me to come to Atlanta to work for the Student Nonviolent Coordinating Committee (SNCC). There is not space enough here to relay how I got from Atlanta to Selma and eventually to Mississippi. But I found more of a home with SNCC (1963–67) than in SDS. SNCC's "ideology" was very close to liberation theology. Liberation theology begins with practice (i.e., working alongside the oppressed in their resistance), resulting in a transformed society that brings those at the margins into the center. The intellectualism I encountered at Port Huron was more theory than experience driven. The theories of social change encountered in SNCC grew out of practice: the nonviolent, love-infused, stress-filled, and conflicted struggles to dismantle US apartheid by nurturing indigenous leaders to develop black power in political, educational, and economic spheres.

The thread that bound SDS to SNCC was the concept of "participatory democracy." It really doesn't matter who first coined this term. What matters is that SNCC's godmother Ella Baker mentored us in the theory and practice of social change based on participatory democracy. She lived the practice of participatory democracy during the decades of her activist life *before* she helped students birth SNCC. If it weren't for her practice, SNCC workers may never have had the motivation or experience to plumb the deep leadership pool of indigenous leaders that Ms. Baker had worked with since the 1940s. It was this pool of veteran leaders working together with young people who changed the nation.

One significant SNCC-initiated change resulted from the Mississippi Freedom Democratic Party's procedural challenge to the seating of the all-white Mississippi delegation at the 1964 Democratic Party Convention in Atlantic City, New Jersey. While the challenge was not successful, one of the commitments won from some of the Democratic leadership was that segregated delegations would, in time, no longer be seated at future national conventions. By 1972, convention rules required that all state delegations be made up of "reasonable representations of women and minorities," as reflected in each state's demographics. Over time, this fruit of our struggles for participatory democracy changed the face and body politic of the Democratic Party and the nation.

Movements are more like nature than science. The tide doesn't ask from which part of the globe the seawaters originate. Movements create a tidal-like synergy that crosses geographic borders, races, ethnicities, classes, and even physical matter. Our activist origins consisted of diverse inheritances, and even with all our divisions, critiques, weaknesses, and strengths, we grew one legacy. In many ways, today we remain one through our diverse activism and mentoring of succeeding generations to go beyond us to achieve a world where "we would replace power rooted in possession, privilege, or circumstance by power and uniqueness rooted in love, reflectiveness, reason, and creativity" in the never-ending struggle for liberation.[4]

5 | Reflections on SDS and the 1960s Movements for Social Justice

by Dorothy Dawson Burlage

Students for a Democratic Society (SDS) was an important part of my young political life, but I had been a civil rights activist for four years before I joined the organization and five years before the Port Huron conference. For me personally, it was not the ideology of SDS that was critical. Rather, SDS was of great significance to me because it was a national network of young idealists with whom I could identify and that provided relationships across the country, a source of information and inspiration, and, most importantly, a community of friends. It connected, catalyzed, and energized social justice organizations worldwide.

It is remarkable that SDS and the many organizations with which it had relationships developed a national network of thousands of students and young people without the aid of cell phones, copy machines, or computers and without the money to make many long-distance phone calls or take many trips. SDS was built primarily with the use of personal connections, mimeograph machines, and what we now call snail mail.

I was not the typical SDS member. I grew up in a very conservative white family in Texas and Mississippi, deeply embedded in the Jim Crow southern way of life. There were contradictions, though, between what I learned about race from living in a segregated society and what I was taught about how people should treat one another. Every week in my Protestant church, for example, the children sang, "Jesus loves the little children, red and yellow, black and white." The contradictions led me to question Jim Crow laws and develop the values that would stay with me for life. By high school I cautiously and fearfully put my toe in the waters of the struggle against segregation by attending an National Association for the Advancement of Colored People (NAACP) meeting and sitting in the "colored" balcony of the theater at a time when that was illegal. Both seem inconsequential now but seemed monumental then.

In 1957, a year after I had transferred to the University of Texas at Austin from Mary Baldwin College in Virginia, I started my career as a political organizer, engaging in activities that eventually led up to my joining SDS. The University of Texas had just been desegregated when I started college, but the public facilities, many of its programs, and all the dormitories were still segregated. As a result, I decided to move off campus into a private dorm because it was interracial. At that time in my life, it felt like a very radical step away from my upbringing—gigantic in fact—and it served to break down the barriers of segregation with which I had grown up.

My views about racism were influenced by working with the student YWCA, a major source of activism on the campus. The Y, which was across the street from the university, was one of the few buildings in Austin where interracial meetings could be held. It was there that many demonstrations against Jim Crow laws and segregation on campus were planned. Though Y members were mostly white, reflecting the student population, there were African Americans in major leadership roles. That was a new experience in my life. The national Y set priorities for students to address, and in my year it was "race relations" and "the changing roles of men and women"; thus the Y helped motivate me to be active in both the civil rights movement and later the women's movement. In 1959, I was chosen by the Y to be part of a student exchange with the Soviet Union. That was when I observed that the Marxist ideals did not match the reality of people's lives, making me skeptical and sometimes inattentive later during prolonged ideological debates and speeches in SDS.

My views were also shaped by my friendship with the muckraking, investigative journalist Robb Burlage and the writers at the *Texas Observer*, all of whom were well informed and thoughtful. Also while at the university, I became involved with the National Student Association (NSA), another source of liberalism on the issue of race. The NSA had a more radical group associated within it called the Liberal Study Group (LSG), which helped spark the growth of SDS. There were interlocking connections among the people active in the Y, NSA, LSG, and SDS.

In 1960, I went to Harvard Divinity School to study philosophy with Paul Tillich and social ethics with Reinhold Niebuhr. As I was starting graduate school, the sit-ins were starting in the South, and I organized picket lines to support them. In 1961, I was a cofounder of the Northern Student Movement (NSM) in Cambridge, Massachusetts, an organization formed initially to support the Freedom Riders and to raise money for the

Student Nonviolent Coordinating Committee (SNCC), which was doing direct action against Jim Crow laws and organizing voter registration projects for African Americans in the South. I invited SNCC staffers to come to Cambridge and speak about their work, where I then sold the first SNCC buttons. The originals were based on the SNCC letterhead logo—two hands shaking, one black and one white. Though NSM continued as a civil rights organization in the North, many of the students involved in that original effort went on to join SNCC or SDS. The three organizations—SNCC, NSM, and SDS—fed each other.

In the same year, I received an invitation through my SDS and NSA connections from Paul Potter, a leader in both organizations. He had a grant from the Field Foundation that was funneled through the southern NSA office for voter registration drives in the South and asked me to be the director. I said yes and dropped out of school to go back to my native South.

My heart was truly in the South. Racism was my battle. I had grown up in the South and I was passionate about desegregation and correcting the wrongs that were being perpetrated against African Americans. I had been taught good values in church, even though they contradicted what I learned by growing up in a segregated society. Those values resonated with those of the civil rights movement—social justice, peace, the brotherhood of man, the love of one's neighbor, care of the persecuted and needy, and the equality of all people in the eyes of God. I was at home in the southern freedom movement and inspired by its concept of the Beloved Community, the idea of living in a society without violence and not defined by race or color. Thus I spent about ten years, in several southern states, working in the civil rights movement as a campus and community organizer.

SDS was primarily a northern organization. I got to know it through my University of Texas friends, Robb Burlage and Sandra (Casey) Cason. It was at her wedding to Tom Hayden in 1961 (when she became known as Casey Hayden) that I met Alan Haber. Alan was carrying little white SDS membership cards and asked me to join the organization. The membership fee might have been $1. With his beatific smile, you would have thought Alan was inviting me to a Sunday school picnic rather than a political movement to change the world. I thought it odd that anyone would be engaged in political organizing at a wedding, but that was Alan and typical of the SDS style in those days. It was also strange, especially for a southerner, when people at the reception talked about the threat of nuclear war instead of what the bride wore and other social niceties. In spite of the overwhelming cultural differences, I joined SDS. One reason was that Robb and Casey were signing up. The recruitment process, taking place through social ties, was typical of how the personal was political and the political was personal in what we called "the movement." Part of the appeal for me was that SDS had a social and political analysis that included class as well as race and that it was mobilizing against the spread of nuclear weapons and later against the Vietnam War.

I attended many SDS meetings in the North, including the Port Huron conference, where I continued to experience culture shock. Many people in SDS, having grown up in left-wing families, spoke what sounded like a foreign language to me, using words I had never heard like LID, SLID, Old Left, New Left, CP, and Trotskyites, sometimes Trotskyists, maybe shortened to Trots. Some people in SDS also had a name for its leaders. They were called "heavies," a term applied only to white men. As an extremely shy and unsophisticated southerner, I was in awe and intimidated by SDS. But I thought the people were amazing—bright, knowledgeable, idealistic, and committed to making the world a better place.

The concept of participatory democracy increased the appeal of SDS for me because it resonated with the slogan of "one man, one vote" in the civil rights movement. I do not remember that participatory democracy was discussed as having any relevance to women's rights or roles, but it was a fundamental and compelling concept in SDS. The idea was not very well defined and elicited varied responses, much like a Rorschach test. Though it changed in meaning from one situation, organization, or person to another, the notion of participatory democracy has been inspirational in many struggles, has endured, and has become global. It seems to touch a deep need that people feel to be heard and have a voice in society, to be treated equally regardless of race or social class, and to be treated with respect.

At the time I joined SDS, I was deeply committed to the idea of nonviolence as the correct path to social change. SDS members seemed to share that view, but there were some moments when I felt I was not on the same path. To quote the words of Dr. Martin Luther King Jr., "Raise no fist, commit no violence." As early as 1963, I was confused when SDS members raised their fists in the air for an SDS photograph. Even though the intent for some might have been determination and assertiveness rather than aggression, that wasn't clear to me and the gesture made me uncomfortable. In later years, some people in SDS branched off into other organizations that became involved in violence, and I was horrified by the harm that resulted from their actions.

In general, women were not in leadership roles in SDS. We were often asked to be secretaries, taking the minutes at meetings and doing office work such as typing and mimeographing. The analyses of political issues and the long speeches were the realm of the men. While I had been raised with the directive that "southern ladies" do not discuss religion or politics "in public," most of the SDS women were northern and politically sophisticated. Many had grown up in liberal or left-wing homes, so they were familiar with SDS language and its style of work. Although I did not see women in major leadership positions in SDS, I found the women associated with the organization to be remarkable. Not only were they extremely bright, but they were quite competent with whatever work they did. It was thought that the SDS women were especially effective as community organizers, skilled at making social connections at the grassroots level, even more so than the SDS men. In spite of the fact that many SDS women were just as articulate and analytical as the men, their voices were usually not heard. Their experience in SDS, both their work and their personal relationships with the men in the organization, influenced some of them to become significant players in the women's movement as it developed in the mid- and late 1960s. It was this dismissiveness of women that I found upsetting and that initially led me to support the struggle of women to be recognized as equals.

My own experience as a woman was not so distressing. Robb Burlage and I were married in 1963, when he was a graduate student at Harvard University and an intellectual leader in SDS. Robb was very supportive of my work in the civil rights movement. He shared housework and chores. We provided hospitality to SDS "travelers," the organizers who went from town to town promoting new chapters, soliciting new members, and leading actions such as demonstrations. We also offered space for SDS meetings. About the same time, women friends of mine, both in SDS and in SNCC, were talking to one another about feeling unappreciated and demeaned by men, developing an analysis of why it happened, expressing their frustration and anger, and building resistance. Casey sent me a memo on women's roles, which she and Mary King had written, and at the same time I was reading books by Betty Friedan, Simone de Beauvoir, and others who influenced the later women's liberation movement. I was at the SDS meeting when women staged a walk-out, and I was amazed at the assertiveness expressed in that act. Personally, I was torn: I wanted to be loyal to my women friends and stand up for a legitimate cause, but I did not want to see SDS split over it. Though I knew that women's issues were important, it was at a time when violence still pervaded the South and blacks were still denied the right to vote, so putting my effort in the south-ern freedom movement seemed much more pressing and urgent to me.

Given my commitment in the South, I did not work in the northern Economic Research and Action Project or in the national office. SDS members were supportive, however, when, in 1963, I helped organize the Southern Student Organizing Committee (SSOC) to reach out to south-ern white students on the issue of race and help them mobilize on south-ern campuses. I also helped them make connections with the members of SSOC, SDS, and SNCC.

SDS and the *Port Huron Statement* had a direct impact on my work in the South. There were only a handful of southern whites, all a generation or two older than members of SDS—Reverend Will Campbell, Myles Hor-ton of Highlander Folk School, Anne and Carl Braden, Jack Minnis, and Lillian Smith come to mind—who offered analyses of class as well as race in the South. One argument was that the "Bourbons," the wealthy land-owning class, were able to dominate workers on farms and plantations, offering horrendous working conditions and wages disastrously below minimum living standards by segregating blacks and whites and encour-aging them to compete for scraps as field workers, tenant farmers, and sharecroppers. The SDS members who were familiar with labor organiz-ing filled in many blanks for me about class and the economic situation of workers in the South, especially in the textile, timber, and coal industries. Because of these influences, I began to see working-class and poverty-stricken whites not only as potential members of the Ku Klux Klan and victimizers but also as victims themselves. This understanding contrib-uted to my desire to work with white people in the South through SSOC not only to combat racism but also to promote alliances along economic interests.

I continued to rely on my SDS network when I organized in a black community on housing and welfare issues, using a pamphlet written by Jill Hamberg, Paul Booth, and other SDS members. During the women's movement in the mid-1960s, I organized a women's consciousness-raising group in Washington, DC, composed primarily of SDS women. When I moved back to Boston to go to graduate school at Harvard, it was discus-sions with SDS women that led me, with other graduate students and fac-ulty, to establish a women's center in Cambridge in 1971, whose purpose was to help women with practical problems such as jobs and childcare.

In the early years, SDS had appealed to the best in us. The causes of the end of SDS, SNCC, and SSOC are much too complicated to go into here. It was heartbreaking to watch the movement collapse. After the end of the organizations as we had known them in the early 1960s, we faced a new struggle—rebuilding our lives. It seemed to be a traumatic time for everyone who had been intensely involved in the movement. Some people fell apart emotionally. Others found ways to continue to express their political beliefs through other venues or organizations. Some turned to violence, some went to graduate school, some got jobs in factories where they continued organizing, and some got professional jobs.

At the time, I was organizing around housing, welfare rights, and education in Anacostia, a predominantly African American neighborhood in Washington, DC, and that helped me deal with the demise of SDS and the other organizations that had sustained me. However, the changes in the political landscape forced me to think more deeply about social change and why, after so much hope and idealism, we had experienced such a sad end. In spite of the extensive and comprehensive analysis of America in the *Port Huron Statement*, something was missing for me. To quote scientist and psychiatrist Wilhelm Reich, "The most burning problem of the 20th century is the abysmal irrationalism and brutality of man . . . why people yield so easily to wrong ideas and to trends of thought which are contrary to their own life interests."[1] In my words, what is in the psyche of the American people that prevents us from making positive, life-affirming decisions? Why are people so drawn to hatred, greed, violence, and war? Why do movements for social justice seem to move society three steps forward and then two steps back? What does it take to create lasting social change?

Feeling that intellectually I needed to expand my understanding of social issues and social movements, I entered a doctoral program in 1971 in psychology and public policy at Harvard. I hoped to get renewed energy, reflect on the movement's successes and failures, and get a new sense of direction. Having become active in the women's movement in the late 1960s, I continued to be involved during graduate school, but that is a story for the 1970s. Studying psychology, I began to understand how crippled we might be from our childhood years and how those early experiences might influence our behavior as adults, thereby affecting our social, political, and economic institutions. My political work, including what I had learned in SDS, had led me to a concern for the welfare of children, parents, and families and the insight that we need not only political and economic reform but also changes in family structure, childrearing, education, and health care. In addition, I realized that if children are to grow up healthy, without damage to their bodies, they must live in an environment that does not pollute their food, water, and air. These insights still inform my political activities and professional work as a clinical psychologist. Both when I was a graduate student and since receiving my doctorate, I have worked as a teacher, researcher, consultant, and clinical psychologist, always keeping in mind the social and economic factors that affect families, women, and children.

I want to close by acknowledging what has stayed with me from SDS as well as from the southern freedom movement. My experience in the civil rights movement left me with a lifelong commitment to fight prejudice and discrimination based on race, ethnicity, country of origin, religion, sexual orientation, and gender identity. The list includes not only African Americans but also immigrants and persons perceived to be of foreign origin, Arab Americans, Muslims, and members of the LGBT community. My experience in both the freedom movement and SDS made me appreciate the significance of civil liberties as the foundation of a democratic society and as a necessity to protect social justice movements. Both SDS and SNCC instilled in me a lasting concern for the welfare of workers and an understanding of how racial issues intersect with class issues. SDS gave me a lasting awareness of the overwhelming power and destructive influence of the military-industrial complex and heightened my awareness of the harm caused by US colonialism and imperialism.

I am grateful for the role that SDS played in my life. I felt that I had been in, but not of, SDS. Even though as a southerner and as a woman I was never totally integrated into the organization, it gave me a network of people who shared my idealism and a community when I was just developing as a political activist and needed mentors. It helped me understand issues that otherwise would never have made sense to me and it had been a critical support system for me for the many years that I worked in other social justice organizations. When SDS ruptured, some of my connections remained strong, and though we have grown and changed, I am blessed to still have good friends from those years. We spent our formative young lives together, becoming deeply attached as we worked and learned together. We tried to take care of each other, though much like any family, we also argued. We shared hopes, accomplishments, frustrations, and disappointments, as well as many happy times. We are bonded as veterans of some of the most significant struggles in the twentieth century in the United States.

6 | Reflections on Women and the Culture of Port Huron

by Barbara Haber

In 1962 I arrived at Port Huron a very fortunate young woman, having lived a string of amazing and life-altering experiences over the previous ten years. When I was twelve I had entered the adult world of painting at the Art Students League in New York City. At sixteen, an unsupervised summer at the League in Woodstock deepened my desire for a life of art and bohemian community. A year later at Brandeis, I studied Marx, Lenin, and other left thinkers with Herbert Marcuse himself, and I adopted a democratic vision of socialism that I learned from my teacher and mentor, Irving Howe. I began, very tentatively, to take myself seriously as an intellectual and was encouraged by some male professors to consider an academic career—not an expected path for women at that time. At Brandeis I also strengthened my sense that the words "never again" called me, as a Jew, to act against oppression.

When four students sat down at a lunch counter in Greensboro, North Carolina, during my senior year, I was galvanized into two years of intense and passionate civil rights organizing. I learned to mobilize large groups for weekly Woolworth department store picket lines. I took nonviolence training. I attended the Student Nonviolent Coordinating Committee (SNCC) founding convention. After graduation, I worked with the Congress of Racial Equality (CORE) in Baltimore. We had weekly sit-ins at segregated restaurants on the Eastern Shore, sometimes followed by a night in jail, where we talked and sang freedom songs from our segregated cells. These experiences allowed me, for the first time, to know African Americans as comrades and friends. Their commitment, intelligence, and courage, laced with humor and kindness, provided me with a template for the kind of person I wanted to be.

Nevertheless, I encountered quite early the growing ambivalence of some Black activists about the role of whites in the civil rights movement. By May 1962 I decided it was time to leave.

I moved to New York, ready to devote myself to a new phase of political work with others who shared my radical vision of social change. I was not at all drawn to the array of old socialist groups I'd learned about at Brandeis. I had in mind a group I'd known of for some time, Students for a Democratic Society (SDS). I'd heard glowing reports about two of SDS's leaders, Al Haber and Tom Hayden, and read some of their pamphlets. SDS seemed to be a fresh and radical hybrid that was not specifically socialist, which I found intriguing. I arrived in New York one week before Port Huron and walked into the SDS office on Nineteenth Street. The office was funky, crowded, and bustling. I met Al, Tom, Casey Hayden, and others, all immersed in preparing for their upcoming convention. Tom handed me a copy of "the manifesto" (as the *Port Huron Statement* was then called) and urged me to come to Port Huron in Michigan. One week later, I found myself past midnight at the FDR Labor Camp, about to have my life changed once again, in ways I could not have imagined.

At Port Huron I felt I had found just what I was looking for. The people I met there were smart, humorous, politically experienced, and energetic. Those of us who gathered at Port Huron believed that through collective thinking we could understand our world and that with passionate dedication we could change it. The exuberance that came from our shared moral purpose and sense of historic mission was exhilarating!

It seemed at Port Huron that we had the elements needed to create a lasting organization and movement. Our task, revising the *Port Huron Statement*, gave us the medium in which to shape our collective political vision and a way to get to know one another. We were aiming to create a piece of literature that would actually be read, reflected upon, and remembered, as it has been. We wanted to envision, freshly, the radical possibilities of political culture; to provide ourselves with a rough map to guide our activist lives; and to fire the social imaginations of our contemporaries.

I came to Port Huron seeking personal transformation as well as political and social change. I believe this was true for others as well (though not for all). The values-driven and courageous lives of civil rights workers were not only our inspiration; they provided a compelling standard by which we judged the stereotypic and conformist social niches that were waiting for us—especially women!—and we were repelled. If my art, academic, and civil rights experiences had evoked in me a vision of a life of meaning, vitality, and adventure, it was SDS, as it seemed at Port Huron, that appeared to offer a community within which I could live that life. I sensed that this dream of a future was shared by others, which made it both more believable and more exciting. By the time I left Port Huron, I certainly expected to spend my life in SDS and "the Movement," our name for something we were creating that was larger than SDS. I was beginning to feel some confidence at last that I had escaped the suburban housewife fate that awaited me and other women in those days, even educated and talented ones.

For many of us, our personal needs appeared, in that fleeting moment of Port Huron and the early days of SDS, to mesh seamlessly with our political goals. We were giving birth to a new kind of organization in which we believed that we could develop skills, carve out our own identities, and become effective agents of radical social change. That we pioneer SDS women felt this was possible testified to our considerable experience as serious students and competent organizers as well as to the unique form of organization and movement that we believed that we, men as well as women, were coaxing to life at Port Huron.

Although the simplicity and near perfection of moments such as Port Huron can never last, several unique elements of SDS culture held promise for a transformative personal and political community.

First, SDS was improvisational. It did not have at its core a full-fledged ideology. The *Port Huron Statement* had (and still has) so much life in it because it never aspired to a unified theory of historical cause and effect. Rather, it said, "Here are the big issues we're thinking about, and here's a guide to how we might continue to elaborate, shift, even change our thoughts over time." About strategies and actions it was even less specific. Improvisation was at the root of the excitement we felt at Port Huron. It signaled a remarkable rejection of old, left ideologies, fully equipped as they were with hierarchy, primary contradiction, and anointed vanguard as the motor of change.

It was also a style of thinking with which many women felt at home. Never invited into the boys' club of megatheory, raised by mothers whose lives were daily improvisations and balancing acts, and encouraged to know the arts and literature, we found this experimental style to be simpatico turf. Intellectually, many of us preferred research and writing grounded in observation and centered on lived experience rather than abstract theory—subject areas that benefit from an improvisational approach.

Improvisational politics demanded of its participants flexibility and personal transformation in ways that traditional politics had not. It opened up creative space in which a rich mix of red diaper babies and children of liberals, dreamy bohemians and middle Americans, Jews and Christians, and practical planners and visionaries could approach one another with curiosity and respect, sometimes even with affection and love. Those outside our movement whom we sought to recruit could see or sense this spirit; it drew them to us and cleared a path for them to join us.

Second, improvisational politics is quintessentially relational, which was also a good fit for many women (as well as for some SDS men). Without ongoing investment in relationships, improv falls apart. Early SDS happened because Al Haber, Tom Hayden, Sharon Jeffrey, and an expanding band of sisters and brothers reached out in the early days, with their ideas and their selves, person by person, group by group.

This small-scale, relatively egalitarian approach to organization building was inviting to women. It drew on experiences and skills many women had. As students, and as young women entering the work world, we had needed to cultivate skills in relational agility in order to impress yet not offend.

At Port Huron, and at our best moments in SDS, we were able to initiate and sustain complex, high-stakes dialog with one another, even those with different political tilts, personalities, and priorities of the moment. Women contributed a great deal to this process.

Improvisational and relational abilities played a large and fluctuating role over the next several years in how we rose and fell, what we accomplished and how we failed, what we saw clearly, and where we were blinded.

The third guiding cultural value of early SDS was community. The civil rights movement idea of the beloved community as both necessary means and ultimate goal had been adopted by many of us early SDSers. At Port Huron and beyond, we were trying to create a community that was sustaining and resilient, that would help us thrive and withstand whatever external pressures and pitfalls came our way. (We could never have imagined the weight of events that would come at us soon and relentlessly.)

We also sensed that community might address the surging alienation that many young white people experienced and attract them to joining us. So community promised both a strategic advantage for recruitment and a sustainability advantage for us.

Women, of course, were leaders in community building. From nuclear and extended families, to neighborhood groups, to faith and civil organizations, to the grunt work that kept unions and political organizations going—all the backroom work, the uncredited weaving of communal fabric—this has been historically the work of women. We'd grown up absorbing those skills and the unspoken understanding that community building was up to us. Although we aspired to intellectual and organizing roles in our movement work, we intuitively and automatically moved to weave that fabric. And the men expected it of us, were comfortable with us being there, thought it was where we belonged, and gave us emotional rewards for doing it.

The fourth defining cultural element of early SDS was participatory democracy, the term most identified with the *Port Huron Statement*. An intellectual and political Rorschach, participatory democracy implied an egalitarian invitation to a movement that would be broad-based, inclusive, and empowering. Amazingly, at Port Huron, and in the days after, we never examined collectively and in depth what participatory democracy meant. Was it something we needed to create, cultivate, and enact in the present, in our own internal processes? Was it primarily a macropromise of a way that individuals and publics would interact with government at some later time, as a result of political and social change? Or did it need to be both? And if so, how would we go about envisioning, creating, and sustaining it? What would it demand of us? Would a focus on it within our community distract from large-scale organizing around important social issues?

I have found myself wondering what might have happened if, at Port Huron, in that rare moment of openness and imagination, we'd had a circle in which each of us put out our visions, our reservations, our hopes for participatory democracy. Even at that early stage, some woman might have said, "Participatory democracy has to be now, here, us, not just a promise for later. It has to mean that we women are listened to, respected, and encouraged to participate fully as organizers, writers, and speakers." And might other women, emboldened by her audacity, have said, "Me too"? Certainly, we women had all tasted moments of being supported, challenged, and included as students, thinkers, and organizers. But experiences in which we were condescended to, ignored, or punished for our outspokenness or ambition far outweighed them. For many of us, our most painful negative moments had come within our political world. SDS and the *Port Huron Statement* had raised our expectations. And what would later come to be called sexism was more deeply hurtful and less tolerable in our chosen community and from our comrades, friends, and lovers.

We expected "our men" to be different and better. But they were at the stage of life in which masculine culture demanded that young elite men make their moves to establish their place in the world. Our wonderful SDS men would have been heavy contenders in the professional, managerial, and mainstream political worlds. Part of what was going on in early SDS was a transfer of male ambition and competition to a higher purpose. Women were not a part of that story for men in or outside of our movement: the competition for place was to be among men. We women were to be their supports. That was just the way it was.

Perhaps had we explored the meanings of participatory democracy, none of us women could have accessed our protofeminist consciousness or dared to rock our lovely boat right then. And had we done so, we might have been met by incomprehension, superficial reassurance, bad jokes, subtle (or not so subtle) rejection—even shunning and isolation. Perhaps such daring would have ruptured the rapport among us women. But maybe, just maybe, the seed of equality would have come into the sun. Maybe the bare beginning of a growing feminist consciousness could have had room to blossom within SDS before years of rancor piled up and led to an explosive and wrenching tearing apart of what was, by then, our not-so-beloved community. It might even have opened space for other groups, which were also silenced, to speak out in the name of participating democratically—gays and lesbians, people of color, members from poor families and rural cultures, and men who were not seen as alpha men.

By 1965, a mere three years after Port Huron, SDS was in crisis, unable to handle its growth in size and diversity, swamped by competing strategic and organizational models, and bedeviled by incompetence and lack of accountability.

The alienation of women in SDS, first voiced formally by Casey Hayden and Mary King in their manifesto, "Sex and Caste," led to a mass walk out by women from a midwinter 1965 meeting that was attempting to set a new course for SDS. The meeting failed, but for women working within SDS and the growing antiwar movement, our terms of engagement changed decisively. The liberation of women, which demanded root changes in gender relationships, now took center stage for us. Many of us continued to work in antiwar, antipoverty, and other mixed-left projects. Naming sexism and making it visible in SDS did open spaces for some women to function more effectively, but by and large our concerns were not addressed. Our working and personal relationships with our male comrades were increasingly stressed and unstable. More and more women opted out of the mixed—or male, as it was often called—left and devoted themselves to creating an independent women's movement.

From 1965 until its demise in 1969, SDS careened from a radically anti-leadership, antistructure, and thus inevitably unaccountable morass into its opposite. A gaggle of Marxist-Leninist groups arose espousing rigid theories of change and seeing themselves, in full-throttle arrogance, as the vanguard. Most disastrous, of course, was Weatherman, Leninist in its vision of change, with a new set of "primary contradictions" that would lead to revolution, an escalating embrace of violence, and a rock-star sexiness that attracted media attention. It was not only SDS, the organization, that they stole. Weatherman waged an attack on the principles and vision that underlay SDS. Damaged and divided, SDS was still the repository of a unique vision; of a willingness to endure the ambiguities of political improvisation; of trust in an imperfect community in which relationships, open dialog, and a democracy of full participation were our best hope; of commitment to creating a new society by winning the hearts and minds of the public; and of radical change as a long-term public and accountable process. This was not a vision of liberalism or reform; this was a fresh, new, bigger-than-we-could-have-imagined template for radical change.

What stopped those of us who still believed in the principles of Port Huron and early SDS from mounting a strong counterargument against Weatherman? A lot was at stake. Why was there no "we" capable of organizing such an enterprise? These are questions worth understanding for the historical record but more important as insight for future young activists who take on projects of major social change.

At Port Huron we had defined a new kind of politics that might have provided us with enough confidence and unity to argue for our vision. But the male-dominant, competitive culture we carried over from the mainstream squashed the impulses among most women and many men to carry out the promise of Port Huron to change ourselves into new kinds of left people and our organization into a culture that prefigured the society we wanted to create.

To withstand Weatherman, COINTELPRO, and other disintegrating forces, we needed a culture in which all members were listened to, respected, and included; their particular abilities nurtured, utilized, and acknowledged. We needed those among us with special talents and skills in process to be recognized as teachers essential to our project just as experts in foreign affairs and power-structure analysis were essential. These teachers, many of whom would have been women, might have helped create a broader political community that would attract people, as we had been attracted, to the taste and smell of a better life, living in community and filled with political purpose.

SDS accomplished much in a short time, not least of which was the spawning of the women's movement and numerous other liberation movements. It played a major role in opposing the Vietnam War, shifting public opinion against it, and placing America's involvement in the larger context of US imperialist policy. It helped raise awareness about poverty and inequality in America. It influenced a generation of young people to consider lives as agents of social change. It transformed many of its participants into people committed to living with their eyes open and fulfilling their obligation to speak and act for change.

Still, our organization died young, leaving a tarnished legacy and, for many participants, memories of a painful experience of movement life that required long years of healing. The death of SDS and the dominance of Weatherman as the public representative of our movement created a decades-long chasm and a discontinuity on the left, within which the right wing rose to great power, while the left shrank and was marginalized.

Of course radical change is always a long shot. Much has been written about the overwhelming impact that assassination, COINTELPRO, the tenacity of racism, and most of all the vicious system revealed by Vietnam had on our perception, our sense of urgency, and our outrage. It often seems as though the shift back to canned ideology and violent tactics that came so soon was inevitable. I do not want to underestimate the impact of these factors.

But history is always mean and unpredictable, and government response to potent adversaries is always full of horrible surprises. So we needed a set of qualities that would maximize our resilience, stability, and wisdom and thus allow us to withstand these without turning into what we had explicitly rejected. Our failure to develop these virtues meant as the sixties moved into the seventies, SDS was unable to evolve into a network of poststudent, varied-but-linked radical change groups, connected by the thread of common principle and longing, held by the bonds of long relationships of trust. It meant that the thread of continuity between us and the next generations of left activists was broken.

I consider myself fortunate to have been a pioneer SDS woman and to have participated in the major movements of the sixties, whatever their personal costs to me and the social limitations they revealed. I remain in awe of the genius with which we began our journey and the deep caring and intelligence with which we attempted to achieve more than was possible. And yet, for me and for so many of my compatriots, there is sadness as well, and always the question "What if . . . ?"

7 | The Evolution of a Radical's Consciousness: Living an Authentic Life

by Sharon Jeffrey Lehrer

Even though I was a child of the Cold War and grew up in deeply segregated Detroit in a country ruled by white men, I was raised by a social activist, feminist mother, who worked for the United Auto Workers (UAW) and took me to a National Association for the Advancement of Colored People (NAACP) convention when I was thirteen. I marched with my mother on union picket lines, and I was inspired by UAW president Walter Reuther's vision and values for a just and secure world. When I was five, I met Eleanor Roosevelt in her home in Hyde Park, New York. From then on I wanted to be like her, an activist for social justice, serving humanity as a strong woman with purpose.

I got my chance when I met Al Haber in fall 1959 at the University of Michigan. Al had a vision for creating a national student political movement months before the sit-in by black students at the Woolworth's dime store in Greensboro, North Carolina, on February 1, 1960. Two years later, after its founders had organized students at campuses around the country, Students for a Democratic Society (SDS) held its famous Port Huron conference.

Standing on the shores of Lake Huron, watching the sun rise after an all-night session, adopting the *Port Huron Statement*, I was in awe of what we had done. We knew we had accomplished something significant. We knew that we were dreamers and visionaries who were expanding the boundaries not only of the traditional left but of American culture as well. We were challenging authority and creating a society of empowered, authentic individuals who would actively participate in the body politic.

We were big thinkers with big hearts and bold visions of a just, fair, and free society. We believed that societal change was possible, that humanity could grow and change. I believed what we wrote in the *Port Huron*

Statement—that individuals are "infinitely precious and possessed of unfulfilled capacities for reason, freedom, and love."[1] That vision lifted my heart and soul then, and it still does today. I wanted to become that realized person. I wanted to live an authentic life, to grow into those values, to live that vision, and to change the world.

It was my desire to "walk my talk," so during summers in college and for two years after graduating, I lived and worked in black communities registering voters in the South, organizing rent strikes in Harlem, and building a community center in Guinea, West Africa.

In 1965 we established an SDS Economic Research and Action Project (ERAP) in Cleveland, Ohio, organizing white and black welfare mothers. Living communally in a poor white neighborhood, we were committed to living our vision. During the day, we explored the meaning of "participatory democracy" by organizing welfare mothers to change the welfare system, and at night we'd have lengthy discussions before arriving at decisions by consensus. I chose Cleveland ERAP because the men there respected the women and the women were strong leaders and organizers.

Wanting to continue my activism, I moved to the South Side of Chicago, where I was the director of a community organization building a stable, racially integrated community. While on a camping trip at Mt. Rainier in 1973, I had a very unusual experience, which changed my life radically. It was what I now understand to be a spiritual experience, but at the time I didn't know what it was. I unexpectedly found myself in an internal dialogue. One part of me affirmed that I had a very successful professional career. Another part posed a question: "But how do you feel in your heart?" I had no idea how I felt in my heart. I had never thought about it. I was an organizer. I didn't know about my feelings. Who had time for that? Then a third part of me suggested that I resign from my job. This was a tremendous shock.

The next morning I awoke knowing that I was going to leave Chicago. It was instantaneous, which was not how I had made decisions in the past, but this time I just knew it was right. Six months later, I flew to California for a vacation.

I was smitten by California's beauty, the ocean, the mountains, and the sense of freedom I felt. Through a series of synchronistic events, I ended up at Esalen Institute, a center for the development of human potential on the Big Sur coast. For someone who was a driven political organizer, whose purpose was to change the world, finding myself sitting in a hot tub gazing at the Pacific Ocean and attending workshops exploring my feelings and inner life was truly the most radical thing I had ever done. I was out of my comfort zone, and at the same time, I was intrigued by the journey. Esalen gave me the opportunity to explore worlds that I didn't know existed. I discovered I had a heart. I discovered my emotions were rich with meaning, language, and intelligence. I discovered that living authentically meant being able to identify and respect my feelings, even the uncomfortable ones. I began to understand the meaning of emotional intelligence.

California completely captured my heart. From Esalen I moved to San Francisco and established a consulting practice for organizations and individuals, applying SDS values and visions while continuing to explore my feelings.

Through a client, I had the good fortune of meeting an extraordinary woman, Dr. Angeles Arrien, a cultural anthropologist who was raised in the ancient wisdom tradition of the Basque culture. From her I learned that not all cultures share our Western worldview. Indeed, some indigenous cultures have profoundly different beliefs about what is real, what matters, and how things change.

The insight I gained about allowing and respecting different cultural perspectives was invaluable in 1981, when I was the consultant for a project organizing Southeast Asians in San Rafael, California. There were Cambodians, Vietnamese, and Laotians, all with different languages, cultures, and histories. Organizing people from these three nationalities to work together to fight for a common goal and services they all needed—despite centuries of mistrust among them—was challenging and exciting. At that time I also consulted with Latino community organizations, food banks, and shelters for homeless families.

In 1982, I became the executive director of the Center for Attitudinal Healing, founded by Gerald Jampolsky, MD, author of *Love Is Letting Go of Fear*. There I saw children facing cancer and opening to love. I witnessed them and their families face their worst fears with grace and dignity. I saw them being healed emotionally, and often physically, by love. (They also continued with their medical treatment.) I saw the limits of Western medicine and the power of positive emotions to transform a person's reality.

I had the opportunity to explore consciousness from a scientific perspective when consulting for the Institute of Noetic Science (IONS), founded by Edgar Mitchell, the Apollo 14 astronaut who had a life-changing experience in space. According to Mitchell's biography, "He was filled with an inner conviction as certain as any mathematical equation he'd ever solved. He knew that the beautiful blue world is part of a living system, harmonious and whole—and that we all participate 'in a universe of consciousness.'" He felt this experience was just as trustworthy as any he experienced in the world of rationality and physical precision: "It represented another way of knowing."[2]

My worldview was evolving, changing, and expanding beyond the political-economic paradigm of SDS. This was a fundamental shift. I was drawn to pursue it because it felt like truth. Yet I was of two minds. My Social Activist Self and my Spiritual Self felt in opposition. It was a paradox that I continued to explore.

In 1979, I fell in love with a beautiful man, Glenn Lehrer, an artist, who touched my soul with the beauty of his being and his creations. When he first showed me his fluid gemstone carvings and precisely faceted stones, I was swept away by their radiance, beauty, and majesty. Marrying an artist, living in California, and being involved in psychological and spiritual development were real stretches for my family and my self-image as a social activist.

Continuing my studies with Dr. Arrien, I learned about child-rearing practices of non-Western cultures. For example, the Basque and American Indian cultures valued, honored, and respected the feminine principle: qualities of being, receiving, listening, cooperating, nurturing, intuiting, feeling, conceiving, organizing, and being in the mystery. They also honored, valued, and respected the masculine or dynamic principle: qualities of doing, implementation, intellect, decision making, focus, will, and action.

Central to these cultures was balance. The feminine energies conceive, the masculine energies implement. Creativity and dynamism in harmony. For both men and women, it meant being in balance with one's inner feminine and masculine qualities. It also meant developing and being in balance with four parts of the Self: physical, mental, emotional, and spiritual. This boggled my mind. Even though I was a feminist, I didn't know about the true feminine. Having never been taught anything at all about my spirituality during childhood, I had never even heard about the concept of a Spiritual Self.

In Dr. Arrien's class, we learned what happens when the masculine and feminine energies are out of balance. In our modern world, the feminine is denied, dismissed, and discounted, while the masculine is elevated to a position of complete authority. The true masculine is replaced by the twisted version that the chauvinistic perspective brings. The masculine is seen as superior; the feminine is inferior. Everything is viewed as a hierarchy, a cosmic pecking order rather than a harmonic whole. This perspective has influenced our entire thinking in the Western world, from philosophy, to religion, to commerce, to our methods of scientific inquiry. Cultures with a more balanced perspective work with nature and maintain harmony. Within our male chauvinistic paradigm, dominance is the name of the game. People, animals, and even the earth itself can be owned, dominated, and manipulated for personal status, wealth, and power. The results of this perspective are evident in our current environmental crisis.

During this time, I learned to take responsibility for my thoughts and feelings. I learned that my thoughts have impact. Thoughts and feelings are energy, and energy travels. Other people are affected, positively or negatively, by what I am thinking. I was learning to take responsibility for my impact, to make a conscious choice. *What is my real motivation?* When I see that my underlying thought is to blame, judge, control, or manipulate, I ask myself, "Is that really who I want to be as a human being?" I choose to take responsibility at this subtle level. As I heal my negativity, fear, anger, jealousy, envy, rage, hatred, and hopelessness, I am reducing the negative frequencies in the collective consciousness, creating a more positive resonance.

Owning my impact also includes recognizing my positive impact. I've learned to pay attention to how people respond to my love and joy, and I am surprised and delighted to see how it inspires and uplifts. As people become more loving, more compassionate, and more understanding, in ever-greater numbers, the positive frequencies in the collective consciousness increase, and this creates a more positive resonance for all of us.

I am continually vigilant as a woman to notice and take responsibility for my own ingrained chauvinism, any of my thoughts or actions that discount or dismiss my feminine qualities or those of another. It's disturbing when I see myself impose my chauvinism. In my efforts to change the world, I sometimes blame, judge, or attempt to control and manipulate others instead of honoring them and their process. I recognize how this ingrained behavior negatively impacts people, how it runs counter to the very results I wish to achieve, and how it violates the values I embraced years ago in the *Port Huron Statement*. When I'm viewing the world through the lens of chauvinism, I'm not being the loving person I want to be. To live the love, SDS's primary value, I have to be willing to continually change and grow into my personal infinite "capacities for reason, freedom, and love."[3] Part of changing the world is changing me. As I let go of the lesser parts of myself, I become more and more free. Dr. Arrien taught the Basque proverb "Walk the spiritual path with practical feet." In other words, to evolve spiritually, one has to become a more loving human being with regard to one's self, one's relationships, and one's actions in the world.

As comfortable as I was with exploring consciousness and spirituality, I didn't feel at ease with how to reconcile this quest with my political, activist self. They seemed to be polar opposites: either I was a spiritual person or I was a political activist. The two lived separately in me, often in open conflict. For years I judged myself and felt guilty that I wasn't doing enough politically, that I had abandoned my commitment to changing the world. I worried about what my family and political friends would think of me. Would they even understand what I was talking about? Would they think I was delusional?

For a long time I struggled with my internal conflict (political versus spiritual) until I finally stopped judging myself and let go of my fear of being judged by others. I opened to loving and accepting all aspects of myself and to knowing that I am loved. Having come to understand that thoughts and feelings are energy that goes out into the world like waves on the ocean, this has led me to a unique form of social and political activism. I started accepting that my work in the spiritual dimensions was positively changing the world. I let it be real. The lenses in my eyes opened. The illusion of separation came down. I no longer felt divided into two irreconcilable selves. A synthesis of all my parts emerged. I now see myself as an Activist for the New World, integrating and utilizing both my Political Self and my Spiritual Self. I am a larger, more whole person. I don't have to give up either part of me. I value all of me and who I am becoming.

I now envision a world where people live in balance and harmony with all that is; where they seek resolution, not just solutions; where they are defined by the quality and quantity of their love, not by how much they own, control, or dominate. My childhood as the daughter of a political activist and my time with SDS gave me a strong foundation for a lifetime of seeking dignity and freedom for myself and for others. So strong is my commitment to live as a free spirit that I am continually compelled to explore all assumptions and beliefs about reality and consciousness, as we did so courageously back in 1962. I continue to learn, grow, and change, always becoming more authentic, closer and closer to my Truer Self. Being part of the founding of SDS and striving to live those values gave me purpose and direction for living a meaningful and fulfilling life.

I see all the changes happening in the world as similar to the transformative process of a caterpillar becoming a butterfly. The caterpillar consumes everything, eating voraciously; it then spins a cocoon within which it dissolves into a liquid substance that scientists call "imaginal cells." Out of these imaginal cells emerges a brand new being, and a butterfly is born. I believe we are in a similar process of transformation. We are consuming everything around us: water, air, oil, money. The old is dissolving, and out of the essence of the substance of the old, the imaginal cells in us are stirring, bringing forth new ways of being, new ways of creating, of thriving, and relating to each other and the earth.

I have great faith in the power of our imagination to envision and birth something new, something beyond what is visible or knowable now. As Albert Einstein said, "We cannot solve our problems with the same thinking we used when we created them." I have hope for the future and for all dreamers, visionaries, and activists around the world. I believe that now, we stand on the precipice of a New World. We are poised at a new frontier for humanity. The new global activism in our world stands on the shoulders of a few brave and visionary students who came together in Port Huron, Michigan, so long ago. That new global activism will fulfill the visions and values of the *Port Huron Statement* and SDS.

8 | Port Huron: Where's the Labor Section?

by Kim Moody

My road to Port Huron began, as it did for so many other northerners, in February 1960, when I heard the news of the student sit-ins in Greensboro, North Carolina. This wasn't just, as the *Port Huron Statement* put it, another one of those "events too troubling to dismiss." It was an action taken by people of my generation, though possibly not "bred in at least modest comfort," as I knew it in Chicago.[1] It was an act that both pointed a finger of shame for inaction and showed that, as we say today, "another world is possible." The road, however, was not to be straight or direct.

In fall 1960, I went to Johns Hopkins University in Baltimore, a city that still had many segregated institutions. Once in Baltimore, I quickly sought out and found the civil rights movement, which was already highly visible there. The group that I contacted was the Civic Interest Group, or CIG, which became a Baltimore chapter of the Student Nonviolent Coordinating Committee (SNCC). That sounds radical, but in fact this chapter was a pretty conservative group. It was an older organization started somewhere in the mid-1950s at Morgan State College, which was the historically black college in the area. Its leader was Clarence Logan, who'd been a founder of CIG.

The Morgan students had been trying to integrate a number of lunch counter chains as well as the segregated movie house and restaurants at the Northwood shopping mall right on the doorstep of Morgan State. The black students couldn't go to the movies and couldn't eat in the restaurants, so they had been trying for years to integrate the mall by demonstrating and lobbying—respectable tactics that didn't work. By the time I got there, they, like everyone else, had discovered the sit-in. So I joined this group. We were "weekend warriors," participating in lunch counter sit-ins like the Greensboro students I so admired.

Well, not quite. At that point I wasn't one of those who volunteered to resist and get arrested. Hopkins said it would expel anyone who got arrested for any reason, and I wasn't prepared to take that chance. We were simply, but firmly, escorted out of the restaurant by the police, while the real heroes stayed behind to be hauled off to jail. I wouldn't actually get arrested until the big Northwood Theater sit-in in 1963, when 350 of us spent four days in Baltimore's Civil War–era jail. There were also mass marches where you could feel the size and power of the movement. Whether it was a sit-in or a mass march, most events started in one or another of Baltimore's black churches. Over the next few years, I spent a lot of time at meetings in these black churches and got a good introduction to African American culture as it was then. The music, the language, the positive spirit of resistance in the face of oppression, and the sense of community made a strong impression on me. It made me more aware not only of the oppression felt by African Americans but also of their resolve to overcome it. It made me more aware, therefore, of what it meant to be part of a mass movement.

The CIG was a student group with a largely middle-class base, or at least a base headed toward the middle class with the sort of outlook that would imply. The Baltimore chapter of the Congress on Racial Equality (CORE) was something very different. It was an adult organization, but more to the point, most of its leading activists were union activists as well. Most were public employees, working for the city or the post office. This seemed significant to me. Here were working-class people, part of organized labor, leading one of the more radical groups in the local civil rights movement. These were activists who had learned organizational skills and the reality of conflict in the unions as well as in the movement. They didn't have the cautious approach and ideas that the middle-class leaders from the Ministerial Alliance or the National Association for the Advancement of Colored People (NAACP) showed over and over. Among other things, CORE focused on employment discrimination, particularly as most of the formal segregation of public accommodations fell to the pressure of the movement fairly soon.

My friend Peter Dawidowicz was active in CORE, so I began to meet some of the CORE leaders and participate in their actions. I was impressed by their union activity as well as their radicalism. Ed Chance stood out as just such a person. I think he was in the American Federation of State, County, and Municipal Employees (AFSCME). CORE activists also talked about the black steel workers' caucus at Bethlehem Steel's Sparrows Point mill, which would later play a big part in helping bring unemployed workers to Washington in 1963. Two things became clear. First, the working class, which much of the literature of that time assumed to be mostly white, was, in fact, interracial—if not always integrated. Second, organized labor was far more dependent on black labor than I had imagined. The connection between labor and the civil rights movement, while by no means simple, was nonetheless a reality not simply in such coalitions as existed at the top but deep in the ranks of African American workers as well.

The next experience that deepened this connection for me came with the freedom rides that CIG, imitating CORE, held on Maryland's Eastern Shore. Today, the Eastern Shore is like a resort area. Back then, it was like Mississippi. This, along with Northern Virginia, had been the birthplace of black slavery in North America in the early 1600s. It was very backward; its main industries were chicken farming and the canneries that packed the catch from Chesapeake Bay. When we went down and demonstrated in Cambridge, the Eastern Shore's main town, or on the roads leading there, that's where you found the most hostile whites engaging in verbal abuse and threatening gestures. Nobody ever really got hurt, but it was scary. We went down to Cambridge to try to integrate some of the shops that wouldn't hire blacks. We were dealing with employment issues early on. So both CORE and to some extent CIG moved into opening employment opportunities for African Americans.

Cambridge, Maryland, had its own civil rights movement, and Gloria Richardson was its leader. The Cambridge movement was working class to the core and believed in armed self-defense. We heard stories about how the Ku Klux Klan had tried to go into the black neighborhood, crossing the dividing line named, of all things, Race Street. Gloria Richardson had organized groups to shoot back and drive the Klan out, which they did. They knew the authorities down there would do nothing to protect the black area of town, so they took matters into their own hands.

We would go down there, nice students from Goucher College, Morgan State, and Hopkins, marching in circles and singing our freedom songs, wondering when the Klan was going to show up to intimidate us. We noticed, all around the edges of where we marched, these big African American guys. We later found out they were cannery workers. Gloria sent them downtown to protect the students. It was said they were "packing." I don't know if that's true, but they were meant to be seen so the white thugs did not bother us. We went down there maybe two or three times. It was important to the Cambridge organizers to have support coming from Baltimore and elsewhere. But the movement in Cambridge was a working-class movement willing to go beyond the norms of nonviolence when necessary. Thus it was that the civil rights movement helped make the working class and the labor movement a reality for me.

My next effort was to find or rather help start the peace movement in Baltimore. Soon there was a little group of us, both at Hopkins and at Goucher. So we contacted the Student Peace Union (SPU), which I had read about, and they sent Dave McReynolds down from New York. I was very impressed with him. He was honest about his politics as a member of the Socialist Party (SP) and extremely articulate. So we set up an SPU chapter. Within the first year, we had maybe thirty to forty people in it, which for Johns Hopkins and Goucher was pretty sizeable. We had a march around town to ban the bomb, with paper hats that read, "Official Fallout Shelter." Norman Thomas, the longtime leader of the SP, spoke at the rally. He was an inspiring speaker, one of that generation of politicos who learned to speak to big crowds in the 1930s. This was the first and only time I had a chance to talk to Thomas. I asked him why the SP did not run candidates any longer. He said it just was not worth the effort; they would only get a tiny vote. On the other hand, he expressed considerable exasperation with the Democrats.

Once I got involved in the affairs of the national SPU as a leader of the Baltimore chapter, I ran across the Young People's Socialist League (YPSL), the SP's youth group. It seemed to me that the YPSLs (i.e., Yipsels, as its members were called) wanted total control of SPU, a practice that I thought would limit its growth. To some extent this centered on one's attitude toward Communism and Communists. When I went to an SPU educational weekend, I heard Michael Harrington for the first time. He was already a well-known socialist—as he put it, "America's oldest young socialist." He had us read from *The God That Failed* and then spent a long time talking about how we can't have the Communists in this movement, dwelling on how horrible they were. Although I didn't doubt the horrors of Stalinism, this seemed to me like a diversion. "We're here to fight for disarmament," I thought. "I don't like the Soviet Union and the fact that it is the other actor in the Cold War, but isn't this kind of beside the point? And anyway, isn't the Communist Party practically a corpse in the United States?" Still, from fall 1960 until spring 1962, we remained a very active SPU chapter, getting fairly big and doing some interesting actions.

My experience in the CIG and SPU, however, convinced me that we needed something more than a "ban-the-bomb" group at Hopkins and Goucher, on the one hand, and a civil rights group based at Morgan State, on the other. We needed something that addressed all the issues facing America, above all the Cold War, civil rights, poverty, and, somehow, the working class, which I had come more and more to see as central to social change. I didn't think that YPSL could fulfil this role because it was too tied up in internal debates over things like the Sino-Indian War. It had the kind of sectarian atmosphere that prevented it from becoming a true mass organization. Then I heard about Students for a Democratic Society (SDS).

In spring 1962, a graduate student at Hopkins, Ned McLennan, told me about a new organization that sounded promising. He said something like, "There's this organization called Students for a Democratic Society, and they're going to have a founding convention in the Midwest. They're sort of 'laborites' like you. I think you'd be interested." There was no SDS chapter yet in Baltimore and not too many elsewhere. The largest SDS chapter by far was that around Tom Hayden and Al Haber at the University of Michigan in Ann Arbor, and it was they who were organizing the conference. So a small group of us decided to go: Diane Ofstrofsky, Arthur Cheswick, and me. We drove out there to the Midwest, to Ann Arbor, and somebody showed us how to find Port Huron. It was just the idea that somebody's starting a student group that is multi-issue and clearly left wing that excited me. I assumed, "Well, they're having their meeting at the United Auto Workers' summer camp, so it must be kind of labor oriented." It turned out it wasn't. But it *was* an important experience.

Port Huron and SDS

Apparently, as late as fifteen days before the famous Port Huron convention of SDS, there was no meeting place. This came at the last minute from the United Auto Workers, who offered their training center on Lake Huron. Some drafts of what would become the *Port Huron Statement* were sent out to actual SDS members beforehand, but we weren't yet members. So in June 1962, we were heading for a convention that had just barely found a place to meet to discuss a document we hadn't seen. Somehow, none of this bothered us.

I didn't know what to expect. Aside from my two colleagues from Baltimore, I didn't know anyone there. Any anxiety I might have had disappeared as we began to mingle with those who were already there. It was exciting because they were approximately my age, in our early to mid-twenties, and looking for the same thing. You got to know people pretty fast, all these new people with radical ideas. What was more, many of those I met in the first days at Port Huron were involved in the same issues I cared most about—above all, civil rights. There were recent veterans of the movement in the South. In addition to Tom and Casey Hayden, there was Chuck McDew and Bob Zellner from SNCC. Those I met were also interested in the Cold War, the anticolonial rebellions abroad, Marxism, C. Wright Mills, Simone de Beauvoir, Sartre, Camus—all the issues we cared about and the works that were standard reading for the New Left that was in the making.

Even more important was this: when we discussed these ideas and the *Port Huron Statement* draft, the polemical style I thought hurt the YPSL so much was entirely absent. It wasn't at all that people agreed on everything but that the debates and discussions there had a more respectful manner. This made a big impression on me and would keep me in SDS even though I was in a small minority of those who questioned the dominant orientation toward the Democratic Party. On top of that, SDS people had a sense of humor.

We at the convention spent five days discussing and rewriting Tom Hayden's lengthy draft. Hayden had strong credentials, having been in Mississippi, probably segregation's most dangerous stronghold, along with his wife, Casey. As the draft statement was very long, we amended it section by section. After everybody got to know each other a little, we broke down into groups according to the chapters of the original draft. To my dismay, there was no labor section. Rather, there was a sort of afterthought on organized labor in the economy section. So I went to the economics panel, where I hoped to learn more about how capitalism worked and see what we could do with the labor afterthought.

The guy who ran the discussion of that section was Robb Burlage from Texas. That alone was pretty unique for this left-wing movement. Moreover, he considered himself a Marxist and was frank about it. I wanted, like him, to push the discussion and the document as far left as we could. I cannot say that in 1962, I had anything like a grasp of Marxist economics. I hadn't read *Capital*, but I had some vague ideas. And under Burlage's leadership, the economics section did push things about as far as we could go. He was explicit about taking on the system: "Let's have a critique of capitalism, as much as we can," I recall him saying. In fact, a lot of the discussion in our group, which went on a long time, was spent reformulating the draft to make its critique deeper. In the end, Burlage presented the revised section to the convention as a whole by famously saying, "We accept the draft of Brother Hayden with certain revisions by Brother Karl Marx."

The economics section also included what little the draft document had to say about organized labor. Hayden had apparently imbibed C.

Wright Mill's dismissal of what Mills called the "labor metaphysic"—that is, the idea that the working class was central to social change. As a result, the draft paragraphs on labor mostly cataloged the growing conservatism of the unions, or they simply acknowledged the institutional importance of the unions in a reformed Democratic Party, as suggested by the draft's main political strategy of "realignment." The *Statement* included a few references to "militant Negro discontents" within organized labor, along with some "sweeping critics" of business-as-usual unionism; these signaled a countertrend to union bureaucracy and conservatism. Perhaps I had a role in adding those notes, since that kind of dissent within the labor movement was precisely what I thought I'd seen through my experience in the civil rights movement. Generally, though, I was pretty insignificant as a player at Port Huron. I was there more to take in what was happening and what possibilities this more or less new organization promised.

I disagreed strongly with the political section on realignment of the Democratic Party—an idea I had rejected when I first came across it in SP discussions. But the critique of American society seemed radical enough at the time. With one notable exception, the atmosphere at Port Huron and at the next two or three conventions was one in which you could disagree without being isolated and without getting into the sort of polemical factionalism I had seen in the YPSL. The debates and the votes that were taken were conducted in normal democratic fashion. Later, with the development of the Economic Research and Action Project (ERAP), a consensus style was introduced that seemed to me both endless and, as meetings went on so long, susceptible to manipulation. At Port Huron, however, we agreed to disagree when necessary and felt the strength of a common purpose.

Despite the lack of attention to organized labor in the *Port Huron Statement* and Hayden's rejection of the "labor metaphysic," a lot of those at Port Huron and Pine Hill the following year saw organized labor as important. Stanley Aronowitz was already an organizer for the Oil, Chemical and Atomic Workers Union when he came to the 1963 Pine Hill convention. In fact, looking back at the labor "section" of the *Port Huron Statement*, I see that it missed one of the great advances of organized labor in the 1960s: the self-organization and unionization of public sector workers that brought millions of African Americans and women into the labor movement. Some of us who were present at Port Huron or Pine Hill, like Paul Booth, Monte Wasch, Peter Dawidowicz, and me, would go on to be organizers in that upsurge.

The exception to the rule of "comradely" if sometimes passionate discussion took the form of a generational dispute, though it was deeply political. This was the by now well-known reaction of the "adult" observers representing the League for Industrial Democracy (LID), the old social democratic think tank that was technically the parent organization of SDS, along with the slightly younger representatives of YPSL's right wing. Most notable was Michael Harrington—once again. The others included Donald Slaiman of the AFL-CIO and Rochelle Horowitz, Dick Roman, and Tom Kahn—all three from YPSL. This was a side of the YPSL I had not seen, one that in its own way was as sectarian as the left-wingers I had encountered earlier. Most of the YPSLs at Port Huron were now followers of Max Shachtman, originally an associate of Trotsky who split from him in 1940 over the nature of the Soviet Union. Obsessed by the dangers of Stalinism, Shachtman had moved far to the right and was now advising AFL-CIO leaders. He had, in effect, replaced the working class as a whole with the trade union bureaucracy as the hope of the future.

Al Haber, who along with Hayden was the main organizer of the convention, belonged to YPSL as well. He was not, however, sectarian in disposition, and he sympathized with the rest of us. Most of the attacks from the right came after the convention, but they surfaced at the meeting as well. The issue again was anticommunism, for SDS, it seemed, was insufficiently so. After all, we had voted to seat the representative of the Communist Party youth group as an observer. Despite the many disclaimers concerning Communism and the Soviet Union in the draft that came out of the convention, these social democratic guardians of the West, a number of whom had not read the document, went "through the roof," as Harrington put it. It was like a rerun of the SPU convention with its stern lectures on the evils of Communism. To his credit, however, Harrington later repudiated the heavy-handed actions of the LID.

Most felt as I did about not being excessively anti-Communist, emphasizing that "we should not focus on this; we've just gotten past McCarthyism and we're still fighting HUAC [House Un-American Activities Committee]." I agreed with that, even though I had a "third camp" analysis that considered the Soviet Union a repressive class society. Of course, most of us had not been through years or decades of bitter fights with the Stalinists that many of the erstwhile Trotskyists-turned-social democrats had experienced.

When I returned to Baltimore, I was determined to pull together an SDS chapter. What then to do with the thirty-member chapter of SPU? It didn't seem to me and some of the other SPU leaders that we could sustain two radical groups at Hopkins. We tried to get the entire SPU chapter to switch to SDS. After all, the bomb and the Cold War were also SDS issues, as well as civil rights. So we set about educating members of the SPU group on the advantages of a multi-issue organization. We had people read the *Port Huron Statement*—in fact, we sold copies in the dormitories. In the end we were successful, and the Hopkins SPU became an SDS chapter. I informed the SPU headquarters in Chicago of what we had done. They said we couldn't do that, and I replied we already had.

I would say that the early SDS, as a whole, was more radical than it is often given credit for. The radicalism of SDS would be tested in practice later that year in October, during the Cuban Missile Crisis, when the world came as close to nuclear war as it ever would. We responded vigorously with a rapidly improvised demonstration at the White House demanding a pullback from the brink of nuclear war—and a long pamphlet explaining how the Cold War led to such a disastrous situation. Soon after that, our Baltimore SDS chapter participated in the huge Northwood Theater sit-in along with more than three hundred students from Morgan. In 1963, many of us in Baltimore SDS signed up as volunteer organizers for the March on Washington for Jobs and Freedom. We played a small role in the debate over getting buses for the unemployed. The Ministerial Alliance opposed this, while CIG, CORE, and SDS were, of course, for it. In the end, A. Philip Randolph, the force behind the March on Washington, came to town and laid down the law—the unemployed would ride the buses to Washington. The black steel workers rented eighty buses just to make sure. Our chapter was on the way to becoming bigger than we could have been as part of SPU and more deeply involved in social issues. Soon, we would participate in debating the community organizing strategies eventually put into practice through SDS's ERAP. That, however, is another story.

Looking at the place of Port Huron and the early SDS in the development of the movements of the 1960s and beyond, it can certainly be said that the first three or four years of SDS produced a significant number of talented organizers, thinkers, and activists in a number of fields: community and labor organizing and the antiwar and women's movements. SDS should also get a good deal of credit for kicking off the mass movement against the Vietnam War in 1965. What is more, as the 2012 Ann Arbor conference on the *Port Huron Statement* showed, many of the veterans of Port Huron are still fighting the good fight. And, of course, there has recently been a good deal of interest among young activists and scholars about SDS. But in many ways, the early SDS and the politics of the *Port Huron Statement* were left behind as the movements took on a more radical direction—though not always a healthy one (as indicated by the Weather Underground).

On the other hand, the realignment strategy soon took a powerful hit when Democratic Party liberals and labor leaders succumbed to President Johnson's refusal to seat the Mississippi Freedom Democratic Party delegation at the 1964 Atlantic City convention. In the light of Black Power, urban riots, massive civil disobedience of the antiwar movement, and other signs of militancy in the late 1960s, the *Port Huron Statement* seems, well, too polite. Nor did its afterthought on organized labor prepare us for the upsurge of public-sector workers or the rank-and-file rebellion that commenced in the mid-1960s and shook the established unions as well as American capitalism through the mid-1970s. This was not because the sages of Port Huron failed to predict these events—nobody could have. Rather, the analysis of organized labor that came out of Port Huron was undermined by the liberal "coalitionism" inherent in the realignment strategy focused on reforming the Democratic Party and by the ghost of C. Wright Mills and his rejection of the "labor metaphysic." Still, I wouldn't have missed Port Huron for all the world.

9 | It's Time to Change the Water in the Fish Tank

by Frank Joyce

Several speakers at the 2012 New Insurgency conference suggested that the *Port Huron Statement* had been a catalyst for profound gains in opportunities for women. I agree. Further, the remarkable shift in the social position of lesbian, gay, bisexual, or transgender (LGBT) people has been even more rapid and dramatic. While there is still a long way to go, there is no denying the evidence of profound improvements in attitudes and policies. At the same time, however, too many of us ignore the continuing reality of black-white disparities in wealth, income, access to health care, longevity, incarceration, employment, and every other aspect of US life. Behind the evasion lies the reality of white racism.

One way or another, struggling with that reality has been my life's work. Like many who came to join the New Left, I was something of a rebel without a cause in my high school years. The year after graduation, I found my cause. In spring 1960, a few months after courageous college students from North Carolina Agricultural and Technical State University made history by sitting in at a lunch counter in Greensboro, I was driving on Detroit's infamous Eight Mile Road when I saw a picket line and news vehicles at the corner of Greenfield. The picketers were protesting the privately owned Crystal Pool denying access to African American children. I made a U-turn, parked my car, and joined the line. My picture was on the evening news. My father, with whom I already had an untenable relationship, saw it. As of the next day, I was out of the house. Fortunately, I had started working when I was twelve years old and have been employed ever since. My factory job paid enough for rent, living expenses, and tuition for the classes I was taking at Wayne State University.

Not long after that, I discovered the Northern Student Movement (NSM) from an article in *Reporter* magazine about its founders, Peter and

Joan Countryman. I wrote them a letter, promptly heard back, and became the founder of a Detroit chapter of NSM. That in turn intersected with the emerging political consciousness at Wayne State and within the religious community. As I became more involved in the national organization, NSM grew, and we had projects and full-time staff in many cities and chapters on many campuses. We supported the Student Nonviolent Coordinating Committee (SNCC) in the South but also developed projects of our own to address the effects of racism in city ghettos. We quickly got past the idea that racism was a "southern" phenomenon.

I helped organize tutoring programs for Detroit Public School students in the Brewster-Douglas Housing Projects, the largest public housing tract in the city, under the auspices of NSM. (One Brewster Douglass resident was a young woman by the name of Diana Ross. Her younger brother Fred was one of my "tutees," as we called them at the time.) The tutorial program grew and was an eye-opening experience for me and many other, mostly white college students. The more involved we got, the more radicalized we became. It became increasingly obvious that the problems of the students were caused by a racist *system*.

Somewhere around 1965, a serious conversation began within NSM about the role of whites in what had always been a multiracial organization. The awareness grew that the more appropriate task of whites was not in helping blacks but rather in taking the antiracist struggle into the white community. This was and still is a very radical idea. To this day, many liberals and radicals think that well-meaning whites should support policies that "help" African Americans. Among other problems, this carries within it the deeply embedded notion that there is something "wrong" with blacks and nothing "wrong" with whites. To put it another way, the problem isn't the *effects* of racism, although they surely exist. The problem is the racism itself. A variation on this theme is the position that the role of whites is to be an ally of the black movement. This too suggests that racism is not itself destructive to whites.

The same conversation about the role of whites in combatting racism would intensify in SNCC too, but before that happened, NSM had already divided into NSM and Friends of NSM. Most of the whites became active in Friends of NSM. Those who disagreed with the decision left. About a year later, the Friends of NSM became People Against Racism (PAR). For a time, PAR flourished. At its peak, we had full-time staff in several cities, chapters on at least twenty-five campuses coast-to-coast, and many individual supporters. We developed a body of literature explaining and exploring racism that was widely circulated.

Often in conjunction with faith-based organizations, we conducted workshops and forums on race and racism. And we participated in the larger movement. After an intense internal debate, PAR decided to oppose the Vietnam War on the grounds that it was racist. The "domino theory" that warned against one country falling to Communism after another—and threatening the "American way of life"—targeted the nonwhite peoples of Southeast Asia. We thought the American way of life was itself racist anyway, and thus every policy decision foreign and domestic was infused with white supremacy. And we noted that those being sent to Vietnam to kill and be killed were disproportionally people of color. On that basis, in 1968 PAR participated in and helped organize many antiwar demonstrations, including those at the infamous Democratic convention in Chicago.

Looking back on 1960s history leads to an inescapable conclusion. Our movement was for all practical purposes racially segregated. SDS was overwhelmingly white. SNCC was mostly black, although whites made great contributions, most notably during Freedom Summer in 1964. For a time the Congress on Racial Equality (CORE) was genuinely interracial. The antiwar movement was a complex coalition but overwhelmingly white, in both its leadership and participation. (Opposition to the war within the military was more complex.) NSM was multiracial but then deliberately separated along racial lines.

My purpose here though is not to rehash the issues of the New Left and race but to look forward. The time for a new abolition movement is at hand. And no, I don't mean the appropriation of the term by those fighting human trafficking or, with all due respect, environmentalists like Bill McKibben who are talking about getting rid of fossil fuels.

I mean the real thing. Now, however, instead of a movement to abolish *slavery*, we have the opportunity to abolish white racism.

The original US abolition movement is worthy of study by any contemporary political activist. I am not aware of any US political movement since that one that achieved so much in such a short period of time, albeit at the incredibly high cost of the civil war.

A good place to start is Adam Hochschild's book *Bury the Chains*, which describes the pioneering work done by the British abolitionists. As Hochschild's book observes, concepts from the abolition movement in Britain shaped concepts of human rights and methods of political organizing that endure to this day. The same is true of the US version of the movement. In fact, the *Port Huron Statement* and all that flowed from it are the linear descendants of abolitionism.

But while chattel slavery was abolished in the United States, racism, white supremacy, and segregation are still very much with us. The United States is now and always has been an apartheid society. Our Constitution, government, economy, and culture rest on a systemic foundation of structural, ideological, and psychological white supremacy. Each successful challenge to that system produced a counterrevolution that reinvented white domination in a modified form. Jim Crow replaced slavery. The end of Jim Crow brought the race-based capitalism that still defines our society today.

The success of each counterrevolution notwithstanding, the social changes that elicited backlash do teach us that change is possible. Otherwise, there wouldn't have been anything to backlash against.

The challenge now is to make a revolution that takes us to the next level. To do so requires that we recognize the critical role white supremacy plays in impeding *any* further social progress. We can no longer be satisfied when some persecuted groups gain rights while another is still pushed down. Nor can we any longer indulge the delusion that we can "fix" this system piecemeal. What we can do is fully embrace the systemic change the *Port Huron Statement* envisioned.

The fact that we find ourselves at the end times of race-based capitalism makes it possible. The ecological threat to the planet makes it necessary. Bending the arc of history toward justice makes it morally compelling.

End times, you ask? Doesn't race-based capitalism look more invincible than ever? Isn't institutional racism so deeply entrenched that it will continue indefinitely, preserving white advantages? And isn't "the 1 percent" ready, willing, and able to intervene if any force threatens to disrupt the loyalty of large numbers of whites to the race-based capitalist system?

Yes, capitalism may appear invincible, and we know that well-meaning leftists have, for decades, predicted its demise erroneously. Pockets of capitalism appear to be thriving. It seems as if young entrepreneurs in the Bay Area have made San Francisco off limits to all but millionaires, and the same goes for cities from Shanghai to São Paulo. On top of that, the communication department of global capitalism devotes no small resources to advancing the view that the system is working just fine. And even if it isn't, they say, "There is no alternative" (TINA). They send that message repeatedly via any and every platform they can find or invent.

But appearances can be deceiving. Capitalism does not really look all that stable and its own press carries daily stories about one crisis or another. More significantly, however, we may have more to fear from the continued success of capitalism than from its decline or collapse. The number of ordinary people acknowledging capitalism's threat to the ecology of the planet is rising. Awareness of capitalism's role in escalating inequality is clearly growing. So is doubt about global capitalism's capacity to provide anything close to "full," let alone meaningful, employment.

Also encouraging are emerging visionary theories about social and economic alternatives, made possible by new technologies and changing modes of production. Grace Boggs, Paul Hawken, Vandana Shiva, Frithjof Bergmann, Gar Alperovitz, Michael Hardt and Antonio Negri, Arundhati Roy, and many others are developing these perspectives. They understand that the kind of economic growth required by capitalism is the problem faced by humanity—not its solution.

Set aside for the moment the strength or weakness of race-based *capitalism*. What are the vulnerabilities of ideological, structural, and attitudinal *white racism*? Why should we think, as I do, that it can be uprooted?

For starters, there is an upside to the myth of postracialism: many whites aspire to get over, under, or around race in a way that is not *simply* a deliberate defense of the status quo. Obviously, I am not talking here about the white supremacist sympathizers who wear black robes on the aptly named Supreme Court. I mean those who genuinely work to rid their daily lives of racial prejudice and discriminatory behaviors. I'm not sure how many of these people there are, but they surely exist.

Second, our communication tools are improved. From a historical perspective, narratives quite different from the ones we learn in school are now more available. In *Fear Itself: The New Deal and the Origins of Our Time*, for instance, Ira Katznelson brilliantly describes the quid pro quo that entrenched white power exacted for its support of the New Deal's social contract: social and economic gains reserved for whites were won at the cost of preserving racial oppression. Jim Crow Democrats provided the necessary votes for passage of the National Labor Relations Act (NLRA) by explicitly exempting the businesses that employed most African Americans. They also gutted attempts to expand voting rights for African American soldiers and veterans of World War II in ways that have provided a template for voter suppression today. In sum, Katznelson has shown the means by which white privilege is created and institutionalized.

In popular culture, films like *12 Years a Slave*, *The Help*, and *Fruitvale Station* have brought the brutal reality of white racism to the attention of large audiences. Increased representation of African Americans in television programs and advertisements counteracts some of the "otherness" that helps perpetuate racism and segregation. For that matter, so does having an African American president. That's why ardent defenders of the racial status quo devote so much energy to delegitimizing Barack Obama.

Beyond powerful historical accounts, scholars and activists alike are better understanding and better explaining why whites now have many incentives to purge white privilege from personal attitudes and from the structure of our political economy. *Washington Monthly* editor Philip Longman has written brilliantly about how racial disparities in health are disadvantageous to both whites and blacks.

Long-held attitudes can change. We see this in the success of dedicated efforts to change public opinion, such as the campaign to publicize the adverse health effects of smoking, despite the tobacco companies' denial; the new knowledge of the head injuries suffered in contact sports like football and hockey; and growing opposition to bullying.

In describing the kind of change needed to establish a sustainable society, environmentalist Paul Hawken said in 2012, "What we're trying to do is not about winning, it's about losing, and it's about losing this burden of having to make it, to be rich, to be comfortable, to be seen, to be famous, to be followed, to be friended, to be known. We don't need all that because it's an upside down world and the winners are the losers. And what we lose is the delusion and suffering that we are here on Earth for ourselves." Likewise, "losing" white racism is liberating. The white man's burden isn't black people. The white man's burden is racism. It's time to lift it.

To be sure, many whites are emotionally invested in preserving their advantages and their deeply ingrained sense of "superiority." Denial and avoidance is their first line of defense. To read the comments section of any newspaper or website post that touches at all on race is to see this attitude writ large. Often the language is explicitly hateful. Even when it isn't, these arguments can be stunningly wrong-headed, self-justifying, and uninformed. Here, for example, is what "Sarah from Brooklyn" said in an online comment to the *New York Times* in June of 2013:

> Young white males are the most discriminated against group in this time of our history. They are not responsible for the racism that existed 50 years ago just as blacks are not responsible for the Irish slaves (the forgotten slaves in our history). Blacks are now overrepresented in all areas of government, unionized workers, city jobs and the list goes on. White males are being turned away for jobs over blacks and Spanish applicants. Community colleges are mostly black. Whites are held to higher SAT scores and turned away routinely. . . . Not all white people are rich and . . . not all black people are poor. Some are children of doctors, lawyers, principals of

schools, teachers etc. Those children have not experienced any poverty or discrimination and would be put ahead of a poor white person simply because they are black. Not fair. Diversity is a good thing but Affirmative Action is not achieving diversity, it is creating an anti-white society and clearly hurting whites.

In response to arguments like that, the antiracist activist Tim Wise has observed whites are oblivious to white privilege in the same way that "a fish doesn't know it's wet." And yet I am convinced that somewhere deep down inside, most whites do know that their skin color alone provides them with many advantages.

In fact a major component of race-based capitalism is a place in the white "brain" that is engineered for willful ignorance and denial. The alleged lack of awareness is a tactic. The tactic is in pursuit of protecting the privilege. This is why many whites claim to be so good at knowing what racism is not and at the same time so poor at knowing what racism is—let alone being interested in doing anything about it.

Whether we acknowledge it or not, there is only so far we can go in overcoming *any* present social injustice if we try to do so without addressing racial injustice. The problems we face, especially reversing the ecocatastrophe that is already well under way, require human unity. Survival recalibrates our priorities. As author Rebecca Solnit argues in *A Paradise Built in Hell: The Extraordinary Communities That Arise in Disaster*, catastrophe or the prospect of it often brings out the best in humans. That's true even in contemporary capitalist society where people have been trained in extreme individualism and all-competition-all-the-time.

All that aside, whether whites currently appear "ready" or not for abolition doesn't matter as much as one might think. Is the deck any more stacked now than when the original abolitionists in England or the United States began their campaign against slavery? I don't think so. Social change is hard to predict. The history is clear that when African Americans intensify their struggle, some whites respond with support.

How might a new abolition movement be organized? Certainly there are existing organizations within both the faith-based and the secular communities that might be mobilized. Many college campuses already have some kind of antiracist organization. For the past twenty-five years, Not in Our Town/Not in Our Schools, an organization that fights hate crimes, has deployed innovative and effective models for overcoming many forms of bigoted thoughts and actions.

This is not the time or place for a fully detailed blueprint. No one person could design such a thing anyway. But a dialogue can begin. We can all start by resisting the formation of segregated organizations for social change. Whatever the issue, multiracial organizations and coalitions should be the goal whether they occur "organically" or because organizers do whatever it takes to bring them about. Moral Mondays in North Carolina clearly meets this standard, and such organizations should be supported in any way we can.

Reducing the grip of white racism is admittedly a daunting challenge. It may seem that "Sarah from Brooklyn" is unlikely to ever change her mind. But remember, women made remarkable gains over the last fifty years, and the LGBT movement brought about stunning changes in hearts, minds, and policies in an even shorter time. Yet patriarchy and homophobia are ancient practices. So surely we can do something about white racism. It's only five hundred years old.

10 | Democracy, Labor, and Globalization: Reflections on Port Huron

by Robert J. S. Ross

Participatory democracy, the central idea of the *Port Huron Statement*, is today more relevant than ever before. The assault on labor rights launched in Wisconsin and other Midwest states during 2011, the rise and fall of Occupy Wall Street as a movement against inequality, and the continuing institutionalization of global capitalism and financial capital's power within it all raise the question "What does the concept of participatory democracy mean in our era of crisis and hardship?" Indeed, questions of organization and decision making are relevant at all times when ordinary people seek to organize themselves for political and social action. So here I shall focus on the meaning of participatory democracy as we founding members of Students for a Democratic Society (SDS) understood it and practiced it, when we first sought to build a movement that could change the world at home and abroad. In the process I want to correct some propositions about that decision-making process that have, in my view, more currency than accuracy.

Some Background

In spring 1960 I joined picketers in Ann Arbor who were supporting the national call for a boycott of Woolworth and Kresge stores. Sit-ins pressing for the desegregation of lunch counters had swept the South after students at the North Carolina Agriculture and Technical College got things started in Greensboro, North Carolina, on February 1. Our picketing showed our solidarity with their cause. After the local picketing had begun, a Conference on Human Rights in the North was convened in Ann

Arbor in April 1960. Robert Alan "Al" Haber had planned this conference *before* the southern sit-ins changed the landscape of social action. This was but one of Haber's farsighted plans that earned him the adjective "prophetic." Al had understood that the "human rights" of Black people—then referred to as Negroes—were a national not just a regional issue.

Haber was a long-term Ann Arborite. His father, Professor William Haber, had been a prominent New Deal economist and would become dean of the University of Michigan College of Literature, Science, and the Arts (1963–68). Al had become involved in SDS's predecessor, the Student League for Industrial Democracy (SLID), through its Michigan chapter, the Political Issues Club, and he had risen to some responsibility in SLID's small national membership.[1] Having been introduced to activism by the spring picketing, I attended the April conference—though only after contacting Haber and asking him to suspend the registration fee, which I could not afford. He did. Afterwards, Haber asked a number of the picketers and those who had been active at the conference to join him in the new incarnation of SLID, which he proposed to rename SDS. Those of us whom Haber recruited were each very young. I was finishing my first year in college and so too was my future roommate and successor as Ann Arbor SDS chapter leader, Dickie Magidoff. Sharon Jeffrey, who would soon be my cochair, was a second-year student. She was the daughter of ex-socialist Mildred Jeffrey, one of the United Auto Workers' key political strategists. Haber had succeeded through long, patient one-on-one conversations in convincing us that democracy itself was a radical idea—the ultimate radical idea—and that on this basis, the schisms and sectarianisms of the past could be laid aside for a new vision.

At the June 1960 convention of the newly named SDS, I became—at the tender age of seventeen—a member of the reconstituted National Executive Committee. Soon thereafter, that body named me vice president, in strict accordance with *Robert's Rules of Order*. I was nominated and voted in to fill a vice presidential vacancy created by the resignation of a member of the Yale chapter who distrusted the new activist turn of SDS. The total number of voters in this election was three.

Back in New York during summer 1960, I was an after-hours volunteer at the national SDS office on Nineteenth Street in Manhattan while holding down a seven-day-a-week job as a lifeguard and tennis court attendant near my home in the South Bronx. I stuffed envelopes and helped with production of newsletters. It was a bit like a summer course in political theory and praxis with Chairman Al, the Socratic seminar leader.

Over the next two years, we organized several chapters, the most vigorous and successful of which was at Michigan, where VOICE, a mass political party campaigned and won leadership with the student government. Tom Hayden and his associates Ken McEldowney and Andy Hawley, all senior editors at the *Michigan Daily*, had been the instigators and first organizers of VOICE, but Sharon Jeffrey and I made it a winner of elections and campaigns. As leaders of the SDS chapter, Sharon and I brought the local group into VOICE and then led VOICE to affiliate nationally with SDS.

Hayden had returned from a summer at the University of California, Berkeley, impressed by the pioneer New Left student organization SLATE, which had done the counterintuitive thing for student radicals and taken student government seriously. Largely the province of the Greek letter organizations, student governments were somewhere between the sandboxes for political toddlers and training grounds for future Young Democrats and Republicans. Hayden saw the possibility of making the student government a representative voice for students in real governance—and Sharon and I thought this was just the right thing to do, if democracy was the centerpiece of your thinking.

Even before Port Huron, then, a local practice was emerging in Ann Arbor and other soon-to-be affiliated SDS chapters, which saw democratic practice as relevant to university governance and educational issues. We butted heads with student government conservatives and centrists, who opposed our desire to have the council make pronouncements on political issues of national and international consequence (e.g., passing a resolution against the Bay of Pigs Invasion). But we were also vitally concerned with campus issues. Thus we campaigned to prohibit racial discrimination in the Greek letter societies that wished to use university facilities (which was all of them). Another issue was our campaign against the principle and practices of in loco parentis, whereby universities acted in place of parents and thus enforced curfews that applied to women and constrained our lives with other regulations we considered far too intrusive. Eventually we won this fight and the dorms were "liberated": dorm hours were eventually abolished, and men and women could entertain visitors of the opposite sex. And, of course, after a while, co-ed dorms emerged.

The experience Sharon and I had as VOICE representatives on the student government council shaped my views on "process," a contentious issue later in the 1960s and beyond. Since the council was a formal body, with a constituency of twenty-five thousand student voters, its proceedings followed strict rules—and thus Sharon and I endured a crash course in parliamentary procedure. From that time on, I became, willy-nilly, one of the Movement's experts on how to run large meetings. Our SDS/VOICE chapter settled decisions—when there was division—by a formal vote at a membership meeting. Mostly we made decisions in small groupings and votes were not required; but when the meetings were large and the decisions weighty, we voted, counted hands, and declared a winner.

I do have one vivid memory of such an occasion. During the Cuban Missile Crisis of October 1962, our leftist community in Ann Arbor was, to say the least, tense. Tom Hayden, Dick and Mickey Flacks, and others were huddled around the shortwave radio of a friend of ours, the social psychologist Bill Livant, listening to an English-language broadcast of Radio Moscow, which they somehow thought would give them new or different information than that which came from US media sources. Mickey headed for Washington, DC, to demonstrate with Women Strike for Peace, which wanted a United Nations–mediated solution. Meanwhile, fully resigned to being momentarily powerless, I drafted the VOICE political party platform for the upcoming elections to student government. My draft of the platform condemned the Kennedy administration threat to start a nuclear war over the Cuban missiles. When the VOICE membership later met to consider the draft, we took formal majority votes on each part.

Our practice as campaigners running for student government office in no way channeled or restricted our practice as social movement activists. Our local organizing in support of the Student Nonviolent Coordinating Committee (SNCC) and our demonstrations against the arms race continued apace. One virtue of the student government campaigns: they caused us to bring our ideas about democracy in the university and democratic participation in the society and economy face to face to thousands of folks who otherwise would never have come to a leftist rally or encountered our ideas.

In the course of reorganizing the old SLID, Haber, Hayden, and the rest of us were making what had been a fairly inert "discussion club" formation into a more activist organization. We also had to deal with SLID/SDS's heritage as an extension of the social-democratic movement, which had staked out an anticommunist and, for better or worse, nonrevolutionary position. In December 1961 at a National Council meeting in Ann Arbor, members aligned with the Young People's Socialist League (YPSL, often pronounced "Yipsel"), the youth group of the Socialist Party, vigorously challenged the "anti-anticommunist" positions the new leadership had taken: rather than prohibiting any collaboration with Communist Party members, we took an "inclusionary" attitude, and we developed a critique of those liberals and laborites who acquiesced in the arms race and the Cold War.

For Tom, Al, and Sharon, each of different heritages but none of Communist parentage, the social-democratic fixation on anticommunist purity on the left was an overly sectarian and narrow view of the need for social reform here in the United States: this old antagonism, which dominated SLID's parent, the New York–headquartered League for Industrial Democracy, was a sea anchor that kept us from moving with the winds of change.

For those of us whose parents had been influenced by the Communist movement (and thus were sometimes called "red diaper babies"), this social-democratic heritage was an insulting and threatening slur and a scary attack on our parents and their friends. We considered our elders— largely rank and filers—to be ultimately democratic; we gave little credence to the Cold War anticommunist charge that they were the carriers of totalitarianism. In fact, the culture that surrounded the young people in, around, and formerly of the Communist movement seemed so committed to democracy that when Haber preached democracy as the bedrock idea for radicalism, we felt comfortable, despite SDS's anticommunist social-democratic parentage.

Port Huron and Participatory Democracy

The YPSL challenge to these emerging SDS attitudes made it apparent that some sort of defining statement, a manifesto, was needed to articulate a vision for a New Left. Tom Hayden, Al Haber, and I were named to a drafting committee, but immediately it became clear that Tom was the writer, and (while I cannot speak for Al) my job was encouragement.

If democracy was the radical umbrella, though, what was wrong with what we—the United States—had then and have now? Our critique of contemporary democratic practice leading up to Port Huron can be summarized briefly: citizenship as broadly understood was part-time and passive. You listened, you voted, and you were done. Democratic rights did not extend to the economy, so power over everyday life was exercised by corporate bureaucracies beyond the reach of workers and community members. Democratic rights were routinely denied to Black people by law and practice, while economic inequality excluded the poor from the community of citizens. And finally, the political parties were morally compromised and politically inert; potential opposition was entombed in Cold War orthodoxy and unable to challenge it—unable, that is, to speak truth to power.

Participatory Democracy

Tom read numerous statements from independent left thinkers. We were all influenced by C. Wright Mills, but Hayden was an omnivorous reader, and among those who particularly influenced him was one of our professors at the University of Michigan, Arnold Kaufman, a social philosopher.[2] At the core of Kaufman's thought was the proposition that we can be more than isolated, self-absorbed, and narrow beings and that democratic participation can expand human capacities. Democratic activism, thought Kaufman, is a kind of redemption. These reflections on democracy and human capacity, which found their way into the very first paragraphs of the *Port Huron Statement* draft, were followed by critique of the economy, of poverty, of segregation, of the danger of nuclear war, and of the stifling of the developing world. A section focused on the segregationist Dixiecrat influence in the Democratic Party and called for the ouster of racist tribunes from that party. This was in fact a part of the social-democratic strategy favored by the Socialist Party activist Michael Harrington: an effort to "realign" the Democrats as a more consistently liberal-left party.[3] Ironically, the Voting Rights Act of 1965—and the Republican Party's strategic choice to become the party of southern white people—did largely accomplish this. It had a historic downside too: persistent Republican majorities in the states of the former Confederacy.

When we assembled at Port Huron, attendees were confronted with the task of absorbing and amending Tom Hayden's forty-nine-page draft—and making it their own. There and at virtually every SDS convention that was to follow, adherence to parliamentary procedure and forms of representation was normal.[4] Early on, the participants decided on a "bones and flesh" strategy of amendment and discussion. The document was broken down to sections, and these were assigned to small committees of three to five members. I participated in the group working on the labor movement and its relations to the student movement. Each group was to break down its section into "bones" (i.e., essential political or strategic points). These were matters to be debated and possibly revised. The bones, and any proposed changes in them, would be brought before a final plenary meeting, which would send instructions to a subsequent (postconvention) drafting committee. (There the "flesh"—or prose needed to elucidate the positions adopted by the plenary—would be added.) The small groups worked more or less informally, but the Port Huron final plenary was composed of thirty or forty people, who voted in a highly formal manner to pass, reject, or amend these bones. It took all night.

One of the moments I found most memorable occurred during the discussion of the section on the arms race and the Cold War. A YPSL member assailed the section and called many of the participants (pointedly myself) "paranoiac anti-anticommunists." A majority vote defeated his attempt to change that "bone."

The idea of participatory democracy was not originally or essentially about how to conduct meetings; it was about how to organize society and to conceive of citizenship. The *Port Huron Statement* contrasted "domination of politics and the economy by fantastically rich elites" with the alternative of "shared abundance." We acknowledged the labor movement, which played a central role in improving workers' lives, as the most democratic institution of the mainstream, but noted too that "'union democracy' is not simply inhibited by labor leader elitism, but by the unrelated problem of rank-and-file apathy to the tradition of unionism."[5] Way ahead of its time, the *Statement* also remarked, "The contemporary social assault on the labor movement is of crisis proportions."[6] In my view at the time, participatory democracy was an American phrase to encompass socialist democracy (and I still hold to that). In early SDS, many of us had a strong interest in worker-oriented democratic innovations abroad, ranging from the German codetermination law (putting union representatives on corporate boards) to Yugoslavian workers councils.[7]

In the period between Port Huron, in June 1962, and the March on Washington to End the War in Vietnam, in April 1965, SDS became steadily more well known through the work of its campus chapters and the writing and speaking of its talented national leaders, including Hayden, Haber, Todd Gitlin, and Paul Potter. Throughout this period—and beyond—internal decisions were made by more or less standard parliamentary procedures and representative democracy. In these few years, SDS grew slowly but steadily. The *Port Huron Statement* was widely circulated through the traditional mimeograph duplication process and also by the photocopying of the first typeset publication of the *Statement* in the Methodist collegiate magazine *Motive*.

The 1963 SDS National Convention considered and adopted (by formal majority votes) a successor to the Port Huron manifesto titled "America and the New Era."[8] Unfortunately neglected by scholars, "America and the New Era" is a better guide to subsequent SDS views and behavior than any other document, including the *Port Huron Statement*. "America and the New Era" identifies the character of the Kennedy administration as "corporate liberalism"—note the parallel to the later usage "corporate globalization"—and calls for a politics of "local insurgency."[9]

Beginning in 1964, most intensely with the Swarthmore College chapter, SDS began to think about community organizing as a radical practice. The Economic Research and Action Project (ERAP) was launched in summer 1964 with groups working in ten cities. About six of these projects survived as multiyear organizations, and two or three were to have long-range impact on their cities and on the left: Newark, Cleveland, and Chicago. The ERAP initiative meant there were ex-student SDSers consisting of a large fraction of the de facto if not de jure leaders of the organization, who were now off campus in nonchapter groupings.

This transition was the setting for a dramatic and critical incident in which the future of SDS and the antiwar movement hinged upon an obscure parliamentary maneuver. I tell this tale both because it is fun to remember it and also because it so thoroughly refutes the idea that SDS advocated a democratic process without strong procedures or majority votes.

Robert's Rules Save the Day

On December 31, 1964, the SDS National Council convened at a union meeting hall in lower Manhattan. Late in the evening, a member from New York, Jim Brook, then working as a letter carrier, made an impassioned call for SDS to initiate a demonstration against the impending escalation of the war in Vietnam. One will recall that in August 1964, the notorious incident in the Gulf of Tonkin had given Johnson and McNamara the excuse they apparently wanted to escalate US intervention. After alleged, and highly contested, attacks upon the destroyers *Turner* and *Maddox Joy*, the United States, for the first time, undertook a massive and openly acknowledged bombing of North Vietnamese targets. Plans for a major escalation in the use of US ground forces were in the works.

Brook came before the council at roughly eleven o'clock at night. Already, some of the women had begun setting up food and drink for a New Year's party at the back of the room. (Yes, that is the way it was then.) In opposition to Brook's anti-imperialist plea for action, a number of the more senior and well-respected leaders of SDS, who were now situated in ERAP community organizing projects, rose to express doubt about the proposal. They argued that antiwar work would make SDS too single-issue, not the comprehensively radical organization it had always aspired to be, and they also thought that the effort to organize antiwar work would not connect to the poor white and black constituents of the ERAP projects and thus would detract from the work of the community organizers.

Among other highly influential people expressing these doubts, Tom Hayden figured prominently. It's more than a bit ironic given his future role as a major leader of antiwar action during the Vietnam conflict and after, but Brother Tom made a Buddha-like intervention, wondering what would happen if we called a demo and nobody came. I note openly that Tom has a different memory of this moment than I do. The motion to sponsor the march failed, with people like me—with one foot in community organizing and another on campus as a graduate student—torn. I voted against.

The meeting recessed for party preparation, and in the interim my former roommate, Dickie Magidoff, then working in the Cleveland ERAP project, urgently brought me to a side conversation. "This is a big deal" was the burden of his whispered plea. We can't let this pass by. We have got to change it. And I was the man to do it, because, as you will recall, I had learned the technics of parliamentary procedure cold when I had been a University of Michigan student government leader. One of *Robert's Rules of Order*'s little miracle escape hatches is this: an individual may move to reconsider a question if and only if he or she has voted on the prevailing side. Dickie knew this, as did I.

As the clock approached midnight and we prepared for partying, the meeting reconvened to finish things off. I moved to reconsider. I cannot claim to have made any important intervention in the debate. SDS national secretary Clark Kissinger, a University of Wisconsin radical who had attended Port Huron, made the last and most persuasive plea about the moral responsibility to oppose an outright imperialist war. On a reconsideration vote, the motion passed and history was thus bent through the use of *Robert's Rules of Order*.

So, on April 17, 1965, SDS led the first big Washington demonstration against the war in Vietnam, the March on Washington to End the War in Vietnam. At that time it was the largest demonstration against an American war policy since the Spanish-American War. The old guard of anti-communist social democrats was scandalized by our nonexclusionary policy: Y'all come, we said, if you agree with the main slogan: "End the War in Vietnam." They were more concerned that Communists would join the March than they were that the March would succeed. That the March did galvanize public opinion and mobilize a new wave of public opposition to the war was perhaps the definitive sign that the Cold War on the left was over—or irrelevant—and that the New Left was now the culturally and politically hegemonic left.

For SDS the march—the very act of calling for the march—was transformative. At the University of Chicago, where I was forming a new chapter in my first year of graduate school, our meetings of fifteen to twenty-five became meetings of one hundred. We sent five buses to Washington from Chicago. We had one chapter in Chicago before the March; by the time the buses returned, we had at least three, including those at Roosevelt University and Northwestern. SDS had become, overnight, a mass organization.

Reflecting on Participatory Democracy

These reflections on how individual SDS chapters governed themselves, and on how the national body came to call for the March on Washington to End the War in Vietnam, set in motion an alternative understanding of what has all too often become a canonical interpretation of what we at Port Huron meant by participatory democracy. In subsequent years many commentators have trivialized the idea of participatory democracy or defined it as impractical and utopian in the worst sense.

While rigorous participation and direct involvement in decisions was the ideal, the notion that no one could or should be *represented*—that voting for a representative was inherently undemocratic—would have been viewed as silly by Port Huron participants. We voted for our national officers; we voted for chapter leaders; we voted for resolutions and for constitutional alterations. Whatever I may say later about the problems of democracy in a global setting, Port Huron veterans and those who joined SDS in later years were not silly. We thought of ourselves as vigorously participating citizens—and some, at times, would have said revolutionaries.

How did participatory democracy come to be trivialized as a meeting rule for small groups? One guess is mistakes by journalists and misinterpretations by new recruits. If a journalist came to a small local chapter meeting, he or she might observe a kind of consensus-seeking process taking place. Given the prominence of the rhetoric about participatory democracy, this might then become what the journalist thought it was all about. By thus reporting it, the idea became a self-fulfilling prophecy. In addition, SDS grew so rapidly that there was little "socialization" of newer members by older members.[10] A kind of naive literalism was fueled, perhaps, by a romantic cultural memory of America's own anarchosyndicalist past. New Leftists venerated the memory of the Industrial Workers of the World (IWW): many agreed with the famous IWW motto "We are all leaders." There was also a sort of cultural affinity between a rejection of representation and the hyperindividualism of parts of American culture at that time: "I am unique; no one can represent me."

By the second decade of the twenty-first century, the notion of participatory democracy as a philosophy of group process had enough currency to be adopted uncritically by the Occupy Wall Street anarchist tendency. They too found an American phrase for a European-origin ideology, but this time it was not socialism but rather a variant of anarchism. This was sustained by a certain cultural ambience that has been a factor of continuity between SDS and successor organizations like Occupy Wall Street that identify with its heritage. Former SDS vice president and quipster Paul Booth once made the semifacetious remark that SDSers think "freedom is a constant meeting." Another time he said we might be "students for a small society." It is assumed that the element of continuity lies in an emphasis on process, community, and participation rather than formal majoritarian rules of debate and decision.

The most trivial interpretation of participatory democracy understands it as a way to conduct face-to-face meetings. Usually this interpretation conjures up consensus seeking as the fundamental goal and invents a variety of procedures for reaching it. What formal standards like venerable *Robert's Rules of Order* do—however dense and forbidding they seem—is to offer procedural safeguards assuring majority rule while also preserving minority rights. In contrast, a doctrine of consensus allows obstinate minorities to obstruct the will of the majority. Cases in point abound, including the highly consequential use of a sixty-vote requirement for cloture in the US Senate. A more absurdist example came during an Occupy Wall Street meeting in Atlanta one morning in October 2011 when an eccentric individual blocked Congressman John Lewis from speaking, an obstruction at variance from what appeared to be the will of an overwhelming majority of those present.

Of course, meeting facilitators and prudent activists will seek consensus under many circumstances. These include situations when there are very small groups of decision makers or when the stakes are extremely high and members of the group risk legal or physical jeopardy. Nonetheless, the national SDS still worked by majority vote when it took up matters that carried legal jeopardy in opposing the Vietnam War draft.

What did participatory democracy evoke as a phrase for the Port Huron cohort that, following Tom Hayden's writing, made it their own? Broadly speaking, my claim—as I mentioned previously—is that it was an American language for socialism and in particular for, of all things, industrial democracy. I can testify directly to the many conversations I had with comrades about worker control, German codetermination laws, the Yugoslav industrial example, and Wobbly syndicalist ideas. If bureaucratic power (in C. Wright Mills's dim view of it) was Satan, and Paul Goodman's simple anarchism was Eden, we were the democratic Adam as yet innocent.

Labor and Participatory Democracy

The *Port Huron Statement* was notable for addressing universities and students as potential agents of democratic change. Yet the document was conscious of the organization's historical ties to labor and the working-class movement. Contrary to the subsequent stereotype of SDS as "antilabor," Port Huron attendees included many with family and other connections to unionism. Some, like myself, came from working-class trade union families or families with trade union officials (such as VOICE cochair Sharon Jeffrey); others came from families of New Dealers with commitments to labor rights (such as Paul Booth). We should remember that SDS evolved from SLID. That the parent League for Industrial Democracy had become ossified in the course of the Cold War did not negate the proposition that workers' enfranchisement at work and in the broader economy was central to any vision of democracy. It remained central in ours.

While the inclusion of the working class and the labor movement in a vision of participatory democracy was near universal among the early founders of SDS, criticism of the labor movement from the standpoint of democracy was also widespread. In some ways the early SDS perception of threats to the labor moment was way ahead of its time. The document anticipates the attack on and decline of the labor movement, even while the social science and big picture political observers of the day were still talking about "big labor." Like AFL-CIO president George Meany, we thought of labor as "big," but in the *Port Huron Statement* we did accurately foresee its incremental defeat as a movement and institution. The initial formation of our consciousness about such matters came from, on the one hand, the liberal-labor coalition itself, embodied, for example, in John Kenneth Galbraith's theory of countervailing powers, which saw big labor, big government, and big corporations as in some sense balancing each other.[11] On the other hand, although we were not fully in contact with the rumblings in the labor movement itself, there were in fact members and places that were—for example, Kim Moody in Baltimore. So the section on the labor movement written and revised in 1962 is strikingly up to date: it bemoans bureaucratic lethargy, notes grassroots democratic discontent, and recognizes movements arising within unions to address these matters. Further, the *Port Huron Statement* notes threats to the existing labor movement from the shift away from manufacturing and toward service-producing industries. Reading it now affirms Haber and Hayden's prophetic insight: if one subjects every institution to scrutiny from the point of view of democracy and participation, much of what is wrong will be clear and much of its development can be predicted.

Substantial fractions of our critique of the labor movement were based on its own understanding of itself as strong, included in power, but—in our view—too conservative. We saw the cliff upon which union influence was so precariously perched, but because most of its official leadership did not, SDS was sometimes characterized as hostile to the labor movement. The discussion was not extended. The urgency of war and then the apocalypse of racial conflict—the urban "civil disturbances" of 1964 to 1968—distracted our attention from so many other avenues of reflection.

In any case the final draft of the *Port Huron Statement* has an amended reference to labor and students at the end. It is terribly written (solely because I wrote the revision), but it actually states a neglected proposition:

> To turn these possibilities into realities will involve national efforts at university reform by an alliance of students and faculty. They must wrest control of the educational process from the administrative bureaucracy. They must make fraternal and functional contact with allies in labor, civil rights, and other liberal forces outside the campus. They must import major public issues into the curriculum—research and teaching on problems of war and peace is an outstanding example. They must make debate and controversy, not dull pedantic cant, the common style for educational life. They must consciously build a base for their assault upon the loci of power.[12]

However clumsily stated, it seems to me ultimately appropriate to focus on the cooperation of young intellectuals, students and faculty alike, with labor, immigrant, and minority interests to remake more nearly democratic institutions and culture. The struggles of the last decade have in fact seen the burgeoning of just such coalitions.

The distance between SDS and the labor movement has usually been exaggerated. SDS had links to and strong sympathy with what would now be understood as "the labor left." That so many SDS veterans gravitated toward all parts of the labor movement is testimony to the central importance it played then and still does in viable visions of a democratic commonwealth.[13] If one takes democratic participation as a keystone value, then where else in American society, outside of the labor movement, do ordinary people have a say in conditions under which they work?

Democracy at Scale

If participatory democracy and the *Port Huron Statement* envisioned both social and economic democracy and envisioned empowered working people in alliance with educated youth, they nevertheless did not have, and the American left still does not have, an adequate response to the problem of scale. It is all very well to say that one wants to have a say in the decisions that affect one's life. Does that mean a group of upper-class property owners on Nantucket Sound should be able to frustrate a state or nation's desire for wind-powered energy? Does democracy mean that a board of selectmen or town meeting in a small village should be able to deny a building or zoning permit to a halfway house for emotionally disturbed juveniles or a Planned Parenthood facility? Leftists hearken when working-class neighborhoods resist toxic waste sites, but we don't have a consistent decision rule for when a small group of the people should decide or when larger aggregations of the people should decide. The *Statement* is not a guide to the problem of scale, and none of us—so far as my own small brain knows—have thought this through to a conclusion. The future of democratic movements and theory is open in other and even more dramatic ways than this.

For all its vision, the *Port Huron Statement*—as did every other midsixties understanding of global affairs—missed the impending change in the structure of global capital. The *Statement* is fairly naive about industrialization and its potential growth in those new nations that were once European or American colonies. It does not contemplate the use of low-income countries to pound down standards of living of workers in those nations bordering the North Atlantic.

So the problem of the race to the bottom is a whole new frontier for today's democratic movements—the reconciliation of workers' needs on a global basis. The matter has become increasingly painful. Oligarchical power elites steer key decision-making institutions: the central banks, the international financial institutions, the financial conglomerates, the regulatory agencies captured by the interests they are supposed to regulate, and transnational political institutions like the European Union or the World Trade Organization. The distance between those rulers and ordinary citizens is truly titanic. Accountability, no less participation, seems more exotic a hope each week. It is clear that democrats everywhere await—or should work to hasten—the day that workers of the world understand and find ways to cooperate so they all lose their chains.

Special edition stamp for the Asia-Africa Conference, Bandung, Indonesia, 1955, the political debut of the third world. Haus der Kulturen der Welt, Berlin, Germany

II.

Contexts

The Making of an American New Left

Unquestionably, the social-justice movements that gained momentum in the United States from the late 1950s on shook the foundations of American life. If not exactly comparable to the Civil War (and emancipation) or the "earthquake" of the Great Depression, these movements nonetheless mounted to the level of a potent seismic tremor that ended up recasting a great many norms governing relations of race, gender, sexuality, family, schooling, religion, city life, attitudes toward nature, economic affairs, and the place of the United States in the world. At many points through the formative period (1955–65), surges and setbacks to social movements left participants uncertain of whether challenges to the status quo would indeed ripen into a new, wholesale opposition; around 1965 and afterward, the trajectory of radicalization became much more evident. In retrospect, we recognize a new insurgency rising before and cresting after the mid-decade. And yet, in some respects, the notion of a "New Left" is misleading. Just as many historians today customarily refer to "the long civil rights movement" stretching across much of the twentieth century, we might better talk of a "long left" in which the distinctions of Old Left (1930s) and New Left (1960s) are less sharp than usually claimed. Christopher Phelps contributes to this kind of border crossing by demonstrating that "the New Left was old, and the Old Left was new"—that is, that older movements and activists remained on the scene in ways capable of wielding influence over the forms of the new insurgency and that the genuinely newer features of 1960s radicalism were not entirely without precedent in decades past.

In another kind of border-crossing move to contextualize the new insurgency, Matthew Countryman relativizes the customary distinction of North and South, demonstrating black resistance to white supremacy as much in the former as the latter and arguing that the New Left can hardly be understood aside from the racial system of the North. Ronald Aronson and Robert Genter, in their reviews of philosophy and esthetics, reinforce how much "sixties" attitudes rested on ideas and practices begun in the 1950s. Aldon Morris points out the unique combination of southern black activism and contemporary social science that shaped the characteristic views expressed in the *Port Huron Statement*.

Another context was quite immediate: Port Huron's time was summer 1962; fall 1962 was the time of the Cuban Missile Crisis. The fiftieth anniversary of that superpower confrontation was marked just a week prior to the New Insurgency conference. Two chapters here consider radical responses to the Missile Crisis, from quarters typically recognized as New Left (Todd Gitlin's recollection of how much the threat of nuclear war prevailed over the early SDS sensibility) and Old Left (Alan Wald's narrative of how activists of the Young Socialist Alliance—the Trotskyist youth wing of the Socialist Workers Party—dared the still-potent Red Scare environment of Bloomington, Indiana).

—Howard Brick

11 | Lefts Old and New: Sixties Radicalism, Now and Then

by Christopher Phelps

Now so familiar as to risk seeming clichéd, "We Shall Overcome" was the paramount song of the civil rights movement. "Deep in my heart, I do believe that we shall overcome some day": the song spoke to a generation's idealism, solidarity, and optimism in the coming triumph over injustice.

It is now practically lost to memory that the song enjoyed an equal vitality within the early New Left. *We Shall Overcome* was the official songbook title of the Student Nonviolent Coordinating Committee (SNCC), a group more important than the better-known Students for a Democratic Society (SDS) in generating sixties New Left radicalism. When Tom Hayden, at age twenty-one, traveled south from Michigan in 1961 to observe SNCC's efforts to register black voters in Mississippi, he returned to write the SDS pamphlet *Revolution in Mississippi*, which, issued in the same year as the *Port Huron Statement*, reproduced all the words to "We Shall Overcome" on its title page. Joan Baez, twenty-two, sang "We Shall Overcome" at the 1963 March on Washington, and Pete Seeger sang "We Shall Overcome" together with SNCC staff in Mississippi during the Freedom Summer in 1964.

So popular was the song that President Lyndon Baines Johnson stated the words "we shall overcome" in a nationally televised address in 1965 to advocate the Voting Rights Act, a striking instance of that curious alchemy by which the radical becomes mainstream. Yet when SNCC's Bob Moses, historian Staughton Lynd, and radical pacifist David Dellinger led a march on the White House later in 1965 to signal the transformation of the civil rights movement into a movement against Johnson's own war in Vietnam, they still sang "We Shall Overcome."

If "We Shall Overcome" seems the quintessential song of the sixties, that is only due to the erasure of its origins in a much earlier left. The song first appeared as sheet music in 1947 in *People's Songs*, a periodical Pete Seeger founded after the demise of the Almanac Singers, which he and Woody Guthrie had created to arouse antifascist spirits on the eve of World War II. One of Seeger's associates, Zilphia Horton, had set down the words and music as "We Will Overcome" in 1947, after she heard it sung by black women in the Food and Tobacco Workers, a Communist-led union out on strike against the American Tobacco Company in North Carolina. Those women, in turn, had adapted it from the old gospel hymn "I'll Overcome Someday."

The song became a staple at rallies for Henry A. Wallace, whose independent Progressive Party campaign in 1948 against Harry Truman protested the Cold War and racial segregation. There the song sustained wishful thinking, since, far from overcoming, the Wallace campaign was the last gasp of a Popular Front left soon to be suppressed by McCarthyism. Around 1955, the year when Seeger was called before the House Un-American Activities Committee, the singer, in an inspired move, substituted "shall" for "will," transforming "We Will Overcome" into "We Shall Overcome." In that iteration the song was taught at the renowned civil rights leadership training center, Highlander Folk School, in Monteagle, Tennessee. There, Rosa Parks, Septima Clark, and Martin Luther King Jr. learned the song and transformed it into a movement anthem as the civil rights tempo quickened with the Montgomery bus boycott of 1955–56.

What, then, was "We Shall Overcome"? Many things at once: a song of the 1940s, a song of the 1960s; a song of the Popular Front, a song of the New Left; a black spiritual adaptation, a folk rendition; a protest song, a crossover hit; a song for the picket line, a song for civil rights marches; a song with a history, a song that seemed, by the early sixties, to be entirely of the moment.

"We Shall Overcome" is emblematic of the 1960s, whose movements radiated newness and youth even as they drew strength from deeper and older currents. This nuanced reality, however, has been occluded by the story sixties radicals told themselves.

Young radicals in the 1960s, seeking to demarcate themselves, adopted a narrative of progression from what they called the Old Left to what they called the New Left. Their story went something like this: In the 1930s and 1940s, there was an Old Left. Centered on the Communist Party, it included Trotskyists, Socialists, and others. Shaped by the Great Depression, the Old Left was organized in political parties, typically vanguard parties.

It saw workers as its constituency, pursued common ownership of production, and espoused economic radicalism first and foremost. Then came 1956, Khrushchev's revelations about Stalin's atrocities, the Soviet invasion of Hungary, and the collapse of the American Communist Party. The Old Left's credibility lay in ruins. A New Left kaleidoscope arose in its place. Movement, not party, was its focal point; affluence, not hard times, its context. The New Left sought to transcend Cold War categories with a radicalism focused on moral and cultural issues—race and war, later sexuality and gender—all of which the Old Left had compromised on by promising to address them "after the revolution." The New Left, by contrast, sought participatory democracy in the here and now.

This account held undeniable power. Radical youth perceived their cause as new in part because *any* left would be new after the fifties. The interruption imposed by McCarthyism in the history of American radicalism had been severe. In calling themselves the New Left, sixties youth sought to conjure up a new sensibility as well, one that reflected political necessity since the revealed record of Stalinism required American radicals—if they hoped to retain moral credibility—to distinguish themselves from the Soviet Union.

In the process, however, the New Left did something not often recognized: it created the Old Left. That category functioned to emphasize discontinuity in the history of radicalism at the expense of understanding the ways in which, as with "We Shall Overcome," that history was actually marbled and layered. Because social movements achieve widest success when they forge solidarity across generations, one of the less-recognized self-imposed limits of the sixties upsurge was the equivalency it presumed between youth and virtue.

"Old Left" was a retroactive appellation, popular among sixties youth, that evoked an image that was at best partial. Certainly, nobody at *People's Songs* in 1947 thought of themselves as Old Left. They were young, too—so young, in fact, that Pete Seeger was still with us when we marked Port Huron's fiftieth anniversary. But into the Old Left's maw all the left's faults and foibles could be tossed. That left was reductionist, mechanistic, dogmatic. It was not radical enough because it was subordinate to the liberalism of the Henry Wallaces and Eleanor Roosevelts. It disguised itself behind terms like "the people" because Seeger and others had failed to be forthright about their Communist Party memberships. In a word, it was passé.

For reasons both explicit and tacit, the vision of a New Left proved attractive. Newness was a prominent value in a society forever trying to move commodities off the shelf, evoking positive associations even in the subconscious of those youth alienated from the shallowness of consumerism and conformity. Red diaper babies sought to succeed where their deflated parents had not, while southern students influenced by existentialist Christianity and northern left liberals each had their own reasons to be suspicious of Communists as well as Cold War anticommunism.

And there *was* something genuinely new and attractive about the New Left. The widespread embrace during the 1960s of an open-ended radicalism, one as much about democracy as political power, about values as much as victory, did represent a break from the Old Left, as was evident when social democrats such as Michael Harrington and Irving Howe chastised New Left youth whom they saw as naive, both in an approach to politics that tended toward utopianism and in their willingness to overlook or downplay Communist malevolence. When socialist elders had the locks changed in New York shortly after the Port Huron convention, barring SDSers from their own office, it underscored the apparent gulf between old and new.

Fifty years later, however, the distinction between Old Left and New Left is of distinctly limited value. Its categories simply dissolve and disintegrate if put to the test—as exemplified by the journey of "We Shall Overcome."

Consider the following criticism of American politics. Speaking of "the unbelievable degree of apathy and uninterest on the part of the American people," this passage reads as if it were taken from the *Port Huron Statement:* "Unless the American people are aroused to a higher degree of participation, democracy will die at its roots." But this was penned by Saul Alinsky in *Reveille for Radicals,* written in 1946. That book drew on what would later be called "Old Left" lexicon in speaking of "People's Organizations." His was a new leftism emerging within the Popular Front of the 1940s.[1]

Or consider, from an entirely different sector of the left, the sardonic writer who mocks the "professional revolutionary": "The deceived masses run away from you and you run after them, yelling 'Stop, stop, stop, you proletarian masses! You just can't see that I am your liberator!'" Such would-be "Marxists," says the writer, believe "sexuality is a petit-bourgeois invention. It is the economic factors that count." This is not Abbie Hoffman but Wilhelm Reich in *Listen, Little Man.*[2]

Or what of the writer dismayed to find radicalism in America "scattered, demoralized, and numerically insignificant"? Because "the present high school and college generation does not remember the depression," a revival will require "new foundations": "Radicalism in America must be recruited from radicals, from strong and independent spirits willing to stand on their own choices. . . . A disciplined, maneuverable army of the left is, in this country, an absurd dream. There is no reason for anybody to join it; those who easily accept orders are in quite different armies already. Communism has failed completely in the United States partly because its adherents have not played a truly radical role." Surely this was produced after 1956? But no, it's Henry F. May, "The End of American Radicalism," in *American Quarterly* in 1950, examining the rubble left after the Henry Wallace campaign.[3]

Other examples abound of an alternative left-wing consciousness sprouting from the cracks of the 1940s. Dwight Macdonald spoke openly of "a new left." The Congress of Racial Equality pioneered sit-ins and freedom rides. C. Wright Mills developed a criticism of bureaucracy that owed much to the opposition to "bureaucratic collectivism," East and West, in Max Shachtman's circle of Trotskyist-derived heretical socialists. Staughton Lynd, the New Left's most noted intellectual by the mid-1960s and himself a product of the early postwar years, once called these 1940s trends "the first New Left."[4]

Or was it the *actual* New Left? After all, in the 1940s such ideas were truly new. By the 1960s, they were long in gestation.

Not only was the New Left old, but the Old Left was new. The Old Left generation was not simply erased by McCarthyism and Stalinism. The Communist Party was discredited, to be sure, but this freed a generation of radicals to chart more independent courses after 1956, making the 1960s left far more intergenerational than is often acknowledged. It's not just that Pete Seeger records spun on many a New Left turntable. Everywhere one looks in the 1960s, one finds an adult left in its middle years, interacting with youth, contributing to sixties radicalism, and collapsing distinctions between Old Left and New.

In Los Angeles in 1950–51, for example, four Old Leftists, still young in heart but rejected by the Communist Party, formed the first sustained American homophile organization: the Mattachine Society. By the early 1960s, the homophile movement had made a significant contribution to the sexual revolution so often credited to the New Left at the expense of the supposedly economistic Old Left.

Those in Britain who hatched the very term New Left—including historian E. P. Thompson, whose *Making of the English Working Class* of 1963 pioneered a "new" labor history engaged with class and culture—were

Communists who quit in 1956. They helped found the journal *New Left Review* in 1960, and it was there that C. Wright Mills published his "Letter to the New Left," saying that students, rather than a "labor metaphysic," were the agents of radical renewal.

Many putatively New Left strategies were spawned by Old Left seers. Bayard Rustin, Ella Baker, Stanley Levison, and other Old Left veterans advised Martin Luther King Jr. and younger radicals in the southern freedom movement. Social democrats in the United Auto Workers helped arrange use of the Port Huron camp for SDS in 1962 and donated money to make its Economic and Research Action Project possible. Hal Draper, a 1930s Trotskyist, gave sage counsel to Mario Savio and other student radicals during the Free Speech Movement in Berkeley in 1964.

What periodicals did New Leftists read? They read *Monthly Review*, the *National Guardian*, and I. F. Stone's *Weekly*, all launched in the 1940s and 1950s by remnants of the Popular Front. Or they read *New Politics*, edited by left-socialist veterans of the 1940s and 1950s. Perhaps they even read the *Dissent* of Irving Howe, onetime Shachtmanite, who clashed with the New Left but published Tom Hayden, Staughton Lynd, and other new radicals.

Malcolm X Speaks, published in 1965, was edited by George Breitman, a member of the Socialist Workers Party, which was practically the only organization to give the black militant a platform in the last year of his life. It was issued by Grove Press, where Harry Braverman, another Trotskyist veteran, was editor. Would Malcolm's views been as influential had not older revolutionaries—Jewish, in this case—arranged for their dissemination?

National demonstrations against the Vietnam War, although initiated by SDS in 1965, were mostly organized by a coalition of older radicals in the National Mobilization Committee to End the War in Vietnam, headed by radical pacifist A. J. Muste, whose activism dated back to World War I. Prominent intellectual opponents of the Vietnam War included Norman Mailer, Noam Chomsky, Howard Zinn, and Sidney Lens, all of whom came of age on the 1940s left.

Even Black Power fits the template. Stokely Carmichael, who popularized that slogan more than anyone else, was a Trinidadian immigrant whose initiation into radical politics came through his close friendship at the Bronx High School of Science with Eugene Dennis, son and namesake of the American Communist Party leader. Black Power radicals James and Grace Lee Boggs came out of Detroit's labor left of the 1930s and 1940s, while Harold Cruse, who did so much to promote black nationalism and stigmatize the Old Left, had once been a Communist. In England, the Trinidadian C. L. R. James, a Trotskyist since the 1930s, counseled black militant pan-Africanists of the 1960s.

Or take the women's movement. It was indubitably new in scale, innovation, and independence in the 1960s, and the left in the 1930s and 1940s did subsume gender within class when discussing "the Woman Question," but New Left men responded with even less comprehension when women began to assert the need for sexual equality in the 1960s. Old Left women, moreover, helped spawn the new feminism in ways direct and indirect. Although McCarthyism buried the memory of initiatives such as the Congress of American Women (CAW), which in the late 1940s pushed for child care, equal pay, and other demands that would later be called feminist, CAW veterans in the 1960s such as Eleanor Flexner and Gerda Lerner pioneered the writing of women's history while Women Strike for Peace, formed by Old Left women, contributed to a rebirth of women's political action.

When the young white civil rights organizers Casey Hayden and Mary King wrote two memos in SNCC and SDS that were the first serious documents on women in the New Left, objecting to sexism within those organizations, they read older women who were making themselves anew: Simone de Beauvoir's *The Second Sex* (1949), Doris Lessing's *The Golden Notebook* (1962), and Betty Friedan's *The Feminine Mystique* (1963). Friedan masked her background in the left-led United Electrical, Radio and Machine Workers of America (UE) with a fable of middle-class suburban life, and her Popular Front ethos was too tame for women's liberationists, but her criticism of rigid Cold War gender norms sowed seeds of radical women's consciousness.

Many recent histories of American Communism fail to register how gravely Stalinism distorted the left of the 1930s and 1940s, a factor just as important as McCarthyism in necessitating the disguises adopted by the Seegers and Friedans of the time. Democratic radicals and revolutionary socialists observed those failings at the time, the fundamental differences among rival camps of radicalism being another reason "Old Left" holds little value as an all-encompassing term. There is, however, ample evidence that even the Communist left was hardly contemptible on every issue, as historians have charted the many positive contributions of 1930s and 1940s radicals on issues of labor, fascism, empire, and especially race—which the Old Left cannot now be said to have waited until "after the revolution" to address.

Ideas bracketed as "Old Left," moreover, remained live options throughout the 1960s, which hardly saw all the older folkways dispelled. One is found in the later New Left's attempt, in a decade of war and revolution, to "name the system," as SDSer Paul Potter put it. That process led many to see "capitalism" and "imperialism" not as stale, musty words but as accurate descriptors at the very moment when the American business class was reclaiming the word "capitalism" and investing it with positive connotations.

Once capitalism and imperialism came into sight again for the Left, as Carl Oglesby observed, it was certain that young radicals would work their way back to Marx and Lenin. In this there was plenty of insight, not only tragedy, for the turn to theory and history signaled recognition of social systems and structures that would not be displaced by moral symbolic action alone. It is also the case, however, that a good part of the New Left in the end succumbed to the Old Left's worst errors and deficiencies: scriptural fundamentalism, bureaucratic centralisms, and simplistic versions of internationalism revolving around a single sun, whether China, Cuba, Algeria, or, worse, Albania or North Korea.

Here again the sunny contrast between New Left innocence and Old Left bankruptcy is shown to be overdrawn. Newness and youth did not guarantee purity. Some errors of the New Left, such as its Weatherman-style adventurism, were catastrophic beyond most of the commonly cataloged faults committed by the once-disdained Old Left. At the same time, the later New Left fostered new liberations in culture, sexuality, and gender beyond those the early New Left had wrested, and much of it came to understand, however belatedly, that working-class majorities are the crux of lasting transformations. Even as the New Left suffered fissures and crises by the 1970s, it showed by that time greater humility toward its older counterparts on the left, recasting them as long-distance runners who faced similar predicaments and challenges.

The 1960s are now two decades older from our time than they were from the 1930s, and the New Left is old in a new way. The times, they have a-passed. The millennial generation inevitably has its own points of reference and perspectives. They do take interest in the flurry of fiftieth-anniversary commemorations now erupting, since the epochal shift of the sixties continues to exert an attraction upon youth as it always has, but we are witnessing the final draining of the wash of '68, and any future American left will have different contours and identities.

For decades in the history of American radicalism, a single generation's myths and legends have held sway over others. Boomer dominance prevailed even as, from South African divestment in the 1980s to AIDS resistance to the global justice Battle of Seattle in 1999, outbursts tossed up newly radicalized youth. No subsequent cohort emerged with numbers or ideas sufficient to surpass the New Left generation, whose glory days, cautionary tales, and power within left-wing leadership bodies held sway over the radical, or once-radical, imagination. The consequences for memory were illustrated when the fiftieth anniversary of the *Port Huron Statement* was marked at events across the country while the hundredth anniversary of the 1912 campaign of Socialist Eugene Victor Debs passed entirely unobserved.

Debs was part of what might be called, to adapt Lynd's phrase, the first Old Left, winning a higher percentage of the presidential vote in 1912 than any American socialist before or since. Many of the assumptions of American socialism in its heyday now seem naive, if not retrograde. It was largely, though not exclusively, male-dominated at a time before women were guaranteed the ballot; it was prone to talk of class unity alone at a time when black Americans were being lynched and stripped of voting rights. Electoral socialism does not resonate so well with a contemporary left steeped more in anarchism than Marxism. In these respects the New Left may still present a fresher model. Other aspects of the Debsian vision, though, surely speak as well, if not better, to our era: its imagining of a fighting left, one opposed to war and exploitation, inclusive of revolutionary visions and social reform alike; its multigenerational combinations; its commitment to effective organization; its bent toward economic democracy against immense inequality. In some respects its old credo is neglected not for its faults and archaisms but because it remains so radical and relevant.

That lineage may revive in trace form in future lefts, now that Occupy, however fleeting, has put class and inequality again on a new generation's radar. It informed even the New Left, however, which for all its affluent context cannot be understood without its roots in a Debsian vision of equality. SDS in its earliest years focused on poverty in the Economic and Research Action Project, and various New Left voices—James Weinstein at *Studies on the Left* and *Socialist Revolution*, Paul Buhle's *Radical America*—sought a socialism rooted in American realities, imbued with the cumulative insights of subsequent liberatory radicalisms. Such is perhaps the vein of radical thought and action now being reclaimed by those seeking alternatives to the bubble-and-bust capitalism of our new Gilded Age.

If the New Left was old, and the Old Left was new, if neither were faultless and neither irredeemable, if both remain attractive but neither can be transferred tout court to our present, if their evaluation and appraisal was never made easier by seeking to box them up tightly in neatly divided chronological compartments, then perhaps this leaves us with a story of a common left, a long left, a left that stretches far back in time all the way up to our present, one subject to tragic flaws but animated, at its best, by the enduring ideals of democracy, freedom, and equality. Contingents of radicals to come will generate their own fables of newness while staking claims to this heritage that arcs back to 1776 and the abolitionists. Always the left has had continuities and ruptures, innovations and borrowings, solidarities and betrayals, legacies to draw upon, errors to discard. If future lefts synthesize the best of the old, experiment anew, draw upon the verve of youth and the perspective of age, and succeed in speaking to their present, casting the left's ideals in a parlance and fashion suited to their moment, then perhaps someday we might well overcome.

12 | Of Little Rocks and Levittowns: The Northern Racial Landscape and the Origins of the 1960s New Left

by Matthew J. Countryman

> We are people of this generation, bred in at least modest comfort, housed now in universities, looking uncomfortably to the world we inherit.
>
> —*Port Huron Statement*[1]

With its opening words, the *Port Huron Statement* implicitly located its audience in the white world of the postwar suburb. The *Statement* was, as Kirkpatrick Sale wrote in 1973, "unabashedly middle class, concerned with poverty of vision rather than the poverty of life, with the world of the white student rather than the world of the blacks, the poor, or the workers."[2] As children of the postwar North, the lives of the student activists of the early New Left had been shaped by the massive spatial and structural reorganization of race that had taken place in northern cities and suburbs in the 1940s and 1950s. Racial bias and segregation, structural inequities and cultural misunderstandings, and the ever-present threat of racial conflict shaped daily life on both sides of the color line in the postwar North.

Since the 1940s, American racial discourse has defined racism and racial injustice along two axes: de jure segregation and individual prejudice. On both of these axes—the imposition of segregation by law and the explicit expression of white supremacist ideologies and attitudes—race relations in the post–World War II North and West appeared infinitely better than in the Jim Crow South. As Jo Freeman put it in her memoir of her years as a student activist at the University of California, Berkeley, white northerners, even left-liberal activists, tended to see racism as a problem that happened in faraway places. "Racial segregation was automatically assumed to be evil, but it was also seen as something *other* people did.

Students protested against apartheid in South Africa . . . against Jim Crow laws, and for passage of laws ensuring civil rights. Racism as something other than racial segregation or discrimination was not part of our vocabulary. Conceptually, it did not exist."[3]

For most of its twenty-five thousand words, the *Port Huron Statement* similarly elided the centrality of race to the economic and cultural landscape of white middle-class communities in the postwar North. The *Statement* organized its catalogue of American social ills on the premise that *race* was a southern problem and that *class* exploitation was the root cause of poverty and ghettoization in the North. Only at one point, deep in the *Statement*, did the Students for a Democratic Society (SDS) writers analyze the overpowering but rarely acknowledged reality of race in their own experience, by highlighting the economic and cultural investment of the northern white middle class in its own forms of racial exclusion. "The majority of Americans," the authors wrote, "fight to keep integrated housing out of the suburbs . . . [T]here are no Negroes except on the bus corner going to and from work." This hostility to the black presence extended beyond the often-expressed concerns about property values. Not only, the *Statement*'s authors continued, do "most Americans persist in opposing marriage between the races . . . [but] white America is ignorant still of nonwhite America—and perhaps glad of it." "White," the section concluded, "like might, makes right in America today."[4]

Northern racial issues are rarely invoked as a factor in the development of the New Left and in the creation of documents like the *Port Huron Statement*, and most historians and memoirists have failed to examine the whiteness of the young radicals' middle-class experience.[5] But it is only in comparison to the South that racial practices in the postwar North appear more liberal. While the North was largely free of laws mandating segregation in education, public transport, and public accommodations, spatial racial segregation and discriminatory practices shaped economic and social life for all northerners. Why, in thinking of the formative influence of the civil rights movement on the early New Left, do we cite the crisis in Little Rock—and not Levittown?

In August 1957, mob violence came to Levittown, Pennsylvania, a suburb of Philadelphia, after the Myers, a black family, moved into town. With the support of a coalition of religious, liberal, and left-wing activists, the Myers survived a month-long siege in which crowds of white residents threw rocks against police protecting their home, breaking most of the house's windows and knocking one officer unconscious. But while supporters of

Levittown's integration were able to recruit a second black family to move into the community a year later, the Myers themselves grew tired of being racial pioneers and moved away in 1959.[6]

The two Levittowns, planned new towns developed by Levitt and Sons home builders on Long Island and in suburban Philadelphia between 1947 and 1958, epitomized the centrality of racial exclusion to the postwar suburban North. The Levitts were as innovative in their real estate marketing practices as they were in their application of Fordist principles to housing construction. In contrast to prewar suburban developers who focused on upper-income home-buyers, the Levitts targeted the new postwar middle-class, particularly the first-generation US-born children of Eastern and Southern European immigrants, with an emphasis on a panethnic white identity largely shorn of the anti-Semitism and anti-Catholicism that characterized prewar racist discourse.[7]

In the postwar North, segregated neighborhoods were maintained through racial covenants, by federally mandated real estate and mortgage industry practices, and, where necessary, by white racial violence. In 1948, the Supreme Court ruled that restrictive covenants were legally unenforceable. And yet, the development of all-white suburban communities—which first appeared on the northern metropolitan landscape in the 1920s—increased exponentially in the two decades after World War II. For example, 98 percent of the new homes built between 1946 and 1955 in the suburban counties surrounding the city of Philadelphia were marketed for white buyers only.[8]

In most suburban communities, exclusionary housing practices were sufficient to ensure white-only schools. In cities and other communities with racially mixed populations, similar results were achieved through the gerrymandering of neighborhood school district boundaries and through ability-based tracking in nominally integrated senior and junior high schools. Even in a university town like Ann Arbor, Michigan, neighborhood school boundaries and a discretionary school transfer policy enabled the maintenance of a single predominately black elementary school—in a city with a black population of about 5 percent—until 1965.[9]

Racial segmentation was also a ubiquitous feature of northern labor markets. The explicit use of racial categories in help wanted ads only began to disappear with the passage in the postwar years of state and municipal fair employment practices laws. These laws, however, were less effective at opening up new job opportunities for black workers than reformers hoped, as employers developed a range of tactics—from seniority-based promotion lists to the token hiring of small numbers of

black employees—to maintain racially segmented workforces. As Philadelphia's Commission on Human Relations put it in 1960, "In the framework of the present-day administration of the fair employment law, the
employer who does not 'refuse to hire' because of race may, with impunity,
continue to conduct his recruitment, training and advancement of employees with only rare and nominal deviation from the traditional pattern."[10] Finally, while most northern states had laws banning racial segregation in public accommodations, in practice there were hotels, restaurants,
and theaters in every northern community that were known not to serve
black customers.[11]

Thus, the white middle-class baby boom generation grew up in communities structured fundamentally by racial exclusion, communities in
which racial covenants and real estate marketing practices were designed
not just to exclude blacks but also to create a cultural environment in
which white ethnic and religious differences were subsumed into a white
American panethnic identity. In the postwar suburb, the black presence
was reduced to domestic servants and other low-skilled workers and to
the urban ghettoes that formed the backdrop for travel to downtown retail
districts. Peter Countryman, the founder of the Northern Student Movement (NSM), a New Left civil rights group, remembered trips on the com-
muter train from his suburban neighborhood to downtown Chicago: "I
would accompany Mom . . . looking down from the [commuter] train on
miles and miles of dilapidated tenements, jammed against each other so
tight it seemed it was only their very crowdedness that kept them from
collapsing, wondering at . . . the groups of raggedy-clothed black children
playing in the slush and refuse of the backyards."[12] Still, as omnipresent as
northern forms of racial separation were, they remained, at least for the
white children of the postwar middle class, hidden in plain sight by liberal
discourses that promoted the ideal of a color-blind society and highlighted
the absence of segregationist laws in the North.

New Left Childhoods

The early recruits to the New Left—the predominately white student activists from northern campuses who were drawn to civil rights and antinuclear activism and to a nonsectarian left-wing critique of Cold War–era
liberalism—included but were not limited to the founders of SDS. Others
gravitated to the NSM, a multicampus network of student civil rights
groups that was strongest in New England and the Mid-Atlantic states; to

the National Student Association's Liberal Caucus, which provided an annual gathering point for students interested in the civil rights and peace movements; to the campus chapters of the Congress of Racial Equality (CORE), which grew rapidly following the 1961 Freedom Rides; and to the coalition of civil rights and left-wing activists on the University of California, Berkeley, campus who would provide most of the leadership for the Free Speech Movement.[13]

Most early New Left activists grew up in one of three kinds of northern communities: all-white suburbs; white urban neighborhoods undergoing or threatened by racial transition; and, if we include the small numbers of black students who joined SDS and NSM as well as northern-born black Student Nonviolent Coordinating Committee (SNCC) activists like Stokely Carmichael and Bob Moses, black urban communities. Whether they grew up in a university town, big city, or, as in the case of SDS President Paul Potter, on a farm, the white activists of the early New Left shared the experience of growing up in a world that was deeply racialized and yet a world in which race—in the form of black people—was distant and invisible.

White Suburbia

Wini Breines, in her study of 1950s suburban girlhoods, *Young, White and Miserable*, captured the way in which the prescriptive conformity of the suburbs served to contain threats ranging from racial integration and communism to feminism and homosexuality by denying their very existence. The postwar suburb operated as a kind of escapist fantasy in which highways and cul-de-sacs operated as shields against a dangerous wider world. Parents, schools, communities, television, and newspapers all conspired to construct a world in which racial homogeneity was compatible with color-blind liberalism, gender conformity was both natural and universal, and the anticommunist and consumerist political consensus was the inevitable outcome of democratic processes. The children raised in this artificial world knew no other way; it was simply the order of things.[14]

On issues of race, the childhood memories captured in most New Left autobiographies evince a sense of being simultaneously oblivious and yet vaguely disturbed. Tom Hayden, for example, has professed to having had little or no awareness of racial issues while growing up in the all-white Detroit suburb of Royal Oak. "I attended an all-white high school," he wrote in his autobiography, "watched black maids waiting for buses on the street corners in the morning and evening, but I had no sense of racism. I only later learned that we had moved out of downtown Detroit because blacks were moving in."[15] "No sense of racism," and yet the evidence was all around him. Throughout the 1950s, blacks were limited to two apartment complexes in one nonresidential section of Royal Oak. In 1954, the Royal Oak Chamber of Commerce published a brochure promoting the suburb as "virtually 100% white."[16] Moreover, Hayden, whose parents were divorced when he was seven, spent his weekends traveling into Detroit, with its rapidly growing black population, to see his father. Following his graduation from high school, Hayden moved onto to the University of Michigan, a campus whose thirty thousand students included less than one hundred black undergraduates. Once on campus, Hayden soon displayed greater consciousness of racial issues than his memoir suggests. As a staff writer for the campus newspaper, he penned a series of exposés of the racially discriminatory membership practices of the officially color-blind campus fraternities and sororities.[17]

Both Jo Freeman and Peter Countryman evinced a similar mix of acceptance of, and disquiet about, the racial status quo in their autobiographical writings about their suburban childhoods. Freeman was raised in Southern California by a single mother who had grown up in Alabama but had become a racial liberal as a result of her experiences in the Women's Army Corps in World War II. When Freeman was seven, she and her mother moved from central Los Angeles to Van Nuys in the San Fernando Valley. As a result, Freeman moved from an integrated school to an all-white one. On the one hand, Freeman recalls being aware of the race and class implications of this move, a point that was driven home when her mother lost her job as a real estate agent for trying to arrange the sale of a suburban home to a black family. On the other, she thrived in her new environment, becoming a top student and eventually winning admission to Berkeley. Like many in her generation, Freeman found herself frustrated by the homogeneity and the sterility of the suburbs, but these were theoretical concerns in comparison with the benefits she accrued daily from living in a postwar suburb.[18]

Peter Countryman's autobiographical sketch contains even less favorable memories of the all-white suburban neighborhood that he grew up in. Countryman grew up in Morgan Park on the far southwest side of Chicago. While still within the city limits, Morgan Park in the 1950s was at some distance from the expanding borders of the black South Side. Countryman's family encouraged and celebrated his academic achieve-

ments even as it struggled with family dysfunction and downward mobility. Growing up, he was deeply aware of the class, ethnoreligious, and
racial divisions that structured community life in Morgan Park and the
surrounding area. In a family struggling to maintain its class status, the
gloss of whiteness could not mask the class tensions in a community that
ranged from the country clubs of Beverly Hills to the working-class en-
claves of Mt. Greenwood and Esmond or the ethnoreligious tensions
that separated his Anglo-Protestant family from their Italian and Irish
Catholic neighbors. And despite his family's professed commitment to
"liberty and justice for all," he also understood that "for the adults
around me, 'the colored' were inferior people." On trips to his uncle's
farm in central Illinois, he got to ride a black horse named "Nigger." And
on drives across the black South Side to watch White Sox games, his father would invariably wonder "how these people can afford such fancy
cars."[19]

Morgan Park's racial, ethnic, and class divisions became most apparent
to Countryman in high school. "Morgan Park High," he wrote, "was a
'melting pot'—but, like the society it reflected, a very stratified one." At the
top were the wealthy, Protestant kids from Beverly Hills who made up the
vast majority of the students in the college prep classes. In Countryman's
memory, these were the kids who received the lion's share of the school's
resources and faculty's attention and "whose achievements and behavior"
set the standard by which everyone was judged. In contrast, students from
his part of Morgan Park "floated somewhere below the elite, half of us
clinging precariously to the higher echelons, the rest taking commercial
prep courses and staring vacantly from the sidelines at their betters' social
and academic whirl." Finally, "the white and black working-class kids
[there was a small black enclave within the district boundaries of Morgan
Park High] . . . had a separate world of their own, literally at the bottom of
the heap—all the trade preparation courses being in the basement." Those
in the basement "became nearly invisible to the rest of us."[20]

Despite not feeling like they fit in with suburban culture, Freeman and
Countryman were both beneficiaries of the suburban institutional system.
Freeman not only earned admission to Berkeley but was able to pay her
own way through school after her mother cut her off as punishment for
getting arrested in a civil rights demonstration. Countryman was admitted to Yale as a scholarship student. Their visible break from the racial
practices of their families and home communities came only after they left
for college and became active in the civil rights movement.

City Kids

While most of the white student activists in the early New Left were middle class, a significant portion of them were raised not in the new postwar suburbs but in big-city urban neighborhoods. Steve Max, Dick Flacks, Todd Gitlin, and Bob Ross of SDS and Mario Savio, Bettina Aptheker, and Margot Adler of the Free Speech Movement all grew up in New York City, while Sharon Jeffrey of SDS and NSM, Frank Joyce of NSM, and Marilyn Lowen of NSM and SNCC grew up in Detroit. To a large degree, the racial experiences of white middle-class city kids differed little from their suburban counterparts. In an autobiographical speech that was published after his death in 1993, Savio described his childhood in Queens using familiar images of the postwar suburb: "The fifties were 'normal'. . . . The man thought he was in charge, the woman let him think that while making certain decisions in the house (she took care of the kids, made sure they were all washed and went to school, everything went just right)." And in this "normal" world, everyone was white. "The only black man they knew was the one who came around collecting money for charity."[21] In his autobiographical history of the 1960s, Gitlin told the story of his New York City childhood in similarly monochromatic terms. Gitlin's 1950s were a time of middle-class prosperity and political conformity in which the Cold War and the threat of nuclear war were the spark that drove his disillusionment with the status quo and that of others in his generation. Despite New York's booming black population, Gitlin made only the briefest mention of the civil rights movement and ignored completely northern racial issues.[22]

What is perhaps more surprising is that the childhood narratives of children from Old Left families, both the red diaper babies whose parents were active in the Communist Party or its Popular Front affiliates and the pink diaper babies whose families were involved in the non-Communist left, differ little in their recounting of their racial experiences from white New Left activists from more mainstream backgrounds. Both groups grew up in largely segregated landscapes and had little to no meaningful interactions with black people their own age. And both groups lacked access to a language for understanding and analyzing northern racism distinct from southern legal segregation.

Sharon Jeffrey came from a trade union family. Her mother was a leading figure in the United Auto Workers (UAW), and Jeffrey has recounted being taken to a National Association for the Advancement of Colored People (NAACP) convention at age thirteen where she and her mother were the only whites. At the same time, Jeffrey grew up in what she has described as "a deeply segregated" Detroit and as a teenager was the only one among her friends who was not horrified by the idea of interracial dating.[23] Bettina Aptheker and Margot Adler both grew up in families within the Communist Party's orbit and have clear memories of their parents' involvement in left-wing civil rights activism. Aptheker, in particular, has described in vivid terms social gatherings hosted by her parents that included some of the Communist Party's leading black figures. In their day-to-day childhood experiences, however, both Aptheker and Adler traversed largely segregated worlds of school and neighborhood.[24]

While residential and school segregation served to isolate most white middle-class northern youth from the realities of northern racial practices, there was one group of northern white youth who were directly exposed to the North's changing racial demography and geography. In urban neighborhoods undergoing racial transition, white male youth were often at the front lines of racial violence, seeking to punish black families who sought housing across racial borders. Few stories of neighborhood racial transition can be found in the autobiographical narratives of white New Left activists, however. In a recent compilation of autobiographical accounts of women from SNCC, Marilyn Lowen has described growing up in the Russell Woods section of Detroit as black families began to move in. Despite her parents' commitment to secular humanism and to remaining "in a changing neighborhood," they reacted with horror when she began dating black boys and attending civil rights demonstrations. Along with Frank Joyce, she was a member of the union-sponsored Detroit Brotherhood Youth Council.[25]

Mark Naison, a CORE and SDS activist who grew up in Crown Heights, Brooklyn, has described a similar reaction among his parents and neighbors as the border with all-black Bedford-Stuyvesant gradually moved closer to their predominately Jewish neighborhood. According to Naison, his parents and the other adults in the community thought of themselves as supporters of the emerging southern civil rights movement. But as the racial border moved closer and closer, his parents and their neighbors reacted with fear and resentment, as if their hard-won middle-class status was under threat. "I was more disturbed," Naison wrote, "by the racial fears and prejudices I saw emerging in my neighborhood and family [than by the influx of black residents]. My apartment was a hornet's nest of tension." Within a few years of Naison's graduation from high school, his parents and most of their neighbors had left for all-white neighborhoods in Queens and on Long Island.[26]

Naison has ascribed his break from the racial attitudes of his parents and neighbors as springing from his idealistic enthusiasm for what he perceived to be the interracial worlds of team sports and rock 'n' roll. His day-to-day world may have been divided spatially along racial and ethnic lines, but he thrilled to the cross-racial interactions he experienced on the basketball and tennis courts in his neighborhood and in Brooklyn's rock 'n' roll dance halls. "For our generation," he wrote, "part of becoming American was becoming culturally 'black.'"[27]

At Columbia, Naison tried out for and made the tennis team, pledged a fraternity, and in his sophomore year joined the campus CORE chapter where he helped organize tenants' associations in East Harlem. But it was in his encounters with the upwardly mobile white Catholics who populated Columbia's athletic teams and fraternities that Naison most directly confronted the distance between the students who were drawn to the movement and most of those who came from white urban neighborhoods like his:

> Most of the [athletes and fraternity brothers] were urban and suburban Catholics whose families had worked hard to pull themselves out of poverty. Like Crown Heights, their own neighborhoods were experiencing an influx of African Americans, and their residents felt the pressure of ethnic succession acutely, especially because many of them owned their own homes. It deeply offended them that the northern civil rights movement had targeted de facto segregation by advocating open housing and school busing. They believed they had the right to protect their investment in their homes by keeping their neighborhoods and schools white. If African Americans experienced social and economic discrimination, they argued, it was a problem for them to conquer through hard work and self-help, the way the Irish and Italians had done.[28]

What then drove Naison to see the world differently? His family too had "lost" a neighborhood they had invested in financially and culturally (though as renters the financial costs of moving to Queens were somewhat less). Naison, Lowen, Hayden, Savio, Countryman, and other lower middle-class white radicals were thus the exceptions that proved that the early New Left's appeal was primarily to students from higher-income, culturally liberal and left families and communities. Most white student radicals came from families better able to withstand the potential financial impact of racial integration and, thus, ironically, from communities less susceptible to integration.

Growing Up in the Black North

One group of early New Left activists for whom the reality of northern racism was part of their everyday experience were African Americans born and raised in the North. A number of key leaders in the southern student movement were northern-born. Some—including SNCC leaders Tim Jenkins from Philadelphia; Diane Nash from Chicago; Charles McDew from Massillon, Ohio; and Stokely Carmichael and Courtland Cox from the Bronx—first moved south to attend college at historically black institutions. Others, like Prathia Hall from Philadelphia, James Forman from Chicago, Bob Moses from Harlem, and Martha Prescod from Providence, were drawn south by the movement.[29] In contrast, the northern New Left was overwhelmingly white, which is not particularly surprising given that black students were distinctly underrepresented at northern elite universities in the years before affirmative action. Still, Carolyn Craven from Chicago and Baltimore's Goucher College and Phil Hutchings from Cleveland and Howard University both played key roles in SDS's development in the years after Port Huron.[30] NSM attracted a somewhat larger group of black student activists. In 1963, Bill Strickland, a Bostonian and Harvard graduate, replaced Peter Countryman as NSM executive director.[31] In addition to Strickland, NSM's leading black activists included New Yorker Byron Rushing (Harvard); Philadelphians Joan Cannady (Sarah Lawrence), Charyn Sutton (Brandeis), John Churchville (Temple), and Carl Anthony (Columbia); and Chuck Turner (Harvard) from Cincinnati.[32]

These activists all shared direct experience with the limited achievements of postwar northern racial liberalism; most had grown up in all-black neighborhoods, whether Roxbury, North Philadelphia, the South Side of Chicago, or Cleveland's East Side. Charyn Sutton grew up in southwest Philadelphia "in an all-black community that went to school at a majority white school where issues of race were there all the time. . . . You had to walk on certain streets because you couldn't walk past the white people's houses." According to Sutton, in fourth grade, her teacher recommended that she skip a grade, "and then all these parents of the white kids came up and wanted to know how a nigger could be skipped." When Sutton was in junior high, her parents joined an ultimately successful campaign led by a local minister to desegregate a nearby city pool.[33]

Joan Cannady's parents took her out of their neighborhood public school because they were concerned that her white teachers were over-looking her academic potential. Eventually, they enrolled her as one of the first black students in a nearby Quaker school. Cannady's parents were avowed integrationists who worked with the city's Commission on Human Relations to pressure restaurants in their section of the city that continued to refuse to serve black customers.[34]

Stokely Carmichael's family migrated from Trinidad to the Bronx in the early 1950s. His father managed to gain entry into a building trades union but complained often that the union favored its white members and that he rarely got jobs from the union hiring hall. Still, he was able to buy a small "fixer-upper" home for his family in a predominately Irish and Italian neighborhood in the Bronx. They were the only black family in the neighborhood for most of Carmichael's childhood.[35]

Many black activists began their involvement in civil rights issues while still in high school. Charyn Sutton joined a high school student chapter of CORE as well as the Philadelphia chapter of the W. E. B. Du Bois Club, "which was kind of communist . . . but they didn't say they were the communist party." Joan Cannady participated in Quaker work camps that sought to fix-up homes for black families threatened by urban renewal. Phil Hutchings participated in the Youth Councils of both the Cleveland NAACP and the Council on Human Relations.[36] As a student at the Bronx High School of Science, Carmichael attended political rallies and social events organized by the children of white leftists from both sides of the Communist Party/Socialist Party divide. But for Carmichael, it was his excursions to Harlem barbershops and to hear the black nationalist street speakers on 125th Street that provided him with a way to understand both the structural and spatial discrimination he saw around him and the paternalism and unconscious sense of white superiority that he experienced at the Bronx High School of Science. In contrast to liberal narratives of black assimilation into whiteness, Carmichael thrilled to the nationalist vision of a decolonized Africa and the Caribbean's limitless future. In his autobiography, Carmichael described the street speakers as "the oral historians of the community, our town criers, waking up the sleeping town and bringing news of distant conflicts. Our secular prophets, they were keepers of the flame, holding aloft our heritage as African people in exile . . . ceaselessly exhorting us to keep historical and revolutionary faith with our ancestors' long history of struggle and resistance."[37]

The New Left and the Northern Civil Rights Movement

A full examination of the ways in which the experience of growing up in the spatially segregated North shaped early New Left activists' involvement in the emerging northern civil rights movement is beyond the scope of this chapter. However, a brief synopsis of the events of 1962–64 demonstrates both the centrality of race to New Left understandings of social inequity and the challenges they faced in trying to bridge the racial gaps that had so structured their childhoods.

In April 1962, NSM hosted a student conference on civil rights in the North at Sarah Lawrence College where Joan Cannady was student-body president. At the conference, NSM executive director Peter Countryman announced that NSM was shifting its central focus from the southern movement to racial issues in the North. Specifically, it would establish tutorial programs in black urban neighborhoods in order to address the debilitating impact of inadequate schooling on black communities.[38]

The spring of 1963 saw the beginning of a wave of protests against employment discrimination in northern cities. In New York, activists from Columbia's CORE chapter and NSM's Harlem Education Project, a tutorial program, helped lead a successful boycott of Sealtest Dairies because of its discriminatory hiring practices. The following summer both groups were crucial to a successful series of rent strikes in Harlem. Similarly, in the Bay Area, Berkeley's CORE chapter recruited hundreds of students to a series of protests against discriminatory hiring in San Francisco's restaurants, hotels, and auto dealerships. Many of these student protesters would go on to form the core of the leadership of Berkeley's Free Speech Movement in 1964.[39]

Finally, in 1964, both NSM and SDS undertook community-organizing initiatives designed to address issues of racism and poverty in the urban North. Believing that tutorial programs perpetuated a culture of black dependence on white altruism, NSM shifted its primary focus to black-staffed organizing projects in Harlem, Philadelphia, Detroit, Boston, and Hartford. At the same time, NSM continued to support a number of tutorial projects as well as white-led antiracism initiatives in Detroit and Philadelphia.[40]

In theory, SDS's community organizing program, the Economic Research and Action Project (ERAP), sought to build "an interracial movement of the poor" that was simultaneously committed to "racial justice and an end to poverty." In practice, however, ERAP's primarily white and middle-class organizers (only its Newark project included a significant contingent of black organizers) struggled to bridge the gaps between themselves and the poor white and poor black communities they were seeking to organize. In the four cities where they succeeded in establishing community organizations in poor neighborhoods—Boston, Chicago, Cleveland, and Newark—they did so in either black or white communities. Only in welfare rights organizing in Cleveland, and to a lesser extent Chicago, were they able to overcome racial divides between poor communities.[41]

By 1967, NSM and SDS's community organizing strategies had been largely superseded by white student involvement in the antiwar and women's liberation movements and by black student activism for black studies programs on predominately white campuses. Despite their best efforts and a number of important successes, the activists of the early New Left proved largely unable to transcend the racial and class divides that they had grown up with in the postwar North.

13 | The Lightning Bolt That Sparked the *Port Huron Statement*
by Aldon Morris

Introduction

The *Port Huron Statement* was completed on my thirteenth birthday. At that time, I moved from rural Mississippi to Chicago, the urban hog butcher of the world. Before leaving the South, I had come to know Jim Crow racism up close and personal. I spent my early childhood in Jim Crow Mississippi, which was among the most racist states in the nation. We were socialized to believe that whites were superior. It was difficult not to accept this racist ideology because all the good things of life that mattered to children—freedom from fear, good housing with inside bathrooms, televisions, glistening toys, attractive school buildings, leisure, and respected elders—whites seem to possess. Even Jesus Christ belonged to white children because his pictures portrayed a tall man with white skin, blue eyes, and long blonde hair. Racial inequality that stretched from high heaven to the red clay of Mississippi was a tangible fact of life.

In this racist atmosphere, it was not possible to see whites as good people. Rather, they were wickedly powerful and mean people like those selfish giants lurking in scary children's books. One of my earliest memories is the 1955 lynching of fourteen-year-old Emmett Till, a Chicagoan who was visiting Money, Mississippi, located just a few miles from where I lived. I became a part of what sociologist Joyce Ladner has called the "Till Generation" because his lynching frightened and angered me. I remember not being able to sleep because I could not understand why grown whites would kill a boy. Were they real people like us, I wondered, and if so how could they do such a brutal thing?

As a child, I was baffled by the whole edifice of Jim Crow. Why were we poor when my young white counterparts had all the good things of life? It puzzled me that we were all "niggers" while our mothers were aunties and our fathers were boys. I couldn't figure out why we had to board the back of the bus and receive ice cream from the rear of the Dairy Queen. I wondered why we went to dilapidated schools and read hand-me-down books that white children discarded. I was perplexed by the discovery that at the beginning of the school year, all my classmates disappeared from school only to return two months after cotton had been harvested. At the tender age of six, I wondered why the sweet Lord Jesus they preached about at church wouldn't stop whites from abusing us.

The Jim Crow system dashed the idealism of young Blacks and destroyed the aspirations of Black adults through brutal economic exploitation and political oppression. Jim Crow was a powerful evil that needed to be destroyed. But in the 1950s, it was not clear how entrenched racism could be attacked. Many African Americans had become victims of a culture of submission that taught them it was natural they occupy the bottom rung of the social order. That culture emerged in the Black community as a result of deadly oppression endured by generations of African Americans. As a result, submissive ideas permeated Black culture of the Jim Crow era. For example, they could be heard in the music, such as when one bluesman moaned he "had been down so long that being down don't seem to bother me," while another cried, "If it were not for bad luck I would have no luck at all."

As the 1950s rolled in, Blacks were still viewed as an inferior race. The racial inferiority ideology was constructed as a justification for centuries of exploitation during slavery and the Jim Crow regime. This thesis claimed Blacks were not fully endowed as human beings and were, therefore, incompetent and childlike. Unlike whites, Blacks were argued to have no cultural heritage to draw upon independent of white culture. Thus Blacks were left with no choice but to copy the culture of their white oppressors. Yet because of mental limitations, Blacks could only produce inferior copies of the dominant culture. As a result of this belief, whites thought Blacks were incapable of making great contributions for their community and the larger society.

American social science embraced the Black inferiority thesis, though by the 1950s, social scientific scholarship softened its view that Blacks were biologically inferior. Yet it clung to the view that Blacks were products of an inferior culture.[1] American social science fostered beliefs that Blacks did not possess the agency to challenge racism and overturn oppression. Black leaders, religion, family, and political and social institutions were thought to be too weak, morally flawed, and disorganized to engage in effective collective action to initiate change. Gunnar Myrdal concluded in his famous and influential study *An American Dilemma* that "the Negro's entire life and, consequently, also his opinions on the Negro problem are, in the main, to be considered as secondary reactions to more primary pressures from the side of the dominant white majority."[2] Social scientists embraced the claim that problems associated with race were properly understood as the white man's burden. Thus social science promoted the view that Blacks were a helpless group trapped in an enduring state of racial inequality. It followed they would forever be subordinates unless whites decided to ease up on the reins of oppression. White leaders of the Jim Crow regime demonstrated no such tendencies for they continued to exploit Blacks economically and control them politically and socially through racial segregation and the lynch rope.

Racial inequality was entrenched outside the South during the 1940s and 1950s, although less formally than it was under Jim Crow. Most northern whites also adhered to views proclaiming Black inferiority.[3] These beliefs were supported by structural arrangements that produced racially segregated housing that forced Blacks to live in urban ghettoes and participate in discriminatory labor markets where whites enjoyed enormous economic advantages. This was the era in which northern, middle-class whites fled to exclusive suburbs, made possible in part by subsidies from the federal government. Segregated neighborhoods produced segregated schools where young Black and white children were not afforded the opportunity to learn from each other and experience the other as fellow human beings. To the contrary, racial segregation, whether in Mississippi or Chicago, generated ethnocentric values that promoted provincial viewpoints, especially those pertaining to race.

During the first half of the twentieth century, American colleges and universities were largely segregated by race. Few African Americans attended private universities, whether public or private. Universities including Chicago and Michigan had so few Black students as to negate the sense of a collective Black presence. Martha Prescod, a Black student at the University of Michigan during the early 1960s, recalls that it was a lonely experience matriculating at an institution where you were expected to assimilate into a sea of whiteness.[4] Given this reality, most Black college students attended historically Black colleges and universities located in the South, such as Fisk University in Nashville and North Carolina Agricultural and Technical College in Greensboro. Although Black and white college students were of similar ages and aspired to receive educations enabling them to build productive careers, their paths seldom crossed because of the racially segregated worlds established by the architects of Jim Crow.

The curriculum offered in segregated schools did not prepare white students to understand the lived realities of Black people. No knowledge was disseminated that prepared them to understand the oppression Black people experienced daily due to entrenched racism. White students were unaware of the humiliation young Blacks experienced while attending college. Thus the treatment that a proud, Chicago-reared Diane Nash endured when she arrived on Fisk's campus in 1959 was typical. Upon her arrival in Nashville, she was introduced to southern racism requiring racial segregation. Nash could not dine in segregated restaurants, watch movies in theaters except in the Negro balcony, and could not relax at a segregated lunch counter downtown. While college years were supposed to be a time when young people sought new experiences, Nash and countless other students at Black institutions of higher learning encountered brick walls of segregation that confined them to narrow, circumscribed walks of life. Moreover, segregation and discrimination attacked the personhoods of these young adults, making them feel as if they were unfit to enjoy privileges available to the average human beings.

White educational experiences did not prepare students to learn the depths of Black agency and what Blacks were capable of achieving. As previously mentioned, the social sciences and humanities shared the view that Blacks were inferior. White students were seldom exposed to Black scholars like W. E. B. Du Bois, who went to great lengths to unravel the agency and creativity that were embedded in Black culture and its institutions. They were unaware of Du Bois's insight into the crucial role that Black soldiers played in the outcome of the Civil War and the many contributions Black leaders made to the nation during Reconstruction.[5] In the curriculum of white universities during the 1950s and early 1960s, typical Black people were usually absent. The writer Ralph Ellison immortalized the condition of Black invisibility in his novel *Invisible Man*:

> I am an invisible man. No, I am not a spook like those who haunted Edgar Allen Poe; nor am I one of your Hollywood-movie ectoplasms. I am a man of substance, of flesh and bone, fiber and liquids—and I might even be said to possess a mind. I am invisible, understand, simply because people refuse to see me. Like the bodiless heads you see sometimes in circus sideshows, it is as though I have been surrounded by mirrors of hard, distorting glass. When they approach me they see only my surroundings, themselves, or

figments of their imagination—indeed, everything and anything except me.[6]

Even the most critical sociological writings portrayed Blacks as lacking in human capacity or ignored them altogether as if they were invisible. This approach was evident in the influential and critical analyses of C. Wright Mills, the famous sociologist who became the intellectual icon of white students seeking to build an American New Left in the early 1960s. Mills attacked the legitimacy of an American power elite, bemoaned the sheep-like behavior of a theorized homogeneous mass society, and advocated for a new revolutionary actor that would fight to create a robust democracy so thoroughly lacking in America. In all his agitation, Mills ignored racial inequality fueled by historic racial oppression. He never envisioned the possibility that Black southerners would revolt and, in so doing, ignite sweeping waves of activism that would challenge the very foundations of American quiescence.

It is odd Mills missed this momentous development given his belief that the "sociological imagination enables us to grasp history and biography and the relations between the two within society."[7] Racism had been a central aspect of America from its inception, and it was deeply intertwined with the biographies of all Americans. If Mills had taken these realities seriously, he would have realized that racism was a major stumbling block standing directly in the path of democratic possibilities in the United States. He would have grasped the existence of a historic Black freedom struggle that first took shape in the slave community and was alive in the first half of the twentieth century. Indeed, that struggle was vibrant during World War II when Black leaders—A. Philip Randolph, Bayard Rustin, and others—inspired by the nonviolent mass movement led by Gandhi to overthrow British domination, organized mass protests. Those protests targeted segregated defense industries and a racially segregated military in which Blacks fought Hitler's forces seeking to spread white supremacy. If Mills had probed the Black community as he looked for new agents of social change, he would have discovered militarily skilled, and angry, veterans returning to America expecting the freedoms they had fought to secure for others across the seas. He would have discovered that these veterans were likely insurgents willing to fight and die to overthrow Jim Crow. Had Mills surveyed thousands of Blacks crowded in New York's Madison Square Garden and other venues in protest against racism in the 1940s, he would have realized that African Americans were becoming agents of social change. It is likely that Mills missed these developments because he shared Myrdal's view that only the actions of whites mattered in America. To be sure, Mills made it clear that he had "never been interested in what is called the Negro problem."[8] Scholar Stanley Aronowitz is probably correct when he argued that Mills ignored race dynamics because he believed racism was a white problem derivative of more basic power relations rather than a systemic structural reality. Given Mills's limited sociological imagination regarding race, he failed to see the presence of potent social change agents even as they launched protests to challenge race inequality, shattering his image of an American mass society teeming with cheerful robots.

It would be unrealistic to expect white college students of the 1950s and early 1960s to be enlightened about racial dynamics if they were ignored by a gifted critical sociologist like C. Wright Mills. Some of these students were not cheerful robots, either, because they had been raised by radical parents whose political backgrounds taught them that inequality, especially class inequality, was rampant in American society and could be challenged. Richard Flacks, who would become an influential sociologist and an architect of the New Left, was one of those "red diaper babies" who was exposed to protest against inequality as he rode in his baby carriage piloted by his parents.[9] Because of the segregated education they received and the image of Blacks as a hapless people, typical white college students had no reason to think that Black students could be major historical actors providing models for them to follow. Ensconced comfortably in racially segregated universities where they pursued the attainable American dream, they knew almost nothing about what their counterparts in Black schools faced and thought little of how the American dream was out of their reach. American social science was of no help, for it left Blacks in the shadows, providing no hint they could be history makers.

Montgomery Bus Boycott and Black Student Sit-Ins

In 1955, Blacks in Montgomery, Alabama, seized the stage and became shapers of history. For a decade, some female professors at the all-Black Alabama State College had concerns beyond campus. In 1946 they organized the Women's Political Council to confront racial segregation in Montgomery, including the segregated buses transporting their students. On December 1, 1955, the college's professors went about their tasks preparing students to navigate a segregated world dedicated to undermining their dignity and limiting their earning capacity. On that Thursday, one of

their activist members—Rosa Parks—violated segregation bus laws by refusing to give her seat to a white man. Members of the Women's Political
Council immediately organized in support of their colleague by calling for
a bus boycott and took the initial steps to organize it by spending the night
at the college, mimeographing thousands of leaflets to be distributed
throughout the Black community.[10] The community mobilized the boycott and sustained it for an entire year. This mass protest resulted in victory when the Supreme Court ruled bus segregation in Montgomery unconstitutional. An unsuspected agency of change had been uncorked,
even though it was not what Mills envisioned as he searched the horizons
for insurgent young white and Third World intellectuals. As the protest
was under way, additional boycotts were being organized in segregated
Black communities. Seasoned Black leaders including Bayard Rustin and
Miss Ella Baker realized the new possibilities and began developing tactics, strategies, and organizational capacity to spread Black insurgency.

The effect that the yearlong boycott and subsequent movements had
on young Blacks has not been fully examined. This is especially true for
Black college students. Some Alabama State students assisted the Women's
Political Council in producing and distributing thousands of leaflets calling for the boycott. It was impossible for students and young people of all
ages to be unmoved by the mass protest in which they participated alongside parents and community leaders. At the time that Dr. Martin Luther
King Jr. was chosen as leader of the boycott, he was twenty-six and had
finished graduate school only six months earlier. To many young students,
King's youth was attractive because they could identify with a leader not
much older than they. Students became involved in movements in other
cities. Many of them were young people active in the National Association
for the Advancement of Colored People (NAACP) youth councils like
those Rosa Parks led in Montgomery before the boycott.

In Tallahassee, Florida, on May 27, 1956, a bus protest developed. Two
students at the all-Black Florida A&M College were arrested for refusing to
move out of the "white section" of the local bus. The student body at the college initiated the mass protest when they voted unanimously to boycott the
buses for the remainder of the semester and monitored them to ensure that
students honored the boycott. Tallahassee's adult Black community organized in support of the student boycott. But it was the students situated on
Black college campuses that took action and sparked the mass movement
that resulted in victory after the Supreme Court ruling in the Montgomery
case. Across the South throughout the late 1950s, Black college students were
being recruited and trained to engage in massive nonviolent direct action.

Indeed, in Nashville, the Reverend James Lawson—who had visited India to study the Gandhi movement in the 1950s—was training students from multiple Nashville colleges to initiate student sit-ins in 1959. Black college students were gearing up in preparation to launch a massive student attack on Jim Crow as the decade closed and the sixties roared in.

The massive student attack on Jim Crow commenced February 1, 1960, when four students from North Carolina Agricultural and Technical College sat in at the lunch counters of a Woolworth department store. They continued the sit-in beyond the first day, making clear that this protest was not episodic. News of the sit-ins traveled rapidly across Black colleges and movement centers throughout the South. Lawson's group in Nashville and students in other communities followed Greensboro's lead. Within two months, sit-ins had spread across the South and ignited a Black student movement.[11] Like all human beings confronting serious danger, the student protesters were nervous: they feared for their lives and worried about being rejected by parents and friends who viewed them as the crème de la crème of the Black community that would prove to whites, through their educational achievements, that Blacks were not inferior and deserved a seat at the table of equality.

Black students did not allow their fears and insecurities to derail their rebellion. While being cursed, spit on, and knocked off lunch counter stools, they remained calm following the precepts of nonviolence. As mustard was splattered across their faces and lit cigarettes rubbed out on their skin, the Black students continued to read Shakespeare, Dante, and the Bible. While their white attackers appeared as if they were participating in auditions seeking parts in the "Devil Reincarnated," Black students wrapped themselves in the mantle of Jesus's love, forgiving their enemies for they knew not what they did. As will become clear shortly, it was also important that a few white students participated in the 1960 sit-ins, as they would in later demonstrations. The student sit-ins were the major development in the civil rights movement in 1960s. Their rapid spread throughout the South and their success in overturning a major aspect of Jim Crow sent a powerful message that nonviolent direct action was coming of age in America.

Black Students' Sit-Ins and White Students' Response

The sit-ins reverberated far beyond segregated establishments in the South. By the 1960s, the majority of Americans owned television sets, making it possible for whites beyond the region to view, in their living rooms, the drama created by sit-ins. In the North, there were pockets of activist-oriented white college students who took notice of the sit-ins immediately. As they witnessed Black students being attacked while sitting at lunch counters, these white students felt a deep connection with their Black southern counterparts. Tom Hayden captured the affinity: "They were in many ways like myself—young, politically innocent, driven by moral values, impatient with their elders, finding authentic purpose through risking 'their fortune, and their sacred honor'—in short, a genuinely revolutionary leadership."[12]

Another southern white student from Texas, Sandra Cason, explained that she was "thankful for the sit-ins if for no other reason than that they provided me with an opportunity for making a slogan into a reality, by making a decision into an action. It seems to me that this is what life is all about."[13] Significant numbers of white students throughout the nation identified with the Black students and the revolt they spearheaded by conducting sit-ins. In addition to watching sit-ins on television, activist-leaning white students began spreading the word of these protests by phone while student journalists chronicled them in campus papers. Moreover, white students organized protests at chain stores in the North whose southern counterparts were racially segregated. Others were also aware that a few white students actually participated in the southern sit-ins at great risks. The actions of southern Black students were beginning to generate movement activity nationally.

New explosive forms of nonviolent protests followed the sit-ins. The student leaders of the sit-ins organized their own protest organization, the Student Nonviolent Coordinating Committee (SNCC), to coordinate nonviolent protests throughout the South to overthrow Jim Crow and enfranchise the Black community. Under the tutelage of Ella Baker, SNCC developed a participatory democracy procedure that rested on decentralized decision making and eschewed the charismatic leadership approach. Additional young whites became involved in the civil rights movement through SNCC, given its interracial character. In 1960–62, major interracial protest occurred, including the Freedom Rides in 1961, that drew young whites directly into the movement. During the same year, SNCC organized a community-wide protest movement in Albany, Georgia, that attacked all forms of racial inequality. There were small numbers of whites who participated in the Albany Movement and were deeply influenced by it. Thus by 1962, the civil rights movement had become a major national force that exposed significant numbers of white students to entrenched racism and nonviolent direct action that employed high-risk activism to attack racism head on.

Enter Tom Hayden

Tom Hayden, more than anyone else, shaped the *Port Huron Statement*. He wrote its first draft and was instrumental in producing it as the polished manifesto of the 1960s student movements. To understand the philosophy and guiding ideas of that document, it is crucial to understand Hayden's early role in the southern civil rights movement. Hayden grew up in a white Detroit suburb of Royal Oak, where he attended elementary and high school, "a model son of the white lower middle class," as he put it later.[14] He knew little about his Black male counterparts in inner-city Detroit except that when four years old, he dimly remembers that there was a racial divide in Detroit. Racial conflict drove his parents to the white suburbs where there existed "homeowners covenants limited to 'white persons of the Caucasian race' except for their Black domestic servants."[15] Consistent with his background, Hayden was on track to achieve his dream of becoming an important journalist.

To ensure his future, Hayden attended the University of Michigan, one of the premier public institutions of higher learning in America. He was a serious student at Michigan, majoring in English and working on the staff of the *Michigan Daily*, one of the best and most prestigious student newspapers in the country. Although clearly gifted intellectually, Hayden possessed one of those rare, probing minds that sought answers to penetrating issues confronting America as it entered the second half of the twentieth century. In 1960 Hayden became editor of the *Daily*, an enviable position enabling him to cover important issues of the period, especially student activism and the young presidential candidate John F. Kennedy. In summer 1960, he traveled to Los Angeles, California, where he observed the Democratic Party national convention. While the Kennedy contingent politicked inside the arena, Hayden met and interviewed Martin Luther King Jr. as he picketed outside, supporting the southern civil rights movement. Hayden was aware of the spring 1960 student sit-ins but had kept his distance covering them as an objective reporter. However, this aloof stance began to change after Hayden interviewed King:

My most significant encounter during the convention week was there on the picket line: I interviewed Dr. Martin Luther King, Jr. "Ultimately, you have to take a stand with your life," he told me gently. I felt odd writing the words in my journalist's notebook. As I left the line, and later as I left Los Angeles, I asked myself why I should be only observing and chronicling this movement instead of participating in it. King was saying that each of us had to be more than neutral and objective, that we had to make a difference. That was something I realized I always wanted to do. Now the way was becoming clearer.[16]

Hayden soon made the decision to become active in the southern civil rights movement. In short order, he was dispatched to Atlanta as the first field secretary of Students for a Democratic Society (SDS), a small organization consisting largely of a paper membership. This assignment landed Hayden in the center of Atlanta's Black community and the southern civil rights movement, as SNCC and the Southern Christian Leadership Conference (SCLC) were headquartered in the city. As a result, Hayden became directly involved in SNCC projects in Mississippi and Georgia aimed at overthrowing crucial aspects of Jim Crow, including dismantling Black disenfranchisement and segregated public accommodations. These activities drew stiff resistance from white segregationists who used violence, arrests, economic reprisals, and intimidation to maintain the status quo. These repressive measures were also levied against whites, especially northerners, who participated in the movement. They were perceived as "nigger lovers" and despised because they violated racist practices by mingling closely with Blacks and joining them in protests that targeted spaces reserved for whites only.

Hayden experienced southern white brutality up close and personally. He participated in SNCC protests to register Blacks to vote in McComb, Mississippi, and in a Freedom Ride from Atlanta to Albany, Georgia. In McComb, Hayden was beaten by whites, who rained blows upon his body. In Albany he was arrested and jailed for violating segregation ordinances at the bus station. These were the negative consequences suffered by anyone challenging southern Jim Crow, including a white college graduate from Royal Oak, Michigan. Yet there were also positive consequences: Hayden generated reams of good copy describing developments in the southern movement and dispatched them to SDS, where they were widely distributed among student activists; he fell in love and was soon to marry a courageous young white woman activist deeply schooled philosophically and programmatically in nonviolent civil rights protests; and the documented brutality he endured, coupled with his coverage of the movement, made him famous in activist circles nationally.

Hayden's involvement in the southern movement was personally transformative. He was able to meet, observe, and work with major young Black leaders and activists in SNCC, including Bob Moses, James Forman, Charles McDew, and numerous others. These activists defied every Black stereotype peddled by white social science and media—they were smart, astute organizers, debonair, creative, courageous, and committed to slaying Jim Crow through disciplined nonviolent direct action if even it meant sacrificing their lives. Hayden was mesmerized by these freedom fighters: "They lived on a fuller level of feeling than any people I'd ever seen, partly because they were making modern history in a very personal way, and partly because of risking death they came to know the value of living each moment to the fullest. Looking back, this was a key turning point, the moment my political identity began to take shape. . . . Here were the models of charismatic commitment I was seeking—I wanted to live like them."[17] Repeatedly, Hayden witnessed the defiance and bravery of his new heroes. Chuck McDew, SNCC's first chairman, epitomized the fearlessness of SNCC's warriors: "McDew was the chairman of SNCC. A former Massillion, Ohio, football player, a combination of intellectual, jock, and playboy, McDew was an instant positive force in any situation. His ear-to-ear grin, white teeth on Black face, and absolutely arrogant fearlessness, drove the segregationists crazy. He laughed at people who wanted to lynch him and goaded the timid into action."[18] Hayden went on to explain how McDew operated: "When we arrived at the Freedom School the next morning, I saw McDew nonchalantly sauntering up the street to the church. Along the sidewalk were a dozen whites yelling curses at him. For the first time in my life, I heard people threatening openly and loudly to kill someone on the spot. McDew flipped them the finger, as if they were just another morning nuisance, and walked safely into the church."[19] Surely, there was no hint of such Black people in Mills's scholarship and that of other scholars Hayden had read.

Witnessing these moving displays of bravery, commitment, and SNCC's strategy sessions, Hayden was transformed. He described the impact that these experiences had upon him as akin to a religious conversion. Hayden and other young whites who participated in the early civil rights movement experienced a sea change. For them, racial leadership shifted dramatically: Black student activists became the exemplars setting the political agenda of elite white student activists. Hayden recalled the shift: "I was more struck by how challenging and revolutionary they were in contrast to those of the white northern students searching for meaning through abstract ideas alone."[20] White women who participated in the early civil rights movement had similar revelations. They were profoundly influenced by Black women activists who served as role models because they were strong and courageous freedom fighters in contrast to meek and domesticated white women with whom they were familiar.[21] Hayden sent out the message that white students should board the freedom bus conducted in the South by young Black activists: "Well, now the southern movement has turned itself into that revolution we hoped for, and we didn't have much to do with its turning at all. . . . Now they are miles ahead of us, looking back, chuckling knowingly about the sterility of liberals, tightening grimly against the potency of the racists. In the rural South, they will be shouting from the bottom of their guts for justice or else. We had better be there."[22] Hayden had learned from his southern activists experiences and willing to follow the lead of his young Black counterparts.

Beyond his mental transformation, Hayden also learned valuable movement lessons and values. Hayden was exposed to the collective action frame the civil rights movement provided. Jo Freeman captured this contribution of the civil rights movement, arguing, "More than any other influence, it ground the lens though which we saw the world. Nationally, as well as among our generation, it had prompted a perceptual shift in how people were categorized and how they were judged."[23] Sara Evans captured this frame innovation, writing that it produced a perceptual shift that contained "a language to name and describe oppression; a deep belief in freedom, equality and community . . . ; a willingness to question and challenge any social institution that failed to meet human needs; and the ability to organize."[24] Hayden clearly understood through his southern activism how the frame changed, and he communicated it outside the movement, declaring, "Most important is the crazy new sentiment that this is not just a movement but a revolution. . . . In our future dealings, we should realize that they have changed down here, and we should speak their revolutionary language without mocking it for it is not lip service."[25]

From the movement, Hayden schooled himself in nonviolent direct action. He came to see concretely that people could organize and act to change social conditions. In contrast to Mills's thesis regarding the permanent lack of agency among most Americans because they were part of an inert mass society, young Black activists revealed that they could organize for change using their very bodies as change agents. Thus the organizing process was highlighted in direct action, for without it the movement stalled. Nonviolence also taught a profound philosophy about the nature of human beings. They were viewed as infinitely worthy, possessing souls that could be perfected—even those of evil segregationists. To be sure, SNCC's founding statement declared, "By appealing to conscience and standing on the moral nature of human existence, nonviolence nurtures the atmosphere in which reconciliation and justice become actual possibilities."[26] In this approach love stands as an ultimate goal in human affairs because love transcends hate. Hayden came to see the importance that his new role models attached to love as a regulating medium through which human beings sought what King called the "Beloved Community."

Finally, Hayden witnessed how SNCC organized itself as a social movement organization. It rejected the charismatic model championed by King's SCLC. It frowned on centralized bureaucracy as existed in the NAACP. SNCC constructed a decentralized model whereby organizers were dispatched to local communities to nurture indigenous leadership, as advocated by Miss Ella Baker. This brand of organizational "participatory democracy" was not lost on Hayden. He recalled that he "advocated this form of 'anti-leader' organization and saw the debate repeated several times in the course of the many movements of the 1960s."[27] Equipped with these myriad lessons absorbed from the southern civil rights movement, Hayden was superbly prepared to draft a manifesto to guide a social movement that young white activists hoped to build. In Port Huron, Michigan, in June 1962, they would debate and refine a statement that was initially crafted in the bowels of the southern movement when Hayden put pen to paper in a jail in Jim Crow Albany, Georgia, just months earlier.

The *Port Huron Statement*

The *Port Huron Statement* is a bold manifesto that ranks as one of the most important American political documents of the twentieth century. Yet without the southern civil rights movement, there probably would not have been a *Port Huron Statement*. The framers of the statement made clear at the outset that racism and the movement to overthrow it were paramount to their efforts at Port Huron: "As we grew, however, our comfort was penetrated by events too troubling to dismiss. First, the permeating and victimizing fact of human degradation, symbolized by the Southern struggle against racial bigotry, compelled most of us from silence to activism."[28] The civil rights movement was seen by the students as proof that an organized social movement could be effective. They made clear their debt:

> In exploring the existing social forces, note must be taken of the Southern civil rights movement as the most heartening because of

the justice it insists upon, exemplary because it indicates that there can be a passage out of apathy. . . . This movement, pushed into a brilliant new phase by the Montgomery bus boycott and the subsequent nonviolent action of the sit-ins and Freedom Rides has had three major results: first, a sense of self-determination has been instilled in millions of oppressed Negroes; second, the movement has challenged a few thousand liberals to new social idealism; third, a series of important concessions have been obtained, such as token school desegregation, increased Administration help, new laws, desegregation of some public facilities.[29]

If there had not been the rise of the civil rights movement, there would not have been a training ground in mass activism for these pioneering white students and a model to follow even by many of them who did not participate directly. But as we have seen, the major drafter of the document, Tom Hayden, had been steeped in the philosophy, tactics, and activism of the southern movement. Many of the white activists became familiar with the movement through Hayden's concrete and detailed depictions of its actual struggles.

Even though the civil rights movement gave the decisive inspiration to the *Statement*, other influences were crucial too. Note that the *Statement* contained twenty-five thousand words, compared to SNCC's founding statement, which consisted of 155, or the recent Occupy movement document, with seven hundred words; it was even seven thousand words longer than the *Communist Manifesto*. Such lengthy manifestoes are generally disastrous organizing tools. Yet this fate did not befall the *Statement* because, in addition to a unifying vision, its guiding theoretical framework was anchored in a critical sociological framework. That framework provided the interpretive lens through which the big ideas—race and class inequality, the Cold War and the nuclear bomb, anticolonial revolutions, political disenfranchisement, American foreign policy, bureaucratic and corporate domination, human alienation, apathy, economic exploitation, and social movements—were analyzed. Without this sociological perspective stressing social forces, social structure, social organization, and social systems the cohesiveness of the document could not have been achieved.

C. Wright Mills's writing stressed the role social structures played in shaping human activities. Mills directed attention to how structural arrangements including bureaucracies, class formations, power structures, and a vast military apparatus dictated the experiences of twentieth-century

Americans. His work revealed how the most negative psychological feelings were the products of social structures. Mills argued that personal troubles were often not personal at all because they resulted from social forces that caused the same personal misery in thousands of people. Even feelings of loneliness and estrangement had structural roots. Thus millions of Americans experienced piercing alienation because they were disconnected from meaningful publics, making it impossible for them to participate in major decisions controlling their lives. The principal framers of the *Port Huron Statement*—including Hayden and Richard and Mickey Flacks—were well versed in Mills's writings, including *White Collar* (1951), *The Power Elite* (1956), *Sociological Imagination* (1959), *Listen Yankee* (1960), and "Letter to the New Left" (1960), and they were highly influenced by his structural analyses. The statement utilizes that approach, whether analyzing intimate personal phenomena or the behavior of gigantic corporations. This structural framework is the glue holding the document together and it accounts for the incisiveness of its analyses.

Although Mills's intellectual influence is apparent throughout the *Statement*, the philosophical and political ideas of the civil rights movement were crucial as well. When Hayden became involved in the southern civil rights movement, he discovered that the writings of the existentialist philosopher Albert Camus were influential among SNCC leaders and activists. Camus advocated that the individual had a moral responsibility to break free of apathy and rebel against unjust human conditions. In so doing, the individual was to remain free from rebelling for the sake of power and vengeance. Camus's philosophy was valuable also because it was consistent with nonviolence, for he rejected violence and elevated the need to construct humane communities. After being introduced to Camus by SNCC, Hayden devoured his writings, reading *The Plague* (1947), *The Stranger* (1942), and others, finding they addressed existential dilemmas and legitimated his push for students of his generation to transcend the apathy so aptly described by Mills. As a result, Hayden thoroughly interjected Camus's philosophy into the *Port Huron Statement* because he witnessed how it favorably impacted SNCC's leaders and spoke to oppressive conditions faced by student activists and how they might challenge them collectively.

The values of love and nonviolence were stressed in the *Port Huron Statement*. These two ideas were foundational in the civil rights movement and advocated by both King and SNCC. Nonviolence and love were the central value set forth in SNCC's founding statement: "Nonviolence, as it grows from the Judeo-Christian tradition, seeks a social order of justice permeated by love."[30] King declared, "We must discover the power of love, the power, the redemptive power of love. And when we discover that we will be able to make of this old world a new world. We will be able to make men better. Love is the only way."[31] The framers of the *Port Huron Statement* struck the same chord as SNCC and King by arguing that "only . . . love of man overcomes the idolatrous worship of things by man."[32] They included in their manifesto, "We would replace power and personal uniqueness rooted in possession, privilege, or circumstance by power and uniqueness rooted in love, reflectiveness, reason, and creativity."[33] Hayden and the framers of the *Port Huron Statement* echoed the civil rights movement's bedrock principle of nonviolence: "In social change or interchange, we find violence to be abhorrent because it requires generally the transformation of the target, be it a human being or a community of people, into a depersonalized object of hate. It is imperative that the means of violence be abolished and the institutions—local, national, international—that encourage nonviolence as a condition of conflict be developed."[34]

Participatory democracy was a key principle advocated in the *Port Huron Statement*. The framers defined it as a condition that exists when an "individual share[s] in those social decisions determining the quality and direction of his life."[35] Miss Ella Baker, the most influential founder and advisor of SNCC, first articulated a participatory democratic approach to achieve community empowerment and the way social movement organizations should organize themselves to struggle for change. SNCC adopted Baker's philosophy of grassroots change and organized itself as a nonhierarchical group-centered social movement organization. Carol Mueller correctly argued that while the architects of the *Port Huron Statement* have generally received credit for introducing the idea of participatory democracy, the fact is that "the basic themes of participatory democracy were first articulated and given personal witness in the activism of Ella Baker."[36] Hayden witnessed Baker espousing the principles of participatory democracy and its organizational manifestations in the operation of SNCC. While not being the only influence regarding this philosophy, Hayden credited this "remarkable forty-year-old Black woman named Ella Baker" as being crucial.[37]

This discussion makes clear that the *Statement* was not a document solely influenced by wide-ranging white intellectuals including Mills and Camus. Although these intellectuals provided foundational ideas upon which the document was based, the ideas and organizational insights of the southern civil rights movement were foundational as well. In this sense, the *Port Huron Statement* bears a heavy Black influence. Given its

184 | A New Insurgency

deep rootedness in the Black experience, the document makes a profound contribution to the understanding of that experience in America and around the world that was not part of popular media and social-scientific scholarship of the early 1960s. In this manner, young white students barely in their twenties broke from their professors and intellectual heroes who failed them miserably in providing analysis of the global color line.

The *Port Huron Statement* and the Color Line

The *Port Huron Statement* presents a bold structural analysis of racism. The analysis contrasted sharply with contemporary social scientific literature of the 1950s that portrayed Blacks as an incompetent people; if they were ever to receive better treatment, social scientists asserted, it would happen because whites decided to act favorably toward their inferior darker counterparts. White social scientists of the 1940s and 1950s had no inkling that a massive civil rights and Black Power movement was gaining agency to explode sociological myths and attack American racism head-on. In this scholarship lurked Amos and Andy stereotypes, not the likes of Ella Baker, Bob Moses, Martin Luther King Jr., Chuck McDew, Fannie Lou Hamer, and Diane Nash.

Yet when young whites, including Hayden, joined the southern movement, they came under the spell of activists not remotely matching the prevalent Black stereotypes. They saw their creativity firsthand and witnessed Black cultural resources housed in churches, schools, and other institutions. These young whites also came face to face with the reality of structural racism—poverty, political disenfranchisement, illiteracy, dilapidated housing, unemployment, poor health, and so on—that Blacks faced routinely. They also learned that their southern white counterparts from the governor to poor white workers were committed to maintaining the racist status quo at all costs. Viewed as "nigger lovers" intent on overturning a noble way of life, the white activists came to understand the pain associated with resisting oppression, including beatings, jail, and even death. They learned that conditions Blacks endured resulted from brutality and the exercise of state power. Once on the ground floor of the movement, these activists realized the absurdity of claims that Black conditions were products of Blacks themselves.

The image of America as a shining democracy was shattered by racial inequality the civil rights movement exposed. The framers of the *Statement* stated bluntly, "While these and other problems either directly oppressed us or rankled our consciences and became our own subjective concerns, we began to see complicated and disturbing paradoxes in our surrounding America. The declaration all men are created equal . . . rang hollow before the facts of Negro life in the South and the big cities of the North."[38] The framers committed a portion of the document to a section labeled "Discrimination," where they specified the huge racial disparities in Black/white literacy rates, salaries, occupational attainment, unemployment rates, housing quality, education, and voting rates. These racial inequalities were argued to be rooted in racist structural arrangements: "Discrimination in employment, along with labor's accommodation to the 'lily-white' hiring practices, guarantees the lowest slot in the economic order to the 'nonwhite.' North or South, these oppressed are conditioned by their inheritance and their surroundings to expect more of the same: in housing, schools, recreation, travel, all their potential is circumscribed, thwarted and often extinguished."[39]

The writers threw cold water on the idea of progress being made toward achieving racial inequality, arguing, "The facts bely it, however, unless it is assumed that America has another century to deal with its racial inequalities."[40] The racial realities Hayden witnessed in the movement enabled him to stare the devil in the face and not be misled by his superficial disguises.

Without guidance from their intellectual elders, the visionaries at Port Huron posited a different causality for racial inequality: "Others, more pompous, will blame the situation on 'those people's inability to pick themselves up,' not understanding the automatic way in which such a system can frustrate reform efforts and diminish the aspirations of the oppressed."[41] In this clear-cut causal claim, the *Port Huron Statement* parted ways with sociologists and other social scientists who blamed Black culture or racial traits as causes for Black subjugation. Although Mills was not helpful for their racial analyses, the authors of the document understood his structural approach too well to miss the opportunity to use it to develop a sociological view of race inequality illuminating its structural roots.

The young activists' analyses went beyond race in America. Like W. E. B. Du Bois, they recognized that racial inequality was global and that America was deeply implicated in racism on a world scale.[42] The *Port Huron Statement* focused attention on the movements of darker people in Africa, Asia, and Latin America to overthrow colonialism. By 1962, numerous anticolonial movements had occurred with a number of them resulting in the overthrowing of their oppressors and independent nations established in their stead. The argument put forth in the document was that America tended to be on the wrong side of history by employing anti-Communist ideology to hide its imperialistic, exploitative interests achieved through propping up right-wing, corrupt oligarchies in the Third World. They argued that by supporting these nondemocratic forces, America separated itself from the colonial revolutions. In so doing, America sided with colonialists rather than social revolutions seeking to establish democratic societies.

In a prescient analytical move, the white students grasped that racism abroad and at home were intricately linked and that these struggles generated reciprocal influences. Acknowledging internal pressures, they wrote, "The advancement of the Negro and other 'nonwhites' in America has not been altogether by means of the crusades of liberalism, but rather through unavoidable changes in social structure. The economic pressures of World War II opened new jobs, new mobility, new insights to Southern Negroes."[43] They went on to connect these changes with global pressures:

> More important than the World War II openings was the colonial revolution. The world-wide upsurge of dark peoples against white colonial domination stirred the aspiration and created an urgency among American Negroes, while simultaneously it threatened the power structure of the United States enough to produce concessions to the Negro. Produced by outer pressure from the newly-moving peoples rather than by the internal conscience of the Federal government, the gains were keyed to improving the American "image" more than to reconstructing the society that prospered on top of its minorities.[44]

Here we observe how twenty-year-old radical students provided a sophisticated analysis of how the Cold War, colonial revolutions, and domestic racial realities intertwined and shaped twentieth-century America.

I close, as I began, on a personal note. When I learned as a teenager about the role young whites played in the southern civil rights movement, it changed my view that all whites were mean exploiters because they oppressed African Americans collectively. I wanted to thank them for helping us, given they did not have to make sacrifices fighting in a war to liberate a people not of their own race. But as I grew older, I realized these young white Americans came to understand they could not be free as long as we remained in bondage trapped by Jim Crow and pervasive race inequality. Although some changes Blacks and whites struggled mightily for have been realized, the roots of structural racism and societal oppression have not been extracted from the land. A disciplined struggle to create a democratic society remains high on the agenda for those committed to building a robust democratic society because the unimaginable is still the devil to be avoided.

14 | A New Left Philosophical Itinerary: Marcuse, Sartre, and Then Camus
by Ronald Aronson

From its first paragraphs describing the paradoxes and contradictions of American society, the *Port Huron Statement* demonstrated that early New Leftists were unapologetically intellectual. The *Statement* itself was an analysis of American society that was anchored self-confidently within its universities: this was after all the launch of a *student* movement. As the movement spread, we continued to devour ideas and analyses, passing around *Studies on the Left, New University Thought, Liberation,* and *Dissent,* talking about our readings of Gandhi, C. Wright Mills, Paul Goodman, William Appleman Williams, Isaac Deutscher, Eric Fromm, Norman O. Brown, Malcolm X, Albert Camus, Jean-Paul Sartre, and Herbert Marcuse.

Among the millions of New Left itineraries, my own centered on the last two thinkers and accordingly was especially philosophical. In 1962 I had entered the graduate program in the history of ideas at Brandeis University in order to study with Marcuse. My courses with him included Plato, empiricism and rationalism, Hegel, nineteenth-century social theory, and Marxism and Communism. After completing my course work, my wife and I moved to New Brunswick, New Jersey, where I participated in a community-organizing project in the black ghetto. After publishing a somewhat Marcusean reflection in *Studies on the Left* on the distance between our New Left political activity and Marxist hopes for revolutionary transformation, I was invited to join the journal's editorial board, where I participated actively for the remaining year and a half of its existence. In spring 1968, having just defended my doctoral dissertation at Brandeis on "Art and Freedom in the Philosophy of Jean-Paul Sartre," I led a discussion group on "bourgeois cultural hegemony" in the Liberation School organized at Columbia University in the wake of the student strike. This mixing of radical academic work and political activism has characterized my life ever since, returning me again and again to my deepest philosophical influences, Marcuse and Sartre, and then, in the last dozen years, encouraging me to undertake a close study of Camus. These three happened to be among the most important thinkers during the period when the New Left took shape. Each of them contributed to the movement but in very different and sometimes opposing ways.

Reading *Reason and Revolution* was what drew me to study with Marcuse. Twenty years after it was first published in 1941, the book was still in print and widely available in a paperback edition. I worked my way through it while my wife and I were teaching in a country schoolhouse in Northern California; I hadn't even gotten to the concluding discussion of how Marx absorbed and revolutionized Hegel when I decided that I wanted to study with Marcuse. I later found out that he had also published a critical and historical study of Soviet Marxism as well as a path-breaking and highly original study of Freud, *Eros and Civilization*.

Those of us who studied with him or heard him lecture recall a commanding presence with a German accent and silver-gray hair. He was simultaneously a Hegelian, a Marxist, and a Freudian, and his writings (and his bearing) seemed to emanate from distant realms, all the way from Socrates, Plato, and Aristotle to a cultural universe that included Beethoven's late quartets and the writings of Rilke and Beckett. I wrote about

> watching wide-eyed as silver-haired hawk-nosed Herbert Marcuse lectured at Brandeis in his grey double-breasted suits. He taught Marxism but also the classics: Plato, Aristotle, Kant, Hegel, eighteenth-century liberalism, and nineteenth-century social theory. And he taught the perspective that integrated them all: the hopes of humankind, from Plato to Marx, were of a piece and must be taken seriously. From Plato to Marx and Marcuse, that is: he sternly and self-consciously saw himself as continuing this great tradition of Western rationalism, referring to each of his predecessors as "the old man." Thus was Marx gilded with the authority of Plato, Kant and Hegel, thus did Marcuse assume their mantle, thus, to us, did he gild Marxism with *his* authority. As he spoke, everything I had been wrestling with, all my interests and needs, and my budding socialism, easily drew together.[1]

Here is how I described the experience in a letter to him presented at the Socialist Scholars Conference in 1969:

> I recall those classes on Plato's *Meno* and Kant's *Critique of Pure Reason*; we prepared hard and long, read the material two or three times, refused to miss even one class, came expectantly, brought our friends and wives. Something was happening in Marcuse's classes. We all sensed it, we were learning how to read, to think. Above all you emphasized the idea of reason: the capacity of thought to understand the existing social reality, to criticize it, to project alternatives. All this meant mastery, disciplined work, knowledge for the sake of changing the world.

I went on to say that he "introduced us to a perspective which was new and revolutionary, which made sense of our lives and helped us to find our way as radicals."[2]

I can't exaggerate how important it was for those of us who knew him, heard him, and read him to have someone of his age and stature legitimizing us and showing solidarity with us. In this sense Marcuse was more a grandfather figure than a father figure to the New Left: older than our parents, he was tolerant and accepting, and he encouraged our activism. Born in 1898, he had participated in the Spartacist uprising in 1919, was one of the first members of the Frankfurt School, and with colleagues Max Horkheimer, Theodor Adorno, and Franz Neumann, he left Germany in 1933, as Hitler was rising to power. To the extent that we were in rebellion against our parents and their generation, Marcuse was first of all "the old man" himself, reaching back well beyond any of our current authorities in connecting us to both revolutionary history and high culture. Second, Marcuse immediately identified himself with the New Left: encouragingly, never patronizingly, lovingly, providing tools for our critique of American society, and clarifying the deepest meanings of our rebellion.

One-Dimensional Man, published in 1964, was a key book of those early years. It was fiercely antiestablishment and gave us a handle for understanding the suffocation many of us felt as we were becoming adults. Anti-Soviet as well as anticapitalist, Marcuse described for us an "advanced industrial society" in which the "interests of domination" ruled over their subjects by creating false needs and meeting them by "delivering the goods." We were coming of age in a "society without opposition," marked by the working class's substantial integration into the Cold War consensus. This deeply negative analysis of American society's soft, administered, consumerist totalitarianism fit our experience, except that we could not accept its pessimistic conclusion about the general climate of hopelessness. Marcuse did not suggest ways to find or create an alternative; we, however, felt we needed to break out of this "society without opposition." By the last pages of *One-Dimensional Man*, it was difficult to think of how we might act against the situation he described, except that it was clear that *we* had to create the alternative. Instead of taking his descriptions of one-dimensional society as meaning that the possibility of struggle was over, as a few of Marcuse's students did, many of us embraced this critique of American society as we located or created the energy to try to change it. And as we did act, he supported us wholeheartedly. More, he supplied us with intellectual tools for projecting alternatives. Some of us found them in *Eros and Civilization*, which, along with Norman O. Brown's *Life Against Death*, reshaped the meaning of Freud, usually read as a pessimistic view of human destiny, to make it part of a utopian vision fitting our sense of historical possibilities. In going beyond Marx, Marcuse was being rigorously Marxist: the kinds of repression demanded by a world of scarcity, and then by the historical project of overcoming scarcity, were no longer necessary in a postscarcity world. Rather, they were maintained, artificially, by the political and economic "interests of domination." Realistically speaking, actual historical possibilities suggested an end of toil and renunciation. By the end of the 1960s, in Marcuse's lectures and in *An Essay on Liberation*, it was not only his stark negativity that inspired us but also his powerful utopianism.

While the civil rights and anti–Vietnam War movements drew us into action, another living philosopher who prodded us to act was Jean-Paul Sartre. A number of things drew us to him. First, he was an activist and a radical. Sartre had been intensely involved in opposition to the just-concluded war in Algeria. His article against torture was banned by the government and then published clandestinely, and he spoke at the first major meeting against the war, went on demonstrations, edited one of the major leftist journals, and supported the Jeanson network aiding the *Front de Libération Nationale* rebels. His apartment was bombed twice by the right-wing terrorists of the *Organisation Armée Secrète*. In 1964 Sartre turned down the Nobel Prize in Literature because he felt it had been used for Cold War political purposes—why, he asked, didn't they award it to him when he was active against the Algerian War? Also, in a strong anti-establishment stand that many of us appreciated, he said that he didn't want "Nobel Prize winner" to be attached to his name and give extra weight to his writings.

In 1967 he became president of the Bertrand Russell Vietnam War Crimes Tribunal and wrote its judgment condemning the United States for committing genocide. The next year, during the May events in Paris, he went to the Sorbonne, not lecturing to the students but in fact interviewing the students' leader, Danny Cohn-Bendit. Rejecting the "star system," he put himself at the service of the New Left not only for a brief moment but as long as he was physically able to be active. Viewing him from across the Atlantic, here was a political intellectual we could relate to, willing to use his fame for our causes and to put himself on the line again and again. If Marcuse might be seen as a grandfather figure, Sartre was too close to our attitudes and values, our radicalism, to be regarded as a father figure. This greatest French philosopher of his generation—the squat, ugly, half-blind Sartre, who came to politics late but now openly identified with us—kept young activists from elevating him to parental status. Because of the simple and direct way he shared our commitments, he seemed more like an approving uncle.

If his example was inspiring, so were Sartre's ideas. His writings were more widely familiar than Marcuse's because of the fame of existentialism and because many of us had read his famous lecture, *Existentialism Is a Humanism*, in college freshman philosophy courses. On the one hand, the argument there fits perfectly with American individualism: we are free to make our own choices and our own lives. If taken out of context, Sartre's key ideas there and in *Being and Nothingness* of freedom, self-determination, responsibility, and bad faith might appear to give the poor responsibility for their poverty and credit the rich for their wealth. But that is not what he meant. He did indeed briefly become notorious on the left as the thinker who wrote that "the slave in chains is as free as his master"—but he labored long and hard to correct any impression that he ignored the weight of social and historical realities.[3]

In fact, *Being and Nothingness* said that human freedom was precisely freedom to encounter these realities; it was never absolute and was always situated. One's situation includes social class, wealth or poverty, race, gender, and family upbringing, as well as previous choices, language, and environment. Indeed, beginning in 1947, Sartre titled his collections of essays *Situations*. In using this term, Sartre announced his commitment to describe both the objective *and* the subjective, both the constraints that shape and oppress us and our freedom and power of self-determination within these limits.[4] A natural agitator, he chided people who insisted that they couldn't help themselves and were determined by forces beyond their control, but Sartre's greatest fury was directed against people and systems that would oppress, dominate, and diminish others. His greatest hatred was directed at those who treated people as things, as nonhumans—at those who would destroy other people's subjectivity. Accordingly, he wrote powerfully against torture, fascism, racism, anti-Semitism, colonialism, and capitalism, and he powerfully described efforts by the oppressed to find their voices and shape themselves despite and against forces that reduced and limited them.

Sartre's words pointed to action. He was the writer who told us that to not oppose an evil carried out in our name is to become its accomplice. If we are citizens of a democratic country that is engaged in colonialism, imperial wars, or genocide, then we sanction those practices simply by not opposing them. Governments depend on our passive complicity. To act or not: this is the demand that haunts many of his fictional characters.

In addition, at the very time the American New Left began, *Search for a Method* was published and discussed in *Studies on the Left*. It joined Sartre's existentialism to the historically most important system of political thought and action, Marxism—and it was among the writings that helped free Marxism from its Stalinist sclerosis and stay alive for another generation. It was originally published during the brief post-Stalinist thaw in Poland in 1957. Its key idea is that the philosophy of freedom, responsibility, and choice was not opposed to systemic social change but essential to it. Sartre called for the end of the stifling Stalinist determinism, "dialectical materialism," labeling it an a priori thought that pretended to have all the explanations for any historical event before the event itself happened. In its place he called for a nondogmatic Marxism that studied the events themselves and that took seriously the dimension of human subjectivity.

Since Sartre's death and especially the collapse of Communism a decade later, there has been much score settling regarding his 1952–56 alignment with the French Communist Party and the Soviet Union, which were irrelevant to us. By the time we first encountered him in the 1960s, Sartre had already made himself into a major independent non-Communist political force because of his creative and undogmatic Marxism, his support for non-Communist and Third World revolutions, and his way of theorizing revolutionary violence—which was precisely what attracted many of us.

During the high point of the Cuban Revolution in 1960, Sartre and Simone de Beauvoir visited the island and wrote a series of articles that were immediately translated as *Sartre on Cuba* and that painted a detailed and glowing picture of Castro's revolution before it embraced Communism. Most interesting to many of us was a chapter in one of the early issues of *Studies on the Left*, "Ideology and Revolution," which prized action over ideology. He claimed there that previous revolutions had begun with an ideology but that the Cuban Revolution developed its ideology in practice, in response to real conditions and demands of its situation. The revolution, he said approvingly and in true existentialist spirit, had "not a minute for theory, not an action which isn't founded on experience."[5] Sartre also understood the violence of revolutionary movements as appropriate responses to systemic violence imposed on the oppressed, even when this was done legally by the authorities. Years of brutal attacks by southern racists, sluggish responses by the federal government, and the dawning awareness of how difficult it was for the African American minority to overcome an entrenched racist system led to growing impatience with both black-white unity and nonviolence. The growth of Black Power coincided with an increasing interest in violence as a tool of social change. This was happening just as Sartre's embrace of revolutionary violence was becoming widely known through the 1963 translation of Frantz Fanon's *The Wretched of the Earth*, published with Sartre's approving preface. There Sartre moved from insights into the structure of colonialism, to sketching its psychic damage—to celebrating the natives' revolutionary violence as therapy and liberation: "To shoot down a European is to kill two birds with one stone, doing away with oppressor and oppressed at the same time: what remains is a dead man and a free man."[6]

In retrospect, it is important to note that Sartre's extreme rhetoric was not simply a momentary excess; that rhetoric can be shown to be rooted in his key terms. And it is also important to note that a few paragraphs later in the preface, almost unnoticed, was an attack on what he regarded as the complicity of those espousing the nonviolence of his deceased former friend, Albert Camus: "The non-violent are looking pleased with themselves: neither victims nor executioners! Come on! If you are not victims, since the government for which you voted, since the Army in which your young brothers have served, carried out a 'genocide' without hesitation or remorse, then you are unquestionably executioners."[7]

While Sartre supplied intellectual ammunition for a direction being taken by one current of the New Left, others remained true to the very different philosophical inspiration of Albert Camus. I myself did not sense his importance in those years, but Camus was a spiritual source for many activists. Many who were already committed and active found in Camus more personal guidance than in either Marcuse or Sartre, and I think few of those inspired by him could have experienced him as an elder like the others. There was an intimacy to the writings of this tragically and recently dead young man, this older brother who left us his thoughts about how we might conduct ourselves in a difficult world—Camus after all died in a car crash in January 1960 at the age of forty-six; he won the Nobel Prize in 1957 when he was barely forty-four. For this reason, he remains young to us, even as we age.

Very few of us knew anything about the courageous and pained political life of this ideologically moderate but deeply committed leftist who had been turned down for teaching and then rejected by the military during the war because of tuberculosis. He had been active all his adult life—as a Communist in Algeria; as leader of a politically oriented theater troupe there; as a journalist and then editor of the foremost newspaper, *Combat*, to emerge from the Resistance; as a neutralist and then anti-Marxist and anti-Communist as East-West tensions were deepening; as Sartre's antagonist in the most spectacular rupture of a friendship caused by the Cold War; and as the last *Pied-Noir* trying to find a way out of the worsening Algerian conflict. All this became widely known to Americans only long after Camus's death.

But his core ideas were accessible to us in the early days of the Movement—in philosophical works such as *The Myth of Sisyphus* and *The Rebel* and fiction such as *The Stranger* and *The Plague*. These books, all written before he was forty, have a special power for those who are trying to figure out the meaning of life and of acting politically. The key themes include absurdity, living intensely despite absurdity, a profound sense of political limits pointing to rebellion rather than revolution, opposition to political violence, the need to struggle against oppression from the left or the right, and solidarity as one of the highest values.

Camus's most powerful ideas are often captured in images. One of these is the unforgettable one of Sisyphus straining to push his rock up the mountain, watching it roll down, and then trudging down after the rock to begin all over in an endless cycle. This "is the hour of consciousness. At each of those moments when he leaves the heights and gradually sinks towards the lairs of the gods, he is superior to his fate. He is stronger than his rock." Why? He is fully aware, and he is defiant. Camus says, "Sisyphus, proletarian of the gods, powerless and rebellious, knows the whole extent of his wretched condition: it is what he thinks of during his descent."[8] This then is Camus's reply to his famous question about whether or not to commit suicide: full consciousness, avoiding false solutions such as religion, refusing to submit, and carrying on with vitality and intensity.

A second image, from *The Plague*, describes the "sanitary squads" removing diseased rats from the city of Oran. As I have written elsewhere, this novel "was Camus's manual of commitment. It conveys the unheroic determination to do what must be done in the face of a total threat, without, as the narrator says, 'attributing overimportance to praiseworthy actions.' Those who participated in the novel's 'sanitary squads' did so because 'they knew it was the only thing to do, and the unthinkable thing would then have been not to have brought themselves to do it.' The situation demanded it; that was all."[9]

Two of the main characters, Rieux and Tarrow, take a break from their labors and swim out to sea. They spontaneously time their strokes so that they would move out and swim back to shore precisely together. Camus writes, "They dressed and started back. Neither had said a word, but they were conscious of being perfectly at one, and the memory of this night would be cherished by them both."[10] This was a communion of combatants, who had no need to say how much they shared. Their silence captured Camus's sense of solidarity. The world might be absurd, as Camus said, but the answer was not to seek to transform it root and branch, looking for total solutions and trying to take the place of the God who wasn't there, but to engage in acts of rebellion against its injustices and to do so nonviolently and in a spirit of solidarity.

What are some of the ways the ideas of the three thinkers might still be relevant to those of us who remain committed to the values and goals that motivated us fifty years ago? What are some of the ways we should be criticizing and going beyond them? To my mind, two issues stand out today: the nature (and evaluation) of political violence and the one-dimensional nature of American society.

By a remarkable prescience, the most significant political-intellectual quarrel of the twentieth century—that of Camus and Sartre—anticipated a major issue of the twenty-first. The main issue dividing them was political violence—specifically, that of Communism.

The core difference between Camus and Sartre surfaced in fall 1946 after Camus's series of articles in *Combat* titled "Neither Victims nor Executioners," where he both equated Marxism with murder and refused to take sides in the looming East-West conflict. In other words, he supplied a key theme of the West's ideology while rejecting the Cold War itself.[11] Although he had reluctantly justified taking up arms against Nazi Germany, he now refused all complicity with violence, becoming known for his anti-Cold War, anti-Communist reformist leftism. Sartre replied to his friend that it was impossible to refuse all complicity with violence. Since violence would take place no matter what, "one must make a choice, according to other principles." For Sartre, the issue was not to concoct what he regarded as an illusory nonviolent path but to decide in this violent world which path brought France closer to realizing a better society.[12]

Their differences came to a climax in 1952 with the sensational row over Camus's *The Rebel* in Sartre's journal *Les Temps Modernes*, and as they continued to jab at each other, often in code, during the rest of the decade, especially during the war in Algeria, a major issue between them became terrorism. The 1957 and 1964 Nobel laureates broke sharply over which kind of violence most urgently demanded to be addressed and attacked—the humiliations and oppressions, often masked, which Sartre described as systematically built into daily life under capitalism and colonialism, or the brutal and abstract calculus of murder denounced by Camus as built into movements claiming to liberate people from capitalist and colonial oppression.

This debate remains pertinent today because, first, if the issue of violence is to be discussed fully and honestly, and if the various forms of the worldwide politics of violence are to be critically understood, *each form* deserves to be placed under the microscope. This means distinguishing rhetorical claims from reality: in what ways, if any, might the War on Terror be described as legitimately defensive violence and in what ways, if any, might today's terrorism be described as legitimately antisystemic violence? Such an approach would include discussing the systemic kinds of violence singled out for attack by Sartre (rigged elections, laws applied unequally, restrictions on political participation) no less than those antisystemic ones described by Camus (political assassination, violence against civilians). Keeping these in mind, the intentional violence of terrorism demands to be interrogated alongside the violence inscribed in routine social practices as well as the violence of wars against terrorism, and these need to be distinguished from other forms of violence masquerading as defensive and emancipatory, including violence carried out for reasons of religious, ethnic, military, and imperial domination. I have written that the Camus-Sartre conflict remains unresolved because when either one appears to win their debate, we all lose. Each man described and denounced a single dimension of contemporary violence, Camus targeting revolutionary violence and Sartre targeting the violence structurally imposed by social systems based on inequality. Each man had a dazzling but partial insight, yet each one was blind to the other's insight.

Today we are not done with their debate because its issues have not yet been resolved. As the sheer facts of contemporary terrorism and the War on Terror have made compellingly clear, we continue to be plagued by denial about core issues. Camus for one would have turned over in his grave to see his ideas used, as indeed they were, to justify the American war in Iraq.[13] His half of the truth about violence played nicely into the hands of the neoconservatives dominating the Defense Department's strategic thinking after September 11. And too often, conversations on the left about terrorism still wind up resting, explicitly or not, on Sartre's claim that it is the "only weapon" available to the weak.[14]

We still live amid the Cold War's obfuscations: on the one side, Camus falsely equated Marxism with murder because it sanctioned revolutionary violence; on the other, Sartre uncritically embraced violence as the only possible path of social transformation. In the years since the Cold War, the victors have continued to taboo any serious talk about their own system's endemic violence, and they self-righteously inveigh against any violence by the world's underclass. The War on Terror still seeks to delegitimize antisystemic violence in advance, even when no meaningful alternatives exist. And no less worthy of censure are those who refuse to make the moral or political distinction between combatants and noncombatants, finding both fair game for violent attacks, as well as those critics of the United States who sometimes go soft on terrorism. Opening their eyes to Sartre's analysis of systemic violence can be a needed antidote to antiterror warriors; for those unwilling to think critically about terrorism, Camus's analysis of the origins and destructive effects of revolutionary violence may be a needed antidote.

Thinking about Marcuse today immediately demands that we ask about *One-Dimensional Man* as prophecy. When Marcuse claimed to be identifying key tendencies of advanced industrial society—specifically, the United States—many of us responded as if he had hit the nail on the head. We resonated with his description of a society without opposition and of individuals who were increasingly suffocated by the integrative force of the economy, culture, and government. To what extent did his analysis anticipate developments over the next fifty years?

In a decisive respect, although in ways he did not foresee, the entire world has grown politically and economically more one-dimensional. I am referring to the victory of capitalism and the collapse of Communism as an alternative. Marcuse grouped them together as advanced industrial societies of similar tendencies, but the Communist version has vanished. Even if it was a bad alternative, it did encourage thinking and acting in noncapitalist directions. It turned out that Communism's disappearance (and in the case of China and Vietnam, their embrace of capitalism) helped cut the ground from efforts of labor and social-democratic parties to combat neoliberalism. Today, only a few countries in Latin America and Scandinavia have been able to resist slightly the stampede toward free-market globalization. As the world has become more one-dimensional, what we now call "the 1 percent" have become more self-confident, more crudely aggressive and ruthless in ignoring limits, dismantling controls, and removing restraints.

In many ways, then, the situation is much worse than fifty years ago. The political-economic-ideological trend has included the rise of neoliberalism, the shrinking of union membership, an increase in inequality, more direct corporate control of the political system, a shredding of the safety net, and privatization of schools and public services. The working class is being moved out of the middle class (most strikingly by the installation of a two-tiered wage system in the automobile industry).

As we know, there does remain a struggle with two sides to it, but it is difficult to speak of either of these being an "alternative" in the sense Marcuse meant. Look at the sides: the most sustained political rebellion of the last few years was not the short-lived Occupy movement but the Tea Party, with its bizarre demand in the midst of the Great Recession (and ever since) for more of the same deregulation and free-market policies that caused the crisis of 2008. For a generation, all advanced societies have been reshaped by a class struggle from above. Those of us opposing the extreme right have joined forces with moderates and liberals, all of us being on the defensive against their demands. Even after Occupy and as in 1964, there is virtually no opposition in Marcuse's sense of posing alternatives that would expand human freedom and possibilities.

A related negative trend demands that we keep the spirit but correct the specifics of Marcuse's description of the society as "totalitarian." Marcuse used that term to describe the political, social, and ideological consensus of the welfare-warfare state, but that consensus turned out to be short-lived and has clearly ended. Still, his sense that capitalism was becoming more and more all-encompassing does help us to understand a crucial dimension of our world: the ways in which the for-profit economy and its logic infiltrate all other dimensions.

The logic of capitalism seeps into and dominates the rest of everyone's life, right down to attitudes and values. The economy totally depends on, and feeds, a sense of constant and endless innovation in the production of goods, services, and marketing. Capitalism depends on creating new wants. But today, we are finding out that we have all become infected by consequences of the drive for profit. Everything we do and touch—and are—seems increasingly informed by the social imperative to compete, grow, develop, and change. Even children are commodified, as the education system is being transformed into a free-market free-for-all. Today, the "bottom line" increasingly subjects all corners of existence, all physical and psychological spaces, to a kind of free-market totalitarianism, a maelstrom of "progress," that sweeps everything in its path. The focus on "the next big thing," the logic of the consumer society, ensnares all of us: its beneficiaries are its victims.

To be sure, we have not reached the totally administered universe Marcuse foresaw. Quite the opposite, he did not anticipate the demands for equality and explosion of identities, sexuality, and other personal freedoms that would change American society, within a generation after the height of the New Left, into a far less repressive and more diverse and livable place. We have participated in and lived through this nonstop transformation, which has changed much of how we think, how we act, and what we do. Its political and social detonators were the civil rights and then black movement, the antiwar and student movements, and the women's movement, followed by the gay and lesbian movement. Their far-reaching demands for political and legal equality were also an attack on the repression and uniformity that not only had stifled us growing up but were once ascribed to civilized life itself. And today? Recently, I've been drafting an essay tentatively titled "Reasons Why There Won't Be a Socialist Revolution in America." It points to the proliferation of freedoms, amenities, and lifestyles unknown fifty years ago: tattoos and pornography, the Internet and smart phones, coffee houses and art fairs, T-shirts and jeans, oral sex and divorce, yoga and foreign travel, Twitter and Facebook, Whole Foods and Trader Joe's, "your comments" on the Internet on everything under the sun and rising interest in gourmet food and wines, and so on. The list keeps growing and reflects the kaleidoscopic and immensely profitable expansion of choice, freedom, and individual expressiveness in our lifetime.

Despite its commercialization, the space in which we move today is far freer, far more inclusive, far more interesting and diverse, and humanly and socially far richer than any of us would ever have anticipated upon closing the pages of *One-Dimensional Man*. It is important to stress that this is largely due to human actors, including ourselves, responding to both the repressions and the possibilities within and around us in assertive ways that significantly changed ourselves, others, and the world. But just as obviously, today's world has also been shaped by capitalism's dazzling ability to meet and generate new needs, to "deliver the goods" and then some. Far from threatening the capitalist system, the new energies released in the 1960s have become vital new sources of its expansion and profits, especially in the crisis-ridden years since 1975. This means that the cultural and social changes in which we participated not only have *not* threatened but have been happily accommodated by the capitalist system. Indeed, capitalists have proven that they can be hip and tolerant: to young people today, being an entrepreneur has some of the same cultural cachet as being a political activist once had in our time.

The Marcusean tone of this last observation gives no solace, but it does at least suggest that the philosophers who inspired the New Left, and the issues they raised, still have much to say to us today. We, and those younger than ourselves, face immense tasks and will obviously make use of recent analyses and newer thinkers. Just as obviously, there is much to be gained from engaging with Marcuse's writings, as there is by engaging with Sartre and Camus. As we have seen, it will be a critical and self-conscious engagement, one keenly aware of how different today's world is from that of fifty years ago but also of how much remains unchanged.

15 | Participatory Art as Participatory Democracy: The American Avant-Garde in the 1950s and 1960s
by Robert Genter

"Art," explained philosopher John Dewey in *Art as Experience*, "insinuates possibilities of human relations not to be found in rule and precept, admonition and administration."[1] In linking art to social transformation, Dewey famously revised traditional philosophical understandings of experience, arguing that aesthetic experience was in part an enhanced form of everyday personal experience but one that encouraged direct participation by individuals in the project of imagining the radical transformation of existing society. In so doing, Dewey provided intellectual inspiration for the founding principle and rallying cry of the *Port Huron Statement*—participatory democracy. For Dewey, participatory democracy was not merely a political project to make government more responsive to public demands or to encourage individual political action but an *aesthetic* principle to help individuals transform themselves and their surroundings and to reshape their lives in more authentic ways. Politics and art, according to Dewey, were fundamentally intertwined, the latter unearthing the transformative possibilities inherent in the former. As he explained, "Works of art are the only media of complete and unhindered communication between man and man that can occur in a world full of gulfs and walls that limit community of experience."[2] The *Port Huron Statement* was shaped by this Deweyan notion of democracy as in part an aesthetic practice not reducible to specific political issues, defining its politics "as the art of collectively creating an acceptable pattern of social relations . . . [and] a means of finding meaning in personal life."[3]

In this sense, the *Port Huron Statement* is just as much a literary work as a political manifesto, one focused on the aesthetic transformation of human beings and their world. It is hardly a poem, to be sure, but many of the claims made by Tom Hayden and other contributors concerning human potential and creativity link the *Statement* just as much to the cultural history of the late 1950s as to the political history of that time. As Todd Gitlin has explained in *The Sixties: Years of Hope, Days of Rage,* "The New Left had a practice and a spirit before—or more than—it ever had an ideology," a practice and a spirit centered on ideas about participation and creative action.[4] For instance, the rise of participatory democracy as the trumpet call of Students for a Democratic Society (SDS) was paralleled by the rise of participatory art as the key artistic practice of the American avant-garde in the late 1950s, led by the innovative work of Jack Kerouac, Jackson Pollock, John Cage, Allan Kaprow, and a host of others. Feeling similarly stifled by powerful economic concentrations, equally troubled by the possibility of a nuclear holocaust, and calling for a revolution in consciousness to overcome feelings of alienation, many artists and writers rebelled against conservative notions of art as somehow separate or sealed off from everyday life; they sought to redefine art as a participatory form predicated upon risk taking and direct action as the path to liberation. "Art," explained Norman Brown in *Life Against Death: The Psychoanalytical Meaning of History* (1959), one of the books that influenced Tom Hayden while writing the early draft of the *Port Huron Statement,* "seduces us into the struggle against repression."[5] For Brown and many others, art and politics had become intertwined by the end of 1950s, as the meaning of liberation acquired both a political and aesthetic dimension.

But the nature of participation in both a political and artistic sense was highly debated at that time, a fact reflected in the language of the *Port Huron Statement* itself. For some, participation as a creative act, whether through the gestural painting techniques of Jackson Pollock or the spontaneous poetic outpourings of Jack Kerouac, was the means through which the individual might escape the shackles of psychological control and rediscover his or her authentic identity liberated from a bureaucratic, militarized society; it was an aesthetic project that drew heavily from twentieth-century modernism. But for others, participation, whether through the chaotic events of Allan Kaprow's "happenings" or John Cage's infamous silent musical composition, was the means by which the individual abandoned the solipsistic search for autonomy, loosened the physical and psychological barriers separating himself or herself from others, and discovered liberation through a form of self-divestiture, an aesthetic project that marked the emergence of postmodernism. Participation in a political sense bore a similar confusion, referring simultaneously to a form of face-to-face political interaction, individual risk-taking through which personal authenticity was discovered, and radical decentralization in which all hierarchies and all structures separating individuals were dismantled. Throughout, the *Port Huron Statement* juggled these conflicting notions of participation, a tension that complicated the vision of liberation proffered by the New Left and that situated the *Statement* on the divide between modernism and postmodernism.

The Artistic Roots of Sixties Radicalism

The political shift in American radicalism from the Old Left of the 1930s to the New Left of the 1960s was marked by a similar shift in American culture, as the social realism of the Great Depression in the form of proletarian literature and New Deal–sponsored art gave way to modernism in the form of abstract expressionism and Beat poetry. But the heyday of American modernism in the 1950s did not mean that the link between art and politics was severed. Instead, their definitions were changed, as art was defined no longer as a piece of revolutionary propaganda but as a medium for a revolutionary change in consciousness, and politics was redefined in more existential terms. Throughout the 1950s, intellectuals such as Herbert Marcuse, Norman Brown, and Paul Goodman, each of whom influenced the New Left, argued that art had an essential role to play in any revolutionary politics by helping end feelings of alienation and reintroduce notions of human connectedness seemingly erased by market relations. Even C. Wright Mills, one of the intellectual godfathers of the New Left, argued that aesthetics played a role in any political appeal or call to arms. Mills always claimed that his writings were a form of "sociological poetry," designed not only to delineate the economic and political forces dominating the American landscape but also to help readers locate themselves within this landscape and persuade them that change was possible.[6] In his 1959 book, *The Sociological Imagination*, Mills encouraged his colleagues to adopt the modernist practices of Kenneth Burke and Friedrich Nietzsche in order to achieve "perspective by incongruity."[7] He instructed sociologists to loosen their imaginations, dispense with their disciplinary biases, and look at the world differently—making unimportant things seem essential, making other things comical or grotesque by exaggerating their features, and inverting established hierarchies. As Mills explained, "You try . . . to let your mind become a moving prism catching light from as many angles as possible."[8] This playful, modernist sensibility, found in

Marcuse and Brown as well, was designed, as the *Port Huron Statement* explained, to overcome the resigned belief that "there is no viable alternative to the present."[9]

Besides the influence of Mills and others, there was a much more direct literary connection between the founders of SDS and the American avant-garde—namely, the Beat poets of the 1950s who overturned the conventions of American writing and, in so doing, initiated a cultural revolution. As Tom Hayden has acknowledged, "The beat poets, such as Jack Kerouac and Allen Ginsberg, had stirred us," offering, through the art of personal revelation, an image of the individual freed from the forces of social control and capable of authentic expression.[10] In his 1957 autobiographical novel, *On the Road*, Kerouac introduced a new form of confessional writing, dispensing with traditional narrative structure in order to transcribe directly his memories and emotions concerning the events of his life. For Kerouac, writing was less about crafted form or didactic moralizing and more about communicating with honesty the essential nature of his own self. He referred to his writings as a form of prosody—spontaneous outbursts that were unchecked by conventional norms or societal demands and that flowed freely from his mind. The goal, as Kerouac explained, was to overcome "the pacification of instincts" and reclaim "the pure masculine urge to freely sing."[11] Prioritizing the unconscious over the conscious and the imaginary over the symbolic, Kerouac and his fellow Beat poets argued that their expressive writings were undistorted markings of their true selves and evidence of their performative powers. This act of rebellion, what Tom Hayden referred to as "the personal instinct to take risks and journey into an emotional and intellectual wilderness," marked Kerouac's importance to the student movement.[12]

This image of the artist as an outsider and a rebel, at least in the postwar period, was also traceable to Jackson Pollock, whose dripped and splatter-filled canvases heralded a revolution in American painting. In a famous 1949 *Life* magazine article, "Jackson Pollock: Is He the Greatest Living Painter in the United States?," Pollock was photographed standing in front of one of his paintings, arms crossed, cigarette dangling from his mouth, and dressed in denim—a defiant pose repeated by other influential rebels from the 1950s including James Dean and Marlon Brando. In challenging both conventional notions of the artistic process and staid images of the role of the artist, Pollock, like Kerouac, shifted the focus from art as an object or a representation of experience to art as a process or expressive gesture. Pollock's work heralded what art critic Harold Rosenberg described as "action painting," seen as a record of the dynamic activities of the artist and as a form of personal revelation. Art was now a transformative practice; as Rosenberg explained, "The act on the canvas is an extension of the artist's total effort to make over his experience."[13] Consequently, Pollock's actions while painting were just as important as the finished project, a claim that famously encouraged filmmaker Hans Namuth to film Pollock painting, something hardly done with artists before. Rosenberg captured the essence of action painting: "A painting that is an act is inseparable from the biography of the artist. . . . The act-painting is of the same metaphysical substance as the artist's existence."[14] Indeed, the goal for artists and writers like Pollock and Kerouac was to merge art and life—to open the artist's studio and the writer's notebooks to their own personal experiences and to the world at large, changing both in the process.

In introducing notions such as action, spontaneity, and self-expression into aesthetic discourse, both Pollock and Kerouac challenged the dominant form of modernist practice within the American art scene in the 1940s and 1950s: high modernism.[15] Found in the literary theory of the New Critics, the art writings of Clement Greenberg, the essays of Lionel Trilling, and the translated works of Theodor Adorno, high modernists in the postwar years looked to safeguard art from any outside contamination—in particular, from the appropriation of art for political purposes by totalitarian movements and from the homogenizing impact of the culture industry. In response, high modernists introduced a formalist bent into aesthetic discourse, arguing that any art object, due to the unique configuration of its elements, was ontologically separate from the rest of the world—from both the artist who created the object and the viewer who consumed it. High modernists rejected efforts to bring extratextual explanations (historical, social, biographical, etc.) to the aesthetic experience, choosing instead to see each object as a unique source of meaning. Although high modernism seemed a legitimate response, albeit a resigned one, to a world torn asunder by global conflict and by oppressive mass movements, the result, as Pollock and Kerouac readily noted, was a calcification of art—art that seemed to lack any dynamism and that seemed inherently elitist and cold.

The effort by high modernists to produce an apolitical understanding of the aesthetic experience, however, resonated in the early Cold War, and, consequently, high modernism was institutionalized in literary journals, art museums, and universities, including, most prominently, in English classrooms where students were instructed, under the auspices of the New Criticism, to engage in close readings of poems. Kerouac, in particular, was frustrated with what he saw as the sterility of high modernism, especially with the reception his work received from his English professors at Columbia University. His prosody, as he explained, was "diametrically opposed to the Eliot shot," his shorthand for the practices of high modernism.[16] In many ways, Kerouac's frustration with higher education prefigured the critique of the university system by the 1960s student movement, which rebelled not only against the top-down structure of university bureaucracies, the practice of in loco parentis, and the influence of military spending on university research but also against the nature of higher education itself. High modernism was predicated upon the belief that individual spheres of knowledge—art, politics, and law, for example—were distinct from one another and needed to develop along separate lines. As the *Port Huron Statement* explained, "The specialization of function and knowledge, admittedly necessary to our complex technological and social structure, has produced an exaggerated compartmentalization of study and understanding."[17] This compartmentalization marked a foreshortening of the true purpose of higher education, which was to offer analytic tools with which to comprehend and change the world. Instead, "academia includes a radical separation of the student from the material of study. That which is studied, the social reality, is 'objectified' to sterility, dividing the student from life."[18] High modernism, no less than the traditional social and behavioral sciences, was guilty of this unfortunate separation.

In this sense, the *Port Huron Statement*, much like the work of Pollock and Kerouac, was centered first and foremost on the psychic liberation of the individual from the false barriers separating art and politics from everyday life. According to Gitlin, "There was an expressive side to the movement culture, rooted in the subterranean ethos of the Fifties, and in a longer-run revolt against the containment of feeling and initiative in a society growing steadily more rationalized."[19] This impulse, however, was not limited to bohemian groups; it was part of a larger intellectual revolt against the administered society of the 1950s. Within psychology, for instance, new movements arose such as "Third Force" psychology that challenged "the dominant conception of man in the twentieth century: that he is a thing to be manipulated, and that he is inherently incapable of directing his own affairs."[20] Criticizing behaviorists for reducing all human behavior to conditioned reflexes and challenging psychoanalysts for reducing all mental life to preordained categories of development, Third Force psychologists focused instead on the unlimited potential within human beings. For instance, psychologist Carl Rogers developed a form of "client-centered therapy" that dispensed with the more authoritarian approach of psychoanalysts, who often fitted the histories of their patients into preconceived narratives. In contrast, Rogers sought to democratize therapy by leveling the patient-therapist relationship and turning the therapy session into a sympathetic client-centered conversation. In *Motivation and Personality* (1954), Abraham Maslow, another prominent humanistic psychologist, argued that human beings were capable of reaching their full potential in all spheres of life, what he termed "self-actualization." Such development, according to Maslow, was based on a hierarchy of needs—ranging from basic physiological needs to more abstract ones such as belongingness and self-esteem—that often were thwarted by society.

Such language, whether directly cited or not, bled into the *Port Huron Statement*, which argued that any political transformation was predicated upon a transformation in the psychic lives of individuals. Echoing the work of Maslow and others, the *Statement* argued that "men have unrealized potential for self-cultivation, self-direction, self-understanding, and creativity."[21] Indeed, the therapeutic ethos of the New Left was quite visible from the beginning, an ethos that borrowed heavily from the writings of Kerouac, revisionist Freudian schools of thought, and existentialist thinkers like Albert Camus. Throughout, the *Statement* called for, in language culled from numerous such sources, "a quality of mind not compulsively driven by a sense of powerlessness, nor one which unthinkingly adopts status values, nor one which represses all threats to its habits, but one which has full, spontaneous access to present and past experiences, one which easily unites the fragmented parts of personal history, one which openly faces problems which are troubling and unresolved."[22] Challenging a reality principle that demanded the repression of desire in the name of social control and therefore distorted any true understanding of the self, the *Statement*, using the framework of this new psychology, called for a form of psychic empowerment, a move that linked the *Statement* to the work of Wilhelm Reich and Erich Fromm, among others. Such heroic transcendence, as the examples of Pollock and Kerouac demonstrated, was accomplished through expressive, creative acts that liberated the individual from social restraints, erased feelings of powerlessness, and thereby restored a sense of authenticity.

Participatory Art and the Postmodern Turn

But action painting and Beat poetry were not the only avant-garde movements in the 1950s, and self-expression through spontaneous poetry or dripped paint was not the only form of cultural rebellion. By the late 1950s, many artists and writers argued that the project inaugurated by Pollock and Kerouac to liberate some authentic subjectivity was merely a form of solipsism, one that stressed the individual self over and above group participation and the larger social world as a whole. Action painting and prosody might lead to personal transformation and might help the individual overcome personal alienation from a bureaucratized, militarized landscape, but it did very little to achieve its original goal of merging art and life. At this moment, modernism, both as a cultural movement and as an aesthetic practice, began to splinter: the long-standing search for a lost wholeness within the depths of the self gave way to a general emptying out of the self into the chaos and disorder of a fragmented world. As Ihab Hassan argued in his 1971 book, *The Dismemberment of Orpheus*, one of the first works to delineate the postmodern turn, modernism was the art of industrialization and the urban landscape that used aesthetic experimentation to reclaim individual autonomy in a fully administered society, while postmodernism was the art of the global village and the computer age, where participation and action defined the limitless spirit of a postindividual world.

In many ways, the *Port Huron Statement* reflected this divide within American culture. While the idea of community as outlined in the *Statement* borrowed much from the social-democratic principles of the Old Left, the *Statement* at times also placed a much more radical spin on the notion of participation that savored of the postmodern aesthetics emerging in the late 1950s. The *Statement* openly recognized that the hardboiled individualism promoted by Kerouac and others often ran counter to the project of building a beloved community and therefore tried to clarify the new image of man that participatory action would create. "This kind of independence does not mean egoistic individualism," the *Statement* argued. "Human interdependence is a contemporary fact."[23] Years later, Tom Hayden would refer to this as the "post-modern style" of his manifesto or what he also called "the Port Huron style"—that is, "the endless improvising, the techniques of dialogue and participation, learning through direct action, the rejection of dogma while searching for theory."[24] This ambiguity was reflected in the debates in the early 1960s over the meaning of participatory democracy. While some of the founders of SDS saw participatory democracy, as outlined by philosopher Arnold Kaufman, as an antidote to the failures of representative democracy or as an American version of socialism, others saw it as a means to overcome egoistic individualism and to immerse oneself into the flux of group experience.[25] Participation meant, in this sense, not the pathway to some pristine self existing outside regulatory structures but a self defined through social relations and social discourse, one with a radically new openness to others and to the world at large. Like many other writings from the early 1960s, the *Port Huron Statement* rested on this uncomfortable divide between modernism and postmodernism.

The harbinger of this cultural shift was the musical composer John Cage, who argued that art should function not as a form of self-expression but, in the tradition of Zen Buddhism to which Cage was attracted, as a form of self-abnegation, helping end the isolation of the individual ego from the world at large. As Cage argued, art was not a means of releasing some hidden, authentic self but a means of "freeing the ego from its taste and memory, its concern for profit and power, of silencing the ego so that the rest of the world has a chance to enter into the ego's own experience whether that be inside or out."[26] The most famous example was Cage's 1952 piece *4'33"*, which entailed the performer sitting at the piano for the duration of the piece but not actually playing the instrument. The resulting silence, according to Cage, was not silence at all. Instead, audience members were awakened, perhaps for the first time, to the noises in the room around them, encouraging them to recognize that there was nothing to which they were not related. Cage's idea for his silent piece came from artist Robert Rauschenberg's *White Paintings*, first exhibited at Black Mountain College in 1951. For Rauschenberg, these paintings, with their monochromatic surfaces, were devoid of any expressive marks or other authorial content, existing merely as passive receptors for the surrounding environment, collecting dust and displaying shadows.

In challenging the notion of art as an expression of the individual ego, Rauschenberg and Cage depersonalized the artistic act, arguing that the primary goal of the aesthetic experience was to overcome the divide between subject and object by loosening ego boundaries and merging individuals together, an argument also found in Norman Brown's *Life Against Death*, Herbert Marcuse's *Eros and Civilization* (1955), and Marshall McLuhan's *The Gutenberg Galaxy* (1962). But Cage was not merely interested in revealing the expressiveness of the world. In using chance methods of composition and relying on randomness as his key principle, Cage wanted to liberate sounds from reified musical relationships and other domineering cultural practices. Cage hoped to release his listeners from the compulsive need to cognitively grasp and thereby dominate the world around them and allow listeners instead to witness on a perceptual level the particular sounds surrounding them. For Cage, such a mode of perception was a direct challenge to modern capitalist society that reduced everything, including human relationships, to simple commodities. "In contemporary civilization," explained Cage, "where everything is standardized and where everything is repeated, the whole point is to forget in the space between an object and its duplication"—that is, to recognize each particular sound before its uniqueness was stripped by the inevitable process of commodification and thereby become attuned, through the erasure of the individual ego, to immediate experience.[27]

This Cagean, pragmatic spirit—centered on openness, selflessness, and flexibility—was part of the cultural revolutions of the 1960s in which the *Port Huron Statement* played an essential role. According to Tom Hayden, "This 'movement spirit' was present everywhere—not only in religion but in music and the arts as well," a spirit that shared similar intellectual sources.[28] While Hayden and members of SDS were reading John Dewey's *The Public and Its Problems* to rethink the nature of modern society, artists such as Allan Kaprow were reading Dewey's *Art as Experience* to rethink the nature of modern art. Both books reflected the pragmatic philosopher's frustration at the lack of any participatory ethos in modern society. Dewey argued that under modern industrial capitalism, art, which in previous centuries had once played an essential role in the ceremonies of religious and social institutions, had been severed from any larger social function and segregated from everyday life within a separate realm called the aesthetic, comprising museums, bourgeois theaters, and elite concert halls. Two unfortunate results followed—first, art objects, deprived of any larger context, were reduced to commodities and subjugated to market forces; second, modern artists, separated from any social function, were now resigned to producing artworks merely as forms of self-expression. Consequently, art lost its critical function of reflecting upon commonly shared experiences. Therefore, "the task," as Dewey explained, "is to restore continuity between the reified and intensified forms of experience that are works of art and the everyday events, doings, and sufferings that are universally recognized to constitute experience."[29] In this way, Dewey's critique of aesthetic formalism echoed John Cage's critique of artistic conventions, a lesson that a younger group of artists, including Allan Kaprow, quickly digested. The key moment was a series of classes taught by Cage in the late 1950s at the New School for Social Research, attended by several members of the emerging avant-garde in New York City, including Kaprow, artist George Brecht, composer Dick Higgins, and several others, in which Cage encouraged them to break down the artificial distinction between art and life.[30]

Participation became the new watchword for these artists. Following the lessons he learned from Cage and Dewey, Kaprow, for instance, outlined his new artistic project in a 1958 *Art News* essay, "The Legacy of Jackson Pollock," in which Kaprow dispensed with formalist readings of action painting and argued instead that the revolutionary aspect of Pollock's paintings was the artist's blurring of the space between the artwork as a solid object and as an experience. Kaprow argued that the experience of "the skein of lines and splashings" of Pollock's paintings was not merely an optical one but an all-consuming one, as viewers became "entangled in the web" that Pollock had spun on his mural-sized canvases.[31] In this sense, the painting escaped its borders and "continued into the room," filling "our world with itself." Painting in the traditional sense no longer seemed possible after Pollock, and Kaprow encouraged other artists to "become preoccupied with and even dazzled by the space and objects of our everyday life, either our bodies, clothes, rooms, or, if need be, the vastness of Forty-second Street."[32] He sought, in other words, to dispense with object-based artworks. Not only were they susceptible to commodification, but they also reified false distinctions between the artist and audience and between the audience and the work of art. After experimenting earlier in his career with abstract collages modeled after Pollock's methods, Kaprow turned in the late 1950s to what he termed "happenings"—quasi-theatrical events that redefined art as a participatory event.

Borrowing from earlier avant-garde movements such as futurism, with its kinetic, sometimes vaudevillian energy, and cubism, with its shifting perspectives and nonlinear style, happenings turned art galleries (and later, random outdoor locations) into a "theatre of mixed means" that dispensed with narrative conventions to present instead a collage of non-related activities, often involving audience participation.[33] In his 1959 piece, *18 Happenings in 6 Parts*, one of his most famous happenings, Kaprow divided the Reuben Gallery in New York City into three separate rooms, divided by plastic and canvases, in which performers followed specific instructions—ring a bell, flash a light, turn on a record player, bounce a ball, and so on—everyday actions that invoked the randomness of contemporary life. In his 1961 piece, *Yard*, Kaprow filled the outdoor space of the Martha Jackson Gallery with used automobile tires, which viewers were encouraged to climb upon and toss freely—mimicking the action painting of Pollock while playing with the debris of modern society. Happenings touched upon various commonplace themes—urban decay, technological changes, societal violence, consumerism, and a host of others—all of which revealed the pressures placed upon the individual in mass society and offered the hope of emancipation. Happenings were, as

Kaprow explained, "a moral act, a human stand of great urgency, whose professional status as art is less a criterion than their certainty as an ultimate existential commitment."[34] Throughout the early 1960s, Kaprow extended this Deweyan notion of art as experience, not only encouraging more audience participation, but also limiting the scope of his instructions and replacing contrived activities with more childlike forms of play.

While Kaprow tried to include audience involvement as much as possible in his happenings, other members of the avant-garde in the 1950s redefined art exclusively *as* participation. No group captured this pragmatic perspective more than Fluxus, the famed artistic collective created in the late 1950s by Lithuanian-born artist George Maciunas, who corralled a number of like-minded artists in New York City into a Dadaist-inflected movement.[35] Trained as an art historian, Maciunas was inspired by the explosion in artistic activity in New York City in the late 1950s and opened the short-lived AG Gallery in 1961 to house performances and exhibitions. Soon, he met fellow artists Al Hansen and Dick Higgins, who had studied with John Cage at the New School and who had formed the New York Audio Visual Group to continue their explorations; he engaged those artists associated with the Chambers Street performance series taking place at Yoko Ono's downtown loft as well. Maciunas organized these artists into a loose association, designed, as he explained, to "purge the world of dead art, imitation artificial art, abstract act, illusionistic art, [and] serial art."[36] The common aesthetic concern for artists associated with Fluxus was to erase the boundary between art and life.

Consequently, most Fluxus artworks were not objects but activities to perform—that is, participatory art that required for its completion some form of audience involvement, either conceptual or physical. For instance, George Brecht developed a number of Event Scores—cards with instructions to perform a specific action such as *Exit* (1961), which had only one eponymous instruction, or *Tea Event* (1961), whose two simple instructions were "preparing" and "empty vessel." In this way, Brecht translated everyday actions and concepts into artistic forms either to be performed or to be contemplated in the hope of awakening participants to the possibility of simple, unmediated experience. *Fluxus I*, the first so-called Fluxkit, was an attaché case containing random objects designed to be used and consumed—musical scores, napkins, latex gloves, bars of soap, rubber balls, photographs, and so on. The goal was to open up participants to the "flux" of experience, helping to overcome ingrained habits and attitudes and to reestablish openness to the sounds, smells, and sights of the world. Fluxus artists hoped to challenge the sterile nature of contempo-

rary life, which had supposedly fallen under the sway of instrumental reason and bureaucratic thinking. Participatory art, as Fluxus members argued, was a form of play and therefore an antidote to modern forms of
alienation.

But Fluxus also had a political project, over and above the fact that Maciunas was a communist who tried but failed to turn the group into a revolutionary, guerrilla movement. Although the more conservative members famously attacked Maciunas's call in 1963 in *Flux News-Letter No. 6* for direct
action against elite cultural institutions, most Fluxus artists did hope to
"purge the world of bourgeois sickness, intellectual, professional and com-
mercialized culture" and promote a new democratic culture.[37] No other art
movement in the early 1960s was as antielitist and anticommercial. Fluxus
performances often took swipes at high culture, including an infamous recital at the Carnegie Recital Hall in 1964. Pieces that night included George
Brecht's "Solo for Violin," in which the performer merely polished his instrument on stage, and Japanese artist Ay-O's "Rainbow for Wind Orches-
tra," in which musicians blew bubbles with their instruments. Many Fluxus
activities required no professional training and sometimes no skill to perform, reflecting Maciunas's argument that high culture was elitist and a
product of class divisions. Similarly, since Fluxus art required some active
physical or conceptual participation by audience members, the artist was no
longer to be privileged, which helped erase the divide between creator and
spectator. In her famous 1964 "Cut Piece," for example, Yoko Ono appeared
onstage, dressed in a robe, and encouraged audience members to cut holes
in her clothing until she was completely naked. Most important, Fluxus artists produced works that were either ephemeral or disposable, such as Alison Knowles's "Making a Salad" (1961), assuring that such works possessed
no commercial value and were incapable of being commodified. "Anything
can be art and anyone can do it," argued Maciunas, the two key themes of
participatory art.[38]

The common thread linking these artistic movements to the radical
spirit of the early 1960s was their anarchist leanings. Indeed, if anything
tied together the political sentiments of the early student movement and
the 1960s avant-garde, it was the radically democratic sensibility of anarchism. As Tom Hayden explained, "The participatory ethic of direct action . . . drew from traditions of anarchism," and many of the intellectual
predecessors of the New Left—Paul Goodman, Norman Mailer, Dwight
Macdonald, and Allen Ginsberg, for instance—promoted anarchism in
the 1950s as the only viable radical alternative in a polarized Cold War
landscape.[39] Similarly, many radical artists including John Cage, Barnett

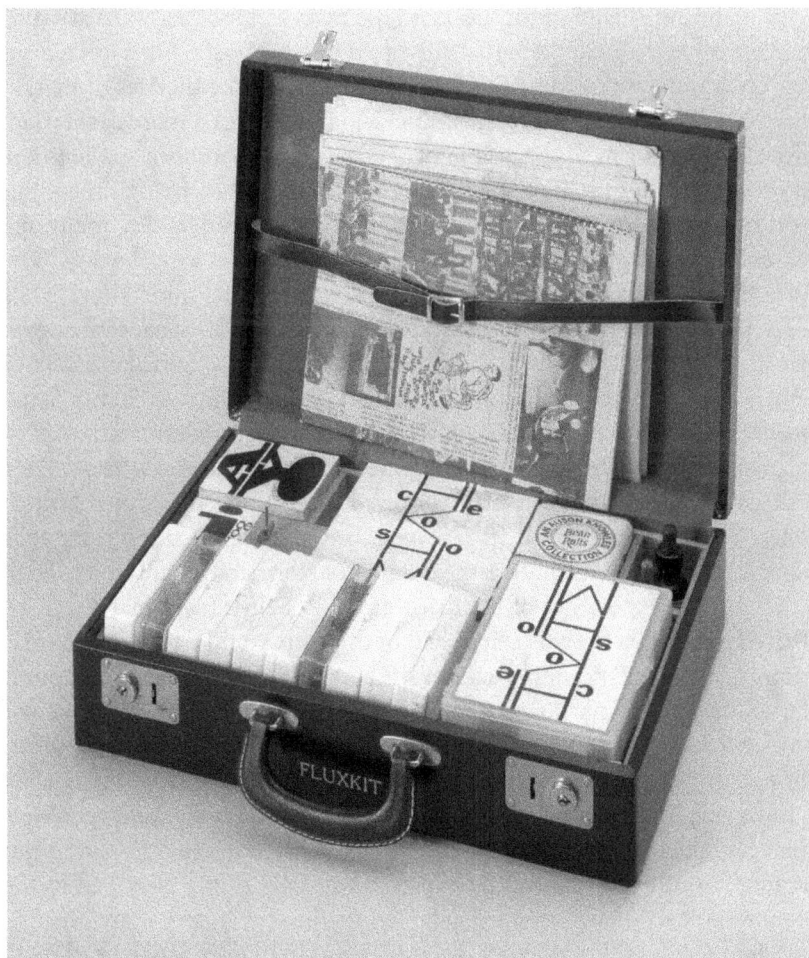

Fluxkit. 1965. Vinyl-covered attaché case, containing objects in various media, overall (closed): 13 3/8 x 17 1/2 x 4 15/16" (34 x 44.5 x 12.5 cm). Publisher: Fluxus Editions, announced 1964. Assembled by: George Maciunas. Designed by: George Maciunas. Edition: unknown. Containing objects by: Eric Andersen, Ay-O, George Brecht, Dick Higgins, Joe Jones, Alison Knowles, Takehisa Kosugi, George Maciunas, Nam June Paik, Benjamin Patterson, Mieko Shiomi, Ben Vautier, and Robert Watts (The Gilbert and Lila Silverman Fluxus Collection Gift). Digital Image © The Museum of Modern Art/Licensed by SCALA / Art Resource, NY

Newman, and Allan Kaprow declared their works "essentially anarchistic," as Kaprow explained.[40] Anarchism served two purposes. First, anarchism spoke to the political dream of a life lived outside the dictates of market forces, state control, and bureaucratic demands and of a more egalitarian, decentralized form of social interaction. Second, anarchism spoke to the personal dream of a life lived outside the forces of psychological control and of a reimagined understanding of human relatedness. For many, the latter often took priority over the former. According to Tom Hayden, "The idea of participatory democracy, therefore, should be understood in its psychic, liberatory dimension, not simply as an alternative concept of government organization."[41] Making little reference to grand narratives of emancipation or to revolutionary agents of change, the *Port Huron Statement* bore the markings of an anarchistic, early postmodern text.

The nature of this liberation was often confused, however. The call for self-cultivation and self-determination in the manner of Kerouac, which often bred narcissistic self-involvement, ran counter to the call for self-abnegation and egolessness in the manner of Norman Brown, which led to "the exalting experience of the fused group."[42] Self-transformation, in either Kerouac's or Brown's sense, had both positive and negative connotations, tensions that ran throughout the counterculture of the 1960s. Similarly, the idea of participatory democracy was built upon a particular understanding of experience—the notion that there were primary forms of experience that existed prior to conceptualization or even outside power relations—an understanding that ran counter to the larger New Left critique of modern capitalist society. "There was," as Todd Gitlin has argued, "a direct line from the expressive politics of the New Left to the counterculture's let-it-all-hang-out way of life."[43] Consequently, the call for democracy and participation, both as abstract ideals, led to hostility to any organizational structures and to any form of hierarchy, a theoretical move that, in the end, had devastating consequences for the overall movement. As the disdain for any formal organizational structure became prominent throughout local chapters by the mid-1960s and national conventions devolved into endless debates about democratic procedures among the membership, SDS struggled, as James Miller has explained, to live up to "its professed ideals of 'authenticity', neighborly community, and rule-by-consensus," until the organization was taken over by the more radical elements of the movement by 1969.[44] Such tensions—between self-expression and self-abnegation, individual action and group participation, and autonomy and egolessness—echoed throughout the political and artistic avant-garde during the 1960s.

The Legacy of Participatory Art and
Participatory Democracy

As the years progressed, this anarchic, avant-garde sensibility became even more prominent within radical political and artistic circles.[45] Most famously, the Diggers, the Haight-Ashbury performance group that served as the conscience of the 1960s counterculture, instilled an anticapitalist spirit into the movement while maintaining a focus on personal, psychic liberation. Created by members of the San Francisco Mime Troupe, the Diggers married avant-garde artistic practices borrowed from Allan Kaprow's Happenings with the antielitist, anticonsumerism ethos of the early New Left. In creating performance spectacles such as the Free Food event, in which participants were required to walk through "The Frame of Reference," a thirteen-foot doorway, to symbolize their awakened consciousness, the Diggers challenged, in a manner similar to early avant-garde groups, the materialism of modern consumer society. The Diggers were just the most famous of numerous cultural revolutionaries in the 1960s with a strong participatory ethos. The Living Theatre, which began in New York in the 1950s with experimental productions of plays by Kenneth Rexroth and Paul Goodman, turned to more participatory and revolutionary forms of theater in the late 1960s with productions such as *Paradise Now* (1968), which not only was communally authored but also involved spectators participating in the performance and ended with a collective march out of the theater and into the streets. Other movements such as the Artists and Writers Protest, the Art Workers Coalition, and the Artists' Protest Committee merged New Left politics, including anticapitalist and anti-imperialist stances, with their vision of participatory aesthetics. Throughout the 1960s, this avant-garde, anarchist sensibility infused antiwar protests in Washington, DC, and antielitist demonstrations at the Museum of Modern Art, among other activities.

Participatory art, in the vein of happenings and other Fluxus-related activities, continued to thrive as well, albeit hampered by some of the complications that faced the counterculture as a whole.[46] Participatory art was built on a sometimes naive notion of human nature, brushing aside, much like the *Port Huron Statement* did, the pessimistic image constructed in the 1950s by intellectuals such as Reinhold Niebuhr, Lionel Trilling, and others of humans as corruptible, often irrational beings. Indeed, participatory art was founded on a belief in playfulness, generosity, and respect, which sometimes was contradicted by the actions of audience members. Gallery owners in the 1960s often discovered that the objects in the participatory works of Robert Rauschenberg and George Brecht were stolen by patrons. One Fluxus artist who set up a Bureau for Democracy, which entailed him sitting in a room waiting for audience members to talk to him, was disappointed when no one spoke to him. Other Fluxus artists who encouraged spectators to physically participate with them, offering their own bodies as canvases for spectators to draw on them, were unpleasantly surprised when spectators became unusually aggressive and sometimes angry in their responses. At times, moreover, participatory art seemed a silly, almost gimmicky kind of art and, at other times, suffered from the burdens placed upon it, which included unattainable hopes of transformation and social change.

But this participatory ethos persisted well past the demise of both SDS and Fluxus, inspiring a range of movements including feminist activists in the 1970s, anti-Communist groups in Eastern Europe in the 1980s, and antiglobalization protesters in the 1990s, all of whom incorporated elements of performance art, theatricality, and direct action into their political movements. Indeed, the effort to merge art and life, to break down artificial barriers between the artist and audience and between the artwork and the spectator, and to aestheticize politics has remained an essential element not only within the current vogue of participatory art today but within American political radicalism too. Overturning the traditional image of the spectator or audience member as a passive observer, the "politics of spectatorship" has infused current artistic and political efforts, ranging from the pedagogic project of artist Paul Chan in response to the devastation of Hurricane Katrina to the confrontational project of Occupy Wall Street in response to the 2008 financial crash—to challenge racial, gender, and class hierarchies through participation in new forms of emancipatory social relations.[47] Such efforts are committed, as was the New Left, to the belief that "there *is* an alternative to the present," one based on the intermingling of art and politics and the aesthetic transformation of everyday life.[48]

16 | Facing the Abyss
by Todd Gitlin

A specter haunted Port Huron: the specter of thermonuclear war. We were war babies, most of us. Around the time we were born, the human situation had changed, changed utterly. From our generation onward, children were being born into a world that had the capacity to destroy itself. We held to a double vision: there was the prospect of extinction, and there was also, alongside it, the emergence of a living resistance. Human *nature* had changed.

For the Students for a Democratic Society (SDS) founders and those who, like myself, read Tom Hayden's draft manifesto before Port Huron and recognized ourselves in it, the new situation was arrestingly put in this single sentence: "Our work is guided by the sense that we may be the last generation in the experiment with living"[1]—the most memorable of the document's references to the edge of the abyss where we lived our lives. We accepted the burden of knowing that the odds were against humanity. For we knew, first of all, that the military-industrial complexes in both the United States and the Soviet Union were committed to the development and knife-edge deployment of thermonuclear weapons. We also knew that our compatriots sensed danger but, at the same time, stashed it away into mental darkness. They were possessed by the phenomenon that had been named, not long before, by social psychologists at the University of Michigan: cognitive dissonance.[2] SDS was acutely aware that in the face of immense danger, the public was paralyzed. The *Port Huron Statement* evoked "the desperation of people threatened by forces about which they know little and of which they can say less; the cheerful emptiness of people 'giving up' all hope of changing things; the faceless ones polled by Gallup who listed 'international affairs' fourteenth on their list of 'problems' but who also expected thermonuclear war in the next few years."[3]

The culture's most sensitive bellwethers knew the score. Science fiction filled up with doomsday scenarios. In 1958, Tom Lehrer recorded "We'll All Go Together When We Go." In a poem called "Fall 1961," Robert Lowell wrote, "All autumn, the chafe and jar / of nuclear war; / we have talked our extinction to death." Scientists collected baby teeth to assess the risk of radioactive strontium released by nuclear tests penetrating their bones, although the report by the *New York Times'* chief science reporter (November 25, 1961) led with the news that "pregnant women and their unborn children absorb radioactive strontium . . . only about 10 percent of the time."[4] One month before the Cuban missile crisis, Bob Dylan performed "A Hard Rain's A-Gonna Fall" (though subsequent rumor had it that he had written it during the crisis itself). During the year 1962, the United States detonated more than ninety nuclear weapons; the Soviet Union detonated more than thirty. While the *Port Huron Statement* was circulating, finding its final form, Nikita Khrushchev was ordering Soviet medium-range ballistic missiles to Cuba. When American intelligence spotted them, Kennedy ordered a blockade (he called it a "quarantine," a kinder, gentler word). He also blocked appeals from his inner circle for bombing and invasion, but of course no one outside the White House knew that at the time. What we knew was the brink. There were pitifully small numbers opposed—and when they did turn out, furies were unleashed in violent counterdemonstrations. Here in Ann Arbor, four hundred gathered by SDS, and a local group called Women for Peace passed out a leaflet urging an end to what they called the "game of Chicken, with mankind on the bumpers"—which was, at that time and since, my favorite metaphor of the week. The demonstrators wanted the Russian missiles withdrawn but also wanted the United States to guarantee Cuba's safety (which, as it turned out, was the deal eventually worked out by Kennedy and Khrushchev to defuse the crisis). Six hundred students jeered at them, blocked their march, hurled eggs and stones.

Later that week, most of the SDS leadership in Ann Arbor—Tom Hayden, Casey Hayden, Dick Flacks, and Mickey Flacks—set out for Washington, to demonstrate. Why not? Nobody had a better idea. From Cambridge, Robb Burlage, Maria Varela, Steve Johnson, and I also drove down. We picketed the White House. We were not a lot of people. In a church meeting hall, in an atmosphere of near-hysteria, we heard I. F. Stone warn that nuclear war could not be stopped. We heard talk about the possibility that Anne Eaton, a wealthy member of Women for Peace, might fly her private plane to Cuba to deposit some protesters to sit down at a Russian missile site as hostages against an American attack. To give you a sense of the small scale of protest at that time, six months earlier, the Cambridge peace group Tocsin, with the support of the Student Peace Union, Student SANE (National Committee for a Sane Nuclear Policy), SDS, and other groups, had been thrilled to attract eight thousand protesters against the arms race, nuclear testing, and bomb shelters to Washington, where they lobbied administration officials and members of Congress.

Around the time in late October when we drove to Washington, none of us knew—nobody knew—that four Soviet submarines off the Florida coast were armed with nuclear-tipped torpedoes targeted on American aircraft carriers. These submarines were not made for the near-tropical temperatures of the South Atlantic. On October 27, the air conditioning on one of these submarines failed, and the temperatures over the course of days surpassed 120 degrees Fahrenheit. The sailors were limited to one glass of water a day as twelve American destroyers circled overhead, dropping depth charges. Unable to contact Moscow, the submarine captain grew frantic. He thought it possible that war had already broken out, in which case it was his duty to launch his Hiroshima-scale torpedo bomb at a nearby American aircraft carrier. He had the authority to order that launch. Technically, it would be easy enough to do: a simple matter of joining together two halves of a key—one in the captain's possession, the other in the hand of the submarine's political officer. The two men were in agreement: they should launch. But the fleet commander, a man named Vasili Arkhipov, was also on board. He was a cooler head. He said no. He said wait until we restore contact with Moscow and find out what's what.[5]

People like ourselves who demonstrated that week were realists. We did not know the details in advance, but we could sense that some confrontation like the Cuban Missile Crisis had been coming. When John F. Kennedy learned of the Soviet missiles, he might have yielded to the importunities of those in his inner circle who thought the United States should attack the Cuban bases. Instead, for the short run, he chose the middle course of "quarantine." He did not know that even this "quarantine" would result in placing a Russian naval officer in a position where he could light a fuse and trigger a nuclear war. Such was the logic of that cycle of retaliation that was built into the supposed-to-be-foolproof scheme known by the antiseptic name of "deterrence."

Many others who did not demonstrate also sensed the magnitude of the danger. (Some got into their cars that week and drove over the Canadian border.) The small movement against the Bomb, briefly mentioned in the *Port Huron Statement*, was dead right. There was a new human condition. There was also an experience of rupture between generations. During those years, for example, I tried (and mostly failed) to convince my parents that nuclear weapons had drawn a bright dividing line across human history and that this was the reason they could not understand me and my friends. They had known a world before the threat of total extinction. We had not and never would. This was true. It was also grandiose. There was another truth: our parents not only had lived through total war but were the first generation to know about Auschwitz—to know that industrialized slaughter on such a scale not only was possible but had actually happened. Still, not unreasonably, we insisted that our generation was marked, unique, conscripted into a struggle that had chosen us. Such a rationale for the perception of a generation gap is a time-honored ritual, a move to justify the feeling that, as Sartre wrote of his own generation, "we thought that the world was new because we were new in the world."[6] This sort of naiveté served our need to break away from the prevailing drift toward global catastrophe.

Before the missile crisis, President Kennedy had been a prisoner of Cold War drift. The missile crisis trauma led him to conclude that the arms race needed to be dampened and a new scenario launched. On June 10, 1963, he launched it with a stirring address at American University. He called for a test ban treaty and "an end to the arms race." He tried to think himself, and the country, out of the trap of endless Cold War confrontation. The tenor of this speech was altogether different from anything he had delivered to date. His war-minded bravado was gone. He called peace "the most important topic on earth":

> What kind of peace do I mean and what kind of a peace do we seek? Not a Pax Americana enforced on the world by American weapons of war. Not the peace of the grave or the security of the slave. I am talking about genuine peace, the kind of peace that makes life on earth worth living, and the kind that enables men and nations to grow, and to hope, and build a better life for their children—not merely peace for Americans but peace for all men and women, not merely peace in our time but peace in all time.[7]

And so the prospect of nuclear war fell out of the headlines. In relief and hope and no small amount of denial, it fell out of our generational consciousness and took up residence in the deep shelters of the unconscious. Miraculously, the nuclear faceoff had gone away. And when, two years later, the war in Vietnam moved from the back to the front burner, and as some residual antinuclear movement continued, most of us became—rightly—obsessed with stopping a war that was not hypothetical but flamingly actual, for bombs of napalm and white phosphorus and so on were going off in actual time and burning the actual flesh of actual human beings.

Now we know that the human power to wreck the world has more than a single way of accomplishing the mission. In 1962, official American doctrine blessed the policy of "launch on warning"—that is, launching nuclear missiles once an intelligence signal had been received to the effect that the Soviet Union had already launched an attack but before any Soviet bombs actually had actually struck the United States.[8] Though the number of intercontinental nuclear missiles has been reduced considerably in the subsequent half century, thanks to treaties, America and Russia each retain more than enough nuclear warheads to obliterate each other and (via nuclear winter) the rest of the planet, many times over.

But the threat of extinction is not always spasmodic. Slow-motion apocalypse is also a strong possibility.[9] Alongside the danger of a spasmodic atomic apocalypse, there is the danger of a catastrophe that would arrive—is already arriving—by fits and starts. Un-self-consciously, humanity has converted the remnants of expired species into fuel—mislabeled "fossil fuel"—that is in the process of driving species into extinction and subject our own to the convulsive floods, typhoons, hurricanes, ice melts, and droughts that already make life more tenuous around the planet. Filling the atmosphere with carbon and other heat-absorbing compounds will suffice to render life as we know it unlivable.

Fifty years ago, it was just beginning to be understood that extinction could arrive in many forms. The movement against the Bomb understood one end of humanity's new condition; Rachel Carson understood another end. *Silent Spring* and nuclear winter both stared us in the face if humanity didn't get off the bumpers and escort the lunatic drivers and their horrendous, annihilationist machines off the road.

The movement against the Bomb knew in its bones, as those at Port Huron did in their own way, that some crazy logic of modernity had led to the institutionalization of mass violence, earth-destroying power, and a live prospect of annihilation. The danger had not materialized overnight. It had been building for decades and centuries. Human beings had learned how to generate immense energy from physical processes. That energy, and the hubris that fueled it, powered the accumulation of wealth and brought, along with much suffering, a great improvement of living conditions on parts of the planet even as huge populations were enslaved. The infrastructure that made many of the improvements possible also, diabolically, set up the conditions for self-destruction. In numbed America, it was considered realistic to appreciate the improvements but unrealistic to appreciate the dangers. The metastasis of human-devised destructive powers had unfolded a crisis that was at once intellectual, spiritual, and political. The New Left was unimpressed by the standard thinking that C. Wright Mills called "crackpot realism."[10] To reject crackpot realism sometimes freaked us out more than a bit. It might have been more fun to be cheerful idiots. But here we are, and the nuclear missiles have outlasted Soviet Communism, and the missiles are still, by policy, poised, ever ready to "launch on warning"—that is, before an actual enemy bomb goes off on American soil.

The early antiwar movement and the early New Left broke with the prevailing institutional default and the drift toward global catastrophe. We thought subversive thoughts and we acted on them as intelligently as we were able. We struggled to harness passion and reason. In the process we contributed to a great reclamation of human powers against the monstrous creations to which our society was, and remains, too much devoted. It wasn't for lack of trying that we failed to rid the earth entirely of nuclear bombs. But we weren't gods and we weren't omnipotent.

So the emergency goes on. The earth writhes under human dominion, even in ways we could not have imagined in 1962. We have, once again, in Albert Camus's great image, to bring everything we have and feel and know to the immense and necessary and beautiful work of rolling the rock of survival back up the hill.[11]

17 | Beyond Port Huron: The Indiana "Subversion" Case Fifty Years Later[*]

by Alan Wald

At two thirty in the afternoon of Wednesday, October 24, 1962, seventeen students, neatly groomed and mostly in their early twenties, walked briskly toward the steps of the main auditorium on the Indiana University (IU) campus. In the conservative ambience of Bloomington, a small city in the southern part of the "Hoosier" state, the clean-shaven men with short hair and the women in modest, long skirts and dresses might have appeared to be rushing to a church social or PTA meeting.[1] Yet the instant this serious, square-looking group hoisted the awaiting picket signs worded "Hands Off Cuba!" and "Stop the Blockade!," the central campus area was transformed into a combat zone.

Since two o'clock in the afternoon, hundreds of right-wing students, fraternity boys, and local thugs, buttressed by four to five thousand mostly unfriendly onlookers, had been forming a mob that now surged forward with cries of "To Hell with Fidel" and "Kill Them!" As some thirty Indiana State Police officers looked on, one of the hecklers grabbed the protest sign held by undergraduate Polly Connolly Smith—most people remember it saying "Hands Off Cuba!"—and tore it to shreds. Her husband, Bloomington lawyer Don Smith (a 1953 IU graduate), futilely attempted to make a citizen's arrest of her assailant. As the beleaguered protesters edged their way along Seventh Street toward downtown, they were subject to continuous physical assaults while the police did little more than apprehend a few people on both sides. The next morning's headline in the *Indianapolis Star* read, "Thousands of Students Smash Cuba Sympathizers' Protest at I.U."

---

[*]This chapter appeared in a different form in Alan Wald, "The Audacity of American Trotskyism: The Indiana 'Subversion' Case Fifty Years Later," *Against the Current*, July-August 2013. Reprinted with permission.

An accompanying photograph showed a twenty-four-year-old radical graduate student in history named Ralph Levitt trading punches with pizza parlor employee Frederick Rice, also in his midtwenties.[2]

This volatile march was the initiating moment of what soon became the celebrated Indiana "Subversion" Case, a separate but related phase in the same process of right-wing political harassment. The protest itself occurred only four months after the completion and ratification of the *Port Huron Statement* at the Students for a Democratic Society (SDS) convention in Lakeport, Michigan, but there is no evidence of SDS involvement in the action or of any SDS members on the IU campus at that time. Although a national council meeting of SDS would be held in Bloomington a year later—producing the iconic September 1963 photograph of radiantly smiling leaders with fists raised—the location was chosen primarily because a number of the national leaders were there to attend a conference of the National Students Association (NSA). The available histories suggest that SDS was then embroiled in an internal debate over its appropriate organizational form and therefore unlikely to pay more than episodic attention to developments outside its own immediate concerns.[3] In the meantime, however, a national radicalization was under way and young enthusiasts in the Midwest and elsewhere were choosing other venues for political expression.

The daring Bloomington demonstration, precipitating phase one of what would snowball into a national political cause, had been planned by the Ad Hoc Committee to Oppose U.S. Aggression, an organization led by members of the Fair Play for Cuba Committee and Young Socialist Alliance (YSA) at IU.[4] It occurred at the height of the confrontation between the Kennedy administration and the Soviet Union known in the United States as the Cuban Missile Crisis and in Cuba as the October Crisis. These thirteen days are now judged to be the time when the Cold War came closest to turning into a nuclear conflict.

Several months later, in early 1963, phase two of the Bloomington events began, when three of the participants in the October protest against the Cuba blockade were indicted under the 1951 Indiana Anti-Communism Act, a state statute carrying a one- to three-year penalty of imprisonment. Ralph Levitt, who had been pictured in the *Indianapolis Star*, was joined by twenty-five-year-old James Bingham, another history graduate student, and twenty-two-year-old Tom Morgan, an undergraduate in government. Dubbed "the Bloomington Three," they were all native Hoosiers and members of the Trotskyist YSA. They were the first students in US history to be criminally charged for their political ideas. Their case was to drag on for four years.

Fifty years later there has yet to be another such prosecution, due in part to the bold professionalism with which these young activists and their supporters in the YSA and the Socialist Workers Party (SWP) responded to the charges. The audacity of the action was combined with the disciplined response that only a functional organization steeped in the traditions of nonsectarian political defense could provide. Through the Committee to Aid the Bloomington Students (CABS), support was mobilized around the country and the indictments beaten back.[5]

Today, Levitt is a retired transit worker living in Indianapolis; Bingham a rancher in Fresno, California; and Morgan a family counselor who raises horses near Terre Haute, Indiana. They and other veteran socialists of the era have provided me with new details to assist in this attempted rescue of the memory of unsung Trotskyist activists of the early 1960s from "the enormous condescension of posterity."[6]

Revolutionaries in the Heartland

The October 1962 protest dominated local and state news in Indiana for days; it was also reported in the national media as a shocking and singular event. Five decades later, the action can be retrospectively assessed as part of the breakdown of the repressive culture of the 1950s and a harbinger of the coming mass radicalization of the late 1960s. Even so, there was a mystique about the Bloomington events. The nature of the Ad Hoc Committee's bold anti-imperialist action and the composition of the socialist protesters appeared at the time to be quite different from the nonviolent sit-ins occurring in the South; the premonitory rumblings about free speech issues at the University of California, Berkeley; and intellectual debates about "participatory democracy" in Ann Arbor.

After all, the city of Bloomington was right smack in the middle of the US conservative heartland, and the male "Reds" who received most of the publicity in the subsequent legal case appeared to be a bunch of athletic-appearing white guys, some of them veterans, much like the sons of working-class people in the region. They also bore little resemblance to the stereotype of East Coast radical students, regarded as Allen Ginsberg–type beatnik intellectuals. For example, the sole identifiable Jewish last name among all the protesters was that of Levitt, and he counted among his relatives prominent members of Detroit's "Purple Gang." (His first name was in honor of Ralph Capone, Alfonso's brother, one-time business partner of Levitt's father.) A widely disseminated photograph of the Bloomington Three depicted husky young men who looked as if they would more likely be among the hecklers than the radicals. Four of the

October 1962 protesters had been members of Sigma Alpha Epsilon, the top fraternity on campus; their former fraternity brothers threw objects at them during the march.[7]

We now know that this hypermasculinist, WASP image of the Bloomington leftists is a bit misleading. A principal element in the case for "subversion" centered on the March 25, 1963, campus visit of an African American revolutionary socialist, Leroy McRae (1940–2013). A national YSA officer, McRae spoke on "The Black Revolt in America," in which he affirmed the constitutional right of armed self-defense against racist attacks.[8] The Monroe County, Indiana, public prosecutor claimed that this constituted advocacy of the violent overthrow of the governments of both the United States and the state of Indiana. Moreover, recent interviews with surviving Bloomington activists indicate that the October 1962 march would never have occurred without the insistence of two of the women in the Ad Hoc Committee. And at least two of the central males in this saga of Bloomington left were gay or bisexual.[9]

The Bloomington YSA was started in 1961–62 by George Shriver (later known as the translator George Saunders), a graduate student at Indiana University's Russian and East European Institute. Arriving as a committed Trotskyist from Harvard in fall 1960, Shriver initially set about organizing a chapter of the Fair Play for Cuba Committee. He and his wife, Ellen, were so involved that they became known as "Mr. and Mrs. Fair Play." Among Shriver's graduate student coworkers in the cataloging of the papers of Boris Nicolaevsky (a Russian Menshevik historian) were Stephen Cohen, the future Russian studies scholar, and Gerry Paul, a graduate of American University, later known as the Marxist journalist and translator Gerry Foley.[10] Foley soon joined the YSA, just after Bingham and Levitt.[11]

After the YSA chapter was established in spring 1962, conservatives on campus tried to deny YSA and the Fair Play for Cuba Committee recognition as official student organizations. The members of the YSA local responded to this harassment with a militancy joined to a sense of humor. A major activity became "tweaking the noses of traditional Hoosiers."[12] Characteristic actions consisted of the composition of wild and wacky leaflets by Gerry Paul that called for proletarian revolution. These were handed out at reunions of conservative IU alumni, football games, and rallies of Fred Schwarz's Christian Anti-Communist Crusade, sometimes resulting in brawls.[13] And rumors spread that the fun-loving Bloomington comrades consumed enough alcohol to render the entire population of one of the smaller Soviet republics insensible.

What is remarkable is how strong the Bloomington YSA quickly became, even in the absence of a nearby branch of the SWP to assist and well before the Vietnam radicalization helped boost YSA membership nationally. In effect, Shriver, Paul, and the others were building a YSA local with SDS-style numbers and impact. Other key players in the early period were Paulann and Bill Groninger, Jack Marsh, Don and Polly Smith, Marcia and Jack Glenn, Joe Henry, Dave and Beverly Scott Wulp, David Fender, Jeff Phillips, Mike McNaughton, and Tom Marsh. George Shriver remembers that sympathizers of the Fair Play for Cuba committee included Bill Lindner, Barry Schatz, Jeff Sharlett, and Rick Congress.[14]

To Cancel or Not to Cancel

On the day of the demonstration, the Bloomington members proved that they were more than mere political pranksters when they faced the hundreds of aggressive hecklers who shouted epithets, threatened violence, tried to grab placards, and kept swinging punches. Simply deciding to show up at the auditorium forced radicals to question whether they would fight for something if threatened with bodily harm.

David Fender remembers the YSA meeting at Don Smith's house where Bingham first proposed a demonstration against the blockade of Cuba. All the members agreed, and, instead of drawing up a full-page leaflet, they decided to do a two-line strip of paper calling for a demonstration against the Cuban blockade, giving the time and the place, and signed by Fair Play for Cuba. With about seven strips to a page, each ream of paper netted thirty-five hundred flyers. They passed these announcements around the campus by leaving them in every conceivable place where students congregated: every table in the cafeteria several times a day, all over the Indiana Memorial Union, popular student bars, and so on. These strip flyers were readily accepted and read on the spot, which in some cases generated instantaneous hostility.[15]

The seventeen or so organizers of the protest, mostly members of the YSA and Fair Play for Cuba, knew in advance that there would be no chance to discuss exactly how they should proceed once the action began. So Bingham, a six-foot-tall handsome man with short brown hair and the build of a football linebacker, was appointed to make on-the-spot tactical decisions that others would follow. Most important, it would be up to Bingham alone to determine whether the group would proceed with the planned march all the way from campus to the center of town, or disperse, after making a showing at the university auditorium, in order to avoid injury.

On October 24, the atmosphere on the Bloomington campus was grim and threatening. Driving the signs and placards in a large, army-green-painted old car (nicknamed "the Tank") to the assembly point, David Fender and Jack Marsh passed right-wing counterrallies at fraternity houses and groups of men chanting, "Where are the Commies?" and "Show yourselves!" A pole with a hangman's noose was displayed. In the meantime, Paulann Groninger, Jim Bingham, Polly Smith, and Ralph Levitt were clustering around a fountain in front of the auditorium. When Bingham surveyed the menacing crowd, a surreal spectacle that extended as far as the eye could see, there seemed to be no choice. The mass outnumbered the protesters two hundred to one, and from its depths came murderous cries. Accordingly, Bingham quickly declared, "Cancel!"

Then two young women stepped forward from the group, Paulann Groninger and Polly Smith—the latter having previously drawn attention among some of the conventionally sexist male activists chiefly because of her "great legs."[16] Facing Bingham, they announced fearlessly that the two of them planned to go ahead with the action regardless of what the others did. Most of the remainder of the group was overcome with dread at the sight of the huge hoard of reactionaries but felt that they couldn't abandon their female comrades.[17] Or perhaps they recalled poet Robert Frost's famous observation, "The best way out is always through."[18]

Thus began the all-day brawl in which the small group made its way in the direction of the center of the city, breaking through human blockades of right-wingers chanting, "Block that ship!" and periodically interchanging blows. A few members of the Young People's Socialist League (YPSL), including the IU wrestling champion Walt Carnahan and a football player named Charlie Leinenweber, joined on "free speech" grounds in efforts to protect the marchers. In the end about twenty people fought off hundreds of antagonists. This was possible because the smaller group was well organized, unified, and had a purpose.

Nevertheless, in the course of the ordeal, every single picket sign was grabbed from the protesters' hands, and Levitt was arrested by police. At the very last stage, just as the group reached the dividing line between campus and town, mayhem broke loose. The protesters ran for refuge at the university library. Smith, Groninger, and some of the others barricaded themselves inside while seventy-five or so of the hard-core demonstrators, ringing the building outside, sang the national anthem and other patriotic songs for several hours.

Young Socialists on Trial

The persecution of Bingham, Levitt, and Morgan got under way in January 1963. Thomas Hoadley, the newly elected Monroe County prosecutor, had dismissed the charges against right-wing thugs arrested by police in the demonstration. Then, on February 18, 1963, he requested that IU withdraw recognition of the YSA, which had been granted late in 1962. After the university refused to cooperate, Hoadley sought an indictment under the 1951 Indiana Anti-Subversive Act. He claimed that Bingham, Levitt, and Morgan—singled out probably because they were listed as officers of the YSA chapter—had attended the March 25 meeting where violent overthrow was advocated by Leroy McRae.

When this was quashed on May 1 due to a technicality involving poor wording, Hoadley went for a second indictment based on the tape recording (by an eavesdropping landlord) of a meeting in a private home where defendants and their attorneys discussed their defense. Hoadley would pursue his crusade for years with an obsessiveness to rival the revenge fixation of Sweeney Todd. In the end, however, Hoadley was revealed to be merely an opportunist seeking to exploit anticommunist fears to achieve political prominence—not unlike Joe McCarthy. When the battle for public opinion went against him, he simply dropped the matter and moved on to an entirely different career in Palm Beach, Florida, where he continues his legal practice to this day.

In 1963, however, Hoadley orchestrated a public smear campaign, accusing the YSA Trotskyists of being Moscow trained, of functioning as part of an international communist conspiracy, and—due to their solidarity with striking Harlan County coal miners in 1962—of "conducting a running gun battle with the Commonwealth of Kentucky."[19] In a separate case, Hoadley arrested and tried an Indiana University student, Nancy Dillingham, for possession of marijuana, and when he learned that her attorney was YSA sympathizer Don Smith, he charged that she was a confidante and marijuana supplier of the Bloomington socialists. Hoadley was not one to fret about fact checking in this laugh-free comedy. In Indiana of the early 1960s, show trials just weren't what they used to be.

At a March 1964 pretrial proceeding, a Bloomington judge declared the section of law under which the students had been indicted to be unconstitutional. Hoadley appealed to the Indiana Supreme Court and obtained a split decision in January 1965 that reversed the ruling. Then the three students filed an appeal in the US district court in Indianapolis requesting an injunction to stop the prosecution as well as a declaration that the law was unconstitutional. In this effort, the Bloomington Three were joined by several faculty and townspeople claiming that the law impinged on their free speech as well.

An Injury to One

CABS grew out of the Bloomington Defense Committee, established in 1962. Since the YSA was in political solidarity with the national SWP, the Bloomington defendants were quickly put in contact with George Novack (1905–92), a seasoned Marxist cadre engaged in political rights defense work for more than thirty years. From 1937 to 1940, at the time of the Moscow Purge Trials, Novack was the National Secretary of the American Committee for the Defense of Leon Trotsky. In 1941 he held the same position in the Civil Rights Defense Committee, which handled the case of the first victims of the Smith Act. More recently, he led the eight-year campaign to reinstate James Kutcher (1912–89), "the legless veteran," in the Veterans Administration job from which he had been fired due to SWP membership. The SWP's founding chair, James P. Cannon (1890–1974), had once headed the Communist Party's International Labor Defense, and the Trotskyist movement was steeped in the conviction that "an injury to one is an injury to all" as well as the necessity of fighting back against all repression. The SWP understood that the issue in the case was not agreement with the ideas of the Bloomington defendants but support of their right to express their views.

From the outset, CABS was guided by the SWP national office, and at the end of 1963, the defense committee formally moved its national headquarters from Bloomington to Manhattan in order to publicize the case and raise money. YSA National Chairman Barry Sheppard and National Secretary Peter Camejo (1939–2008) hurled themselves full time and selflessly into the defense effort and won the undying gratitude of the defendants. Fund-raising, distributing literature, securing a legal team, attaining prominent sponsors, and organizing several national and regional tours of the three defendants were all coordinated from New York with the help of local CABS chapters elsewhere that generally consisted of YSA activists. By 1965, more than thirteen hundred faculty members on ninety-five college campuses signed the defense campaign's appeal as sponsors.

Among the YSA members on the Bloomington campus was Gregory Hildebrand, a graduate student who was also an active folksinger. He had joined the YSA a few years earlier in Boston under the influence of the painter Arnold Trachtman and singer Joan Trachtman. Hildebrand was at the October 1962 demonstration, and when CABS was launched, he composed a number of songs that were sung at rallies in defense of the Bloomington Three. His biggest hit was inspired by an Ewan MacColl lampoon, "Barratty-Parratty," which was in turn set to the tune of the Scottish folksong "The Wee Cooper O' Fife." Two of verses went as follows:

There's a
lawyer in town with just one aim,
Hoadily toadily piddily poo, to
bring publicity to his name.
Hoadily toadily full of mendacity, rattling verbally, none of it
true.
There's
just one office he thinks he's worth,
Hoadily toadily piddily poo, attorney general of the earth.
Hoadily toadily, etc.[20]

The other song was more of a ballad in the style of the left-wing People's Songs artists with the tune adapted from a children's song, "The Good Ship Ragamuffin":

1. Well, our
    student body prez was on hand or so he says, and our
    rights were all respected on that day. Now, I'm
    going to set you wise to that hypocrisy and lies, 'cause the
    business really happened this-a-way.

2. Now, we
    made a bunch of signs, thought we'd stand up in a line—said it's
    foolish to blockade a foreign land. By the
    fountain where we met, such a turnout did we get—There were
    crowds of people there on every hand.

3. They had
    signs written so: Yankee, Si! and Cuba, No! to the
    cheering of a thousand head or more. Though we
    had but twenty-two, we decided that we'd do just the
    same thing that we'd planned to do before.

4.   So we
held our signs up high, looked those hecklers in the eye, and we
started up the street in single file—while our
upright campus youth, acting shockingly uncouth, followed
after us, just screaming all the while.

chorus I:
    Yes, the
hoodlums all were there, and their screaming filled the air, as they
tried to take our civil rights away————————We
were a great sensation in our Cuba demonstration, though we
feared we might not survive the day.

5.   Now, they
kicked us from behind, and they tore up all our signs. They threw
rocks at us and called us dirty Reds. They were
brave as all the world when they were picking on the girls. If they'd
been alone they doubtless would have fled.
Chorus I again, if you feel like it. Then:

6.   But in
Berkeley Cal today, and Wisconsin by the way, and at
Wesleyan and Antioch, you'll find that they're
marching just the same, and we ought to feel ashamed, that our
campus is so very far behind.

chorus II:
    But we
did survive the day. Got some bruises, that's okay, 'cause they
won't forget our line of twenty-two————————had their
say and stood up straight against a thousand full of hate, and that's the
story, folks, and you can bet it's true![21]

The events of October 24 were similarly described in chapter 10 of the novel *The Translator* (2002) by John Crowley, an acquaintance of Hildebrand, the Groningers, Gerry Paul, and others involved in the demonstration. The story concerns an exiled Soviet poet teaching at a Midwestern university in the early 1960s, Innokenti Falin, and his affair with a student, Kit Malone, who translates his work. In a magical realist narrative, Innokenti appears at the October 1962 demonstration against the blockade, then vanishes—perhaps assassinated or kidnapped. Kit's circle of friends includes activists in the Fair Play for Cuba Committee, including one non-student (Jackie) who may be a police or even Soviet agent. According to Crowley, the character Saul Greenleaf in the novel was based on Gerry Paul, and Max (no last name) was based on Joe Henry. Moreover, Crowley and documentary filmmaker Lance Paul made a moving picture of the demonstration itself.[22]

Tom Morgan later recalled that Communist Party (CP) backing of the case was remarkable in light of its past antagonism toward Trotskyists. He asserts that the CP provided CABS activists with multiple contacts, speaking engagements, financial aid, and press coverage. Support was especially noticeable on the West Coast and in Chicago. In one of the annual "Buck Dinners" (a fund-raising event serving venison) held in Detroit by lawyers close to the CP, the CABS campaign was featured along with support for the Student Nonviolent Coordinating Committee. In Morgan's view, collaboration on the case induced a temporary thaw in the historical "chill" between the CP and the SWP, but this ended in 1964 when the CP launched its own new youth group, the W. E. B. Du Bois Clubs of America, which judged the YSA to be divisive.[23]

On the other hand, evidence of official SDS involvement in the case has not come to light, although Todd Gitlin does not exclude the possibility that some sort of motion of support might have been passed or that SDS-ers may have sought an endorsement from the NSA.[24] Tom Hayden recalls no connections at all between SDS and the Fair Play for Cuba Committee nationally, although some SDS chapters did organize protests during the Cuban Missile Crisis.[25] Richard Flacks believes that SDS distance from Fair Play for Cuba was due to a "broad aversion to taking stands on international matters" at that time.[26]

The national cochairs of CABS were Herbert J. Muller, a historian at IU, and Mark DeWolfe Howe, a law and history professor at Harvard University who died during the course of the case. Lord Bertrand Russell was honorary chair of CABS, and other prominent backers included A. J. Muste, James Baldwin, Warren Miller, John Lewis, Linus Pauling, Germaine Bree, H. Stuart Hughes, and Malcolm Sharpe. Hundreds of thousands of leaflets, pamphlets, and brochures explaining the issues and reprinting the allegedly seditious speech by McRae were distributed across the country; speaking tours of Morgan, Bingham, and Levitt extended to more than one hundred campuses and were often combined with radio and television interviews; the NSA and British Labor Party Youth passed resolutions in behalf of the Bloomington Three; and even the *New York*

Times published several editorials deploring the threat to free speech if the prosecution were victorious. Fund-raising came through rummage sales, cocktail parties, dances, art auctions, hootenannies, and performances by the San Francisco Mime Troop.

Although the Bloomington affiliate of the American Civil Liberties Union (ACLU) initially refused to support the case and even red-baited the defendants, the Bloomington Three were able to secure the services of a local attorney named James Cottner. Then Cottner abandoned the case and an unsuccessful search ensued for a lawyer admitted to the Indiana bar. This led to the defense team contacting a Louisville, Kentucky, attorney named Daniel T. Taylor, who arranged to be qualified. In the meantime, the Emergency Civil Liberties Committee provided the defendants with its esteemed general counsel, Leonard Boudin (1912–89), and eventually the ACLU provided an amicus curiae brief for the defense.[27]

The case began to wind to a conclusion when, on March 20, 1964, a county circuit court judge found the Indiana Anti-Subversive Act unconstitutional and dismissed the indictments against the three students. Prosecutor Hoadley appealed the ruling to the Indiana Supreme Court, where the indictment based on the tape-recorded private meeting was reinstated on January 25, 1965. In November 1966, a hearing on the constitutionality of the Indiana Anti-Subversive Act was to be held in a federal court but was cancelled, evidently in response to the decision of Prosecutor Hoadley to resign his office and depart Indiana. After some delay, the new county prosecutor decided not to pursue the case. CABS issued its final communication to its sponsors and contributors in February 1968.

Smashing through the Mask

The historical framework of the Cold War era is crucial to assessing the events in Bloomington. The 1950s and early 1960s were years of notorious political repression. The Indiana antisedition laws were part and parcel of the apparatus of blacklists and investigating committees. As a new radicalization began to emerge among students and African Americans, authorities targeted the most militant as a means of intimidating others.

The SWP of that era knew, almost as an immediate reflex, exactly how to start up and sustain an effective political defense. Its skills made the Bloomington case into the most significant civil liberties case of its day, helping to turn what might have been merely a rising summer storm of episodic revolts into the national climate change known as "the sixties."

The strategy should be studied and remembered as crucial for securing the right of students of all political opinions to discuss, deliberate, and debate political ideas simply on their merits—and for the right to form organizations to promote those ideas without fear of police reprisal. Deprived of such an option, the claims of "academic freedom" at universities are a sham.

Why did this happen in Bloomington? Perhaps the Bloomington YSA just rushed in where the more experienced feared to tread. Decades later, Levitt observed that it could be explained by no single factor: "For us it was totally natural, a convergence of pro-Cuba politics, stupidity, militancy, inexperience, and a desire to fight."[28] Other radical groups were present on the IU campus, including the much larger YPSL, but none seemed capable of inaugurating a similar action. The Communist Party had to be hypercautious due its long-standing connection to Moscow, and it had little credibility among those seeking a new radicalism free of the Stalinist legacy.

Perhaps most important, the YSA at that time, in contrast to later years, was relatively unencumbered by a bureaucratic party organization orchestrating matters from afar or sending in sniffer dogs of orthodoxy to quash creative action. Several defendants recall that, while both the YSA and SWP leaderships had counseled members against holding "risky" demonstrations at the time of the Cuban Missile Crisis, the organizations took no steps to impose specific advice on the local level.[29] Once the crisis erupted, any hesitancy to fully support the young radicals in Bloomington would have been nullified by the strong insistence of national secretary Farrell Dobbs (1907–83) that the SWP provide full backing. The mechanisms of such a campaign were second nature to the SWP so that this one was run brilliantly along standard SWP lines.

Still, the original audacity of the action was equally crucial to the blend of creativity and self-discipline that allowed a tiny band of revolutionary socialists to punch above its weight. Led by a woman previously known by sexist males for her "great legs," the Bloomington Trotskyists met the contingencies of their own period with fortitude. They faced down a reactionary mob, smashing through the ugly mask of the bully of US Cold War culture. Fifty years later, historians as well as activists should be alarmed by the widespread memory loss that has occurred in regard to these and similar events in the record of the far left. What occurred in Bloomington could have been a hideous mess but can be savored today as a perfect cocktail. Those who forget their own history are rewarded by having it forgotten by pretty much everyone else.

Three Puerto Rican nationalists, including Lolita Lebrón, seized by Capitol police after firing into the House Chambers from the gallery and injuring eight congressmen. Washington, DC, March 1, 1954. © CORBIS

III.

Connections

The Sixties Movement of Movements

It has become common coin in radical activist circles of the past fifteen years to emphasize the plurality of causes that mobilize protest, no longer speaking of "the Movement" as many did fifty years ago but rather of what Naomi Klein called, when describing the globalization protests starting in 1999, a "movement of movements."[1] In fact, that characterization applies as well to the new insurgencies of 1955–65, and this collection aims to highlight the multiple forms and causes that coexisted at the time, often intersecting in ways that served to inform each other and enhance momentum, sometimes operating in distinct channels, and occasionally inducing strains or conflicts with which organizers tried to cope. In these chapters we see how varied currents—anticolonialism, pacifism, feminism, black liberation, and more—interacted with each other. And yet it was also the case that things close at hand may have gone unnoticed: we do not know how much, if at all, the (largely white) university activists of Ann Arbor were aware of the dramatic developments in Detroit's black radical politics, when James Boggs and Grace Lee Boggs helped convene the Grass-Roots Leadership Conference (November 1963) that played host to black nationalist Malcolm X almost as he was breaking from his organizational home, the Nation of Islam, toward an independent activist career with a much wider audience. (See Stephen Ward's chapter on the emergence of James Boggs's distinctive Black Power politics.) In another case, somewhat surprising connections *were* made, as Andrea Friedman narrates the activities of radical pacifists after World War II, showing solidarity with Puerto Rican nationalists, even though that entailed the discomfiting defense of agitators who took up arms. Marian Mollin describes radical pacifist challenges to the nuclear arms race.

Ramón Gutiérrez reveals how the urge to assimilate different causes (and regional cultures) into a common movement could obscure the specificity of one strand of Mexican American mobilization. Daryl Maeda illuminates the long-overlooked engagement of Asian Americans in New Left activism, which would lead, in time, toward an independent movement of ethnic self-assertion; Paul Chaat Smith's reflections on the American Indian Movement (AIM) recognizes the distinctive conditions and rhythms that made AIM both linked to and apart from other new insurgencies. Ruth Rosen and Marian Mollin explore the dimensions of women's consciousness within and without protest organizations in the 1950s and 1960s. Richard Mann, one of the organizers of Michigan's innovative Vietnam teach-in of March 1965, describes the evolution of academic dissent. Not included here but part of the 2012 conference was Kevin Mumford's intriguing account of black and gay/lesbian identities ("Subversive Perversion: Notes on James Baldwin, Lorraine Hansberry, and Bayard Rustin") well before the Stonewall "riot" of 1969 boosted gay liberation into public recognition as yet another insurgent dynamic.

—Howard Brick

18 | Refugees from the Fifties
by Ruth Rosen

In fall 1952, my parents pinned an "I Like Ike" button on my Brownie uniform. In 1957, I sat glued to the television as I watched nine brave black students desegregate Central High School in Little Rock, Arkansas. It was a turning point in my life; I not only was inspired but learned a new meaning of bravery. Fast forward to the early sixties when I worked for a variety of civil rights organizations. And in spring 1965, after an all-night bus trip, I arrived bleary-eyed in Washington to protest the Vietnam War. There I marched with twenty-five thousand people, wept as World War II veterans wheeled themselves to the rally, and experienced immense relief that others shared my anguish over the Vietnam War.

Standing in front of the Washington Monument was Paul Potter, president of Students for a Democratic Society (SDS), who challenged me with his unforgettable speech. What kind of society, he asked, could promote so much injustice and cruelty? What kind of society, he asked, "consistently puts material values before human values—and still persists in calling itself free and still persists in finding itself fit to police the world? We must name that system. We must name it, describe it, analyze it, understand it and change it." Only a social movement, he said, could change a system that daily violated its own ideals and values.

The Vietnam War and then the women's movement shadowed my entire adult education. A few years later, as a graduate student at the University of California, Berkeley, both of these movements continued to consume my political activism. By 1970, I was teaching the first course in women's history, demanding gym facilities, child care, and education that was relevant to women's lives.

We were refugees from the fifties. The media called it "the generation gap." Like so many young people in my generation, I suffered a sense of extreme alienation. My spiritual and moral compass was at odds with the

I AM FURIOUS

(FEMALE)

This essay originally appeared in RIPSAW.
It is an attempt to formulate perspectives
for the Women's Caucus of the New University Conference.

published by
Radical Education Project
Box 561-A Detroit, Mi 48232

Cover, I Am Furious (Female), Radical Education Project, Detroit, 1969. University of Michigan Library (Special Collections Library) materialistic and militaristic culture of a nation that daily violated its ideals of equality.

Not all young people felt alienated, nor did all those who felt alienated become activists. Some, like Sharon Jeffrey, got their language from their parents. What was unique about those who led and joined the civil rights, antiwar, women's, gay, and environmental movements was that they politicized their feelings and became committed to changing the world in which they lived. As Paul Potter had rightly hoped, those movements gave activists individual purpose within the solidarity of a social movement.

Where did the language of these movements come from? Some young people had already learned the language of injustice from their families—activists in the Old Left and the civil rights movements in the 1930, 1940s, and 1950s. Still others, like myself, reinvented themselves and learned the language of opposition from their friends within the Movement.

The brilliance of the *Port Huron Statement* is that Tom Hayden and the people at the Port Huron convention captured that alienation. They understood that those of us who politicized our alienation were hungry for a new world and idealistic enough to believe that we could create it. They understood that many of us felt like refugees from another time and that we wanted to replace our sense of helplessness with becoming engaged members of a participatory democracy. In commemoration of the *Port Huron Statement* more than fifty years later, I discuss how those young men and women—mostly white, college-educated, and part of the dominant culture—entered the sixties with overlapping but varying expectations and anxieties and created something—captured so well in that *Statement*—that impacted men and women, of different classes and ethnicities, in dramatically different ways.

The young men and women of the fifties had much in common. The colonial struggles for independence and self-determination, especially in Africa and Cuba, inspired them to champion social movements for popular democracy. In their search for a language expressing their alienation, they read the same books, saw the same films, and read the same magazines. They rejected David Riesman's "*Lonely Crowd*" and William H. Whyte's "*Organization Man*," and they identified instead with Ralph Ellison's "*Invisible Man*." They had read the existentialists and knew they had to find a larger purpose in life. On a more personal level, many searched for a way to escape the lives laid out for them.

For young men, hints of that escape began to appear when *Mad* magazine, first published in 1952, satirized the popular culture of the fifties. One year later, Hugh Hefner began publishing *Playboy*, which encouraged bachelors to enjoy a sybaritic sexual life. For the upscale man, an elaborately appointed apartment—complete with revolving bed, rotating lovers, and reflecting mirrors—offered all the pleasure of sex without the burden of a family.

Only a small number of young men could afford Hefner's lifestyle, and it was mostly a few "wannabes" who followed the Beats into coffeehouses or out on the road, leaving behind crabgrass, marriage, and a mortgage. Still, as the alienated sons of the fifties entered a new decade, they had models of revolt, intellectual analyses of their alienation, prophetic mentors, and fantasies of escape, if only they dared.

Their female counterparts, influenced by the same intellectual and political legacy, had fewer examples of female rebellion and nonconformity. Like educated women before them, they lived in a dual culture, experiencing life as a woman but learning to interpret what they read as a man. They absorbed critiques of materialism and conformity through men's eyes. They learned to view society's conformity through men's analyses and tried to shed the prudery of the fifties by inventing themselves as the free-spirited women young men increasingly expected them to be.

In the short run, the male literary and sociological tradition of dissent unleashed dreams of freedom and a critical distrust of authority, encouraging in their place a taste for nonconformity. All of this created a foundation of sorts for a future women's movement that would question all conventional wisdom. In the civil rights movement, both black and white women fought against racial supremacy, which raised the question of what justified *male* supremacy. From Paul Potter and other SDS intellectuals, these women learned the need to "name the system" and to find language for the injustices they experienced in the Movement and identified in American foreign policy.

Women don't appear in the *Port Huron Statement* because the path they needed to forge had not yet been articulated. Hardly anyone could have anticipated how differently the Movement would affect young women activists.

For female activists who worked in the civil rights, New Left, and antiwar movements, the generation gap between parents and children was far more complicated than it was for Movement men. Elsewhere, I have called it the "female generation gap." The immediate past conjured up images of claustrophobic marriages, coercive motherhood, and constrained chastity. Most of these young women had had personal acquaintance with what would later be described by Betty Friedan as "the feminine mystique": they recoiled from the role of housewife, even if their own mothers had worked on an assembly line or engaged in activism. The ghost haunting these young white women was not an "organization man" but a woman wearing an apron and living vicariously through the lives of her husband and children. Much of the women's liberation movement would be forged in opposition to this image.

This was not the case for black young women, whose mothers had rarely enjoyed the luxury of avoiding work outside the home. Their rebellion was not against domesticity but rather against exploitative work, racism, and an older generation that had avoided direct confrontation with the white vigilantes who enforced segregation. These young women became leaders in the civil rights movement and demonstrated their organizational brilliance. They were angered by watching black men lust after white women. And later, in the late 1960s and 1970s, they reflected upon the sexism they had experienced in the Black Power movement.

Although young white women had been influenced, too, by what their male counterparts had read, they had precious few intellectual mentors who addressed them as women. Aside from Simone de Beauvoir's *The Second Sex*, which did travel through movement circles, there was no C. Wright Mills or David Riesman to help them analyze their fears and dreams. In fact, some of the male mentors could be hilariously wrong. In the July 21, 1967, issue of *Time* magazine, the well-known sociologist David Riesman, who had taught me to seek authenticity, wrote authoritatively, "If anything remains more or less unchanged, it will be the role of women."[1] It was probably the worst prediction he ever made in his career.

As they entered the sixties, many young women began searching for ways to avoid becoming a traditional housewife. The birth control pill, of course, did something historic: it ruptured sexuality from reproduction for the first time in human history. New books addressed questions they hadn't even articulated. In 1962, Helen Gurley Brown published *Sex and the Single Girl*, which mirrored Hugh Hefner's "playboy" philosophy and encouraged single women to "swing" with men, whether they were married or not.

Like Hefner, Brown encouraged young women to leave crabgrass and domesticity behind, enjoying sex for their own pleasure. The few women who joined the Beats or who spent a few years in the urban sex scene soon discovered the fundamental inequality that shadowed their sexually liberated lives. If they waited too long, they could risk ending up with no husband and bumping up against their biological clocks. Without perfect contraception or legal abortion, women literally risked their lives if they became pregnant. And given that both young men and women were relatively ignorant about sexual relations, some women began to realize that more encounters did not necessarily result in better sex.

By 1964, the sexual revolution entered the circles of the antiwar and New Left movements. Some women felt the same ambiguity as those who had followed Helen Brown's advice. Sexual liberation seemed an ideal form of rebellion, but some feared being treated as dispensable playmates by movement men. In addition, many still wondered how they would work, have a family, and yet not end up being a housewife responsible for all child care and homework. When movement men treated them as housewives, they had no idea what a hot button they were pushing.

At the time, there were few answers to the questions movement women began to discuss among themselves. The conventional narrative of the women's movement is that sometime between 1965 and 1967, women began to leave the New Left and the antiwar movement because their work was undervalued and involved too much mimeographing, typing, and making the coffee rather than writing position papers or speaking to the press.

There is some truth to this story, but it hardly captures what is a far more complicated history. Movement men had grown up in the fifties. They had therefore inherited traditional views of women that began to irritate young women who were gaining confidence in their own abilities.

It may be hard to believe this, but before the women's movement, the president of Harvard University saw no reason to increase the number of female undergraduates because the university's mission was to "train leaders." As a result, Harvard's Lamont Library was off limits to women for fear they would distract male students. Newspaper ads separated jobs by gender; employers paid women less than men for the same work. Bars often refused to serve women; banks denied married women credit or loans, a practice that did not change until 1974. Some states even excluded women from jury duty. Radio producers considered women's voices too abrasive to be on the air; television executives believed that women's voices didn't carry sufficient credibility to anchor the news; no women ran big corporations or universities, worked as firefighters or police officers, sat on the Supreme Court, installed electrical equipment, climbed telephone poles, or owned construction companies. All hurricanes had female names due to the widely held view that women brought chaos and destruction to society. As late as 1970, Dr. Edgar Berman, a well-known physician, proclaimed on television that women were too tortured by hormonal disturbances to assume the presidency of the nation. Few people knew more than a few women professors, doctors, or lawyers. Everyone addressed a woman as either Miss or Mrs. depending on her marital status, and if a woman wanted an abortion—legal nowhere in America—she risked her life, searching among quacks in back alleys for a competent and compassionate doctor. The public believed that rape victims had probably "asked for it," most women felt too ashamed to report it, and no language existed to make sense of what we now call domestic violence, sexual harassment, marital rape, or date rape. Just two words summed up the hidden injuries women suffered in silence: "That's life."

This was the culture that formed most of these young men. What the conventional narrative misses is that these men, like their female counterparts, had traditional gender expectations and didn't see them as a violation of their commitment to equality. As comrades, moreover, women and men were more or less equals. After the sexual revolution intersected with the Movement, around the middle of the decade, relationships became more problematic. Some young men even thought that the sexual revolution was the same thing as women's liberation. Some women felt exploited.

The truth is, the Movement was a tremendous gift to young women. Nowhere in America could they find such opportunity and freedom. It was in the Movement that young women learned to clarify their ideas, analyze their grievances, and organize people for social justice and against the war. By 1967, the Movement promoted token women to speak at rallies, to head up committees, to write reports and position papers, and to take leadership positions. Many of these women would become leaders, writers, and organizers of the women's movement. And given the influence of other liberation movements, it was hardly surprising that they dubbed the new movement they were creating "the women's liberation front."

In short, the common belief that men in the civil rights, New Left, and antiwar movements treated women badly ignores the historical context and erases a far more important story. These movements inspired a group of young women to seek their own independence and self-determination.

Why, then, did women gradually begin to discuss their grievances in consciousness-raising groups and write memos, position papers, and pamphlets that crisscrossed college campuses with new interpretations of women's lives? There were many reasons. Black Power activists had asked white activists to organize their own communities. Some women denounced the revolutionary violent fantasies and self-implosion of the late New Left into sectarian groups. Many women no longer experienced the late New Left as a community that supported their growing desire for self-determination and their wish to speak about their own lives.

Between 1955 and 1965, then, these women activists had learned the skills they needed to create a national movement. The civil rights movement inspired them to question male supremacy. The spirit of Port Huron reflected their alienation and challenged them to carve out an individual purpose within the solidarity of a social movement. From those New Leftists who celebrated expressive and cultural politics, women learned that the personal is political and that there are political dimensions in all personal relationships. From the very beginning, the women's liberation movement embraced the idea of participatory democracy. It was not, however, immune to the kind of sectarianism and "trashing of leaders," influenced by Mao's cultural revolution, that led some activists in women's liberation to denounce talent and leadership.

These were the movements that gave women an opportunity to fight for equality as well as social and economic justice—an opportunity that would turn their lives upside down. From these movements, women inherited a sophisticated and substantive intellectual legacy. Networks were already in place and women knew how to organize. That is why the women's liberation movement swept so swiftly across the nation and why pamphlets, poetry, memos, essays, and books poured out of movement presses and publishing houses so quickly.

Men were blindsided by the women's movement. Shaped by their childhood in the 1950s, they thought they had been good comrades. And in many ways they had. So women's anger shocked them. Women's fury confused them. They didn't realize that it was precisely the Movement in which female activists had first realized their subordination in American society.

For the first time, these young activists organized a movement around their own lives. Once they saw inequality, they saw it everywhere. And it was everywhere. But like fish in water, it had just seemed normal. As Paul Potter had said, they needed to name the system and to find language for what I have elsewhere described as "the hidden injuries of sex."

Creating a Movement

On August 27, 1970, fifty thousand women marched down Fifth Avenue, announcing the birth of a new movement. Their three demands included legal abortion, universal child care, and equal pay for women and men—preconditions for women's equality with men at home and at the workplace. These are not what SDS founders would have demanded in 1962, but they mirrored the values and vision of the *Port Huron Statement*.

Turns out, there were plenty more hidden injuries, which activists soon discovered and publicized. Rape, once a subject of great shame, became redefined as physical assault that had little to do with lust. Date rape, for which there was plenty of experience but no name, opened up a national conversation about what constituted consensual sex. Few people had ever heard the words marital rape. "If you can't rape your wife," Congressman Bob Wilson of California said in 1979, "then who can you rape?" Thus began a new conversation about the right of wives to have consensual sex.

Sexual freedom without legal abortion inspired women's liberationists to join the abortion rights campaign of the sixties. Determined to repeal laws against abortion, New York feminists testified before the legislature and passed out copies of their model abortion bill—a blank piece of paper. Through "public speak-outs," they admitted to having undergone illegal abortions, and they explained why they had made that choice. In Chicago and San Francisco, activists created their own clandestine organizations to help women seek qualified doctors. Some learned how to do it for their comrades. And then, in 1973, the Supreme Court's *Roe v. Wade* decision ignited the endless abortion wars.

Activists also began to share their sexual ignorance and disappointment. Embarrassed to discuss sexual matters, many young women had faked orgasm for fear of being labeled frigid and wanting to be viewed as "good in bed." It was no surprise, then, that the faked orgasm became a metaphor for the many ways women hid their private anxiety and anguish from others, especially men.

Arguably, the women's health movement was the greatest accomplishment of what was increasingly called "the women's movement." Women knew too little about their own bodies and passively allowed physicians to treat them as ignorant children. In 1971, the Boston Health Collective published a booklet that would become *Our Bodies, Ourselves*, now translated all over the world. Inspired by the barefoot doctors of China's Cultural Revolution, the book not only disseminated biological knowledge but also questioned why doctors controlled women's reproductive decisions and why medical researchers only used male subjects when they tested new medicines. When activists in Los Angeles decided to teach each other to do gynecological exams with mirrors, they were arrested. As one activist famously wrote, "What man would be put under police surveillance for six months for looking at his penis?"[2]

In time, feminists—as many activists soon called themselves—questioned the safety of the birth control pill and the dangers of drugs intended to prevent miscarriages. They created women's health centers all over the nation and established the National Women's Health Network, which asked researchers tough questions and testified before Congress.

Given the homophobia of the time, it was inevitable that much of the mainstream media and public would try to smear women activists as lesbians. Why else would they complain about male behavior? To dilute this constant accusation, women began to discuss and write about compulsory heterosexuality. Together with the burgeoning male gay movement, feminist lesbians formed the gay liberation front. What feminists had achieved, in the spirit of the *Port Huron Statement*, was the courage to call a custom a crime. Perhaps one of the greatest hidden injuries was the sexual predatory behavior of those who abused their power. Some called it sexual blackmail, but when renamed as sexual harassment, it became illegal because it created a hostile atmosphere where women worked and thereby violated their right to earn a livelihood.

When feminists reframed wife beating as domestic violence, women now had the right to be safe in their own homes. Battered women's shelters, moreover, gave women a place to escape violence and possible death.

This is only a short list of the achievements of the early women's movement. It doesn't even include creating one word, "Ms.," to replace Miss or Mrs. Nor does it reflect the struggle to ordain ministers and rabbis or to challenge the academic disciplines and change socially accepted behavior.

Sometimes these successes came from legal cases that ignited national debates. The movement also sued the textile, telephone, and airline industries for better working conditions for women.

But we shouldn't underestimate how much the countercultural New Left had taught feminists about publicizing their grievances. In the streets, activists used agitprop and guerrilla theatre to satirize a male-dominated society. They whistled at men's tight buns, loudly admired men's bulging arm muscles, and heckled construction workers with shouts and whistles. They invaded bars that would not serve them; sat in at magazines, newspapers, and libraries that still quarantined them in special women's sections; and posted stickers like "This ad insults women" all over American cities. One group, Women's International Terrorist Conspiracy from Hell (WITCH), decided to deploy their magical powers by hexing Wall Street. The stock market inexplicably declined.

In 1968 they satirized the Miss America Pageant in Atlantic City, which exclusively valued women's appearance. These activists, by the way, were rather good looking—check out the pictures—but they wanted to be valued for more than their appearance. To make their point, they decided to burn "instruments of oppression," including bras, girdles, and hair curlers. But when the fire chief told them they might start a fire on the wooden boardwalk, they complied with his request. Nevertheless, by the next morning, the national media had spawned the myth that women's liberationists had burned their bras at the Miss American contest.

Just as Tom Hayden had condemned materialism in the *Port Huron Statement*, women activists targeted the marriage industry for trying to turn young women into consumers of all kinds of domestic products. On February 15, 1969, on both coasts, feminists invaded two gigantic bridal fairs that featured gowns, furniture, appliances, and honeymoon trips and denounced the profits from the "sale" of marriage.

The inspired and disillusioned women who began the women's movement had come a long way in less than a decade. And their excavation of the injuries of sex spread quickly to women in all occupations, professions, and unions through the media's endless fascination with what they still viewed as a fad.

At the same time, minority women began to discover sexism in their own liberation movements. As early as 1967, women in the Chicano movement, for example, challenged the sexism of movement organizations. For them, however, the struggle was aimed not mainly against the housewife's role, which seemed like a luxury, but against poverty, violence, racism, and the obstacles that kept their men from supporting families. Even though they bristled at sexism, they understood they were struggling to end the abuse of Mexican Americans, to preserve the survival of indigenous people, to support the independence of Puerto Rico, and to fight racism against Asian Americans.

Many felt divided loyalties. To preserve cultural tradition resisted the dominant culture. But tradition also limited women's opportunities to live more independent lives. Elaine Brown, of the Black Panthers in the 1970s, wrote, "I had joined the majority of black women in America in denouncing feminism. Now I trembled with fury long buried. The feminists were right. The value of my life had been obliterated as much by being female as black and poor."[3] Gradually, they formed their own feminist organizations dedicated to helping the most vulnerable women in their communities.

The women who had grown up in the civil rights and New Left movements had absorbed a political culture and intellectual legacy that gave them the skill and spirit to create a new women's movement, arguably the most transformative force of our time because it eventually reached half the world's population.

At long last, activist women had begun to see their lives through their own eyes, and they came to understand that the state must protect their rights—as mothers, wives, union workers, and, of course, as citizens.

In turn, they altered mainstream political culture, as we still see in a nation polarized over women's reproductive rights, equal pay, and same-sex marriage and in the emergence of a gender gap that rests mostly on the votes of African American women. You could say they helped kick off the cultural wars and you wouldn't be wrong.

As Paul Potter had urged, they had found language for the world in which they lived and loved. In the spirit of the *Port Huron Statement*, they had sought independence and self-determination. Nothing less would do. Rage replaced shame. Entitlement supplanted despair. Activism led to pride.

Nothing would ever be the same again.

19 | The Empire at Home: Radical Pacifism and Puerto Rico in the 1950s

by Andrea Friedman

The *Port Huron Statement* begins with the recognition of paradox. Kids who grew up believing in America's goodness had matured into young adults who now saw "complicated and disturbing paradoxes in our surrounding America. The declaration 'all men are created equal' rang hollow before the facts of Negro life in the South and the big cities of the North. The proclaimed peaceful intentions of the United States contradicted its economic and military investments in the Cold War status quo."[1] If the authors of the *Port Huron Statement* named many contradictions in US democracy, they missed many others, including in their analysis of American foreign policy. They railed against the "warfare state," denounced alliances with the "old colonialists," and especially condemned US policy toward Cuba, but they were completely silent about the fact that America itself remained an imperial power. What scholars have called the "Puerto Rican paradox" was born at the turn of the century, when Puerto Rico was deemed an "unincorporated territory" that was "owned by" but not included within the United States. This paradox was exacerbated in the interwar years when Puerto Rican residents were accorded US citizenship but lacked rights to national representation or many of the protections of the Constitution, and it was heightened during the Cold War when the US government collaborated with Puerto Rican officials to create the impression that it was no longer a colony at all. The *Port Huron Statement*'s silence on Puerto Rico is testament to their success.[2]

Nonetheless, long before youthful white radicals embraced the Young Lords Party and the Fuerzas Armadas de Liberación Nacional (FALN) in the late 1960s and the 1970s, there was a North American solidarity movement advocating Puerto Rico's independence. Its adherents were radical pacifists, and many of them went on to work in pacifist organizations that were key to the creation of the New Left and antiwar movements, such as the Committee for Non-Violent Action, *Liberation* magazine, and the Fair Play for Cuba committee. The story of Puerto Rico's important role in helping to make possible a more visible and more widespread North American anti-imperial solidarity movement has not yet been told. But organizing in support of Puerto Rican independence activists during the early Cold War years not only helped consolidate personal and organizational connections that sustained the antiwar movement of the sixties but also, crucially, yielded an analysis of the role of solidarity workers in anti-imperial struggles that was necessary to the emergence of that movement.

In certain ways, the emergence of 1960s anti-imperialist movements from radical pacifism was itself paradoxical, as it required those who were committed to absolute nonviolence to support the efforts of oppressed peoples who used violence to free themselves. And it was here that the Puerto Rican solidarity movement was key, for it was loosely aligned with the Nationalist Party (NP), which during the early 1950s pursued acts of "self-sacrifice and valor" to draw attention to the US occupation of the island. In 1950 NP members launched an island-wide armed uprising that led to pitched gun battles between insular police and NP supporters, the bombing by the National Guard of two mountain towns, and upward of two dozen deaths. Simultaneously, two NP members, seeking to "make a demonstration" against colonialism, attacked President Truman's temporary residence in Washington. One of the gunmen and a presidential guard died as a result, and three other men were wounded. In 1954, four Nationalists, led by Lolita Lebrón, fired on the House of Representatives, injuring five Congressmen, a protest that was met with the imprisonment of almost all NP leaders in Puerto Rico and the continent.[3] Their pacifist allies sought to put this violence into a broader context, arguing that it had to be compared to the structural violence of the US empire. I suggest that it was in this moment that US activists began formulating a new model of anti-imperial struggle, one that insisted that a radical peace politics could stand in solidarity with those who use violence in national liberation movements.

The Beginnings of a Solidarity Movement

The Puerto Rican paradox had long generated disquiet and discontent on the island, but the demand for independence from the United States proliferated in the desperate days of the Great Depression, when it was voiced across the political spectrum. No advocate was more outspoken than Pedro Albizu Campos, president of the NP. Arguing that Puerto Rico's territorial status was nothing more than an illicit military occupation, he organized quasi-military local units and called for armed struggle—if necessary—against the United States. Federal authorities' unrelenting efforts to suppress the NP, through surveillance, political persecution, and criminalization, produced even greater political turmoil. A series of violent encounters between the Nationalists and colonial officers ended in Albizu Campos's 1937 incarceration in federal prison in Atlanta.[4]

When US officials decided to imprison Albizu Campos on the mainland, they could not know that this would provide the spark for an organized proindependence movement in North America. In 1943 he fell ill and was transferred to a New York City hospital, where he remained until 1947, when he returned to Puerto Rico. A number of intellectuals and activists had protested his arrest and conviction, and on his arrival at Columbus Hospital, Albizu Campos became something of a celebrity. Many progressive New Yorkers sat at his bedside during these months, among them Vito Marcantonio, Pearl Buck, and Dorothy Day. Joining them were the activists who congregated around the Harlem Ashram, founded in 1940 by Jay Holmes Smith and Ralph Templin, both former Methodist missionaries who had been expelled from India for their support of the proindependence movement there.

The Ashram served as home and organizing center for a number of radical Christian peace activists. Many of its residents were affiliated with the Fellowship of Reconciliation (FOR), an international antimilitarist organization whose members had worked since World War I in support of conscientious objectors as well as civil liberties and economic and racial justice. FOR members were early participants in the growing civil rights movement, helping to found the Congress of Racial Equality (CORE) and to pioneer some of the movement's key strategies of nonviolent resistance. Because of these commitments to racial justice, the Ashram was organized as an interracial community. Among those who lived there were African Americans Pauli Murray, James Farmer, and Wilson Head, as well as white pacifists John Swomley, Ruth Reynolds, Abraham Zwickel, and Jean Wiley (later Jean Zwickel). Others, like Dave Dellinger, Bayard Rustin, and lawyer Conrad Lynn—also African American and a former member of the Communist Party—were frequent visitors. The Ashram hosted meetings of the New York branch of CORE and the March on Washington Movement. Its members worked to desegregate the YMCA; marched from New

York to Washington, DC, to protest poll taxes and lynching; and established a play co-op for neighborhood children. Reflecting its founders' earlier experiences in India, they also conducted annual "Free India Day" pickets at the British Embassy.[5]

Living on the border between central and East Harlem, Ashram members worked within the Puerto Rican as well as the African American communities, and some of their Puerto Rican neighbors pushed residents to attend to US as well as British imperialism. In summer 1943, Ashram member Al Winslow brought Nationalist activist Julio Pinto Gandía to dinner. Both draft resisters (Gandía, in accord with an NP policy of noncooperation with the US government, refused induction in the Army), they had met in prison. Gandía urged Ashram residents to visit Albizu Campos in his New York hospital room. Jay Holmes Smith accepted the invitation, and soon after, Ashram residents decided to add the demand to "Free Puerto Rico" to their annual Free India Day demonstration. On January 26, 1944, armed with posters condemning US empire in Puerto Rico as well as British empire in India, they marched through Harlem and then took the subway to the British consulate, where about a dozen were arrested when they set up a picket line. Among them was Ashram assistant director Ruth Reynolds, to whom leadership of the action had fallen because Smith was in Washington conducting a fast for Indian independence. Reynolds's picture made the paper, and Albizu Campos asked that she come to see him. Their meeting changed her life.[6]

Reynolds was a young white woman who had "fallen in" with pacifists while studying in Chicago. Born in North Dakota, she had trained as a teacher but was unable to find a steady job during the depression. In any case, she was more drawn to a life of the mind, so she went off to Northwestern University, where she received a master's degree in English. While there, she volunteered at a settlement house on Chicago's South Side and read Gandhi. In 1941, she completed her degree and moved to the Ashram to take a "training course in total pacifism" offered by FOR. She became one of its most dedicated residents, and while there she developed an uncompromising pacifist stance, accumulated organizing experience, and built relationships with New York and national activists. Her meeting with Albizu Campos reshaped her pacifism in crucial ways. Reflecting later in life, she remembered that "within a month or so of knowing Don Pedro, I really felt that I had to commit myself to the struggle for the independence of Puerto Rico." Many of the radicals she knew were working on behalf of the black freedom struggle, but few were aware of the plight of Puerto Ricans denied their independence. Reynolds believed that as a citizen of the United States, she bore personal responsibility for this injustice. For the next thirty years, she dedicated her life to rectifying it.[7]

In January 1945, Reynolds helped organize the American League for Puerto Rico's Independence (ALPRI). Its members pledged to work for federal recognition of the island's independence, immediate amnesty for all political prisoners, and "full and speedy reparations." The commitment to independence kept ALPRI relatively small, for some whom Reynolds approached were not convinced that granting Puerto Ricans freedom would be good for them, since it would deny them US military protection and financial aid. About fifty people joined, but active members numbered less than a dozen, and almost all were closely associated with the pacifist movement. Many of them also knew Albizu Campos and their ties to him came to shape the positions taken by the group. ALPRI members testified before Congress, monitored United Nations debates about decolonization, and lobbied President Truman. Although Jay Holmes Smith was president, Reynolds and several women close to her—particularly pacifist Thelma Mielke—did most of the work. ALPRI steadfastly rejected any proposed reforms that aimed to make US control over Puerto Rico more palatable, arguing that while these might pave the way to economic development, they also required islanders to "barter away [their] birthright of full freedom" for nothing but a "dependent independence and a dominated dominion."[8]

ALPRI disbanded in 1950, divided over opposition to Nationalist violence, but through the 1950s and into the 1970s, Reynolds went on to organize a number of successors that advocated independence for Puerto Rico, including Americans for Puerto Rico's Independence and the Committee for Justice to Puerto Ricans. She also drew other groups into this campaign. Pacifists were always at the center, including some little-known women such as Mielke, nurse Yolanda Moreno (who would marry Conrad Lynn), Lula Peterson (later married to James Farmer), and Jean Zwickel, as well as men with names familiar to historians of the Old and New Lefts: Dave Dellinger, A. J. Muste, Julius Eichel, Ernest Bromley, Jim Peck, and others who were active in the "revolutionary pacifist" group Peacemakers and the War Resisters League (WRL). Their activism was guided by their recognition, as Reynolds wrote at the time, that only by admitting "individual and corporate responsibility for every act of our government—a sense of responsibility without which democracy is nothing but a lie" could American citizens "begin to free ourselves from the racial and national arrogance that is making our nation a curse in the earth."[9] They believed that advocating Puerto Rican independence was an act of patriotism, intended to make the United States live up to those ideals—a love of freedom and commitment to self-government—that it daily betrayed as a colonial power.

Puerto Rico, Militarism, and the Global Cold War

Ruth Reynolds helped draw pacifists' attention to Puerto Rico, but it was the Cold War that kept it there. Puerto Rico's status as a US possession was especially troublesome at this time, when colonialism and decolonization resided at the center of the struggle between the United States and Soviet Union for the allegiance of the global South. Puerto Rico was crucial to this struggle, as US and Puerto Rican officials collaborated to make it an exemplar of the promises offered by capitalist development to emerging nations as well as a signifier of American support for decolonization. Puerto Rico's majority political party, the Popular Democratic Party (PPD), depended heavily on US support. PPD head Luis Muñoz Marín built his reputation on the foundation of economic development. His highly touted development plan for the island sought to manage systemic unemployment and underemployment by industrializing with the help of US government aid and corporate investment while relying on US citizenship to facilitate unimpeded migration to the continent. American authorities, on the other hand, needed to maintain control over Puerto Rico not only to help them convey the benefits of US-style development to other Latin American nations, nor simply to guard the value of substantial corporate investments on the island, but also because of its continuing and rapidly expanding strategic importance as a site for US military bases. Both the PPD and the Truman and Eisenhower administrations agreed that the colonial relationship should be maintained, then, but they also recognized that its image needed to be recast.[10]

To these ends, they sought to portray Puerto Rico as a "showplace of democracy," but this was no easy task. The island's anomalous status meant that its residents—nominally citizens of both Puerto Rico and the United States—lacked many of the basic rights of self-governance.[11] To resolve this problem, the US government implemented a series of political reforms between 1946 and 1952, all intended to provide Puerto Ricans a greater degree of home rule while leaving imperial power substantially untouched. These included appointing the first indigenous governor in 1946 and then passing an elective governor bill in 1947, followed by the inauguration of Muñoz Marín as governor the following year. In 1950,

Congress passed legislation enabling Puerto Rican officials to write a constitution that island residents could ratify (although Congress also exercised its authority to change that constitution before allowing a ratification vote). The creation in 1952 of the Commonwealth of Puerto Rico (or
Estado Libre Asociado, Associated Free State) accorded Puerto Rican officials authority over a range of domestic policies while depriving them of
control over trade, defense, foreign affairs, currency, and like matters. In
1953, federal and territorial officials declared that, with these reforms, "the
last vestiges of colonialism [have] disappeared in Puerto Rico." After a
rather contentious UN debate, in which Communist states and some
newly independent nations argued that the United States was actually creating "a new form of colonialism," the United Nations endorsed the position that the people of Puerto Rico were now "self-governing."[12]

These moves did help to consolidate both domestic and international
support for US policy, but they also spurred NP members to new levels of
militancy and did little to convince a core of solidarity workers that island
residents were free. Indeed, if the Cold War context prompted limited reform of Puerto Rico's status, it also contributed to intensified pacifist activism on the issue. The cause of Puerto Rico's independence was important to
pacifists precisely because it was vitally connected to their broader concerns
about civil liberties, militarization, and nuclear technology. Once again, it
was Ruth Reynolds—arrested and imprisoned on the island in 1950—who
provided the link between the pacifists' general political commitments and
the specific case of the American empire in the Caribbean.

Reynolds had been living in Puerto Rico for several years while writing
a book about government repression of a 1948 student strike. During that
time she was drawn increasingly into the NP community, attending meetings and befriending its members, although she denied ever joining the organization. In the wake of the 1950 revolt, Reynolds was arrested on charges
of promoting the overthrow of the Puerto Rican government, convicted
under Puerto Rico's Little Smith Act (known locally as *la mordaza*, the "gag
rule"), and sentenced to two to six years in Puerto Rican prisons. Her imprisonment both divided and mobilized the pacifist community. Some of
her erstwhile colleagues in ALPRI abandoned her for betraying pacifist
principles, while others, particularly the radicals in Peacemakers and WRL,
joined together to create the Ruth Reynolds Defense Committee. They organized picket lines and public meetings, arranged for Conrad Lynn to serve
as her legal counsel, published accounts of her case, alerted international
networks, and spoke to audiences in numerous cities on the East Coast and
in the Midwest. From agitating on behalf of Reynolds, whom all of them

had known through the radical pacifist movement, they moved more generally to work in solidarity with supporters of Puerto Rican independence. During her trial, for example, Ernest Bromley, Wally Nelson, and Harlem Ashram cofounder Ralph Templin traveled to San Juan to witness against US empire. They distributed a manifesto in which they apologized for North America's "continuous violence" against the Puerto Rican people, denounced conscription and the militarization of the island, and urged "the people of both the United States and Puerto Rico to rise and, through the power to be found in non-violence, to end one of the worst imperialisms in recent history." "Imperialism," they proclaimed, is "the Real Violence."[13] Reynolds served twenty months in Puerto Rican jails before making bail and appealing her conviction, which was ultimately overturned by the Puerto Rico Supreme Court.

The central contention of Puerto Rican Nationalists had always been that the US presence in Puerto Rico amounted to nothing more than military occupation, and their opposition to conscription of Puerto Rican men during World War II and the Korean War appealed to radical pacifists. After all, members of the two groups first encountered each other in prison as draft resisters during World War II. This confluence between NP and pacifist interests only increased in the early Cold War years as Puerto Rico was militarized in new ways. During World War II, the US Navy and Army both built large installations on Puerto Rico, and between 1942 and 1950, the Navy seized three-quarters of the island of Vieques, encompassing it within an immense military complex in eastern Puerto Rico. Vieques was used for munitions storage and air-to-ground training, including live fire exercises, resulting in the displacement of much of the island's population and severe social and economic dislocation. By the early 1950s, Ramey Air Force Base (originally Borinquen Field) had been transferred to the Strategic Air Command; it housed some of the most advanced weapons of the Cold War, including surveillance aircraft and nuclear-equipped B-36 bombers that could reach into the Soviet Union. Radical pacifists made condemning the US military occupation one of the keynotes of their solidarity work, endorsing the NP position that Puerto Rican men were subject to "conscription without representation" and denouncing militarization of the island as an "act of war against the people of Puerto Rico."[14]

As Puerto Rico's military significance expanded from an outpost overlooking the Panama Canal to an important staging ground for the atomic-age Cold War, the NP placed US nuclear capacity at the center of its rhetoric. In the months before the 1950 uprising, Albizu Campos toured the island, accusing the US of making Puerto Rico its "atomic base and the base for [its] most advanced weapons. . . . Ostensibly, they are inviting the enemy to attack Puerto Rico, which has come to be the Pearl Harbor of the Atlantic." Warning that the island was being transformed into an atomic arsenal that could be used against all of Latin America as well as other "enemies," he railed against US officials' "cynical" belief that "because they possess the atom bomb they can sit on the heads of all human beings. Theirs is a power which respects nothing but brute force."[15]

This rhetoric tallied with pacifists' concerns about the dangers of nuclear technologies. Groups such as the WRL had opposed atomic weapons since the bombing of Hiroshima and Nagasaki. After President Truman's announcement in early 1950 that he had approved development of the hydrogen bomb, radical pacifists ramped up their protests against preparation for atomic warfare, staging fasts, holding public meetings, and conducting civil disobedience. Simultaneously, many of these same activists began speaking out against the nuclearization of Puerto Rico, endorsing Albizu Campos's accusations that the United States had made Puerto Rico an inevitable target for atomic annihilation. And when Albizu Campos personalized these charges, accusing US officials of using atomic weapons to torture *him*, radical pacifists were drawn even further into the Puerto Rico solidarity movement.[16]

During his incarceration after the 1950 uprising, Albizu Campos alleged that electronic or atomic rays were being aimed at him, causing debilitating physical injuries, including weight loss, edema, burns, and fever. Government officials insisted that he was mentally ill and his symptoms self-inflicted, but Albizu Campos countered that he was the victim of "lynching at the height of the atomic era." His health continued to decline, and in 1953, international pressure forced Puerto Rico's governor to release him from prison. When he returned home, his visitors told of seeing blue, silver, or rose-colored rays of light in his bedroom, and his symptoms grew worse. This news was credible to the Nationalists who surrounded him, in part because other prisoners had complained of similar incidents. During summer 1952, for example, Ruth Reynolds and NP women, incarcerated in the same jail as Albizu Campos, told authorities that they experienced electric shocks, temporary paralysis, "vibrations," mental confusion, and "oppression." Nationalists also knew that the US government had a history of using Puerto Rico as a scientific and medical laboratory, and this knowledge shaped their understanding of Albizu Campos's illness. Radical pacifists may not have been cognizant of this history, but as critics of nuclear technology, they did not find such reports incomprehensible, although some of them remained somewhat skeptical.[17]

As concerns grew about Albizu Campos's health, pacifists and NP members worked furiously to determine if he was suffering from radiation sickness, sending a Geiger counter to San Juan and appealing to prominent scientists to investigate. In February 1954, Dave Dellinger wrote to Albert Einstein, asking for his opinion on the matter. Dellinger confessed that he had "considerable reservations" about Albizu Campos's allegations but thought it important to find out whether such an attack was possible. He was delayed in mailing the letter, as a postscript made clear: "The violence in Congress erupted between the time I wrote this letter and the time I got it out. About all I can say is that this probably underlines the urgency of the situation. Apparently those who made the attack are amongst those who accept Albizu's charges." And, indeed, Lolita Lebrón sought to bring Albizu Campos's "barbarous torture" to light when she and her compatriots fired on Congress. Their belief that their leader was being subjected to medical and possibly nuclear experimentation and might die created a context within which the most dramatic action seemed necessary.[18]

The 1954 attack on Congress, which brought together radical pacifist concerns about military and imperial violence, atomic technology, and civil liberties, proved pivotal in the development of US solidarity movements. In its wake, federal and local authorities rounded up Puerto Rican activists in New York and Chicago and on the island, and pacifists organized the Committee for Justice to Puerto Ricans (CJPR) to help defend the dozens who were arrested, tried, and ultimately convicted. This was an exceedingly difficult task given the political context. Bemoaning the state of American civil liberties at the height of the domestic Cold War, the members of this committee worked "to prevent violation of civil rights and all efforts to deepen the atmosphere of hysteria and to extend a regime of repression" in Puerto Rico as well as the United States. Organized a decade after Harlem Ashram residents began to protest US occupation of Puerto Rico, the CJPR included (mostly) men who spanned pacifism from the 1920s to the New Left. Among them were A. J. Muste, who had joined the Fellowship of Reconciliation before the United States entered World War I; World War II–era conscientious objectors like Dellinger, Bayard Rustin, Roy Kepler, and Julius Eichel; and Norman Mailer, Waldo Frank, and Sidney Lens, all of whom would work with the Fair Play for Cuba Committee half a decade later. Some of them—Dave McReynolds and, of course, Dellinger himself—would go on to lead opposition to the war in Vietnam. Although Ruth Reynolds was specifically asked not to join because her close ties to the NP made her a controversial figure, she and her longtime comrade Thelma Mielke did much of the legwork.[19] At the height of McCarthyism, and at a moment when popular support for the politics of the expanding national security state was still very strong, the CJPR consolidated an anti-imperial network and argument, helping to make possible the articulation of a more generalized anti-imperial critique of US policy by the end of the decade.

Still, defending those who engaged in violence posed a real dilemma for radical pacifists, and there were sometimes bitter conflicts within the movement over the decision to assert solidarity with the Nationalists. Many of these pacifists were committed internationalists, and they saw nationalism itself as divisive and archaic—a position that conflicted with the impulse toward nation building among colonized peoples that was rapidly transforming the postwar world.[20] This was a contradiction that would have to be resolved were pacifists to play a role in postcolonial solidarity movements. Another and more fundamental contradiction resided in the willingness of radical pacifists to support those who used violence against the US government. Even if Nationalists understood their efforts as targeted attacks against their oppressors, the predominant response in the United States and abroad was that they were "terrorists" killing (or trying to kill) innocent men. Focusing on civil liberties and political repression provided some cover, allowing activists to sidestep the question of whether NP violence was justifiable.[21] But many radical pacifists drew more broadly on antimilitarist and anti-imperialist principles, situating Nationalist violence as a response to the massive violence of US occupation. For example, the revolutionary pacifists of Peacemakers picketed the Foley Square courthouse where Lebrón and her compatriots were being sentenced. The flyer they distributed made clear that they did not "condone the use of violence by anybody" but pointed out that "the United States is . . . condemning the violence of Puerto Rican Nationalists while practicing violence herself. We believe that, instead of sending Puerto Rican patriots to prison, the American government should TAKE ITS ARMY OUT OF PUERTO RICO." Ruth Reynolds was dismayed and infuriated by the shooting at Congress, but she did not waver in her belief that "empire is in itself the basic violence, and that to oppress with violence is worse than to resist oppression with violence." This was a position that she defended before the grand jury investigating the shooting, a body before which she was summoned about a dozen times. Similarly, activist Julius Eichel wrote Jim Peck, "It is not sound pacifism to hate terror and war, and then close our eyes to the terror and oppression practiced by our own government against a helpless people."[22]

These were lessons that came hard to the pacifist movement. Eichel's letter was written in response to an article in the WRL *News* in which some pacifists defended US policy toward Puerto Rico as critical to establishing democracy and prosperity on the island. Some of these disputes continued in later years. In 1958–59, for example, members of Peacemakers staged a hundred-mile Peace and Good Will Walk, from Guanica, site of the 1898 US invasion, to the American military headquarters in San Juan. Several expatriate pacifists living in Puerto Rico criticized the action because they viewed it as either too supportive of the Nationalist agenda or too critical of US policy.[23] Such outright opposition to solidarity protests was unusual, but many pacifists struggled with the proper way to do such work. Ruth Reynolds consistently argued that pacifists should oppose US empire nonviolently but that it was wrongheaded to lecture Puerto Ricans about the appropriate methods to fight for their freedom. Others took longer to accept this position. Reynolds remembered that Dave Dellinger was "always for me" but that nonetheless it wasn't until the Cuban Revolution that Dellinger truly understood "it's not our duty always to go in somewhere and convert people to pacifism."[24] Her remark suggests that in their engagement with the Puerto Rican liberation struggle from the mid-1940s right up to the time of the Cuban Revolution, pacifists worked out their relationship to national liberation movements. Reynolds played a key role in accomplishing this reconciliation. But she is essentially absent from the historical record, often meriting not even a footnote in accounts of postwar radical pacifism.

Reynolds's invisibility mirrors the continuing silence of US historians— not to mention politicians and pundits—on the American empire in Puerto Rico. Even as historians of the United States have sought to be more attentive to our imperial history, much interest has focused on the Philippines, safely securing US colonialism in the past. Histories of the New Left have reproduced this evasion. When Puerto Rican liberation struggles do appear in these histories—for example, with the founding of the New York branch of the Young Lords in 1969 or the underground revolutionary FALN in the early 1970s—they are often interpreted not as a harbinger of transnational solidarity but as an extension (or imitation) of Black Power, or else as an example of the end of radicalism in misguided forms of violence and even terror.[25] Today, few Puerto Ricans support independence, but they continue to reject the imperial status quo, even as US citizens outside of Puerto Rico and its diaspora seemingly remain oblivious to the injustices and inequalities created there by US policy. Puerto Rico has always had much to tell us about the contradictions of American democracy. As we look forward to new insurgencies, it may serve us well to think again about the Puerto Rican paradox.

20 | Radical Pacifism in the Long 1950s: Forging New Forms of Protest and Dissent

by Marian Mollin

The activists who gathered in November 1960 to protest at the Electric Boat shipyard in New London, Connecticut, considered themselves the wave of the future. There, in the heart of southern New England's military-industrial complex, and after months of organizing peace walks, pickets, and vigils, they came together to oppose the ceremonial launching of the *USS Ethan Allen,* the newest Polaris-class nuclear missile–carrying submarine. As the crowd held signs and sang songs of peace and disarma-

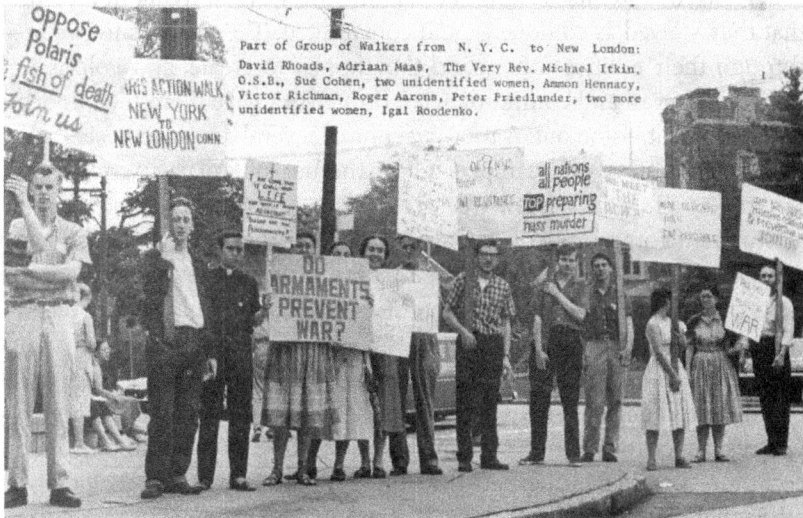

1960 New York-New London Polaris Action Peace Walk. June 1960 *Polaris Action Bulletin* (Marian Mollin)

ment, a small group of young pacifists broke off to make a daring assault on what they identified as "the evil and dangerous policies" of the US government. Jumping into the filthy, icy water of the Thames River, activists Bill Henry and Don Martin swam to the submarine and, despite the retinue of sailors assembled on top, used the red, white, and blue bunting adorning the vessel's hull to pull themselves aboard. Authorities quickly arrested them, as well as seven other activists in a nearby skiff, but the damage had been done. The next day, startling photographs and film footage of swimsuit-clad pacifists scaling the most powerful emblem of US military might immediately appeared on the front pages of the nation's newspapers and in cinema newsreels. Activists and their supporters were elated. After months of staging peace marches and disarmament vigils, leafleting workers, and engaging in community outreach, their dramatic protest had successfully turned Henry, Martin, and the radical pacifist movement they represented into visible symbols of "living protest" against the Cold War. It was a portent of things to come.[1]

Equally important were the less visible dimensions of what was called Polaris Action, the ongoing organizing campaign that had set the stage for this mediagenic event. Since June of that year, hundreds of volunteers had passed through New London to participate in Polaris Action's innovative experiment in nonviolent action and nonviolent living. Some were seasoned veterans of earlier radical pacifist protests. But many others were college-aged students seeking more authentic ways of living in a culture that they viewed as conformist and constrained. They wanted to live in— through their politics—the world they hoped to create, and Polaris Action's egalitarian and communitarian framework gave them the opportunity to try that vision out. A rotating crew of several dozen activists staffed the project's office and camped out at the nearby Polaris Action Farm, staying for a few days, a few weeks, or even a few months as they formed an itinerant community of resistance. Together they shared the drudgery of work and the excitement of risk-taking protest. They divided up the tasks of cooking, cleaning, staffing the office, and organizing demonstrations. They learned the finer points of consensus-based decision making. And as they shared meals together, folded leaflets together, risked arrest together, and engaged in endless discussions of everything from nonviolent resistance to civil rights to vegetarian cooking, they became an action community, a living alternative to the depoliticized and individualistic ethos that defined much of the world around them. In doing so, they believed that they stood at what organizer Brad Lyttle called the "cutting edge" of wider efforts for social and political change.[2]

The Polaris Action campaign of 1960 exemplified two critical components of the radical pacifist movement that it had grown out of: an unswerving determination to publicly confront and challenge the basic tenets of the Cold War and a parallel commitment to do so by creating an idealistic, communitarian, and egalitarian culture of dissent. These priorities grew out of almost twenty years of struggle—beginning with the protests of World War II–era conscientious objectors—to build a revolutionary pacifist movement that would challenge the institutions and practices of violence in all ways, shapes, and forms. Since the early 1940s, this small but influential group of activists had protested against conscription, racial inequality, economic injustice, and the development and deployment of nuclear weapons by using an evolving array of nonviolent direct action and community-building techniques. Although this movement was always small in number, the prominence of its membership—which included such activist luminaries as A. J. Muste, Bayard Rustin, David Dellinger, and Barbara Deming—helped push these ideas and practices into the broader currents of American political dissent.

Historians and scholars have described the radical pacifists of the postwar era as a bridge between the Old and New Left, as a political force that connected the movement to ban atmospheric nuclear weapons testing with the soon-to-be mass opposition to the Vietnam War, and as a movement halfway house that shared skills and resources with other social movements. The writers of the *Port Huron Statement* characterized these radical pacifists, and the larger peace movement that they were a part of, as one of the few "alternatives to helplessness" in the United States. Here, I endeavor to cast them as something a bit different. Through its determination to challenge the Cold War while creating a new kind of culture of dissent, radical pacifism became more than just a bridge between movements or a welcome voice in the wilderness of Cold War conformity. In fact, it established a model of protest and dissent that, as an oppositional undercurrent in the political culture of the postwar years, prefigured the key concerns and values of the New Left.

Challenging the Cold War

Radical pacifism's efforts to challenge the Cold War, the first of these prefigurative qualities, were best exemplified by the increasingly dramatic campaigns the movement waged against nuclear weapons and nuclear weapons testing from the mid-1950s on—culminating with the Polaris Action campaign of 1960–61. Directly inspired by the Gandhian model of nonviolent resistance, which they adopted and translated onto American soil, radical pacifists of the 1940s, 1950s, and early 1960s experimented with a range of direct-action techniques. They organized sit-ins and stand-ins against racial segregation through their work with the Congress of Racial Equality (CORE), held hunger strikes for peace, led marches and pickets for nuclear disarmament, and, in more recent parlance, "occupied" sites directly linked to the Cold War nuclear arms race: the Nevada Test Site, the Pacific Nuclear Test Zone, intercontinental ballistic missile (ICBM) bases, and, in 1960, Polaris submarines. Thus by the late 1950s, they had begun to target the most potent symbols of the Cold War.[3]

These efforts began in earnest during summer 1957, when a group of almost three dozen activists traveled to the Nevada nuclear test site in order to solemnly commemorate the twelfth anniversary of the US atomic bombing of Hiroshima at the end of World War II. They held an overnight vigil in the desert, believing that their presence would force the government to halt a nuclear test planned for that very day. Eleven of them, in an act of civil disobedience, also approached the main gate and attempted to walk onto the site. Federal authorities quickly arrested this smaller group, but the remaining activists stayed at the site until the next morning, when they witnessed a nuclear blast firsthand. By combining several forms of risk taking—arrest, imprisonment, and nuclear contamination—the group hoped to bring attention to their demands for nuclear disarmament. Extensive news coverage of the demonstration, on the CBS and NBC television networks, Fox Movietone, and numerous regional and national newspapers, suggested that the strategies of these "Atom-Lopers," as they were dubbed by the local press, could increase the movement's visibility and provide publicity for its demands.[4]

Radical pacifists followed the Nevada action with a series of increasingly more audacious campaigns. In the winter and spring of 1958, the group attempted to send a ship, manned by a crew of activists, into the Pacific test zone during a planned nuclear test. Their goal was simple: through courage, daring, and sacrifice, they hoped to "arouse the conscience of the world" and generate public outrage over the dangers of nuclear testing. Government antagonism toward the project aided their efforts. As the group's tiny ship, named the *Golden Rule*, made its way through the first leg of its journey, US officials responded by issuing regulations and court injunctions to keep the ship and its crew on land. The men of the *Golden Rule*, however, defiantly refused to obey, and their ongoing attempts to set sail from Hawaii into the test zone sparked repeated arrests, several Coast Guard chases, and even imprisonment. Although they never made it into the Pacific test zone themselves, their ongoing conflicts with the Coast Guard and federal courts led to an unprecedented degree of news coverage and a heightened awareness of their call for an end to nuclear arms. Subsequent efforts included blocking trucks trying to enter a missile plant in Wyoming; camping out for an entire summer at the Strategic Air Command base in Omaha, Nebraska (where activists held nonstop around-the-clock vigils and scaled the fence twice a week); and, beginning in summer 1960, the Polaris Action campaign. Each experiment in civil disobedience brought creative new techniques, as well as their open opposition to the Cold War, into the public eye.[5]

Radical pacifists not only challenged US military policies but directly and publicly questioned the legitimacy of the Cold War framework itself. On the home front, they vocally opposed the anticommunist red baiting that characterized much of American politics at that time—occasionally going as far as picketing in support of imprisoned Communist activists— even though they were openly critical of the Communist Party itself. More important, radical pacifists acted as "equal opportunity" critics who openly condemned the militarism and nuclear policies of both the United States and the Soviet Union. One of their favorite slogans of this time, "No Tests East or West," which appeared on the banners, leaflets, and placards that they held at all of their demonstrations, exemplified this position. By trying to chart an independent path between capitalism and Communism, radical pacifists challenged the notion of a binary Cold War world and instead promoted a radical and nonaligned vision of global peace.[6]

Through all of their nonviolent direct action efforts, radical pacifists of the 1950s helped disrupt the domestic culture of postwar conformity. During a time when few Americans spoke out against the dangers of nuclear war and nuclear testing, instead accepting what historian Laura McEnaney describes as the "militarization of American life," this small but vocal movement highlighted opposition to US policies and, more important, demonstrated to other citizens that it was possible to engage in political dissent.[7]

Building Radical Community

Underneath the more public protests against the Cold War lay the development of an equally radical but less visible experiment in interpersonal politics and political culture that, in important ways, prefigured the "prefigurative" politics of the New Left. Like the writers of the *Port Huron Statement* and the early members of Students for a Democratic Society (SDS), radical pacifists based their movement on the idealistic belief that actually living out their vision of the kind of society they hoped to create would lead to the changes they wanted to see. From this perspective, means and ends were inextricably linked: if activists wanted to construct an egalitarian world, free from violence and exploitation, then they needed to live, work, and act in a nonhierarchical, nonviolent, and cooperative manner. What makes the radical pacifists noteworthy is that they initiated their utopian experiments well over a decade before the founders of SDS began considering such possibilities.[8]

Radical pacifists rooted much of this idealism and utopianism in their various efforts to build community, a tactic they considered necessary to help develop and sustain political resistance. On the most basic level, they did this through the formation of extended activist communities: local, regional, and national networks that provided support and encouragement for activists who found themselves isolated and alone on the fringes of society. Building such communities was a pragmatic organizing strategy for members of a movement that most Americans of the World War II and Cold War eras considered cowardly, disloyal, and treasonous. Radical pacifists had long recognized the importance of creating intentional bonds of solidarity and camaraderie. Despite their hope that they could spark a mass nonviolent movement on par with Gandhi's campaign for Indian independence, they quickly recognized that such a following would not materialize anytime soon and that they were essentially out there on their own. In response, during the 1940s and early 1950s, they focused on forming local fellowship groups, holding regional and national gatherings, and creating mutual assistance plans in the event of imprisonment or arrest. Such endeavors played a central role in sustaining individuals' commitment to the struggle and supporting their collective survival as a movement.[9]

A number took this commitment to community a step further and in the 1950s founded several politically focused experiments in communal living where activists came together, as couples and families, to live in the same household or on a shared piece of land. Often they shared finances in some way, working together in a cooperative business or pooling their economic resources in order to make ends meet. They also shared the essential domestic duties of cooking, cleaning, and childcare. As with the extended activist communities, the goals of these intentional communities were simultaneously practical and idealistic. On the one hand, communal living could facilitate political activism and mobilization by bolstering morale through the ongoing support of an extended household and—through pooling the resources of time, money, and skill—freeing community members up to organize campaigns, risk arrest, and go to jail. On the other hand, the activists who lived in these communities valued them as physical embodiments of the new society they hoped to create. In this way they served, as Dave Dellinger explained, "as examples of alternatives to the existing social set-up."[10]

Then there were the itinerant action communities that sprang up around the prolonged campaigns of protest that characterized the radical pacifist movement of the late 1950s and early 1960s. Focusing their resistance on the most visible symbols of US nuclear policy inevitably meant taking their protests on the road—to Nevada, Omaha, New London, and beyond. And as activists moved, for the duration of these campaigns, away from their homes and hometowns, they created temporary action communities whose members lived and worked together for days, weeks, and sometimes months. Within these communities, activists shared the day-to-day duties of writing press releases, running the mimeograph machines, and organizing demonstrations. They slept and ate as a group, and together they engaged in acts of protest and dissent. Although these communities dispersed when the campaigns they had organized were completed, they created a strong sense of solidarity that helped those involved feel part of something larger than their individual selves.[11]

The Opportunities and Limits of Brotherhood

Finally, one can't discuss postwar radical pacifism without highlighting its egalitarian ethos, the commitment to "brotherhood" and equality that pervaded every aspect of this movement's vision. Reflecting pacifism's historic roots in the Quaker peacemaking tradition, radical pacifists felt called to defend what they described as an egalitarian "human brotherhood." In the world of the 1940s, 1950s, and early 1960s, these activists used "brotherhood" as a gender-inclusive term to signify the creation and preservation of horizontal relationships that deliberately disregarded differences due to race, class, ethnicity, religion, and nationality. It shaped all dimensions of their work.

This egalitarianism served as the foundation of the movement's broad political agenda. It motivated their deeply held revulsion to militarism: in their eyes, violence against another human being was akin to fratricide, an immoral and unconscionable act. But it also led them to embrace other struggles. Radical pacifists believed that in order to uphold the sanctity of "brotherhood," one had to resist all the forms of violence that shaped American life, including economic inequality, political repression, and racial injustice. It brought them into the labor movement, the civil liberties campaigns, and, most notably, the black freedom struggle.

Although radical pacifists claimed "brotherhood" as a gender-inclusive egalitarian ideal, they did not always translate these beliefs into practice. Despite activists' best intentions, their movement's political culture was defined by the fetishizing of what one scholar calls "the masculine spectacular," or what I define as a conflation of masculinity and militancy that rendered women invisible, even when they stood (or swam) side by side with men on the front lines of protest. This was a dynamic that harkened back to the movement's earliest days, when imprisoned war resisters struggled to overcome the public stigma that linked the pacifist refusal to fight to an effeminate form of cowardice that made them less than men. In response, they turned nonviolent risk taking into an alternate form of masculine heroism and courage; they may not have been willing to fight a war, but they were willing to go to jail. But as radical pacifist men worked to create what they literally called a "virile" and comprehensive program for social change, they did so at the expense of the women alongside them. For how could they hold onto their manhood if women's heroism and resistance surpassed their own? Within such a framework, the movement's male leaders viewed courageous and militant female activists as an incomprehensible yet potent threat to their newfound definition of radical pacifist masculinity.[12]

In the 1940s, this attitude took the form of dismissal and exclusion. During World War II, the movement celebrated those who took the greatest risks—who were, by definition, those men who refused to cooperate with conscription and thus ended up in jail. But even in the immediate postwar era, women's participation was not always welcome. In 1947, for example, radical pacifists organized and led a project they called the Journey of Reconciliation. The journey, like the 1961 Freedom Rides that modeled themselves after this early endeavor, sent interracial teams of black and white activists across the states of the upper South on Greyhound and Trailways buses, where they defied Jim Crow seating arrangements, often at great personal risk. All those chosen to participate in the journey, however, were men, even though quite a few women wanted to go. There were practical reasons for the women's exclusion. Organizers expressed the fear that "mixing the races and sexes would . . . exacerbate an already volatile situation." But when women expressed a desire to organize an all-female journey as a follow-up project, one woman recalled that the men "just put their collective feet down." While male activists at the time celebrated women for their inherently peaceable nature, they did not see fit to promote opportunities for female militancy and leadership. It went counter to their understanding of the heroic pacifist male.[13]

By the late 1950s, things had shifted ever so slightly, as radical pacifists found room to accept and acknowledge female militancy but only when it accentuated women's difference from men. When the all-male crew of the *Golden Rule* sailed into the Pacific nuclear test zone in 1958, for example, a predominately female group of supporters, including many of those men's wives, staged an extended occupation and hunger strike at the headquarters of the Atomic Energy Commission that turned into a pacifist celebration of Mother's Day. One year later, after repeated arrests at the gate of the Strategic Air Command in Omaha, Nebraska, another radical pacifist woman gained widespread attention—including a prominent article in the women's magazine *Redbook*—for her willingness to spend six months in prison, separated from her husband and four young children. Her sentencing judge chastised her as a "bad mother." But her fellow activists celebrated "the completeness of her sacrifice" for going to jail to protect her children from the perils of nuclear war. By conflating pacifism and maternalism in this way, and thus highlighting accepted notions of gender difference, male activists could embrace women's protests without undermining their own sense of militant manhood.[14]

The college-aged women of the Polaris Action campaign, however, did not fit easily into this mold, and their experiences reveal the contradictions that pervaded radical pacifism's egalitarian vision. As young single women in revolt against the Donna Reed world of the 1950s, the maternalist frame held little appeal to begin with. Instead, they did their best to highlight the values and motivations that they shared with their male associates and to demonstrate through their actions that they took these values as seriously as did the men. These women took numerous risks during Polaris Action's first summer, fall, and winter. They "manned" the picket lines, acted as public "spokesmen," and became known as the most vigorous and diligent leafleters in the group. One young woman took pride in her ability to withstand being "cursed at, propositioned, and . . . [targeted by] snowballs and stones" while she distributed fliers that winter to workers at the submarine shipyard. And when, in summer 1961, Polaris Action organized civil disobedience demonstrations against the very same submarine that Don Martin and Bill Henry had climbed aboard the previous fall, women took the lead: they defied Navy frogmen as they swam to the vessel and attempted to climb on board, they resisted arrest so defiantly that officers literally had to tie one woman down, and they staged a hunger strike once they were arrested and in jail. One male companion candidly remarked that these female resisters had "left us men in the shadows." Except that they hadn't. Instead, Polaris Action's publications that summer either described these women as "our pretty girls" or, more aptly, literally left them "unidentified" and unnamed. Despite their accomplishments, women's militancy clearly remained too problematic to be embraced by the movement to which they belonged. Neither men nor women protested this marginalization. It simply did not fit the gendered frame of protest that they had come to accept.[15]

As one of just a few models of protest from the long 1950s, radical pacifists provided a simultaneously inspiring and limiting vision of how to achieve social change—although not limiting in the way that many scholars have inferred. This chapter does not hold this movement indirectly responsible for the so-called nihilism of the late 1960s, nor does it subscribe to the paradigm of radical declension that so many other writers have advanced.[16] Radical pacifism, in fact, contributed much of positive value to the political culture inherited by the writers of the *Port Huron Statement*. The radical pacifist commitment to confront and challenge the Cold War through nonviolent direct action visibly highlighted cracks in the mold of postwar political consensus and helped pave the way for a broader critique of US foreign policy. Similarly, by advancing a political culture defined by idealistic, communitarian, and egalitarian values, the movement served as a bold counterweight to the depoliticized individualism celebrated by so much of postwar America and as a potential model for organizing and action. At the same time, the marginalization of the movement's female activists highlighted contradictions in radical pacifism's egalitarian vision, contradictions that it passed on to activists who followed in their wake. It was a complicated heritage that helped shape the struggles of the next generation.

21 | An Ending and a Beginning: James Boggs, C. L. R. James, and *The American Revolution*
by Stephen M. Ward

In August 1967, the venerable black radical C. L. R. James delivered a speech in London on the much-discussed topic of "Black Power." The slogan had generated considerable debate since it erupted onto the American political scene one year earlier, and James felt well suited to interpret its meaning and significance for his British audience. "I believe this slogan is destined to become one of the greatest political slogans of our time," he began. "What I aim to do this evening is to make clear to all of us what this slogan Black Power means, what it does *not* mean, *cannot* mean."[1] Drawing on his vast knowledge of black political struggles and his extensive experience in Pan African and radical politics, including the fifteen years he spent in the United States (1938–53), James proposed to break through the fog of confusion—"from both the right and also the left"—that surrounded the concept of Black Power. The slogan was not, he insisted, empty rhetoric or racial chauvinism, as some critics then charged, nor was it doomed to political futility. "Too many people see Black Power and its advocates as some sort of portent, a sudden apparition, as some racist eruption from the depths of black oppression and black backwardness," James declared. "It is nothing of the kind. It represents the high peak of thought on the Negro question which has been going on for over half a century."[2] Yet James did not shed much light on the specific character or unique sources of Black Power thought, and he offered little insight into the range of activists, thinkers, and ideas that animated the movement.

His failure to do so is noteworthy, since one of his former political comrades, James Boggs, was an influential and well-respected figure in the Black Power movement. Boggs had already helped create an infrastructure for the movement, including the short-lived Organization for Black Power in 1965—before Stokely Carmichael and his Student Nonviolent Coordinating Committee (SNCC) colleagues adopted the term in 1966—had published several theoretical essays, and frequently delivered speeches or participated in public discussions on this new trend. In early September 1967, the month after C. L. R. James delivered his London speech, Boggs served as chair and commentator on a panel regarding Black Power at the third annual Socialist Scholars Conference in New York City. His remarks described Black Power not solely as a movement against racial oppression but as one arising from broader historical dynamics and thus holding a deeper revolutionary potential. "At the very heart of the concept of Black Power," he asserted, was the recognition that the black population represented "the growth of a force inside this society that is in fundamental antagonism with this society." This antagonism was "based upon the historical development of production inside the U.S.A." that was making the black masses expendable as laborers. This, he said, compelled the black movement to push beyond the struggle for rights toward a struggle to claim political power. "Black Power," Boggs declared, "raises the fundamental question of the concrete organization and mobilization for taking power" and thus can "lay the basis for creating a new political and social order."[3]

Speaking in London, James saw Black Power as the natural continuation and maturation of black political thought inside and outside of the United States, whose leading figures such as W. E. B. Du Bois, Marcus Garvey, George Padmore, and Frantz Fanon emphasized pan-Africanism and anticolonial revolt. By contrast, Boggs understood Black Power as an outgrowth of specific conditions and changes within the United States and of African Americans' position within it, making them "the chief social force for the revolt against American capitalism."[4] This thesis, developed at the start of the decade when Boggs was a prominent member of James's organization, known as Correspondence, had initiated a political break between the two during 1962—after which Boggs and his wife and political partner, Grace Lee Boggs, came to play an independent role lasting decades more in Detroit's black left.

Correspondence

In 1951, after a decade working within the American Trotskyist movement, C. L. R. James and his political collaborator Raya Dunayevskaya established their own independent Marxist organization under the name of Correspondence. The group relocated its base from New York to Detroit, the center of the American industrial working class, and set out to publish a "worker's" newspaper (also called *Correspondence*) dedicated to presenting the ideas, experiences, and desires of the American working class. Correspondence rejected the idea of a vanguard party—that is, a political group whose task is to conceive of a program for the workers and to guide them in their struggle—arguing instead that workers have the capacity to organize themselves and create their own methods of social transformation, without the leadership of radical parties or even labor unions. It was this idea—the spontaneity and self-activity of workers fulfilling their historical role as agents of revolution—that Correspondence considered their distinctive contribution to Marxist practice and revolutionary theory. James Boggs, an auto worker and union activist who joined Correspondence soon after its arrival in Detroit, in many ways personally embodied the group's vision of revolutionary agency.

Boggs's political trajectory had its roots in his upbringing in rural Marion Junction, Alabama, where his experiences with family, black community life, and the racial codes of the South largely conditioned his worldview and set the stage for his eventual political outlook.[5] Upon his graduation from Dunbar High School in the mining town of Bessemer outside of Birmingham, Boggs left Alabama for Detroit. Having just celebrated his eighteenth birthday, Boggs was following family members and others from his community who had gone to the Motor City in search of employment in the auto industry. Finding such jobs hard to come by during the Depression, he went back out on the road, traveling by freight train through the western states and to the South again. He returned to Detroit during World War II and landed a job at the Chrysler Jefferson factory, joined his plant's local union of the United Auto Workers (UAW), and started a twenty-eight-year career as auto worker and labor activist. His work experience during World War II allowed Boggs a chance to explore a range of radical political organizations, including the Communist Party, and to grapple with Marxism. At the same time, he participated in local black community struggles against various forms of segregation. Over the course of the 1940s, these three distinct but at times overlapping spaces— the union, civil rights activism, and radical politics—fostered Boggs's intellectual and political development. By the end of the decade—as the UAW purged its leftists and the existing radical groups had lost their appeal—he was a black radical in search of new opportunities for political activism and intellectual engagement. Correspondence, both the organization and the newspaper, provided these opportunities, and over the course of the 1950s, they became the primary venues for his intellectual and political work.[6]

The political tensions that would eventually lead to the 1962 break with James had their roots in the group's responses to major political developments in 1956–57. This was precisely the moment at which Boggs assumed leadership of the organization. James, who had been forced to leave the United States due to his immigration status in 1953 just as the group launched its newspaper, remained the group's central figure, attempting to exercise leadership of the organization through frequent and often lengthy letters from London to his American comrades. Moreover, Correspondence suffered a severe blow in 1955 when an internal conflict led Dunayevskaya and about half of the organization's seventy to seventy-five members to split off and form a rival group. The remaining members suspended publication of *Correspondence* as they reorganized—and the Boggses emerged as the group's primary leadership, with Grace Lee serving as editor of the newspaper and James elected chairperson. The group's reorganization coincided with three momentous political events of 1956–57—the Hungarian Revolution, the independence of Ghana, and the Montgomery bus boycott—that energized the organization and renewed its members' faith in their specific vision of revolutionary change. Everyone in the group believed that this was a moment of great revolutionary potential and that as revolutionary Marxists they had a contribution to make toward realizing that potential. However, there existed subtle differences within the group regarding how they understood this moment, and in these differences there existed the early signs of political division between James and Boggs.

Hungary, Ghana, and Montgomery

When spontaneous antigovernment protests broke out in Budapest, Hungary, and quickly spread across the country in late October 1956, James immediately and excitedly championed the uprising as a great leap in the world working-class movement. He wrote to his American comrades instructing them to orient their theoretical work around this most significant development. What excited him most were the workers councils, which industrial workers formed during the revolution as their own rank-and-file organizations; James saw this dimension of the revolution as a historical validation of Correspondence's most central ideas—namely, their belief in the spontaneous organization of the working class, their unequivocal opposition to bureaucratic state management, and their faith in the capacity of working-class self-activity and workers' self-governance not only to expose the bankruptcy of the oppressive bureaucratic elite but also, ultimately, to replace it. On November 4, 1956, six thousand Russian tanks entered Hungary and put down the revolt, but this did not temper James's assessment of the revolution's historical significance. The day after Soviet troops crushed the rebellion, James wrote to the group again, making his point in even stronger terms: "I don't think you all recognize what the Hungarian Rev'n means . . . *Since 1917 nothing has so shaken the world.*"[7]

Such allusions to the Russian revolution of 1917 appeared frequently in James's assessments of Hungary, and he did not use them lightly. Since James's earliest days in the Trotskyist movement (which defended the Bolshevik revolution while decrying the dictatorial state Stalin constructed afterward), the Russian revolution loomed in his consciousness as the singular event in modern world history and undisputed flashpoint in Marxist theory. It was his key reference point and benchmark for assessing Hungary's historical significance as a revolutionary workers' revolt against the Stalinist state, even though it was suppressed. He also repeatedly said Hungary represented something new in the theory and practice of revolution. "I hope you realise that the present crisis is one of the greatest turning points of history," he wrote in one of his letters to the group. "The Hungarian Revolution is the ultimate. There cannot be a future revolution that can surpass it. I doubt if there will be many to equal it."[8]

James's celebration of Hungary and elevation of it over other struggles is striking given cotemporaneous developments. He was, for example, writing in the shadow of the 1955 Bandung conference, in the midst of the Suez crisis, and on the cusp of liberation movements across Africa. Moreover, the surge of the civil rights movement in the mid-1950s was beginning to threaten the racial order of the United States. Of these and other spaces of political ferment he was well aware. But in asserting Hungary's singular significance, he was also asserting Correspondence's singularity. That is, he believed that Correspondence had a unique role to play in interpreting Hungary as part of a world revolutionary advance.

Boggs, however, did not share this enthusiasm. Writing to James at the end of November 1956, Boggs took issue with Correspondence's nearly singular focus on Hungary over the preceding month, and he sharply called into question the group's excitement over Hungary relative to popular insurgencies in Africa and Asia: "The whole organization is reading and talking about the Hungarian revolution night and day as if this is all that is happening in the world. . . . Now, with me, I am excited over any revolt. I don't care if it is only a sporadic one in the shop that lasts only half a day. But I can't get half as excited over the Hungarian revolt as I can over the colonial revolts." Boggs urged a fuller appreciation among his comrades of the revolutionary potential in the Afro-Asian states and liberation movements. He saw in this rising Third World, with its nationalist ferment and Bandung-style spirit of nonalignment, a political creativity and the potential to reconfigure global politics and fashion revolutionary change the world over. Moreover, Boggs regarded the potential of Hungary to shape the contemporary political situation as limited. "So far as I am concerned the Russians only had the Hungarians for about 12 years, but the British have had the Egyptians and all these countries for over a hundred years. I feel that the colonial question is going to go far beyond the Hungarian question," he wrote. "The Hungarian revolt is small and isn't going to have the world-wide repercussions that the colonial revolts have. It just isn't," he insisted. "That colonial question is going to shake up the whole world."[9]

Boggs insisted that the nationalist uprisings, because of the colonial peoples' historically constituted subordinate position in the world political economy, offered something that the other uprisings could not. "All I can see that Russia and the West can give to the world is technological advancement." On the other hand, anticolonial revolts were fighting for "a new form of organization of life," a struggle that included but went beyond economic arrangements or relations of production. "Western civilization has been geared to production and all I see coming out of it is some psychological attempt to reorganize production. We have been so tied up in materialism in Western civilization." The colonial nations, by contrast, had the potential to break from this. Admittedly, they have "a few corrupt puppets," he said, who have "been paid off by both the U.S. and Russia" and who remain committed to the patterns and values of the existing order. "But the public in these countries have not been raised up in materialism and they have a much better chance to find a better civilization that isn't directly wrapped up in production." To amplify his point, Boggs offered a comparison between "Nkrumah's country" and its West African neighbor Liberia. "Liberia has its puppets from America and they are Negroes and they are profiting off the country. Nkrumah isn't doing that."[10]

Boggs knew that his reference to "Nkrumah's country" would be meaningful to James. Kwame Nkrumah was the leader of the anticolonial movement in the Gold Coast, the West African nation that, at the time of Boggs's writing, was less than four months away from achieving independence from Britain. James and other members of Correspondence (including Grace Lee) had met Nkrumah during World War II when Nkrumah was a student in the United States and an aspiring anticolonial leader. Despite James's connections to Nkrumah and his long-standing interest in the Gold Coast struggle, however, he apparently paid very little if any attention to it during the months leading up to independence. During this period there seems to have been no discussion within the group about the Gold Coast revolution or its impending independence. This is surprising, given James's work since the 1930s theorizing and struggling for African independence. As he would proudly recall in the preface to the 1963 edition of his book *The Black Jacobins*, the closing pages of the study, originally published in 1938, "envisage[d] and were intended to stimulate the coming emancipation of Africa." When the book originally appeared, he boasted, "Only the writer and a handful of close associates thought, wrote, and spoke as if the African events of the last quarter century were imminent"—that is, precisely the post–World War II upsurge of nationalist politics and mass protest in colonial Africa, resulting in dozens of newly independent states.[11] Ghana was the first of these south of the Sahara, and under Nkrumah's leadership, the new republic self-consciously became a touchstone for a renewed Pan Africanist project and vision of African liberation that owed no small debt to James and his labors.

The September 1956 announcement of the date for Ghana's independence preceded the uprising in Hungary by a month; most of the group's activity during the end of 1956 centered on the significance of Hungary and the need to project the group's analysis of it by drafting, collectively, a special pamphlet on the subject. Then at the end of January 1957, James received an invitation from Kwame Nkrumah to attend Ghana's independence ceremonies in early March. His initial response showed limited interest or enthusiasm, though he added, "I am sure I ought to go. . . . How big the occasion is in the minds of the political world is shown by the fact that Nixon is going."[12] He left for the Gold Coast on February 24, and his experiences during the two-week visit deepened his appreciation for Ghana's independence movement. He "spent a social evening" with Nkrumah, his cabinet, and the Central Committee of the Convention People's Party (CPP). James found the building of the CPP to be the most significant historical aspect of the (Ghanaian) revolution, even describing it as "the greatest political achievement in Africa for a hundred years."[13]

Shortly after his return to London, James gave his strongest statement yet about the importance of Ghana and its priority in his and the group's work. "I propose to postpone the Hungarian pamphlet for 4-6 weeks," he wrote to the group, "and do instead a 70,000 word book on Ghana." This reprioritization reflected the lofty expectations he had for the book. For one thing, he anticipated that it would at once be a commercial success. He also believed it would serve as an articulation of "our *whole program* in a most concrete context, for Ghana and for everybody else." As such, the book would be "a flying start for the general publicizing" of the group's ideas in Europe, the United States, and colonial Africa.[14]

James proposed to build on his past work, particularly *Black Jacobins*. Here he would show how he had in that book anticipated the African revolution that Ghana represented, but he would also revise the theory of colonial revolution articulated in *Black Jacobins*. Whereas the earlier work had linked the success of the colonial revolution to European proletarian mass movements, this new book would assert that "the African Revolution (as a process) is no longer to be seen as supplementary to or subordinate to the revolution in Western Europe." This was very close to the position that Boggs had articulated the preceding fall when the organization began to analyze the Hungarian revolution.[15]

James wrote to the group again the very next day, this time introducing a new point of focus to his analysis of Ghana. He would soon be meeting Martin Luther King Jr., and he hastened to point out that "Nkrumah has worked on much the same ideas as Luther King." Both, he said, had accomplished something "profoundly" revolutionary. The Ghana book would include a section on the Montgomery bus boycott that "should make both sides of the Atlantic aware of what is involved."[16] This letter, dated March 21, 1957, clearly shows that James had an appreciation for the Montgomery struggle before he met King, but this appreciation would grow even stronger three days later when they met.

On the afternoon of March 24, 1957, James and his wife Selma welcomed to their London home Martin Luther King Jr. and Coretta King for lunch and conversation. The Kings related the remarkable story of the bus boycott, giving a firsthand account of the mood occasioned by Rosa Parks's act of defiance, the response of local leaders, the rallying of the black community, and the building of a mass movement.[17] The next day, James penned a letter to his comrades in the United States eagerly recounting the meeting. "I have stopped everything to do this," he began, "because in my opinion it is extremely urgent that you study it and penetrate as deeply as possible into what I have been trying to say over the last week or two."[18] James related in some detail the events of the boycott's initial days, focusing especially on the process by which King emerged as the leader. James then offered commentary on the movement's political and theoretical implications. Throughout the six-page letter, James issued unreserved praise for the boycott. Ranking it as "one of the most astonishing events in the history of human struggle," he implored his comrades not to miss the profound historical statement registered by the Montgomery movement. "I hope no-one underestimates the tremendous inner power of a movement which results in 99% of a population refusing to ride in the buses for over a whole year. . . . It is one of the most astonishing events of endurance by a whole population that I have ever heard of."[19]

James, however, did not see Montgomery as singular. The true significance of the boycott, as he saw it, derived from the connections and parallels between Montgomery and Ghana—and both of them to Hungary—and it was these connections that most interested and excited him. "The more I look at this," he wrote, referring to the parallels between Montgomery and Ghana, "the more I see that we are in the phase of a new experience which demands the most serious analysis."[20] He urged his American comrades to see Hungary, Ghana, and Montgomery as an interconnected whole, one that posed a "warning to all revolutionaries not to under estimate the readiness of modern people everywhere to overthrow the old regime."[21]

On the face of it, the attention that James devoted to Ghana and Montgomery during spring 1957 seemed to suggest that the distance was narrowing between his and Boggs's positions as they had appeared the prior fall. The historical and theoretical significance that James assigned to the Ghanaian revolution—declaring it a milestone in world revolutionary activity, linking it with Montgomery, a major event in the black American struggle, and placing it on par with (rather than subordinate to) Hungary—could easily be read as James answering Boggs's plea for the group to give more attention and weight to the anticolonial revolts. But James's analysis rested in a political framework that Boggs found increasingly restrictive. The core of their differences was this: Boggs highlighted the *racial assertion* at the heart of these two movements, while James stated their most salient feature to be *popular insurgency* as such. James surely recognized these two movements as marking major advances in black and Pan African political struggle, but unlike Boggs, that was not the framework within which he analyzed or approached them.

By 1957 Boggs and James were moving along divergent theoretical paths. While both men remained committed to the project of building a revolutionary Marxist organization, they developed competing and ultimately incompatible interpretations of the revolutionary process that led them to identify different sources and spaces of revolutionary change, both as a theoretical question and as an analysis of the contemporary political world. Boggs urged Correspondence to see Ghana and other anticolonial revolts as a revolutionary breakthrough precisely because they wrote the newest and most transformative chapter in the struggle against colonialism and the domination of Western Europe over racialized people in the Third World.

Boggs embraced Marxism but never to the same level of theoretical depth and commitment as James. The difference in the two men's relationship to Marxism became more pronounced over the next four years, as Boggs's political engagements and experiences led him to move away from, revise, or reject aspects of Marxist theory. In particular, he focused his intellectual and political work in two areas during the late 1950s and early 1960s that significantly influenced his thinking about Marxism: the rise and impact of automation and the evolving black struggle in the United States. He identified these social and historical forces as producing the most fundamental contradictions in American society, and this analysis became central to his vision of a distinctly American revolution to come.

The Real Question Is the American Working Class

Boggs's interest in automation derived from what he saw and experienced. As an auto worker, a union member, a resident of an East Side Detroit neighborhood, and a member of the *Correspondence* publishing committee, he engaged the impact of automation on the auto industry and the city of Detroit from multiple angles. He saw how the implementation of the new technology at Chrysler led to the elimination of an entire shop (and its eighteen hundred jobs) at his factory; he took note of automation-related job loss at factories across the city, including the impact on suppliers and independent manufacturers who were forced to close; and he talked to fellow workers, often reporting on or soliciting their first-person narratives about their responses to automation and the changes it brought in their plants, lives, and communities. Moreover, Boggs witnessed the failure of the UAW to craft any substantial response to all this.

He began thinking and writing about automation during the early 1950s, just as a national debate was emerging about the meaning and potential impact of this new technological advance in production. He grappled with the main concerns in this debate, which revolved around the problems of worker displacement and unemployment. But he also posed larger questions about production and the deeper social implications of automation: What did automation mean, as a social question, for the next generation of would-be auto workers who would likely face obsolescence? Rather than simply taking a defensive posture of protecting jobs, how should auto workers respond to automation? If automation signaled a new era of production (as he came to believe it did), what new roles should workers and unions assume in production? What new social possibilities could this new productive capacity open up?

Boggs and James agreed that the advent of automation was pushing society toward crisis. However, the book that James completed in 1958, *Facing Reality*, came to a very different conclusion than did Boggs regarding the ultimate meaning of automation for workers and social transformation. "It is from the growing realization that society faces total collapse," James wrote in *Facing Reality*, "that has arisen the determination of American workers to take the control of total production away from the capitalists and into their own hands. Up to now American workers have only organized to defend themselves from the machine inside the individual factories. Now, in defense of all society, they are being driven to organize themselves to regulate total production . . . far more than in any country, the automation of industry in the United States is creating the actual conditions for a Government of Workers Councils."[22]

Boggs's experiences as an autoworker inspired no such confidence in the acumen or political vision of American industrial workers. He saw no indication that workers would seize the control of production and respond to automation in the way that *Facing Reality* predicted. To the contrary, based on what he saw happening in his plant and in Detroit generally, Boggs argued that automation was further weakening workers' power. Moreover, he feared that it would deepen their participation in and ideological commitment to consumption-driven progress, a topic he lamented in one of his early *Correspondence* articles on the impact of automation. This underscores a growing difference between Boggs and James regarding the role of the American working class. For James, automation would propel the working class to assume its historic role: by taking control of production and then creating structures of self-government in the plant, workers would lead the way for transforming society and thus fulfill the role assigned to them in Marxist theory as the agent of revolutionary change. By contrast, Boggs argued that automation represented a new stage of production that was causing the reduction rather than expansion of the industrial workforce, thus compelling a rethinking of Marx's scenario of revolution. In place of the industrial working class, Boggs inserted

African Americans—who as group, he said, were being made expendable by automation and whose escalating political movement was throwing the nation into crisis—as the social force best placed to lead a revolution in the United States.

Not surprisingly, Boggs's theoretical projections about the revolutionary potential of the black movement paralleled his activist trajectory. Over the course of the 1950s, he steadily devoted less energy to the union and more to black activist politics. By 1961 Boggs was thoroughly immersed in a network of black radicals, both in Detroit and locally, that operated outside of and often challenged the racial liberalism of the mainstream civil rights movement.

In April 1961, *Correspondence* ran a front page story titled "Tide of Afro-American Nationalism is Rising," which captured some of this political current. The article also illustrated how, under the editorial control of James and Grace Lee Boggs, the paper was transitioning from its original identity as a *worker's paper* to what we might call a *black movement paper*—that is, one devoted to chronicling and advancing black activist politics. The article, which carried no byline but Boggs likely wrote, reported on the rising membership and influence across the country of new nationalist groups whose significance "lies in the fact that they do not want integration into American society as it is. By the totality of their rejection of existing society and their refusal to compromise with it, they are bringing the American revolution closer."[23]

The explicit articulation of this vision of revolution—led by the black struggle and not the working class—in the pages of *Correspondence* called forth a full blown crisis in the organization. The conflict actually erupted in January 1961. The group decided to publish an issue on the Cuban Revolution, but Boggs and Martin Glaberman, a committed member of the organization going back to the early days of James and Dunayevskaya, proposed contrasting formats. Glaberman proposed running an all-Cuba issue with the back page in Spanish. Boggs opposed this idea, arguing that the issue should contain some continuation of the paper's analysis of "the American situation"—that is, the black struggle and other expressions of popular protest in the United States—which he believed was the paper's primary responsibility. Glaberman succinctly captured the gathering conflict, writing to James that "the special Cuba issue has brought out certain substantial differences among us. . . . The real question involved is not Cuba but the American working class."[24] At the end of the year, Boggs wrote and submitted to the organization a document articulating his thinking regarding these now hotly contested ideas. Its focus was to be "the potentialities of the American revolution," by which he meant an examination of the prospects and likely character of a distinctly American revolution. He offered an analysis of the recent historical, political, and economic development of the United States, a reappraisal of the Marxist scenario of revolution in light of this analysis, and finally a call for a theory of an American revolution appropriate for the time. "I have felt that there was a great need for such a document," Boggs wrote to the group at the end of 1961, "because America itself now stands as the citadel of capitalism and it is here more than any place else in the world that the question of whether society will always be governed by capitalism has to be tackled."[25] The document that Boggs produced, titled "State of a Nation—1962," drew considerable fire from James, Glaberman, and others in the group for its departure from Marxism. This provided the final push toward the split.

In January 1962, C. L. R. James brought a close to his long political relationship with James and Grace Lee Boggs by declaring, "Henceforth I break all relations, political and personal, with all who subscribe to that resolution."[26] By March, James and Grace Lee Boggs had formally left Correspondence (though they maintained control over *Correspondence* newspaper), marking the end of one stage of their activists careers and the beginning of another.

"State of a Nation" became the basis of Boggs's first book, published in the following year. James and Grace Lee Boggs shared the document with various people in their widening network of associates and friends, including W. H. "Ping" Ferry, vice president and cofounder of the Center for the Study of Democratic Institutions and initiator in 1964 of the Ad Hoc Committee on the Triple Revolution in Cybernation, Weaponry, and Human Rights (of which James Boggs was a member). In April 1962, Ferry brought the manuscript to the attention of Leo Huberman and Paul Sweezy, the editors of the socialist journal *Monthly Review,* who agreed to publish the work. It appeared first as the ninety-six-page July–August 1963 double summer issue of *Monthly Review* and then as a paperback book, *The American Revolution: Pages from a Negro Worker's Notebook,* published by Monthly Review Press in October.[27]

Amid an eruption of books on "the Negro revolt" and a similarly exploding body of writing on poverty and economic production, *The American Revolution* arrived at a pivotal moment in the civil rights movement, and its unique and thought-provoking assessment of the movement's meaning and possible trajectory established its author as an original and penetrating analyst of the black freedom struggle. The book, however, is not only or even principally about the civil rights movement or black protest. Its starting point, both narratively and analytically, is the labor movement and its failure in the face of changes in the industrial economy brought on by automation. Boggs argued that automation was making black labor obsolete, turning a generation of young people into "outsiders"—a group of people who had no real prospects of entering the system. This fact, he said, meant that the civil rights movement would be pushed beyond a struggle for rights to the question of the reorganization of society, and this would involve the struggle for black political power. By emphasizing the need and prospect for black political power in relationship to the historical development of the United States, the book catapulted Boggs into a national debate during the early 1960s about automation and the future of the industrial economy and set the stage for him to emerge as a key figure in the Black Power movement.

22 | The Religious Origins of Reies López Tijerina's Land Grant Activism in the Southwest

by Ramón A. Gutiérrez

In the history books that chronicle the ethnic Mexican experience in the United States, two men are hailed as its most important civil rights leaders: César Chávez and Reies López Tijerina. César Chávez is often compared to the Reverend Dr. Martin Luther King Jr. as an activist who demanded better wages and working conditions for farmworkers through peaceful, time-tested unionization strategies. Chávez's practice of nonvio-

Reies López Tijerina and supporters, 1969. Photograph by Mark G. Bralley

lence, his fasts, and his pilgrimages, along with his nationwide boycotts of different crops (table grapes, lettuce, strawberries), led to his sanctification as the Mexican American Gandhi, a legacy that is now more hotly contested.[1]

Reies López Tijerina is probably a name many have never heard before. In the historiography, he is depicted as the *mecha*, as the spark that unleashed the militant Chicano struggle for national liberation in the 1960s. He took up arms and seized federal lands, thus emboldening young Chicano men to advocate a militant nationalism throughout the Southwest, demanding jobs, educational reform, and an end to the exercise of arbitrary and unwarranted state force. Some Chicanos even harbored the utopic dream of building an independent nation-state called Aztlán and took their inspiration for regaining lost lands from the Alianza Federal de Mercedes (Federal Alliance of Land Grants), the organization Tijerina founded in 1963 to seek the return of communal lands taken by the US government after the Mexican War in 1848. In 1967 both *Newsweek* and the left-wing *Militant* called Tijerina the "New Malcolm X." On April 20, 1968, the *Saturday Evening Post* went further, transforming Tijerina into a caricature by translating his name into English as "King Tiger." The intent was clear: the magazine meant to link Tijerina to the frightening image of the Black Panthers.[2]

Reies López Tijerina was born into a sharecropping family near San Antonio, Texas, in 1926. As a boy, he regularly migrated with his family to Michigan, following the crop cycles of cotton and sugar beets. At the age of fifteen, he had a religious conversion and decided to become a preacher, and in 1946, he began his public life as a fundamentalist Pentecostal affiliated with the Assemblies of God. For several years, he crisscrossed the Southwest staging revivals and preaching a fiery end-time theology. How did this conservative religious restorationist get transformed into a violent revolutionary? How did this itinerant preacher railing against the corrupting influences of modernity, heralding the millennial return of Jesus Christ and offering salvation, healing, Holy Spirit baptism, and tongues speech, become a cultural nationalist seeking the creation of the Chicano nation of Aztlán? The short answer is that the historiography on Tijerina is simply wrong. In their fervor to write a useable history, a history that would inflame the popular imagination to national revolution through racial revolt, a whole generation of Old Left and New Left historians fundamentally distorted Tijerina's ideology, secularized his religious message, and elevated a carefully planned citizen's arrest gone wrong as a major act of Chicano warfare, as the *mecha*, the spark of the revolution.[3]

* * *

Histories of the 1960s, New Left studies of the opposition to the war in Vietnam, and Chicano and Chicana historiography of the last forty years myopically begin the narratives of the Mexican American civil rights movement with two moments. The first is the September 16, 1965, strike against growers in California's Central Valley. Led by César Chávez, it was followed by a pilgrimage from Delano to Sacramento, California, in 1966 and a series of fasts by Chávez to bring attention to his unionization campaign. I want to focus on the second moment, a June 5, 1967, courthouse scuffle in Tierra Amarilla, New Mexico, led by members of the Alianza Federal de Mercedes, a group of land grant heirs and sympathizers, which Tijerina began and served as its president. This courthouse fracas is now seen as the catalytic event that birthed Chicano radicalism.

The courthouse incident was the climax of an ongoing struggle between the Alianza and its archenemy, District Attorney Alfonso Sanchez, that dated back several years. On October 15, 1966, with great fanfare and glaring national television cameras recording, Tijerina and members of the Alianza seized portions of the Kit Carson National Forest, claiming that the land had been fraudulently stolen from their ancestors at the end of the nineteenth century. While personal familial plots, which constituted one part of the land grant Spain (and later Mexico) awarded colonists for the settlement of the realm, could indeed be bought and sold as personal property, the second part of these *mercedes*, the ancient commons (known as *ejidos*), were inalienable communal property vested in the town. At the end of the nineteenth century, however, the US federal government declared that these communal lands belonged to the sovereign, not to the towns, and as the area's new sovereign was the United States, formally established by victory in war, the lands now belonged to the federal government.

That was precisely the reasoning challenged by the Alianza members whose communal lands had been appropriated by the federal government to form the Kit Carson National Forest. They invaded the space en masse, intending to restore the original land grant of 1706, given by Spain's king to Francisco Salazar as the site of a new town, San Joaquin del Rio de Chama. Reclaiming that heritage by declaring the forest tract to be the Free City-State of San Joaquín del Rio de Chama, Tijerina and his followers elected a mayor and deputized several marshals to patrol the town. When National Park Service rangers eventually arrived, they were arrested, tried by the members of the town, found guilty of trespassing, and released with death threats. For two weeks, the Alianza maintained the occupation, arguing that they were the legal owners of the land, and if the federal government wanted to evict them, then the government would have to prove the validity of its claim.

The federal authorities were unwilling to do that. District Attorney Alfonso Sanchez repeatedly warned the Alianza and its president that the title to northern New Mexico's lands had been adjudicated in the 1890s and that little could be done to address those dispossessions now. But when the national press moved on to their next news story, so too did the Aliancistas, ending the standoff.[4] Sanchez, in any case, was determined not to allow the Alianza to seize more land or to declare the formation of another independent city-state, fearing it would provoke further conflict in the area. Between 1965 and 1967, large tracts of land had been incinerated in northern New Mexico. Anglo farms, haystacks, and fences had been torched, livestock had been slaughtered, and farm equipment had been smashed. A US Department of Agriculture field station had been set ablaze. By attacking both symbols of Anglo and federal authority, the Hispanos of northern New Mexico were demonstrating their anger over the alienation of their ancestral lands and the severe shrinking of permits for the grazing of livestock on federal lands. Much as African Americans had burned down their ghettos in American cities those same summers, so Hispano passions over the historic loss of their communal lands in the 1890s had become particularly incendiary. Of course, the Alianza was not the only group capable of such vandalism, but no one could persuade Sanchez of that.

On June 2, 1967, he thus ordered the state police to block all the roads leading into the village of Coyote, where an Alianza meeting was scheduled. Eight Alianza members were arrested, were charged with inciting to riot, and spent the weekend in jail, awaiting their arraignment scheduled for Monday. Tijerina escaped arrest that day because he arrived at the event late, warned that a dragnet was in place.

On Monday, June 5, 1967, at about three o'clock in the afternoon, some fourteen to twenty Alianza members (accounts vary) entered the Rio Arriba County courthouse in Tierra Amarilla, a small village about thirty miles north of Santa Fe, hoping to post bail for jailed Alianza members. Alianza's leaders, angry that the district attorney had violated their right to assembly, also intended to make a citizen's arrest of Sanchez and have him face a jury of his peers in San Joaquín del Rio de Chama, the free city-state they had declared in 1966.[5]

When the Alianza members entered the courthouse, they scurried through the building trying to find Alfonso Sanchez. When they could not, some became particularly irate and violent. Several were trigger-happy from the start and needed little provocation. Business in Santa Fe had kept Sanchez from appearing at the scheduled arraignment, but the Aliancistas suspected that they were being lied to and that he was actually hiding somewhere in the building. They systematically surveyed the courthouse, bludgeoning several employees to learn where Sanchez was, seriously wounding two court workers as their bullets flew about. The blaring sirens of approaching state police cars led to a quick retreat. They fled with two hostages, whom they quickly released. Whether Reies López Tijerina was actually present during the melee was much disputed for a time and was never proven in a court of law. His presence was later confirmed by Tijerina's daughter, Rose, who was a participant and eyewitness to the day's events, but it was always denied by her father.[6]

In the months that followed the June 5 failed citizen's arrest of Sanchez, Tijerina was quickly hailed by New and Old Left leaders as a revolutionary hero. Elizabeth Martinez and Beverley Axelrod, women who had long been leaders in SNCC, moved to northern New Mexico, convinced that the struggle by poor farmers to regain their lost lands held the potential for revolutionary change. Was this the new Sierra Madre? By July 1967, Elizabeth Martinez had started the newspaper *El Grito del Norte* with the explicit goal of publicizing the glories of the Cuban Revolution and the necessity to construct a "new Man" and to tie local New Mexican struggles over land to other Third World national revolutionary struggles, particularly the one in Vietnam. Old Left newspapers reported on the New Mexican land grant struggle in similar ways, as the beginnings of a class struggle that would surely spark a proletarian revolution.[7]

On October 21, 1967, slightly more than four months after the attempted citizen's arrest at Tierra Amarilla, Tijerina, now out of jail on bail for federal charges stemming from the occupation of the Kit Carson National Forest, convened the annual convention of the Alianza in Albuquerque. Present on the stage with Tijerina were the Hopi Indian chief Tomas Ben Yacya; Ralph Featherstone, SNCC's program director; Maulana Ron Karenga, the founder of US Organization (i.e., "Us Black People"); and a number of Black Panther Party and Congress of Racial Equality members. Ralph Featherstone entered the auditorium with a sign that read, "Che [Guevara] Is Alive and Is Hiding in Tierra Amarilla." The audience broke out into enthusiastic applause and listened to his harangue about black-Hispano commonalities and the urgency of "tak[ing] back what is ours by any means necessary." Karenga likewise ended his speech, titled "People of Color: We Shall Survive," by shouting out in Spanish,

"¡Viva Tijerina! ¡Vivan los indios! ¡Vivan los hombres de color!" (Long live Tijerina! Long live the Indians! Long live men of color!). The conference ended with the ratification of treaties of "PEACE, HARMONY, AND MUTUAL ASSISTANCE BETWEEN THE SPANISH-AMERICAN FEDERAL ALLIANCE OF FREE CITY STATES" and the organizations represented, vowing mutual assistance, respect, and understanding.[8]

By the end of 1967, a significant mythology had taken shape about what had transpired at Tierra Amarilla earlier that year, but most Americans remained woefully ignorant of what Reies López Tijerina believed, how he had risen to national visibility, and what his movement was about. In 1969, Rodolfo "Corky" Gonzales, the person most responsible for forging a host of Mexican American student groups into a unitary national Chicano identity, proclaimed Tijerina the leader of the Chicano nationalist revolution who would restore the homeland of Aztlán. Interestingly enough, I have found no printed document or archival manuscript in which Tijerina has said that his 1960s activism was on behalf of Chicanos, Mexicanos, or Mexican Americans. Nor did Tijerina ever mention this in any of my personal interviews with him. He consistently explained that his activities were to improve the lives of Indo-Hispanos, an invented panethnic political identity that would be forged by Indians and Hispanos working together to regain the lands they once had under Spanish and Mexican rule.

Who was Reies López Tijerina? What was his lifelong message? Why did he go to New Mexico in the first place, and what did he accomplish there?

Reies Lopez Tijerina spent his childhood living in poverty with his family on the outskirts of San Antonio. They routinely followed the crops between Texas and Michigan as agricultural laborers. In summer 1941, he met an itinerant Baptist preacher named Samuel Galindo, who gave him a copy of the Bible in Spanish.[9] "I read it all," Tijerina explained. "Then I got my brothers around the table and read it to them a second time. I noticed the word 'justice' used as many times as words like 'love.' So I read about Abraham, David, Ishmael, and the prophets. I found many words in there to reach my heart." Mercy and truth, justice and peace: these were the keywords that resonated most in his imagination, prompting what he described as a "yearning of my heart for justice." At the age of eighteen, Tijerina enrolled in the Assemblies of God Latin American Bible Institute in Saspamco, Texas, from which he graduated in 1946.[10] Together with his classmate and later wife María Escobar Chávez, they committed themselves to the salvation of souls.[11]

From 1946 to 1956, María and Reies Tijerina crisscrossed the United States staging revivals. They preached in homes, in halls, in tents—virtually anywhere people congregated. Never did he tire of spreading the word of God. His services were never short events and often consumed an entire day. They were exuberant gatherings full of singing and clapping, sobbing and shouting, with fits of anger and punching motions into the air to banish evil and Satan from their midst and guttural, other-worldly, seemingly ghostly speaking in tongues. Tijerina constantly announced that the living God would soon arrive and that it was time to repent and be saved.

The sermons Tijerina preached between 1946 and 1956 had a burning urgency to them. He called to repentance a generation he believed was lost to the vulgar materialism of modernity. As a person who obeyed the laws of God and who had been sent as a prophetic clarion, Tijerina was certain that the world was in its latter days and that one could already see the dawn. That dawn was the day of the millennium when Jesus Christ would return to earth anew. On that day God would welcome into his kingdom the righteous and the moral. It would be a day of salvation and a day of great rejoicing.

Tijerina's sermons were simple in form. They were lyrical and melodious with a thunderous cadence and often pure poetry to the ear. Their delivery was equally spellbinding. Eyewitnesses attest that Tijerina was an extraordinary orator who could expound for hours without pause. His classmates at the Latin American Bible Institute selected him as their graduation preacher in 1946 precisely because of this skill. He spoke extemporaneously with ease, moving audiences to enthusiastic laughter and cheers and, in a flash, flipping their emotions to dread and tears.[12] His call to action was hard to ignore. Indeed, his sermons were moving, and his auditors were equally moved.

Tijerina was a radical restorationist who wanted both the Assemblies of God and society to return to a purer and simpler time, to the apostolic time of Christ, to that moment before corruption. Between 1946 and 1950, he tried to lead his followers to holiness, offering them caustic sermons against sexual promiscuity, drinking, dancing, smoking, watching television, and listening to the radio, which were all products the media was selling. He condemned all of this as the wiles of the "sinful and wicked whore of Babylon." This same whore was also ensnaring the leaders of the Assemblies of God, who had also become materialistic and increasingly bureaucratic and had forsaken their commitment to the poor, to orphans, and to widows.

By 1950 the leadership of the Assemblies of God had heard enough of Tijerina's searing critiques of their behavior and expelled him from the church, withdrew his license to preach, and ordered him shunned. After his expulsion Tijerina continued to preach throughout the West and Midwest, mostly to Mexican and Mexican American migrant workers. His message was an end-time theology, urging those who would listen to follow the example of Christ and to seek their own holiness. In 1955, with a group of seventeen families, he started a short-lived utopian community in Arizona, near Phoenix, which they called the Valley of Peace. A year later, largely because of an apocalyptic dream he had, he traveled to northern New Mexico, to villages he had visited before in the late 1940s. There he learned how the area's Hispano residents had lost the communal portions of the land grants given to them by the kings of Spain and the presidents of Mexico. On hearing these stories, Tijerina concluded that they had a holy, just, and sacred cause.[13]

Having spent his adult life pondering and preaching the laws of God, Tijerina now threw himself into the study of the laws of man, having concluded, "I learned that there's no mercy in churches, no justice in religious people."[14] At the end of 1957, he and a cadre of about thirty followers settled in Albuquerque and, on February 2, 1963, incorporated the Alianza Federal de Mercedes. He threw himself anew into another restorationist project: the recuperation of the *mercedes*, the lost land grants. His message was a simple one: the charters of incorporation that Spain's kings had given the Hispanos to establish towns also bestowed upon them writs of nobility and aristocracy that modernity had eroded. Their honor, their culture, and their lands had been lost and now could be restored if they joined the Alianza. The government had stolen their lands and given them nothing in return except powdered milk, a reference to the commodities distributed as food aid at the time.

Between 1963 and 1966, Tijerina traveled throughout New Mexico and much of the Southwest using the ritual formulas he had mastered as a revival preacher: reading law, bearing witness, healing. He told old women and men about their lost dignity and lost lands and promised to restore them. Where previously he would have begun his revival by reading from the Bible, now he read from the Laws of the Indies and the Treaty of Guadalupe Hidalgo. Much as congregants would have given personal testimony about their sinfulness at a revival, at Alianza meetings, men and women would explain how their families had lost their lands and describe their lives of utter poverty and unemployment. They would then sing and pray, party and commune, and contribute the $2 monthly membership dues to advance the cause, exactly as they would have at a revival. By the end of 1963, the Alianza was said to have registered five thousand members; by the end of 1964, it had fifty thousand members. By Tijerina's own count, he had some eighty thousand dues-paying members by 1966, and they were ready for some dramatic action, the type District Attorney Sanchez feared and undoubtedly the type emboldened by the radical nationalism of other American ethnic groups in those years.[15]

It was then, on October 15, 1966, that 350 members of the Alianza took their bold step of occupying a portion of the Kit Carson National Forest. Eight months later, they would attempt their citizen's arrest of Sanchez.

Tijerina and the activist members of the Alianza spent several years embroiled in litigation. Tijerina and several others faced federal charges stemming from the arrest of the US agents at the Kit Carson National Forest on October 15, 1966. The charges against those arrested for illegal assembly at Coyote on June 2, 1967, were dropped. But the courthouse scuffle of June 5 resulted in 584 collective counts against twenty participants. Charges were dropped against eight for insufficient evidence, with twelve, including Tijerina, being tried by the state of New Mexico. The big break in this case occurred when presiding judge Paul Larrazolo issued his jury instructions: "Anyone, including a state police officer, who intentionally interferes with a lawful attempt to make a citizen's arrest does so at his own peril, since the arresting citizens are entitled under the law to use whatever force is reasonably necessary to effect said citizen's arrest and to use whatever force is reasonably necessary to defend themselves in the process of making said citizen's arrest."[16] On December 13, 1968, Tijerina and his codefendants won complete acquittal, though the state retried the case against him and eventually won convictions on two lesser charges.

Tijerina took his newly found sanction for citizen's arrest to Washington, DC, in April 1969. By the authority of the citizens of San Joaquin del Rio de Chama, he tried to arrest Warren Burger, then chief justice of the Supreme Court, for refusing to intervene in their land grant claim. Before a gaggle of television cameras and newspaper reporters, Tijerina theatrically put a lasso around the court building; Burger didn't even see the commotion and was shuttled out by guards through a side door. Tijerina next tried to arrest Sid Hacker, then the director of the Los Alamos National Laboratory, for building atomic bombs. Hacker was out of the country and Tijerina ultimately left a printed arrest warrant in Hacker's mailbox.[17]

The event that finally landed Tijerina back in jail occurred on June 8, 1969. Tijerina, his second wife Patsy, and a number of Alianza members entered the Kit Carson National Forest that day, burned the US Forest

Service sign marking the park's entrance, and constructed a makeshift sign announcing that one was entering San Joaquin del Rio de Chama. They were immediately arrested, found guilty of the destruction of federal property, and sentenced on January 5, 1970, to two to five years in the federal prison in Springfield, Missouri.

While Tijerina sat in jail, from June 1969 to December 1973, most of what mushroomed into the Chicano student movement had its genesis. On March 28, 1969, Rodolfo "Corky" Gonzalez hosted the National Chicano Liberation Youth Conference in Denver. Tijerina did not hear about the conference nor did he see a copy of *El Plan Espiritual de Aztlán*, the conference manifesto, until several months later, while awaiting trial for the sign burning. But on hearing that he and the Alianza's land grant struggle was being announced by Gonzalez as the beginning of the armed revolution to create the Chicano homeland of Aztlán, Tijerina wrote his "Letter from the Santa Fe Jail," explaining to his followers that the cause of the Alianza had been to recuperate lost lands through litigation, not violent revolution.[18] The Mexican American political activism into which Tijerina tapped in the late 1940s—as did César Chávez in the early 1960s—was rural, class based, and committed to the poor and to farmworkers who worked for a pittance under brutal conditions. They both invested their movements with the language of religion, largely to escape the accusation that they were Communists; they were indeed both devout Christians. They criticized racial discrimination obliquely by focusing on its class iterations.

El Plan Espiritual de Aztlán, in contrast, had committed itself to the formation of a national identity-based movement that addressed the plight of urban youth: police harassment, unequal treatment by the courts, residential segregation, educational neglect, poverty, and vulnerability to the draft.[19] Far removed from the land, young city-based Chicanos and Chicanas depicted their segregated barrios as exploited colonies and articulated a theory of internal colonialism that called for a revolutionary nationalism to overthrow their oppressors. To challenge the racism they experienced daily at the hands of the police, the courts, and schools, they fashioned notions of racial pride rooted in the brown color of their skin at the same time denouncing racism, white skin privilege, and racial supremacy. Drawing on Tijerina's failed attempts to regain communal lands, students radicalized his vision, proclaiming the need for an independent Chicano nation of Aztlán—something Tijerina deplored because he wanted Indo-Hispano incorporation into the American body politic, not separatism or independence.[20] Eventually, feminist demands for sexual liberation, reproductive rights, and gender equity made their way into the Chicana/Chicano student agenda. These rankled Tijerina to the point of a breach. He wanted no part of sexual liberation or gender equity. His was a gospel of family order, the sanctification of the body, and the holiness that abstinence from the blandishments of "the evil whore of Babylon" guaranteed. He wanted to restore patriarchal authority and familial honor, not destroy it, which quickly put him at odds with Chicana feminists and queer nationalists who accordingly found him too old and too out of touch when he was released from prison in 1973.

Reies López Tijerina's Pentacostal origins in the Assemblies of God gave the Mexican American civil rights movement a number of ideas that have advanced the cause of social justice. First and foremost, Tijerina preached a social gospel that focused on the poor and dispossessed in the society. He never wavered from this commitment. As an Assemblies of God preacher, he taught his followers to appropriate their individual and direct access to God. Anyone could read the Bible and interpret it for himself or herself without the assistance of trained intermediaries. Tijerina left the Latin American Bible Institute in 1946 with a stack of Bibles written in Spanish that he would give to anyone willing to take one, encouraging them to read the word of God for themselves and hopefully to be as moved by the words justice and love as he had been. When Tijerina took up the cause of the land grants he cultivated the same reading practice among the members of the Alianza, urging them to pore over the Laws of the Indies and the Treaty of Guadalupe Hidalgo. If they were to regain their lands, they had to understand the laws of man and to act, militantly, to ensure the words were honored at least in letter if not in spirit. The laws and the treaty said *ejidos* could not be alienated; they had been. Now the Aliancistas' sacred duty was to contest this fact in the courts of law, as they did.

The Assemblies of God inspired the organizational form that the Alliance of Free City States took under Tijerina's leadership. Since the founding of the Assemblies of God in 1914, they consciously avoided the word "church" in their name precisely to allow individual religious communities the freedom to define themselves and their uniqueness, free of the hierarchy and bureaucratic structures of organized Protestant churches. Tijerina imagined city-states in much the same way. They were free to do as they pleased, without interference from other cities, acting as an alliance when needed but governed by themselves.

Reies López Tijerina died on January 19, 2015, at the age of eighty-eight. The final days of his life were spent in Ciudad Juárez, Mexico, just across the border from El Paso, where his modest Social Security benefits went much further. He lived there with his third wife Esperanza, to whom the US Department of Homeland Security refused (until recently) to issue a green card so they could live together in the states. Reies López Tijerina never got a single acre of land returned to anyone, but he did politicize the history of land tenure in New Mexico, which is still very much alive and contested there to this day.

23 | Before the Birth of Asian America: Asian Americans and the New Left[1]

by Daryl Joji Maeda

The historiography of Asian American activism in the 1960s is dominated by studies on the Asian American movement, a social movement for racial justice that arose in the late 1960s.[2] The Asian American movement conceptualized Asian Americans as racially oppressed subjects; was committed to multiethnic, multiracial, and transnational coalition building; and adopted rhetorics of power and self-determination over assimilation and equal rights. It organized within Asian American communities and framed issues—ranging from lack of housing and health care, omission from college and university curricula, and the Vietnam War—as particularly salient to Asian Americans. Because the Asian American movement did not have significant ties to the Old Left but instead grew out of the antiwar and Black Power movements, its participants tended to create new, specifically Asian groups rather than working within existing organizations (though by the mid- to late 1970s, many Asian American organizations merged into multiracial parties). Although studying the Asian American movement has revealed a panoply of previously obscure Asian American activism, concentrating on the movement itself has simultaneously obscured activism that did not conform to the movement's dominant ideologies. Individual Asian Americans did join the New Left prior to 1968, but not the Asian American movement per se.

This chapter considers two case studies of Nikkei (ethnic Japanese) activists who participated in the New Left prior to and outside of the Asian American movement: Tamio Wakayama, a Japanese Canadian who joined the Student Nonviolent Coordinating Committee (SNCC) in the South and then returned home to Vancouver to become a community activist, and Patti Iiyama, the daughter of Old Left radicals who became a longtime member of the Socialist Workers Party. I argue that Wakayama and Iiyama emblematize the divergent avenues of activism that participating in the early New Left opened up for Nikkei before the movement era. Although their cases cannot be taken as representative of Asian American activism in the early to mid-1960s, I would surmise that substantial similarities might be found with Chinese American and Filipino American activists during this period.

Given the location of this conference in Ann Arbor and its focus on Students for a Democratic Society (SDS) and the *Port Huron Statement*, I thought it would be fantastic to track down T. Robert "Lefty" Yamada, whom Alan Wald told me about years ago. According to James Miller, Yamada was a "dedicated democratic socialist" who had attended the University of Wisconsin but, by the late 1950s, was a "fixture on the Ann Arbor scene" where he worked at a bookstore in town, ran the extracurricular Political Issues Club on campus, and was a member of the Ann Arbor chapter of the Student League for Industrial Democracy (SLID). One of Yamada's achievements was convincing his friend and Michigan student Alan Haber to join SLID.[3] Miller mentions that Yamada had been incarcerated during World War II but provides no further details. Similarly, Maurice Isserman describes Yamada as a "former University of Michigan student and a mover and shaker in Ann Arbor radical circles" and suggests that he was a member of the Young People's Socialist League.[4] Yamada was born in Seattle in 1925 and was in high school in 1942 when he, along with his family, was incarcerated at Puyallup and Minidoka during World War II. He earned a degree in sociology from Michigan, attended Wisconsin for graduate school for a time, and then returned to Ann Arbor. This timeline verifies Miller and Isserman's characterization of Yamada as older than students like Haber, for he would have been around thirty-one in 1956. In 1961, Yamada departed Michigan for California, where he worked in the bookstore of the well-known Berkeley institution called the Co-op, founded the Berkeley Historical Society (BHS) in 1978, and served on the board of the Berkeley Public Library. He was a longtime and active member of the Berkeley chapter of the Japanese American Citizens League (JACL) and curated an exhibit, "The Japanese American Experience: The Berkeley Legacy, 1895–1995," at BHS.[5] Yamada passed away in 2004.[6] Although I had hoped to track Yamada down for an interview, what I find intriguing about his trajectory (at least as revealed in the sketchy story I've uncovered so far) is that he stands out as an extraordinary Japanese American for his 1950s radicalism, but his path eventually converged both with the mainstream of Japanese American politics in the

1970s and also with radicals like Ernie and Chizu Iiyama (the parents of Patti Iiyama, discussed later).

Tamio Wakayama

Tamio Wakayama (known as "Tom" during the movement era) is far from a typical Japanese American. In fact, he's not Japanese American at all, but rather is a Japanese Canadian, born near Vancouver on April 3, 1941, to Issei (immigrant) parents.[7] Along with all other Japanese Canadians, the Wakayama family was expelled from the West Coast during World War II by the Canadian government.[8] Because his family was exiled from Vancouver when he was a mere infant, Wakayama's earliest memories are of growing up in Chatham, a farming town in southwestern Ontario. The Wakayamas and a few other Japanese families settled into the only area of Chatham that they could afford: the black neighborhood. His father, who upon arrival in Canada had labored in sawmills, had scrimped and saved to become a shopkeeper in Vancouver but in Chatham could only find the gruesome work of processing the carcasses of diseased cattle.[9] Wakayama's childhood produced a complicated sense of race. He recalls the comfort and safety of the Japanese cultural bubble created by the small Nikkei community—Oshogatsu (Japanese New Year) stands out in his memory—but also felt the sting of racism.[10] In the youth culture of Chatham, Japanese kids played and aligned with black kids on the nonwhite side of the racial divide.[11]

Wakayama was not politically active before college nor during his matriculation at University of Western Ontario. However, while home for summer 1963, he began following news of the growing civil rights movement in the United States broadcast on the Canadian television news. He was transfixed by the March on Washington for Jobs and Freedom in late August and was particularly drawn to the oratory on display—but it was John Lewis, not Martin Luther King Jr., who captivated him.[12] He made the fateful decision to go south with hardly any conscious thought. He remembers that the southern struggle "gripped my imagination" at a moment in which he was searching for some meaning in life, and above all else, he intuitively felt that the civil rights movement was something that he desperately needed to understand.[13] His oral history interview and his written memoir make clear that this intuition that the civil rights movement was integral to his own survival reflected an inchoate but powerful sense that it offered a way to address his own place in the racial hierarchy. He writes, "And where, I wondered, is my own rightful place in this monolithic white world and these thoughts awoke the distant hope that perhaps, within this black movement for freedom, I could locate the matrix of my own liberation."[14]

With no real plan, no contacts, and no set destination, he loaded up his trusty Volkswagen Beetle, hugged his mother good-bye, drove north across the bridge from Windsor to Detroit, and then headed south. By the second day of his trek, Wakayama had made it to Nashville and heard news over the radio about the Ku Klux Klan bombing of the Sixteenth Street Baptist Church in Birmingham, Alabama, which killed four African American girls. He immediately set off toward the troubled city. When he arrived, he got lost and wandered into a black neighborhood, where an angry crowd of youth surrounded his vehicle. When they spied a light-skinned driver behind the windshield, they began rocking his car, but Wakayama surprised them when he climbed out and proved to be not white. He mollified the crowd by expressing "outrage" at the bombing and offering "condolences" for the victims. They sent him on his way with directions to the YMCA and a warning to get there quickly, "for this was not a night to be wandering the streets of Birmingham."[15] The centrality of this incident in Wakayama's recollection signals his marginality in the South, light enough to arouse suspicion from blacks and yet nonwhite enough to be a potential ally. His narrative underscores the latter point: before arriving at the YMCA, he stopped at a black restaurant where he was greeted guardedly, but he broke the ice by trading a Canadian du Maurier cigarette for a Lucky Strike with the counterman. In the ensuing conversation, he learned about what it was like to be black in the Jim Crow South and, fatefully, discovered the location of headquarters of SNCC.[16]

The next morning, Wakayama arrived at the A. G. Gaston Motel, where he met John Lewis, Julian Bond, and Annie Pearl Avery, who took him under her wing. He and Avery joined eight thousand mourners at the funeral service for three of the four girls killed in the bombing, where he heard for the first time the spellbinding oratory of Dr. King. Afterward, an elderly deacon apologized for the open displays of emotion during the ceremony, which in Wakayama's narrative triggers a related recollection: that having grown up in a black neighborhood, he was familiar with the expressiveness of black worship. He notes further that an Issei friend of his family had married a black woman and preached occasionally at a Methodist church. This aside functions to underscore Wakayama's closeness to black culture. In contrast, he recalls humorously how disoriented his Issei mother (who was Buddhist and Shinto) had been when she visited the raucous black service.[17]

Wakayama owned a valuable resource: a working car, which granted him quick entry into SNCC circles. From Birmingham, he drove Bond, James Foreman, and photographer Danny Lyon to SNCC headquarters in Atlanta. Initially, he worked as a janitor and driver but soon graduated to working on the SNCC newspaper, the *Student Voice*, and was put on the SNCC payroll. His newspaper work entailed layout, and he learned how to develop film. He also developed a good eye for images and began experimenting with photography. At first he was the only Asian in SNCC, but he was joined for a time by "Brother Ed" Nakawatase, a Sansei (third-generation Japanese American) from Seabrook, New Jersey, who later joined the antiwar movement, became a socialist, worked for the American Friends Service Committee on American Indian matters, and was active in the Redress and Reparations movement.[18] But he recalls that despite being unusual, being Asian wasn't particularly notable, for this was the period in which SNCC welcomed workers of all stripes. In the South he experienced both white racism, from a hostile police officer who called him a "Jap," and white graciousness, from a shipping clerk who went far out of his way to rush out SNCC promotional materials because his brother had been a member of the "Lost Battalion" rescued by the famous Japanese American 442nd Regiment during World War II. But mostly he felt like an "anomaly." During 1964, he had the opportunity to put his photographic skills to work as he toured the Mississippi backcountry during Freedom Summer with Bob Moses, whom he deems to have been his most lasting influence.[19]

Wakayama's reflection on SNCC's transition from beloved community to Black Power provides an invaluable index into his understandings of race, identity, and nationalism. He attended the 1964 Waveland, Mississippi, SNCC retreat, most famous for Casey Hayden and Mary King's critique of sexism but also an occasion on which racial schisms grew more visible.[20] Wakayama recalls his ambivalence on the question of Black Power:

> As a Nikkei, I was torn on the issue of Black Power and for once, my racial neutrality was of no help. On one hand I could well understand the call for the black pride and I personally took it to heart that the first step towards any real change was to cast off the historically imposed slave mentality and replace it with a new and proud self image grounded in an affirmation of their African heritage and pride in their historic courage that enabled them to survive centuries of slavery and segregation. On the other hand I felt

the leap from there to the Black Power political agenda of a separate and independent black state in America was not only logically invalid but also illusory.[21]

Shortly after Waveland, Wakayama returned home to Canada for the 1964 winter holidays. It was the end of his active work with SNCC. In a sense, he fled before the oncoming storm, for he believes that in the 1965 SNCC split, he would have been expelled, his nonblackness overriding his nonwhiteness.[22]

In the aftermath of his southern civil rights activism, Wakayama spent the next few years wandering through the Canadian New Left, participating in the Student Union for Peace Action (SUPA), a Canadian analog to SDS, in which he frequently found himself to be the only person of color. He photographed First Nations reserves and the Doukhobor (a Russian minority) and traveled to Cuba. He meandered between Toronto and Vancouver and through a number of romantic relationships and experimented with 1970s-style diversions, all the while searching for his photographic muse. During this period, he experienced the growing Orientalism of the left, going from being seen as a "dirty Jap" to being regarded as some sort of Zen guru, and realized that his romantic liaisons with white women had often positioned him as an "exotic Asian morsel to be sampled in order to fuel their rebellion."[23]

The event that precipitated Wakayama's transformation from a stranger in someone else's movement to a protagonist in his own came when he embarked on "a pilgrimage to the ancestral land" of Japan.[24] There, for the first time, he experienced being in the majority—a sensation he found both comforting and disquieting for its novelty. While he enjoyed looking like everyone else, Wakayama found out how distant he was from Japanese culture: he was bewildered by the complexity of social rituals, made some cultural blunders—such as emptying the *furo* (a soaking tub in which the water is kept hot for several days) after his bath—and studied the language assiduously. He also began studying the *shakuhachi*, a Japanese flute. Given that Oshogatsu was a major celebration of his community in Canada, he eagerly anticipated an elaborate celebration but was disappointed by the cursory rituals in Japan—the expected *mochi* pounding, *soba* eating, and neighborly visits were all missing. This experience made him realize that Japan had undergone radical changes over the decades, and Nikkei in Canada could rightfully claim their place as preservers of the "cultural flame." This revelation constituted an important step in Wakayama's journey of understanding, for as he writes, "Japan was the bridge that brought me home." Critically, he credits the African journeys of SNCC leaders like John Lewis as inspiration for his own pilgrimage to Japan, which enabled him to find a new home in the Japanese Canadian community.[25]

Wakayama returned to Canada, living in Toronto and in assorted rural places, before settling in Vancouver. Having improved his Japanese language skills in Japan, he had begun writing letters to his mother in the simplified katakana and hiragana syllabaries but had great difficulty decoding her replies. In search of an interpreter, he visited Language Aid, an immigrant aid center, where a woman named Michiko Sakata translated his mother's letter and, upon learning that Tamio had studied shakuhachi in Japan, directed him to a shakuhachi master in downtown Vancouver. Tamio found himself at Tonari Gumi, a drop-in center for Japanese elders, where he made a second home volunteering and hanging out. He writes, "I had just entered a world that would consume all my energy and bring closure to my life's journey."[26] He also continued to work on his Japanese with Michiko.

The next leg of Wakayama's journey began when Michiko approached him in 1974 with the idea of creating an exhibition to document the history of the Nikkei in Canada. She reasoned that his expertise as a photographer would make him the perfect partner, but Tamio refused, having established a lucrative studio that took up much of his time. Despite his rejection, she persisted, until he finally agreed not only to participate but also to take on the role of director and curator. Wakayama and a crew of about twelve, evenly divided among Sansei and new immigrants, threw themselves into the task of archival and photographic research, interviewing Issei, gathering photographs from the community, creating a coherent narrative, laying out images, and writing captions. For these intrepid volunteers, creating the exhibition amounted teaching themselves and writing the history of Japanese Canadians, for they had no textbooks to draw upon. The intensity of the work drew the group together. Wakayama recalls, "Not since my time with [SNCC] had I felt such a bond with others but my ties to my brothers and sister[s] in this new coalition was stronger and more intimate for we were dealing with issues that went to the very core of our being."[27] In other words, adding racial commonality strengthened the bonds of commitment that he had previously felt in his prior social movement communities. After two years of labor, "The Japanese Canadians, 1877–1976" opened in Vancouver. Wakayama and his coworkers took great satisfaction in seeing the reaction of elderly Issei as they viewed the exhibition: expressions of joy, excitement, and sorrow. The exhibition went on to be displayed in Ottawa at the Museum of Man and eventually was exhibited in forty venues in Canada, the United States, and Japan. Working on the exhibition immersed Wakayama totally in the Japanese community in Vancouver. He became an integral member of the Powell Street Festival organizing committee, which put on what has become an annual celebration of Nikkei history and culture held in the historic heart of Japanese Vancouver. The festival overcame political and generational rifts in the community to become a rallying point. Wakayama's dedication to preserving and rebuilding a sense of cultural belonging in Vancouver paralleled efforts by the mainstream Asian American movement in the United States to defend affordable housing, provide cultural resources to communities, and build a sense of pride among Asian Americans in cities as far flung as Honolulu, San Francisco, Los Angeles, and New York. Critically, for Wakayama, his search for his Japanese Canadian identity had begun with working with SNCC in the South. Reflecting on his personal journey from Vancouver to Ontario to the Deep South to Japan and back, Wakayama concludes, "After three decades of exile, I had found my way home."[28]

Patti Iiyama

In contrast to Wakayama, who began his activist trajectory as a curious but apolitical naïf, Patricia "Patti" Iiyama is a classic red diaper baby, the daughter of longtime leftists Ernest and Chizu Iiyama, who trace their radicalism back to the 1930s.[29] Ernie belonged to the Oakland chapter of the Young Democrats, an organization of about ninety liberal to progressive Nisei in three chapters in Oakland, San Francisco, and Los Angeles. The Young Democrats supported the labor movement and the New Deal; organized politically among Nisei and cooperated with Chinese Americans to allay anti-Asian discrimination; opposed fascism at home and abroad (including Japanese fascism); and criticized the Japanese American Citizens League, the center-right Nisei political formation.[30] He also belonged to the Communist Party (CP) before Japanese American members were unceremoniously expelled from the party at the outset of World War II.[31] Chizu Kitano met Ernie while both were incarcerated at the Topaz concentration camp in Utah, and Ernie introduced her to his political circles, which included leftists and Young Democrats like Mine Okubo and Kazu Ikeda Iijima.[32] Chizu recalls the camp and her conversations with the Young Democrats as the beginning of her political education, as she learned the history of racism and labor exploitation in the United States and connected those histories to Japanese American experiences.[33]

The Iiyamas left camp to resettle initially in Chicago, where they worked in the Chicago Resettlers' Committee, a social service group that helped Nisei find housing and jobs. Around 1943, they moved on to New York City, where they were integral members of the Japanese American Committee for Democracy (JACD), a progressive organization that both Ernie and Chizu headed at different times. The JACD did not limit its fight to equality for Japanese Americans but instead forwarded a broad-based critique of racism writ large as antidemocratic. JACD members participated in civil rights actions demanding fair housing and voting rights for "Negroes."[34] Patti was born in New York in 1945, ensconced in this network of progressive Japanese Americans.[35] When the Iiyamas returned to Chicago around 1948, they again immersed themselves in political activism, especially around civil rights for African Americans. Chizu recalls writing letters, picketing, and protesting for fair housing and employment in collaboration with the National Association for the Advancement of Colored People (NAACP) and Urban League.[36] The family moved often, always living on the edge of the black ghetto; because Ernie's leftist politics had resulted in him being blacklisted by employers, the family frequently found it difficult to make rent.[37] Some of Patti's earliest memories involve going to the beach on Lake Michigan with her parents, but these were no ordinary outings. They admonished her to always keep an eye on them and be ready to run out of the water if they called her. Their caution stemmed from the fact that these outings were part of a campaign to desegregate the public beaches of Chicago, and her parents were wary of being attacked by segregationists.[38] With that kind of upbringing, it is not surprising that she went on to lead a life of activism.

The Iiyama family returned to California in 1955, settling in the predominantly white suburb of El Cerrito. Patti was but one of a handful of Japanese or Asian Americans at El Cerrito High School, where there were virtually no African Americans.[39] Perhaps surprisingly, Ernie and Chizu joined the Contra Costa chapter of JACL, an organization of which they had been critical in prior decades. Nevertheless, they became active JACL members, and Ernie eventually served as president of the local chapter. Joining JACL did not mean abandoning their progressive politics, however. Patti recalls picketing at the Woolworth store in Berkeley in support of the civil rights movement's attempts to desegregate the chain's facilities in the South (sometime around 1960). Furthermore, Ernie became head of the Human Rights Commission of El Cerrito.

At the age of sixteen, Patti graduated from high school and enrolled at the University of California, Berkeley, in 1961. She immediately joined the political scene on campus and was eventually arrested for her participation in the Free Speech Movement (FSM). Unsurprisingly, given her civil rights activism, Patti was drawn to the SLATE coalition for its dedication to supporting the civil rights movement. She ran for student senate as a representative of Women for Peace and a member of the SLATE and won a seat.

Patti was there on Sproul Plaza when the police took Jack Weinberg into custody for staffing the Congress of Racial Equality (CORE) table and participated in the thirty-two-hour-long standoff in which students surrounded the police car holding Weinberg and refused to let it leave the plaza. Although she was politically active, she was not one of the students who stood atop of the police car to deliver an oration, because, as she recalls, she was still too shy to speak out in public at that time. During the FSM, Patti served on the executive committee and was one of the 773 students arrested for occupying Sproul Hall. When the police came to arrest protesters, she remembers going limp in order to force the police officers to drag her from the building. Though the police had begun their offensive in the middle of the night, this strategy slowed the removal of protesters so much that they were still being cleared when classes resumed in the morning. Although she was bailed out of jail almost immediately, the next summer a judge tried and convicted her of trespassing and resisting arrest. She refused probation as a matter of principle and as a "ringleader" received a sentence of thirty days in Santa Rita Jail, an experience she describes as "horrible" for the regimentation and total loss of freedom. Patti does not remember any other Asian Americans active in the FSM, certainly none as centrally involved as she was, but believes that two other Japanese Americans were arrested. All three had their pictures published in the local Japanese American community newspapers, and her own grandmother told Patti that she had shamed the family by being arrested (Grandma Kitano was only grateful that Patti bore her father's last name of Iiyama). Patti's takeaway from the FSM was that it is possible to change people's minds, to educate them on issues, and to mobilize them for social change.[40]

Patti developed her belief in the efficacy of mass demonstrations during this period as a part of her work in support of civil rights. She recalls participating in one of the major demonstrations in San Francisco:

> The first largest demonstration I went to, where there were several thousand people, was when we were picketing at Sheraton Pal-

ace . . . [in 1964], because Sheraton Palace was discriminating against blacks in their hiring practices. We went there in San Francisco and the first time, our demonstration surrounded the entire hotel. So it was like four blocks around, you know, we were able to go all the way around, our picket line went all the way around. I had never seen anything that big before, and it was a wonderful feeling to know that you were not alone, that other people were with you on this. It gives you such a feeling of strength and empowerment.[41]

Here she offers a concise statement about organizing tactics: that mass demonstrations not only demonstrate the strength of a social movement to its opponents and targets but also build solidarity within the movement for further action.

After the conclusion of the FSM, Patti cast about for a new cause and found it in the antiwar movement. Inspired by the Vietnam teach-in in Ann Arbor, she joined the Vietnam Day Committee (VDC) in Berkeley and helped organize the May 1965 teach-in, which was billed not as an antiwar event but as an educational opportunity to learn about Vietnam through lectures and debates. She found this framing valuable because it enabled antiwar activists to try to change the minds of other people. A few months after the teach-in, the VDC organized a demonstration on Telegraph Avenue in Berkeley to express solidarity with the South Vietnamese people. On April 12, 1966, when the police attempted to shut down the unpermitted demonstration, about half the crowd marched on city hall, with Patti leading a contingent of about one hundred women.[42]

Iiyama was also active in organizing Stop the Draft Week, in which thousands of protesters attempting to stop buses carrying draftees from reaching the Oakland induction center clashed with police. SWP leader Fred Halstead recalls her remembering October 20, 1967, as the greatest day of her life. She said, "For a change it was the cops, not the demonstrators, who were on the run."[43] Most importantly, Patti believed in the tactic of mass demonstrations. As more and more people hit the streets, it would become easier for ordinary citizens to shed their aversion to protest and their fears of being branded as unpatriotic. In her recollection, this was exactly the case: "I remember the first demonstrations I went to, they were very small of course, they were really really tiny. We would be lucky to have maybe a hundred people at them. And then as they grew larger, you started thinking 'Yeah, more and more people are starting to believe like I do.'"[44] Although she was critical of the "ultraleft actions" that provoked police violence against protesters, she also later came to recognize that excessive police brutality garnered attention and sympathy for the antiwar movement—growing the demonstrations from a few thousand to ten or fifteen thousand within a week.

As with the FSM, Patti found herself to be the only Asian American within antiwar organizations. Patti opposed the war in Vietnam because she believed that the Vietnamese people were struggling for self-determination and independence from colonialism. Iiyama thought, "To my mind, to be free of colonialism, you have to have a socialist revolution," but she understood it to be the purview of the Vietnamese people to decide what form of government they would institute, even if it was not socialism. She also recalls that the stories of Asian American veterans were filtering back to the antiwar movement in the United States— experiences such as being harassed for looking like the enemy and being called "gooks." Patti interpreted the experiences of the vets as evidence that the war was a racial, as well as capitalist and colonialist, enterprise. In this aspect, her view was remarkably similar to the Asian American movement's position on the war.[45]

During her VDC days, roughly 1965–67, Patti joined SDS but was alienated by what she perceived as its lack of focus, operation by consensus, and problematic gender politics. I interpret her critique of SDS's lack of focus as impatience with the inexactitude of its political line, meaning that the organization's loosely defined oppositional stance did not lead to ideological coherence. This criticism applied as well to SDS's operation by consensus (rather than majority rule), which rankled Patti as an insufficiently disciplined way to run an organization. Finally, she chafed at the male chauvinism rampant within SDS. However, her opposition to sexism did not mean that she was necessarily drawn to the women's liberation movement either. To the contrary, though she considered it good for women to organize as women, she found the women's movement to be too subjective and objected to the use of consciousness raising as personal "therapy."

Patti was a founding member of the Peace and Freedom Party (PFP) in 1968 and organized the Black and Brown Caucus along with Eldridge Cleaver, whom she found "terrible to work with" because he was "dictatorial" and preferred "a lot of rhetorical bombast rather than debate." However, she became disillusioned with the "washed out" politics of the PFP, which she regarded as shying away from true radicalism. Thus she formally joined Socialist Workers Party (SWP) in January 1968. She was attracted to the SWP, which she admired both for its outright socialism and for its explicit Marxism. She stipulates that in her mind, "Marxism is a method, not a Bible. . . . Marxism is a methodology, a way of looking at things, it's a way of analyzing what is happening right now to try to figure how to go forward and what to do next." It is valuable for showing "how you win over the vast majority of people into understanding why the basis of society right now is no good for us." Patti was also drawn to SWP's operating principle of democratic centralism—not, she clarifies, the "fake" democratic centralism that tended toward authoritarianism and was on display in "many of these Maoist groups," but a democratic centralism that valued debate but moved in a unified direction once a majority was reached. To Patti, this was unlike SDS, where you did what you felt like doing, and unlike the Maoist groups, where you did not have input on actions and simply did what you were told.[46]

Today, Patti continues to view the SWP's unbending insistence on single-issue, peaceful mass marches as a compelling tactic.[47] She argues that building a mass movement requires that children and families feel safe at events and that creating situations that incite police violence is thus counterproductive. In addition, she was and continues to be critical of Maoism, which she characterizes as a "variant of Stalinism" that is "repellent" for its cult of personality, "intolerance for differences of opinion," "thuggery," and "anti-intellectual" bent.[48]

Given her hostility toward Maoism, it is unsurprising that Patti was uninterested joining any of the Mao-inflected Asian American organizations that popped up around the Bay Area—groups like the Asian American Political Alliance (AAPA) and the explicitly Maoist Asian American movement organizations Wei Min She and I Wor Kuen, which flourished in the early 1970s. She recalls, "I didn't have a relationship with any of them until the [Third World Liberation Front] strike [at Berkeley]." She did attend a political education class of a Maoist group (not AAPA but another group that she cannot recall) but was turned off by the emphasis on memorizing selections from the "Little Red Book"—*Quotations from Chairman Mao Tse-tung*—which she says discouraged people from thinking for themselves.[49]

During the 1969 Third World Liberation Front (TWLF) strike at Berkeley, which called for the institutionalization of ethnic studies on campus, she found herself to be in a peculiar position due to her race and politics. She recalls that "they wouldn't allow [her] to be a part" of TWLF because she wasn't a member of one of the constituent organizations, which were organized by race. As mentioned previously, she was not a member of any of the Asian American organizations because of her political line. Although she attended a couple of the early meetings of the AAPA, she recalls being "basically kicked out" for her politics. She said of the first meeting, "I spoke a couple of times and they didn't like what I had to say. I spoke saying that the meetings should more open and that we should try to open them up to as many people as possible, and we should try to get as many Asians as possible involved in making the decisions." These statements were not well received, and when Patti returned for the second meeting, she was not welcome.[50] Though excluded from the TWLF, she did participate in the Support Committee in which she helped organize white student support and wrote and distributed leaflets.[51]

In the early 1970s, Iiyama cotaught the first Asian American studies class at the University of California, Davis, along with Frank Chin (a Chinese American writer and advocate of Asian American literature whose perspectives differed dramatically from hers) and taught a Third World women's course at Merritt College in Oakland.[52] She also worked as a staffer in black studies at the University of California, Los Angeles, but was unable to obtain a position in Asian American studies there. When the SWP turned to industrial unionism in the late 1970s, Iiyama became an oil worker, airline baggage handler, and garment worker in far-flung places from San Diego to Houston to Alabama to New York. Her purpose in joining the working class was to educate workers about the possibilities for participatory unions, which she sees as alternatives to the labor unions that have become partners of management rather than representatives of workers. It is difficult to imagine a four-foot-eleven-inch and ninety-five-pound woman performing some of these physically grueling jobs, but it speaks to her indomitable spirit and determination. Today she describes herself as "a retired oil worker." She continues to believe that the SWP provides a useful path toward building a just world and serves as a part-time copy editor for the SWP publisher, Pathfinder Press.

Patti Iiyama was one of a handful of Asian American activists in the New Left of the early 1960s, but a new cohort of Asian Americans arose in the power movements of the late 1960s and eventually coalesced into the Asian American movement. Yet she did not follow the trajectory of Alex Hing, who participated in Stop the Draft Week and Free Speech protests at San Francisco City College before joining the Red Guard Party and eventually the Asian American group I Wor Kuen. Nor did she move from the PFP to AAPA (one of the first and most important Asian American organizations of the period) like Yuji Ichioka, who founded the latter based on the former's membership rosters.

What differentiated Iiyama from Asian American activists of the 1960s and 1970s? As a member of the highly disciplined SWP, Iiyama was committed to a number of approaches and ideologies that were both similar to and different from the Asian American movement's main trends. First the similarities: Iiyama was (and continues to be) convinced that race and class are integrally interconnected. In the aftermath of the 1960s, her path converged with the one traveled by many veterans of the Asian American movement. In the early 1970s, like innumerable movement activists, she worked in the burgeoning field of ethnic studies as an instructor and staffer. When the SWP turned to industrial unionism in the late 1970s, she entered the working class. Asian American movement veterans like Steve Louie and Alex Hing also moved into industrial unionism after the end of the movement era, reflecting the stances of Maoist groups like the Revolutionary Union and League of Revolutionary Struggle, both of which contained substantial proportions of Asian American activists.

As for differences, Iiyama's journey began prior to the rise of the Asian American movement, which was far more closely linked to the power movements of the late 1960s than to the Old Left. A red diaper baby, she was accustomed to disciplined party membership, which was certainly at odds with the freewheeling culture of many New Left organizations (at least until the era of party building began in earnest in the mid-1970s).[53] (Predictably, given the heated CP-SWP rivalry, Patti's father Ernie reacted apoplectically upon learning that she had joined SWP.) The early Asian American movement was marked by flexibility, with activists floating easily among organizations and causes such as AAPA, antiwar coalitions, and TWLF chapters, but Iiyama's membership in SWP anchored her in place. And when the center of Asian American radicalism coalesced in Maoist organizations, Iiyama's SWP membership rendered her as an outsider.

In the late 1970s and early 1980s, a movement to obtain redress and reparations for Japanese Americans incarcerated during World War II gathered considerable steam across the political spectrum of Japanese American communities. Radicals and veterans of the Asian American movement who formed the National Coalition for Redress and Reparations worked alongside members of politically mainstream groups such as the JACL. Ernie and Chizu Iiyama participated from within the JACL, an organization they had opposed before World War II, but Patti never actively took part despite being supportive of its aims. The best explanation is that among her priorities of work within the SWP, the ethnically specific grievance of redress and reparations probably did not rank highly.

Conclusion

This chapter has just begun to scratch the surface of understanding Japanese American and Asian American activism in the 1960s and 1970s outside of the Asian American movement. Its brief portraits of Tamio Wakayama and Patti Iiyama are meant to be suggestive rather than definitive, but these cases raise questions about the political trajectories and avenues available to Japanese Americans and Asian Americans in the early 1960s. Chinese, Japanese, and Filipino Americans (the three most populous Asian ethnic groups in the United States prior to 1965) were all portrayed as undesirable racial others in the early twentieth century and then subsequently had decades of racial oppression denied and whitewashed by the Cold War discourse of Asian Americans as a laudable model minority. How did progressive Asian Americans locate themselves within a racial hierarchy most often understood through the black-white binary? How did they build their own identities as racial, cultural, and political subjects? How did they reconcile their commitments to fighting racial and class inequality? And perhaps most importantly, how did they interact with the larger social movements of the early to mid-1960s? As the cases of Wakayama and Iiyama show, there is no single answer to these questions.

Steven Kiyoshi Kuromiya provides a final example of a political journey that began with participation in the civil rights movement. Like Tamio Wakayama, Ed Nakawatase, and Patti Iiyama, Kuromiya's origins trace back to the era of incarceration and exile for Nikkei. Kuromiya was born in 1943 at the Heart Mountain concentration camp in Wyoming. A Sansei, he attended the University of Pennsylvania in the early 1960s, where he joined SDS and led CORE-sponsored sit-ins at segregated restaurants in Maryland. He met Martin Luther King Jr. in 1963 and worked with King in Montgomery, where he was beaten unconscious by sheriff's deputies while registering voters in 1965. Later he marched with King in Selma and cared for the King children after their father was assassinated in 1968. Kuromiya was also an early activist in the gay liberation movement, participating in a 1965 demonstration at Independence Hall in Philadelphia. In 1970, he spoke on behalf of gay rights at the Black Panther Party's Revolutionary People's Constitutional Convention and formed the Philadelphia chapter of the Gay Liberation Front. He critiqued both the racism of gay activists and the homophobia of radicals of color. During the same period as his early gay activism, Kuromiya participated in the antiwar movement, sometimes in theatrical ways. For example, at the University of Pennsylvania, he publicly announced that a dog would be napalmed and then admonished the crowd of two thousand who showed up to protest that they should be as concerned about the plight of the Vietnamese people. He was arrested in 1971 for participating in the massive antiwar demonstrations in Washington, DC. In the 1980s, Kuromiya founded several key Philadelphia AIDS organizations, including AIDS Coalition to Unleash Power (ACT UP)/Philadelphia, and characterized health care as the "new civil rights battleground"—a label that highlighted how he saw his activist strands as interwoven. He protested against policies that prevented medications from being affordable in poor communities and advocated medical marijuana usage. Kuromiya passed away in 2000 from complications of AIDS and cancer, but his trajectory, like those I've discussed earlier, began with civil rights and extended to include activism around other identities.[54]

In addition to Wakayama and Iiyama, figures like Lefty Yamada, Ed Nakawatase, Ernie and Chizu Iiyama, and Steven Kiyoshi Kuromiya all richly deserve much fuller study. Widening the focus of scholarship on post–World War II Asian American progressive politics to include individuals who were active before the advent of the Asian American movement and/or operated outside of the movement is certain to lead researchers to uncover rich legacies of activism, commitment, and political evolution.

24 | The Ann Arbor Teach-In and Beyond: An Oral History

by Richard D. Mann

My purpose here is to touch briefly upon several forms of opposition to the war in Vietnam in 1965: the teach-ins, including the Ann Arbor teach-in, the national teach-in, and the televised debate on CBS with McGeorge Bundy, President Lyndon B. Johnson's national security advisor.

I want to begin by honoring the person whose deep understanding of Vietnam inspired and guided my involvement with the teach-ins, Merrill Jackson. He was a graduate student at the University of Michigan in the fifties. He was one of the two Michigan students who successfully urged candidate Kennedy to propose the Peace Corps. His parents were missionaries in Vietnam, and he was interned with them by the Japanese. After the French left Vietnam, he began a correspondence with Ngo Dinh Diem; when Diem cancelled the elections in 1956, they were no longer on friendly terms with each other. He not only taught me about what was going on in Vietnam from 1956 onward but also was the first person I ever met who received the Congress of Racial Equality (CORE) newsletter, which at the time was filled with news about lunch counter sit-ins in Baltimore and other East Coast cities.

My own political involvement started in 1959, when my wife and I moved to Cambridge, Massachusetts, and joined a tiny little group called Boston CORE. We attempted to employ the techniques of Gandhian nonviolent direct action. We would test whether realtors and rental agents were being honest in telling potential renters what properties they had to offer. When they offered a much fuller and better range of possibilities to white renters, we would negotiate with the realtors to see if they would let the black applicants see all the open apartments. None ever did, but some of them did indicate that their preference would be passage of a fair housing bill.

One of my colleagues in those early days of CORE was Bill Gamson, another great figure in this whole story. We were, successively, chairmen of the Boston CORE group. Then we both moved to Michigan, Bill first to teach sociology and me afterward to teach psychology. In early 1965, when the Gulf of Tonkin resolution (passed by Congress the prior August) was used to justify the bombing of North Vietnam after the attack on Pleiku, Bill and I could talk of nothing else. Over dinner one night, we realized we had to do something about this. Our political history led us to imagine engaging in some appropriate, nonviolent direct action. Our modest idea was to stand up on the steps of Angell Hall and object to the war in Vietnam. We would cancel our classes. That was crucial.

But the notion that we would cancel our classes for such a purpose aroused great alarm in the state of Michigan. Radio and television reported that Governor Romney and various state senators denounced the professors who planned to cancel their classes as un-American; they threatened to cancel the tenure of any professors who actually did so. On the other hand, as the days went by, we talked to more and more faculty members who were going to join us. The list got longer and longer. My chairman, Bill McKeachie, would drop by my office, and I would tell him, "Well it's up to 85, Bill" or "Oh, 112 now, Bill." The potential showdown seemed increasingly ominous, but before long there was a move within our group. Maybe we ought to get together and talk about what we were doing? There was a meeting at Bill Livant's house, where six or seven people came forward with a new idea. What could we do instead of cancelling classes and facing such a showdown?

This subgroup, as I recall, included Anatol Rapoport, Ted Newcomb, Frithjof Bergmann, Arnie Kaufman, and a few others. I gather it was Frithjof who proposed, "Why don't we not do what we're planning? Instead, why don't we do what we really do well, which is to teach?" My memory of the formulation that moved things in a new direction was this: "They're on the radio all the time telling the people of Michigan that we don't want to teach. Well let's not teach less, let's teach more. Let's teach all night. We could call it a teach-in." This new proposal split the planning group more or less in half.

The other more radical members of the group, including some from the Students for a Democratic Society (SDS), were, on the whole, in favor of continuing with the original project, but most of the people were beginning to peel off and decide the teach-in was actually a clever and effective move to make. Bill Gamson was very close to the SDS members on campus, and he was definitely in favor of continuing on with the project. In fact, we walked home that night somewhere between three or four o'clock in the morning, with him saying this was really in effect the end of the whole movement against the war in Ann Arbor and me thinking, "No, it's still . . . let's just try it." From that all-night meeting came the plan for the teach-in.

I can only imagine that the idea of us transitioning away from trying to call the bluff of the senators and governor was met with great delight in the dean's office. It was probably the best news they had had in weeks, so they were beyond generous. They said they would allow us to use all the necessary classrooms, auditoria, and audiovisual equipment. They even offered to suspend the "parietal rules" limiting female students' curfew, which meant co-eds could attend the entire night. In the weeks before the Ann Arbor event, many faculty—especially professors in the anthropology department—called colleagues around the country with the result that other teach-ins were being planned even before the night appointed for the event, March 24, 1965.

We thought that maybe two hundred people would come to Angell Hall Auditorium A, but as a sort of a "just in case," we lined up audio backup for Auditoriums B, C, and D, all of which filled up that night. It was a very cold, snowy, late-March night. The halls were packed. A thousand students, faculty, and townspeople showed up. We invited somebody from the State Department to come and present their side of the discourse, and he was treated very respectfully. He wasn't very convincing, I didn't think, but at least he was there.

At one point during the night, a bomb threat was called in. We were told in the middle of the presentations that we had to clear the auditorium. Hundreds of people streamed out into the Diag or the library steps, only to be greeted by snowballs thrown by members of several fraternities who were provoked by this "unpatriotic" gathering. When no bomb was found, we trickled back into the auditorium. We divided into groups and met for the rest of the night in smaller classrooms in Mason Hall. At eight o'clock the next morning, we held a ceremony on the steps of the library. By then there were still two hundred people left to hear the final benediction for our effort. "What next?" became the question at hand.

I want to go on beyond that first teach-in, because there were more events that followed directly from this event. Before long, we met at Bill Gamson's house, and the question was, "Well, now what will we do?" I don't know who came up with the idea; maybe I did or maybe somebody else, but we thought, "Well, why don't we challenge McGeorge Bundy himself to a debate? If we're going to have a campus teach-in, why don't we have a national teach-in in Washington?" We got a whole bunch of professors from around the country to sign up for what we came to call the Inter-University Committee for Debate on Foreign Policy. I was the executive director of that short-lived organization. We all contacted national figures from other schools and listed them down the left side of the letter we wrote McGeorge Bundy, even though the general tenor of the discussion at Bill's house was, "That's the most ridiculous idea anybody has ever heard," "They are going to laugh in our face," and "They are going to throw it in the wastebasket."

Two days later, McGeorge Bundy called me on the phone. "Hon," my wife said, "the White House is on the phone." He said he would agree in principle to debate the war on Vietnam with one main speaker on our side and an academic panel to back up both speakers. He suggested we should proceed to start arranging it. He asked, "Who do you have in mind for presenting your case?" I said, "We've got in mind Hans Morgenthau, the political scientist." He said, "Well, that would be unacceptable. I would not be willing to debate with Hans Morgenthau." I said, "Why not?" He said something like this: "Well, it's a very complicated story, but he almost got to be a professor at Harvard and I . . . he thinks that I nixed the whole deal for him to be hired and so he would . . . there would be a personal animosity behind his presentation." So Morgenthau was off the panel. But some among us felt that this was exactly the kind of Washington-style manipulation they knew would come to the fore.

I flew down to Washington to set up the details with Chester Cooper, Bundy's primary assistant. We tried to arrange a series of balanced discussions. Cooper presented Bundy's nomination of three people who would support the administration's side of the argument during the panel discussion after his talk: Bob Scalapino from University of California, Berkeley; Zbigniew Brzezinski from Columbia University; and Wesley Fishel from Michigan State University. For the smaller panel discussions, he proposed progovernment spokesmen, such as Daniel Elsberg, formerly of RAND (and subsequently renowned, once he had turned against the war, for releasing the Pentagon Papers).

As the national teach-in began on May 15, 1965, I was sitting beside Ernest Nagel. We were in the auditorium listening to Arthur Schleslinger Jr. give a long rationalization for the war in Vietnam. However, at the same time, because he was anti-Johnson and pro-Kennedy, he spent time attacking Johnson's intervention in the Dominican Republic. As we were listening, I was tugged on the sleeve to come quickly. We were hurried out of the room, out into the street. There was a limousine waiting there. Nagel and I went sailing through the streets of Washington, and the gates leading to the West Wing of the White House swung open.

We walked into what was obviously Bundy's office, only to be met by someone who said that Mr. Bundy was not going to be able to come to the teach-in. We asked, of course, "Well, why not?" His answer was delivered in an intimidating, Camelot style that brooks no opposition: "Well, I'll tell you, but if you tell anyone else, they will come and carry me out of here on my shield." We were told that Bundy was, at that very moment, in Puerto Rico talking to Juan Bosch to see if he could work out some arrangement to forestall President Johnson's plans for the US occupation of the Dominican Republic.

The spokesman conveyed Bundy's choice to replace him in the teach-in: Wesley Fishel, whose expertise about Vietnam included getting federal grants for designing Diem's military training. When Scalapino heard who had been nominated to defend the government's position, he and Brzezinski huddled privately and, before West Wing officials had even been consulted, announced that Scalapino would replace Bundy.

The whole teach-in, from morning until late at night, was broadcast on Educational TV, the fortuitous result of a relative of University of Michigan anthropologist Marshall Sahlins, who worked for this network. We had our side for the debate: Mary Wright from Yale University, Robert Browne from Fairley Dickenson University, and George Kahin from Cornell University. What impressed me and depressed me at the same was to see how utterly authoritative Scalapino could appear. All sorts of tribal names were rattled off as if to assert that if you didn't know all this material, you just couldn't enter the debate. It was intimidating, or so it seemed to me. I recall Scalapino, with gusto, asking our team, "Well, what about Cao Dai, Hoa Hao, and Binh Xuyen in the Mekong Delta?" My memory is that we were quite off balance the whole time. We were the academic outsiders, they were the academic insiders. Academics they certainly were, but with such access and polish. To my mind, they just talked circles around us.

Nonetheless, we returned to Ann Arbor quite exhilarated by the success of the teach-in. Over the course of a very full day, dozens of experts made clear how deep and extensive the opposition to the administration's Vietnam policy was. The question, once again, was, "OK, now what do we do?" There was a long meeting at Bill Gamson's house. Some people were still insulted that Bundy had failed to show up, and their contempt for his duplicity and cowardice was manifest in several interviews published in *Ramparts* magazine. The idea of challenging Bundy to a debate on television came up, and I was assigned the job of writing a letter to him that expressed some regret over the published comments but still might lead him to accept. Again he called and said, "OK, come to Washington," and so we did.

Jonathan Mirsky from the University of Pennsylvania and I went to the White House. As we walked into his office in the West Wing, Bundy took one look at me and my striped repp tie and said, "You know, that's the official tie of the British Intelligence Service." (Small detail, I realize, but it did throw me off balance quite effectively.) Besides Bundy, there was Fred Friendly and Eric Sevareid from CBS. We arranged the half-hour television debate, prime time, and for this round Morgenthau was allowed to be on the team.

I think we got clobbered again. I really do. The people who sat around the television at our house were all depressed after it ended. It wasn't as if we were voting up or down. We were just bummed out by how, for example, Bundy got to say to Morgenthau, in effect, "Where do you get off attacking the administration's policy in Vietnam when you supported exactly the same policy in Laos?" They just had a nimble, self-assured way of countering most if not all our arguments. I think our eventual discouragement indicates just how invincible and convincing we had thought our arguments and our champions were. We were overmatched, perhaps not in terms of the merit of our views but in terms of the kind of debating style Bundy and his colleagues could sustain.

The issue of who won was not, of course, the most important aspect of the debate in the context of the antiwar movement. For starters, hundreds of thousands of people had now heard deeply critical assessments of the Vietnam policy of both Kennedy and Johnson. They heard their country associated with such words as aggression and imperialism. These entries into the mainstream of public debate breached the administration's seemingly self-evident story that justified America's mounting mobilization for war. In all probability, many of the arguments raised by the teach-in speakers constituted what Bundy was referring to when he conceded, many years later, that the antiwar critics evidently had it right all along.

In our different ways, we moved from there to new tactics designed to stop the war. Ed Pierce, Barbara Fuller, and I helped create Vietnam Summer in 1967. It involved going door to door, trying to get people to sign a statement that they were against the war. To our surprise, it turned out that even Ann Arbor was quite anti-antiwar. This was a dispiriting thing to find out so emphatically, and what emerged in our city at least was a strong desire to talk mostly to like-minded people and to move toward a more confrontational style. We organized a stadium-size rally. We lay down on US-23 to stop traffic. And in 1969 there was the Mobilization against the War, with "the Mobe" getting eight hundred thousand of us to show up in Washington and do what we could to force Nixon to pay attention. True enough, by that point the Tet Offensive had deflated the general notion that for sure we were going to win this war, and soon.

Somehow, in its early stages, the impact of the teach-ins had something like the effect of those first crucial, anti-inertia turns of the prayer wheel. We couldn't just do nothing in 1965, and toward the end of the war, eight years later, we just couldn't walk away from the ongoing air war in Cambodia. By 1973, when our troops had been brought home and "the movement" seemed dead, my colleague Tom Weisskopf and I joined in with the Indochina Peace Campaign. Tom Hayden and Jane Fonda led Ann Arbor and other scattered groups in saying that flying over the rice fields at very high altitude and unloading an obscene tonnage of bombs was no different from the time we bombed the North.

Finally, in January 1973, there was a peace agreement. What the teach-ins had helped start, "the antiwar movement," was what we might then have called "a good action."

25 | New Indians in the New Frontier
by Paul Chaat Smith

I began preparing for the New Insurgency conference during the prior week, about the time that Sandy, the storm of the century, went up the coast. I did two things. First, I watched *The Big Lebowski*. Not as good as I remembered it, but you know what, it's still pretty good. Second, I read every word of the *Port Huron Statement*.

What a strange document! The thing ranges over a bewildering number of topics at a length that tries the patience of many a reader. We go from detailed critiques of university administration to the role of Dixie-

Alcatraz dock during the Indian occupation, 1969-71. Golden Gate NRA Park Archives (Creative Commons)

crats in the national Democratic Party to speculation on Adenauer's next move in Germany to goofball riffs on the wonders of atomic energy and mass migrations of people from those alienating cities to the countryside.

For a contemporary reader, what really stands out is the sense of urgency and utter lack of cynicism. The *Statement* is fueled by a tangible fear of impending apocalypse. It is important to recall how pervasive, how immediate the Cold War felt in 1962. People really did build bomb shelters in their basements. Children really did duck and cover under their desks. The Soviet Union and the United States really did come close to nuclear war over Cuba. When the Students for a Democratic Society (SDS) framers concluded their massive text by saying, "If we appear to seek the unattainable, then let it be said that we do so to avoid the unimaginable," everyone knew exactly what they were talking about.[1]

I was in elementary school when all that manifesto writing was going down in the Michigan woods. I grew up mostly in the Washington, DC, suburbs, and my father worked at the University of Maryland, so I had a front-row seat for the antiwar moratoriums in Washington. I read the *New Republic* (don't laugh) and started an underground newspaper in high school. I must have heard of SDS around that time. In fall 1973, I enrolled at Antioch College in Ohio, and through Antioch I soon found my way to South Dakota and the American Indian Movement (AIM).

AIM was on trial, and not just any trial. More than two hundred people were under federal indictment and facing juries in Iowa, Nebraska, Minnesota, and South Dakota for the seventy-one-day occupation of Wounded Knee. The trials went on for three years, and even though most ended in acquittals, the effort halted AIM in its tracks and essentially bankrupted the movement.

It was then, during the mid-1970s, that I learned about the American left. There were few Indian lawyers back then, so the legal teams were mostly young white folks, many of them with the National Lawyers Guild, and they often had left-wing, even revolutionary politics. Approximately a thousand years had passed since 1962. Port Huron was old news. I didn't know anyone in the Weather Underground, but I knew people who knew people who were once in the Weather Underground. Truthfully, I didn't want to know very much, but I will admit this was kind of thrilling. There wasn't much discussion of the Democratic Party or the Cold War. The massive antiwar demonstrations were over and it didn't feel like the streets were full of democracy. It was depressing. The name said it all: Wounded Knee Legal Defense/Offense Committee, but everyone knew the "Offense" part of the name was just a brave front.

By then I was reading Carl Oglesby, Todd Gitlin, James Miller, and V. I. Lenin, and *The Guardian* had replaced *The New Republic*. I was getting up to speed.

On the second night of the New Insurgency conference, we heard Tom Hayden matter-of-factly explain that SDS wasn't trying to be the coolest New Left group or outwit its opponents or prove how smart they were (maybe I'm not convinced on that one), but they actually were trying to shape national policy—as in, winning voting rights for disenfranchised blacks, building alliances to end the Cold War, and defeating poverty. They wrote thinking the White House would read their words, and in fact, the White House did read their words.

I have to say this was news to me. My time as an activist never included moments where I, or anyone I knew, actually imagined we could shape national policy.

But during my years with AIM, and later its international arm, the International Indian Treaty Council, I discovered that I found failure and failed revolutions subjects of endless fascination. I wasn't a very good activist and never did much; technically, I edited a newsletter and helped out on conferences. Mainly, I just was hanging out, watching a failed revolution unfold in all its mesmerizing glory. I had missed all the key events, but the aftermath was fascinating enough.

I began studying other failures. I remember zipping through James Forman's *The Making of Black Revolutionaries* like a teenage girl inhaling *The Hunger Games*. I loved *Famous Long Ago*, Raymond Mungo's telling of the rise and fall of the Liberation News Service. Somewhere along the way, it occurred to me to write a book about the failed revolution I knew best.

The Indian movement never really took off until the final weeks of 1969, and the signature event happened in 1973. So we were late to the party. Indians are never directly mentioned in the *Port Huron Statement*, which is probably a good thing. What would SDS have said about Indians in 1962? The same thing we would have said, which is Indians are invisible and irrelevant. That would soon change, at least for a while. Anyway, Indians are present in the *Port Huron Statement* because Huron is the name of an Indian tribe.

The Indian movement was terrible at almost everything it attempted and lights-out brilliant at precisely one thing. That one thing was a killer ability to stage occupations in a way that performed a pretty neat magic trick: the invisible became visible. The first was in 1969, at the abandoned prison Alcatraz, conveniently located in shouting distance from San Francisco. What would drive people to take over an empty maximum security prison? Exactly. The second was in fall 1972, as a ramshackle group called the Trail of Broken Treaties made their way to Washington, hoping to meet with President Nixon. He was kind of busy, this being days before a presidential election. And among the skills the Indian movement severely lacked was anything to do with planning or logistics. The promised housing in Washington was a mirage, so the hungry Indians went to the Bureau of Indian Affairs and didn't leave for a week. In fact, they ended up trashing the place. The occupation was entirely the result of incompetence, but this became movement lemonade as they set up a tipi in front of the colonial headquarters and built gasoline bombs on the roof.

AIM's marquee event was an armed occupation that took place five months later, at a village on the Pine Ridge reservation called Wounded Knee. In 1973 everyone in America had heard of Wounded Knee, but most never thought about Indians who were still around. The takeover at Wounded Knee won network television coverage for weeks. This was before satellite trucks and meant that television reporters had to film their reports and send their film by jet to the networks.

Indians occupying Alcatraz. Indians occupying the Bureau of Indian Affairs. Indians occupying Wounded Knee. And scores and scores of lesser known occupations—of Nike missile sites, national monuments, and government offices—that collectively involved thousands of people. Each event, however briefly, made Indians famous at a time when Indians were anonymous.

Occupations by their very nature are a desperate strategy, nearly always doomed to failure. The state has time on its side, and the occupiers can only hold out so long.

Some argue the Indian movement was the most underachieving movement of its time, and I find this to be true. Yes, there were extraordinary moments of courage and heroism, but they are offset by massive collateral damage and a failure to turn visibility into anything more than visibility. We had no victories like the Voting Rights Act or Fair Housing Act. Our leaders don't appear on postage stamps, never won Nobel Prizes, and never had national holidays. Instead, three of the most prominent—Russell Means, Dennis Banks, and John Trudell—have among them a score of television and film credits as actors—actors playing Indians.

So what do we make of this, that at the end of the day, when we look back and see that even with all those brilliant mistakes, nothing since has come close to winning attention for the most invisible population in the country? How much is that attention worth? Would Indian activism have been stronger without the shambolic takeovers?

A New Insurgency charged us with thinking about the *Port Huron Statement* in its time and also Port Huron in our time. And what we really meant is not the words in the manifesto but the question of what activism and a left agenda looks like around 2012.

My answer is I have no idea. But the question forced me to think about the Occupy movement. Like most people at this conference, I've spent a fair amount of time critiquing Occupy. And why not? It's easy, fun, and free. Here's what I found most annoying about Occupy Wall Street: the human microphone. Creepy! Also, the so-called decision-making process. As Homer Simpson asked recently, when will people finally realize democracy doesn't work? Also super-icky were those drumming groups. Basically, I really hated the whole Phish concert vibe.

Occupy didn't accomplish anything either. It didn't end wars or segregation. The police rousted them in the end as everyone, except maybe some of those drummers, knew they would.

But the one smart thing they did, amid the many stupid things, was freaking genius. The 1 percent and the 99 percent. Holy moly, how awesome was that? Very, very awesome.

And what if that genius phrase is the only thing that survives? It's still pretty amazing, and many activist movements have accomplished far less. And here's another uncomfortable question: is it possible the reason I'm so harsh about Occupy Wall Street is because it was so similar to AIM? The AIM I wanted was an indigenous version of the Student Nonviolent Coordinating Committee. But AIM was eerily similar to Occupy. Both were one-trick ponies with way too much drumming and disorganization and ultrademocracy. Neither group could ever learn when it was time to get off the stage.

Conclusion: OK, so one is tempted to speak of these moments—Port Huron, Wounded Knee, Occupy Wall Street—as platforms rather than campaigns that won or lost, that it is up to those who come later to make what they will of those moments.

The Velvet Underground (interesting name!) is famously remembered as a group that sold few records, but everyone who purchased one started their own band.

I think SDS and AIM were the Velvet Underground of activist organizations. Those outfits could inspire you for a lifetime, whether your dream was being a US senator from California, an urban guerilla, or a Hollywood movie star.

Platforms or dead ends? I can't say. I end up in a familiar place, the land of honest confusion, and maybe that's not such a bad thing.

London to Aldermaston march by the Campaign for Nuclear Disarmament (CND), 1958. Committee for Nuclear Disarmament

IV.

Comparisons

Global New Lefts

The largest context of the new insurgency was global. Most generally, the social and political realities of the Cold War and decolonization, as those became intertwined, shaped the world the New Left inhabited. We can recognize a more particular nexus of relations, still profoundly transnational, that fostered the rise of a New Left in exchanges between writers and activists in the United States, Britain, France, and Germany—as we learn from Michael Vester's first-person testimony and Rita Chin's historical survey. The political incitements to protest in these sites, we know, reached beyond that "Western" center—to Eastern Europe, due to the catalytic effect the Soviet suppression of the Hungarian revolution had on Western European Marxists (as well as the influence of Polish dissidents of 1956 on them); to what came to be called "the Third World," via the imperialist imbroglio of Suez, the Algerian war and its effect on France itself, the Cuban Revolution, the movement into Britain of people from its prior colonial possessions (particularly the West Indies and South Asia); and to the war in Vietnam. The mutual affinity between African independence movements and the African American freedom struggle set another essential coordinate to the period.

The new lefts arising in that time around the world could be found near and far. In the Caribbean, aside from Cuba, a current of West Indian radicalism stimulated by the independence of former British possessions, stretching from Jamaica to Trinidad and Tobago in 1962, strove for genuine decolonization—that is, social, cultural, and economic autonomy, free of the great powers, as described here by Paul Hébert. A Mexican left also sympathized with the Cuban Revolution circa 1960, though a full-blown student movement only emerged there later, in the wake of government repression (and mass murder) of protesters in 1968, as Louise Walker shows us. Further afield, and with fewer direct reverberations on the US scene, young militants in Japan from the student associations known as Zengakuren set themselves off from the Communist Party around 1960 and commenced a new left there. In this volume, Leslie Pincus discusses a unique element of new dissent in Japan that reflected postwar pacifism and an orientation toward the transformation of everyday life interestingly akin to American counterculture.

—Howard Brick

26 | The German New Left and Participatory Democracy: The Impact on Social, Cultural, and Political Change*

by Michael Vester

In this chapter I focus on the impact of the comprehensive movement of societal change identified with participatory democracy. I go back to 1961–62 when, as a Fulbright scholar in the United States, I took part in the development of Students for a Democratic Society (SDS). At the Port Huron convention, I represented a "fraternal organization," the West German Socialist Students' Federation, *Sozialistischer Deutscher Studentenbund* (hereafter abbreviated as German SDS). In the *Port Huron Statement*, the German contribution appeared particularly in the section concerning how to end the Cold War. As a whole, the *Statement* represented our common ambition to end the sectarian isolation of the Old Left by adopting new perspectives on recent changes in the nature of capitalism and embracing a vision of participatory democracy. In this chapter, I will also show how the new ideas of the British and American New Left and of left-leaning liberals came to Germany, where they sparked passionate controversies and helped inspire the mass youth movements of the 1960s.

On the political level, the German developments differed from those in the United States. In Germany, a strong base of employees' participation in enterprise governance and welfare-state provision had developed after the fall of the Nazi regime. By the late 1960s and afterward, as American movements suffered demoralizing setbacks due to the assassinations of the Kennedys and Martin Luther King Jr., the German movements took advantage of new political openings. Consequently, under the governments of Willy Brandt, many movement aims were translated into participatory reforms.

*This essay appeared in a different form in *The Port Huron Statement: Sources and Legacies of the New Left's Founding Manifesto,* ed. Richard Flack and Nelson Lichtenstein (Philadelphia: University of Pennsylvania Press, 2015).

The Making of the *Port Huron Statement*

When I arrived in New York in October 1961, I had just finished my year on the national board of the German SDS in Frankfurt. As its vice-chairman I had been responsible for developing a new international network of socialist student and youth organizations. We understood ourselves as parts of a new, unorthodox political current that came from England and, already in 1958, had named itself a "new left."[1] As Edward Thompson wrote retrospectively in 1970, this "British 'new left' was among the first of this international family. It began in the mid-fifties as a strongly political movement, taking hostile views of both orthodox social democracy and communism, and since 1960 it has gone through many mutations."[2]

In 1961, the New Left current consisted of dissidents inside and outside the old socialist international organizations in the developed countries, in the newly independent nations of the Third World, and in communist Eastern Europe. All these activists of a younger generation sensed that a new political opening had occurred, following the advance of decolonization and John Kennedy's election, which, at that time, encouraged the hope for new, progressive electoral majorities in many countries. The activists were eager to contest the bureaucratic stalemate and authoritarian domination in the countries of the Eastern as well as the Western bloc. The new mood was manifest in the protest movements of Japanese and Turkish students, of the English and German Easter marches for nuclear disarmament, and by the antiracist civil rights movements emerging in the United States and in South Africa.

They did not expect change to come from powerful organizational structures, theoretical credos, or charismatic leaders like Kennedy. Instead it would arise from real social movements and mobilizations that were a product of the contemporary situation. But there *was* also a new appreciation of social theory. Most important in this respect was the British journal *New Left Review*. Simultaneously, in Germany and Italy, many dissidents of the early twentieth-century revolutionary left were rediscovered, among them Antonio Gramsci, Rosa Luxemburg, Wilhelm Reich, and Karl Korsch.

Arriving with this background, I got in touch with like-minded organizations in the United States. My most important contacts were Al Haber, president of SDS; Bob Ross, the vice president; and Dick Flacks, also engaged in transforming SDS into a New Left organization and movement. I also met socialists such as Michael Harrington and representatives of the Young People's Socialist League.

In discussions with Al Haber I immediately found out that both of us were enthusiastic about a 1960 British collection of New Left essays edited by Edward Thompson.[3] This book offered to the amorphous currents of the New Left a common definition of the historical situation and the role of a New Left to "find a way out of apathy."[4] It was not a declaration of principles but a concrete analysis of the manifold social contradictions that defined the new "'bastard' capitalism" (as Ralph Samuel called it in the book) and an analysis of the possibilities of renewed class conflicts and socialist movements.[5] When the book appeared in Europe, it immediately became the most important signal of a new and liberating practical *and* intellectual departure. It reached a wider international audience than even C. Wright Mills's famous 1960 essay, "A Letter to the New Left," which was read mainly in Britain and the United States.[6]

In early December 1961, Al Haber told me that SDS was planning its own public statement, which would apply the new ideas to the American situation. Tom Hayden produced a first draft of nine pages, circulated for discussion in March 1962. After months of discussions, in which I also took part, Tom transformed his first draft into a fully developed preconference draft of a manifesto. At the Port Huron conference in June 1962, we had no alternative but to understate our ambitions, calling it simply a "statement" named for the locale where we met to discuss and formulate the final draft.

The ambitious stance of the *Port Huron Statement*—to express the political perspectives of a whole younger generation—was not just intellectual hubris. It was encouraged by the new movements rising around the world. Its new language, markedly different from the stereotypical slogans of the Old Left, provided a fresh but erudite diagnosis of the historical situation. Given the rhetoric of reform that accompanied the new president's administration—so different from the age of Eisenhower and Joseph McCarthy—the authors felt encouraged to proclaim the possibility of social change going well beyond Kennedy's "New Frontier." The *Statement* became a great synthesis of what was discussed in the international New Left. It analyzed the new social and political contradictions of the advanced, "affluent" capitalist societies. Moreover, it recognized the ways that these contradictions took the form of a generational conflict—as a conflict that broke out within social classes and within gender and ethnic groups.

But the *Statement* also went further. The term "participatory democracy" was offered as an integrative formula for the emerging movements. It allowed us to look back to a long tradition of emancipatory, communal, and labor movements in many countries that advocated economic democracy as well as personal freedom. The term became a common denominator for the manifold new movements renewing those traditions of genuine democracy. For us, at that time, there was no necessary contradiction between unionist, socialist, antiracist, emancipatory, and youth-cultural movements and organizations. This combination was symbolized by the fact that we adopted this manifesto at a camp on Lake Huron built by the United Automobile Workers (UAW) in the Detroit area during the Great Depression.

Indeed, the formula of participatory democracy brought together the different movements for personal and political emancipation. These would come to include gender emancipation as well as nonauthoritarian pedagogy, the emancipation of ethnical and cultural minorities, the establishment of democratic publics and popular control in politics and economics, and the ecological and pacifist reflections on the destructive consequences of one-dimensional modernization.

Today, after decades of neoconservative restoration, the spirit is still here, recently manifested by the international chain reaction of new democratic movements. In the Spanish May manifesto of 2011, protesters rediscovered the term "genuine democracy" along with the notion of "democratic participation." To me, this continuity of emancipatory movements stems not only from a heritage of ideas but also from underlying changes in everyday culture and social structure. The slow but steady spread of grassroots activities among the younger generations today gives participatory democracy the appearance of what Raymond Williams once called a "long revolution" in his famous analysis of the revolution in culture, which unfolded alongside the democratic and industrial revolutions since the nineteenth century.[7]

The German Contribution to the *Statement*

Al Haber took a central role in organizing, motivating, and discussing the contributions to the manifesto draft and its different chapters. With his encouragement, I contributed two documents regarding the analysis of the Cold War and a possible disengagement of the military blocs. The key themes of those memos were included in the preconference, forty-nine-page draft of the manifesto that was circulated shortly before the Port Huron meeting. Also, a general comment I wrote on that long draft was circulated as well. There I raised the key question of who should bring about the social changes we demanded. I argued that Hayden, following Mills, may have put too much emphasis on the role of intellectuals as agents of social change. In my view, the intellectuals by themselves could only be mediators "but *not the agency*, the moving power itself." That was still a task for the labor movement.

My main contributions, however, were the two papers on ending the Cold War. The first paper offered the perspectives of German SDS on the Cold War, adopted by our national conference in October 1961.[8] This motion had been formulated by our group in Berlin, where the division between the Eastern and Western blocs had been "cemented" by the infamous Berlin Wall since August 13, 1961.

Our proposal for ending the Cold War by diplomatic negotiation challenged the West German government's Hallstein Doctrine, which refused diplomatic recognition of the East German state, the *Deutsche Demokratische Republik*, on the grounds that this would grant moral support to an undemocratic regime and raise an insurmountable obstacle to future German reunification. To study the problem of diplomatic recognition more fully, I took part in a course on international law at Bowdoin. Advised by Professor Arthern Daggett, I wrote a paper demonstrating that, by the criteria of international law as well as by selected cases, diplomatic recognition had nothing to do with moral or political approval; rather, it had been, historically, a way to ease tensions. I integrated that perspective into a ten-page political analysis, "Berlin: Why Not Recognize the Status Quo?" On February 6, 1962, I sent the paper to Al Haber, and within a week, he had passed it on to Bob Ross for comments. He told me he would also "have it included in the TURN TOWARD PEACE packet," produced by a coalition of sixty peace and liberal internationalist organizations chaired by Norman Thomas. Later, Haber told me that the National Student Association also distributed my Berlin paper.

The second paper was titled "A Hungarian Proposal for Depolarisation." Its authors, the Hungarian émigrés Géza Ankerl, a political friend of mine, and Lazlo Huzsar, had been members of the Revolutionary Student Committee during the Budapest rebellion of 1956. Their plan for a military and political withdrawal of both military blocs in Europe, which concretized the much-discussed idea of disengagement, had already gained the attention of George Kennan, Adlai Stevenson, and other prominent politicians.

The ideas presented in those two papers regarding diplomatic recognition, military disengagement, ending nuclear tests and armament, and creating demilitarized zones between the Eastern and Western blocs were integrated into the final text of the *Statement*. Reflecting the views of West Germany's non-Communist left, the *Statement* remarked, "We should recognize that an authoritarian [West] Germany's insistence on reunification, while knowing the impossibility of achieving it with peaceful means, could only generate increasing frustrations among the population and nationalist sentiments which frighten its Eastern neighbors."[9] To avoid this, we advocated mutual diplomatic recognition of the two German states and of Berlin's divided status in order to diminish Cold War tensions.

Moreover, following my suggestions, this section of the *Port Huron Statement* emphasized that the Cold War was not merely a problem of Soviet-American conflict: "Even if Washington and Moscow were in favor of disengagement, both Adenauer and Ulbricht would never agree to it because Cold War keeps their parties in power."[10] Our solution to this problem included a series of "disarmament experiments," of which the most important would be the military disengagement by both world powers from Poland, Czechoslovakia, and the two Germanys. By undermining the Russian argument for tighter controls in East Europe—that is, the "menace of capitalist encirclement"—such diplomacy, "geared to the needs of democratic elements in the satellites," would develop a real bridge between East and West.[11] All of this resembled the Ostpolitik that Social Democratic Party (SPD) leader Willy Brandt began to pursue seven years later.

On my contribution, Tom Hayden later commented, "We saw the cold war only inside of the United States; United States versus Soviet Union. We weren't thinking of the people on the ground in between the superpowers. So if you read the Port Huron Statement, you'll see a German SDS influence on this long section about why the Cold War had to be ended and why it had to be ended with the involvement of European social movements. . . . I credit [Michael Vester] with conceiving and writing the entire Cold War section of the Port Huron Statement."[12]

The *Statement*'s text made clear that politically, "as democrats," its authors were "in basic opposition to the communist system"—which, of course, was also the position of the German SDS. However, this did not help us much in Germany, where we said "blind anticommunism" and hostility to the Soviet Union was used to shore up a conservative and constrained political culture at home. There, in an atmosphere of Cold War polarization, the SPD was in the process of expelling German SDS members from party membership on the pretext that we were Communists, which we definitely were not. Reconciliation did not take place until after 1969, when Willy Brandt became head of a new government and the spirit of a new departure finally spread to Germany. Brandt received the Nobel Peace Prize in 1971 for his efforts to lower Cold War tensions, almost exactly the same politics of détente and mutual diplomatic recognition that we had advocated in the early 1960s.

Frankfurt and the Historical Success of Workers' Participation in Germany

As happens in wonderful friendships, the transport of ideas also went into the other direction, from the United States to Germany. Soon after Port Huron I returned to Frankfurt, where my colleagues and I continued building the new international network of New Left youth and student organizations.[13] Our collective efforts were made all the more urgent by the radically unstable times: the continuing Cold War confrontations in and over Berlin, the nuclear tests conducted by both the Soviet Union and the United States, the conflicts in Algeria and South Africa, and the eruption of movements against dictatorial regimes around the world.

Frankfurt in the early 1960s was a city where the New Left and the international socialist movement exchanged ideas and developed plans for action. The "critical theory" of the Frankfurt Institute for Social Research was very important for us, but so was the left wing of the labor movement, which had a strong base in the city. Frankfurt was home to many left-wing democratic socialists of the older generation who had been persecuted or driven into emigration during the Nazi years. In such a milieu, ideas and ideologies devoted to building workers' democracy and fostering antiauthoritarian education were all part of an undogmatic socialism that posed an alternative to both authoritarian communism and the right-wing mainstream of Germany's postwar social democracy. In particular, the rediscovered ideas and ideals of Rosa Luxemburg and Wilhelm Reich were extremely important.

Frankfurt's socialist students sought to enhance democratic participation, both civic and industrial. In the pursuit of this aim, we relied not only on the new youth and intellectual movements of that era but also on the working-class intelligentsia (i.e., functionaries in the big industrial unions who had played important roles in the antifascist resistance).

After the war, strikes by the industrial unions had laid the foundation for a strong welfare state and helped ensure a voice for organized workers in the governance of the enterprise for which they worked. In 1949, big organized demonstrations of the metal workers and the miners moved

West Germany's parliament to concede the *Mitbestimmungsgesetz* ("Participation Act") of 1951, which gave employee representatives 50 percent of the seats on the supervisory boards of the big coal and steel corporations.[14] One year later, the same majority conceded the *Betriebsverfassungsgesetz* ("Enterprise Constitutional Act"), which did not include employee representatives in the supervisory boards but gave strong minority rights to boards of elected employees' representatives (*"Betriebsräte"*) in *almost all* enterprises in Federal Germany. Astonishingly enough, this working-class progress came when conservative governments were in power. From 1949 to 1963, Chancellor Konrad Adenauer tried to develop a new conservatism that was responsive to working-class demands and therefore a bulwark against the appeals of Communism or the return of the Nazis. In order to avoid severe social and political ruptures, Adenauer also ensured that Germany would remain a nation wedded to parliamentary institutions and formal democratic rights for its citizens.

The striving for workers' participation after World War II followed in the tradition first established by the democratic workers' councils of the 1918 German Revolution. Those councils had been decisive in introducing full parliamentarian democracy and the idea of industrial democracy to Germany after World War I. Many of the leftist union activists who now fought for *Mitbestimmung* ("Participation") had been influenced by the legacy of 1918 and by their experience in the resistance to the Hitler regime. After World War II, such participatory workers' movements were not limited to the Federal Republic. They remained a strong strain within the European and Latin American labor movement, especially in Italy, France, Britain, and Chile, as well as in the Portuguese and Nicaraguan revolutions of the 1970s.

The introduction of Mitbestimmung served as a key example of participatory empowerment in Arnold Kaufman's famous essay of 1960, "Participatory Democracy and Human Nature," which gave the *Port Huron Statement* its central slogan.[15] In an ambitious assault upon the work of Walter Lippmann, Sigmund Freud, Melanie Klein, Erich Fromm, Joseph Schumpeter, Robert Michels, and others skeptical of the human capacity for democratic and rational decision making, Kaufman argued that the main justification for a "democracy of participation" is the "contribution it can make to the development of human powers of thought, feeling and action. In this respect it differs, and differs quite fundamentally, from a representative system incorporating all sorts of institutional features designed to safeguard human rights and ensure social order. *This distinction is all-important.*"[16] Only by recognizing the distinction, he suggested, could the contributions of *both* participation and representative systems be understood and combined in practice.

Kaufman's intervention came in a historical situation where, since the 1950s, the possibility of workers' participation was again discussed internationally as an alternative to authoritarian structures in state-socialist as well as capitalist enterprises. This discussion was spurred by the widely noted "experiments in Germany, Yugoslavia, Poland and elsewhere."[17] Kaufman referred to an international symposium on Workers' Participation in Management held in 1956 by the International Sociological Association. The question was whether "workers could assume managerial functions with good results both for the workers themselves and for the larger society."[18] While the German sociologist Ralf Dahrendorf asserted that "the appointment of workers to managerial or quasi-managerial positions is bound to defeat its own ends," another participant considered "the possibility of eliminating conflict through an extensive rotation of managerial jobs."[19] To resolve such debates, Kaufman called for an empirical program to study practical examples of democratic participation defined by the criteria that it "essentially involves actual preliminary deliberation (conversations, debate, discussion) and that in the final decision each participant has a roughly equal formal say."[20]

In fact, the research Kaufman proposed was pursued already by West German sociologists of labor relations.[21] In Dortmund, Popitz, Bahrdt, and others had conducted a famous empirical study on how Mitbestimmung had reshaped authority relations in the industry and how workers' social consciousness was now structured. In Frankfurt, the Institute for Social Research was responsive to the city's radical political culture in its research on the democratic potentials within the West German population. Our underlying common aim was to prevent a return of fascism in Germany. In cooperation with the labor union left, professors Ludwig von Friedeburg, Gerhard Brandt, and Manfred Teschner coordinated substantial research in industrial sociology and on workers' mentality. Jürgen Habermas, von Friedeburg, and others conducted influential studies on students' attitudes toward democracy and on educational opportunities. Helge Pross initiated the institute's work in feminist studies. In all these fields, former Frankfurt students developed further research when they won posts in many German universities during the movement years until the 1970s.

Important impulses came from the studies on authoritarian and democratic personality formation initiated in the 1930s and 1940s by Theodor W. Adorno, Erich Fromm, and Wilhelm Reich, who had emigrated to the

United States. They motivated many of us to become active in promoting democratic, nonauthoritarian pedagogy. Monika Seifert-Mitscherlich and her friends founded the first antiauthoritarian kindergarten in Frankfurt, which was soon replicated all over the country.[22] Since the 1970s, the Frankfurt School studies of changing attitudes toward democracy and of class mentalities were carried on especially at the University of Hannover, where the approaches of Adorno, Fromm, and Reich were combined with the approaches of Pierre Bourdieu and with New Left cultural studies.[23]

Preparing a New Participatory Mobilization

Around 1960 in Germany, the participatory elements of Mitbestimmung were still embedded in a societal context with many constraints, including a paternalistic family model and the conservative consensus fostered by the Cold War. In our view and the view of the unions, the participatory reforms achieved so far were strong but not sufficient.

How could we break that oppressive sense of constraint? When, around 1960, most of the local German SDS groups began to consider themselves part of a New Left, we developed a multilevel idea of how to mobilize people for participatory politics. Many SDS members became active in workers' education and the politics of the big industrial labor unions. We also tried to build a national "left wing" or "labor wing" inside the Social Democratic Party. And we joined forces with the most critical and active parts of all progressive democratic organizations. These were not only the labor union and SPD youth and the leftist socialist youth organizations (the Red Falcons and the Friends of Nature) but also other activists who had turned left during the Cold War conflicts: student government leaders, activists from the student press at high schools and universities, and even activists of the different scouting organizations.

By combining these different levels of engagement, the German SDS mobilized and coordinated working-class and general youth activities, especially in the fields of labor movement education in the high schools and universities. In the early 1960s, this was a rather slow process, but after the mid-1960s, it gained momentum by merging with the broad, worldwide cultural revolt of youth directed against authoritarianism of all kinds. This historical coincidence of sociostructural changes and active political groups finally, in 1969, led to the sweeping electoral victory of Willy Brandt, which in turn opened space for many institutional reforms demanded by the social movements of the New Left.

These beginnings were connected with a socialist-inflected, transatlantic labor internationalism. One outstanding representative of that tradition was Hans Matthöfer, a friend of German SDS, an official in the Frankfurt headquarters of metal industry employees' union IG Metall, and the grandson of a Polish immigrant. Matthöfer had spent a year working in the United States with the UAW. From 1960 to 1972, he organized the large educational program for the 2.2 million IG Metall members. After the left-wing Frankfurt Social Democrats sent him to the Federal parliament in 1961, he helped build the nationwide party left and then became its voice in the governments headed by SPD chancellors Willy Brandt and Helmut Schmidt from 1969 to 1982.

On the theoretical and political level, Peter von Oertzen from Göttingen was a most important partisan of participatory democracy. His studies of workers' councils and on workers' participation proved influential in German SDS as well as in the field of union education. Ludwig von Friedeburg from Frankfurt became similarly influential for a new generation of radical industrial and educational sociologists at German universities. After 1968, both became ministers of culture and initiated radical participatory reforms in the school and university systems of the SPD-governed states, von Oertzen in Lower Saxony and von Friedeburg in Hesse.

Responding to Liberal and New Left Ideas from the United States

After returning from the United States, I served as an editor of *neue kritik*, the national magazine of German SDS, published in Frankfurt. I wrote a series of comprehensive articles on the United States for the journal, with special attention to the peace and civil rights movements and to the changes and problems of postwar American capitalism.[24] These articles helped initiate discussions that, as historian Martin Klimke has put it, extended the "range and intensity of the American influence on the German SDS."[25]

Even before my US sojourn, Anglo-Saxon developments were important to us. In 1961, the journal published a review of Thompson's *Out of Apathy* by Gerhard Brandt of the Frankfurt Institute.[26] Those New Left essays responded to new challenges that had rendered the Old Left helpless: the astonishing revival of capitalism and conservatism after 1945 and the improvements of working-class living standards, developments suggesting to some observers that capitalism now could provide endless growth and a material and mental integration of the working class into petty bourgeois or consumerist schemes. Contrary to that view, the *Out of Apathy* authors maintained that there were still contradictions in capitalism and conflicts between classes but that these could only be grasped by developing an undogmatic understanding of Marx and openness to what could be learned about Keynesian economics and the everyday culture of the working class.

Thus we paid attention to left-leaning Keynesian analyses of changes in capitalism since the Great Depression and New Deal. Especially important were John Kenneth Galbraith's studies of American capitalism, especially his views on the countervailing power of labor unions and the contradiction between private affluence and public-sector poverty. I contributed to the discussion and criticism of Galbraith in a broad analysis of the new phase of capitalist development, in light of new debates on the American left.[27]

In this respect, C. Wright Mills—whose books were first published in German in 1962 and 1963—had a great influence on many of us.[28] *The Sociological Imagination* was enthusiastically welcomed by younger sociologists, who endorsed Mills's criticism of both the positivist empiricism identified with Columbia University's Paul Lazarsfeld and the grand sociological theorizing of Harvard's Talcott Parsons. We also welcomed Mills's *The Power Elite*, which struck us as a new, sophisticated way of explaining how a contemporary ruling class exercises power. Although we doubted Mills's claim that intellectuals were now a prime agent of social change, we did not question Mills's idea that a Keynesian war economy had helped generate a new ruling elite composed of an alliance of big corporations, the state apparatus, and the military, an uneasy constellation that offered the world an irresponsible risk of nuclear war. Nor did we question his assessment of widespread apathy toward politics.

Consequently, my articles on the American scene described the apparent stabilization of postwar capitalism by Keynesian state intervention (combined with rising armament and partly welfare expenditures) and the rise of mass consumption (connected with a "colonization" of everyday life by capitalism) and showed that this stabilization was not definite but produced new risks, instabilities, and social conflicts. My critique was summed up with a Millsian flourish: "The countervailing powers are like hyenas fighting for prey. The hegemony of the power elite remains untouched."[29] The discussions were continued in Frankfurt, especially in a seminar held in 1964–65 by Jürgen Habermas, who was generally very interested in efforts to import left-wing American scholarship to Frankfurt.

We differed with Mills, however, because we did not see all this as a one-dimensional and irresistible tendency in either America or Europe. Like the authors of *Out of Apathy*, we insisted that capitalism was still contradictory and that participative action on the part of the working classes was still a possibility. For us, the role of critical intellectuals in the media and in politics was not to *replace* the working classes but to help them to understand that their private grievances had political causes—a formula borrowed from Mills himself.

We revisited this question in 1964, when Herbert Marcuse visited from the United States to present his new book *One-Dimensional Man*. At a meeting with the Frankfurt SDS group, Marcuse passionately attacked our position and especially a paper of mine that argued there was still a potential of socialist change within the working classes. Considering my position on a surrender to the right-wing leadership of a reformist social democracy, Marcuse insisted that radical change could only come from those who were oppressed by or excluded from the benefits of the affluent society, such as racial minorities and colonial subjects.

Thus we found ourselves in conflict with someone we had earlier considered our mentor (particularly for his philosophical writings on Marx). In our view Marcuse may have been influenced unduly by the disappointing recent history of trade unionism in the United States. He was not at all familiar with the new situation in Europe, where space seemed to be opening up for a social and political mobilization of the working classes. Marcuse would gain a certain influence later in the decade of the 1960s, especially among movement activists a half-generation younger than us, whose hopes for a revolutionary transformation were linked to Third World insurgencies and the awakening of racial and ethnic minorities still marginalized in the nations of the First World.

Nonetheless, the working-class-oriented New Left remained strong in Germany and the rest of Western Europe. In contrast to both Marcuse and the old, social-democratic left, we argued that economic immiseration was hardly the only injustice facing the working class, because the experience of social injustice in *all* its dimensions, not only the economic but also the moral and the political, was decisive in shaping consciousness. For this approach, our discussions of Anglo-Saxon scholarship again became influential, especially monumental works by E. P. Thompson and Barrington Moore. At the same time, there was substantial European research on structural change within the working class, showing that the "affluent workers" and the growing groups of technical experts and white collar workers did not represent an end of class but a new stage of class

society, in which institutionalized conflicts and a more rational understanding of class interests became important. Consequently, militant conflicts might still take place.

The Effect of American Direct Actionism in Splitting the
German Student Left

Movement politics in the United States had an enormous impact on the
young left in Germany and helped precipitate a split in our organization
from top to bottom. Until 1965, German SDS had been an explosive but
unified mixture of changing and controversial orientations, many connected with the new international movements. The big groups in Frankfurt, Berlin, and Göttingen were now the leaders of a new majority that
wanted to break free from small intellectual ghettoes and bureaucratic
organizational forms in order to explore a new antiauthoritarian and participatory movement strategy. I was asked to formulate these basic principles for the SDS majority in an article for *neue kritik*. It appeared in June
1965, in the midst of ardent debates that preceded the national SDS conference of that year. It was titled "The Strategy of Direct Action."[30] It developed the perspective that the still prevailing apathy of the popular majority toward politics could not be overcome by propagating, from above,
abstract intellectual ideas or doctrines. The left could only leave its ghetto
when it tried to mobilize people by raising issues germane to their everyday experiences and grievances. To gain moral support and to carry the
cause into politics, nonviolence and grassroots democratic participation
would be the best approach.

The essay developed a sociological approach based on a narrative analysis of the US demonstrations, marches, and participatory movements up
to spring 1965. The American SDS, now growing rapidly, seemed to offer
the German New Left an example of democratic and emancipatory mobilization. Of course, in Germany and Great Britain, nonviolent protests
such as the Easter marches against nuclear armaments had not been unknown. But in the United States, protest movements seemed fresh and
new, if only because they attracted a much greater number of participants
and went beyond an audience of those who were already convinced.

My *neue kritik* article reported on three kinds of new, "direct" actions
in the United States. First, the civil rights movement had made massive
civil disobedience a powerful weapon, initially in the Montgomery bus
boycott, then in the lunch counter sit-ins, and finally in the effort to regis-

ter black voters in the South. Second, I described how issues of poverty, slum housing, poor schools, and political powerlessness in the urban North were brought to public attention when SDS began its community organizing work, sometimes involving rent boycotts, in working-class and African American ghettos of the North. A third leap forward involved the incorporation of civil rights methods into the universities. In February 1965, Günter Amendt had already reported on the Berkeley Free Speech movement, which mobilized thousands of students and won support from part of the liberal public. In my article on direct action, I reported a further breakthrough: the American peace movement within the universities—particularly, the invention of the antiwar teach-in at the University of Michigan. With the help of student radio stations all over the United States, the Ann Arbor initiative had caused an avalanche of coordinated teach-ins on America's foreign policy at universities in thirty-five states.

My advocacy of direct participatory action evoked enormous controversy inside German SDS. The organization polarized into two coalitions or camps. These were the "Traditionalists," who had much support in Marburg, led by SDS national chairman Helmut Schauer; and the "Anti-Authoritarians," whose leadership came from the Frankfurt, Berlin, and Göttingen student groups. Schauer saw himself as a traditional socialist and a Marxist who wanted SDS to form a set of alliances with parties, unions, and other organizations. At the SDS national convention in October 1965, our Frankfurt group therefore broke with the traditionalists and made a majority coalition with the Berlin group, which had turned to the antiauthoritarian left by admitting Rudi Dutschke and his friends to membership. We also allied with a Munich group whose members were influenced by the provocative Situationist International. Situationist confrontations and occupations would soon create a stir in Berlin. But as this coalition could not yet present a candidate for the German SDS presidency, Schauer was reelected and used his term to defend socialist traditionalism (in its noncommunist strain, of course) starting from the view that capitalism was bound to collapse in a crisis and that it was an illusion to appeal to the left-liberal mainstream. Instead, SDS, as the only socialist organization in Germany, should mobilize and expand its membership by developing a program and an organizational nucleus with a clear socialist outlook. This implied that in the end, an economic crisis would enable a socialist party to win a parliamentary majority and thereby introduce socialist change by political measures from above.

This seemed to me a battle plan taken right out of the nineteenth century. It reproduced the German Old Left socialist tradition, which differed markedly from what I had seen at Port Huron, where a flexible combination of Marxism, Keynesianism, and John Dewey's pragmatism—together comprising a participatory and humanist tradition—became the basis for a set of principles deployed not as a dogmatic blueprint but heuristically (i.e., as the tools for a fresh experience- and data-based analysis of the situation). At the 1966 national convention of German SDS, Schauer was replaced by Reimut Reiche, a young Frankfurt activist who had analyzed the social-structural dimensions of the Berkeley and Berlin student revolts in *neue kritik*. His election as chairman signaled a fundamental change away from programs and parties and toward movements and participation. Now the antiauthoritarian majority transformed SDS into a real social movement with all sorts of public actions and campaigns.

In Frankfurt we developed two sorts of campaigns that soon spread all over the country. On the one hand, we were highly active in support of anti-imperialist and anticolonial movements in the Third World, especially in terms of our opposition to the US war in Vietnam. The other dimension was the everyday experience of the younger generation to which our actions were directed. German SDS activists founded the first antiauthoritarian kindergartens and supported new movements of high school students and of apprentices in their opposition to authoritarian structures and conservative sexual morals. Books on sexual liberation by Günter Amendt and Reimut Reiche sold many hundreds of thousands of copies. Activists conducted sit-ins in the universities and on tramway rails, occupied empty houses as part of the squatter's movement, and welcomed the rise of late 1960s feminism, including those protests directed against male leaders of SDS. From Berlin came the more spectacular political actions. Very soon, the protests against the shah of Iran and against America's war in Vietnam made the German student movement a mass phenomenon, one that would challenge the established social and political powers until at least the 1980s and even then remained a force that resisted the neoliberal rollback in the decades that followed.

It should be kept in mind that these enormous escalations of participatory movements of all kinds cannot be explained as the mere product of voluntaristic group activism. Our earlier experience as activists had taught us modesty. The ingredients for a radical oppositional movement—the ideas and potential leaders—were present in Germany from 1960 on, but they did not get a wider hearing until after 1965. That change depended on the experience of the younger generation, mediated through changes taking place in the fundamental structure of society. Even the spectacular student rebellions of the late 1960s were only the tip of a huge iceberg, consisting of radical changes in everyday culture, particularly a youth culture that was increasingly antiauthoritarian, participatory, and solidaristic. For us, this change of everyday culture, the end of the economies of scarcity, the potential for the emancipation and development of all individuals was also a product of capitalism in its contradictions. The young generation that the *Port Huron Statement* spoke for—whether political or not and whether intellectual or working class—had the feeling that the old rules of social order and discipline and hierarchy were outdated. This impetus of youth culture was largely supported by new developments of rock music, especially the Beatles. In all this, there was an opening of social space that translated into politics, too. You could feel this every day when you opened the papers: you saw that things became possible that had been unthinkable before.

This change toward participation also included the working classes as productive forces (i.e., the culture at work). The waves of spontaneous movements for workers' participation that accompanied the new movements until the mid-1970s can also be explained by this deeper structural change. Capitalism needed a better educated labor force, which implied higher competences and more autonomy at work. Industrial workers as well as the growing number of service employees had experienced the rising possibilities of participation in everyday culture and politics; they wanted the same to be realized at work.

Opening the Political Field for Participatory Change: The Making of a New Political Camp in Germany

In Germany, these social changes coincided with a remarkable political opening for the left. Here we find a striking contrast to the experience of the United States. When reading the historical accounts of the 1960s by Todd Gitlin, Dick Flacks, and Tom Hayden, I was again shocked by the series of demoralizing political setbacks that took place during that decade.[31] These started with the assassination of John F. Kennedy in 1963, the subsequent refusal of the Democratic Party to incorporate the political wing of the civil rights movement into its structure, and the progressive entanglement of Lyndon Johnson in the Vietnam War. In 1968, hope was again destroyed when Robert Kennedy was shot just a few months after Martin Luther King Jr.'s assassination. As the Democratic Party failed to mobilize its progressive potential, a Republican, Richard Nixon, became president. And this came only one year after Ronald Reagan, who was to crush the student movement at Berkeley, was elected governor in California.

Developments in Germany contrasted sharply with this demoralizing sequence of setbacks in the United States. Until the 1970s or even the 1980s, many authoritarian initiatives could be turned into public mobilizations that significantly enlarged the ground for alternative politics. This pattern appeared first in 1962, when the conservative government's arrest of editors at the liberal weekly *Der Spiegel*—charging them with treason for investigative reporting on security issues—provoked an outcry that led to an expansion of civil liberties and a shift away from the Federal Republic's authoritarian political culture. Consequently, in October 1963, Chancellor Konrad Adenauer was forced to resign. With him fell the architect and symbol of authoritarian conservatism. While social space would soon be closed for the American movements, it opened in Germany.

Similarly, in 1967, when a police bullet killed a student protester, Benno Ohnesorg, an avalanche of direct student and civic protest actions followed; the same pattern recurred in spring 1968 when the Berlin student leader Rudi Dutschke was shot and gravely injured. The Springer press, fount of reactionary attacks on the radical student movement, was confronted with huge demonstrations. In contrast to the right-wing backlash in the United States following the 1968 Democratic National Convention, Germany saw relatively few government reprisals, legal or political. Instead, the German movements could translate into new political majorities in regional elections and especially in Willy Brandt's electoral win in 1969 and his more sweeping victory in 1972.

How had this been possible? Of course, the burning memory of the incredible crimes in Germany's Nazi past inhibited a return of right-wing extremist politics in West Germany. Moreover, the new conservatism designed by Adenauer, though gradual and incremental, had done much to replace German nationalism with the project of European integration, while at the same time taming a capitalist economy through the construction of a robust, though conservative, welfare state offering the working class a set of participatory rights in industry governance.

This political context had helped open a space for New Left action in Germany. Because there was not such a sustained and successful backlash from the right or from the conservative center, the strivings of the social movements could be increasingly translated into influence in democratic institutions. Thus did movement activists become increasingly well organized in the left-wing youth section of the SPD, the Young Socialists or so-called *Jusos*. They determinedly pursued antiauthoritarian, participatory politics and successfully began to conquer many sections of the party. This had started in Frankfurt already very early, in 1961, when the *Jusos* had helped elect Hans Matthöfer to the Bundestag. This policy accelerated from the mid-1960s on. It resulted in the growth of a strong, mainly *Juso*-based left wing in the SPD and in the Social Democratic factions of the federal and state parliaments. This was combined with a successful mobilization of the liberal intelligentsia—journalists, writers, actors, film makers, and so on—as C. Wright Mills had envisaged.

This joint liberal and left mobilization was the precondition for Willy Brandt's electoral victories, which many of us thought paralleled the effect of Kennedy's 1960 election in symbolizing an opening to the left. The Brandt years brought a remarkable expansion of welfare state and civil rights politics. Hans Matthöfer stuck to his antifascist and participatory convictions even when he became a member of the Brandt and Schmidt SPD governments. Actively supporting the resistance against Franco's fascist regime in Spain, he was honored with the nickname the "Deputy of Barcelona." In 1973, when he was parliamentary secretary in the Ministry of Economic Cooperation, he publicly attacked the military putschists of Chile as a "gang of murderers"—and helped many people get out of Chile with the assistance of the German embassy. In 1974, he became minister of research and technology, launching a huge research program on the "humanization of work."

Not unlike the Swedish developments of that time, the early 1970s in West Germany also translated many movement aims into legislation, ending legal discrimination of women and the criminalization of homosexuality and of abortion; enlarging the participatory rights of pupils, apprentices, and students; expanding and opening the schools and universities for the popular classes; raising welfare state benefits; and enlarging the rights of employees at their work places. But there were also politics of containment. Already under Brandt, measures were taken to keep so-called extremists out of educational institutions.

After Brandt's resignation, the governments of the right-wing Social Democratic chancellor, Helmut Schmidt, from 1974 to 1982 systematically continued these containment politics. Students' and employees' rights to participate in the self-government of universities were cancelled. Also, the *Mitbestimmungsgesetz* of 1976 was a brake and containment on employees' participation in management. The right-wing majority of the SPD defended the construction of nuclear power plants and, in the late 1970s, cooperated with the United States when highly controversial plans were made to station medium-range nuclear missiles on German soil.

As a consequence, the left and liberal forces that had brought Brandt to power now lost influence in the political parties—even though they had gained ground in the growing social movements, in the alternative youth cultures, in liberal public opinion, and in the mass media. By this time, the organized student left had broken apart. Several distinct currents within German SDS differed on how to respond to the extremely contradictory scene of 1968: defeats in France and Czechoslovakia that showed the strength of "the establishment," a still-growing mass support for student movements and spontaneous strikes, and electoral victories for reformist social democratic parties. In 1971 German SDS formally dissolved. The movement's main current—focused in the new organization, the Socialist Bureau (SB)—consisted of left-wing reformism, Third World internationalism, and emancipatory antiauthoritarianism, though it also included smaller groups that did not survive the 1970s, such as the Situationists. Other currents emerged in the form of Maoist fundamentalism as well as a small, increasingly isolated minority that engaged in underground terrorist activities.

Although the German left was deeply divided in the 1970s, it was not defeated or marginalized. Because of its New Left principles—its commitment to participatory democracy and nonviolence—the SB found rising general support for its programs. This political tendency joined forces with the left-liberal mainstream when, after the 1973 oil crisis, rising civic mobilizations responded to the ecological and social risks of modernization and growth, recurring unemployment, insufficient civic rights and participation, urban and infrastructural problems, and nuclear armament and energy. And, of course, with its participatory principles, the SB current also constituted an attractive alternative to the Maoists and the terrorist cells. When, after 1977, those groups collapsed, the SB current gained an uncontested hegemony on the left. From 1979 to the early 1980s, a huge peace, intercultural, antinuclear, and ecological movement arose, often linked to feminism and a "second youth revolt." It was widely supported by the growing left currents in the churches, in the labor unions, and among liberal opinion leaders.

This progress provoked an escalation of the existing conflicts between the different wings inside the established political parties. In these confrontations, the movement activists began to form their own political camp, separated by deep cleavages from the old party majorities. Since 1980, they began to form a separate "green" party, which soon commanded a stable electorate between 5 and 10 percent of the voters. Many movement sympathizers also remained inside the old parties, forming strong "green" wings, especially within the SPD. Simultaneously, civic participation was professionalized and institutionalized. Acceptance by the left part of the mainstream implied an increase of political realism, of institutionalization, and of adapting utopian idealism to practical everyday ways of life.

This progress, however, also provoked more countermobilizations from the right, encouraged by the electoral victories of Thatcher in Britain and Reagan in the United States. The Free Democratic Party (FDP) became the spearhead of neoliberalism in Germany. In 1982, it left the government of Helmut Schmidt to form a majority government with the Christian Democrats (CDU), headed by Helmut Kohl until 1998. Kohl promised "a spiritual and moral turn." But as in the decades before, German development again took a course that differed markedly from the British and US developments. As in Britain and the United States, welfare state securities were whittled down, but this occurred at a much slower pace due to the resistance of the labor unions, the labor left wing, and voters of the CDU itself. A return to authoritarian politics (in the fields of gender, immigration, civil rights, democratic participation, ecology, and foreign politics) was limited by strong counterpressures from the "Greens" and the "green" wings in all political camps.

The scales were tipped only gradually toward the neoliberal side, but that tilt was accentuated through the 1990s. After 1989, the external confrontations of the Cold War, which had in fact given the German New Left much of its appeal as an alternative, were replaced by a different political constellation in which any alternative to global capitalism appeared to be absent. For a time a neoliberal current proved near hegemonic. But much remained of the democratic culture generated by the participatory New Left in the 1960s: with its large base, that current retained its role as one factor among a plurality of camps.

27 | European New Lefts, Global Connections, and the Problem of Difference

by Rita Chin

The milestone anniversaries of the 1960s have occasioned a flurry of scholarship on the protest movements that have long been synonymous with that decade. For historians, approaching the fifty-year mark has placed the events of the 1960s squarely in the past and made them legitimate objects of study. It should come as no surprise, then, that a wave of scholars has recently begun to scrutinize this period from a number of critical perspectives, seeking to understand the roles of multiple actors (famous and otherwise) and the highly complex causes and consequences of their actions. This new work moves well beyond the myriad personal accounts offered by veterans of the student movements that have dominated the histories of the New Left, the 1960s, and 1968.[1]

The fiftieth anniversary of the *Port Huron Statement* offers an opportunity not only for activists and participants to revisit one of their signature achievements but also for scholars to take stock of the latest historical work on the New Left that has expanded our understanding of the movement both temporally and spatially. Many people familiar with the early history of the New Left in the United States know that members of Students for a Democratic Society (SDS) gathered in late spring 1962 at a United Auto Workers retreat in Port Huron, Michigan, to draft a manifesto. The *Port Huron Statement*, as it was later called, sought to identify the "complicated and disturbing paradoxes in our surrounding America" and proposed "truly democratic alternatives to the present."[2] It laid out a "youth agenda for the 1960s"—including active participation in policy debates, grassroots mobilization, and public protest—that served as the political road map for the US student movement.[3] Less well known is the fact that Michael Vester, a leader of West Germany's *Sozialistischer Deutscher Studentenbund* (German Socialist Student League), attended the conference at Port Huron, participated in drafting the statement, and served as an important conduit between German and American activists. The conversations and collaborations between Vester and Tom Hayden, universally recognized as the chief author of the *Statement*, bespeak the crucial role of transatlantic networks and exchanges in shaping the politics and strategies of 1960s New Left–inspired student radicalism.

This chapter assesses the recent push to take seriously the global aspects of the New Left, a body of work that has extended our geographical perspective not only from the US to Europe but also across the world. Focusing specifically on European contexts, I examine how attention to the global has altered scholarly approaches to 1968 and fundamentally transformed our understanding of the larger movement. I ultimately suggest that global networks must be pursued even further because at least two major postwar developments—the process of decolonization and the economic demand for foreign labor migrants—brought the world to Europe in unprecedented ways. By following the exchanges among activists engendered by these twin developments, an understudied and largely unacknowledged strand of New Left engagement becomes visible. Questions of "difference," in short, emerge as a constitutive element of the European New Left's formation and legacy.

Although contemporaries widely acknowledged the eruption of student protest in the late 1960s as a worldwide phenomenon, the story of New Left political radicalism has traditionally been told through a national lens. For instance, the volume *1968: The World Transformed*, whose publication coincided with the thirtieth anniversary of the events in 1968, devoted an entire section to "challenges to the domestic order"— with separate chapters on the United States, Poland, France, and Germany—as well as a final chapter on the Third World.[4] This insistently national framework—albeit one in which many national stories appeared side by side—made it difficult to see connecting threads across the Atlantic, across the Iron Curtain, and across the globe. My point here is not to suggest that international connections have been entirely absent in previous scholarship. Some early histories, of course, noted that the events of 1968 spanned the globe: the Tet Offensive began in late January, just as the Prague Spring was gaining momentum; the West Berlin Vietnam Congress took place in February, followed by the twenty-five-thousand-strong antiwar march in London; and the May student uprisings and worker strikes in France followed quickly on the heels of the student takeover of Columbia University.[5] Other histories have pointed to the key role of someone like Michael Vester.[6] But until the last few years, scholarly narratives have often presented such connections as self-evident chains of reaction requiring little explanation or as exceptional exchanges, facilitated by exceptional individuals.

In many ways, this predominantly national frame has been reinforced by the best-known images of the New Left. For the European scene, there is perhaps no more iconic event than the student demonstrations in Paris during May 1968 and no more iconic figure than Daniel Cohn-Bendit, or "Danny the Red" (figure 1).

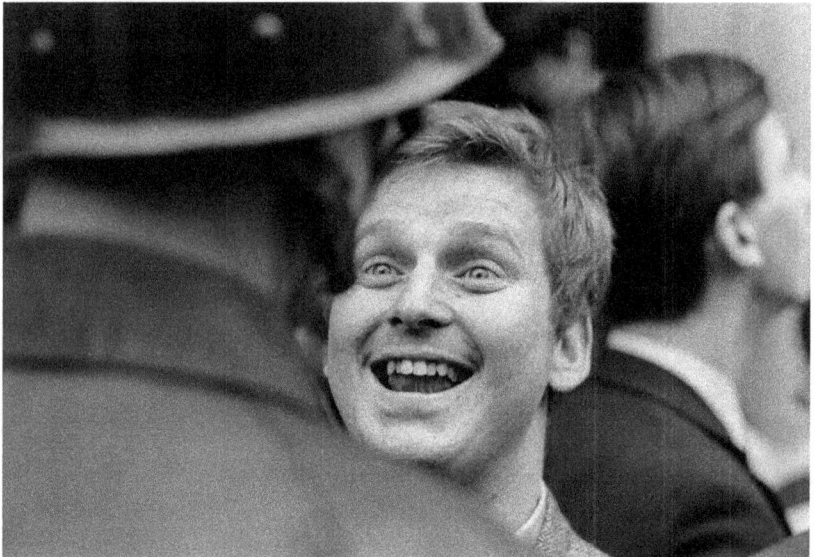

Figure 1: Student leader Daniel Cohn-Bendit surrounded by police officers in front of the Sorbonne, May 3, 1968. © Jacques Haillot/Apis/Sygma/Corbis

In this photograph taken by Jacques Haillot on May 3, 1968, near the Sorbonne, Cohn-Bendit confronts a member of the French riot control forces (*Compagnies Républicaines de Sécurité*), wild-eyed and laughing as if to provoke a reaction. The news photo was quickly transformed into a revolutionary poster—"Nous sommes tous 'indésirables'"—by the *Atelier populaire des Beaux-Arts* (figure 2).[7] Plastered on the walls of Paris during the student demonstrations and worker strikes that paralyzed the country for six subsequent weeks, the ubiquitous face of Danny the Red became synonymous with May 1968. This image evocatively captures many of the

Figure 2: Atelier populaire poster, 1968. Collection Stedelijk Museum Amsterdam

defining elements of a broader history: the centrality of the "youth" generation's perspective; the confrontation with state authority and its enforcers; and the commitment to taking democracy into the streets. But it is also a strikingly *national* image: a French student leader in the midst of French protesters confronting a French policeman on the streets of the French capital photographed by a French journalist. Of course, the actual circumstances were more complicated. For one thing, the French president Charles de Gaulle wanted to expel Cohn-Bendit as an "undesirable" and German citizen, even though the radical had spent his childhood in France and was attending university there. But the larger point still holds: this picture depicts a historically specific movement within a singular national frame.

By way of contrast, consider a second image that is far less known, even though it portrays an event that is arguably just as important for understanding this history (figure 3). Here, Rudi Dutschke, a central figure in the Berlin chapter of the German *Sozialistischer Deutscher Studentenbund* (SDS), is flanked by the Pakistani Tariq Ali (at far left), the American Dale Smith, and the Chilean Gaston Salvatore. Arm in arm, they lead an antiwar demonstration through the streets of West Berlin in February 1968, marking the end of a two-day international conference on the Vietnam War. If we expand our geographical frame—not only from Paris to Berlin but across the globe—we might conclude that this photograph is more representative of the European New Left. But to appreciate the significance of this image, it is useful to begin by examining the new perspectives opened up by recent attention to the global.

One major effect of widening the geographical purview on 1968 has been a rethinking of chronology. Earlier narratives of the student protest movements generally took 1968 as their focal point. This approach had at least two historiographical effects. First, it tended to treat the first waves of New Left activism as a mere prelude to the spectacular upheavals of that annus mirabilis. Second, it placed undue emphasis on big events. Even in its broader application, "1968" has often served as useful shorthand or metonym for the major moments that took place over the course of the decade. This event-driven mode of analysis has frequently produced a lack of attention to questions of process: How did the student protest movements develop? Which ideas and actors were instrumental in shaping their evolution? What consequences did these movements produce? Yet, as Timothy Brown has pointed out, the term "1968" "operates not merely as a temporal designation but as a spatial one": it suggests "a world-historical conjuncture, centered roughly around the year 1968, which took

Figure 3: Rudi Dutschke, in Berlin, flanked by Tariq Ali (at far left), Dale Smith, and Gaston Salvatore, February 18, 1968. Foto: Landesarchiv Berlin/Bert Sass, F Rep. 290_0125494

place over a sufficiently large expanse of the globe—from Paris to Mexico City, from Berkeley to Dhaka, from Prague to Tokyo—so as to figure as a 'global' event."[8] The concept of 1968, in short, enfolds the temporal and spatial together.

Recent efforts to take seriously the global character of 1968 have necessarily shifted attention away from singular moments and toward longer patterns of cross-pollination. This approach, moreover, has resulted in an expansion of the temporal timeframe. Indeed, much of the latest work on the New Left's transnational connections has adopted versions of Arthur Marwick's "long sixties" periodization, extending backward as early as 1954 and forward as late as 1978.[9] The broadening of frames, in turn, has opened up new kinds of questions about the development and trajectories of the European New Left: How, for example, did the networks established in 1957 between the National Union of French Students and the Algerian National Liberation Front (FLN) influence French students' efforts to gain the support of factory workers in May 1968? In what ways did the exchanges between American sociologist C. Wright Mills and the editors of the British journal *New Left Review* in 1960 shape the emergence of cultural Marxism within the British New Left?[10] How did interactions between the Black Panther Party and West German student activists help radicalize splinter groups in the Federal Republic? What kinds of influence did the Weather Underground and the Red Army Faction (RAF) have on each other in the early 1970s?[11] In what ways did the early 1970s French *Tel Quel* group absorb the principles of Mao's Cultural Revolution?[12]

Somewhat paradoxically (though not, perhaps, surprisingly), these temporal and geographical expansions have also pushed scholars to concentrate their focus, to examine a more limited set of actors or activist groups in order to trace how the exchanges actually worked. First-wave efforts to consider the New Left's global dimensions emphasized a wide-angle perspective, pointing to—among other things—the crucial impact of new kinds of communication technology. Satellites, for example, gave television and other news media the potential to spur action around the world through the instantaneous transmittal of a single searing image.[13] But beyond noting the synchronicity of protests in multiple countries, these early observations offered little explanation of how such parallel actions transpired. Several years ago, Martin Klimke bemoaned precisely this absence, arguing that the "exact processes through which activists from numerous countries established contact, shared ideas, and adopted each other's social and cultural practices are still largely unexplored."[14] His own recent study of the relationship between the American SDS and the West German SDS, however, has begun to fill the gap.

In *The Other Alliance*, Klimke tracks the unexpectedly close—even personal—connections between the American and German SDSs, shedding light on the specific ways these groups supported and influenced each other. German exchange student Michael Vester, for instance, was an active recruiter for the American SDS from his home base at Bowdoin College. Not only did he attend the Port Huron conference in 1962, but he offered a detailed response to a preliminary draft of the celebrated statement. He encouraged Tom Hayden to be more explicit about the "societal contradictions pointed out by socialist analysis," highlighting in particular "the gaps between political democracy and economic concentration of power."[15] Vester further provided an international perspective on the concerns that the two SDS groups shared. As Hayden later recalled, "We were very interested in what Michael Vester . . . had to say about the cold war and its effects on Europe. He helped internationalize our understanding of what we faced."[16] At the same time, the American SDS took a keen interest in the struggles of its West German counterpart. When American SDS president Al Haber learned from Vester about the German Social Democratic Party's decision to expel all members of the German SDS (its own youth wing) from its political organization, he wrote letters in defense of his West German colleagues. Klimke concludes that the American and West German SDSs "openly supported one another in the face of massive institutional pressure from their parent organizations as well as attacks by international socialist associations on a New Left ideology that both groups could identify with."[17] What emerges here is a far more nuanced picture of transnational New Left connections, one in which the American and German SDSs not just were vaguely aware of each other but forged close personal bonds that facilitated the exchange of theoretical ideas as well as practical collaborations.

In tracing the global dimensions of the New Left, scholars have been forced to pay closer attention to the particular *networks* that traversed national borders. Here again, the recent work has been instructive. Maria Höhn has examined West German student radical K. D. Wolff's efforts to establish Black Panther Solidarity Committees in late 1969. A major goal was to connect with politicized African American GIs stationed in the Federal Republic in order to forge a revolutionary alliance that would "unseat the centers of American empire in both Germany and the U.S."[18] Höhn details the strategies used by student activists to garner the attention and interest of African American soldiers. These included protesting in front of US military barracks, adopting the Black Power salute, frequenting bars and discos that catered to African American GIs, and participating in Black history study groups on the bases. Such initiatives led to joint rallies across West Germany to criticize the Vietnam War and demand freedom for Black Panther leader Bobby Seale. They also led to collaboration on an underground newspaper, *Voice of the Lumpen*. The solidarity between American GIs and West German students culminated in a joint effort to gain the acquittal of the "Ramstein Two," a pair of African American former GIs who were arrested in a shooting incident that injured a German security guard at Ramstein Airbase. Höhn's work, moreover, provides a crucial backstory for Klimke's argument about the US Black Power movement serving as role model for the radicalization of the West German New Left and specifically the RAF, which, he claims, applied Black Panther notions of "armed struggle" in the Federal Republic during the 1970s.[19]

This rich and fruitful exploration of New Left networks has largely focused on intra-European or transatlantic exchanges.[20] Less well understood are the connections between the European New Lefts and those in the so-called Third World. In the US context, by contrast, the Third World angle has received considerable attention. Historians have explored the early involvement of foreign students of color with the civil rights movement; the active engagement of African American activists and intellectuals with independence movements in Africa and Asia; the importance of anticolonialist networks between the United States and Africa; and the impact of the Cuban Revolution and the Bandung Conference on activism in the United States.[21] By and large, this body of scholarship takes the US context as its center of gravity, but it has also opened up new perspectives on the complex ways that global politics informed domestic American issues and concerns.[22]

To the extent that scholars previously acknowledged the European New Left's relationship with the Third World, they tended to interpret it as a kind of "screen" onto which European radicals projected their own national and generational psychic dramas.[23] This line of argument has been especially prominent in the scholarship on West Germany, due in no small part to the long shadow cast by the Holocaust. Here, activists' interest in Third World revolutionaries or internationalism has been read as an attempt "to exonerate themselves as Germans and claim a position that transcended national sins" or as "a means of escaping from a despicable skin, the skin of being a German."[24] Even Richard Wolin's recent book on French Maoists asserts that China of the Cultural Revolution "became a Rorschach test" for the "innermost radical political hopes and fantasies" of these *gauchistes*. "By 'becoming Chinese,' by assuming new identities as French incarnations of China's Red Guards," he writes, "these dissident Althusserians sought to reinvent themselves wholesale. Thereby, they would rid themselves of their guilt both as the progeny of colonialists and, more generally, as bourgeois."[25]

The most compelling recent work has sought to treat the European New Left's links to the Third World more seriously, investigating institutions that fostered contacts between European leftists and people from around the world. One crucial nexus was the university. In *Foreign Front*, Quinn Slobodian focuses on the social milieu of West Berlin's Free University (FU), noting that more than ten thousand foreigners from Asia, Africa, and Latin America were studying on West German campuses by the early 1960s.[26] Some, like the Nigerian student Adekunle Ajala, were funded by the German Academic Exchange (*Deutscher Akademische Austauschdienst*); others received support from the Fulbright Commission; still others relied on family money for their German education.[27] It was in such contexts that German SDS leaders Rudi Dutschke and Bernd Rabehl formed an "international working group" in 1964 to discuss Marxist and critical theory with fellow students from Latin America, Haiti, and Ethiopia.[28] They held their meetings in the "student village" near the FU in Dahlem, where some of the Latin American and Caribbean students lived. Through his regular visits to the student village, Dutschke also became friends with the Chilean activist Gaston Salvatore, the two ultimately collaborating on a German translation of Che Guevara's final speech.[29] These concrete relationships impressed upon Dutschke the need for an "internationalization of strategy for the revolutionary forces" as well as pushed him toward a search for revolutionaries within West Germany who could serve as "domestic counterparts to Third World insurgents."[30] By elucidating the personal connections and intellectual exchanges between Dutschke and foreign students such as Salvatore, Slobodian effectively counters the notion that the Third World was a mere projection—or fetish object—of German radicals as well as the paternalistic assumption that German students merely served as "mentors" for their international peers.[31]

Indeed, many foreign students were politically active in freedom movements, decolonization efforts, and national liberation struggles in their home countries. As genuine dialogue partners with German activists, they had a major impact on how members of the West German New Left came to understand revolutionary action. When Moïse Tshombe, Congolese prime minister and former Katanga secessionist, paid an uninvited state visit to West Germany in December 1964, the FU's African Student Union led by the Nigerian Ajala spearheaded a public protest.[32] The action was supported by members of the SDS, the Latin American Student Association, and FU-based Argument Club.[33] Dutschke was among the eight hundred demonstrators in West Berlin, where the original plan of a silent march turned into "an assault on public order involving catcalls, thrown tomatoes, and scuffles with the police."[34] Acknowledging the foreign students' impact on how this protest played out, Dutschke noted in his diary, "Our friends from the Third World stepped into the breach and the Germans had to follow."[35] With such collaborations in mind, scholars now view foreign students as a central catalyst for the internationalist consciousness that shaped the antiauthoritarian wing of the SDS and came to dominate the West German student movement after 1965.[36]

In actual practice, though, the university served as an important setting for contact and exchange between leftist activists and foreign students well before the 1960s moment. In Britain, for example, foreigners from the various colonies began to matriculate at Oxford and Cambridge in significant numbers in the 1870s.[37] By 1960, there were nearly fifty thousand overseas students in the United Kingdom.[38] As Jordanna Bailkin has argued, postwar Britain became a "crucial hub of international education," and the British government actively encouraged foreign students to study in the United Kingdom because it viewed their education in Britain as a way to "monitor" and "manage" the process of decolonization.[39] Of course, the British state could not fully control the political orientation and activities of its New Commonwealth charges. Among the early waves of postwar exchange students was Stuart Hall, who came from Jamaica in 1951 to study at Oxford as a Rhodes scholar. At first, his social circles predominantly consisted of the small number of Oxford Third World students who shared an interest in "colonial" questions. But he quickly came into contact with members of the "Oxford left" and began to weigh in on a range of contemporary issues—the future of the Labour Party and the left, the nature of the welfare state and postwar capitalism, the impact of cultural change during the age of British affluence—through his collaborative work on the journal *Universities and Left Review* in the late 1950s.[40] From there, Hall went on to become the first editor of *New Left Review* and the father of British cultural studies.[41] In both roles, he was uniquely positioned to initiate questions on race and ethnicity, racism, and decolonization as part of the broader effort to renew the British left through a "radically new analysis of the social relations, dynamics and culture of postwar capitalism."[42]

Tariq Ali played an equally important role in the trajectory of British New Left radicalism during the late 1960s. Ali arrived at Oxford from Pakistan in 1963 and quickly began meeting with the Socialist Group inside the Oxford Labour Club. In 1965, he was elected president of the Oxford Union, the university's debating society, and began to concentrate his political activism on the Vietnam War, establishing a Vietnam Committee on campus and organizing a teach-in on the conflict.[43] A founding member of Britain's Vietnam Solidarity Committee (VSC) as well as its most prominent spokesman, Ali initially sought to challenge the Labour Party's support of US intervention in Southeast Asia but eventually articulated a much broader critique that fused strenuous anticolonialism (abroad) with a desire for radical social transformation (at home).[44] Throughout 1967, he orchestrated several demonstrations against the Vietnam War in London, culminating in a massive VSC-sponsored protest in March 1968. Assessing Ali's central part in this event, a reporter for *India Abroad* noted in 2008, "The 1967 [sic] student revolt that nearly toppled the Charles De Gaulle government in France was led by home-grown radicals. Across the Channel, around the same time, 25,000 students were marching on the American embassy in London, protesting the Vietnam War—and they were led not by an Englishman, but by someone who was not even born in that country."[45]

This reporter's characterization brings us back to the contrasting images of the European New Left with which I began—and especially the photo from Berlin (figure 3). This picture was taken at an antiwar demonstration that was part of the West Berlin International Vietnam Congress in February 1968. As noted earlier, flanking Dutschke are the Pakistani-born Oxford student Ali, representing the London-based Vietnam Solidarity Committee; the African American Vietnam veteran Dale Smith, representing the Student Nonviolent Coordinating Committee; and the Chilean-born FU student Gaston Salvatore, a nephew of the future Chilean president Salvador Allende. Each of these figures, we might say, represented a connecting thread between the New Left in Europe and the wider world. Their very presence—and collaborative efforts—force us to recognize the ways in which an event that has previously been read as West German was, in fact, the product of multiple lines of influence—from the United States to Asia by way of the United Kingdom and Latin America. As Ali explains in his memoir, this event was "an important turning point for the Vietnam movement in Europe. It was the first real gathering of the clans and it reinforced our internationalism as well as the desire for a world without frontiers."[46] More effectively than the iconic image of the May events in Paris, this photograph of the Vietnam Congress in Berlin captures the global exchanges that were crucial to the development and evolution of the New Left in Europe.

By way of conclusion, I want to suggest a few of the ways in which a global line of questioning might be pursued even further. For the most part, the new work stressing transnational and global connections has focused on well-known figures, collaborations, and networks, clustered between about 1964 and 1970. But this line of inquiry needs to be taken further, extended to less obvious actors and organizations but also to less established moments in the larger history. We would do well, for example, to consider the years when the political category of the Third World was gaining discursive traction.[47] Starting in the second half of the 1950s, left activists in both France and West Germany served as couriers (of money and information) for the Algerian FLN. The underground network organized by Francis Jeanson in 1957 is already familiar to scholars, in large part because of his coauthored book denouncing French policy in Algeria and because of his highly publicized arrest and trial in 1960.[48] Historians of postwar France make passing reference to Jeanson, Alain Krivine, Henri Curiel, Félix Guattari, and the cartoonist Siné as supporters of the

Algerian cause.[49] But we know very little about how the courier network itself functioned in practice. And we know even less about transnational connections established elsewhere in France, in cities like Marseille, Lille, and Lyon. The Lyon organization is of particular interest because it facilitated contact between the FLN and West German leftists such as Reimar Lenz and Hans Jürgen Wischnewski, who also acted as couriers for the Algerians.[50] Recently, Christoph Kalter has written a remarkable book on the French left's engagement with decolonization, focusing in particular on François Maspero's leftist publishing network. Maspero owned a Latin Quarter bookstore that sheltered Algerians during the October 1961 massacre, and his Maspero publishing house brought out the first edition of Frantz Fanon's *The Wretched of the Earth* as well as other landmark books critical of the Algerian war.[51] Filling out this history of postwar anticolonialism—not just in France but also in West Germany and Britain—would help answer some crucial questions: How did engagements with the Algerian and other independence movements transform young European leftists' understanding of politics? Of leftism? What influence might their experiences have had on their conceptualizations of former colonies that would eventually come to be known as the "Third World"? And how did these ideas shape an emerging "new" Left?

On the other side of the conventional periodization, we would do well to look more closely at the early 1970s, a moment of expanding encounters between left activists and foreign workers located squarely within European borders. Even amid the New Left's search for an alternative revolutionary subject, there were numerous activists who continued to identify the working class as the key to radical social transformation and directed their organizational energies into the factories. These included students who occupied factories with workers throughout the Paris region in May and June 1968; members of the Maoist *Gauche prolétarienne*, who helped mobilize protests at the Renault-Billancourt factory in 1970 and 1972; and Marxist-Leninist oriented communist cadres or "K-groups" and informal spontaneity groups (later known as Spontis), which participated in the 1973 wildcat strike at the Ford factory in Cologne.[52] Through such actions, French and West German radicals encountered—many for the first time—large numbers of laborers from former colonies and guest workers. In many respects, these encounters suggest another dimension to the European New Left's internationalist turn, one that has had major implications for postwar European society. And yet we know virtually nothing about how the early lines of collaboration developed between French and West

German activists and immigrant workers or how these alliances may have transformed the thinking and priorities of a fragmenting New Left.

Accounting for the global in our narratives of the European New Left significantly alters the contours of the story of postwar leftism—not just in terms of key actors, groups, or events but also in terms of the larger story. What the global frame insistently underscores is the central place of "difference" in shaping the concerns, engagements, and actions of the New Left in Europe. This engagement can no longer be relegated to a handful of distant issues such as the US civil rights movement and the Vietnam War or downplayed as a peripheral set of concerns. In assessing the European New Left in view of its global connections, what becomes clear is that engagement with various forms of cultural, racial, and ethnic difference began as early as the transnational courier networks for the FLN, continued with exchanges between the American and West German SDSs, and was deepened through dialogues with foreign students. These dialogues, in turn, facilitated collaborations around the Berlin Vietnam Congress, produced new forms of solidarity with the Black Panthers and African American GIs, and included cooperation with a wide range of immigrant workers in factory actions. Acknowledging that questions of difference constituted an ongoing and evolving concern within New Left politics pushes against our conventional narratives of a neat and easy shift from class to race or from material conditions to questions of culture, ethnicity, or religion. More accurately, it seems to me, these issues have always been overlapping and mutually constitutive within New Left politics. Thus far, we have yet to consider how the New Left's engagement with questions of difference changed over time—a crucial issue if we are to make sense of our current political climate, a moment when public pronouncements on the "failure" of multiculturalism have become increasingly commonplace across the wider region.

28 | "Thought Is Action for Us": Lloyd Best, New World, and the West Indian Postcolonial Left

by Paul Hébert

The colonized subject is ineffectual precisely because the colonial situation has not been rigorously analyzed.

—Frantz Fanon

During the first half of the twentieth century, West Indian thinkers living under British colonial rule, including Marcus Garvey, C. L. R. James, George Padmore, and Eric Williams, theorized and militated against the effects of racism, capitalism, and imperialism on West Indians and the broader African world. In the 1960s, as West Indians gained independence and confronted their position in the neocolonial order, a new generation of activist intellectuals drew on the Caribbean's rich intellectual history and on new currents in pan-African, anti-imperialist, and antiracist thought to develop New Left critiques rooted in both the realities facing the West Indian people and global currents of radical praxis.

An important part of this West Indian New Left tradition was the New World Group, a pioneering intellectual collective that, under the leadership of the Trinidadian economist Lloyd Best (1934–2007), had a profound impact on Caribbean scholarship and politics. In their publications, notably the *New World Quarterly*, a journal the group published from 1963 to 1972, New World's members worked to understand the West Indian past and present in order to shape a democratic and egalitarian vision of the region's future. Responding in part to development planning that they believed would serve only to perpetuate metropolitan control of the Caribbean people and their resources, New World analyzed the dynamics underpinning West Indian political marginalization, economic underdevelopment, and poverty and theorized alternatives to neocolonialism. In his contribution to a 2012 retrospective collection of essays on the New World Group, Norman Girvan, the prominent Jamaican economist and a member of the collective, called New World a "form of resistance . . . to Eurocentric thinking" that "waged a kind of intellectual guerrilla warfare" and became, along with Rastafari (a political, cultural, and spiritual movement that, in the words of historian Horace Campbell, "challenges . . . the entire Western world to come to terms with the history of slavery, the reality of white racism and the permanent thrust for dignity and respect by black people") and the Caribbean Black Power movement of the late 1960s and early 1970s (most visibly manifest in the 1970 "Black Power Revolution" in Trinidad), an important component of West Indian attempts to address the effects of a history of imperial domination.[1]

New World's thinkers often evoked West Indian values as a necessary foundation for the region's postcolonial social development. The value that New World thinkers did the most to elucidate, and the concept driving much of their work, was that of independence, defined as broadly as possible to encompass the political, economic, and cultural spheres. In that spirit, New World put the question of epistemic sovereignty—the freedom to think outside the structures imposed by metropolitan power—at the center of their analyses of the West Indian situation. For the intellectual spearhead Lloyd Best, the valorization of locally rooted epistemology meant rejecting many of the categories typically assumed in studies of the West Indies, including an emphasis on class analysis as well as concepts of the "Third World" or the global "South" that limited West Indian intellectual freedom by circumscribing attempts to understand the region on its own terms. This rejection of many of the categories central to Western progressive thought presents a challenge to talking about the thought of New World without reproducing the very concepts that much of the group's work reacted against.

Taking to heart the Fanon quotation that provides the epigraph to this chapter, New World worked from the assumption that no political, economic, or social vision of the West Indian future was appropriate unless it was grounded in a detailed study of the region on its own terms, not through the conceptual lenses inherited from an imperial past. Without analysis rooted in West Indian epistemologies, political action to break away from the constraints imposed by imperial or neoimperial power was impossible.

In the early 1960s, as the colonial administration known as the West Indies Federation fell apart and the British Caribbean moved toward self-government, West Indian intellectuals and activists shifted their focus from pushing for formal independence to dismantling the political, economic, and intellectual structures inherited from the empire. This shift in orientation from pursuit of independence alone to the achievement of full decolonization coincided with the establishment of the Faculty of Social Science at the Mona (Jamaica) campus of the University of the West Indies (then called the University College of the West Indies), which provided an infrastructure for research into regional social and economic issues.[2]

A 1959 lecture series at Mona on the future of the West Indies—including a talk by the Marxist and pan-Africanist Trinidadian writer C. L. R. James that "lit the place afire," according to the economist Girvan—helped set the tone for West Indian thought in the decade to follow.[3] Lloyd Best, a young economist at Mona, hosted meetings of students and lecturers to continue the conversations started by the lectures; they formalized their sessions as the West Indian Society for the Study of Social Issues (WISSSI). WISSSI united a number of prominent or soon-to-be prominent West Indian intellectuals, including Girvan; the economist Alister McIntyre; the political scientist Archie Singham; and historians Roy Augier, Orlando Patterson, and Walter Rodney.[4]

WISSSI's discussions focused on political independence and the question of how to decolonize the social, economic, and political spheres in order to promote the development of a democratic and egalitarian West Indies. Of particular importance was their desire to move popular visions of the region's future development beyond the false dichotomy posed by the two Cold War power blocs—US capitalism versus Soviet communism—and thereby allow the West Indian people to chart their political and economic paths guided not by the demands of foreign power but by their desire to "build a society appropriate to our collective needs," as an early *Quarterly* editorial put it.[5]

In 1962 Best went to Georgetown, Guyana, as a UN economic advisor to Premier Cheddi Jagan's Peoples' Progressive Party (PPP) government. There he continued the work started by WISSSI with like-minded intellectuals; in a 2005 interview with Girvan and the historians Brian Meeks and Anthony Bogues, Best called the Georgetown group "a tremendous intellectual mobiliser."[6]

Participants in the Georgetown meetings collaborated to produce the first edition of what would become the most important print forum for 1960s West Indian progressive thought. *New World Quarterly* debuted in 1963, and it published regularly until 1968 and then sporadically until 1972. A companion publication, *New World Fortnightly*, which focused on Guyanese issues, ran from 1964 to 1966. *New World Quarterly* drew on a broad spectrum of Caribbean thinkers—including economists such as Best and George Beckford, historians such as James Millette and Elsa Goveia, and literary figures such as George Lamming and Jan Carew—to present lively exchanges of ideas within a framework committed to a genuinely independent intellectual life.

The desire of an emerging generation of West Indian intellectuals to free themselves from the confines imposed by metropolitan structures of thought was a key element in the conception of the *Quarterly*. In a 1997 interview with the anthropologist David Scott, Best recalled his frustration with West Indian scholars who felt obligated to publish in "reputable" (meaning foreign) journals. "If we don't put our statements into our own papers and journals," he asked, "how will our papers and journals ever become reputable?"[7] Besides the journals, New World produced studies and pamphlets addressing regional issues including currency devaluation, sugar production, unemployment, and Jamaica's attempts to limit the free movement of academics.[8]

Building on the dynamic established by the Mona and Georgetown groups and taking the name of the journal for an independent Caribbean intellectual collective, Best and his colleagues established chapters of the New World Group throughout the Anglophone Caribbean and in Montreal, Canada, where a cohort of West Indian students would play a prominent part in Caribbean and black Canadian political activism.[9]

David Scott describes New World's project as "the interrogation *from within* of the meaning of Caribbean sovereignty."[10] Interrogating sovereignty "from within" meant examining the history and the present conditions of the West Indian people on their own terms, free from conditions and constraints imposed by foreign political, economic, or cultural influences, in order to create an intellectual space from which the West Indian people could decide what to do with their independence, as opposed to allowing foreign interests to define the possibilities open to them.

New World embraced a loosely nationalist vision of a multicultural and multilingual Caribbean, unified in its desire to advance the interests of the Caribbean people. While there was an overwhelmingly large Commonwealth Caribbean contingent in the makeup of the membership and in the subjects they addressed, New World's vision of a democratic West Indies encompassed the entire region, regardless of language or colonial past. The broadest definition of "the Caribbean" came from Best, who in 1966 argued that it was the historical experience of the plantation, and not geographic location, that determined if a place was part of the Caribbean.

In this vision, the Caribbean included Caracas (Venezuela) and the Carolinas as much as it did Kingston and Puerto Rico—though, as we shall see later, Best was not always consistent with this framing.[11]

New World's intellectual approach drew extensively on the radical decentering of the region's history pioneered by figures such as Eric Williams and C. L. R. James, who in landmark works such as *Capitalism and Slavery* (1944) and *The Black Jacobins* (1938) framed the West Indian people as a dynamic force in the development of modernity.[12] The desire to develop a progressive mode of analysis that put West Indian people and their ideas at the center of any study of the region reflected Best's conviction that radical intellectualism did not require allegiance to any conventional ideology but rather developed organically as the response to the particular challenges facing a people. Best saw New World's work as something that grew out of "a sustained application of thought to the matters that concern [West Indians] deeply."[13]

Debates about the future economic development of the West Indies were an important part of New World's work. Economists writing about the region in the 1960s proposed a number of means by which to address the region's chronic poverty and unemployment, including developing the tourism trade, promoting emigration, and using foreign aid to create industries that would allow for import substitution.[14] The most prominent West Indian development economist, the Nobel laureate W. Arthur Lewis, created the so-called Puerto Rican model as a way to address regional unemployment. The model called for using foreign capital and expertise to launch export-oriented industries that would absorb unemployed workers. A key factor in the plan was low wages to maximize profitability and encourage foreign investment.[15]

Best and his colleagues strongly criticized development plans, like Lewis's, that increased West Indian reliance on foreign markets, capital, and initiative. They saw such plans, which they dubbed "industrialization by invitation," as a force that would undermine the ability of the West Indian people to chart their own destiny. Relying on foreign firms would place agency and initiative in the hands of donor countries and would not necessarily lead to increased local investment or the development of local skills. Furthermore, the metropolitan cultures, values, and living standards that came as by-products of foreign investment would potentially undermine West Indian economic and cultural independence.[16]

With an eye to such issues as the role of the sugar industry in perpetuating dependence on overseas markets, the role of bauxite mining in the extraction of Caribbean wealth for the benefit of the industrialized nations, and the domination of the regional financial sector by foreign banks, New World's theorists interrogated the postcolonial West Indian economy in terms of the historical legacies of centuries of colonial rule. New World theorists proposed a variety of initiatives to undo the dependence created by imperialism and to move the West Indian people toward a future in which they had the maximum control of their own resources. A study on Jamaican unemployment called for massive reforms in agriculture, mining, and education and industrial development based on processing domestic resources rather than assembling imported parts.[17] Much of economist George Beckford's work focused on the need to empower small-scale producers to stop producing cash crops for export and to start producing crops to satisfy local needs.[18] Girvan wrote a brief that informed Guyana's decision to nationalize its bauxite mines.[19]

At the 1966 Conference on Caribbean Affairs, one of a series of annual meetings of writers and activists from the Caribbean and its diaspora held in Montreal, Best argued that a principal roadblock for people trying to enact social change was their failure to conduct analyses derived from the study of local phenomena. Given the extent to which the West Indies' problems stemmed from policies built on metropolitan ideas, the destruction of "the intellectual, philosophical and psychological foundations of current politics" was a necessary precondition for meaningful independence.[20] In the spirit of Marcus Garvey's appeal to black people to "emancipate [themselves] from mental slavery," New World's concept of complete sovereignty extended to the realm of epistemology.[21] New World pushed the study of Caribbean society past what Best called "tourist social science"—analyses based on cursory visits to a given country that failed to engage in a substantive manner with local conditions but merely confirmed preconceived notions—so as to address regional issues in their specific historical, economic, and cultural contexts.[22]

In 1968, Best argued that since West Indians controlled their own political systems, the only thing preventing them from "creating an economy appropriate to their own needs" was "the state of their own consciousness."[23] The need for the West Indian people to craft epistemologies free from concepts inherited from their imperial past—in order to create a future society that was free and fair—was a constant theme in New World's work. Economist Alister McIntyre, in a 1966 analysis of West Indian trade policy, tied the failure of the region's leaders to come to an agreement on a customs union to their failure to embrace new ideas because of a persistent "belief . . . that Britain, Europe, and North America possess a monopoly over ideas."[24] In his 1973 essay, "On the Teaching of Economics,"

Best attacked economics departments for reproducing the rationales behind regional economic exploitation.[25] Beckford, in *Persistent Poverty*, argued that any potential improvement of West Indian living conditions required a shift in the consciousness of the West Indian people that would enable them to conceive of new possibilities. The "precondition of all preconditions for change and transformation," Beckford wrote, "is a restructuring of the minds of the people to accommodate change."[26]

It is crucial to note, however, that New World's desire to resist the imposition of alien epistemologies did not imply that a narrow nationalism guided their intellectual orientation. Reflecting the "bricolage" that defines much of West Indian culture, New World drew inspiration from intellectual traditions from Africa, its diaspora, the rest of the Third World, and other relevant intellectual traditions.[27] The critical acceptance of the ideas of pan-Africanists such as Ghana's first president Kwame Nkrumah, African American figures such as Malcolm X, Latin American dependency theorists like Raúl Prebisch and Celso Furtado, and the Swedish economist Gunnar Myrdal was as important to New World as the work of figures such as James, Garvey, Fanon, and Williams.[28]

Best worked closely in the mid-1960s with Kari Levitt, a Canadian economist and founding member of the Montreal chapter of New World who had worked extensively in the West Indies. Together, they developed the "plantation model," a *longue-durée* historical analysis of West Indian development. *Essays on the Theory of Plantation Economy*, which was completed in 1967 but only published in 2009, took the slave plantation as "the original and generic economic institution of Caribbean economy" and analyzed how the institutions, structures, and behaviors produced by sugar production set the stage for centuries of West Indian economic exploitation. Best and Levitt concluded that the plantation's legacy included economic dependence, instability, rampant poverty, inequality, and a political economy in which the state's limited ability to enact independent policy stymied the possibilities for transformation. The modern plantation economy perpetuated the legacies of colonialism insofar as the region was still in a one-way economic relationship with metropolitan power, meaning that "accumulation, technological change and taste formation" were driven by foreign priorities, not local ones.[29]

In his 1972 book *Persistent Poverty*, Beckford expanded the concept of the plantation economy to address the "plantation society." More than a regional economic study, this was a general theory of social, political, cultural, and economic underdevelopment. Beckford argued that modern iterations of the plantation system, notably the multinational corporations, which

Beckford called "vertically integrated corporate plantation enterprises," hindered the economic, political, and cultural development of the West Indies and the rest of the formerly colonized world by alienating people from their resources and hindering the establishment of locally oriented economic links that would encourage structural transformation.[30]

In his interview with David Scott, Best maintained that he had consistently rejected any intellectual approach that did not allow for the study of the West Indies in terms of the region's own specific histories, that relegated the West Indies to a peripheral position in any sort of global framework, or that advocated ideologies that developed in reaction to situations in distant nations. Best stated that he had "never accepted" overarching frameworks such as the "Third World," "developing countries," or "the South" and that he had always "repudiated all isms whether from left or right."[31] Best's critique of imported epistemologies included a critique of Eurocentric conceptions of resistance to that exploitation, arguing that, like the development planning that perpetuated the domination of the region, Marxism and some schools of left-wing "dependency theory" were not based on dedicated studies of the West Indies and were thus of limited use in challenging foreign domination of the region.

Best rejected modes of analysis developed in resistance to European capitalism because they assumed that the social categories created by European capitalism were a universal analytic lens. Best argued that specific economic systems gave birth to specific formations of "group solidarity and group interest." While the plantation economy shared the exploitative nature of capitalism, it lacked its specific historical and cultural dynamics. Specifically, it was entirely geared toward export and not local markets; it relied on imported labor; and the people who controlled the means of production typically lived overseas and were thus not embedded in the same social realities as the people they exploited. Thus the socioeconomic dynamics that led to the development of class and class consciousness in Europe were never at play in the Caribbean.[32] Best's experiences in Guyana, where political fragmentation occurred along ethnic lines, pitting Afro-Guyanese against Indo-Guyanese and black against white—with disastrous results for the nation—helped him to see racial identity as more salient than class conflict in the shaping of West Indian political identities.[33] New World's analyses of economic inequality focused on the racial divisions at the heart of plantation slavery and its successor regimes. Black dispossession and not class exploitation was the ultimate legacy of the plantation economy.[34]

Best was strongly critical of Marxism, rejecting it as a doctrine that, contrary to its universalistic pretensions, was of limited use even within its own European context. At the 1966 Conference on Caribbean Affairs, he noted that Marxism left little space to develop critiques independent of the categories established by metropolitan thinkers, preventing activists from seeing a "wide and constantly changing range of possible social objectives and of feasible social action."[35] Three years later, Best wrote that, in trying to impose European categories and precepts on non-European situations, Marxist thought had "[ridden] rough-shod over local sentiment, [ignored] local possibilities and local limitations," and worked to "inhibit rather than to promote radical reform."[36]

Best's critique of Cuba's Marxist regime reveals he saw how a failure to understand a Caribbean nation through a locally rooted epistemology led to a failure to secure meaningful independence. Best was sharply critical of Cuba's decision to, as he wrote in 1966, "exchange imperial masters" by "entering into voluntary association with the Marxist-Leninist Church" and taking up close association with the USSR.[37]

In his conversation with Girvan, Meeks, and Bogues, Best elaborated on his criticism of Cuba, arguing that Castro had not understood Cuba as a West Indian nation, one whose history had been, like the rest of the Caribbean, shaped by sugar. For Best, "the most important, single thing about Cuba was that it came to be dominated by Afros, and the sugar plantation." Had Castro understood Cuba in terms of the legacies of the plantation, Best argued, he could have made a "vital connection" to other West Indian people who "understood the exploitation of sugar," and thus he could "upset all the politics in the region." Best criticized Castro for orienting Cuba toward Latin America, where, he argued, the lack of a shared history created by sugar kept his message from resonating. Best recalled how, while he was working briefly in Chile during Allende's rule, people would tell him that Castro was "*mas tropical*," which, Best said, really meant he was "too Caribbean," and "thus nobody paid him any mind." Castro's failure to see what was obvious to his Chilean critics prevented him from seeking strong ties with West Indians, which ultimately meant aligning Cuba with Moscow and provoking an American siege that prevented the development of democratic politics.[38]

Alongside critiques of Marxism, New World thinkers modified and expanded the dependency-school approaches like those of Raúl Prebisch, Celso Furtado, and Andre Gunder Frank that informed many critiques of the relationship between former colonies and their metropoles; unique elements of the West Indian situation, they believed, meant they should exercise caution in borrowing from any school of dependency thought that put the region on the periphery of world affairs.[39] Much as he did with Marxism, Best criticized what he saw as a tendency on the part of many dependency-school thinkers to see capitalism as a force that worked the same way everywhere. While Best agreed that it "makes a lot of sense to treat the world as one entity," he believed that approaches such as Wallerstein's world-systems analysis needed to do much more to "disaggregate the world into different civilizations, and into different systems and subsystems." Without doing so, he reasoned, such frameworks risked becoming a "straitjacket" that prevented analyses of the Caribbean from discovering "how it works and how it fits into the world system."[40]

By dividing the world into hard categories of "core" and "periphery," dependency thought risked erasing both the history and the potential of the West Indian people. There is an important tension between New World's framing of the West Indies as a region that had developed, and continued to exist, in a dependent relationship with metropolitan political and economic power and their vision of the West Indian people as a dynamic force in world history and as the only force that could liberate the region from its dependent relationships. On the one hand, as Best wrote in 1973, the West Indies had "been dominated by *total institutions*" that sought to control every aspect of the region's social, political, and economic life.[41] On the other hand, New World thinkers embraced a strong optimism rooted in the creative potential of the West Indian people, who were the only ones who could undo the effects of centuries of imperial rule on the region's development. As Alfie Roberts, a member of the Montreal chapter of New World, wrote in 1966, the West Indians were "a modern and international people" who needed "no lecturing on the virtues of any system or philosophy" but wanted "to be left alone to work out [their] own destinies in conjunction with all [their] people, and thinking and analyzing [their] problems from an independent premise."[42]

Although Best argued that colonialism had left the West Indies lacking a "cultural solidarity" found in other nations, he also saw West Indians as "a distinctive people with [their] own creative will and a determination to build a society appropriate to [their] collective needs."[43] His vision of West Indians as a dynamic force for social change, even as they had been, and continued to be, marginalized and oppressed, reflected C. L. R. James's strong belief that while they had been "mis-educated" and had their "political consciousness . . . twisted and broken," the West Indian people were "the most rebellious . . . in history" and could craft a new society from the intellectual, ideological, and cultural artifacts that their historical circumstances had left them.[44] Like James, New World thinkers put the West Indian people at the center of their visions of the region's future. Beckford once wrote that there could be "no escape from poverty without freeing the creative power of all the people."[45] In a 1996 tribute to Beckford, Best wrote, "We are deciding. We are not the Third World. We are the First. We are in charge, and if it is a mess . . . we have got to clean it up because we are in charge."[46]

New World's focus on epistemic sovereignty, their decentering of Eurocentric analyses, and their desire to affirm the ability of the West Indian people to chart their own course all draw attention to the role of the intellectual in the decolonizing world. In 1960, Arthur Lewis, speaking as principal of the University College of the West Indies, called on the institution to work to improve "the 'image' of West Indians into one more acceptable to the rest of the world." Walter Rodney, then an undergraduate at Mona and a regular at WISSSI sessions, heard in Lewis's words a vision of the university as an institution committed to creating a class of intellectuals who would "go into the business of mystification" and contribute to the perpetuation of (neo)imperialist domination while paying lip service to an empty West Indian nationalism.[47]

In *The Wretched of the Earth*, Frantz Fanon argued that states emerging from colonial rule faced political turmoil in part because their intelligentsia was alienated from popular intellectual currents. He also argued that emerging national elites who inherited economies that had developed outside of their control did not understand how those economies worked. Independence thus did not bring about fundamental change, as the national bourgeoisie, out of touch with the masses, positioned itself as an intermediary for foreign capital and became nothing more than the local representatives of Western multinational firms. Newly independent nations thus remained focused on extracting primary resources for the benefit of the metropole.[48]

Fanon contrasted the behavior of the colonized bourgeoisie with the stance taken by what he called "an authentic national bourgeoisie," meaning those intellectuals who turn their backs on the roles that the colonizers had planned for them in order to be in close touch with the people so that they may learn from the masses while passing on "intellectual and technical capital."[49] Those intellectuals, Fanon wrote, had the potential to "[open] up the future," "spurring [the people] into action and fostering hope."[50] Read through the lens of Fanon's critiques of postcolonial intellectuals, New World's work can be understood as a self-conscious attempt on the part of an educated class to create, from the ground up, a new intellectual tradition. This tradition, rooted in the work of previous generations of

West Indian thinkers and based on a detailed study of West Indian history, economy, society, and culture, was to be a bulwark against the reproduction of imperial modes of analysis that supported an economy predicated on extraction and exploitation.

But while their orientation was deeply political, New World was not actively so. The historian Bert Thomas describes the group as more of a regional conscience than a political actor.[51] As New World developed a body of theory addressing the struggles of the West Indian people, the question of what to do with that theory was a factor in the group's dissolution.

The New World Group fell apart gradually between 1968 and 1972. While the history of its demise is, in the words of Brian Meeks, "controversial" and "hotly contested," one factor driving its disintegration was a tension between Best's wishes to keep New World exclusively focused on intellectual activity and a desire on the part of many members to engage in direct action. This tension, Meeks writes, "robbed New World of people and energy."[52] Of particular importance in pushing many members' focus from analysis to action was Jamaica's refusal to allow Walter Rodney, then a professor of African history at Mona, to reenter the country upon his return from the October 1968 Congress of Black Writers in Montreal. Rodney's banning provoked a strong reaction from both students and marginalized urban populations, such as the Rastafari, whom Rodney had been teaching in informal settings known as "groundings" since arriving in Kingston in January 1968. One account of the protests that followed the ban describes students marching in downtown Kingston from the Mona campus in their academic robes, "led by the radical 'New World' group of lecturers."[53]

Even before Rodney's ban, stress had begun to show between Best's desire to keep New World a strictly intellectual venture and the desires of more activist-oriented members. The Montreal branch of New World was a site of debate about the group's direction; Alfie Roberts and Tim Hector, two of the more activist-minded members, had been pressuring Best to, in his words, "[go] out to the people, what I call agitation"—a notion that Best rejected in part because he did not see a divide between "the people" and the work of intellectuals.[54] This refusal to see the masses as something apart from the work of intellectuals reflected an approach to popular intellectualism outlined in Fanon's depiction of the authentic bourgeoisie that was also put into practice in Rodney's groundings. Perhaps more important, in terms of Best's vision of a politics that was built on a sustained study of local history, society, and culture, he believed that much work needed to be done before concrete action could be taken on New World's ideas. At the 1966 Conference on Caribbean Affairs, he urged his compatriots to understand the need to develop "the intellectual capital goods" that were a necessary precondition for meaningful action. Without a strong theoretical base rooted in local realities, activists would not be able to dismantle the "intellectual, philosophical, and psychological foundation of current politics" and would risk reproducing those politics. "Thought," Best argued, "is the action for us."[55]

Alongside internal pressures arising from the question of political action, another factor in the dissolution of New World was, perhaps ironically, the formal independence of individual Caribbean states, which drew young politically minded individuals away from regional politics toward more narrowly focused nationalist frameworks.[56] As New World fell apart, its members and its ideas contributed to the development of numerous left-wing Caribbean political projects. In Jamaica, New World members were involved in Abeng, an intellectual and activist collective that produced a newspaper of the same name, as well as in Michael Manley's People's National Party. The socialist Antigua Caribbean Movement was founded by Montreal chapter member Tim Hector in 1968. Guyana's Working People's Alliance, which started as a political pressure group in 1974 and became a political party in 1979, counted a number of people associated with New World, including Walter Rodney and economist Clive Thomas. Trinidad's National Joint Action Committee, the student-based movement that was the catalyst of the 1970 Black Power uprising (very nearly overthrowing the government of Eric Williams), drew extensively on New World's analyses. Best founded Trinidad's Tapia House Movement, which began life as an intellectual project in 1968 but became a political party in 1976. Many of these intellectuals and the movements with which they worked explored analytic frameworks from outside of New World's focus on specifically West Indian conceptions, including Marxism and Black Power from the United States. However, this greater openness toward foreign ideas did not imply the abandonment of a focus on the specific political, economic, and social dynamics of the West Indies; it was often tempered by the desire to make these modes of thinking relevant to the West Indian situation.[57]

The role of New World's concepts and people in so many progressive political projects speaks to its importance in the development of modern West Indian radicalism. Yet while New World was a key factor in the development of postcolonial intellectualism, helping to create a generation of progressive political activists, it is hard to dismiss those who see the group's history in terms of a larger story about the inability of popular politics to overcome external pressures keeping the West Indies economically exploited. In the 1970s, many West Indian states, especially Jamaica under Michael Manley, directed their energies toward protecting national sovereignty, alleviating poverty, and eliminating racism, all values advocated by New World. In the 1980s these priorities were replaced by market liberalization, debt repayment, and the undoing of the social safety net.[58] The popular radicalism that came into public consciousness with the banning of Rodney was ultimately short-lived, as his assassination in June 1980 and the electoral defeat of Michael Manley a few months later marked the start of a decline for West Indian radicalism that culminated with the collapse of the Grenada revolution in 1983.[59]

Taking advantage of a relatively free intellectual climate, New World's ideas became part of the mainstream of Caribbean thought in the 1960s. That intellectual freedom, however, was one of the many victims of the neoliberal turn that began in the 1980s; both Kari Levitt and James Millette, a historian and a founding member of New World, argue that the hegemony of neoclassical economics and World Bank and International Monetary Fund logic delegitimized New World's brand of independent thought.[60] But the neoliberalism and globalization that overwhelmed the West Indian New Left failed to improve the circumstances of many West Indians. As the false choice between Western capitalism and Soviet communism has been replaced by one between global neoimperialism and total marginalization, the concepts developed by Best and his comrades have taken on renewed relevance, offering tools to analyze the underpinnings of the industrialized world's contemporary exploitation of the West Indies.[61]

Speaking in Toronto in 2001, Lloyd Best argued that West Indians, as they had done forty years earlier, needed to address the issues that confronted them through the lens of "a whole new interpretation, derived organically from Caribbean history and set in Caribbean institutions and culture." Best saw the New World Group's legacy in a new generation of West Indians who reject "the idea that the Caribbean is not its own first world but somebody else's third." This generation, he noted, sees themselves as "the subject and makers of history, not the object and takers."[62]

29 | On the Shores of Japan's Postwar Left: An Intimate History

by Leslie Pincus

> Never let go of the fact that we are living our lives right here, right now.
>
> —Nakai Masakazu[1]

For the past three decades, Tokumura Tokiko and Tokumura Akira have made their home in the interior woodlands of Japan's northernmost island of Hokkaido. They live among a community of family, friends, and assorted young people and children—some longtime residents and others temporary sojourners. Each summer, scores of children migrate up to "Children's Village" for a rare summer camp experience that borders on creative anarchy. In the "Autumn Forest Schoolhouse," a smaller group of adults gather to experience the forest along with the Tokumuras and share ideas on a range of subjects from organic farming, ecological systems, and planetary ethics to children's initiatives, social movements, and prospects for peace. Twice a year, Akira and Tokiko travel widely through Japan's main island to talk to small groups of old friends and new acquaintances about the knowledge they have gained over years of interacting with children and inhabiting the northern forests. On these trips, Akira often spends several weeks at a time walking the remaining beech forests of Akita and Iwate, occasionally joined by friends who hope to experience firsthand what Akira describes as the "wonder" of the forest and the myriad living beings that inhabit it.

The way of living that the Tokumuras have embraced over the past half century—an evolving experiment in fostering a child-centered and ecologically conscious community—might not appear to be political in the strict sense of the term. Even so, the threads of their own lives are intertwined with the history of the Japanese left in the second half of the twen-

Tokumura Tokiko and Tokumura Akira, 2012. Leslie Pincus (personal photo)

tieth century. The legacies of that larger history lend texture and direction to their convictions and engagements.

In the past, scholarship on the Japanese left, both "old" and "new," focused closely on organizational taxonomies, charting the vicissitudes and schisms that divided the histories of the established leftist parties and New Left "sects." Recently, a new cohort of scholars has taken on these boundary issues, looking beyond organizational divisions to discover continuities and connections among a diversity of progressive and leftist movements. These scholars hope both to rescue the history of Japan's New Left from opprobrium and to situate it within broader contexts. Their work brings to light the New Left inheritance from earlier progressive traditions as well as its legacy (some would say an ambiguous one) for newer forms of collective action in the late twentieth century and beyond.[2] Rather than retrace these new histories, I have borrowed their insights in my own exploration of the narrative itineraries of Tokiko and Akira as they traverse the war years, old and new lefts, local social movements, and more. Both are creative foragers of memory, culling what is relevant to their current engagements even as they continue to make meaning out of their pasts. Their documented lives—whether in print, conversation, correspondence, or, most recently, texted free verse—add up to a small but revealing archive of conviction and practice on the shores of what Howard Brick has called "the long left."

For their generation, that narrative begins by necessity with a calamitous war—the history that "must never be repeated" and the ground zero of leftist and progressive politics in postwar Japan. Akira (b. 1928) first found his political voice in the student self-governing associations that sprang up in the wake of defeat; in 1948 these coalesced into *Zengakuren*, a nationwide federation of student movements identified closely with a revived Japanese Communist Party (JCP). Tokiko, five years his junior, traces her storylines through the cultural circles that flourished in the early 1950s—groups that encouraged participatory democracy, organizational autonomy, and utopian political aspirations. At the end of the decade, these circles and a dynamic student movement converged, in loose association with organized labor and the established parties of the left, to mount a massive, nationwide protest against the 1960 renewal of the US-Japan Security Treaty (commonly known in its abbreviated Japanese form as "Anpo").

Until Japan's surrender, Akira had been a young cadet in Imperial Japan's elite military training institution, the Naval Officers' Training School on Etajima (an island just off coastal Hiroshima Prefecture), where he suffered the routine brutality of Japan's wartime military culture. Had the war continued beyond August 1945, he might have been inducted into the "special attack forces" only to meet his end in a *kaiten*, a manned underwater torpedo. As part of a distinctive generational cohort reprieved from death by Japan's surrender, Akira must have returned to his provincial home in Kanazawa with a mixture of feelings: guilt toward his seniors who *did* die in the war, a sense of being betrayed by the wartime regime, and distrust for an older generation that hastily refashioned itself from fascist to democratic.[3] His activist career began in an elite preparatory higher school where he helped organize one of the many student self-governing associations that emerged with encouragement from a still-progressive Civil Affairs section of the Occupation administration in the wake of defeat. In 1949, newly admitted to Tokyo National University, Akira arrived in the midst of student demonstrations against rising tuitions and early signs of an Occupation-backed "red purge" as US Cold War policies sharpened political divisions in a Japan still wracked by scarcity and inflation. The student protests would have been organized by the Tokyo University branch of Zengakuren (All-Japan Federation of Student Self-Governing Associations) in which all students on campus were automatically enrolled. But for a large part of the student body, allegiance to the JCP-allied Zengakuren was no mere formality: many of this postdefeat student generation were drawn to the Communist Party for its record of opposition to fascism and militarism before 1945 and its commitment to democracy after. And Akira was no exception. By his own account, he kept his distance from the more doctrinaire leadership of Zengakuren, devoting his energies instead to the Japan Memorial Society for Fallen Students, an antiwar organization inspired by the 1949 publication of *Kike, wadatsumi no koe* (*Listen to the Voices from the Sea*), a compilation of posthumous writings by seventy-five student-soldiers who died in the war, some in suicide missions.[4]

For Akira, the antiwar stance had a special salience: on August 6, 1945, he and fellow cadets at the Naval Academy on Etajima watched from five miles across the Inland Sea as Hiroshima and its inhabitants were annihilated in an atomic cataclysm. Less than two weeks later, he crossed over to Hiroshima to pick his way through the ruins in search of a train out of the city. A gifted conversationalist, Akira is uncharacteristically reticent on this topic. Only after the recent Fukushima nuclear disaster sixty-six years later did Akira describe the scene in writing: "What I saw before my eyes was a scene of cruel tragedy: People, near naked, their flesh burned away, wandered the city in search of relatives. It was too much to bear. Right then and there, the worldview of this 'militarist youth' was forever shattered."[5] It was also after the Fukushima disaster, when the issue of *naibu hibaku* (internal radiation exposure) came to the fore, that Akira first realized that the chronic illness that plagued him throughout his adult life was likely the result of his exposure in Hiroshima.

In 1951, Akira returned once again to Hiroshima, this time as part of a production team for a documentary film with the same title as the epistolary anthology *Listen to the Voices from the Sea*. His promotional efforts—tacking up posters with the injunction "Never again repeat the tragedy of Hiroshima"—drew the ire of Occupation authorities who placed the atomic bombings at the top of their covert list of censored topics. In hopes of evading the American military police, Akira made a fateful decision to go underground.

Akira himself attaches little importance to his memories of these early postwar years: "I wasn't acting out of my own conviction," he says. "There was just this powerful tide, and the views of those above me in the organization [JCP]." From my perspective, Akira's retrospective self-doubt seems to run parallel to Zengakuren criticism of the JCP in the late 1950s for its authoritarian organizational tactics, erratic policy shifts, and recent embrace of parliamentary politics. The conflict between the JCP and many of the leaders of the student movement would lead the mainstream of the Zengakuren to break from the Communist Party in 1958 and form an independent, radical left "Bund"—an event that coincides with the early beginning of the New Left in global history. For his part, Akira contrasts this early period of his political life to his more recent engagements with children and ecology, to which he brings endless reserves of initiative, imagination, and passion.

In 1952, still at risk of arrest, Akira was smuggled out of Japan by boat, a clandestine departure most likely arranged and funded by the JCP.[6] His own intention, he explains, was to attend the Vienna Congress of the Peoples for Peace in December 1952 and return to Japan. But once the Congress was over, reentry proved difficult for a Japanese national who had left the country illegally. Akira never clarifies exactly why he remained outside Japan for nearly a decade. He spent most of that period in the People's Republic of China (a safe haven for Japanese Communists in the early 1950s), another subject on which he has little to say—only that he was treated as an "esteemed representative of the Japanese Student Movement." He reveals this fact with some discomfort as if he now believes he was in China under false pretenses. Whatever admiration he may have had for revolutionary China has been blunted by his disillusionment with the orthodox left and the new hierarchies it installed, whether in China or Japan.

For Tokiko (b. 1933), news of Japan's surrender came in Onomichi on the Inland Sea, the Nakai family hometown and refuge from Kyoto, where food had become scarce and bombing raids likely. During the 1930s, To-kiko's father, Nakai Masakazu, had combined a brilliant academic career in philosophy with antifascist, Popular Front activism; for the latter, he was arrested and prosecuted for "dangerous thought" under a sweeping Peace Preservation Law, spending most of the war years in prison or under surveillance. In the wake of defeat, the Nakai household quickly became a center for cultural enlightenment and democratic activism. Tokiko's accounts of those first few years in Onomichi after Japan's defeat are filled with a sense of elation and liberation—a feeling not unique to her but nevertheless intense, colored as it was by a child's experience of the war only understood after the fact. Of the war itself, she invokes a small number of memories with a clarity that suggests a photographic imprint, sharpened rather than dulled with each narrative iteration. These include the kinds of everyday privations shared by many families during the war but also the distinctive suffering visited upon the child of a "thought criminal." Until the eve of defeat, the Nakai children knew little of their father's oppositional views. On rare excursions, Tokiko and the other children, dressed in their finest, were told that the police prison where they were taken to visit their father was his university office.

Tokiko calls up another wartime picture of her father, now released from detention but enduring the enforced idleness of house arrest. Occasionally, the family would pack lunch and head out to Lake Biwa, not far from Kyoto: "One day we rowed out and, as our boat floated in the middle of the lake, a naval training plane happened to fly overhead. My father looked up toward the sky and yelled 'bakayarō' (stupid fool). He was able to say it out loud only because we were out in the middle of the lake. At the time, we kids thought it was a game, so we imitated him."[7] It was only years later, Tokiko explains, that she understood her father's invective, aimed at a regime of violence that had rendered him powerless.

In 1947, when Nakai was appointed by the Diet, Japan's legislative body, to help establish the new National Diet Library, the family relocated to Tokyo. By then a high school student, Tokiko aspired first to the study of Russian literature and then to a career in classical music—both foreclosed by her father's untimely death in 1952 (a tragedy not unrelated, in Tokiko's view, to the rise of a virulent anticommunism and its red-baiting tactics). Compelled to earn a living wage at age seventeen, she found employment at a major bank in Tokyo: "Not a place to spend a life," she decided—and enrolled in an evening course at Tōhō Gakuen College of Music with the hope of redeeming her musical talents for a teaching credential.[8]

In between a day job and night school, Tokiko also found time to participate in several "circles"—small-scale, cultural gatherings devoted to literature, song, group study, or life writing that flourished in the 1950s, often with links to leftist politics. Many of these circles were initiated on the shop floor as part of a JCP effort to educate workers and build mass organization. However, as in the case of circle organizer and theorist Tanigawa Gan, some on the left chafed under the yoke of top-down direction from the party.[9] This more independent stream in the circle movement developed a different organizational philosophy from the established leftist parties. In place of the demand for unity, exclusivity, and compliance with directives issued from above, Tanigawa and other organizers encouraged free expression, internal diversity, participatory democracy, and exchange with other groups. While small in scale, these circles became a touchstone for both the New Left and the new social movements that emerged in 1960s.[10]

Tokiko was especially active in a flourishing *utagoe* (singing voice) movement—workplace choruses often linked to union politics. The choral connection proved to be her ticket out of the bank and into the labor movement. Not long before the 1960 Anpo protests, she took a job as secretary in Kurōkyō, a federation of labor unions established in the early postwar years to support working people in Tokyo's twenty-three wards. Tokiko's entry into labor politics came at a critical juncture: the late 1950s witnessed the last stage of a long struggle of militantly political unions against management efforts, backed by a powerful economic bureaucracy, to reassert control over labor and rationalize the workplace. During these same years, an ultraconservative government led by Kishi Nobusuke, an accused war criminal "de-purged" at the end of the US occupation, pushed a legislative agenda that included remilitarization, strengthening domestic police powers, and reasserting central control over school curricula. For new constituencies who had placed their hopes in Japan's fledgling postwar democracy (unions, women, students, progressive intellectuals, and the leftist parties), Kishi's administration raised the specter of a fascist revival. As the June 1960 deadline for renewal of the US-Japan Security Treaty in the National Diet approached, these new constituencies came together in a coalition to oppose renewal and the binding of Japan to US strategic interests in East Asia. But what ultimately galvanized the millions of ordinary people who took to the streets in protest in May and June 1960 was less the long shadow of US imperialism than the antidemocratic tactics Kishi used to overpower the opposition and force renewal through the Diet.

In the offices of Kurōkyō, Tokiko found herself at the organizational hub of labor strikes and the massive protests against the Security Treaty. This is how she describes her days on the front lines:

> It was my job to go out in support of the strikes; we would go to the Anpo demonstrations too. I'd run off the copies with directives for each of the unions—the electric workers, the teachers union, bus drivers. Each was ordered to send a certain percentage of their members. Those of us from the Kurōkyō brought our red flags; we'd yell out slogans and march on the Diet. Everyone would gather together there—workers from Fukushima and grandmothers from citizens' movements. We'd repeat our slogans, yell "tax thieves," and then go home, still riding high on the day's events. Then the next order would come down. . . . It wasn't too long before I began to wonder whether we could really win the struggle with this kind of command structure.[11]

For Tokiko, the Anpo protests exposed the bureaucratic, hierarchical, and coercive aspects of the orthodox left and raised doubts about the efficacy of its leadership. In search of alternatives, she turned to the most proximate and dramatic exemplar of social transformation: the Chinese Revolution, an event that loomed large in the progressive imagination during the years leading up to 1960 Anpo. "How could it be that the masses of people who brought about a transformation on that scale had acted simply on command from above?" she said. "I wanted to know how each individual actively took part in the movement."[12] Tokiko was especially curious about a term that circulated widely among progressive intellectuals in the 1950s: *taishū rosen* (the mass line), a key concept in the early stages of PRC revolutionary policy. At the suggestion of a friend, she addressed her question to Akira, just back from China. His response, in the form of a letter, served a dual purpose: it offered clarification on the concept of the mass line *and* it ignited a romance. The letter no longer exists, but at my request, Akira attempted to recreate his explanation of the mass line, tempering memory with recent reflection: "Even then I had this sense that it meant drawing on the popular will from below, those freely formed sentiments and ideas, and then gathering them together into a single force." He contrasted this approach with an entrenched tendency in Japanese leftist movements toward top-down organization. "Those above always try to control and manipulate those below, which is why the movement inevitably fragments."[13]

The year 1960 (when Tokiko and Akira's paths converged) marks the culmination as well as the endpoint of the grand coalition of progressive forces in the early postwar era. The ultimate failure of the movement to prevent the renewal of the Security Treaty or to fundamentally transform governing structures led to the disintegration of the antitreaty coalition and widespread disillusionment with the established left (soon to be labeled "the loyal opposition"). Although this history of post-Anpo disaffection has lent itself to a narrative of "the decline of the left," the 1960s actually witnessed a dynamic reconstellation of progressive organizations and movements. Moreover, as the Tokumuras' stories from the 1970s suggest, there are other possibilities for imagining the historical trajectory of the left in late twentieth-century Japan. In the words of Fernando Coronil, the loss of a "monopoly on the future" by the established left "opened spaces for the imagination and experimentation" where a diversity of groups were free to pursue "alternative paths to alternative futures."[14] In the Tokumuras' case, these "alternative paths" have taken unassuming form—a children's library, a collective child-centered community, and, most recently, visionary organizing in the field of deep ecology. These, too, represent one of the byways of Japan's "long left."

The Tokumuras were largely absent from Japan's turbulent social politics of the sixties, no doubt because of Akira's persistent maladies. In 1963, with hopes that his condition would improve with convalescence, the couple moved from Tokyo to Hiyoshi, a semirural suburb at the northernmost edge of Yokohama City. When they *did* reappear in the early 1970s, it was on ground that had been tilled by the New Left and small-scale citizens' movements, both of which had come into their own in the 1960s. At the beginning of the 1960s, Japan was poised on the cusp of phenomenal economic growth driven by developmentalist and technocratic state policies. The more conciliatory politics of the Ikeda administration—with the promise of affluence captured in the slogan "Double your income"—were designed to subdue the widespread desire for radical change of the early postwar years. That desire was also restrained by the extraordinary degree of uniformity imposed on social life in the course of the 1960s. To facilitate Japan's high-growth economy and contain the social energy manifested in the Anpo protests, government and industry coordinated efforts to rationalize the workplace, discipline the workforce, and standardize pathways from school to work.

It was this more affluent and intimately oppressive society that became an object of criticism for the New Left student groups that emerged from the organizational dispersion after 1960. Even as they sought an ideological foundation for a radical left independent of the Communist Party, these new student activists cultivated a critical awareness of how their own everyday lives were implicated in the systemic coercion that operated just below the surface of "Japan's glamorous, consumer-driven society."[15] Armed with the conviction that transforming "everydayness" would lead to social and political change, this generation introduced a new degree of reflexivity into the revolutionary struggle.

On the larger stage of geopolitics, the New Left students saw Japan's rising economic power and wealth as inextricably linked to the Security Treaty system with the United States—a system under which Japan, now a junior party in America's Pacific Asia strategy, had moved to rearm under a thin veil of pacifism. The outlines of that system became disturbingly clear in the mid-1960s as the United States stepped up its intervention in Vietnam and Japan became a staging ground, a manufacturer, and a morgue for the American war in Indochina. Criticism of Japan's complicity in American Cold War policy extended beyond the student movement to engage the political passions of a wider public: between 1967 and 1970, an estimated eighteen million people took to the streets calling for the reversion of Okinawa to Japan and an end to the war in Vietnam—the latter under the banner of Beheiren (Citizens' Federation for Peace in Vietnam), a nonpartisan alliance of hundreds of antiwar groups.[16] One of several large "people's movements" in the later 1960s, Beheiren developed organizational principles that paid tribute to the earlier, independent circle movement—nonalignment, organizational pluralism, voluntary participation, and direct democracy. A similar organizational ethos defined the campus revolts at the end of the decade under the auspices of Zenkyōtō, a loose network of independent, nonaligned "joint struggle councils."

The 1960s also saw the dramatic rise of small-scale, local movements, often in response to environmental depredations caused by intensive modernization policies and industrial recklessness. Scholars have tended to draw clear lines of demarcation between these new forms of collective action and the large-scale movements organized around powerful ideological programs that culminated in the 1960 Anpo protests. The "new social movements" of the sixties and seventies, they suggest, were distinct from the left (new and old) in both organization and objective—smaller in scale, more autonomous from established parties, more pragmatic in purpose, and less ideologically driven.[17]

The 1960s may indeed represent a watershed in movement culture, but that divide proves to be negotiable. Recent scholarship has highlighted continuities among these different movement genres, whether in the activist itineraries of specific individuals, in common aspirations for social justice, or even in movement styles. By the early 1970s, more than a few veterans from large-scale movements on the left had chosen to pursue social change on a smaller scale and in various forms—environmentalist and feminist movements, cooperatives and consumer movements, and alternative communities.[18] While these more local initiatives for social change might not present their ideological credentials in established form or directly confront the state, they often rose on radical ground.

The Tokumuras' plans in the early 1970s for a small, community-based, cultural initiative coincided with this shift in the scale, locus, and affiliation of social movements. It is hard to say whether their choice was a consequence of practical limitations on their lives at the time, disaffection with the established left, or a fundamental rethinking of strategies for social transformation. What *is* clear is that the projects they and other veterans of organized opposition politics undertook in the 1970s sprang from a desire to begin anew—to return to the foundations of everyday life and create a radically democratic and egalitarian way of living, person by person. For Tokiko and Akira in particular, this meant returning to the early postwar moment when the passion for democratic revolution was at its height. As it turned out, it also meant beginning with the child.

The occasion for their renewed activism came in 1971 in the form of a bleak prognosis for Akira's chronic maladies. Confronted with his own mortality, Akira was determined to leave no regrets, and so he and Tokiko considered how to live what remained of their life together. This is where the idea of a children's circle first makes its appearance, and it does so through the mediation of Nakai Masakazu and the culture movement he helped organize in the wake of Japan's defeat in World War II. As a young girl in Onomichi, Tokiko experienced her father's experiment in grassroots democratic transformation firsthand. Akira discovered the movement in print—in Nakai's accounts of how he had converted a small-town library into the headquarters for cultural organizing and a people's university, all intended to nurture a revolutionary democratic subjectivity among farmers, workers, and demobilized soldiers in the towns and villages of Hiroshima prefecture. "I was especially drawn to these essays from the immediate post-defeat era," Akira writes. "However small in scale, we wanted to create a library of our own—a place where we could engage with young people in the neighborhood."[19]

While the couple traced their inspiration back to that postdefeat moment of radical democratization, they found practical advice in a recently published book by children's author Ishii Momoko, an overview of Japan's first wave of children's libraries beginning in the late 1960s. These community-based, volunteer initiatives (typically organized by local parents concerned that the test-driven educational apparatus was diminishing the creative and imaginative worlds of children) aimed to reintroduce the rewards of reading.[20] Though far less conspicuous or contentious than the environmental protests that epitomized the grassroots citizens' movements of this mid-postwar era, the "children's library" initiative also takes its place in the new social movement culture of the 1960s and 1970s.

Most of all, it was Ishii's simple prescription for creating a children's library that drew the Tokumuras' attention: "When we thought of a library, we assumed that a building was necessary; and since we had no resources to build one, we were convinced that our plan was impossible. But Ishii Momoko's book showed us that it was possible to create a 'library' right here and now. . . . All we had to do was *open up* our home."[21] Here they use the Japanese word *kaihō*, which means both "to open" and "to liberate." In the years that followed, the Tokumuras *did* liberate their home—along with their energies and aspirations—as part of a collective enterprise in social transformation. But to be more faithful to their story, I should say that the children liberated these sanctums for them. Akira and Tokiko maintain that they underwent a radical "reeducation" as they learned from the children who literally took over their home and their lives. Ultimately, this reeducation took them far beyond the modest ambitions of the children's library movement. But what made them so receptive to this radical venture were the legacies they inherited from the left, both old and new.

In the first of their coauthored chronicles, *Kodomo ga shujinkō* (The child is the hero), Akira and Tokiko describe the first stage of that venture in the early 1970s as a dialogic process between adult and child that compels both to change; but it is the more socialized adults, steeped in everyday common sense, who must transform themselves to the core: "We started with the expectation that a manageable number of adorable little children would appear; that they would sit and read quietly to themselves or listen with their eyes aglow as we adults read to them. All we had to do was expose them to the gems of children's literature and their minds would be enriched."[22] As if in defiance of their intentions, "Sunflower Library" opened to a mob scene—from sixty children that first Sunday to more than five hundred bona fide participants six months later.[23] Not only did the children take over the house, but their play spilled out the doors into the side alley, on the roof, and out to the hill in back. They yelled at the top of their lungs and overstayed their welcome, and when they finally went home, they forgot to take the books they meant to borrow.

Despite repeated acts of sabotage, the children kept coming back to Sunflower Library, and the Tokumuras wanted to know why. The most likely explanation went something like this: children were constantly reprimanded and exhorted—not to make noise, not to run around, not to go outside, to study hard. In the unfettered environment of Sunflower Library, they raised a ruckus simply *because they could*. But Tokiko and Akira were also convinced that the children "found something here that they couldn't find elsewhere, whether at home, at school, or in the community." In the words of one articulate sixth-grader, "Sunflower Library is like a 'zone of freedom'—that's why I come here!"[24] The children's testimony suggests that Sunflower Library was a rare exception to the rule.

And what was that rule? *Kodomo ga shujinkō* offers a glimpse of some of the new arrangements impinging on children's lives at the culmination of Japan's high-growth era. By the 1970s, towns like Hiyoshi had become bedroom communities for nearby metropolitan centers, their neighborhoods and fields replaced by high-rise apartment complexes where families lived in confined proximity. With this reconfiguration of social topography came the loss of spaces where children could play. At school and at home, children were increasingly subject to hyperregulation: "In a society that keeps its children under constant surveillance," the Tokumuras observed, "where there is no escape from the eyes of parents, teachers, and adults, what drew these kids [to Sunflower Library] was the freedom from supervision."[25]

This trend toward regulation was particularly striking in the field of education: over the course of the 1960s, the Ministry of Education, in league with the powerful Ministry of International Trade and Industry, exerted increasing control over the national education system in the interests of "making it more responsive to the manpower requirements of Japan's economy and industry." In the view of education scholar Horio Teruhisa, the litany of reforms imposed by the central government—from universal scholastic testing and standardized student ranking to a reconstituted course of study (including the return of pre-1945 "moral education")—was designed to control the content of education and produce a compliantly segmented workforce for the diversifying needs of Japan's high-growth capitalist economy.[26] Increasingly, children were measured according to a single education-based standard, one that overwhelmingly determined the officially sanctioned path to their future. In turn, the aspirations of children and parents for educational success became a primary mechanism for discipline.

While these larger forces formed the backdrop to Sunflower Library, Akira and Tokiko seem to have been engaged in a struggle against more subtle and intimate forms of coercion. Here is Akira writing in a self-critical mode: "There was a part of me that was dead set on 'doing good,' on performing a service for these children. But my 'good intentions' didn't necessarily correspond to what the children wanted. I told them to come to Sunflower Library, but only on my terms, in a structure of my making. The kids were trying to go beyond the structure."[27] Significantly, this personal process of critical self-reflection retraced the arc of more public debates of the early postwar decades over the role of progressive intellectuals in relation to the masses—whether to lead the masses as an elite vanguard or to learn from them in pursuit of a mass line. The Tokumuras pursued their own version of the mass line in their early engagement with the children who came to Sunflower Library. But their struggle to dislodge the authoritarian disposition that had taken up residence in their own minds also evokes the more introspective quality of the New Left conviction that self-transformation in the everyday would lead to social change.

In essence, the Tokumuras conducted a sustained experiment in the redistribution of power, in relinquishing the authority that adults normally claim over the lives of children. That experiment would lead to the collective creation of a community where children could make a place for themselves, learn on their own terms, and create things of their own making.[28] In a letter addressed to "Ojiji" and "Obaba" (referring to Akira and Tokiko as grandpa and grandma), Yamada Yūko, a middle-school student at the time, got to the heart of the matter: "What is Sunflower Library, really? In a word, it's sort of like a wide-open field. Since there are no boundaries, no walls or chain-link fences, anybody can walk right in, from anywhere. And as soon as you step inside, that's where you belong; you join a large circle of friends and play to your heart's content."[29]

As Tokiko and Akira tell it, the Sunflower Library community developed spontaneously and incrementally—from games and hand-crafted toys to a "children's bazaar" and a summer camp—all typical activities for any children's circle. Yet there was something unusual about the qualities the Tokumuras brought to this enterprise: first, a rare degree of tolerance for unruly behavior and a willingness to withhold judgment; second, a readiness to listen attentively to those whose voices were often dismissed or discounted; and third, a capacity to resist appeals to social convention and common sense—this last is remarkable in a society where the pressures to conform to the social "common sense" can be both subtle and formidable. I once asked them how they saw their own role in this evolving enterprise.

By way of an answer, Akira drew a pyramid on a piece of paper and explained: Power usually works like this; the few at the top rule over the many below. We've tried turning the pyramid upside down, but see how difficult it is to balance. Whenever the pyramid shows signs of tipping over, from our position at the bottom, we give it a little nudge, just enough to keep it from falling.

In effect, Sunflower Library summer camp was the "testing ground" for Children's Village in Hokkaido—a term-limited experiment in collective living without hierarchy or bureaucracy. As the Tokumuras describe it, "The process by which the camp, through the children's own initiative, became a site of independence and freedom rarely seen elsewhere, was, at the same time, a process in which we grownups struggled to overcome our 'adult common sense'—the 'management mentality' that is part and parcel of summer camp—and all the old ways of thinking that we still harbored."[30]

Early in their Sunflower venture, Akira and Tokiko began to make claims that went against the grain of the children's library movement: "Children will grow up even without books"; "no book can substitute for play."[31] These claims—based on the recognition of the significance of play and an appreciation of different ways of learning—brought the censure of the movement down upon the Tokumuras. Perhaps their most serious offence against the conventional wisdom about raising and educating children was a steadfast refusal of the "management mentality" so pervasive in late twentieth-century Japan. Criticism of the Tokumuras for their failure to provide "sufficient guidance" was a recurrent refrain throughout the history of Sunflower Library. Tokiko and Akira used the opportunity to articulate their own principles of "genuine guidance": (1) Adults need to recognize that each child is an "individual human being with his or her own world"; (2) they must "release their hold"; (3) they should allow children the freedom to make mistakes because this is when they learn the most; and (4) adults must learn in tandem with children.[32]

No doubt it was ideas such as these that provoked critics to describe Sunflower Library and its founders as "extreme"—a word that has easily lent itself to red-baiting, particularly at critical turning points in the history of this unusual children's community. The Tokumuras willingly accept the label, but on their own terms: As they define it, "extremity" is the moment *when the self is shaken to its core*, creating the possibility for profound change—a turn of phrase that evokes a history of the postwar left, from Nakai Masakazu's call for a "revolution of consciousness" in occupied Japan to the New Left call for self-transformation.

The accumulated experience at Sunflower Library encouraged both children and adults to seek alternatives to conventional education, beginning with a series of "Science Symposia" initiated by the children and culminating in the involvement of the Sunflower community in the creation of a "free school" (among the earliest of such educational experiments in Japan). The initial appeal of this alternative school lay in its founding commitment to "freedom and autonomy." Rather than "suppress the individuality of each child in the name of test preparation and supervision," teachers would "value the children as human beings." The plan called for an "open school" with no divisions among grade levels and no classes or exams. Students would learn through hands-on experience and fieldwork in a self-sufficient, cooperative community located in the mountains north of Tokyo.[33] But once the school opened, conflicting expectations among students, teachers, administrators, and parents were ultimately settled in favor of a model too conventional (and too remedial) for the Sunflower Library community, especially the handful of middle-schoolers who had taken the gamble and enrolled. Nevertheless, the "visionary organizing" for this revolutionary educational endeavor helped crystalize the themes that would animate Children's Village, the next chapter of the Tokumuras' story: the idea that "place" is integral to everyday life and that learning is best done in close connection to a specific site and its local inhabitants; the notion that children learn from necessity; the preference for inclusivity across open borders; and the conviction that common sense is something to be overcome.

The new school experiment marks a crucial point in the process that eventually led Tokiko and Akira, along with a number of children and young people, to leave the metropolitan center in 1983 and head north. They describe that process as "protean"—the term itself harks back to the early postwar understanding of the circle movement as an autonomous, spontaneous, bottom-up form of participatory democracy.[34] The decision to move to Hokkaido, Japan's northernmost island, was partly an economic one: housing in the depopulated villages of rural Hokkaido was cheap by most standards, and the town of Takinoue offered Children's Village a swathe of forestland along Bear Creek for use as a summer camp. Nevertheless, the Tokumuras' chronicle suggests other, less quantifiable factors that stirred the collective imagination of the Sunflower Library circle: an extreme environment demanding renewed attention to the foundations of everyday life; a remote location offering the freedom of the periphery; and a land now populated by recent Japanese émigrés, thus easing the burden of settled custom.

In the prose from the time of the relocation, the lure of the "frontier" is palpable. (Hokkaido was, in fact, Japan's first modern settler colony, its nineteenth-century development modeled closely on the settlement of the American West and at a similar cost to the indigenous inhabitants.) It colors both praise for new friends in Hokkaido and an emergent vision for Children's Village. In an exuberant vision of their new location, the Tokumuras imagined a generous landscape of "wide open fields and forest, river and mountains," invoking nature's bounty and man-made development, an egalitarian community of children and adults in a self-sufficient outpost of civilization.[35]

That ebullient frontier spirit has been greatly tempered by time and experience, yielding to a way of life that is less enterprising and more attuned to the contours of the place they have made their home. What has remained constant, however, is a vision of Hokkaido as a space where revolutionary transformation is possible—in the words of Akira and Tokiko, a space "where we can fundamentally rethink human values and ways of living, a place where we can live intensely and mindfully, and, in so doing, go beyond our old selves."[36] But rather than building an outpost of modern civilization, the community has chosen to radically rethink the fundamental principles of civilization on new ground. Over the years, the resettlement in Hokkaido has given rise to a new ecological awareness extending the reach of Children's Village in unanticipated directions.

In the early years, the community put in days of hard labor cutting the ubiquitous bamboo grass and clearing tent sites along Bear Creek. Even so, this continues to be a much wilder affair than the typical summer camp in Japan (or elsewhere, for that matter). Initially, the "facilities" consisted of a bare minimum: a makeshift outhouse, a well for drinking water, a rustic shed for provisions, and, scattered here and there in the woods, tents and tarps for shelter from the rain and mist. In the summers, the kids make themselves at home in the forest, scampering down the foot-worn paths that connect tent sites, supply station, creek-side and campfire circle. Over time, as Akira and Tokiko began to live year-round in the forest (no easy feat in the severe winters of Hokkaido), they have, with collective help, built several improvised structures: a couple of outdoor bathtubs in the form of huge cauldrons heated by wood fires and a few small wooden structures that do service as dwelling, study, studio, guest house, and firewood shelter. In recent years, the community has done less "clearing," allowing trees, plants, and grasses to grow in relative profusion. While people inhabit this small woodland, they live in it lightly: no gas or electricity and no tap water or sewage system. The forest is left largely to its own devices, with human intervention at a minimum. Nevertheless, the site, affectionately referred to by regulars simply as *mori* (forest), has the familiar feel of home rather than a provisional campsite.

Gradually, over the past two decades, Akira and Tokiko have extended themselves beyond the perimeter of the children's circle to embrace a wider community that includes all beings, human and nonhuman. This expansion of conviction and affinity has unfolded within overlapping contexts: on the one hand, a half century of environmentalist activism against an entrenched political economy fueled by development and "public works" and, on the other, an accumulation of personal experience that has illuminated the ubiquity, the interconnectedness, *and* the precariousness of life.

In a series of essays collected in two volumes, both published in 2003, the Tokumuras document continuing commitments and new directions. Here, Akira emerges as an advocate for the forest and a deeply ecological vision of the world. "Over the past several centuries," he writes, "we have come to see trees either as extractable lumber or as aesthetic form; and, from this limited perspective, we assess the value of a forest for its 'health' or its beauty to the human eye. Presuming to understand the forest, human beings thin it or cut it down at their own convenience."[37] But as he reminds his readers, even in the relatively young forest at Bear Creek, many of the trees are longer lived than the oldest surviving human beings. How can we be so presumptuous, he wonders, to believe that we understand the lives of these trees? How can we know which saplings will thrive, which will become ancient trees? Who decides which trees are undesirable? Which grasses, which weeds? The rotting trees that the forestry agency insists on clearing make good habitat for insects and the woodpeckers that feed on them. The wild mushrooms growing at their base rise from vast mycelial networks beneath the ground that connect soil and trees in mutually nourishing, wild systems.[38] From this more ecocentered position, the value of a forest rests not in its appeal as economic or aesthetic resource but rather in the sheer diversity and interrelatedness of the living beings it embraces. Pressing the point, Akira asks, "What *is* the meaning of 'wealth and abundance'"? The word at issue here is *yutakasa*, commonly used to describe the affluence of Japan's postwar consumerist society, but Akira offers a different answer to his rhetorical question: "The *real* meaning of *yutakasa* is diversity (*tayōsei*)."[39]

Based on an intimate and relational knowledge of the forest, Akira has distilled a set of ecological principles, radical in their simplicity: (1) All living beings are equal; there is no living being that doesn't matter. (2) All living beings are connected to one another. (3) What we call an ecosystem is precisely this concatenation of living beings, each playing a role that cannot be filled by any other. (4) If just one of those living beings is missing, the ecosystem begins to unravel from that place. This ecological ethos has its origin in "a more concentrated empiricism" made possible by years of living on the banks of Bear Creek.[40] But, as Akira insists, it only gains cogency when one has "fallen head over heels in love with the forest."[41]

In recent years, the Tokumuras have taken this ecological ethos on the road. With the support of a network of acquaintances spread throughout the Japanese archipelago, they have held hundreds of "gatherings to talk about the forest." I wonder if these intimate gatherings are a form of organizing—or if it is even fitting to call the Children's Village a *movement*. There is no membership roster, only a few cell phones and a carefully maintained, handwritten address book; no initiation fees or treasury, but a running invitation to contribute (in any form whatsoever); no official leadership or fixed agenda, just a core community of people who cooperate together and occasionally make things happen; and a hand-produced newsletter (*mini-komi*) that comes out when it is ready. This is not the conventional repertoire of organizing but rather a movement ecology of a different kind—one that operates on the conviction that encounters among people and between people and the natural world can change hearts and minds and ultimately transform the way people live in a world reconfigured in a less human-centered mode. "It's not that I reject petition drives, demonstrations or strikes that mobilize large numbers of people," writes Akira. "I think they are important. But now, what I most want to do is bring people together in small circles, one by one."[42]

30 | Ashamed of Being Middle Class: Mexico's 1968 Student Movement and Its Legacy

by Louise E. Walker

The 1968 student movement has become one of the most chronicled episodes in recent Mexican history.[1] The outline of events is often presented as a heroic narrative: young people took to the streets against an ossified regime, the one-party rule of the Institutional Revolutionary Party (*Partido Revolucionario Institucional*, PRI).[2] Faced with the possibility of arrest, injury, and even death, the students' enthusiasm grew until the tragic evening of October 2, 1968, when government forces massacred hundreds at a peaceful protest. In many ways, this is an accurate interpretation; its enduring power is a testament to its precision. Its enduring power is also a testament to political imperatives—to hold the PRI accountable for the repression, to uncover the details of the massacre, and to sustain the political longings of the people who joined the protests in 1968.

It is time, however, to move beyond this heroic narrative. It is intellectually irresponsible to lionize the student movement; doing so magnifies its significance and distorts our understanding of Mexico's recent past. This chapter analyzes the class tensions that riddled the rebel generation (politically active leftist students in the late 1960s and early 1970s). Focusing on the aftermath of the massacre in the early 1970s, I use secret police reports to unearth the conflicts that middle-class privilege created between students, workers, and the urban poor—and to examine how students were ashamed of their class status.

These spy reports, declassified in 2002, offer richly detailed accounts of public meetings and private conversations. But excitement over this historical source must be tempered: reports are sometimes inaccurate, and the analysis they provide often only scratches the surface. In theory, intelligence organizations should serve the state and not any one party or politician, but in Mexico the agencies served the PRI and the president. From their beginnings in the 1920s, the intelligence agencies functioned as a political police, shadowing friends and enemies of the regime, and international studies scholar Sergio Aguayo argues that their activities often reflected the personal interests and insecurities of the president. In the 1960s, President Gustavo Díaz Ordaz's (1964–70) anticommunist paranoia sparked a massive growth in the number of agents and informants; in one agency, numbers soared from approximately 120 agents with some informants in 1965 to 3,000 agents with 10,000 informants in 1981.[3] These growing numbers of government spies focused much of their attention on rebellions against the regime, such as the 1968 student movement and the leftist and conservative protests of the 1970s. Agents watched individuals and groups: they eavesdropped on private conversations, infiltrated opposition groups, tapped telephones, intercepted letters, and controlled a network of informants. These intelligence reports often tell us as much about state obsessions as they do about the activities of groups deemed subversive, revealing how the PRI perceived its own vulnerability. The documents also capture everyday political culture of groups under surveillance—including the class tensions and anxieties that pervaded the leftist movements in the 1960s and 1970s.

Understanding these tensions is a crucial step toward writing a critical history of the radical 1960s and 1970s. While other scholars have described the chauvinism that pervaded the student movement, advancing arguments about gender politics, they have largely replicated the heroic narrative of students challenging authoritarianism.[4] But university students belonged to an elite, and their politics vis-à-vis the status quo were more complicated than simple rejection. Analysis of class politics reveals how leftist students reckoned with their complicity in an unequal and undemocratic system.

After briefly outlining the heroic narrative, I examine how middle-class privilege shaped the politics of moderate students who worked with the PRI to reform the political system, of radical students who began organizing with workers and the urban poor, and of students on the far left who formed urban guerrilla groups. Finally, I describe how examining tensions and anxieties about social class helps move toward a more critical history of the rebel generation.

The Heroic Narrative of 1968

The outline of Mexico's 1968 student movement is well known. It began with a seemingly apolitical, routine skirmish between students from several *preparatorias* (higher-education institutions between high school and undergraduate studies) and vocational schools. On July 22 a fight broke out between students from Vocational School 2 and the Isaac Ochoterena Preparatoria. The next day, there was another fight. There was nothing particularly unusual about any of this. But on July 23, the city government sent in two hundred riot police, who confronted students with violence and arrested approximately twenty.

In the following days, street battles occurred in the center of Mexico City. *Prepa* and vocational students, now joined by students from National Autonomous University of Mexico (*Universidad Nacional Autónoma de México*, UNAM) and the National Polytechnic Institute (*Instituto Politécnico Nacional*, IPN), fought the police, riot police, and military. Students blockaded avenues and the military barricaded streets, and on July 30 government forces occupied several secondary schools. Although precise numbers are unknown, newspaper reports estimated that, by the end of July, four hundred students had been injured and one thousand arrested; students claimed that more than fifty of their peers had been jailed, killed, or disappeared. In less than ten days, a wide array of middle-class students found themselves in direct confrontation with the government.[5] In the following weeks, student groups from various schools issued demands, including freedom for political prisoners; elimination of Article 145 of the penal code, which mandated a sentence of two to twelve years for spreading sedition; abolition of the riot police; dismissal of the Mexico City police chief; indemnification for victims of repression; and justice against those responsible for the repression.[6] Student groups also organized tactical responses to the aggression. Young men and women formed unarmed guard units to protect their schools from invasion. Student strikes began on the IPN and UNAM campuses and then spread to other schools in the capital city and beyond.

Conflict escalated in August and September. The protest threatened the PRI because Mexico was hosting the Olympics that fall, the first Third World nation to do so. The opening ceremonies were scheduled for October 12 in Mexico City. Widespread protest would undermine the image the PRI had been cultivating as an effective government for a prosperous Mexico. Faced with the possibility of arrest, injury, and even death, the students' enthusiasm grew until the tragic evening of October 2. Just ten days before the opening ceremony, hundreds of students gathered peacefully in Tlatelolco, a plaza in the heart of Mexico City, to discuss strategy and plan their next steps. Instead, when government forces began shooting from the rooftops, the movement was quashed in a few bloody hours.

Middle-Class Privilege and Leftist Politics

After the Tlatelolco massacre, the Olympics took place without political protest on Mexico City's streets, a success for the PRI. Indeed, for many years, association of the 1968 Olympics with political protest was largely limited to the Black Power salute given by Tommie Smith and John Carlos at the medal ceremony for the 200-meter race. But discontent persisted among students who sought reform, and soon after the massacre the PRI attempted to reach out to the left. The party chose Luis Echeverría Álvarez as its candidate in the 1970 elections. Echeverría was considered a compromise candidate: he had one foot inside the conservative wing of the PRI, owing to his role in the Tlatelolco massacre (as minister of the interior, he condoned the attack). But he was also considered a liberal, because his brother-in-law had been jailed in the 1959 railway worker conflict.[7] Echeverría designed a series of reforms. His so-called democratic opening granted amnesty for many political prisoners arrested during the student movement. He lowered the voting age as well as the minimum age for members of congress and senators, a move he hoped would placate students and intellectuals. His administration also attempted to reconcile with students through the educational reform program, which increased the education budget fourteenfold, opened new schools and university campuses, raised salaries for professors, and introduced new financial resources for students, especially scholarships to study abroad.[8] By shoring up support for education, Echeverría and his advisors hoped to appease students. Echeverría proclaimed an end to the old way of doing politics—repression—and announced that politics would now embrace dialogue.

Students responded in myriad ways. Their middle-class backgrounds defined the parameters of their response. Some students, ashamed of their middle-class identity, opted to *proletarizarse*, to "become proletarian," as they mobilized workers and shantytown residents. A few students reformulated revolutionary theory so that they themselves—students—would supplant workers or peasants as the vanguard of a socialist revolution and, within this theoretical framework, formed armed guerrilla groups to overthrow the state. Still others sought to protect their middle-class status and worked for reform, working with the PRI to rebuild bridges between the party and the student population while demanding material improvements in their schools as well as respect for the rights guaranteed in the 1917 Constitution.

Many students accepted, if tentatively, Echeverría's olive branch. In an article for a university newspaper, one student expressed hope and skepticism: "[Echeverría] seems like an honest man but, you know, it's a question of waiting to see if his actions live up to his words."[9] Moderate students began to organize for improvements in their schools. For many, their protest was fundamentally about middle-class insecurity and responsibility, and their demands were liberal democratic in nature, not radical. After all, university and prepa students either belonged to or aspired to join the status quo. Taking advantage of the increased education budget, they demanded more teachers and staff; higher salaries and better training for teachers; buses for the schools; more books, calculators, and other equipment; more scholarships; and new classrooms. They also demanded more participation in decisions about the budget and the curriculum.[10] These moderate students wanted reform, not revolution. According to historian Herbert Braun, most students felt they had an obligation to ensure that political leaders acted responsibly and for the betterment of conditions for all; their middle-class status "filled them with a sense of purpose and obligation to the social order."[11]

Echeverría's reforms mollified many of the student protesters. With these reforms, the president addressed the material and political concerns of many students—some of whom were incorporated not only into mainstream channels of negotiation but also into the PRI itself. In doing so, Echeverría continued one of the PRI's most entrenched hegemonic strategies: to co-opt dissent. Through the democratic opening and other strategies, Echeverría preyed upon divisions among the students and sought to bring many of the more moderate, reform-minded students (back) into the party. Leftists excoriated this tactic, as it undermined their support among students. For example, the urban guerrillas, discussed later, described education reform as a bourgeois project that enabled capitalist exploitation.[12] But despite many points of contention, there was a good deal of overlap between the PRI and moderate student protesters. (Importantly, only some sectors of the PRI and some sectors of the student population shared this common ground; the consensus was neither stable nor all-encompassing. The president may have espoused a conciliatory rhetoric, but he continued to rely on repressive tactics when he met resistance.) Reform-minded students negotiated and compromised with the president and his administration, often benefiting from the process.

Radical students, in contrast, rejected Echeverría's offer of dialogue, a position made plain in political banners protesting continued repression in the 1970s: "Mr. President, we have been familiar with this dialogue you propose since Tlatelolco 2 October" and "Honor the dead students. A minute of silence—no; a life of struggle—yes."[13] Many radical students took this "life of struggle" to factories and shantytowns. They left the universities and sought contact with workers and residents to organize a broader coalition against the PRI. When they did so, their middle-class backgrounds generated tension for the radicals. (Exploring the tensions between students and workers—or students and shantytown residents—does not diminish the value of the work that they accomplished together, nor does it take away from the satisfaction many experienced when working together. There exist many studies of the positive aspects of their struggles; analysis of class tensions adds to our understanding of this history.)[14] While reform-minded students sought to protect their privilege, radicals faced difficult questions about revolutionary "authenticity." Outside the arena of the university, they encountered resentment from workers and from the urban poor, who accused students of casting themselves as leaders of the revolution, of acting as though they owned the Marxist knowledge necessary to make revolution.

These students also confronted their own existential insecurities. Questions of moral legitimacy arose as the radicals fretted over their relationship to the Marxist or socialist revolution they wanted to foment. Obsessions over authenticity begin with the act of reading Marx: a certain amount of education is required to grapple with *Das Kapital*. (In the late 1960s and early 1970s, leftist students began to read Marx in earnest, both in informal reading groups and in their classes. Changes in the curriculum of the economics faculty at the UNAM gave Marx a sudden prominence in the syllabus.) But within a classical Marxist framework, it is ultimately the workers (or, in a Maoist framework, the peasants) who are at the forefront of historical change; ideological identity and class position are at odds. Radicals, militants, and the denizens of the far left were not proud to be middle class. Indeed, according to revolutionary theory in the 1960s and 1970s, a middle-class individual would have to renounce his or her background in order to develop a revolutionary consciousness. Radical agronomist and Guinean and Cape Verdean independence leader Amílcar Cabral argued this in an important speech in Cuba in 1966: "The petite bourgeoisie has only one choice: to strengthen its revolutionary consciousness, to reject the temptations of becoming more bourgeois . . . to identify itself with the working classes." Then Cabral went further: "The revolutionary petite bourgeoisie must be capable of committing suicide as a class in order to be reborn as revolutionary workers."[15] In Mexico, radical students undertook various strategies to shed their class condition;

committing class suicide meant living in a turmoil of doubt, arrogance, and self-loathing.

Groups of students channeled their political activism into proletarian neighborhoods. They went to the "lost cities," the large shantytowns on the periphery of the capital and other cities. These neighborhoods often lacked basic services such as electricity and clean water. The public health situation was dire. The contrast between the shantytowns and the students' home neighborhoods cannot be overemphasized, nor can the rampant paradoxes created. Often meeting at an outlying metro station, they took buses to the shantytowns. En route they sang protest songs against the government. Other times they would drive to the neighborhoods in cars, sometimes luxury brands like Mercedes-Benz (although it is most likely that few students came from truly wealthy families). Once they arrived, they helped build or improve houses and gave out clothes and toys. Students who had been trained as engineers worked on the design and layout of newly formed squatter settlements. As they did this work, they told residents that the government had forgotten them and that it was only the students who worried about them.[16]

Students in the preparatorias and universities either came from or aspired to join the middle classes. "Middle class" refers to a set of material conditions, a state of mind, and a political discourse. As a set of material conditions, it can be measured by income and class stratification. As a state of mind, it is an identity, lifestyle, and cultural world that can be longed for—and lost. Some of the fiercest political battles in twentieth-century Mexican history are struggles to acquire and defend the socioeconomic and cultural markers of class, which do not always coincide, as illustrated by the popular descriptions *con dinero sin cultura* (with money but without culture) and *con cultura sin dinero* (with culture but without money).[17] Middle class is also a political discourse. Ideas about the nature and function of this group have been used (usually by cultural, political, and academic elites) to create influential narratives about Mexico's past, present, and future, narratives that serve ideological and political purposes. While this three-pronged approach—socioeconomic, cultural, and political—helps to outline the class status of Mexico's rebel generation, the cultural dimension is especially useful for contextualizing the prepa and university students.

Education enabled upward mobility, and during the midcentury economic boom (often referred to as the Mexican Miracle), it had become an important marker of privilege, as only a minority of citizens completed basic schooling. For instance, of the population over fifteen years of age living in Mexico City, only 41 percent had completed primary school in 1970; this figure decreased to 34 percent in 1980.[18] In the context of such inequality, students who made it to postsecondary institutions were either maintaining their middle-class condition or entering the middle classes (though a small number would have belonged to the wealthy). Through education, students acquired cultural capital; as theorist Pierre Bourdieu argues, education is a material and symbolic good that is sought after and exchanged, ultimately conferring power and status.[19]

When they entered the shantytowns, students became uncomfortably aware of their privilege. In the shantytowns, questions about the complicated position of the middle classes in the revolution emerged (not the Mexican Revolution, whose legacy the PRI claimed to represent, but the socialist revolution that students and residents were making). At one community meeting, residents complained about how these students imagined themselves as the leaders of the revolution. And one of the community leaders accused the intellectuals of claiming theoretical ownership of Marxism: "These illusions are a result of the Marxism taught in the universities, because Marxism is in the hands of the petty bourgeoisie or middle class."[20] Faced with this criticism, students responded by attempting to deny their middle-class condition. They decided that it was necessary to "live like and with the working class in proletarian neighborhoods."[21]

Conflict over class identity also erupted when students and leftist leaders contemplated forming a political party and entering electoral politics. In a series of meetings in November 1971, prominent intellectuals, student leaders, and labor activists—including Octavio Paz, Carlos Fuentes, Demetrio Vallejo, Carlos Sánchez Cárdenas, Heberto Castillo, and Tomás Cervantes Cabeza de Vaca—gathered to discuss forming a political party. In these meetings, student leaders admitted a general feeling of frustration within the movement; they described weariness among the student population, who, they claimed, were tired of being manipulated by existing political groups.[22] At one of the meetings, a cobbler challenged the intellectuals present to "set aside their vanity" and approach the workers and the *campesinos* (peasants) as equals, so that these groups might teach the intellectuals about revolutionary struggle. Students and intellectuals, he argued, had much to learn from workers. In response to this challenge, labor activist Heberto Castillo argued that the best option would be for students, intellectuals, and some sectors of the bourgeoisie to integrate into the worker sector, to *proletarizarse*, or "proletarianize themselves."[23]

When students and intellectuals faced class resentment from workers and the urban poor, their response was to purge themselves of their class identity, to become proletarians. This solution was met with skepticism. No doubt, class structures can change over time, and some individuals might lose privilege. But moving down from the middle classes to the lower classes as a political choice is hardly the same as being forced down by economic realities. The complex matrix of cultural components that make up a social class, such as education, values, and expectations, cannot simply be discarded. Leaving aside the question of whether it is possible to proletarianize oneself, middle-class leftists attempted to do so in various ways. It was part of a political strategy to challenge the authoritarianism of the PRI that they embraced after other forms of political action—such as demonstrations and protests—had met with repression.

In his memoir, former guerrilla Alberto Ulloa Bornemann describes how radicals competed among themselves to be less bourgeois. Some strategies were relatively superficial, such as his adoption of "'proletarian' attire"—denim shirts of the sort worn by railroad workers.[24] Other strategies involved inconvenience and discomfort. For example, Ulloa Bornemann elected to take the bus rather than driving his car, even when it entailed catching three buses followed by a long walk to attend his guerrilla warfare training sessions. "All of these complications," he wrote, "stemmed from a guilty eagerness to proletarianize myself and to provide an unsolicited demonstration of revolutionary political decisiveness in the face of [a fellow guerrilla's] accusations of my petty-bourgeois behavior."[25] In another instance, Ulloa Bornemann, dirty and dusty after changing a flat tire, expressed relief when he washed his hands and face in a nearby stream; his companion "went nuts, going on and on about how I should not clean up and should avoid all such 'bourgeois impulses.'"[26]

At times, the ways in which middle-class students tried to "be poor" provoked disbelief among those whom they were trying to organize. For example, Ulloa Bornemann describes how the campesinos they were working with looked on in "astonishment" when two radicals opted to return to Mexico City by bus rather than by automobile, at night, and with a newborn child.[27] In a chronicle of political movements in proletarian neighborhoods, public intellectual Elena Poniatowska describes the work of university students in the Rubén Jaramillo neighborhood in the state of Morelos. There, students sold their newspaper *El Chingadazo* (which roughly translates as "The Big Punch" but also carries the obscene connotation of "The Big Fuck") on street corners, shouting, "Buy your chingadazo; thirty cents, a chingadazo." Residents, although smiling when they heard this, commented to Poniatowska, "With all their education they end up shouting obscenities on the street corner; just because we speak like that, doesn't mean they have to."[28] These students faced the daunting task of convincing the workers and urban poor (as well as themselves) of their authenticity.

The most radical students formed urban guerrilla groups. Like the students who organized in the factories and shantytowns, the guerrillas had been politicized by continuing state-sponsored repression and the apparent elimination of legal means of social change. The guerrillas rejected Echeverría's olive branch, turning to violence to achieve a socialist and egalitarian society. Clandestine revolutionary guerrilla activity erupted in the streets of Mexico's main cities during the early and mid-1970s. Bombs went off in banks and bomb threats disrupted events; men and women assaulted city police officers and stole their weapons; groups of students, divorced housewives, and workers robbed pharmacies, "expropriating" money for their revolutionary aims; and factories became sites of intense political struggle as students, who had joined groups such as the *Liga Comunista 23 de Septiembre* (September 23 Communist League), clashed with private security and the police while they distributed pamphlets and newsletters to workers. Though only a very small number of students joined guerrilla cells (the Liga likely had no more than five hundred members), they acquired national significance through their dramatic acts.[29]

The far-left guerrillas came of age during an international moment when decolonization movements inspired middle-class youth around the world. Régis Debray's *Revolution in the Revolution?* was read in Latin America and beyond and became a manual for a struggle based on armed insurrection.[30] The Cuban Revolution, Salvador Allende's Path to Socialism in Chile and, later, the Sandinista Revolution in Nicaragua animated leftists across Latin America and generated high expectations for social change.[31] In Mexico, these high expectations generated tensions for many radicals who confronted disturbing contradictions between their class background and their Marxist or Maoist political ideologies.

The far-left guerrillas attempted to resolve the tension between their class position and their ideology by reformulating revolutionary theory. They proposed what they called the university-factory thesis (*tesis universidad-fábrica*).[32] In their analysis, the university became an arena of capitalist mass production, another sector of the economy alongside extraction and manufacturing. According to the thesis, moderate students ("bourgeois democrats") who participated in Echeverría's democratic opening and education reform were the enemy: "bourgeois democrats—always conciliatory and opportunistic with regard to the one-party system—argue that students are petit bourgeois; bourgeois democrats emphasize the class origin of the students and the 'democratic' and 'progressive' character of the student movement as a fight for 'respect for the 1917 Constitution and bourgeois law.'"[33] In contrast, the university-factory thesis posited the university as a factory; education was the commodity produced. Students, who had previously simply consumed this commodity, became, in the late 1960s and early 1970s, workers who produced it. Students were transformed from passive consumers into producers through their participation in seminars, in social service, in practicums, and in laboratories; in the university-factory, students and professors were the primary labor force.[34] Through this reformulation of revolutionary theory, students joined the proletariat: "students are part of the proletariat, and as such have the same needs and face the same fundamental problems as the rest of the working class."[35] The university-factory thesis proposed a new revolutionary protagonist: the middle-class student. In this regard, the guerrilla groups were more creative than those who advocated proletarianization.

Much of the information about the Liga and other groups comes from the interrogation of captured members. Often acquired by the use of torture, these testimonies must be read with caution. While it may be impossible to ever gauge the truth of such accounts, they do illustrate the realm of the plausible. They reveal what those captured believed the Ministry of the Interior agents wanted to hear; they also reveal what the agents considered plausible—at least plausible enough to send these reports to their superiors.[36]

The ultimate goal of most of the urban guerrilla groups was to overthrow the government and install a socialist system in Mexico. But they also had ties to similar groups in Latin America and elsewhere. An intelligence report detailing the activities of a young couple from Mexico City, Alfonso and Jazmín, illustrates how this international context informed many urban guerrillas and set them apart from their rural counterparts. In April 1971, intelligence agents intercepted a love letter from Alfonso to Jazmín, who was studying English in New York City. After professing his love and erotic desire, he asked her to buy guns and books on guerrilla campaigns and far left ideologies. One week later, when government spies arrested Alfonso and searched their Mexico City apartment, they found a mimeograph, walkie-talkies, tape recorders, maps, and "communist propaganda."[37]

Alfonso and Jazmín saw themselves as part of an international revolutionary vanguard, not a provincial Mexican movement. Their self-fashioning did not always square with their Maoist-inspired ideology, and sometimes led to tensions with the contemporaneous rural guerrilla movements in

Mexico. For instance, Alfonso and Jazmín, together with colleagues, made a film about Genaro Vázquez Rojas, one of Mexico's most prominent rural guerrilla leaders, intending to showcase it at a youth film festival in West Germany. If these urban guerrillas sought membership in an international cultural politics, their rural counterparts had other things on their minds. While urban guerrillas often turned to their counterparts in the countryside in search of support, training, approval, and legitimacy, they also derided the rural guerrillas as unsophisticated and lacking ideology.

The urban guerilla groups belong to a history of the middle class. They were formed by middle-class youths disposed to sacrifice their lives to redress conditions of exploitation in Mexico. These groups also belong to a history of the rebel generation, alongside the more moderate students who accepted Echeverría's olive branch and the radicals who organized in shantytowns and among workers. These students and former students all struggled with their middle-class identities, and it shaped their decisions and strategies as well as their desires and their shame. The history that emerges here is one of self-doubt, anxiety, and contradictory paths.

Toward a Critical History of the 1960s

The middle-class background of the leftist students, and the tensions it generated, is an important part of the history of the rebel generation. Given the educational inequality in 1970s Mexico, there can be no doubt that the vast majority of university students belonged to the middle classes (or, by virtue of attending university, were entering the middle classes). The public intellectual Elena Poniatowska's collection of testimonies concerning the 1968 student movement, now a classic, abounds with examples of the privilege enjoyed by the students and the resentment it generated among some members of the broader public. "They're so thick between the ears! What a laugh—politicizing workers!" said one student.[38] "Workers don't know the first thing about anything," said another participant.[39] A bus driver, however, complained, "I didn't get any kind of formal education because my folks couldn't afford to send me to school. But if education nowadays is the sort that produces students like that, I'm glad I didn't go to school. I've never in my life seen such disrespectful, vulgar, foul-tongued people."[40] Likewise, a restaurant owner felt that students should be grateful for their privilege: "University students are the future solid middle class of the Mexican Republic. So what reason do they have to be doing all this?"[41] At a demonstration in 1968, students carried a banner with the following offer, which, depending on one's perspective, could be considered generous or condescending: "Free tuition for *granaderos* [riot police] enrolling in literacy classes."[42]

While former student activists and former guerrillas have willingly discussed the class tensions that pervaded leftist politics in the 1960s and 1970s, these tensions are not privileged in academic and popular analyses of this history. Scholarly reluctance to analyze the students as middle-class historical actors might be connected to a reflexive association of "middle class" with conservative politics or the status quo (as though the term itself were an insult, as it was for many radicals at the time). But students' struggles to square their class status with their politics shaped the everyday history of the rebel generation. Their doubts and frustrations shed light on the political context in which they lived and help to explain the decisions that they made. It is especially important to tease out this tension and turmoil because the student movement has become one of the most written about events in modern Mexican history. Accounts of the movement, most of them focused on the events of 1968, exert a major influence on how we understand the rebel generation more broadly—from the moderate students to the radical students to the armed guerrillas. Almost immediately after the Tlatelolco massacre, a series of books were published, forming the basis of what would become the 1968 canon. The custodians of this canon are former student leaders, activists, and sympathizers, many of whom became Mexico's leading public intellectuals in subsequent decades.[43] The narrative that emerged, as described earlier, is a heroic one: at great peril to themselves, students took to the streets to demand more meaningful democracy.

The heroic narrative persists. At the fortieth anniversary of the 1968 student movement, there were hundreds of talks by academics and public intellectuals, artistic events, and marches to commemorate the student protests. While a few individuals, mostly from the public, asked provocative questions about the events of 1968 and their legacy, most speakers reproduced the heroic narrative.[44] On the morning of October 2, 2008, around one hundred people had gathered in the UNAM's cultural center for a program of academic discussion, and in a revelatory moment, one young woman in the audience lamented that we might need to wait until the fiftieth anniversary for a critical history.[45]

With the opening of new archives, it is a good moment to begin this endeavor. The declassification of Mexican intelligence archives provides a fuller picture of the radicalism of the 1960s and 1970s. If a critical history of this radicalism involves moving beyond a heroic narrative, it also involves moving beyond a condemnation of the 1960s and 1970s radicals, especially of the urban guerrillas who turned to violence. The most troubling manifestation of this tendency blames the guerrillas for provoking the state-sponsored torture, murder, and disappearance of tens of thousands of citizens in Latin America.[46] It is time for a critical history of the rebel generation and its legacy: not a history that is necessarily critical of the leftist students and urban guerrillas but one that analyzes them as historical actors in a historical moment. New narratives emerge from new archives: the politics of middle-class privilege shaped the different paths taken by students after the Tlatelolco massacre.

The leftists of the rebel generation were not saints. The moderates were not sellouts, and the radicals were not deluded. They were middle-class students, full of doubt and frustration, who tried, in different ways, to improve the world in which they lived.

Paul Potter, 1964. Leni Wildflower (personal photo)

Shulamith Firestone at Kibbutz Ma'agan Michael, Israel, 1968. Photo by Andrew Klein

V.

In Memoriam

There are many ways to think about the end (or endings) of the 1960s new insurgency as well as its effects and consequences. Many observers were already writing postmortems on the New Left in 1970, given the break-up of both Students for a Democratic Society and the Student Nonviolent Coordinating Committee by that time and the more repressive atmosphere set by the Nixon administration—though in fact the largest antiwar rally of the Vietnam era took place April 1971 in Washington, DC, American Indian activism was still rising at that time, and the powerful gay liberation and women's movements were generating new ideas and forms of action through the 1970s. Nonetheless, many activists—particularly of the Port Huron cohort—sensed some kind of retreat. As Michael Szalay points out in his chapter, socialist Michael Harrington writing in 1974 recognized "a collective sadness" descending on the country. Yet even a retreat need not be flight or surrender; it can also mean stepping back from, or outside, everyday routines, to reflect on recent experience and contemplate next steps. That seems to have been the experience of people like Al Haber, Sharon Jeffrey Lehrer, and Paul Potter, among others. Potter wrote fluently about that experience in his essays, *A Name for Ourselves*, published in 1971, and here Szalay analyzes Potter's reflections in light of a more recent discussion of so-called left melancholy, a mood among radicals chastened by defeat and beset by mourning. That isn't to say that members of the Port Huron group as the 1970s began were mired in depression or inactive. Leni Wildflower, Potter's widow and donor of his personal papers to the University of Michigan's Labadie Collection of radical literature, does not see Potter's experience in those terms at all, since the turn toward concerns of culture and consciousness somewhat distant from street protest could also mean an emotionally enriched personal experience congruent with persistent efforts to spur change. Potter's reflective writings circa 1970 showed, among other things, a fresh and growing affinity for feminism and environmentalism.

The experience of radical feminist Shulamith Firestone, who died alone and poor in New York City two months prior to the opening of the New Insurgency conference, was more clearly one of retreat (or exile) and disappointment. In some ways analogous to Szalay's interpretation of left melancholy, Firestone's personal troubles, Alice Echols suggests, stemmed from the experience of "social defeat," an extreme kind of isolation and separation from community (not only from the feminist milieu that had fostered her remarkable, youthful intellectual innovations but also from her family of origin). It is a phrase that evokes as well the disappointment of radical hopes, the confrontation—which many seasoned left-wing activists today sense—with a world that has, decades afterward, fallen so far short of the aspirations for freedom, equality, democracy, and peace that fueled, and flourished within, the new insurgency.

—Howard Brick

31 | New Left Melancholia, or Paul Potter Swallows Television

by Michael Szalay

In "Left Melancholy" (1931), an essay on the German poet Erich Kästner, Walter Benjamin decries a "left-wing radicalism" that inheres in an "attitude to which there is no longer in general any corresponding political action."[1] Kästner's poetry is a representative instance of a literary movement, Benjamin explains in a subsequent essay, that "has made *the struggle against poverty* an object of consumption."[2] Kästner makes peace with the failure of revolutionary struggle and sells the inevitability of that failure to a bourgeoisie eager to savor the passing of a radical spirit to which it was never in fact fully committed. His work constitutes "the metamorphosis of political struggle from a compulsory decision into an object of pleasure, from a means of production into an article of consumption—that is this literature's latest hit." A wistful if finally disingenuous sadness characterizes this literary hit making. Schooled in "a curious variety of despair" and a "tortured stupidity," Kästner addresses himself to "those mournful, melancholy dummies who trample anything or anyone in their path." His "is the fatalism," Benjamin concludes, "of those who are most remote from the process of production and whose obscure courting of the state of the market is comparable to the attitude of a man who yields himself up entirely to the inscrutable accidents of his digestion."[3]

Benjamin's essay has become a touchstone for recent considerations of the structure of feeling that characterizes the contemporary left. Wendy Brown argues that "*left melancholy* is Benjamin's unambivalent epithet for the revolutionary hack who is, finally, attached more to a particular political analysis or ideal—even to the failure of that ideal—than to seizing possibilities for radical change in the present." As Brown sees it, "Sentiments themselves become things for the left melancholic, who 'takes as much pride in the traces of former spiritual goods as the bourgeois do in their material goods.'" Brown characterizes the contemporary left as one in which "we come to love our left passions and reasons, our left analyses and convictions, more than we love the existing world that we presumably seek to alter with these terms or the future that would be aligned with them."[4] Jodi Dean takes issues with these claims. In a rebuttal to Brown, she emphasizes Benjamin's account of Kästner's capitulation to the market: "He is not attached to an ideal [as Brown argues]; he has compromised revolutionary ideals by reducing them to consumer products." Accordingly, for her, "Benjamin compels us to consider a left that gave in, sold out."[5] As Dean sees it, the contemporary left "has given way on the desire for communism, betrayed its historical commitment to the proletariat, and sublimated revolutionary energies into restorationist practices that strengthen the hold of capital." The melancholia of today's left, she maintains, "derives from the real existing compromises and betrayals inextricable from its history, its accommodations with reality, whether of nationalist war, capitalist encirclement, or so-called market demands."[6]

This chapter aims not to adjudicate this debate but to evaluate the applicability of its terms to a moment on the American left now closer to Benjamin's time than to our own. What follows takes up the case of Paul Potter, an important early member of Students for a Democratic Society (SDS) and an essayist whose writings shed considerable light on the declension of the American New Left in the years following its great successes of the 1960s. Potter is most famous for having popularized the phrase "the system," an epithet so abstract in its calculated displacement of "capitalism" and so promiscuously widespread in the years immediately following the sixties that it might seem on its own to have given rise to a strain of clichéd fatalism attendant upon the waning of the movement: prominent among the many things that period radicals learned about "the system," this line of thinking might suggest, was that you could not fight it. But that was not Potter's lesson, and I'm interested less in whether Potter or any of his peers ever "sold out," as Dean has it, than in his relation to a radical "attitude," to recall Benjamin, that became melancholic as it was severed from "any corresponding political action." I will argue that Potter misunderstood something essential about his lost relation to the kinds of action organized by SDS: that action was for him, as it was for SDS in general, mediated—made legible and coherent, to a surprising degree—by television coverage that became in some sense indistinguishable from or constitutive of his most personal experiences of the movement.

Accounts of how television harnessed the antinomian energies of the New Left and counterculture—and thus in effect transformed "political struggle" into "an object of pleasure" and "an article of consumption"—began to appear during the sixties and have since become an essential part of popular folklore about that decade's radicalism. In 1967, the San Francisco Diggers held a funeral for "Hippie, devoted son of mass media." A year later, Hearst launched a psychedelic magazine, and Columbia Records ran an advertisement that announced, "But The Man can't bust our music." Norman Mailer's *Armies of the Night* (1967) and Haskell Wexler's *Medium Cool* (1968) analyzed the difference television cameras made to radical demonstrations. Later, Paddy Chayefsky's *Network* (1976) lampooned a left that had become beholden to those cameras. In that film, a news executive finds the edgy fare for which she's been looking on the extreme left, representatives of which she recruits to host *The Mao Tse Tung Hour*. A self-described "bad-assed commie nigger" serves as the executive's link with the left. After initial protestations that she'd never work for the establishment, the quondam communist throws herself into the enterprise with gusto. "Don't fuck with my distribution costs!" she yells during a preproduction meeting. "I'm getting a lousy two-fifteen per segment, and I'm already deficiting twenty-five grand a week with Metro. I'm paying William Morris ten percent off the top!"[7]

The system exacted its price, in more ways than one. Prominent members of the left often found themselves in front the cameras. At the same time, they experienced themselves as consumers as much as producers of prime-time television drama about the movement. As Todd Gitlin argues in *The Whole World Is Watching* (1980), even as SDS used television to get its message out, the organization came to understand that message as a function of how television news outlets decided to portray it. "As the spotlight kept on burning," he writes, "media treatment entered into the movement's internal life. The media helped recruit into SDS new members and backers who expected to find there what they saw on television or read in the papers." Claims like these speak directly to Paul Potter's essay collection, *A Name for Ourselves* (1971), which offers a rich and complex elaboration of the impact of television on "the movement's internal life."[8] In Potter's hands, that internal life is suffused by sadness and dejection; in fact, his essays display the characteristics attributed to melancholia by Freud and others on an almost point-by-point basis. My ultimate interest is in the process of "incorporation" by which an individual, confronted with a loss sustained by the psyche, ingests or swallows the image of a love object. Transfixed by that image, the melancholic misperceives and thus cannot mourn the loss that occasioned its ingestion. "The problem with the book," Potter tells us in *A Name for Ourselves*, "is that it presents 'images' of me and the world and us rather than getting at the real hard conflicts I feel in myself." Potter knows that these images derive in good measure from television. Watching television, he explains, is not simply "observation of the wrong thing." It's akin to swallowing and taking inside an image that obscures and prohibits understanding of a "maggot-infested wound."[9]

The Revolution Inside

Paul Potter was twenty-six and the president of SDS when, on April 17, 1965, he addressed some twenty-five thousand people gathered in Washington, DC, to protest the Vietnam War. He stood before the protesters and exhorted them to "name," "describe," "analyze," "understand," and "change" the "system" responsible for US atrocities in Vietnam and the American South and in so doing invoked what was at the time a term of art within the nation's newly ascendant research universities.[10] According to Howard Brick, the phrase "the system" was then appearing "widely in the natural and applied sciences, denoting the orderly processes at work in any complex array of multiple, interacting variables."[11] Eschewing the term "capitalism" in favor of one that he hoped would have a wider appeal, Potter nevertheless meant to locate in the nation's politics and economy a similar complexity; "there is no simple plan," he argued, "no scheme or gimmick that can be proposed here."[12] In essence, he called on the left to develop a new if still largely inchoate critical vocabulary for anatomizing US society.

Potter's phrase achieved a wide appeal indeed, but in the service of ends other than those he imagined. In the years that followed, invocations of "the system" turned into something of a gimmick. Its generality opened it to derision and scorn—Arundhati Roy reminds us that nothing conjures the "sixties hippie dropping acid . . . or a paranoid schizophrenic with a persecution complex" quite so quickly as the phrase "It's the System, man!"—and to laughably broad application. Explaining that Darth Vader was really just a "bureaucrat" who didn't know how to live for himself, Joseph Campbell would argue that the Star Wars character made manifest "the threat to our lives that we all face today. Is the system going to flatten you out and deny you your humanity, or are you going to be able to make use of the system to the attainment of human purposes?"[13] Even during the sixties, the term was often used to transform radicalism into something inoffensive and harmless. As Aniko Bodroghkozy explains in her account of sixties-era television, "'The System' was something vague and generally indefinable, but something that all liberal interests, not just dissident youth, could oppose."[14] It was, we might hazard, a defining feature of the brand image that popular culture had begun to produce of the movement even as the movement began to lose its direction and animating energies.

The subsequent centrality of his famous phrase to popular understandings of the left notwithstanding, major news outlets ignored Potter's speech almost entirely. No television network covered the speech, nor had any covered the picket of Chase Manhattan Bank that Potter had helped organize the month before (the picket protested the bank's open revolving credit to South Africa and was held on the fifth anniversary of the Sharpeville massacre, when police officers killed sixty-nine demonstrators and injured hundreds more). Nevertheless, Potter's Washington speech was a galvanizing event and a watershed in the history of the New Left. As Todd Gitlin recalls, "To the SDS elite and to a considerable portion of the crowd . . . Potter's speech closing the rally . . . was the first public and eloquent articulation of a radical position on the war, insisting that because the war had been generated by the entire American social order . . . the whole system had to be uprooted."[15] Potter's stirring rhetoric was, for that moment, pitch perfect: it allowed opponents of the war in Vietnam to find common cause with members of a potentially larger population dissatisfied with postwar American life, and its call for systematic analysis radicalized the movement at the same moment that it cast figures like Lyndon Johnson and Robert McNamara as banal exemplars of a lethal bureaucracy. These were not "evil" men, he averred; they would no doubt "shrink in horror" if asked to "throw napalm on the back of a ten-year-old child."[16]

Potter was born in Champaign-Urbana on March 25, 1939, to a mother who was a pro-Communist Jewish American and a father who was a pig farmer supposedly descended from Martha Washington. Potter was raised in small towns across the Midwest and educated at Oberlin College. Shortly after graduating, he traveled to Cuba in 1960 and 1961 to demonstrate solidarity with the revolution there. In 1961, he and Tom Hayden were in Mississippi attending a Student Nonviolent Coordinating Committee (SNCC) protest when the two were dragged from their car and beaten. In 1962, he began graduate school in anthropology and sociology at the University of Michigan, where he wrote a number of influential articles on intellectuals, social change, and the Cold War university. In 1964, Potter was elected president of SDS and split his time over the course of the next year between his administrative duties with SDS and his work in

Cleveland, where he lived among and advocated on behalf of the poor and unemployed as part of SDS's Economic Research and Action Project (ERAP).

Potter's contributions to the movement over the second half of the sixties are less well known. He spent the years following his speech in the Northeast, teaching and writing. He attended the 1968 Democratic National Convention and testified in the trial of the Chicago Seven that followed. By the end of the decade, he was living in a commune that he had organized with Al Haber and Potter's partner Leni Wildflower. The three had reconditioned an old resort hotel outside of Santa Cruz called Felton. He spent his days working in a frozen food plant (Wildflower recalls him coming home smelling of Brussels sprouts) and volunteering in the mental ward of a hospital in San Jose. (Tom Hayden would later help get Potter hired at San Jose State University, where he taught a course on political autobiography.) Wildflower recalls long evening conversations, many of them anguished, in which the two debated "love, sex, and what to do with your beer cans."[17] In 1970, she and Potter adopted the child, named Kathy, of a woman in the Weather Underground. (The couple later had a son, Jesse, in 1973.) In 1971, the year his collection of essays appeared, Potter's mother died of cancer.

When giving his famous address in 1965, he averred that the movement needed people "willing to change their lives."[18] Potter's *A Name for Ourselves* offers moving testament to just how seriously he took this admonition. *A Name* offers nothing like a comprehensive catalogue of Potter's trials and tribulations as an organizer or protester. It does recount his efforts with the Cleveland ERAP and at the 1968 Democratic National Convention. More substantially, however, it dwells on the feelings produced in him by these and far less newsworthy events—like, for example, his relationship with Leni, his experience watching television, or his struggle to join friends on the dance floor at a community gathering. On the whole, it's less a full accounting of his experience with the left than a series of reflections about the importance of inwardness to the authentically revolutionary life.

His sense of what it might mean to live and feel in an authentically revolutionary fashion had changed since 1965. Thus, for example, he ventures, "If I was forced to give the system a name now, I would not call it capitalism." He didn't call it capitalism in 1965 either, but his interests had changed with the times, all the same: "I would perhaps say that it was hate and we are love. That it is unattended fear, and we are the courage to attend it."[19] In his use of such terms Potter drew heavily from Herbert Marcuse, who had offered the left an account of the sublimation, guilt, and sexual repression required by advanced industrial society. But *A Name for Ourselves* is neither theoretical nor systematic in its treatment of emotions like love and hate, and while it is valuable as an informal transposition of arguments like Marcuse's, it is most revealing in the severity of its self-scrutinizing commitment to personal experience. Potter is roundly skeptical of his earlier efforts with the ERAP, for instance. Primarily, he faults the program for its monolithic assumptions about "the poor" and for its failure to speak to the inner life of its "guilt-ridden" middle-class volunteers.[20] The "economic analysis" at the core of ERAP, he writes, did not offer "an ideology we could internalize, because it was not about our insides."[21] He set great store by the assistance he and other volunteers were able to offer, but he writes how he blames himself and the program for not having found a way to reconcile that assistance, which strikes him as an expression of academic ideology, with the feelings and experiences of the volunteers. "The goals of an organization I would want to be a part of," he reasons, "would have to be goals that I could see as having flowed from or originated inside me and the other people in the organization."[22] Again and again, he longs for "the presence of a movement that told people the revolution was inside them, inside their real and potential breakaway experience."[23]

Viewed uncharitably, statements like these might seem to warrant the scorn dispensed over the course of the seventies by right-wing journalists like Tom Wolfe, whose essay "The Me Decade" (1976) lampooned the "alchemical dream" of revolutionizing the self by "dwelling on the self," or by disaffected Marxist academics like Christopher Lasch, whose *Culture of Narcissism* (1979) lamented the manner in which "politics degenerates into a struggle not for social change, but for self-realization."[24] Seen in these terms, Potter's essays might be understood to describe a shift in how portions of the American left understood political engagement. As Sean McCann and I have argued elsewhere, in what we hoped was a less accusatory vein, Potter's emphasis on the "breakaway experience" of protesters and activists captured the manner in which some on the left forswore programmatic action in favor of the self-realization and actualization then important to the counterculture. Potter, we claimed, advanced a version of the "magical thinking" that took hold among some members of the counterculture in the late sixties and early seventies and that would later take root among radical humanists within the academy eager to champion the frame-breaking, therapeutic powers of cultural analysis.[25]

Versions of this criticism were warranted; the late sixties and seventies

426 | A New Insurgency

did witness a widespread turn toward the politics of self-realization. But it would be perverse indeed to attribute the failure of the New Left to maintain its momentum to the introspective bent of a figure like Potter, who spent the better part of his life working on behalf of meaningful political change. Perhaps more important, castigating Potter for his inwardness leaves us tone deaf to what makes his collection worth our continued attention. We must, rather, try to make some sense of the extraordinary anguish that suffuses *A Name for Ourselves*. For if it is true, as Lewis Coser and Irving Howe once put it, that socialism is an "act of pain," then Potter's collection is a central text in postwar socialism.[26]

Potter's pain, I'll argue, is particular to his experience and yet possessed of an undeniable generality. His essays are self-lacerating and grief stricken, their pain an expression less of mourning than of melancholia. "The distinguishing mental features of melancholia," Freud writes, "are a profoundly painful dejection, cessation of interest in the outside world, loss of the capacity to love, inhibition of all activity, and a lowering of the self-regarding feelings to a degree that finds utterance in self-reproaches and self-revilings, and culminates in a delusional expectation of punishment."[27] *A Name for Ourselves* displays these characteristics in spades: on its pages, the world often falls away, as Potter confronts his isolation and his ongoing difficulty to love as he thinks it should be possible to love. "I am in trouble. We are in trouble," he writes, about both his relationship with Wildflower and the fate of the New Left. "There is enormous tension. There are enormous fights. There is awful depression."[28] As moving as they are, lines like these are not themselves dispositive. Freud adds, however, that all the symptoms of melancholia save one are present likewise in the person experiencing healthy mourning, and that is the "extraordinary diminution in his self-regard" and "distressing self-denigration" that characterizes the melancholic.[29] Potter's collection is extraordinary and distressing in just this way: it describes the "punitive, immobilizing shame and guilt" that he feels in his efforts to live authentically.[30] "One part of me wishes that the other part would go fuck itself," he writes.[31] Typically, such anger stems from his failure to expunge from himself the habits of heart and mind that he associates with "the system" as he now understands it. But his self-censure is severe and visceral. When he speaks of feeling torn up inside, he says, "The tearing feeling is very literal; it feels like someone has been tearing at my guts or pounding on them."[32]

We must, before doing our best to determine the ultimate source of this anguish, recognize the problem that it presents (a problem anticipated by Benjamin when he invokes "the attitude of a man who yields himself up entirely to the inscrutable accidents of his digestion"). Potter builds his project on a faith in the individual's capacity to feel her way toward truths about herself and the world. Personal authenticity, he believes, stems from an individual's careful attention to her inner state. "Even though human nature, which I am calling the capacity to love, has been defiled," he writes, "our experience still gives us an intuitive recognition that we have been oppressed."[33] He values intuition a great deal. "The instruction I'm looking for," he writes, "is intuitive, not academic"—it must come from what he calls "gut feelings."[34] But how to learn from gut feelings when it "feels like someone has been tearing at [your] guts"? What kind of guide to the authentic are such self-lacerating feelings? Potter acknowledges a version of this problem. "What we must do," he writes, "is learn to reason out of our own experience." Yet "we can reason out of our experience," he adds, "only when we are no longer divorced from it, only when we have begun to be vividly connected to it."[35]

Reading these essays, we can't be confident that Potter overcomes this divorce, in large part because the source of his abjection feels obscure to him. And that, of course, is symptomatic of melancholia, which, Freud tells us, "is in some way related to an object-loss which is withdrawn from consciousness, in contradistinction to mourning, in which there is nothing about the loss that is unconscious." Reading A Name, we feel the lingering effects of an object loss that has been withdrawn from Potter's consciousness and for which he has no name. Potter cannot, as Freud puts it, "see clearly what it is that has been lost."[36]

It's plain enough on some level that, even as he advocates on behalf of inwardness and personal experience, Potter feels the absence of a sustaining collective life—perhaps the one he experienced when a part of SDS and the movement in the mid sixties. Leni Wildflower reports that he was absolutely lost and "melancholic" when the movement began to fragment and lose its momentum, not knowing "where to go or what to do."[37] Freud allows for such a loss; he claims that melancholy might result from the loss not simply of a person but of "some abstraction which has taken the place of one, such as one's country, liberty, an ideal, and so on."[38]

What's particularly challenging about A Name for Ourselves, however, is its tendency to conflate Potter's alienated insides with the kinds of collectivity we might associate with the movement. In his introduction, he writes, "This book is written in many voices" and is as a result "an atrocity"—the very word, we might recall, that he used in 1965 to describe the effects of "the system" on Americans and Vietnamese alike.[39] His collection, he suggests, is a shattered collective made up of the many individuals that he himself now contains. That internal fragmentation mirrors an external one. "What I feel," he writes, "is not that 'we' are coming to-gether, but that we are falling apart, falling away from one another—falling into isolation, hiding, prison."[40] Language like this makes it hard to distin-guish between individuals and the collectives from which they come. "We have been broken and internally fragmented," he writes, "torn apart from each other and ourselves."[41] Potter's unconsolidated "we" requires scare quotes; barely contained, the pronoun does double duty as it refers to lost forms of physic and social wholeness, for individuals as well as for the groups they together make up. It must have been hard indeed to give a proper name to such an entity.

All of this mirrors the way in which, for Freud, the melancholic cannot distinguish between a loss in an external object and a loss inside himself. For the melancholic, "self-reproaches are reproaches against a loved object which have been shifted away from it on to the patient's own ego," one part of which "sets itself over and against the other, judges it critically, and, as it were, takes it as its object."[42] The melancholic hates himself because it is the only way he can express an antipathy for an object whose loss he can-not fathom and for which loss he feels himself responsible. The melan-cholic who hates himself instead of the collective of which he was once a part—or, better, who cannot distinguish between his antipathy toward himself on the one hand and that collective on the other—transforms his ego into that collective in a second sense: punishing itself, his ego renders itself still more internally fragmented and thus numerous.

Freud's account of melancholia is in this instance compatible with the argument advanced by Richard Sennett and Jonathan Cobb in *The Hidden Injuries of Class*. The two argue that, for members of the working class, systemic inequality had come by the seventies to seem an issue of personal rather than collective responsibility. "The burden of class today is . . . a strange phenomenon," they write; "social inequality is maintained by cre-ating a morality of anxiety," and "the logic of discontent leads people to turn on each other rather than on the 'system.'" Still more damagingly, people turn on themselves and partake in what Sennett and Cobb call an "inner class warfare." Members of the working class, they note, tend to take responsibility for their own alienation; this splits the worker in two. "The real impact of class," they argue, "is that a man can play out both sides of the power situation in his own life, become alternately judge and judged, alternately individual and member of the mass. This represents the 'internalizing' of class conflict, the process by which struggle between men leads to struggle within each man."[43]

Equally relevant to Potter are terms offered by Michael Harrington, who attributed the malaise of the left at the start of the seventies less to the worker's loss of class solidarity than to the left intellectual's loss of once-sustaining institutions. In a kind of despair, Harrington writes, "We proposed that men and women find their purpose within themselves, that they disdain all traditional crutches, like God and flag. But were we then to blame because many seemed to have heard only that the old constraints had been abolished and ignored the call to find new obligations of their own?" These remarks, Jefferson Cowie argues, expressed Harrington's sense that the left was foundering due to the loss not of God and flag but of "the New Deal, [which,] he believed, had not just been an amalgam of programs but a way of making sense of the world—it gave order, vision, architecture, and direction to social life." The erosion of that order and architecture resulted in a waning of solidarity that, Harrington writes, "privatize[d] social struggles and [made] people sad" and that led, moreover, to what he termed "A Collective Sadness."[44]

Wendy Brown reconciles a version of this argument to Freud's account of melancholia. She describes a recalcitrant sadness that stems from the contemporary left's failure to understand the nature of its attachment to the welfare state now everywhere under assault and to the "liberal democracy" that Brown associates with that state's social mission. I quote from her account at length: Freud's account of melancholia

reminds us to consider how left melancholia about liberal democracy would not just be a problematic affect but would constitute a formation of the Left itself.

Incorporating the death of a loathed object to which one was nonetheless attached often takes the form of acting out the loathed qualities of the object. . . . So this is one danger: that we would act out to keep alive those aspects of the political formation we are losing, that we would take up and perform liberal democracy's complacencies, cruelties, or duplicities, stage them in our own work and thinking. This behavior would issue in part from the need to preserve the left identity and project that took shape at the site of liberal democracy, and in part from ambivalence about liberal democracy itself. In response to the loss of an object both loved and loathed, in which only the loathing or contempt is avowed, melancholy sustains the loved object, and continues to provide a cover for the love—a continued means of disavowing it—by incorporating and performing the loathsomeness.

There are other ways ambivalently structured loss can take shape as melancholic, including . . . remorse for a past of not loving the object well enough and self-reproach for ever having wished for its death or replacement. . . . In this guilt, anxiety, and defensiveness over the loss of liberal democracy, we would feel compelled to defend basic principles of liberalism or simply defend liberalism as a whole *in a liberal way*, that is, we would give up being critical of liberalism and, in doing so, give up being left. Freud identifies this surrender of identity upon the death of an ambivalent object as the suicidal wish in melancholia, a wish abetted in our case by a more general disorientation about what the Left is or stands for today.[45]

These terms might explain the emotional turmoil of a radical who embraced inwardness at the very moment that he rejected liberalism—which has, even in the broadest of terms, as a historical formation encompassing much of the nineteenth and twentieth century, tended to insist on the sanctity of inwardness. Potter's politics of experience might be considered an effort, in Brown's words, to "act out to keep alive those aspects of the political formation [that he was then] losing"—and was in some general sense responsible for killing. Unable to avow his love of liberal individualism in its devotion to the inner life, or his implication in its demise, Potter incorporates an agonized form of that individualism into his radicalism. In this scenario, his feelings of guilt and ambivalent attachment lead to his ultimately crippling sense that his emotions and feelings were in some sense tied to if not responsible for the larger fate of the left.

The problem with this analysis is that it is potentially reversible: Potter's melancholic relation to liberalism might readily be described as a melancholic relation to radicalism, especially insofar as he might have understood his movement toward inwardness as complicit in the waning of the left's collective life. Here we might note that Potter's pro-Communist mother was dying of cancer as *A Name for Ourselves* went to press. Did he perceive in her death a more general symbolic loss, one in which she stood for the forms of working-class solidarity then in retreat across the left? Did her loss contribute to in Potter a version of the blocked "communist desire" described by Jodi Dean, a blockage brought on more generally, she argues, when a member of the left "sublimates revolutionary desire to democratic drive, to the repetitious practices offered up as democracy (whether representative, deliberative, or radical)"?[46] We cannot know, though it is worth pointing out that Potter's essays consistently question assumptions like Dean's, in which a Leninist political party becomes the chief agent of revolutionary struggle and the guarantor of what will count as "political action." At the same time, we needn't accept Dean's absolutism or her accusations of selling out to recall the by now familiar argument that a radicalism romanced like Potter's by "breakaway" experience was in some respects the mirror image of a "political liberalism," as he called it, romanced by but not structurally committed to utopian visions of collectivity.[47] In fact, we might conjecture that Potter's melancholia stems precisely from the degree of confusion that he and the movement allowed between liberalism and radicalism: the loss of one must necessarily indicate, even as it obscures, the loss of the other. Moreover, I'll suggest in the next section that it's difficult to determine the ultimate nature of that melancholia to the degree that the movement from which he had been separated had become—for him as well as for others—impossibly confused with television images of it.

Swallowing Television

Three weeks after the 1965 March on Washington, CBS featured a "takeout" on SDS that ran for more than three minutes and included a conversation with Potter, dressed in a suit and tie, who explained the objectives of the Chase Manhattan demonstration and the recent march. "You say you aren't affiliated politically," the interviewer asked. "Aren't you really taking a political line?" Potter replied, "We're searching. . . . Political liberalism is not doing the job."[48]

Potter and other members of the "old guard"—the founders of SDS who'd helped draft the *Port Huron Statement* in the early sixties—continued to search as television coverage of the movement began gradually to increase and as the nation turned with perplexed fascination to the growing student dissent. The coverage provided a kind of legitimacy but also produced flattening effects. Todd Gitlin argues that while SDS had up until this point propounded no integrated platform or program, one was forced upon them by the media and by the Johnson administration, each of which overlooked the multiple issues raised by the *Port Huron Statement*, for example, and instead understood the movement as primarily antiwar and antidraft, as opposed to more systematically critical of US society. In addition, he argues, the media's increased attention to the movement corresponded with and in some sense hastened the exit of "the first-generation elite" who had begun the movement in the early sixties. Far more "ambivalent about formal leadership" than the so-called Prairie Power generation that eventually took its place, the Old Guard looked on with some dismay as television coverage especially hastened precipitously the movement's progress, providing it with publicity that ran far in advance of the organization's ability to mobilize at the grassroots level.[49]

Thus even as the media's attention to SDS emphasized "*violence, counterdemonstrations,* and *official statements,*" its coverage polarized the SDS mission, Gitlin argues, inflating movement rhetoric and making it more extreme, producing "generational and geographical strain among both rank-and-file members and leaders," pushing SDS more vigorously toward university activism, and consolidating a politics of celebrity.[50] This last was especially pernicious, Gitlin thinks: the press required colorful personalities willing to speak for the movement, and it anointed them with lavish attention, whether or not they spoke for the organization as a whole. "SDS had not started out seeking the spotlight," Gitlin writes, "but, caught in the glare, the SDS responsibles decided to make the most of it" in a way that changed fundamentally the scope and purpose of the organization: "A movement hell-bent on militant action, and a rock-and-rolling, star-worshiping, media-dependent youth culture alongside it, glared at their celebrity leaders without clear criteria for criticism or coherent principles for selective participation in the spectacle: neither celebrities nor constituents could help the other."[51]

"You can't be a revolutionary today without a television set," declared Jerry Rubin, one of the left's television-made celebrities. The Free Speech Movement "created [the uprisings at] Columbia," he argued. "The kids who watched FSM were ten, eleven years old. Five years later, campuses were up all over the country. And it wasn't through traditional political organizing—reading books, and getting leaflets and hearing arguments. It was through being turned on by something they saw on television."[52] According to Gitlin, there's truth to claims like these: just as television coverage of the civil rights movement brought images of cattle prods and police dogs into the homes of Americans otherwise unconcerned with the plight of black Americans, so too television coverage of the marches and demonstrations organized by SDS helped grow the movement exponentially. But these powerful images came at a price. When in 1966 the House Un-American Activities Committee subpoenaed Rubin, he showed up in an American Revolutionary costume. A son of one of President Truman's economic advisors and a committed radical, R. G. Davis advised him on the choice and recalls, "It seemed to me that *they might not report what he had to say, but they would take a picture of him.*"[53] Television coverage imposed its own terms. The networks would "*cover the event, not the con-*

dition; the conflict, not the consensus; the fact that 'advances the story,' not the one that explains it."[54] In sum, by the end of the decade, it was almost impossible, Gitlin argues, to distinguish the movement proper—its ideas, plans, and strategies—from the movement as a media phenomenon, so thoroughly had television images "entered into the movement's internal life."[55]

When Potter gave his famous speech in 1965—the year that SDS "went public," as Gitlin puts it—that process was just getting under way.[56] On October 11 and 12, the *CBS Evening News* ran two more long takeouts on the movement, each of which focused on antidraft activities and exaggerated accounts of how SDS was mobilizing the nation's high schools. The tone was sensationalistic and intended to stoke public anger. As the producer of the shows told Gitlin, "A dramatic piece is a dramatic piece. You wanted to get what Fred Friendly [then president of CBS News] used to call a 'fire in the belly,' an emotional event with emotional people." Television news programs chose stories that would "fly in the face (or gut) of the audience."[57] The television news certainly impacted Potter's "gut feelings," his sense by the end of the sixties that it felt "like someone ha[d] been tearing at my guts." In an essay on the demonstrations at the 1968 Democratic National Convention—the television coverage of which provided, Abbie Hoffman famously said, "advertisements for revolution"—Potter writes, "We all had been involved in the media business at some level, had been aware that the drama that had been going on in Lincoln Park and Old Town had been played on national television one night, and that the 'whole wide world had been watching.' But we failed to think hard enough about the difference between *seeing* the drama and *being in* it."[58] By the end of the decade, Potter thought the drama had changed venues. He was still in it, but it was now all around him, even though the cameras had seemed to disappear. "I don't even have to leave my house to know real danger," he writes. "It is right here, in me. . . . The objectification/recognition that was going on in Chicago is going on here. We have simply dispensed with the organizing committee and the TV cameras."[59] These lines suggest that the stage of Chicago had become the world and that the cameras, though gone, continued in some panoptic fashion to exert their self-disciplining effects. But Potter more frequently replaced these extensive registers with intensive ones: it wasn't so much that the stage upon which he once acted had enlarged and swallowed the world but rather that he had swallowed that stage, and the cameras once trained upon it. Having swallowed that image, he loses the ability to see what lies beyond it and thus access to important parts of himself. After watching television, he

writes, "What I felt was a more decisive, deadening emptiness . . . a sense
that shards of content and meaning that had been strewn around in my
depression had been washed out of me—a sense of being almost physically diminished."[60] When "we turn off the TV," he writes, "we are empty"
and "the consumer is consumed."[61]

As concerned as he is with that emptying out, he seems doubly concerned with "the method of resistance" that young consumers had developed in response, one that "seems to be a determination to swallow mass
culture whole." It's worth quoting at length from the remarkable passage in
which Potter describes this process:

> The word for swallowing whole is "groove." Kids turn the television
> set into a light show, or sit on a street corner and watch cars go by
> all day, or go into a plastic restaurant and order a cup of coffee and
> sit for hours and watch the plastic people come in and out—and all
> of these things and many more are a kind of swallowing whole of
> the culture in the sense that the whole idea of a TV as a cultural
> symbol which has certain meanings attached to it is consumed. The
> TV is taken as a whole piece and "grooved on" in the sense that its
> essence, its essential quality, is understood apart from its cultural
> meaning. You swallow a TV by turning off the sound and crossing
> up the vertical and horizontal tuning and then turning off the lights
> and feeling all those electrical dots move around inside you; and in
> doing that, you come as close as you can to comprehending its es-
> sence, thus destroying its cultural meaning, or its power as a cul-
> tural symbol to oppress you. . . . [Doing this] gives you a certain
> insight into the nature of the way things in your world work on you
> and it gives you a capacity to survive in that environment by keep-
> ing it under penetrating observation.[62]

Television has become an ambience or pervasive condition that the young
seek to contain by way of ingestion: they seek to inure themselves to the
widespread influence of television by transforming its content and specific
"cultural meanings" into "electrical dots" that transmit no identifiable images. There's a strange literalism implicit in the practice; in place of swallowing the particular images and stories transmitted by television, the
young swallow the machine itself.

It's clear enough that Potter is skeptical of the practice; swallowing television becomes just another way to cavort with Frank Zappa's "plastic
people." Indeed, he goes on to explain why he thinks it built upon a funda-

mental misrecognition. Taking nonreferential images into themselves, the young who groove on television misunderstand something about television and their relation to it. "But what makes me uneasy or makes me feel this is the observation of the wrong things," he writes, "is that I do not think people keep so cool if they were looking right at the thing that had disfigured them."[63] That thing might be the war in Vietnam, racial oppression in the South—or even, he suggests earlier, "middle-class culture."[64] The problem with swallowing television, in other words, is that it impedes understanding a social relation and the particular species of loss that organized the experience of the young. In the same way, it impedes any understanding, on the part of the young, that they too had suffered a terrible loss with the collapse of the movement. Perhaps they swallowed television to better avoid acknowledging their own crippling separation from what might have been sustaining forms of collective life. And perhaps, also, Potter turns to the young to better discuss his own relation to "the thing" that had "disfigured" him. Here we might hazard that Potter's "system" was an image packaged for easy ingestion, one that impeded full understanding of the social relations then organizing global capitalism. However redolent of trends within the social sciences, Potter's "system" was far simpler—and easier to swallow—than even the native theory of capitalism implicit in these lines from Paddy Chayefsky's *Network*, offered by the CEO of the conglomerate that owns the eponymous network: "There are no nations!" he bellows. "There are no peoples! There are no Russians. There are no Arabs! There are no third worlds! There is no West! There is only one holistic system of systems, one vast and immane, interwoven, interacting, multi-variate, multi-national dominion of dollars! Petro-dollars, electro-dollars, multi-dollars, Reichmarks, rubles, rin, pounds and shekels! It is the international system of currency that determines the totality of life on this planet!"[65]

Potter writes that, "in some sense, we are waiting for a decision to be made as to whether or not they will be willing to risk getting on about the business of looking deeper into their own oppression, right down inside the maggot-infested wound."[66] Why was Potter waiting at all, and who is the "we" for whom he speaks? Did something about the process of swallowing television speak to his own felt risk? Why would he—feeling "melancholy" over what he perceived to be the failure of the movement, not knowing "where to go and what to do," experiencing "awful depression," and feeling "torn apart from each other and ourselves"—turn his attention to the young and how they consumed television? Perhaps because the young grooving on television offered him a way to think about and even begin to work through his own melancholic relation to the end of the movement. Perhaps, having begun to understand that loss as the loss of a part of himself—of the energies he invested in the movement—and having begun to distinguish between those energies and the media images that attached to them over the course of the decade, Potter saw something personally meaningful in the manner in which the young, seeking to sidestep the pervasive influence of television, ingested what they took to be a nonreferential image of it and were instead taken in.

Elaborating Freud's account of melancholia, Nicholas Abraham and Maria Torok describe "incorporation" as a process of failed or refused mourning in which a melancholic chooses "photographic images" over language itself. Typical mourning involves a substitution of language for the void occasioned first by the removal of the mother's once nourishing breast and, later, by the loss of the mother herself. Incorporation is antifigurative to the extent that the melancholic, unable to fill the emptiness of her mouth with words, instead ingests the whole of the lost object as an image. Resistant to the substitutive logic of language, the incorporated object acquires what Abraham and Torok call a "magical" power and becomes an "encrypted" presence within the melancholic—as Potter suggests the television set itself had become an encrypted presence within the young of his moment. For Abraham and Torok, encryption accompanies "*demetaphorization* (taking literally what is meant figuratively) and *objectification* (pretending that the suffering is not an injury to the subject but instead a loss sustained by the love object)."[67]

It makes sense that Potter would attach great significance to the swallowing of television. The movement had internalized the media, Gitlin writes, and television above all; it had taken television images of itself inside and come to understand those as constitutive of a shared collective enterprise. Movement members didn't do this out of any personal failing or shortsightedness. It was simply impossible, Gitlin avers, to use television without becoming colonized in turn by it. It follows, then, that some members would respond to the loss of the movement—of the personal energies and shared collective life that sustained it—by internalizing or swallowing the television images of protest by which the movement lived and died or, indeed, by swallowing televisions as such. As Abraham and Torok explain, the process of incorporation means misrecognizing the nature of what has been lost. "In order not to have to 'swallow' a loss, we fantasize swallowing (or having swallowed) that which has been lost, as if it were some kind of thing."[68]

Potter's heartfelt and soul-searching ruminations on the personal and intimate dimensions of revolutionary life become particularly interesting in this context. According to Abraham and Torok, "Incorporation is the refusal to reclaim as our own the part of ourselves that we placed in what we lost, a loss that, if recognized as such, would effectively transform us."[69] Potter longs for that reclamation and transformation, even from within what I have described as his melancholia. The very title of his collection gestures to these processes and to the vital importance of finding, as he puts it, "a name," not simply for ourselves, but for the losses attendant upon slow collapse of the movement. Abraham and Torok write that, "failing to feed itself on words to be exchanged with others, the mouth absorbs in fantasy all or part of a person—the genuine depository of what is now nameless."[70] We can only hope that, by looking with withering honesty "right down inside [his own] maggot-infested wound," Potter had begun to find those missing words and names.

32 | Shulamith Firestone, Social Defeat, and Sixties Radicalism

by Alice Echols

> This sort of person appears . . . at the beginning of movements.
> Magnificent and stunned by insight, they tell us . . . the way we
> live is intolerable. Then they stagger off, leaving [the rest of us]
> to try to live the insight out.
>
> —Ann Snitow, "On Shulamith Firestone"[1]

In September 2012, as I began to work on my talk for the 2012 New Insurgency conference, I was still absorbing the news of Shulamith Firestone's
death just a few weeks earlier. An architect of the women's liberation
movement, Firestone had died alone in her East Village apartment, a
sixty-seven-year-old recluse who had spent much of her adult life in poor
health and with very little money. It had not always been like that. Firestone helped shape the women's movement, both on the ground in New
York City and in her 1970 classic *The Dialectic of Sex: The Case for Feminist
Revolution*. Dubbed "the little red book for women," *Dialectic* was for
many of us the breakthrough text. Over the years in both my writing and
my teaching, I have returned time and again to her audacious manifesto of
women's liberation.

I chose to make Firestone the subject of my talk even though in many
ways she is not an obvious choice for a conference commemorating the
Port Huron Statement. After all, the *Port Huron Statement*'s obliviousness
to women—emblematic of early 1960s *Mad Men* America—embodied
precisely what Firestone so memorably identified in the first line of *Dialectic*: "Sex class is so deep as to be invisible."[2] As for Firestone herself, she
was not among the many women whose feminism was forged in complicated ways through their long-term, committed participation in the New
Left and the civil rights movement. To the best of my knowledge, she was

never a member of Students for a Democratic Society (SDS), the group that produced the 1962 manifesto. In fact, Firestone had only limited contact with New Left groups, and those experiences left her feeling exasperated and fed up. In the wake of one particularly disastrous encounter with the left, the 1969 counterinaugural protest, where feminist speakers were taunted and harassed (cries of "Take her off the stage and fuck her!" drowned out one speaker), Firestone argued that the left had blown its last chance with feminists. In an article in the left-wing paper, *The Guardian*, she wrote, "Women's liberation is dynamite. And we have more important things to do than to try to get you to come around." And then she cut to the chase. "Fuck off, left. You can examine your navel by yourself from now on. We're starting our own movement."[3]

Despite the role that she played in forging an autonomous women's movement, Firestone's story is a part of the history of the left—or it should be. And that's because her analysis made socialism integral to radical feminism. However, it is not primarily her political investments that interest me in this chapter; rather, it is her life and in particular her relationship to the women's movement and what that can tell us about the sixties. Firestone's relationship to this movement was fraught, and I don't want to suggest that her life was typical. Nonetheless, her life can open a window onto the ways in which the political movements and countercultural scenes—however transformative they may have been at the level of the social—were sometimes downright debilitating to participants themselves.

Firestone grew up in a large Orthodox Jewish family in the Midwest, first in Kansas City and then in St. Louis. The eldest daughter, she was precocious and feisty and often found herself battling her controlling father, who insisted that the family keep to a strict Orthodox regime. Shulamith may have felt embattled in her family, but she was extremely close to her older brother, Daniel. So strong was their connection that she skipped a year of high school in order to be with him at Washington University, where he was already a student. By her sophomore year, however, she was no longer observant, and that led to an irreparable, possibly violent end to their friendship. Daniel never spoke to her again. Rather than remain in St. Louis, she transferred to the School of the Art Institute of Chicago, where she earned her bachelor of fine arts in 1967.

During her college years, Firestone protested racial discrimination through her connection to a friend in the Catholic Worker movement. Still, by comparison to many early women's liberationists who had extensive resumes of political activism, Firestone had only a slim dossier. That would change in 1967 with the National Conference for a New Politics (NCNP), held in Chicago during Labor Day weekend. The NCNP was an ill-fated attempt to unite the disparate factions of what was then called the "Movement." Women's liberation was not yet one of those factions, but Movement women were already meeting to talk about what they soon took to calling "sexism."

The NCNP marked a turning point in these fledgling feminists' relationship to the left. The failure of conference organizers to address women's issues anywhere in their agenda led a group of nearly fifty women to come together as a caucus and to produce just such a resolution. When representatives of that group took their resolution to the conference's resolution committee, they were told that the conference already had its resolution on women, which the peace group, Women Strike for Peace (WSP), had submitted. The WSP resolution concerned peace, not women, and Jo Freeman, a member of the women's caucus and veteran of the Berkeley Free Speech Movement, knew that and was steaming mad. Still, she believes nothing more would have happened had she not run into Firestone on her way out of the hall. Feeding each other's anger, Firestone and Freeman stayed up all night drafting an alternate resolution, which grew more and more radical the more they talked. In it, they called for the revamping of marriage, divorce, and property laws, and they condemned the mass media's sexual objectification of women. But they didn't stop there, arguing that women should have "complete control" over their bodies, including access to abortion and birth control information. When the two women tried to present their resolution to the assembled participants, they were shoved aside, and the chairman of the proceedings patted Firestone on the head and said, "Cool down, little girl; we have more important issues to talk about here than women's problems." Furious at being dismissed and with such imperiousness, Firestone and Freeman channeled their anger. They managed, in the words of feminist Ann Snitow, to "invent an indignation and a new vision of how women are oppressed," which, as she recalls, "we all embraced ten minutes later."[4]

Within a week, Chicago's first women's liberation group formed, but Firestone only stayed in Chicago for another month. Many thought she was moving to New York to pursue her art, and she herself wrote that she moved there to pursue a career in painting and writing.[5] Some who knew her in Chicago have since said that she moved away to escape an abusive boyfriend.[6] Whatever the reason, upon arriving in New York, she helped form New York City's first women's liberation group. Almost immediately Firestone became a force to be reckoned with in that group—a group with no shortage of strong-minded and opinionated young women in its ranks. It was this group of mostly left-wing women, New York Radical Women (NYRW), that pioneered consciousness-raising (C-R). C-R, which would become enshrined in the movement as the essential feminist practice, was meant to both pull away the blinkers of women's accommodation to the system and form the basis of theory. It was not intended to be therapy, although C-R did have a therapeutic effect, and, over time, it did indeed evolve into a therapeutic practice.

NYRW staged actions as well as engaging in C-R sessions. In August 1968 its members were among the women's liberationists who made headlines when they protested the Miss America Pageant in Atlantic City. It was on the boardwalk that demonstrators startled onlookers by throwing various "instruments of torture," including bras, into a "Freedom Trash Can." Despite reports of bra burning, no bras were even singed that day. Earlier, in January 1968 NYRW agreed to take part in the Jeannette Rankin Brigade, a women's antiwar protest in Washington, DC. NYRW opposed the war, but members of the group also opposed the march, at least in the way that older women in the pacifist left had conceived it. Firestone was among those who most forcefully took the position that the march was wrongheaded in presuming that being a woman had anything at all to do with opposing war. And in a separate action, she and others in NYRW staged a Burial of Traditional Womanhood—meant as a rebuke of the left-leaning Women Strike for Peace, the group most involved in the planning of the march. (This is one of the moments in the history of the second wave that underscores that as much as women's liberation borrowed from the first wave, it was distinct from it, much like the New Left was indebted to but distinct from the Old Left.) It was in a leaflet for this demonstration that the expression "Sisterhood is Powerful" first turned up, followed by the exhortation "Humanhood the Ultimate."

Ultimately, the exploration of "humanhood" would be pursued without their brothers on the left, as Firestone and other women's liberationists emulated the separatist path recently forged by Black Power activists. This was perhaps an easier road for Firestone to take than for many others, for whom an autonomous movement felt like nothing so much as treachery against long-term, cherished comrades, especially at this moment when the country seemed to teeter on the brink of revolution.

Eventually, feminism's divorce from the left would have serious consequences for the prospects of making change in the United States. Women's liberation *was* dynamite, and the left could have benefited from feminists' energy and analysis. Instead, the left floundered and collapsed as sectarian madness and vanguard posturing won the day. As for the radical feminism that Firestone helped create, it carved out oppositional understandings of marriage, the family, sexuality, gendered violence, and gender itself, much of which is today completely taken for granted. As a movement, radical feminism flourished for a few years, but its disconnection from the left had a downside, too, as strategies for structural change lost ground to schemes of self-transformation. Activist and writer Meredith Tax recalls that about three years into women's liberation, she began to question whether the movement's understanding of politics hadn't grown too capacious. What did it mean, she wondered, when activists believed that repairing their cars was a matter of political significance akin to, say, participating in a demonstration? "I worried about what else was going to happen," she recalled. "This wasn't going to be the whole thing, was it?"[7]

Whatever its long-term consequences, the break with the left had an energizing effect on the women's liberation movement. Throughout parts of the country, but perhaps nowhere more intensely than in New York City, the months that followed featured demonstrations, speak-outs, sit-ins, proliferating manifestoes, and an intensity that is today hard to capture. Throughout it all, Firestone was like a girl on fire. Snitow worked alongside her in this period and remembers Firestone as "aflame, incandescent," someone whose company she found "thrilling."[8]

Firestone was an artist, and a highly articulate one at that. She wrote for and edited a crucial 1968 collection called *Notes from the First Year*, a record of the first year of women's liberation. (It is worth noting that, as the title suggests, Firestone understood from the very beginning that they were making history.) This annual journal was Firestone's "baby," recalls veteran women's liberation activist Carol Hanisch.[9] It was in *Notes from the Second Year* (1969) that Firestone and her coeditor Anne Koedt called on women to "dare to be bad"—that is, to refuse the habituated niceness that was the bedrock of femininity. It was in this period that Firestone came up with her idea of a "dream" feminist action: a smile boycott, an idea that has lost none of its currency, as evidenced by Tatyana Fazlalizadeh's recent art project "Stop Telling Women to Smile."[10]

With journalist Ellen Willis, also of NYRW, Firestone went on to found Redstockings, which, in contrast to NYRW, was meant to be an explicitly radical feminist group. There would be no more wafflers in this group. After organizing a number of important actions, including two around abortion, the group shifted focus and concentrated on C-R. Firestone was not the only Redstockings member made uneasy by the C-R turn, but it was the emerging concern with movement elitism that soured her on the group. As spokeswomen for women's liberation emerged from the ranks, so did the worry that the new movement would be hierarchized like every other movement. Soon Firestone and Willis found themselves attacked as "elitist" for allowing the media to single them out as the quotable leaders of this new movement. Firestone, who was unapologetically intense, articulate, and brainy, found herself pretty much always under attack. She had refused to capitulate to the self-abnegation that her family and the larger culture had pressed on her, and she wasn't about to capitulate now because her so-called sisters were calling for it. In contrast to many other feminists who shut up and went along with the feminist reworking of the nice girl, Firestone did little to disguise her impatience with what she judged "all the noodling over egalitarianism," according to her friend and feminist coconspirator Ellen Willis.[11]

Firestone left Redstockings to form another group with Anne Koedt, a friend and the author of "The Myth of the Vaginal Orgasm," perhaps the most "impactful" article to emerge from the women's liberation movement. Their ambition was to create an organization that would not end in acrimony and division but that would generate a mass-based radical feminist movement. They called it New York Radical Feminists (NYRF), and they devised a structure for the group that they believed would be both democratic and structured, one that would "seed itself" with small groups or "brigades," as they called them in sixties fashion. The founding brigade named itself Stanton-Anthony after that famous and dynamic first-wave duo—Elizabeth Cady Stanton and Susan B. Anthony.

Two years of the women's movement also made Koedt and Firestone wary of dogma and hardened lines. "WE DO WHAT WORKS" was the way Firestone summed up their approach. However, what didn't work, at least for some of the group's newcomers, was the group's explicit hierarchy, in which new brigades went through a six-month probationary period in which members spent three months reading and discussing feminist literature and another three months engaged in C-R. "Why must we defer to the group's founders?" some might have asked. "What makes them better or wiser feminists than us?" Tensions came to a head early on when the members voted to strike down the brigade structure. Firestone and Koedt declined to fight and with some others in the founding brigade decided to walk away from the group. After the meeting, Firestone reportedly showed up at a friend's place and said, "They threw me out and that's it."[12] Tired of perennially returning to square one at each and every meeting, weary of attacks on her leadership, Firestone opted to write about feminism rather than to participate in any of its organizations.

Certainly, the attacks on leaders, which her onetime ally Jo Freeman later dubbed "trashing," made the movement a tricky, destabilizing place for Firestone. According to her editor at William Morrow, members of one of the groups of which Firestone was a member actually demanded that the group rather than Firestone own the copyright to *Dialectic*. While it seemed to some that Firestone had ditched NYRF and the larger movement, she understood her experience quite differently—as one of exile. "It was like she had been rejected by her family," said one friend.[13] Maybe a better way to put it is that the family she had chosen had rejected her just as her biological family had.

By the time *Dialectic* appeared in bookstores in fall 1970, Firestone had been out of the movement for a good six months. However, readers would not have known that its author felt herself an exile from the movement she had helped create. She wrote as an impassioned partisan, noting only that, for strong women, the movement created the dilemma of "having to eradicate, at the same time, not only their submissive natures, but their dominant natures as well, thus burning their candle at both ends."[14]

Dialectic was a thrilling read. Years ago in a review of the book, on the occasion of its reissue, I characterized her feminist reworkings of Freud, Marx, and Engels as "always bold, sometimes breathtaking, and occasionally weird," and I would stand by that judgment.[15] What was most nervy (and problematic) about the book was her contention that families are where dominance and submission are learned and come to feel familiar. She credited Marx with the insight that the "family contained within itself in embryo all the antagonisms that later developed on a wide scale within society."[16] Like a good deal of radical feminism, her theorizing about the family, which, as others have noted, operates as a bulwark against racism even as it reinforces gender asymmetry, was obtuse about its own racial specificity.

Radical feminism of the sort advanced by Firestone in *Dialectic* insisted on feminism's organizational autonomy from the left but took for granted that theoretically socialism was central to the radical feminist project. Even as she dismissed Marx and Engels as knowing next to nothing about women's oppression, she embraced Marxist method and accepted much of their wisdom about class oppression. At the time of its publication, this was hardly an unusual stance among radical feminists, but over time, left analysis would drop out of radical feminism.

There was nothing cautious about *Dialectic*, and her more dubious bits of analysis gave its critics ammunition to dismiss the whole book. Reviewers across the political spectrum savaged parts of her analysis—her characterization of pregnancy as barbaric, the promotion of artificial reproduction as the key to women's liberation, her advocacy of sexual freedom for women and children. As for her conviction that heterosexuality could be harnessed to revolutionary ends through women's boycotting of sex, that would soon become outdated in many radical feminist circles as lesbianism became the revolutionary way forward.

Although *Dialectic* had its defenders, and some of its prescriptions for change have come true, the book was disavowed even by many in the movement. It stood accused of multiple sins, but two stood out. One was that its analysis was male identified in its embrace of socialism, technology, and polymorphous sexuality. The other criticism lodged against it was that the utopia it advanced could usher in a cybernetic Brave New World. Firestone anticipated many of the criticisms against her, including the charge—one that resonated across feminism's political spectrum—that she wanted to transform women into men. She explained she didn't want to "draft women into a *male* world" but rather she wanted to eliminate the gender distinction altogether.[17] Today, Firestone's conviction that getting rid of nature is the way forward is the stuff of gender studies classes. Before Donna Haraway rejected the goddess for the cyborg, before Judith Butler began troubling gender, there was Firestone and, before her, of course, the writer who helped inspire *Dialectic*, Simone de Beauvoir. But Firestone's orientation toward collective solutions and her commitment to socialism increasingly dropped out of the radical feminist analysis and came to reside solely within socialist feminism, which increasingly became an academic orbit.

The immediate reaction to her book, in many ways the most daring of all the women's liberation books yet published, would have challenged even the most emotionally resilient. First there was the avalanche of publicity it generated, which Firestone reportedly found "unbearable."[18] And then there were the reviews. In *The New York Times*, critic John Leonard acknowledged her "brilliant mind" but sneered at the extremity of her formulations.[19] And closer to home, there was her father who called *Dialectic* "the joke book of the century" and refused to read it.[20]

Firestone continued to have ideas, but book and art projects went uncompleted. She grew reclusive, and her behavior became increasingly erratic. Her older brother Daniel's suicide in 1974 was a key event in her emotional unraveling, which would eventually be diagnosed as something more serious and debilitating than the generic nervous breakdown. She was diagnosed with schizophrenia. In 1981 the death of her father, her antagonist and perhaps, as her sister Tirzah suggests, her "ballast" as well, precipitated her further decline.[21] By 1987 she was in and out of hospitals. There was, according to those movement friends whom she consented to see, a medicated mellowness about her, antithetical to the fiery activist they remembered. In the mid-1990s, a support group of younger women broke through her reclusiveness, and for a while they managed to make a difference. At their urging she wrote *Airless Spaces*, her memoirish book of stories about her medicalized, hospitalized life, which was published in 1998. But when her support group slowly came apart, Firestone's condition deteriorated, and she found herself once again in those airless spaces. Still, some old movement friends reported seeing her occasionally until 2010.[22] In late August 2012, when her building superintendent discovered her tiny body face down in her apartment, she had reportedly been dead for several days.

> Too tired, brother sister, to hold my fist so high
> Now that it's gone far away
>
> —Los Lobos, "Revolution"[23]

Firestone's life and the larger story of "second-wave" feminism raise a number of questions that pivot on the relationship between political movements and trauma. Were the movements of the "long sixties" uniquely traumatizing to participants? Was the women's movement unusually bruising? And was there something about postwar US culture that made sixties rebels especially vulnerable both to the contentiousness and divisiveness of movement life and to the feelings of loneliness and despair that sometimes haunted them following movement collapse?

In her eloquent and thoughtful 2013 *New Yorker* article, "Death of a Revolutionary," Susan Faludi comes at this somewhat differently. She asks why it was that Firestone and so many other feminist leaders of her generation were "unable to thrive in the world they had done so much to create." In Firestone's case, Faludi believes that schizophrenia was the culprit. However, in her discussion of the disease, she emphasizes that the key risk factors for schizophrenia all involve chronic isolation and loneliness—a condition that two experts on schizophrenia have called "social defeat." Faludi goes on to explicitly connect the researchers' idea of social defeat with the devastating social defeat that many radical feminists experienced, especially as the movement did what movements always do—that is, wind down and die. She quotes Kate Millett, who in 1998 mourned those pioneering feminists who had "disappeared to struggle alone in makeshift oblivion or vanished into asylums."[24] Faludi so lingers on the failed sisterhood of second-wave feminism that readers cannot be blamed for thinking that, however much social good feminism achieved, the movement was nothing short of a disaster for many of the women who created it.

The idea that sisterhood was powerfully destructive has proven to be the most controversial aspect of Faludi's essay. Her account of trashing led some, such as the left-wing writer and cultural critic Eli Zaretsky, to conclude that the radical feminist milieu in which Firestone moved was "truly mad."[25] Longtime feminist writer and activist Susan Brownmiller, who refused to speak with Faludi for her article, criticized her for not emphasizing NYRF's many (post-Firestone) accomplishments and observed that long-term participation in *any* political movement requires nothing short of "nerves of steel." Lest anyone think that incivility had died with the women's movement, Brownmiller demonstrated otherwise when she accidentally tweeted a private wish, that Faludi "burn in hell."[26]

I was one of many people whom Susan Faludi consulted in researching Firestone's life. In our conversation, she sounded almost haunted by how much misery marked the lives of so many feminist veterans. In her essay she notes their "painful solitude, poverty, infirmity, mental illness, and even homelessness."[27] Some thirty years earlier, when I was working on my dissertation on a history of radical feminism, I met and interviewed about twenty-five veterans of New York women's liberation. Some were doing just fine, particularly those who were working as academics and/or writers. But almost as many appeared to be just scraping by. That they were even able to make ends meet in a rapidly gentrifying city had everything to do with the fact that they had not budged from their rent-controlled apartments in many, many years. But that occurred to me a long while later.

At the time I believed that what I was seeing was a determined and admirable bohemianism, and that was likely a part of it. But as a thirty-something grad student accustomed to living on the margins, I never thought about old age and how that might upend their carefully calibrated lives, driving some from near poverty into the real thing. But then, to me they seemed resilient and plucky. At times I felt exasperated by the wariness with which some responded to me, but given the media's many mischaracterizations of the movement, this did not seem entirely unreasonable. It is true that the laser-like precision and righteous certitude with which activists recalled fifteen-year-old debates left me wondering how much else had happened in their lives since those turbocharged early years of women's liberation. More disquieting was the discomfort caused by mentions of Firestone. No one was specific, but I understood she was not in good shape. Still, I did not see the point of dwelling on the casualties of the movement. I didn't want my book to become yet another occasion for an attack on the movement and the women who made it. After all, by this point—the mid- to late 1980s—we were already deep in backlash territory with book after book proclaiming the folly of feminism, the movement that they argued had managed to hurt women more than it had helped them.

Thirty years later, we are in a different place. We have nothing to gain from remaining silent. And if we don't have these discussions now, when will we? This seems to me an ideal occasion to launch these conversations since it was the *Port Huron Statement* that argued for a politics that "give form to the feelings of helplessness and indifference, so that people may see the political, social, and economic sources of their private troubles."[28] Let's take seriously that exhortation and apply it to movements that were meant to bring us comfort, bring us together, and create community where there had been loneliness and anomie. It is time we recognized that what Faludi terms social defeat is best understood not as a personal concern or individual failing but rather as a collective phenomenon with social roots.

My interest in this subject owes something to my career-long engagement with the long sixties. As the author of two monographs about different parts of the sixties—women's liberation in *Daring to Be Bad* and the hippie counterculture in *Scars of Sweet Paradise: The Life and Times of Janis Joplin*—I've thought a good deal about the shared territory of rebellion in the sixties. The quest for "real life," the embrace of frame-breaking experiences, the search for personal authenticity, the reinvention of self, and the twin (and competing) desires for greater community and a more full-bodied individualism were not uniquely the province of the boomer generation, but they were given full-throttle expression in the sixties. Of course, these movements and scenes were distinct phenomena— countercultural hippies and political activists did not always regard each other as allies, for example—nonetheless, there exists considerable common ground. My aim is to tackle the fallout from the sixties and its aftermath with a focus on the lives of those who put their bodies on the line in all the many ways in which people in that period did. I don't mean in any way to foreclose further discussion of how government repression undermined radicalism. What follows is not a recanting but a reckoning, a melancholy one at that. After all, the incompleteness of what we achieved and the feelings of social defeat that this engendered owe a lot to what happened next.

That feeling also owes a lot to what happened before. Sixties radicals saw themselves engaged in a great refusal of the 1950s, but they were profoundly shaped by that period. Even though the 1950s were not nearly as quiescent as some would have it—for example, change was already afoot with the civil rights movement, the Beats, and rock 'n' roll—for many kids, particularly white, middle-class kids marooned in the suburbs, these were years of an adventure shortage. Their desire for real, authentic life, full of connection and meaning, represented a kind of blowback against the low-wattage lives of their parents, whose experience of the Great Depression and World War II led them to construct circumscribed lives in which security and comfort were paramount.

This generational conflict is repeated time and again in accounts of the sixties. "I'd rather have 10 years of superhypermost than live to be 70 by sitting in some goddamn chair watching TV" was how Janis Joplin described it.[29] For Peter Coyote of the Diggers and the San Francisco Mime Troupe, the point was to "lay life."[30] Huey Newton of the Black Panther Party counseled "revolutionary suicide," and members of the SDS splinter group Weatherman managed to achieve something like that in the disastrous Greenwich Village townhouse explosion that left three of its members dead. But even in the early part of the sixties, activists were putting their bodies on the line in sit-ins and freedom rides. For many activists and counterculture freaks alike, the feeling was, "If you've got a light, burn it out."[31] Firestone put it differently, but there's no doubt that she wanted to burn. In a documentary about her, the twenty-two-year-old Firestone worried she hadn't yet accomplished enough: "I want to do something. Instead of beauty and power occasionally, I want to achieve a world where it's there all the time, in every word and every brushstroke, and not just now and then."[32] Life with the amp set at thirteen was a risky, sometimes scary enterprise that not everyone survived. There's no way to make sense of our penchant for high-risk living without understanding how much it was shaped by the postwar years and our parents' zeal for living small.

Just as the adventure shortage encouraged life at full tilt, so did feelings of isolation drive the desire for relatedness and community. Indeed the *Port Huron Statement* made the case for politics as the vehicle through which community would be forged and isolation banished. The civil rights movement succeeded in some measure because of the bonds of community it forged. Firestone looked for a way to undo the tyranny of marriage and the social oblivion it visited upon singles in *Dialectic*. "Only in Manhattan is single living even tolerable," she observed, "and that can be debated."[33] The desire to make women—single women—a part of the fabric of social life is central to the text. Circumstances varied, of course, but for many young radicals, the search for community—whether on the dance floor at the Avalon Ballroom in San Francisco, at an antiwar march in Gainesville, or at a C-R group in St. Paul—was made all the more pressing because their own family ties were so attenuated and their own nonconformity had left them isolated and alone. The yearning for community and the desire for heightened experience made the collapse of these movements and communities all the more difficult for participants to accept and to absorb. Recalling the period when the counterculture of San Francisco began to crumble, one scenester says, "There was such pain and suffering it's almost beyond bearing."[34]

However much sixties rebels desired community, they also had an equally strong desire for unfettered personal freedom. How many communes and countercultural enterprises fell apart over this tension between the community and the individual? Even rock music impresario Bill Graham maintained that it was a "tragedy" that the San Francisco bands—the Grateful Dead and Big Brother and the Holding Company among others—"never really did anything communally."[35] In more explicitly political movements, community faced other impediments, particularly because of the way in which politics came to be practiced. The impulse to *live* one's politics was there from the very beginning and was manifested in a willingness to take risks—whether that meant confronting the police or becoming a poorly paid community organizer, all the while subjecting oneself to a steady diet of peanut butter and jelly sandwiches. But as advanced in the *Port Huron Statement*, the idea that the personal is political was more of an organizing strategy, a way of getting people to connect their dissatisfaction with, say, police harassment or inadequate city services, to systemic discrimination and injustice.

Women's liberation originally used the idea of personal politics in that way, too, suggesting that personal circumstances—say, who did the dishes, made the beds, cared for the kids, or enjoyed the orgasms—needed to be reframed not as an individual problem but as a social problem that needed to be addressed through collective political action. But here's the thing: once personal politics crossed over into feminism, it came to entail an analysis of personal life itself and the power that inhered within it. Much of the power of women's liberation lay in its rendering of personal life as political. But in practice "the personal is political" came to sanction the personal as the foremost site of political change, which in turn opened up everything from hairstyles to sexual styles and sexual partners to critique. With personal life corralled to conform to ever-shifting notions of political purity, is it any wonder that trashing became so endemic and so terrifyingly personal?

Social movements are ephemeral, and there was no *one* reason for the decline of women's liberation or any other movement of the 1960s. Faludi emphasizes the inability of Firestone and some other early feminists to live in a world they had transformed. It's true that Firestone et al. set in motion changes that transformed our landscape; it's perhaps even truer that what didn't change was what proved their undoing, contributing to the terrible feeling of social defeat.

Just as vexing was the way in which parts of the sixties, such as personal expressiveness and do-it-yourself ingenuity, were appropriated in ways that made movement harder and that seem horribly ironic today. Think of the hippie maxim "Do your thing" or those San Francisco anarchists, the Diggers, and their bit of wisdom, "Today is the first day of the rest of your life," whose resonance one bank recognized and lifted for a "hip" ad campaign. Think of all that affordable co-op whole-wheat bread and what it eventually became: artisanal bread at $6 a loaf. Think of feminism's advocacy of control and empowerment—through gynecological self-exams, masturbation, and the strategic deployment of sex toys.

And consider how this program of self-empowerment was hijacked and given a neoliberal spin. Others have written about this, and they disagree about the extent to which feminism is at fault by allowing what Hester Eisenstein calls the "political economy of feminism" to fall away.[36] Angela McRobbie, for example, focuses instead on the way in which the neoliberal privatizing of everything in conjunction with consumer capitalism appropriated the feminist discourse of empowerment, choice, and freedom, all the while discrediting feminism as a social movement.[37] But as I have indicated, feminism was not the only sixties movement to find parts of its rhetoric and agenda taken up by the forces it opposed and in ways that both changed and maintained business as usual.[38]

None of this could have been predicted. Who knew that "do your own thing" and "do it yourself"—taking control of your body and your life—would prepare the ground for a very different ethos in which the collective good and social responsibility were overwhelmed by something parading as freedom, choice, and empowerment? Shulamith Firestone didn't know this either, but she knew that the Movement could not lose sight of the need for transformative structural change. When the Movement collapsed—and we're still feeling its collapse—she, and many others, were unprotected. Kate Millett said about Firestone that she was someone who, having lived her adult life in the Movement, was not prepared for the "real world"—especially, I would add, one in which a vision of solidarity and social responsibility no longer much figured, a world in which "do it yourself" had given way to go it alone.

Occupy Wall Street, New York City, day 14, September 30, 2011. David Shank-
bone (Creative Commons)

VI.

Insurgency Anew

Participatory Democracy at Fifty

Planning for the New Insurgency conference did not begin in a melancholic mood. To be sure, recent decades have not, for the most part, stirred buoyant hopes on the left for the achievement of great social change—despite many stunning successes in winning official recognition of rights for racial, ethnic, and sexual minorities, women, the disabled, and others. At the same time, inequality in many dimensions grows, as current statistics on disparities of wealth—or (finally) some public acknowledgment of the gross racial bias built into the US archipelago of penitentiaries—indicate. In the meantime, surges of protest have lit up the times—1999–2001, on behalf of social justice across the globe; 2003, in mammoth demonstrations against the impending US invasion of Iraq; and then, toward the end of 2010, the first signs of large-scale protest against drastic government cuts in social services in many of the countries badly hit by the Great Recession of 2008.

Then in the early months of 2011, protest activism suddenly swept across the face of the globe. Following a democratic revolt in Tunisia, stirring convocations in February filled giant Tahrir Square in Cairo, leading to the deposition of the autocrat Hosni Mubarak after decades in power. This was the Arab Spring, in which democracy movements moved, infectiously, from one country to another. When a few months later, unions led spirited rallies in Madison, Wisconsin, against a conservative governor's attack on the collective-bargaining rights of public employees (see Paul Buhle and Mari Jo Buhle), messages of solidarity went back and forth between the Wisconsin capital and Egypt. The summer witnessed protests against government austerity campaigns in Europe and rallies calling for democracy in Russia. By the fall, the unusual protest called Occupy Wall Street began in New York and inspired large and small city-center "occupations" across the country by critics of economic inequality who protested on behalf of the democratic many, the "99 percent," against rule by the superrich "1 percent." While the onset of winter—and harsh police attacks on protesters—led to a tailing off of Occupy agitation, *Time* opened the year 2012 with a cover dubbing 2011 "the Year of the Protester." It was under that aegis that celebrations of Port Huron at fifty began, as "democracy" was again the watchword of dissent.

Contrary to the experience of 1955–65 (and from 1965 into the 1970s), the left today manifests a pattern that is less obviously cumulative but rather exceedingly episodic. Despite expectations that Occupy 2011 would be resumed with spring 2012 in a greater crescendo, that movement and its rallying cry "We are the 99 percent" has waned, while gains for democracy have been brutally reversed in many countries of the Middle East and the lingering economic malaise incited in a number of countries more growth on the political right than left (though the strength of the antiausterity left in Greece was another story). The measures of success and failure and the balance of victories and defeats in the history of social-justice movements remain difficult to determine. Here we include a number of commentaries describing the movements of 2011 and assessing their aftermaths: Juan Cole on the Middle East, Sarah Leonard and Sarah Jaffe on US Occupy, and Marina Sitrin on "horizontality" in practice. The radical left in modern history, however, has often striven both to face squarely the facts of defeat and to uphold the vision of victories that are possible in the future.

—Howard Brick

33 | Envisioning Another World: Port Huron's Continuing Relevance

by Dick Flacks

For me, the most original and influential passages in the *Port Huron Statement* are these:

> As a *social system* we seek the establishment of a democracy of indi-
> vidual participation, governed by two central aims: that the individual
> share in those social decisions determining the quality of his life; that
> society be organized to encourage independence in men and provide
> the media for their common participation.
>   In a participatory democracy, the political life would be based in
> several root principles:

- that decision-making of basic social consequence be carried on by
  public groupings;
- that politics be seen positively, as the art of collectively creating an
  acceptable pattern of social relations;
- that politics has the function of bringing people out of isolation and
  into community . . .
- that the political order should serve to clarify problems in a way instrumental to their solution . . . channels should be commonly available to relate men to knowledge and to power so that private problems . . . are formulated as general issues.

The economic sphere would have as its basis the principles:

- . . . that the economic experience is so personally decisive that the
  individual must share in its full determination;
- that the economy itself is of such social importance that its major

resources and means of production should be open to democratic participation and subject to democratic social regulation.

... [All] major social institutions—cultural, educational, rehabilitative ... should be generally organized with the well-being and dignity of man as the essential measure of success.[1]

Unlike European New Leftists, those of us who met at Port Huron did not explicitly speak of "socialism" and its revitalization as a goal. Some have argued that the absence of the word *socialism* masked the real intent of the authors (i.e., to advance a socialist agenda that would not be burdened by the deep American aversion to the word), and no doubt some who attended saw the matter in these terms. Some right-wing critics, particularly David Horowitz, claimed to have identified a Marxist-Leninist subtext in the statement. But the notion that the language of the *Port Huron Statement* is a kind of "cover" for socialism misses the fact that the stress on participatory democracy and individual self-realization was intended, by Tom Hayden and others present, to articulate a social vision that incorporated the *full* range of American radical traditions, not just the socialist legacy. Students for a Democratic Society (SDS) descended from the early twentieth century Intercollegiate Socialist Society, which became the student wing of the social democratic League for Industrial Democracy, but at Port Huron, many of us were eager to embrace anarchism, pacifism, radical democracy, and libertarianism—and to deliberately efface the historical cleavages among these. One meaning of *New Left* was precisely to transcend the dead-end internecine warfare of the Old Left—and to find, in the left tradition, a core of values and a structure of feeling that might be a foundation for the left's reconstruction. Participatory democracy, although an unwieldy phrase, condensed those values and impulses and, I submit, still expresses the transformative vision and practice embodied in the left tradition.

Hayden learned the phrase and got some of its sense from classes he took with Professor Arnold Kaufman at the University of Michigan. Kaufman, then a young philosopher, might be labeled a radical pragmatist. He clearly had been influenced by John Dewey, who, despite his fame as "America's philosopher," had worked much of his life to figure out how there could be a new American left. Dewey's writings include many passages about participatory and decentralized education and governance— passages that seemed to be echoed in the *Port Huron Statement*. Kaufman's classes also provided entrée into the writings of C. Wright Mills, himself strongly influenced by Dewey, who, in the 1950s, hungered for a revitalized American left that would challenge and seek alternatives to the mass, bureaucratic, authoritarian societies he saw in both the East and the West. Hayden and the other Michigan students who initiated SDS and organized the Port Huron convention were consciously aiming to fulfill such hopes.

These folks were attuned to academic sources of wisdom, but they were experiencing those ideas in the context of a profound moment of history that they were hoping to help make. They had the benefit of witnessing the early days of the student-led southern movement, whose vision and practice seemed to be a living embodiment of participatory democracy. Indeed, for those of us at Port Huron, that experience—embodied by the Student Nonviolent Coordinating Committee (SNCC) workers in attendance, such as Chuck McDew, Maria Varela, Bob Zellner, and Casey Hayden—provided the flesh-and-blood evidence for the radical vision inscribed in the previously quoted passages.

Looking for Political Strategy

The *Port Huron Statement* was much more of a manifesto than a guide to political action. But a second SDS statement, adopted at its 1963 convention and called "America and the New Era," did offer a more politically strategic outlook. That document (which I helped draft) argued that the main political threat to democratic possibility in the United States was not the traditional right but rather the consolidation of a highly flexible reformism by the dominant political, corporate, and institutional elites, typified in the early 1960s by the Kennedys and figures ranging from progressive industrialists like IBM's Tom Watson to mandarin intellectuals such as Arthur Schlesinger Jr., John Kenneth Galbraith, and Robert McNamara (first of Ford Motor Company and an Ann Arbor resident, then of the US Department of Defense, and still later head of the World Bank). It was a point that Mills had already anticipated in *The Power Elite*, in which he argued that the national elites had appropriated liberal rhetoric and accommodation to the welfare state to justify their policies. His analysis was greatly extended by students at the University of Wisconsin under the tutelage of William Appleman Williams. The Madison work, much of it first published in *Studies on the Left*, launched in 1959, argued that, early in the twentieth century, a "corporate liberalism" constituted the ideology and praxis of key business leaders and their intellectual allies. Their purpose was to blunt grassroots protest through a combination of moderate reform, timely concession, and subtle repression, and the same perspective had been utilized to justify and advance American global empire. SDSers and others in the early New Left observed that the same strategy was being applied by the Kennedys to channel and contain the southern civil rights struggle.

As defined by the early New Left, corporate liberalism referred to the emergence of an advanced, bureaucratically organized technique and expertise to anticipate discontent and engineer consent. Participatory democracy provided the basis for a moral and practical critique of corporate liberalism. That critique was embodied in the manifestoes of SDS as well as in the eloquence and activism of SNCC in the Black Belt, insisting on a political voice for the poor as an integral feature of welfare state reform, challenging the legitimacy of top-down styles of leadership, and making use of civil disobedience and direct action alongside efforts to use the ballot box. "Let the people decide" was the slogan of struggles in both the South and North. In September 1964, the Free Speech Movement (FSM) at the University of California, Berkeley, challenged what it explicitly labeled corporate-liberal management of the "multiversity." Indeed, university president Clark Kerr, the liberal, prolabor theorist of managerial capitalism came to symbolize much of what FSM sought to challenge. In the mid-1960s, the SDS organizing efforts in poor communities of the North aimed to create community unions of the poor to challenge the bureaucratic welfare state and emerging corporate partnership with urban political machines.

"America and the New Era" saw such "new insurgency" as the key to a strategy for change. Not only might such an insurgency compel democratization of public institutions and state bureaucracies, but it also might help transform the global position of the United States: "A serious effort by serious men attacking our domestic problems with the pressure of a popular movement behind them would be nothing less than a reordering of priorities for our society . . . [It] would require a vast shift of resources away from the arms race and away from efforts to implement an American Grand Design on the world . . . The poor and dispossessed could force a cessation of the arms race. The objective meaning of their demands . . . would be to make continued support for massive military programs untenable."[2]

We assumed that what some have called the welfare-warfare state was going to continue to be the governing model for the ruling elites. Both the warfare and welfare aspects of the equation contributed to a Keynesian framework for government-corporate partnership that would stave off economic depression, promote technological development, and maintain full employment and growth. It was a working recipe for US global domination and domestic stability. The strategic and moral stance of the New Left was to challenge this model, in part because its benefits were distributed inequitably but more fundamentally because it was inherently a framework for an increasingly bureaucratic, authoritarian state. We certainly supported further development of the welfare state—as promised by President Lyndon B. Johnson's War on Poverty, Medicare, federal investment in education, and other Great Society measures. But our strategy was to press not only for "more" public sector benefits but also for democratic participation and community control of such programs for the building up of grassroots self-organization (like the community unions SDS sponsored in northern poor neighborhoods) and for democratic governance of social institutions (starting with "student power" in the schools).

We had reason to hope that by initiating such grassroots organizing in the spirit of SNCC, established labor and liberal leadership would be moved to support such movement building. One start along this line was made by the United Auto Workers (UAW), which began a program to support organization of community unions. This soon was incorporated into the War on Poverty as the federally funded Community Action Program, headed by veteran UAW staffer Jack Conway. Religious institutions were also interested (the Catholic church had for some years been a key sponsor of the Saul Alinsky neighborhood organization efforts). The federal War on Poverty legislation included requirements for "maximum feasible participation" of the poor in antipoverty programs—language that gave considerable leverage in some cities for grassroots organization and leadership development.[3] Meanwhile, the Welfare Rights Organization, sparked by sociologist Richard Cloward's analysis of the potential power of the poor, was mobilizing welfare mothers to claim their entitled benefits and to democratize welfare offices. The authoritarian character of the welfare state and its marked budgetary constraints were creating the space and the impetus for a movement that would seek to move beyond its confines and become a force for economic as well as social democracy.

Meanwhile, the southern movement, one hundred years after emancipation, was finally achieving its immediate goal. The federal government was now compelled to enforce the Constitution in the Deep South, ending all forms of legalized segregation, pushing for desegregation, and protecting the right to vote. The political enfranchisement of southern blacks was about to be achieved. Johnson's War on Poverty was at least a token appreciation that the struggle for equality was shifting toward economic justice and opportunity and that its terrain would be national rather than regional. The promise and the weakness of the Great Society programs were soon dramatized by explosive urban rebellions all across the country. These rebellions for a time spurred some elite support for an expanding public sector, expressed in the Kerner Commission and other elite "reports" advocating structural change and public investment (as well as more effective policing). For the New Left, the promises made in this fashion provided further impetus for grassroots organizing. Self-organization of minority and poor communities seemed increasingly possible and promising, with experiments and ideas swirling for new forms of enterprise and new political leadership to challenge entrenched urban machines and power structures. The expression of these efforts took many forms, most visibly in varieties of "nationalism" and a rhetoric that, by the later 1960s, was often wildly inflamed.

In long retrospect, the thread of participatory democracy ties together a great deal of the movement upsurge throughout the decade. And—to emphasize my starting point for this historical recollection—all of this was based on the assumption, then taken for granted, that the welfare-warfare state was inherent to corporate liberal public policy. Our job was to find the means to create an authentically democratic alternative.

The concept of "corporate liberalism" turned out to be an inadequate guide to either the ideology or the politics of the US ruling class. Even when the warfare-welfare state was evidently flourishing in the 1950s and 1960s, the ruling elites were probably more deeply divided on the welfare state than it appeared to us then. Clark Kerr, for example, never held the confidence of California's business elite, and even as he fought student radicals at Berkeley, he was the object of investigation and defamation by J. Edgar Hoover's FBI.

The corporate liberal paradigm began to unravel in the early 1970s as the relative prosperity that had characterized American capitalism in the early postwar decades was replaced by a far harsher economic climate. Major US-based corporations faced new global competition and sought to reduce labor costs. At the same time, costs of financing both a warfare and welfare budget were increasingly resisted by corporate elites. Contrary to SDS hopes in the mid-1960s, it was warfare rather than welfare that was preferred by the power centers of the corporate elite.

As the 1960s turned into the 1970s, the alleged liberalism of corporate elites was being replaced by a turn away from the welfare state and corporate-labor collaboration and toward a more classic commitment to state-assisted profit maximization—what many would later call "neoliberalism." By the 1980s, the once moribund far right had been restored to political viability, and Ronald Reagan's election as president (something that would have been thought unimaginable a decade earlier) helped crystallize a drive to roll back the welfare state.

Accordingly, many of the political activists who had grown up in the early New Left turned their energies to a defense of welfare state policies they had once thought both oppressive and inadequate. Likewise, they sought to defend or restore a social contract that, in the 1960s, they had believed to be a source of elite collaboration and managerial hegemony.

In the decades since Reagan's advent, being "left" in the United States has come to represent advocacy and action on behalf of "government" as a necessary vehicle for promoting equity and the regulation of "private" activity in the broad public interest.

In these years, the left has been defined, first of all, by support for equal rights for marginalized and subordinated social identities: demands for full equality between the sexes, for gay rights, and for advancement and protection of rights of racial/ethnic minorities. In the 1960s, the New Left tried to envision how such struggles would go beyond goals of inclusion and integration by inspiring cultural revolution—transformation of consciousness and values. In recent years, inclusion and integration and a more modest vision of multicultural mutuality defines left political discourse on these matters.

A multicultural United States seems within reach because a successful politics of inclusion has achieved major victories in policy and in the hearts and minds of the American majority. This, however, does not match the cultural revolution SDS had imagined—one that would challenge corporate values and bureaucratic institutions. That vision is now hardly remembered.

The second defining theme of the contemporary left revolves around defending and completing what in the United States is thought of as the "New Deal agenda" and in Europe is labeled "social democracy." Veterans of the 1960s New Left have taken the lead in staunchly defending Social Security and other established components of the social wage against the intense and heavily financed drive to reduce the safety net for the aged, the unemployed, and the poor. In the 1960s and 1970s, some SDS veterans went on to lead labor organizing, especially among public-sector workers; gains made by such unions are now prime targets of conservative attacks. Meanwhile, millions of people who graduated from college in the heyday of student activism embarked on careers in public service. The sixties students who envisioned, with both fear and hope, some kind of revolutionary apocalypse went on to serve in the front lines of social amelioration. They became schoolteachers and social workers, urban planners and government staffers, public interest lawyers, community organizers, public health educators, nurses, and nonprofit administrators—working in public agencies or creating their own NGOs with the conscious purpose of combining their hope to make a better world with some means of livelihood. But as economic growth stalled and the fiscal crisis intensified, their work entailed helping people cope and thereby helping maintain a fraying social order. These are people who were experiencing firsthand what the right-wing agenda meant for the society and for people's lives. Instead of a language of revolution, the New Left generation learned how to justify and explain the welfare state and to initiate and support politically possible reforms that would make its institutions more effective and life a bit more livable for working people as corporate and financial elites were undertaking a new class war.

Thus 1960s activists who had begun as sharp critics of the national state of bureaucratic labor unions and liberal lobbies and had dreamed of a democratic march through the institutions of society have devoted their minds and hearts, out of necessity, to a struggle to defend those institutions. As a result, some key institutions are in fact more democratic and leftward today than they had been forty years ago. Likewise, despite the numerical shrinkage of organized labor, the union political and social agenda is now far more inclusive and progressive, in part because some sixties activists ascended to top leadership positions in the labor movement. University curricula are, in our time, far more reflective of the cultural and social impacts of social movements, and university policies regarding admissions, governance, and staffing are far more inclusive than at the time of the 1960s student revolt. Mass media, despite corporate consolidation, are far more culturally and ideologically pluralistic because of the ways the Internet and other technological developments have created forms of media access and usage that undermine corporate control. In many communities, a more genuinely pluralist politics has developed, in part because of the thousands of post-1960s activists who embedded themselves and organized within towns and cities once thought to be bastions of conservative culture and business domination. At the same time, the new social movements of the 1970s and 1980s—especially feminism, lesbian, gay, bisexual, and transgender (LGBT) rights, and environmentalism—have become established centers of political influence locally and nationally. And most importantly, demographic change coinciding with grassroots organizing and activism has provided the basis for a new majority coalition whose base is nonwhite, nonmale, and "millennial." This is the coalition that elected an African American president, and its potential numerical strength is growing.

A political history of the last few decades, when it is written, will therefore note not only the rightward turn of the corporate elite, and accordingly of national public policy, but also the ways that some of the institutional aims first charted at Port Huron have, in fact, continued to be advanced by forms of political activism and cultural expression rooted in the movements of the 1960s. The ideologically defensive posture of today's lefts—and not only in the United States—has meant, however, that there is lately little left-wing capacity to articulate larger societal and institutional alternatives. Even if the antiglobalization movement carries banners reading "another world is possible," it is hard now to find ideas about what that other world might look like.

Participatory Democracy as Cognitive Praxis

Fifty years later, the central theme of the *Port Huron Statement* remains, I think, highly relevant to any effort to redefine a radical vision and program.

It is often claimed that the New Left conceived of participatory democracy as the fostering of small-group, face-to-face interaction as its political ideal—and therefore failed to figure out how to make participatory democracy a basis for practical action at the national and global level. But such notions miss a great deal about the thinking and practices of new social movements during the last several decades as well as about the discourse at Port Huron and in the early New Left more broadly.

Some of us Port Huron veterans have always resented the conflation of participatory democracy with methods of decision making internal to movement organizations. That issue has certainly been an important one since the 1960s, revived recently by the group processes used by Occupy Wall Street and its offshoots, which resulted in a great deal of debate within and criticism of the Occupy movement. But the *Port Huron Statement*'s uses of the term, in fact, referred to society and its institutions. The intention was to provide a framework useful for the articulation of core values and defining features of social transformation.

In the years since, the term itself—and the social relations it condenses—continued to animate a wide range of social movements and programs.

Participatory democracy, in the first instance, points to impulses and ways of thinking that seem to come naturally when people in large numbers step out of their daily routines and private lives and join together to challenge conditions and make demands. By naming those impulses as expressions of a participatory democratic vision, those who challenge authority are able to frame their claims and grievances not only in particular and immediate terms but also as part of a more universal struggle for human emancipation. In the last few years, seemingly local mass occupations and uprisings are understood by many involved in them as expressions of a global democratization process. Indeed, the language of participatory democracy seems to enable international solidarity far more than the language of socialism and class struggle once promised to do. It speaks for commonalities among uprisings rooted in very different religious, ethnic, racial, class, and generational identities.

But the uses of participatory democracy as a foundation for constructing societal alternatives go well beyond the rhetorical. Participatory democracy provides a standard by which existing social arrangements can be judged and criticized. It calls on us to push for arrangements that allow for voice, for direct participation or empowerment, and not just for security or equity. It poses questions such as these: To what extent do those affected by decisions and operations have a voice in governance? To what extent are the rules by which members' activity is controlled set by them? To what extent are members free to express dissent or challenge institutional authority?

In our time, the legitimation of institutional authority structures depends on providing some semblance of a democratic response to such questions. Established authority is particularly vulnerable to questions about voice and participation because even small groups can take actions that make such questions potent. These questions serve as guides for activists and organizers in the practice of making transformational demands. They inspire and sustain action and help shape the substance of structural reform. They are, in short, stimuli for envisioning how and why another world is possible.

One should provide a detailed listing of concrete examples of these points. Instead of such a list, I want to refer to the work of two intellectuals who are documenting (and theorizing about) a vision, strategy, and program rooted in principles of participatory democracy. In both cases, a youthful connection with SDS had some significance in inspiring their current projects. Both projects are ambitious and yet have received little attention in the media of both mainstream and left-wing awareness. Looking at their work will prove rewarding for those wondering how participatory democracy has played out in the practice and potential of community-based activism.

Erik Olin Wright, recently president of the American Sociological Association, began a project in the 1990s to develop systematic thinking about alternative institutional models and strategies. This is the "Real Utopias Project," which is described this way: "The basic idea is to combine serious normative discussions of the underlying principles and rationales for different emancipatory visions with the analysis of pragmatic problems of institutional design." Based in the University of Wisconsin sociology department, the project has published six books and a number of conferences, resulting in a wealth of studies and ideas and providing material for revitalizing visionary politics. How to enable this material to be utilized by activists and organizers is, of course, a continuing problem.[4]

More politically and strategically focused are efforts led by Gar Alperovitz, one of SDS's early mentors, to describe and promote locally based initiatives that go "beyond capitalism" by democratizing wealth and fostering social enterprises at a local level. Alperovitz argues that it is unlikely that capitalism can be reformed simply by hoping to win electoral and legislative gains at the national level. Corporate power at national and global levels captures the state and promotes austerity. But he is hopeful that deepening economic and environmental crises are compelling a search for alternatives. He sees many promising efforts actually happening below the radar. Important examples include community and public banks, participatory budgeting, community development strategies that promote local stability and reinvestment, worker-owned enterprises and consumer cooperatives, and environmental rules that force corporate producers to pay for toxic waste they create. He has embarked on an ambitious effort to promote these ideas. His most recent book, *What Then Must We Do?*, is deliberately designed to reach progressive activists with a usable intellectual framework and concrete ideas for transformational action—ideas rooted in the democratization of wealth and community empowerment.[5]

These projects have documented the many ways that the dream of the early New Left for a worldwide democratization movement has shaped much of the history of the last half-century. These projects are also fulfillments of the *Port Huron Statement*'s call for people housed in universities to provide some of the theorizing, the information, the language, and the space for imagining and experimenting with possibilities for alternative institutional and community structures and processes.

If we wrote the history of the last fifty years in the United States and globally in terms of the theme of democratization, such a history might reveal that more democratic gain has been won in this half-century than is usually acknowledged. And such a history might help identify the intellectual and political strategies needed for possible breakthroughs. Perhaps the celebration of the *Statement*'s fiftieth anniversary will further advance that project. Speaking as a veteran of Port Huron, I of course hope so.

34 | The Wisconsin Uprising and Women's Power: Report from Madison[*]
by Mari Jo Buhle and Paul Buhle

As the historian looks at things, the present is always history in the making. In a deeply personal sense, we look back at the Wisconsin Uprising of 2011 as one of the most exciting moments of our time. As an extended phase of social mobilization, it was important in itself, but it was also fascinating because it both reminded us of and so starkly contrasted with the mobilizations some forty years before.

Teaching Assistants' Association rally at the state capitol, Madison, Wisconsin, February 14, 2012. Peter Patau (Creative Commons)

---

[*]Portions of this essay appeared in a different form in Mari Jo Buhle, "Women and Power in the Wisconsin Uprising," *Dissent*, Winter 2013, 70–73. Reprinted with permission of the University of Pennsylvania Press.

467

When Wisconsin governor Scott Walker opened his assault on collective bargaining in February 2011, few people realized it would open the door not only to stirring protests but also, in their wake, to the 2012 election of Tammy Baldwin, the first woman to represent Wisconsin in the Senate and the first openly gay senator in US history. She had been backed by many women's organizations since her first run for Congress in 1998, but Walker's successful attempt to roll back the collective bargaining rights of three hundred sixty thousand public-sector workers brought together an unprecedented coalition of labor and women's groups behind her.

Walker's bill, the 2011 Wisconsin Act 10, also called the "Budget Repair Bill," exempted some unions—those of safety workers, the police, state troopers, and firefighters—whose members were mainly men. Instead, it focused on unions where women predominated: teachers, health workers, and public-sector clerical workers. Nationally, by 2011, women represented 57 percent of the public-sector workforce. More than 80 percent of teachers, nationally and in Wisconsin, were female, and 90 percent at the elementary level were women. In 2010, there were 54,510 registered nurses employed in Wisconsin; 95 percent of them were women.

Women unionists quickly took their place at the forefront of the 2011 Wisconsin Uprising. The president of the Wisconsin branch of the National Education Association, the Wisconsin Education Association Council, set up a phone bank and e-mail system and reached out to other unions, including those in the private sector. The American Federation of State, County, and Municipal Employees (AFSCME), representing sixty-eight thousand members, started running busses to Madison from distant parts of the state. Meanwhile, Madison Teachers Inc., the city's major union in education, considered its options. On Wednesday, February 16, 2011, as protesters were filling the capitol rotunda, about half of Madison's forty-seven hundred teachers called in "sick" so they could join the demonstrations at the statehouse.

The teachers—as well as health workers—objected most strenuously to the de facto destruction of their power to negotiate nonwage terms of their contracts as they had for decades. Excluded from bargaining, then, were workplace issues such curriculum, class size, schedules, and support staff—in short, the daily life of the classroom.

Huge contingents of students showed up—not so much college students as middle- and high-school students. They marched miles to Capitol Square, interspersing chants of "We are the students, the mighty, mighty students!" with cries of "Union power!"

Alongside the unions, members of women's organizations entered the fray. Prominent was Planned Parenthood of Wisconsin, which early on recognized Walker's longstanding opposition to reproductive rights. Amanda Harrington, the organization's spokesperson, had reviewed Walker's nine-year record as a member of the Wisconsin Assembly and correctly concluded that he would act aggressively to show "across the board opposition to women's health" and fulfill his long-standing anti-choice agenda.[1] Harrington was joined by members of the Wisconsin Alliance for Women's Health and 9to5 Milwaukee, a grassroots organization helping to shape policy making about the transition from welfare to paid labor. Members of the Wisconsin National Organization for Women also turned out in large numbers.

The protests continued as the "Recall Walker" movement shaped up. Women mobilized to collect nearly one million signatures supporting a new election to oust Walker from office. Nonetheless, throughout the protests and recall efforts, the significance of gender in the Wisconsin Uprising remained under the radar.

As we looked around in spring and summer 2011 at crowds gathered in Madison's Capitol Square, numbering as many as one hundred twenty-five thousand people—and at other big rallies held as late as spring 2012—we saw a large contingent of the sixties generation. It was rather like looking at ourselves, and not only because of the college-looking types on hand. Union retirees were heavy in number and celebrated by fellow unionists and the rest of us; considerable numbers came from neighboring states or distant northern zones of Wisconsin. Among the thousands of aging figures, quite a few had the 1960s demonstrator look, or at least we thought so. Perhaps it was because absolute strangers would say things such as "I've been waiting forty years for this" or even "If it never happens again, I'm happy to have lived long enough to see it."

During the great antiwar mobilization in Washington of April 1965, when we were in our twenties, we remember looking around at how many people around us looked *old*, or seemed to, in our eyes. Actually, they were veterans of the 1930s and 1940s social movements—some of them, amazingly, marching in their World War II military uniforms. It wasn't much like that in US antiwar demonstrations of the later 1960s, except in some big cities. There were always peaceniks working hard in the community here, and they could be found in Milwaukee, Waukesha, La Crosse, and Superior, especially as the public views of the war changed and blue-collar America turned against continuing the invasion of Vietnam. But the Democratic Party—even most of its liberal edges, including the editorial board of Madison's *Capital Times*—disliked campus demonstrations at least as much as they disliked the war, and they did nothing to encourage the Movement, except to urge calm until the next election. Mostly, at that time, we were the young, the restless, and the longhaired—not to mention the smell of marijuana and the sounds of antiwar music coming from the neighborhoods just off the University of Wisconsin campus.

Coming back to Wisconsin 2011 and our moment in the sun, it is surely impossible to overestimate the multigenerational nature of the crowds: women in their nineties being pushed by their daughters or granddaughters and babes in arms, perhaps our strongest defense against the threat of official or unofficial violence.

It is likewise impossible to exaggerate how unsixties this made us feel, in the sense that we were not a bunch of antiwar and antiracist youngsters cut off from the bulk of an older population. Back then, Madison was the place many Wisconsinites, particularly rural and suburban, looked upon as the epicenter of sin, sodomy, and socialism. But now, we—the crowds of 2011—looked normal to us.

One year later, though, the broader Republican agenda had become even bolder and clearer. By the winter and spring of 2012, women's rights were evidently at the center of things, not only in Wisconsin, but in many of the states that had a solidly Republican majority in their legislatures. Republican legislators introduced bills cutting or eliminating funds for family planning programs; allowing employers to deny health insurance coverage for contraception for religious reasons; requiring mandatory transvaginal ultrasounds for women seeking abortions; and introducing "personhood" amendments that defined life as beginning with conception (or, in a proposed Arizona bill, two weeks before conception), thereby jeopardizing *Roe v. Wade*. As women began to mobilize against what came to be known as the GOP's "War on Women," the leadership of women and the significance of gender in the protest movement became more visible.

Almost immediately after taking office, Walker had targeted Planned Parenthood. His "Budget Repair Bill," which passed finally in June 2011, blocked state and federal funds from going to any of Planned Parenthood's twenty-seven health centers around the state, which had served seventy-three thousand women annually. These new restrictions cut off general health care, not abortion services, which were already barred from receiving public funds.

In December 2011, Walker targeted the Wisconsin Well Woman Program, which for seventeen years had provided uninsured women aged forty-five to sixty-four with no-cost screenings for breast and cervical cancer and multiple sclerosis. Administered by the state Department of Health Services, the program had contracted with Planned Parenthood, which then became, in four counties, the only provider available to approximately one thousand women. Walker decided to end this relationship.

Wisconsin joined Indiana, Kansas, and North Carolina to become the fourth state to enact such legislation. The Guttmacher Institute, which collects data on this subject, reported that in 2011, in the fifty states combined, legislators introduced more than eleven hundred reproductive health- and rights-related provisions, nearly 70 percent of them intended to restrict access to abortion services.[2]

These bills went far beyond abortion policy: they reined in sex education in the public schools. Wisconsin was one of several state legislatures that passed bills including "abstinence only" clauses. In Wisconsin's case, individual school districts could choose to inform students of contraceptive methods but were required to state that abstinence is the preferred and only truly effective means of preventing pregnancy.

A Wisconsin state senator introduced Senate Bill 507, a measure designed to "emphasize nonmarital parenthood as a contributing factor in child abuse and neglect." Wisconsin Republicans also rolled back the mechanisms for women to file claims against employers for wage discrimination.

Thanks to the investigatory work of the Madison-based Center for Media and Democracy, many are aware that the uncanny similarity among the bills being introduced in state legislatures nationwide stems from the relationship between legislators and the American Legislative Exchange Council (ALEC), which was founded in the mid-1970s to provide Republicans with drafts of model legislation. ALEC-drafted bills included voter identification, concealed carry, right-to-work laws, bans on collective bargaining for public employees, the loosening of charter school regulation, rollbacks on environmental protections, and a host of other probusiness policies. Although Walker denies it, his "Budget Repair Bill" and many other measures passed in the 2011–12 Wisconsin legislative session drew directly from ALEC's template.

At its meeting in December 2011, some six months after the Wisconsin Uprising, ALEC presented its members with a package of six model bills restricting women's reproductive rights, and these bills continue to make their way through various legislatures. The chief GOP sponsors in Arizona and Virginia—the states that have passed the most dramatic bills—are high-level ALEC functionaries. In fact, David and Charles Koch, the petrochemicals tycoons notorious for their vast contributions to diverse conservative causes, have invested heavily in ALEC. That association is telling. Women's health, it turns out, is not merely a "social issue"—it's an economic one, under direct attack from organized labor's biggest enemy.

Thus, during spring 2012, women who had mobilized in the Wisconsin Uprising took an openly feminist stance against the "War on Women."

Through Facebook, Twitter, and several key blogs, particularly Unite-Women.org, women followed the developments in the states where Republicans held legislative majorities and began to organize as women. UniteWomen sponsored more than fifty events nationwide and encouraged women to vote in the fall elections. In Wisconsin on March 13, about six hundred women quickly mobilized at the state capitol to protest the Wisconsin legislation that effectively took abortion coverage out of the Obamacare insurance exchange. Their "Mad as Hell Rally" was called by Planned Parenthood under the slogan "Women Watch, Women Rally, Women Vote" with the support of a broad alliance of health professionals and advocates. On that day, the Republican-controlled state assembly brought up for a vote several measures to further curtail abortion rights and to end comprehensive sex education in schools. By this point, recall efforts begun by the Wisconsin Uprising had successfully narrowed the Republican edge in the state Senate, and the "Recall Walker" campaign was in full swing—leading to the disappointing June 5 loss by Democratic Milwaukee mayor Tom Barrett as Walker beat the recall.

Still, there was momentum. By fall 2012, a neighboring state provided another example of the ability of women working in the public sector to push back. More than 76 percent of Chicago teachers are women. As successors to the nation's first teachers-only union, founded in 1897, and to the nation's first teachers' strike, waged in 1902, Chicago teachers attracted nationwide attention when they walked out and won a new contract that included pay raises and a new evaluation system. The Chicago teachers' strike in September also showed the power and leadership of Karen Lewis, a unionist known for her street-fighting smarts and her determination to block Mayor Rahm Emanuel's plan to take over the Chicago public school system and pave the way for privatization. In Wisconsin, public-sector unions found common ground with their Illinois counterparts. Wisconsin teachers rallied in Madison and Milwaukee to show solidarity and then went by bus to Chicago's lake front to join what was described as a "Wisconsin-style rally."

On November 6, 2012, the enthusiasm of the election-night gathering of Senate hopeful Tammy Baldwin's supporters could hardly be contained. Thousands massed to watch the results, cheering for every state called for Obama and going wild when Ohio fell into line. By this time, Baldwin led in the Wisconsin polls, but her opponent, former governor Tommy Thompson, would not accept defeat and delayed conceding. Finally, he had to admit the triumph of the woman his campaign repeatedly maligned as "the most liberal member of Congress." Baldwin was gracious in accepting her victory but did not back down. She had run on a pledge to represent the powerless against powerful interests and now stepped to center stage. "Make no mistake," she shouted over the raucous crowd, "I am a proud Wisconsin progressive."

The rest of Wisconsin proved not so progressive, lining up once again with other purple states. Although Obama and Baldwin won, Republicans took back the state legislature, overturning the gains made with the earlier recall elections. The new Republican redistricting map, along with huge campaign chests, took some of the luster off the moment.

On that front, we were defeated in much the same way that the most democratic and radical impulses of the 1960s and 1970s were defeated. Due to the Wisconsin Uprising, the state's Democrats were prodded forward, and some of them boldly took the initiative and deserve credit for opposing Walker. But then the normalizing power of big money, along with the dull, unidealistic, unappealing, centrist quality of what can be called the "business Democrats," failed to offer the kind of alternative that might have won the Walker recall and shifted the political momentum of the state in another direction.

Our movement was not large enough to encompass the thirteen poorest counties of the state, whose voters chose Walker at the cost of endangering the public schools and health services that they urgently needed. The voice of Rush Limbaugh and the television ads in football season—paid for by the Koch Brothers—were more powerful than anything we had to offer. It wasn't 1932. The system had not failed dramatically; it was only wound down from factory towns to ex-factory towns, and Tom Barrett, running against Walker in spring 2012, was no Franklin Roosevelt, to say the least.

The Wisconsin Uprising was an extraordinary exercise in popular democracy. It brought back to mind Obama's extraordinary popularity in 2008 and the sense that a different America was possible. But it also brought back countless smaller efforts, from support movements for Third World struggles to ecological initiatives (halting an open-pit mine adjoining Indian lands was one of the last big, short-term effects of the 2011 mobilization) to student struggles. The chancellor of the University of Wisconsin had conspired with the new governor to protect our institution to the detriment of others in the state and also at the expense of the teaching assistants' association, which was as much as abolished. And she had worked to militarize the Madison campus, bringing Pentagon-related cash and personnel. We protesters were, as in 1968, struggling to save the university and surrounding community from corruption and subtle devastation, and that struggle continues.

Despite the setbacks that followed, the mobilization to stop the GOP's

"War on Women" brought feminist activism to the center of US politics in a way not seen since the 1970s. Much remains to be done. Baldwin presented herself as a candidate who has fought for justice and equality for women not only in the United States but throughout the world. And she had a record to back her claim, having represented Wisconsin in Congress for fourteen years. As a member of the Congressional Caucus on Women's Issues, she focused on pay equity, domestic violence, reproductive rights, and women's health care. She won her Senate race with a 10 percent gender gap. She is now one of a record number of twenty women elected to the Senate. But as she said at her election-night victory party, she entered this campaign not to make history but to make a difference.

35 | Democracy and the Arab Upheavals of 2011 and After

by Juan Cole

The progressive youth movements that staged the 2010–13 political up-heavals in the Arab world had increased democracy as one of their goals. They were reacting against the widespread systems of authoritarian elections in the Arab world and aiming for more democratic polls. They did not, for the most part, however, merely have in mind Joseph Schumpeter's notion of procedural democracy, in which there are regular multiparty elections, the losers go home, and elected elites make the decisions without much further public input. Rather, their slogan was "bread, liberty, and social justice." Most of them were social democrats or democratic socialists, and they saw free and fair elections as a means to greater social and economic equity. Some developed a Jeffersonian vision of democracy, inflected by Leon Trotsky, of continued popular pressure and street action as a contributor to the political process along with elections.[1] The youth leaders hoped to initiate a transition to democracy, but the following three years saw that aspiration meet with substantial disappointments. What made for greater or lesser success in these transitions?[2]

The youth movements of 2010–13 were diverse, but left-of-center groups with a vague Marxist or proworker orientation took the lead in many countries. In Egypt, the proworker April 6 Youth Movement was an important player, as were the Trotskyite Revolutionary Socialists. Other liberal and Muslim fundamentalist organizations played a role as well. In Tunisia, the nationwide *Union Général des Étudiants de Tunisie* (UGET) university student union had many leftist leaders at the provincial level. The masses of youth who demonstrated at Tahrir Square in Cairo or on Habib Bourguiba Avenue in Tunis were not themselves, for the most part, movement activists, and many did not have a strong set of democratic

values; rather, their main aspiration was to see positive economic and political change. The opinion leaders and organizers, however, did tend to be
democrats.

Most Arab states are either monarchies or authoritarian republics.
Most of them hold elections, but before 2011 (and in many cases after),
these were "authoritarian elections" that functioned as pageantry advertis-
ing the regime's power, handed out patronage to favorites, and sometimes
provided a safety valve to regime challengers deemed moderate and un-
threatening.[3]

Authoritarian elections, held one after another for decades, however,
can have the opposite of the safety-valve effect their sponsors hope for. In
Egypt, one of the impetuses for the 2011 mass demonstrations was the way
in which the government of longtime dictator Hosni Mubarak (in power
1981–2011) stole the parliamentary elections of November 2010. His National Democratic Party, which functioned as a vehicle for the president's
political cronyism, almost completely shut out the opposition, in contrast
to the very slightly more open elections of 2005, when eighty-eight members of the Muslim Brotherhood and some twenty leftists and independents were elected to a parliament of roughly 450 members. Young Egyptians wrote that after videos circulated of police openly stuffing ballots
during the 2010 election, they despaired of change.

Protests broke out in most of the twenty-two states of the Arab League in
2011. Even where they had little long-lasting political impact, as in Jordan
or Algeria, they often involved large numbers of youth and extensive demonstrations. In Morocco, youth groups, leftists, and Muslim fundamentalists, inspired by Tunisia and Libya, began protesting in northern cities on
February 20, 2011. They were unable to reach a critical mass but could
sometimes bring four to six thousand people into the streets in any one
city and as many as one hundred thousand nationwide. Some demanded
an overthrow of the king, Mohammed VI (r. 1999–), and these were put
down violently. Others saw the then ruling loyalist party, the Party of Authenticity and Modernity (PAM), as corrupt and wanted it dissolved.

The Moroccan protests led to a significant overhaul of the constitution,
overwhelmingly ratified by a popular referendum in summer 2011. Hence-
forward, the king would appoint the prime minister from the largest party
in parliament. (Before, he could appoint a technocrat if no party had a
majority.) The power to dissolve parliament was invested in the prime
minister instead of the king. Freedom of speech and of the press was guaranteed, at least on paper, and the rights of women and minorities were

made explicit. The king retains substantial power as commander in chief of the armed forces and the intelligence services, and he approves the cabinet and appoints judges to the judiciary and ambassadors. Reformists were not satisfied with the new constitution, which was crafted by a council appointed by the court, but it did take steps toward a more democratic system.[4] The nationwide demonstrations helped discredit PAM and its leadership. In the parliamentary elections of November 2011, the religiously inflected Muslim Justice and Development Party (French acronym PJD) received 27 percent of the seats and became the largest single party. It went into coalition with the Koutla, a coalition of three secular parties. This outcome of a party of the religious right forming the government in coalition with secular nationalist and leftist parties was also seen in postrevolutionary Tunisia.

Youth activists feel that they failed in their quest to make Morocco a constitutional monarchy.[5] In contrast, King Mohammed VI's new constitution convinced many Moroccans to give the new system a chance, undercutting the activists. The new freedoms, however, were observed more on paper than in practice. The regime followed, harassed, or jailed members of the February 20 movement who continued to launch trenchant criticisms of the court or the government on Facebook and Twitter; the government often broke up peaceful protests.[6] Still, the changes in the constitution gained by the youth protesters are not trivial.

In Tunisia, leftist and liberal student organizations and youth Internet activists effectively intervened in the political debate on several pivotal occasions after doing so much to overthrow Zine El Abidine Ben Ali on January 14, 2011.[7] On several occasions, youth mobilization and interventions were consequential. By repeated demonstrations at the Casbah square, they ensured that figures from the old regime were excluded from the transitional cabinet. Youth kept the pressure on the transitional team to hold elections for a constituent assembly in fall 2011, and they won that aim.

While subsequent high politics came to be dominated by the al-Nahda (Renaissance) Party, which is center-right and has Muslim religious commitments, the youth did not entirely demobilize. In the elections of October 2011, al-Nahda gained 42 percent of the seats but had to form a government in coalition with a secular liberal party, which was given the presidency, and a socialist proworker party, which was given the position of speaker of parliament. Critics charged that the religious right party dominated key cabinet posts and put its people in influential positions in media and the civil bureaucracy. Secular urban Tunisians often demonstrated and expressed unease at what they saw as a creeping Islamization of their society.

The national student union elections of spring 2012 saw a lively contest between leftist, secular students and supporters of the Islamist al-Nahda Party. The secularists won a crushing victory. Around the same time, al-Nahda renounced any attempt to enshrine the sharia or Muslim religious law in the new constitution that the assembly was crafting. Youth activism and protests reemerged in a big way after two political assassinations of prominent leftist politicians in 2013, putting pressure on the al-Nahda government to resign to pave the way for new elections.[8] In summer and fall 2013, youth sit-ins outside the parliament building at Bardo Palace in Tunis and elsewhere throughout the country kept the discontents visible. The protesters charged that the al-Nahda Party was soft on the small terrorist group Ansar al-Sharia, which was suspected in the assassinations and other violence. They also saw the ruling party as insufficiently committed to norms of freedom of speech and conscience.

The youth demonstrators and citizen journalists allied with the General Union of Tunisian Workers. By September 2013, the ruling al-Nahda Party agreed in principle to step down in favor of a technocratic government of national unity. By early January, al-Nahda had actually followed through. The text of the new constitution crafted by the constituent assembly (which doubled as a parliament) was approved by a majority in that body in January 2014. Had any articles not passed, the whole text would have gone to a national referendum, but the compromises made inside the constituent assembly had been sufficient to forestall that possibly divisive outcome. A technocratic cabinet was installed to oversee elections for a full-term parliament, setting the stage for consolidation of the country's fledgling democracy.

The new constitution guarantees women's rights. It safeguards freedom of speech and conscience. Internet censorship, the bane of youth activists under the Ben Ali dictatorship, was abolished. Political parties can be formed freely, as can trade unions, and the right to strike has been upheld. Youth demonstrations and the labor unions, along with women's and other nongovernmental organizations, vigorously lobbied for the more progressive articles of the constitution. Studies show that a persistent economic downturn in the five years after a democratic transition begins is often fatal for the success of that transition.[9] In this case, despite a crisis in 2011, Tunisia saw nearly 3 percent growth in 2013, and foreign investment was up. High youth unemployment, especially of educated young people, remained a significant problem.

* * *

In contrast to Tunisia, with its strong, longstanding urban institutions, Libyans had to reconstruct their country from scratch after the fall of the dictatorship of Muammar Gaddafi in August 2011.[10] The Gaddafi state had been fluid and personalistic—and deadly—to any political or civil society rivals. Local revolutionary committees loyal to the person of the dictator actively spied on the populace, assassinated critics, and ruled with an iron fist. For decades, private property was disallowed and remained constricted even after minor reforms beginning in the 1990s. There was no independent judiciary and few trained jurists. The military was dominated by ideological cadres and mercenaries willing to kill the people for Gaddafi.

The militarization of the anti-Gaddafi revolution was provoked by the regime's deployment of armor, artillery, and helicopter gunships against civilian noncombatant populations often guilty of no more than peaceably assembling in protest—and it left a deadly legacy to the transitional period. The country's third-largest city, Misrata, was besieged for half a year by tanks and artillery, which reduced the main avenue and the buildings along it to rubble and killed large numbers of children, women, and noncombatant men. The city's youth militia, some of them steelworkers at the major steel mill and others longshoremen at the port, used their specialized skills in mounting a defense, welding armored sides onto trucks or deploying moving equipment to place shipping containers in the path of tanks on the wider streets. In the aftermath, the Misrata militia took part in the invasion of the capital, Tripoli, and insisted on remaining mobilized there and making a claim on national resources, in part to compensate for what Misrata's denizens had lost and sacrificed. The Misrata militia turned toward political Islam, in contrast to that of Zintan, a western Arab city that also helped invade Tripoli in August 2011 but that tended to support more secular politicians.

Libya had a transitional government from fall 2011 until summer 2012, when the country held elections for a constituent assembly and parliament, charged with drafting a new constitution. Of two hundred seats, only eighty were set aside for party competition. Nationalist parties heavily won those constituencies, with the Muslim Brotherhood receiving only 10 percent of the vote. Many of the independents, however, supported political Islam, and the nationalists and religious forces were fairly evenly matched in the national legislature. The parliament elected nationalist Ali Zeidan as prime minister, but he proved a weak figure with little support from the militias, which still played an outsized role in the county.

The nationalists were weakened in parliament in May 2013, when militias successfully demanded that parliament members bar former members of the Gaddafi government from high office even if they had defected early in the revolution. This move forced out a secular speaker of the house and paved the way for a more pro–political Islam speaker of Berber heritage, Nouri Abusahmain. The Muslim fundamentalist bloc in parliament, however, found itself still short of a majority and made numerous attempts to unseat the secular, left-of-center prime minister, Ali Zeidan. He ultimately lost a vote of no confidence in February 2014, but not mainly because of ideological considerations. The General National Council (GNC), despite being widely seen as ineffectual and as having failed in its major charge of crafting a new constitution, voted in early 2014 to extend its mandate until late in that year. This move provoked repeated demonstrations all over the country, and by February 2014, the GNC appeared to agree to go to early elections and to consider ways of creating a stronger central government.[11]

The main problems in the consolidation of democracy in Libya derived not from the politics of the constituent assembly but from the inability of the government to create a new set of security forces after the collapse of the Gaddafi state apparatus. The militias formed in the revolution of 2011 declined to demobilize and were not successfully integrated into a military or police line of command. Factions of politicians in the GNC were beholden to militias the way US congressmen are often in lobbyists' back pockets. In November 2013, civilians demonstrating against militia lawlessness were attacked by the Misrata militia, provoking a political crisis that ultimately passed and left the Misratans still influential in the capital.[12] Militiamen often demanded stipends from the state, feeling that the nation owed them for their sacrifices. Some took public facilities hostage to secure these emoluments, including oil facilities. Although in 2012 Libya's oil production largely recovered to prerevolution levels of 1.5 million barrels a day, in 2013 it was cut to half or sometimes a third of that by militia actions at facilities and by strikes by oil workers who maintained that they had been working for slave wages under Gaddafi. A few facilities were also closed from time to time by autonomists from Benghazi who sought a loose federation of Libyan regions with greater decision making resting in the east, what was historically known as Cyrenaica. Libya also suffered from a small but significant terrorism problem, especially in the east, as extremist groups engaged in assassinations and bombings.

By early 2014, there were more than three thousand registered civil society organizations in Libya, whereas under Gaddafi there had been almost none. These groups were mainly staffed by youth and were devoted to a wide range of cultural and social goals, including improved rights for women, job training, minority rights, and the shaping of the new constitution.[13] As for the shortfall in oil production, it was outweighed by the substantial cushion Libya enjoyed because of the $120 billion in foreign currency reserves it held at the beginning of 2013. The government brought in about $40 billion in income in 2013, suffering a $10 billion shortfall compared to projected income because of separatist and other interference with oil fields. While the problem needs to be addressed, it did not threaten stability in and of itself in 2014.[14]

Libya's transition away from authoritarianism has been troubled. Consolidation of democracy starts becoming apparent when there are two successful elected governments in a row and the general rules of the political game achieve widespread recognition and consent. Three years after its revolution began, Libyans were far from achieving such a record. More than high politics, the big problems facing the new government were continued militia intransigence and the failure to build a new army and gendarmerie quickly enough to begin taking charge. A related problem was the way insecurity interfered with oil production and export, the profits of which are the major source of government income. Deep political divisions over nationalism versus Muslim fundamentalism made compromise difficult. Given the extreme authoritarianism of the long decades of Gaddafi rule and the lack of established institutions, it was predictable that Libya would have a hard ride back to stability after its revolution.

Yemen's is the only one of the democratic transitions leading to the fall of the old head of state that can be characterized as "pacted" (i.e., the result of a political bargain or pact among the country's elites when presented with a revolutionary situation, rather than deriving from an actual overthrow of the old regime).[15] Yemen had begun a political opening in the 1990s, holding multiparty elections. These elections were not considered entirely fair and never unseated the ruling General People's Congress (GPC) of President Ali Abdullah Saleh. Still, for instance, the ruling party received 58 percent of the vote in the parliamentary election of 2003 and faced competition from nineteen other parties and hundreds of independents. In particular, the Muslim fundamentalist party, Islah, supported by a number of important tribes, became well established. By the outbreak of the revolutionary youth movements in 2011, the long decades of dominance by the GPC and its president for life had produced substantial discontents. Youth conducted huge demonstrations and sit-ins at "Change Square" in Sanaa throughout 2011, despite having to face sniping and other regime violence.

Saleh initially declined to stand down. He was wounded in a bombing in June but received treatment for extensive burns in Saudi Arabia, then coming back as president. Ultimately, the Gulf oil monarchies conducted successful negotiations with him, and in January 2012, Saleh finally stepped down as president. His vice president, Abed Rabbo Mansour Hadi, became president and submitted himself to a nationwide referendum on the change in February 2012, when 80 percent of the electorate voted positively. Mansour Hadi formed a government of national unity, giving about half of the cabinet seats to the Joint Meeting Parties, the opposition coalition. Members of the revolutionary youth organizations complained that they were not offered cabinet seats despite their key role in the transition. The GPC continued to dominate parliament, and Saleh remained chairman of the party, which gave him substantial continued power.

In November 2013, Mansour Hadi began a national dialogue conference aimed at finding compromises to some of the most contention issues facing the country in preparation for new elections in 2014. In part as a result of the dialogue and in the face of longstanding severe regional conflicts with the center, he announced early in 2014 that Yemen would become a federal state with six regions. Observers worried that some of these regions might attempt to become all but autonomous, weakening the central state further.[16]

Yemen's political transition has been a series of hard-won bargains. There was more violence in 2011 around the demand that Saleh step down than in the similar tumult in Egypt and Tunisia, but it was on a relatively small scale. Even Saleh's injury in a bombing was not politically decisive. His January 2012 resignation paved the way for a national unity government and a weak transitional president who, despite his relative lack of power, did take steps to remove Saleh's relatives from key governmental and military positions (a demand of the revolutionaries). If the next multiparty elections are held in a free and fair manner, the new government could achieve legitimacy.

Unfortunately, Yemen's greatest problems are not narrowly political and not closely related to the makeup of the cabinet or parliament. It is the poorest Arabic-speaking country in the twenty-two-member Arab League. Some ten million of its twenty-three million people suffer from food insecurity (being one step away from chronic hunger), with half of those often actually going hungry. The population has very little water, and a looming water crisis threatens the country's future. It is riven by sectarian, regional, and tribal conflicts. In the north, the extremist Zaidi (a form of Shiite Islam) Houthi movement has mounted rebellions against the state and engaged in faction fighting with Salafis (hard-line Sunni Muslims). Some provinces have seen a rise of Sunni extremism, with some organizations announcing an affiliation with al-Qaeda (attracting US drone strikes and likely intelligence penetration). Some southerners formed a secessionist movement and fought for autonomy. (South Yemen was an independent socialist state from 1967 to 1990, when it joined North Yemen in a single country. The union was not smooth, and a civil war broke out in 1994, which the north won by force.) These various contentious social movements and the government response have displaced about half a million people, contributing further to problems of food and water scarcity.

The three remaining countries in which a significant attempt at democratic transition was made in 2011 are Egypt, Bahrain, and Syria. In all three, as of early 2014, the transition failed. In Bahrain, the Shiite majority sought greater representation and access to good jobs and education from the Sunni monarchy, which discriminates in favor of Sunnis. Their demands were rebuffed, and the government launched a severe crackdown, with more than a hundred killed and hundreds jailed and allegedly tortured. Because of the military support of Saudi Arabia and the United States (which maintains the headquarters of its Fifth Fleet at Manama), the monarchy felt secure in crushing the movement, which the Sunni Bahrain elite saw as a cat's paw of Shiite Iran (a view that is inaccurate).[17]

In Syria, the Baath government (a one-party state, combining nationalism and socialism, which had turned to neoliberal corruption) decided to crush popular demonstrations with brute military force. The opposition, which had been peaceful through summer 2011, at length responded by militarizing in turn. The government attracted support from Iran, the Russian Federation, and China. The rebels were politically supported by Turkey, tepidly by the United States, and financially by wealthy Gulf oil millionaires. A civil war ensued. Sectarian issues played a role, but the real divisions were economic. The Baath state is dominated at the upper echelons by the Shiite Alawite sect (about 10 to 14 percent of the population). It also has the support of most Christians (another 10 to 14 percent). The secular-minded Sunni urban middle and upper classes likewise supported the state, which provided them government contracts and other benefits. Likely more than half the population was with the regime through early 2014. The rebels were disproportionately rural or from smaller towns and cities and mostly Sunni Muslims. As the revolution turned into a civil war and as the civil war ground on, the Sunni rebels came to be dominated on the battlefield by extremists, some of them announced al-Qaeda affiliates. The aspirations of Syrian youth for greater personal freedoms and economic opportunity, expressed in demonstrations and on the Internet in 2011, had three years later been roundly disappointed. The death toll marched toward one hundred fifty thousand, with millions displaced internally or abroad.

In Egypt, weeks of massive nationwide demonstrations unseated long-ruling dictator Hosni Mubarak in mid-February 2011. What took his place, however, was a military coup. While the military and the remnants of the Mubarak elite in the judiciary and bureaucracy allowed elections in 2011 and 2012, they repeatedly overturned the results of those elections because the winners were the fundamentalist Muslim Brotherhood. The Brotherhood and the Salafis (even more right-wing) dominated the parliament elected in late 2011. Egypt, however, has a French-style presidential system, and the parliament was not allowed to choose a prime minister or form a cabinet. Instead, these were appointed by the Supreme Council of the Armed Forces, a twenty-one-member body of high officers that functioned in 2011 and much of 2012 as a collective presidency.

In June 2012, a presidential election was held between the Muslim Brotherhood candidate, Muhammad Morsi, and former air force general Ahmad Shafiq, Mubarak's last vice president.[18] Morsi won and formed a Muslim Brotherhood cabinet, also appointing fundamentalists as provincial governors. He pushed through a constitution that many Egyptians saw as having theocratic overtones, so the Coptic Christians (10 percent of the population), the left-of-center youth who made the revolution, many women, and the more secular-minded middle and upper-middle classes turned against him. In early 2013, he appeared to be making preparations to pack the judiciary with Muslim Brotherhood jurists. Beginning in April 2013, a youth movement, Rebellion, mobilized to collect millions of signatures on a petition demanding a recall election. On May 30, 2013, millions of Egyptians came into the streets demanding that Morsi run again for his own position, since he had lost the confidence of the people (opinion polling confirmed that his favorability numbers had fallen below 20 percent). General Abdel Fattah al-Sisi, whom Morsi had appointed minister of defense, demanded that Morsi compromise with his critics. When the president declined, al-Sisi launched a coup on July 3, having Morsi and other high Brotherhood officials arrested. Later in July, al-Sisi asked the permission of the people to launch a "war on terror," taking a leaf from former US president George W. Bush. Millions responded, and al-Sisi began conducting a witch-hunt against the Muslim Brotherhood and its civil party wing, the Freedom and Justice Party. Hundreds were killed when al-Sisi brutally cleared Brotherhood sit-ins from squares in August. Late in 2013, the civilians appointed by al-Sisi to serve in a supposedly transitional government declared the Muslim Brotherhood a terrorist organization. They implemented a law forbidding protests and demonstrations unless permission is applied for and gained from the Interior Ministry (to be fair, Morsi had backed a similar piece of legislation). Dozens of leftist and liberal bloggers and activists were jailed under this legislation (some for protesting the antiprotest law) and sentenced to three years' hard labor. In spring 2014, the enormously popular al-Sisi announced his candidacy for the presidency. The tradition of military presidents in Egypt that began with the 1952 young officers' coup appeared likely to have been interrupted only briefly by Morsi's tenure, as Egypt's urban economic and political elite regrouped and reasserted itself after the loss of Mubarak and the (to them) distinctly unpleasant Muslim Brotherhood interlude. Although Egypt, in the three-and-a-half years after its January 25, 2011, revolution, had several referendums and elections, the rules of the game were never agreed upon, and the election and referendum results were all undone by the military or the courts.

Outcomes were diverse in the three years after the Arab youth upheavals. In most of the affected countries, the economic elite of the old regime largely survived, though wealth was so concentrated in the hands of ruling families and their cronies that in the cases of Libya, Tunisia, and Egypt something like a social revolution took place. (In Egypt, however, a counterrevolution on this score had occurred by 2014.) Syria fell into civil war. Morocco remained a monarchy with a strong king at the head of its security forces, despite small openings toward greater liberties. Egypt veered back toward praetorian authoritarianism in 2013–14. Bahrain crushed its dissenters. Libya, despite successful elections, suffered from institutional fragility and militia lawlessness. Yemen achieved some success in a pacted transition away from its president for life, with a multiparty government of national unity leading a transition to new elections in 2014. Its economic and social problems are so extensive, however, that they cast a pall over its not unimpressive political achievements.

Tunisia had the greatest success in its democratization process. The fact that al-Nahda did not have a parliamentary majority and the willingness of its political partners to challenge it played an important role in sustaining the party's flexibility. The summer 2013 military coup in Egypt also likely impelled the al-Nahda leadership in nearby Tunisia to seek compromise. Unlike in Egypt or Syria, Tunisia benefited from a refusal of its small military to intervene in civilian politics. In part, the army was so small (some thirty-five thousand men in a country of 10.5 million) that it did not have much capacity to assert itself.

Tunisia's success and Morocco's and Yemen's partial successes underscore what was necessary for democratic transition in the Arab world. The military had to be willing to allow change and an opening to more freedoms. The Alawite Syrian officer corps declined to allow that to happen, in part because they represented a minority regime that would lose perquisites in a majoritarian democracy. Political elites had to be willing to bargain and compromise with one another. Sectarian or ideological divisions, as between nationalism and political Islam or between Sunnis and Shiites, had to be susceptible to being bridged through these compromises. This area was one in which the Bahrain monarchy failed, as did the Muslim Brotherhood when it held power in Egypt. Institutions had to be strong enough to deliver services but not so overwhelming as to stifle innovation and dissent. (Libya, despite substantial resources, severely lacked governmental capacity.) The economy had to give reason for hope, which did not happen in Egypt, but this was a sphere in which Morocco and Tunisia saw more hopeful signs.

While the democratic transitions in the Arab world in the three years after 2011 had many failures and few assured successes, this time period is too short to allow a definitive judgment on the phenomenon. The protests of 2011 were overwhelmingly mounted by youth movements of twenty-somethings, the millennial generation. That generation will not come to political power for another twenty or thirty years, and the most significant impact of their mobilization may well be yet to come.

36 | Post-Occupy

by Sarah Leonard and Sarah Jaffe

We have two reports from journalists who were directly engaged with Occupy Wall Street (OWS) and present at the encampment protesters maintained for four weeks in fall 2011 at Zuccotti Park in downtown Manhattan.

The call to "occupy Wall Street," starting September 17, 2011, as a nonviolent protest against corporate power (initially issued by the Vancouver magazine Adbusters), *was directly inspired by the mass democracy rallies in Egypt's Tahrir Square and Spanish antiausterity demonstrations earlier that year. Similar encampments cropped up in scores of towns and cities across the country, notably including Oakland, California, where protest marches and attempts to shut down operations of the city's port occasioned clashes with police. Police evictions of the camps brought the most visible actions to an end by December 2011, though Occupy groups and assemblies continued organizing well into 2012, and some offshoots (as described here) have persisted to this day. Although people of all ages took part in Occupy manifestations, most participants in the encampments were young, often identifying with the condition of "precarity," or uncertain employment and minimal security, which is considered a feature of the recent social scene worsened by the Great Recession of 2008.[1]*

Generally committed to ideals of social equality, economic justice, and the practice of democracy, Occupy protests typically avoided posing discrete demands for particular changes or reforms. Critics (on both the right and the left) saw this "no demands" posture as a sign of political immaturity, though many activists justified Occupy's freewheeling character—focused simply on the grievance that the economic elite of "the 1 percent" lorded power over the great bulk of the people, "the 99 percent"—on the grounds that particular demands would blunt the movement's broad, radical impulse; narrow its welcome to diverse dissenters; or imply a rigid program imposed by a hierarchical leadership. Occupy's commitment to a democracy of free and equal participation in decision making militated against establishing "leaders" or officials in the movement, yielding a "leaderless" ethic that also attracted both sharp critique and ardent affirmation.

A whole set of distinctive practices—the best known being the "human microphone" used in large public assemblies to convey speech to an audience without electrified PA systems—became associated with Occupy's "horizontal" culture. In that vein, crying out "Mic check!" would announce a speaker's wish to address the assembly. In other venues, when Occupy protesters confronted representatives of power, shouting "Mic check!" from within the crowd could be a kind of heckling that intended to seize the floor from the authorities.

Sarah Leonard, an editor at Dissent *magazine when OWS began and now an editor at the* Nation *magazine, helped produce one of the movement's newspapers, the* Occupy! Gazette. *Speaking in Ann Arbor during fall 2012, when the enthusiasm of the prior year had begun to wane, she warned against simplistic views of the movement, its virtues, and its flaws.*

The "no demands" position was good when Occupy was holding open a new, altered discussion space by the sheer force of its existence. As long as the protests were in the news—as long as they were surprising, offering unmeetable goals and unpredictable actions—inequality was discussed. That was strategic. But it's time to get beyond that mode because it isn't strategic anymore.

There's a whole genre of article now about the "death" of Occupy that I think makes it hard to see what comes next. The most recent is Thomas Frank's article in *The Baffler*, which I think is totally awful. He lays responsibility for the death of Occupy at the feet of capital *T* Theory. We like Theory too much and spend too much time talking about Giorgio Agamben's notion of the "state of exception."[2] And he counsels us to "try Mississippi in the fifties instead. Reenact Flint, Michigan, circa 1937 and you could get somewhere. Look to Omaha, 1892, and things could work out differently."[3] This embodies most of what I hate about post-Occupy criticism, largely because it asks us to hark back to politics built on the strength of, say, small agriculture or the auto industry. We're going to have to figure out somewhere new to go. I daresay we're going to have to do better than calling up William Jennings Bryan on some sort of activist Ouija board.

There's one thing about Frank's article that I've seen repeated in other "death of Occupy" stories that I'd just like to clear up because it's important: Frank, like other writers, manages the extraordinary feat of attributing none of the end of Occupy to the police. The police not only moved literally all the Occupiers from the park to jail but picked up activists at their homes before May Day 2012, beat them to the point of seizure at Zuccotti, pepper sprayed them, and rounded them up. You can't talk about the death of Occupy without talking about the police. And yes, if you leave them out, it seems plausible that Occupy just dissolved by virtue of discussing Agamben too much. If you don't leave them out, you have a clearer sense of what we're up against. If you leave them in, you understand some of the challenges we face.

Port Huron took a lot of care to identify agents and locations—the social base for its movement. (A notable new constituency was students on university campuses.) The Occupy statement did not, though it listed many grievances. One agent that has been identified by activists is the debtor. This is huge. David Graeber's book on debt became a bible of the Occupy movement.[4] And the group called Strike Debt is kicking off a "Rolling Jubilee" of debt forgiveness this November 15. Their goal is to buy people's debt from banks and then, instead of collecting it from debtors, abolish it, free them, and continue to accept donations to buy up more debt.

This is interesting and in line with the "autonomist" approach of many Occupiers. Indeed, many of the organizers tend more toward anarchism, since the goal is not to build better institutions but to free people from institutions (e.g., the state, the bank) as much as possible. It's a concept that has gotten a lot of people excited because, in the absence of a unionized working class and with the increase in precarious labor, this seems like a category that will encompass many people and perhaps even endow them with some power and agency.

This strategy does, however, have some obvious problems. Will Americans really be into paying off each other's credit card debt? Debt is still a source of shame, but furthermore, if you've been paying off your mortgage your whole life, do you really want a jubilee? There's a related asymmetry: most Americans hold somewhat moderate debt compared to the most hard-up debtors and young people with college loans. Debt varies hugely. How do you make it function as a unifying quality, not a dividing one? Furthermore, debt is a symptom. To quote Marxist economist Doug Henwood, "The focus on debt is classic American populism—focus on finance rather than fundamentals. Debt should be a point of entry into a bigger conversation. Student debt is high because education should be free. Mortgage debt is high because housing inflation used to be the national religion. Consumer debts are high because wages and incomes are stagnant to down but the cost of living isn't. Debt is more a symptom than a cause."[5]

A second place to watch—and one that might be more fruitful—would be the progressive end of union organizing, particularly the Walmart workers who are striking, the Guestworker Alliance, DWU, UNITE HERE in New Haven, and others. The Walmart workers mic-checked their bosses. Maybe this is just a floating cultural meme now, but maybe not. The work that Occupy did with labor was always overlooked—they reached out from the start, and they absolutely made a difference for the Teamsters striking at Sotheby's whom they went and marched with and drew attention to over and over and over again. Neither labor nor Occupy has it all figured out right now, but there are new organizational forms arising in the labor movement that post-Occupy kids are getting on board with. For all our focus on precarity, most Americans still have a boss they report to every morning who screws them over, and this might still be the brightest hope for post-Occupy organization.

Sarah Jaffe, cohost of Dissent *magazine's "Belabored" podcast and a writer on labor, social movements, gender, media, and student debt, reflects on Occupy in 2014.*

Occupy is a Rorschach; it has been since the beginning. To the question "Where is Occupy now?" one receives as many answers as there are activists, as many definitions of Occupy as there are offshoots across the country. Occupy was a formative moment for the twenty-first-century American left and for young people growing up under austerity, unsure how to act politically on their debt and frustration. Occupy's 99 percent versus 1 percent sloganeering was a bracing retort to mealymouthed paeans to the "middle class."

In 2011, Occupy felt huge and magical: Mary Clinton, a labor organizer and OWS planner now says,

> I remember, I wish[ed] I had more of an imagination, because it seemed like whatever idea we had in that space [Zuccotti Park], we could make happen, and we did. After the eviction, where did we go? We went back to workplaces; we were in schools; we were in communities; we were in the streets; we were occupying homes, doing eviction defenses—workplace organizing, things that are arguably even more challenging to capital, to the economic order, and the power of wealth.

The magical moment, however, is long gone and no one disputes that; its organizers have settled into longer-haul projects that often do, in fact, have measurable goals.

The paradox of Occupy is that many of the things that made it succeed also made it splinter. The attraction to a "leaderless" movement was palpable, and the lack of demands made it possible for anyone to join in as long as they agreed with the basic premise that a tiny elite has too much power. Yet the idea of leaderlessness, as so many have written, masks the ways power continues to operate—at large in our society and among activists, too—and the lack of demands wound up as a refusal, oftentimes, to deal at all with existing systems.

Nonetheless, there are concrete gains that can be credited, at least in part, to the Occupy movement of 2011–12. The most high-profile legislative success belonged to an Occupy working group called Occupy the SEC. Alexis Goldstein, a former Wall Streeter turned Occupier, helped write that group's comment letter to the Securities and Exchange Commission (SEC) that is cited repeatedly in the final version of the Volcker Rule, one of the many rules required by the Dodd-Frank Wall Street Reform and Consumer Protection Act that finally went into effect in December 2013. The Volcker Rule's aim is to prevent banks that receive taxpayer backing from making risky trades—or, as Goldstein wrote for the *Nation*, "banks that have a taxpayer-provided parachute don't get to BASE jump off of mountains for the thrill (and profit) of it."[6] In Goldstein's view, Occupy the SEC shifted the policy debate "a little bit to the left." Regulations about hedging and the level of bank oversight, documentation provided to regulators, and more made it into the final rule, which at points cites Occupy the SEC directly. "The banks didn't get what they want because we wanted something else from the other extreme," Goldstein explains, "and so the result was something in the middle." The work of dissenting finance wonks was backed up by a movement in the streets, focusing anger on the banks and bringing media attention to the Occupy policy letter in a way that a small group of concerned citizens could never have achieved.

Goldstein also thinks the rise of Kshama Sawant, Seattle's new socialist city council member, is in part an Occupy victory; Sawant was part of Occupy Seattle and helped relocate that group to the community college where she teaches. Less radical politicians, too, may owe some thanks to a movement that targeted banks. The popularity of Senator Elizabeth Warren—called a "populist" on the left end of the Democratic Party—and the moves of Senator Sherrod Brown and others to introduce new regulations on the size and power of Wall Street banks stem partly from Occupy sentiment. One can count successes, too, in homes defended from foreclosure by activists emerging from Occupy formations in Minneapolis and St. Paul, Minnesota, and in Atlanta, Georgia.

All this may sound like a far cry from the original vision of Zuccotti

Park, where any demand was seen as too small. If Occupy's critics demand larger wins than these, it is only partly in bad faith. It is also because the moment did really feel grander, bigger, as if anything was possible, and now we have had to bring our expectations back down to earth. No, capitalism wasn't overthrown; Wall Street's power still remains; CEOs Jamie Dimon at JPMorgan Chase and Lloyd Blankfein at Goldman Sachs still have their jobs. And the perpetual refrain of "Occupy changed the conversation" can feel like cold comfort when each month's unemployment numbers hit.

The first iteration of Occupy dealt with the issues of community and democracy and building collective spaces that reflected activists' values. The second iteration's two most public faces were Occupy Sandy—which mobilized to aid the most vulnerable city residents battered by Superstorm Sandy in fall 2012—and Strike Debt. Both tried to organize through mutual aid.

After Superstorm Sandy hit New York and New Jersey, the OWS network jumped back into action, building community hubs in Brooklyn and Queens that distributed food, clothing, and other supplies to survivors in the immediate wake of the storm and raising money to help with rebuilding efforts. Skills first honed in the park—feeding hundreds and distributing supplies and divvying up donations—translated easily to filling the gaps left by the failures of state and federal agencies and the major NGOs.

The movement attempted to operate out of "solidarity, not charity." These Occupiers tried to stay aware of the power relations inherent in most charity work, distinguishing mutual aid from do-gooderism. Staten Island, Red Hook, and the Rockaways contain some of the poorest parts of New York City; particularly in the Rockaways, nursing homes, long-term care facilities, and halfway houses for the recently incarcerated are concentrated. For residents there, many of them people of color, health care services and access to food after the storm were sparse. Occupy Sandy raised more than $1 million to help hundreds of New Yorkers—an initial success far beyond Occupy's dreams.

Through its "Rolling Jubilee" campaign, Strike Debt aimed to buy up personal debt on the secondary market for pennies on the dollar—and then abolish it. Strike Debt organizers Astra Taylor and Pam Brown felt that something had been unleashed with the Jubilee—something that proved that debt was an issue that people connected to but felt was outside their control. "We got so much more money than we ever anticipated," Brown says. "More than ten times the amount that we thought was a far reach." Critics honed in on the processes for buying debt, raising questions about whether people whose debt was abolished would have to pay taxes on the "gift" and about accountability for the money raised. But the idea of the Jubilee had never been that massive debt forgiveness was possible this way. Debt in general is a massive problem, and only certain types of debt are available on the secondary market—such as medical debt, which wound up being the type of debt the Jubilee abolished. Rather, the organizers wanted to raise awareness of the issue (which the success of the Jubilee certainly did) and create some room for organizing. Through an act of mutual aid, they hoped to bring new debtors into the movement. However, although many people donated, few of them joined and became organizers. In this case, a tighter-knit core—compared to the wide-open Zuccotti Park encampment—doesn't necessarily translate into a broad-based movement.

That became a key question for both Strike Debt and Occupy Sandy. Shawn Carrié had come out of OWS: he brought a lawsuit against the New York City Police Department claiming he'd been stalked by police officers and his thumb had been gruesomely broken—he says intentionally—which ruined his future as a pianist. He won a settlement of $82,500, only one of the payments the city has been compelled to make. Carrié went on to work with Occupy Sandy but concluded that the effort wound up distracting from, not contributing to, political organizing: "It's important work, but the situation is a crisis, and it's a crisis of capitalism, and [hurricane relief work] is not changing our relation to the economy and society." Pam Brown articulates a similar critique of many second-generation, Occupy-related projects: "People start to feel really good about the aspect of helping others and forgot that it was actually a political project and not a charity." Doing charity wasn't a bad thing—it saved lives. Thousands of volunteers and thousands of dollars came through Occupy Sandy, and most of those volunteers knew next to nothing about organizing. But charity replacing state action is deeply embedded in right-wing ideology that privileges individual choice over collective responsibility—and white people going into communities of color to give aid looked to some like an assertion of racial privilege.

It didn't matter that people of color were directly involved in founding many of these working groups; still, the Occupy movement as a whole was perceived as a white movement. Did Occupy really grasp the racial dimension of power? Pam Brown worked on a report on the debt burden carried by people in areas hardest hit by Sandy; she points out that debt intersects with other forms of oppression, particularly racist oppression. Eventually, she quit Strike Debt when she felt that it failed to prioritize those most impacted by financial disaster: the poor of color.

Just as in the first iteration of Occupy, the masses faded away and left a small core building for the longer term. Astra Taylor wondered, "Where does power hook up with spectacle? Where does power hook up with good deeds and abolishing individuals' debt?" About Occupy, she said, "We're pretty good at spectacle; we're pretty damn good at charity. We're good at constructive action. The real interesting question is the question of power and how you have that."

Building New Institutions: Occupy Power

Other movements have followed. Occupier and longtime organizer Nelini Stamp suggests that Moral Mondays, the series of sustained, weekly actions in North Carolina that protest the moves made by the right-wing government, learned important lessons from Occupy's slipups. "Just one time a week, people got arrested, but it was very loving: 'We have the moral right to do this,' it wasn't angry," Stamp says of Moral Mondays. And in Florida, the Dream Defenders, a movement built by young people—some of whom came from Occupy Tallahassee—calling for justice after the killing of Trayvon Martin, took the capitol building but made the decision to leave when morale started to slide—before a brutal crackdown or visible failure. If the original power of Occupy was in part the power of surprise, that is gone. The masses who were drawn in by the original explosion of Occupy or by the second generation of Occupy Sandy and the Rolling Jubilee are also mostly gone, without an obvious way to tap into a movement other than Facebook pages and Twitter hashtags.

So what now? Minnesota activist Nick Espinosa says that the key is figuring out how to create new institutions: "I think there's a natural tendency to be anti-institutional and to want to dismantle systems of power because they've been used to exploit and colonize and destroy community all over the planet," he says. "The reality is that we can't change the world without institutions that are democratically accountable to the movement and that have real power."

Building power for the movement means understanding the way power is wielded in the world right now; it means understanding, Pam Brown notes, not just the state and not just corporate power but the relationships between the state and corporations, between laws and economic interests and the 1 percent. Power is an infrastructure all its own, and to fight it, a movement needs infrastructure as well.

A project called Wildfire, begun by Yotam Marom, Samantha Corbin, and other Occupy organizers in January 2013, hopes to help strengthen social justice campaigns by offering political education, organizer training, and group development advice. In the Rockaways, organizers have met people where they live and focused on building an institution that will last and earn tangible wins; together they have created the community organization Rockaway Wildfire, which pushes for development projects benefiting the residents there whose lives were devastated by Sandy. Wildfire has gone on to collaborate with Occupy Homes Atlanta and Occupy Homes MN (Minneapolis-St. Paul). As Marom puts it, "A lot of these groups are post-Occupy groups: they're coming out of a similar political moment; they speak a similar language; they want similar things; they're all relatively radical; they use direct action; they're groups that are confronting crisis or are emerging from crisis." Most importantly, Wildfire wants to build a network to put the groups they work with in conversation with one another for the sake of longer-term movement building.

Wildfire's next project is working with the Dream Defenders, which mobilized after the trial of George Zimmerman for killing Trayvon Martin. One of the most visible groups working on criminalization and racial justice, the Dream Defenders took lessons from Occupy as well as civil rights organizing. Their leadership, Nelini Stamp notes, is made up of young people of color—those most impacted by mass incarceration and unequal access to education and jobs.

Frontline communities are also leading the work around foreclosure and housing. Espinosa, whose family home was one of those saved by Occupy Homes MN, says, "I think bringing the energy of the plaza to neighborhoods was one of the best things and the thing I'm most proud of in terms of the work and our accomplishments since Occupy started." Occupy Homes MN has scored eleven victories over banks to keep homeowners in their homes. The group has been fine-tuning its strategy for saving homes from foreclosure and is starting to occupy vacant homes as well. (As of this writing, they hold five.)

According to Espinosa, Occupy Homes MN combines physical occupations of the homes with public pressure campaigns, neighborhood organizing (getting the neighbors to support the occupied home in their midst), and political organizing to build a base of support. "We think homes should not sit vacant, that they should be used to house people, especially in a Minnesota winter where people are freezing to death and there are more empty houses than homeless people," he says.

This kind of home-protection work combines a big-picture vision of long-term systemic change with the challenge of making reforms that will benefit people immediately and, in some cases, save lives. The work in particular of reclaiming vacant homes, of helping people have a home who never had the ability to buy one in the first place, is meaningful in terms of whose needs are being foregrounded. "It's a different base and a different flavor of organizing than we've done before," Espinosa says. The people driving the effort are the people who live in or will live in the homes. Those people too are becoming a political power bloc within Minneapolis. Collaborating with local organizations, particularly Neighborhoods Organizing for Change (NOC), Occupy Homes MN has helped elect a progressive mayor and came within a few votes of being the second city to put a socialist candidate, Ty Moore, on its city council.

The labor movement in the post-Occupy moment is also taking tentative steps toward change. Industry-wide campaigns targeting fast food and Walmart have embraced the one-day strike and civil disobedience and have brought community members into the labor campaign, promoting an analysis of how low-wage jobs hurt the entire economy. Occupiers like Mary Clinton have returned to full-time day jobs organizing workers and have created within New York a solidarity network called 99 Pickets, which supports labor struggles in the city and engages in direct actions that would be too risky for unions to try.

Clinton points out that labor organizing is still time-consuming, hard work that doesn't have the immediate payoff of a march in the street, but by building unions, it builds long-term power for workers: "We know what capital cares about, profits and money, and we know we're in a globalized economy. So how do we challenge that? How do we impact their profit margins, push within that space for real gains for working people? Simultaneously, how do we develop alternatives that don't just withdraw from the system but that build power—how do we build those institutions so that we can support the alternative?"

Do all these various avenues of work add up to a "movement"? The technology that helped Occupy and other recent uprisings spread the way they did also allows Occupy offshoots to function, Stamp notes, as a sort of informal crisis network, responding to things like the George Zimmerman verdict or Hurricane Sandy in a way that simply wasn't possible only a short time ago. But movements have to be made up of deep commitments as well as loose ties. Or, as Marom says, networks have to be made up of groups that are in turn made up of people who have a longer-term commitment and stake in the process.

That means building for a long game while at the same time responding quickly to crisis moments, planning for five or even fifty years in the future rather than expecting a few months to create major changes. Espinosa says, "I think the challenge of our generation is to reinvent what institutions mean and create new versions of institutions that have failed movements in the past that are truly democratic and that stick to our values."

Putting Down Community Roots

On the night after Christmas 2013, I danced in a Minneapolis basement nightclub to a who's who of local hip-hop, performing under a banner reading "Occupy Homes." It was a fundraiser for the Minnesota group—ten dollars at the door and a bucket being passed among the crowd would go to help sustain the home defense work.

Occupy Homes embodies the shift of a movement away from its origins in a park, where demands were seen as too limiting, to the longer, slower, harder work of setting goals and meeting them, of building community power.

"Occupy," in this community, is a verb. Occupy is a tactic—just one of many. The movement claimed to speak for the 99 percent, and to really represent the 99 percent, it had to get out of the parks and into neighborhoods, put down community roots, and listen to what people needed. Occupy Homes MN has a core group of organizers and a network of more than a hundred who respond to emergency texts and face down the police when they come to evict. At the center of this work lies the concerns of people, many of color, who are losing or have already lost their homes; members have a political analysis of both the local problems and the broader national fight; they belong to a network of groups doing home defense work around the country.

In the post-Occupy moment, we can talk about capitalism as a system, and we can talk about class; we can elect a socialist or a movement organizer to office; we understand that inequality is the problem. We have learned some painful lessons: that something that can feel in a heady moment like revolution may not turn out that way and that our tactics will not always work. As Frances Fox Piven noted in the earlier days of the movement, protest doesn't evolve in a linear fashion: "It's much more interrupted, dispersed, there are periods of discouragement—1959–1960 the civil rights movement, people thought it was over," before a new surge, and they were dispirited by the failure of the Albany, Georgia, campaign of 1962 before other gains were won. "This movement is going to be like that too," Piven argued.[7]

The idea of Occupy, artist and organizer Mark Read thinks, is still out there: "[It's] like a ghost; I don't know how to make it physical." But as Stamp says, we should not be worried about reviving it. The problem with disruptive movements is that most people can be disrupted only for so long; participants trickle back to their lives, and those being disrupted learn to adapt. Movements have to adapt and change, come up with new tactics, and draw attention (and numbers) back to themselves. A networked movement is better able to do this quickly, and groups that have a real base in communities have a better idea of what people really need. There is no substitute for the organizing: the hard work it takes to build a real movement.

Movement moments like Occupy in 2011, Marom points out, "don't come from nowhere. There's no such thing as spontaneous. They come through hard organizing and conditions and some magic dust that you can't really explain." What happens next depends on how prepared people are to choose a direction and how ready they are to push.

37 | Movements for Real Democracy: "The People Must Rule!"

by Marina Sitrin

"Marx says that revolutions are the locomotives of world history. But the situation may be quite different. Perhaps revolutions are not the train ride, but the human race grabbing for the emergency brake."[1] Who would have guessed that Walter Benjamin's suggestion that revolutions might mean pulling the emergency brake, written more than seventy years ago, would be used by contemporary movements to describe what has been spreading across the globe since 2011. These are movements shouting "No!" to an increasingly untenable situation—movements that are refusing to pay the social cost of the economic crisis, movements that are refusing to have a future determined by a market, and movements that are beginning to create something else in this refusal. In this way, they pull the emergency brake, declaring "Kefaya!" ("Enough," as was shouted in Tahrir Square). What is being created in this space of the "no" is yet to be decided; for sure, it will be something created collectively, horizontally, and with care.

In this chapter, I explore some of the ways that people in the movements have responded to the crisis, and I describe the various forms of organization with which people are experimenting. I have selected those forms that are most common and consistent globally. I end by questioning the way to assess the success of these movements; I propose ways of understanding what success can mean based on the expressed desires of the movement participants. I rely on the voices of the movement actors themselves based on interviews I have conducted over the past two-and-a-half years as a participant and researcher of these movements.[2]

Crisis

"The 15-M is an inflection point, a total breaking point—in the way there are crisis moments in a positive way. It makes you rethink yourself, your political activity, and then situate yourself in another place." That's the way Ernest, a housing-defense activist in Barcelona, Spain, described the 15-M movement, a series of social-media-driven protests that began on May 15, 2011, and called for a radical reformation of the Spanish economic and political system in the wake of the country's continued economic crisis.[3] Among the offshoots of 15-M were local collectives known as PAH (*Plataforma de Afectados por la Hipoteca*—i.e., those affected by the mortgage crisis), which organized against the economic emergency and opposed foreclosures by direct action. Ernest's sentiments have been echoed around the world, from Portugal, Brazil, Turkey, and Greece to Occupy in the United States.

The language of crisis has been used to describe what people around the globe have been suffering for at least the past few years. While many think immediately of economic crisis, for people in the movements, it is that and much more, ranging from a crisis of the environment to one of their health, their culture, and their very future. This could be seen as students in Quebec and Chile called for a "social strike" against cuts to education, thereby challenging austerity in general; as workers blockaded workplaces and banks on May Day; and as artists occupied galleries and museums, usually at the same time the public squares were occupied, to show that all things were being retaken. Rather than demand a future that people know will never be given to them by others, they are beginning to create their own futures together. What this looks like is not predetermined by any program or platform, yet it intentionally prefigures relationships that many desire for the future, conceived in terms of horizontality, affective relationships, diversity, and emancipation. As Ana, from the Observatorio Metropolitano (an independent collective focusing on radical urban planning issues in Madrid) and 15-M in Madrid, reflected, "The greatest problem we have is that we can't imagine any alternative. And that is the challenge: to invent, create, and think as if we were living just after the collapse, if there is a collapse of capitalism, and how we will organize."

Democracy

The beginning point for the movements is a rejection of the "multiple crises" that began in 2008. This meant a refusal of representation—specifically, the representative democracy embodied in neoliberalism. Slogans around the world, accompanied by the formation of directly democratic assemblies, expressed that refusal: "No nos representan" and "Democracia Real Ya!" in Spain; "We are the 99 percent" in the United States; "You can't even imagine us" in Moscow; and "The people must rule" in Portugal.

Huge segments of the world's population feel that they have no influence over decisions made regarding their lives, that they are not heard or taken into consideration by those who make decisions, and that these "representatives" do not act in the people's interest. "Democracy has lost its initial meaning," commented Fani, from the neighborhood assembly of Ano Poli, a district in Thessaloniki, Greece. "It is said that we have democracy right now in Greece. This is not democracy. We have no real power." If democracy is to mean that "the people rule," then the relationship of the meaning of democracy to established forms of representative democracy is a very distant relation. Politicians make decisions based on what they deem to be best at the time, and the influence of economic interests is far greater than those of the general population. A 2014 study by two political scientists found that the United States is in fact not a democracy but an oligarchy.[4] The global movements have been claiming that we do not live in a democracy; perhaps the study sought to prove them wrong but in the end found they were correct: "When a majority of citizens disagrees with economic elites and/or with organized interests, they generally lose."[5]

While many in the movements have theoretical explanations for the rejection of representative (as opposed to direct) democracy, this rejection does not always come from an ideological place. If the state responded to protests and did not cut people's livelihoods, protesters might not reject the representational form; but because the state has been ignoring the people, the people are looking to and for something else—together. This is how Anestis, a participant in the neighborhood assembly of Peristeri in Athens, Greece, puts it:

> During the last two years, different forms of struggle, mobilization, and organizing have been tested. If you had asked people, even from the movement, two years ago, "If we have a massive demon-

stration in the center of Athens with half a million people, would we succeed in canceling the austerity measures?" most people would have said yes. We did that four times, five times, and austerity continued. I am not implying that we should stop having massive demonstrations in the center of Athens. I am just saying that we have experienced the limits of what we do. The fact that for eight months [from November 2011 to June 2012] we had a government that no one elected was a message. They were telling us that they will continue to manage the capitalist crisis against us, without pretending that the state is democratic.

This mistrust of politicians and political parties extends to institutional politics per se and the forms of institutional power. Most of the new movements over the past several years are practicing forms of direct democracy and are doing so in public spaces, from Tahrir Square in Egypt to the plazas and parks of Spain, Greece, Brazil, Turkey, the United States, and elsewhere. In each of these movements, there was first the occupation of central squares and plazas, creating microcosms of a future possibility. Then, in many of these locations, the movements either were evicted or intentionally chose to leave the main square and subsequently formed assemblies in neighborhoods. These local assemblies, while less visible and often less well known than the large occupations, are more directly effective both in helping to meet people's needs and in creating a more profound experience of democracy. Here, two participants far apart from each other—Luis from the 15-M in Madrid, Spain, and Fani from the neighborhood assembly of Ano Poli in Thessaloniki, Greece—describe the experience similarly:

Luis: For the movement to be real-life, and everyday life to be the movement, it has to intersect with people's lives. One important path for getting here has been to move from the plazas to the neighborhoods. In the neighborhoods, I think it works better because there is a base with what people have in common, and it is on the micro level with everyday life, we can put more issues on the table, like jobs, housing.

Fani: When you're facing so many problems with your social reproduction [maintaining and replenishing the social infrastructure of everyday life], you have to find new ways to resist. It is a question of survival. The answer lies in smaller-scale initiatives. Neighborhood assemblies started multiplying exactly because they were trying to cope with the problems of social reproduction. It was difficult for the movement in the squares to get involved with the electric bills or the electricity cut-offs in different neighborhoods. It was a more central organizational form. In a neighborhood assembly, on the other hand, the neighbor can come and say, "My electricity's been cut off; we have to do something." So we act immediately. It was the decentralized organizational project that helped us confront social reproduction issues.

That there is a rejection of representation in government, and instead experimentation with various forms of direct and participatory democracy, does not mean in any absolute sense that people in the movements around the world now want to establish direct democracy, as practiced in the squares or otherwise, as the new form of government. The use of direct democracy is an integral part of the movements and the creation of new social relationships; it is very much a response to not being heard in society and by those in government. How these new forms will shape up in the long term is still a question—a mode of action that is under construction.

Horizontal Relationships

Along with forms of organization that have been replicated in different places across the world is a common language to articulate these new forms. This language entails ways of using words as well as various hand signals and body language used in the assemblies to facilitate a more participatory process.

The use of *horizontalidad*, or horizontality and horizontalism, has become widespread as a description of the new relationships. *Horizontalidad* was first used to describe the relationships that emerged in Argentina after the 2001 economic crisis there. Hundreds of thousands of people at that time went into the streets, without political parties or unions leading them, and formed neighborhood assemblies, reoepend and reorganized ("recuperated") workplaces, and set up massive barter networks—all as a part of horizontal self-organization. These initiatives were established without relying on the state's "vertical" or representative structure.

Horizontalidad became one of the main ways people described what they were doing. It is a social relationship that implies, as its name suggests, a flat plane upon which to communicate. *Horizontalidad* implies the use of direct democracy with a focus on people actively listening to and hearing one another, with each person speaking. The participation of everyone is key. There is a striving for consensus—that is, the coming together of ideas and agreement, not necessarily a specific form of decision making. People in Argentina would often use *horizontalidad* and then vote at the end of the discussion. The heart of it is that people speak and feel heard. This process is not just about decision making; rather, it is about the way conversations take place and the new relationships created as a result. This form of relating is not an end; it is seen as a tool to help facilitate new relationships—ones grounded in trust, sharing and open communication.

And this relationship, described similarly in the many assemblies around the world, also extends to the creation of prefigurative spaces in the plazas and the neighborhoods. Here's how PAH activist Ernest described the early days of the large assembly in Plaza Catalunya in Barcelona:

> It was like—the way you can imagine another possible world—everyone discussing issues that the media and politicians never talk about—it was awesome. If you took a walk around, maybe even at midnight, you would say, "These people are crazy." There were groups of five or six people who didn't know each other, talking about the energy crisis, nuclear treaties, or discussing labor issues. People who had never met before were there, having discussions, more and more people adding themselves to the discussions, something like miniforums. It came out of a need to express, to communicate, and to imagine other worlds that never existed in the reality before 15-M.

Direct Action and Mutual Aid

Horizontal relationships and the shift to the neighborhoods and villages have addressed matters such as eviction prevention and foreclosure defense; solidarity health clinics and free health care; the reconnection of electricity; direct relationships with the exchange of goods (barter networks or purchasing goods directly from the producers); and horizontal, self-organized production.

We see this at work in downtown Thessaloniki at the movement center, Micropolis, a large building where a large network of groups and movements function. Among the things it houses are a large café and bar, meeting spaces, a children's play space, an animal rescue center, a library, and an organic shop with food coming directly from local producers. The groups that meet there range from people organizing conferences and workshops, the network fighting to keep water public, the Solidarity Initiative that supports the recently reorganized workplace of Vio.Me (a factory whose workers occupied, controlled, and continued production after the owners abandoned the site), and a network to defend health care and create alternative clinics. At Micropolis, Theo said,

> We would like to have this principle of horizontality and direct democracy applied to all areas of life, and a very important area is consumption. Right now, the market is organized in a hierarchical way, so our relationship is as consumers. But here, we want to promote a different sort of consumption. So, we are in touch with people who produce food and all different types of things, and we have a direct relationship with them, and we want to know what sorts of things they are producing [and] how they are producing it. We want to have as much control over what we consume as possible. . . . There is no intermediary, no middleman, and this works in many different ways. It also helps us to create new productive cooperatives so as to help meet our needs. So we begin with our needs, and from there we decide what we want.

Similar principles apply to free clinics and actions in the hospitals organized by neighborhood assemblies. One of the many ramifications of the Greek government accepting conditions from the International Monetary Fund and European Community was a move from free health care to a mandatory five-euro payment for each visit to the doctor, not to mention repeated payments for follow-up treatments or medicines. Neighborhood assemblies responded by mobilizing people to physically block the cashiers so that people who need medical attention are not put in the position of paying, even if they could. The assemblies often stamp the name of the assembly on the form to show payment, which is then given to the doctor by the patient. Almost all doctors respect these actions and treat the patients. In other areas, doctors and neighbors have come together to form free clinics with surplus medicines donated from around Greece and other parts of Europe, as Debbie in Thessaloniki describes:

> We attend to people who have been excluded from the medical system. In six months of activity here we had more than 1,000 people coming to the dentist and more than 700 people have been attended by the other specialists we have, which include pediatricians, neurologists, psychiatrists, psychologists, general practitioners, cardiologists, dermatologists, and ear-nose-throat specialists. And if you need a special-

ized doctor we give you a referral paper and you go to external doctors and to their private practices or to hospitals where we have people working that have shown their solidarity. Everything is free here and where we send you.

We are self-organized and operate in a horizontal way. We have a general assembly where everyone—no matter whether it is a medical practitioner, a secretary or a technical engineer—is equal in the decision-making. We are not trying to help the state out in this time of crisis. We are trying to show a different path by being quite autonomous in the way we operate.

Another of many examples is the defense of housing. The antiforeclosure and antieviction movement that evolved in response to the 2008 crisis has been rapidly growing around the world. Spain is the most well known, with its PAH groups, but many other countries have strong movements. Diverse approaches to challenging the banks and keeping families housed have appeared in the United States, Italy, and Germany. In Italy, for example, where there is a history of occupations, hundreds of homeless families in November 2013 simultaneously took over empty homes and schools that had been closed in towns and cities, including Rome, Palermo, Naples, Milan, and Turin. The actions of families are generally coordinated and have the support of the antiforeclosure activists both during the actions and after. In urban areas in Germany, neighbors organize to help prevent evictions, but if they are not successful, they make sure the homes are impossible to rent by direct actions that prevent the showing of foreclosed houses, such as putting glue in locks. If that is still not successful, and a home is about to be rented, they use social or political pressure, such as explaining to the potential renters that the neighborhood is opposed to their renting or buying the home and that they would be ostracized. This social pressure sometimes leads to new renters agreeing not to move into the home.

In the United States, dozens of groups are organizing and carry out a wide variety of actions. Some, such as Occupy Homes, in places such as Atlanta and Minneapolis—often direct spin-offs from Occupy of 2011—organize neighbors and together physically defend homes at risk of foreclosure. Often the result is that the banks do not go forward with the eviction, and the group helps families renegotiate mortgages. In Chicago's poverty-stricken neighborhoods, community groups make public claims on abandoned homes, work with families still living in the neighborhood, and then collectively move homeless families into them. And then there are the dozens of groups that disrupt the auctions of homes that are to be foreclosed. These actions include singing in courtrooms in the boroughs of New York City or the San Francisco Bay area, thereby disrupting the proceedings so that a home that is supposed to be sold has to be put again on the docket. This usually means additional months to mobilize in defense of the home. The tactics of the various groups are many, expanding, and contagious. For example, in October 2011, a YouTube video of a foreclosure disruption went viral, and within weeks, similar actions were taking place in towns and cities around the United States, using even the same song as was written by the activists in the initial action.[6] In Spain, the PAH has expanded its actions to occupying hundreds of homes as well as empty buildings for homeless families in a style closely resembling that of the Italians. Ernest of Barcelona describes the antiforeclosure work in Spain and its relationship to the new movements:

The *Plataforma* [PAH] is a pre-15-M movement, but it was given impetus by the 15-M. Before the 15-M, there was an assembly of the Barcelona *Plataforma* and another in Terraza, and after the 15-M, in just a short period of time, there were forty-four *Plataformas* [in 2013, there were one hundred fifty], plus other neighborhood assemblies that have the same action guidelines as protecting families from evictions. They give them some kind of counseling or they bring them to the *Plataforma*, but above all, when there are announcements of foreclosures like this next Monday in their neighborhood, they get active and call the neighborhood together so that they can all go to prevent it, knocking on doors to mobilize people to prevent the foreclosure from occurring.

Molly from Occupy Homes in the Bernal neighborhood of San Francisco describes the early process of neighborhood antieviction work:

We'd go out, mostly on Sundays, and knock on doors to find out who these people were. And the stories varied. But for sure there's a lot of shame people have to overcome. Some people we had to go back and talk to many times. We didn't push people. We just said, "Look, if you feel like you need help, we're your neighbors and we're here to help you, and we have some ideas about what we can do to keep you from losing your home."

And we worked with them, and found partners to work with, because most of us didn't know anything about foreclosures. What happens? We didn't know. You get foreclosed on, and you get evicted, and your home is sold at auction. And the auctions take place on the steps of city hall. I didn't know that. Every day, they're auctioning off people's homes on the steps of city hall.

So, now we've stopped a lot of auctions—that's kind of a last-ditch effort, once the home is getting auctioned off. We're trying to stop the foreclosures before that.

Goals without Demands

The previous examples of various forms of organizing are carried out with direct action and clear collective goals, yet they are not based on systematic demands made upon an institution. The fact that there are goals and not demands does not mean there is no relationship to forms of institutional power, whether governments, banks, or insurance companies. Rather than assuming the traditional position of protest movements making a claim on an institution, self-organized groups are making things happen, such as physically preventing the eviction of a home, which then often leads to the bank negotiating. Thus a relationship is formed between bank and movement. The goal is keeping the family housed, which is done. This is distinct from organizing a protest in front of a bank demanding that they not evict a family or protesting their bad loaning practices. It may seem like a question of semantics, but it is far from it. The location of power is crucial here, and the movements see power as something one has: something exercised from below, not something to ask for from above. Matt from Occupy Wall Street in New York City reflected, "I guess, for me, I am a firm believer in the power of direct action and basically creating conditions where one would force the state to come to the negotiating table and consequently making these changes, rather than the framework of demands, which is perhaps a slightly less passive form of begging or petitioning, which I think often relegitimizes the power of the state."

Logic of Care, Not Capitalism

This power being created in the movements does not accept the value system of capitalism, in which the market determines the worth of a person's house or bodily health. The movement refuses to participate in that logic.

Instead, the logic is that of taking care of one another, grounded in prefigurative forms of democracy: forms that enact *now* what we would like to see generalized in the future. The movements in effect declare a different value system—one based in solidarity and democracy—in which each person is respected and heard and his or her opinions matter: this is real democracy. These new relations break with capitalist production rules and create something new. They are creating new values. The "rule" of the movements is not accumulation of capital or surplus but rather of affect and networks of solidarity and friendship. This new value is seen on the subjective level, in the change in people and their relationships to one another. This new value is enacted, concretely, in new ways of surviving and helping others survive based on these relationships.

The movements are young. In a short time, they not only have changed social relationships and created new, horizontal forms of democracy but also have begun to address people's day-to-day lives, making them more livable. These forms can go much farther, not only to keep people in their homes or to make sure they have access to health care, transportation, and education; they can also begin to address questions of the production and circulation of goods. We can see the beginnings of this with the few workplaces that have been taken over in the past year: from Thessaloniki, Greece, to Chicago, inspired in part by the recuperated workplace phenomenon in Argentina. We also see this with the growing barter networks and direct exchanges of goods between producers and consumers. These various actions, using directly democratic relationships, create the basis for new ways of relating that, if expanded, can create more cracks in the capitalist form of relating. As these cracks expand and are filled with more alternative ways of surviving and relating, the alternatives to capitalism expand. While not a "total" answer, these forms create more possibilities to go against and beyond capitalism. The proposition is not to create an alternative mode of production parallel to the state but rather to create forms that meet our needs—to develop deeper forms of democracy and real participation and thus become better able to take on the state, to take what is ours from it, and eventually to replace it with something else: something that we are still developing.

Success

Have these movements been successful? In part, that depends on how one understands and measures "success." While there are measurable "successes"—such as Greek assemblies taking over hospital cashiers so that health care is free, or reconnecting electricity that has been cut off, or the tens of thousands of people who have not lost their homes in Spain, Italy, and the United States due to the action of the housing groups—the thing these projects have in common with direct action is their form of organizing—it is not just *what* they are doing but *how*.

The focus of the organizing is people directly participating, speaking to their neighbors, forming assemblies, and together deciding what to do and then doing it without hierarchy or the election of representatives of parties. People around the globe continue to organize and do so in horizontal ways, attempting to prefigure the world they desire, and in the process, they are creating themselves anew. Participants in these new movements around the globe often speak of having been changed, of experiencing a new confidence and dignity. The shame people felt for losing jobs or houses has now become anger, combined with the knowledge, gained from experience, that they are not to blame. In fact, they know they are the majority, the 99 percent, that can do something about this crisis—a crisis that they did not create. They/we can organize with one another and create an alternative—not ask for one, but make one. That is power.

Contributors

Ronald Aronson is the Distinguished Professor Emeritus of the History of Ideas at Wayne State University.

Howard Brick is the Louis Evans Professor of History at the University of Michigan.

Mari Jo Buhle retired from Brown University in 2009, where she taught US women's and gender history.

Paul Buhle, retired senior lecturer at Brown University, was an SDS member in Champaign-Urbana, Illinois; Storrs, Connecticut; and Madison, Wisconsin.

Dorothy Dawson Burlage cofounded the Northern Student Movement and joined SDS in 1961. She holds a doctorate in psychology from Harvard (1978) and practices in Newton, Massachusetts.

Rita Chin is associate professor of history at the University of Michigan.

Juan Cole is the Richard P. Mitchell Professor of History and director of the Center for Middle Eastern and North African Studies at the University of Michigan.

Matthew J. Countryman is associate professor of history and American culture at the University of Michigan.

Alice Echols is professor of English and the Barbra Streisand Professor of Contemporary Gender Studies at the University of Southern California.

Dick Flacks, research professor of sociology at the University of California, Santa Barbara, was an early leader of SDS and a participant in the Port Huron convention.

Andrea Friedman is associate professor of history and women, gender, and sexuality studies at Washington University in St. Louis.

Robert Genter teaches in the Department of History at Nassau Community College.

Todd Gitlin, SDS president, 1963–64, is professor of journalism and sociology at Columbia University.

Ramón A. Gutiérrez is the Preston and Sterling Morton Distinguished Service Professor of American History at the University of Chicago.

Alan Haber, founding SDS president, 1960–62, and organizer of the Port Huron convention, is a cabinetmaker and activist in Ann Arbor.

Barbara Haber, participant in the Port Huron convention, practices psychotherapy in Berkeley.

Casey Hayden, SNCC and SDS activist and participant at Port Huron, lives with her family in Tucson, where she practices awareness and harvests rainwater, aloe vera, and mesquite beans.

Tom Hayden, SDS president, 1962–63, and lead writer of the *Port Huron Statement,* served in the California state legislature from 1982 to 2000 and directs the Peace and Justice Resource Center in Culver City, California.

Paul Hébert is a doctoral candidate in the Department of History at the University of Michigan.

Sarah Jaffe, cohost of *Dissent* magazine's "Belabored" podcast, writes about labor, social movements, gender, media, and student debt.

Frank Joyce, Northern Student Movement activist and a founder of People Against Racism in the late 1960s, is the board president of The Working Group (TWG), a nonprofit media production company supporting the antihate movement Not In Our Town (NIOT).

Sharon Jeffrey Lehrer, founding member of SDS, is a partner in Lehrer Designs, Inc., with her husband, Glenn.

Sarah Leonard is an editor at the *Nation* magazine.

Daryl Joji Maeda is associate professor and chair of ethnic studies at the University of Colorado, Boulder.

Richard D. Mann, an organizer of the 1965 Vietnam teach-in, is professor emeritus of psychology and religious studies at the University of Michigan.

Marian Mollin is associate professor of history at Virginia Polytechnic Institute and State University.

Kim Moody, participant in the Port Huron convention and longtime labor journalist, is senior research fellow at the Work and Employment Research Unit at the University of Hertfordshire, UK.

Aldon Morris is the Leon Forrest Professor of Sociology and African American Studies at Northwestern University.

Martha Prescod Noonan, SDS member and a SNCC field secretary, taught African American history at Wayne State University, the University of Toledo, and the University of Michigan.

Gregory Parker is administrator at the Eisenberg Institute for Historical

Studies at the University of Michigan.

Christopher Phelps is an associate professor of American history at the University of Nottingham, UK.

Leslie Pincus is associate professor of history at the University of Michigan.

Ruth Rosen is professor emerita of history at the University of California, Davis.

Robert J. S. Ross, a founding SDS member, is professor of sociology and director of the International Studies Stream at Clark University.

Marina Sitrin, visiting scholar at CUNY Graduate Center, was an active participant in Occupy Wall Street.

Paul Chaat Smith writes books and curates exhibitions on issues of Indian space and representation.

Michael Szalay is professor of English at the University of California, Irvine.

Maria Varela, participant in the Port Huron convention, was a SNCC field secretary working in Alabama and Mississippi, 1963–68, and taught at the University of New Mexico and Colorado College.

Michael Vester is professor emeritus of political science at the University of Hannover.

Alan Wald is the H. Chandler Davis Collegiate Professor Emeritus of English Literature and American Culture at the University of Michigan.

Louise E. Walker is assistant professor of history at Northeastern University.

Stephen M. Ward is associate professor in Afroamerican and African studies and the Residential College at the University of Michigan.

Notes

Introduction

1. Laurel Thatcher Ulrich, *Well-Behaved Women Seldom Make History* (New York: Knopf, 2007).

2. Nelson Lichtenstein, *A Contest of Ideas: Capital, Politics, and Labor* (Urbana: University of Illinois Press, 2013), 29–30.

3. Lee Marks, "Students on Diag Debate 'U' Faculty Suspensions," *Michigan Daily*, May 14, 1954.

4. Doris Lessing, "A Small Personal Voice," in *Declaration*, ed. Tom Maschler (London: MacGibbon and Kee, 1957), 185–201; Iris Murdoch, "A House of Theory," in *Conviction*, ed. Norman MacKenzie (London: MacGibbon and Kee, 1958), 230; E. P. Thompson, "At the Point of Decay" and "Revolution," in *Out of Apathy*, ed. E. P. Thompson (London: New Left Books, 1960), 3–15, 287–308.

5. Dick Flacks, personal communication to the author, March 7, 2014.

6. Paul Potter, quoted in James Miller, *"Democracy is in the Streets": From Port Huron to the Siege of Chicago* (New York: Simon and Schuster, 1987), 232.

7. Michael Löwy, *The Marxism of Che Guevara* (New York: Monthly Review Press, 1973); Potter, quoted in Miller, *"Democracy,"* 232.

Prologue

1. *Port Huron Statement*, reprinted in Tom Hayden, *The Port Huron Statement: The Visionary Call of the 1960s Revolution* (New York: Thunder's Mouth Press, 2005), 45.

2. Ibid.

3. Juan Gonzales, well known today for *Democracy Now!* and his columns in the *New York Daily News*, is a brilliant historian of our immigrant history. Less known is the fact that he was an SDS leader at Columbia University before joining up with the Young Lords Party in the late 1960s.

4. "A holy time" is the phrase of Sandra Cason (a.k.a. Casey Hayden), my wife at the time, who cast a vast charismatic spell over the early SDS and SNCC workers.

Convention Document #1

1. William Faulkner, "On Privacy (The American Dream: What Happened to It?),"
Harper's, July 1955, 34.
2. "Things are in the saddle" is a line in Ralph Waldo Emerson's "Ode, Inscribed to
W. H. Channing," in Stephen Whicher, ed., *Selections from Ralph Waldo Emerson* (Boston: Houghton Mifflin, 1960), 440.
3. Iris Murdoch, "A House of Theory," in *Conviction*, ed. Norman MacKenzie (London: MacGibbon and Kee, 1958), 227.
4. Ibid., 228.
5. C. Wright Mills, *Causes of World War III* (New York: Simon and Schuster, 1958),
130.

Convention Document #2

1. Quotation of the American satirist H. L. Mencken (1880–1956), *Notes on Democracy* (New York: Octagon Books, 1926), 148; reprinted in Andrew M. Scott, *Political Thought in America* (New York: Holt, Rinehart and Winston, 1960), 485.
2. Sheldon Wolin, *Politics and Vision: Continuity and Innovation in Western Political Thought* (Boston: Little, Brown, 1960), 389.
3. Scott, *Political Thought in America*, 475.
4. In his 1911 book, *Political Parties: A Sociological Study of the Oligarchical Tendencies of Modern Democracy*, trans. Eden and Cedar Paul (Glencoe, IL: Free Press, 1949), German sociologist Robert Michels (1876–1936) declared his "iron law of oligarchy," claiming that even revolutionary socialist parties inevitably fall under bureaucratic leaderships whose interest in organizational survival leads the party to collaborate with the political status quo.
5. Wolin, *Politics and Vision*, 353.
6. A. A. Berle, *The 20th Century Capitalist Revolution* (New York: Harcourt, 1954), 182–83. Berle (1895–1971), coauthor with Gardiner C. Means of *The Modern Corporation and Private Property* (New York: Macmillan, 1933), was a prominent Democratic Party liberal who belonged to Franklin Roosevelt's "Brain Trust" and headed President John Kennedy's task force on Latin American Affairs.
7. Philip Selznick, *The Organizational Weapon: A Study of Bolshevik Strategy and Tactics* (New York: McGraw-Hill, 1952), 284, 291. In the 1950s, Selznick (1919–2010), a Berkeley sociologist and one-time socialist, became a prominent organizational theorist and critic of authoritarian practices in Communist parties.
8. Herbert Blumer, "Collective Behavior," in *New Outline of the Principles of Sociology*, ed. A. M. Lee (New York: Barnes and Noble, 1946), quoted in Daniel Bell, *The End of Ideology: On the Exhaustion of Political Ideas in the Fifties*, rev. ed. (New York: Free Press, 1962), 23.
9. The phrase derived from José Ortega y Gasset's 1930 book *The Revolt of the Masses*, which criticized the conversion of the modern democratic idea of popular sovereignty into the "sovereignty of the unqualified individual, of the [generic] human being as such," as opposed to highly motivated individuals who sense they are "special" and thus

different from "the mass." See Ortega y Gasset, *The Revolt of the Masses* (New York: Norton, 1932), 23. In *The End of Ideology*, Daniel Bell presents Ortega's phrase as "judgment by the incompetent." Bell, *End of Ideology*, 23.

10. Selznick, *Organizational Weapon*, 277.

11. Erich Fromm, *May Man Prevail? An Inquiry into the Facts and Fictions of Foreign Policy* (Garden City, NY: Doubleday, 1961), 234–35. Fromm (1900–1980) was a German-born émigré social psychologist in the United States and member of the Socialist Party of America in the 1950s, known for his 1961 book advocating "Marxist humanism," *Marx's Concept of Man* (New York: Frederick Ungar, 1961), and his advocacy of nuclear disarmament with the organization SANE (National Committee for a Sane Nuclear Policy), formed in 1957 and winning the support of Martin Luther King Jr. in 1958.

RE: manifesto

1. Michael Harrington (1928–89), prominent young socialist, renowned for his book *The Other America: Poverty in the United States* (New York: Macmillan, 1962), and informal "adviser" to SDS in its first years. He represented the parent group, League for Industrial Democracy, at the Port Huron meeting and criticized SDSers for their "anti-anticommunism."

2. "Realignment" was the political program promoted by Harrington and Harrington's mentor in the Socialist Party, Max Shachtman. It sought to exclude the segregationist "Dixiecrats" from the Democratic Party, their traditional home, which would then enable the Democrats to fully represent the labor movement. As a result, US politics would be "realigned" along a clear divide—a determined reform party on the center-left, expected to be the majority party (Democrats), versus a conservative party on the center-right (Republicans).

3. See C. Wright Mills, *Causes of World War III* (New York: Simon and Schuster, 1958), 81–89.

4. Erich Fromm (1900–1980), social psychologist and Socialist Party member who had a prominent public profile and influence in liberal circles, particularly through his work with SANE, the National Committee for a Sane Nuclear Policy.

5. C. Wright Mills (1916–62), sociologist known for his self-consciously radical critique of the "power elite" in the United States, who had influence on both the British and US New Lefts; he suffered a fatal heart attack on March 20, 1962.

6. Father Charles Coughlin (1891–1979), Roman Catholic priest in Royal Oak, Michigan, and radio preacher of the 1930s, known for assailing the New Deal in "populist," anti-Semitic, and quasi-fascist terms.

7. Dean Rusk (1909–94), secretary of state under presidents John F. Kennedy and Lyndon B. Johnson, 1961–69.

8. Reinhold Niebuhr (1892–1971), Protestant theologian known for "neoorthodox" theology emphasizing the reality of human evil and his related doctrine of political "realism"; he was a left-wing socialist in the 1930s and a prominent public advocate of liberal anticommunism during and after World War II.

9. Nicolas de Condorcet (1743–94), French philosopher of rational progress in human betterment, a moderate republican in the French Revolution.

10. Southeast Asia Treaty Organization (1954–77), Cold War military alliance initiated and maintained by the United States.

11. National Executive Committee of SDS.

12. Erich Fromm wrote "The Case for Unilateral Disarmament," *Daedalus* 89 (Fall 1960): 1015–28, which was, however, not a pacifist call for complete nuclear disarmament by the United States (without awaiting international negotiation) but rather a proposal for "graduated . . . unilateral initiative in taking practical steps towards disarmament."

13. Speaking at Westminster College in Fulton, Missouri, March 5, 1946, former British prime minister Winston Churchill helped define Cold War politics when he declared that an "iron curtain" divided Soviet-dominated Eastern Europe from the West.

14. US Arms Control and Disarmament Agency, established in 1961.

15. A lawsuit begun in the Tennessee county including Memphis claimed that failure to redraw legislative districts according to federal censuses gave undue political power to depopulated rural areas. The suit led to the landmark Supreme Court decision *Baker v. Carr* (1962), which opened state apportionment to federal court scrutiny; subsequently, the Supreme Court's *Reynolds v. Sims* (1964) mandated redistricting on the principle of "one person, one vote."

16. European Common Market, formed in 1957.

17. January 21, 1962, meeting of the Organization of American States (OAS) in Uruguay, where the United States secured a measure excluding Cuba from OAS representation.

18. Referring to the *Congressional Record*, a ten-day filibuster in March 1962 by southern senators that delayed passage of a constitutional amendment banning poll taxes as a requirement for voting, later ratified as the Twenty-Fourth Amendment in 1964. Senator Thomas J. Dodd (Democrat, Connecticut) was one of a few northern senators who cooperated with southern Democrats in maintaining the filibuster to block passage of the poll tax ban. He spoke on irrelevant matters of judicial salaries and the United Nations.

19. A public debate over the effects of automation as a new stage of mechanization and labor-saving technology was at its height in the early 1960s. Tom Hayden signed a 1964 statement known as the Triple Revolution Manifesto, warning that automation could either lighten labor and reduce the work week for all—or result in mass unemployment. See Stephen Ward's chapter in this volume, "An Ending and a Beginning: James Boggs, C. L. R. James, and *The American Revolution*."

20. According to some radical critics beginning in the 1940s, a "permanent war economy" derived from a need of the capitalist economy to check tendencies toward depression by maintaining high government expenditures on arms. Although first coined in 1944, the phrase in later use implied that the US government sustained the Cold War for reasons of economic stability.

21. Joseph S. Clark Jr. (1901–90), a liberal supporter of civil rights from Pennsylvania, and James Eastland (1904–86), a Mississippi segregationist, were both Democratic senators. Senator Jacob Javits (1904–86) of New York was long known as a liberal Republican.

22. Universal Military Training (UMT), the name given to the peacetime military conscription system, from 1951 to 1967, by an act of Congress.

23. CD, or Civil Defense, is the government-mandated measures preparing for nuclear war—from air raid drills to fallout shelters—that peace activists assailed for encouraging the false notion that civilians could survive a battle of nuclear arms.

Part I

1. Casey Hayden and Mary King, "Sex and Caste: A Kind of Memo" (1965), reprinted in Timothy Patrick McCarthy and John McMillian, eds., *The Radical Reader* (New York: New Press, 2003), 417–20.

Chapter 1: A Call, Again

1. *Port Huron Statement*, reprinted in Tom Hayden, *The Port Huron Statement: The Visionary Call of the 1960s Revolution* (New York: Thunder's Mouth Press, 2005), 169.
2. Mark Rudd, *Underground: My Life with SDS and the Weatherman* (New York: Harper, 2010).
3. David Gilbert, Robert Gottlieb, and Gerry Tenney, "Port Authority Statement," in *Revolutionary Youth & the New Working Class: The Praxis Papers, the Port Authority Statement, the RYM Documents and Other Lost Writings of SDS*, ed. Carl Davidson (Pittsburgh: Changemaker Publications, 2011), 52–127.

Chapter 2: Experiencing the Sixties at the Intersection of SDS and SNCC

1. IF I HAD A HAMMER (The Hammer Song), words and music by Lee Hays and Pete Seeger, TRO-© copyright 1958 (renewed), 1962 (renewed) Ludlow Music, Inc., New York, New York. International copyright secured. Made in U.S.A. All rights reserved including public performance for profit. Used by permission.
2. I did not enter these professions, but two of my sons did become doctors employed at the University of Michigan Medical System and the third became a practicing attorney.

Chapter 3: Returning to Ann Arbor

1. Constance Curry et al., *Deep in Our Hearts: Nine White Women in the Freedom Movement* (Athens: University of Georgia Press, 2000); Faith S. Holsaert et al., eds., *Hands on the Freedom Plough: Personal Accounts by Women in SNCC* (Urbana: University of Illinois Press, 2012); Tom Hayden, *Inspiring Participatory Democracy: Student Movements from Port Huron to Today* (Boulder, CO: Paradigm Publishers, 2012).
2. Casey Hayden, "The Movement," *Witness* 2, nos. 2–3 (Summer/Fall 1988): 244–48.
3. Casey Hayden, "Port Huron: A Template of Hope," in *Inspiring Participatory Democracy: Student Movements from Port Huron to Today*, ed. Tom Hayden (Boulder, CO: Paradigm Publishers, 2012).

Chapter 4: Many Inheritances . . . One Legacy

1. Pope Leo XIII, *Rerum Novarum* (1891), published as *Rerum Novarum: Encyclical Letter of Pope Leo XIII on the Condition of Labor* (New York: Paulist Press, 1940).
2. *Port Huron Statement*, reprinted in Tom Hayden, *The Port Huron Statement: The Visionary Call of the 1960s Revolution* (New York: Thunder's Mouth Press, 2005), 52, 53.
3. Tom Hayden, *Reunion: A Memoir* (New York: Random House, 1988), 96.
4. *Port Huron Statement*, 53.

Chapter 5: Reflections on SDS and the 1960s Movements for Social Justice

1. Wilhelm Reich, *Where's the Truth?: Letters and Journals, 1948–57* (New York: Farrar, Straus, and Giroux, 2012), 17.

Chapter 7: The Evolution of a Radical's Consciousness

1. *Port Huron Statement*, reprinted in Tom Hayden, *The Port Huron Statement: The Visionary Call of the 1960s Revolution* (New York: Thunder's Mouth Press, 2005), 51.
2. "IONS Directory Profile, Biography, Edgar D. Mitchell," Institute of Noetic Sciences, accessed May 18, 2014, http://noetic.org/directory/person/edgar-mitchell.
3. *Port Huron Statement*, 51.

Chapter 8: Port Huron

1. *Port Huron Statement*, reprinted in Tom Hayden, *The Port Huron Statement: The Visionary Call of the 1960s Revolution* (New York: Thunder's Mouth Press, 2005), 45.

Chapter 10: Democracy, Labor, and Globalization

1. SLID was the distant offspring of a 1905 organization—the Intercollegiate Socialist Society—started by prominent intellectuals including the novelists Upton Sinclair and Jack London and the great lawyer Clarence Darrow. In the course of its historical evolution it had become the student group of the social-democratic League for Industrial Democracy (LID).
2. A. Javier Trevino, "Influence of C. Wright Mills on Students for a Democratic Society: An Interview with Bob Ross," *Humanity & Society* 22, no. 3 (1998): 260–77; Robert J. S. Ross, "At the Center and Edge: Notes on a Life In and Out of Sociology and the New Left," *Critical Sociology* 15, no. 2 (1988): 79–93.
3. Maurice Isserman, *The Other American: The Life of Michael Harrington* (New York: Public Affairs, 2000), 105–74.
4. Richard Rothstein, "Representative Democracy and SDS," in *Toward a History of the New Left: Essays from within the Movement*, ed. R. David Myers (New York: Carlson, 1989), 49–62.

5. *Port Huron Statement*, reprinted in Tom Hayden, *The Port Huron Statement: The Visionary Call of the 1960s Revolution* (New York: Thunder's Mouth Press, 2005), 85.

6. Ibid., 82.

7. Immanuel Ness and Dario Azzellini, eds., *Ours to Master and to Own: Workers' Control from the Commune to the Present* (Chicago: Haymarket, 2011).

8. "America and the New Era," Students for a Democratic Society, 1963, http://archive.lib.msu.edu/DMC/AmRad/americanewera.pdf.

9. Dick Flacks was the lead drafter of "America and the New Era" with, according to Kirkpatrick Sale, "considerable help from the theoretical apparatchik: Booth, Haber, Hayden, Ross," *SDS* (New York: Vintage, 1973), 90, http://www.antiauthoritarian.net/sds_wuo/sds_documents/sds_kirkpatrick_sale.pdf.

10. Robert J. Ross, "Primary Groups in Social Movements: A Memoir and Interpretation," *Journal of Voluntary Action Research* 6, nos. 3–4 (1977): 139–52.

11. John Kenneth Galbraith, *American Capitalism: The Concept of Countervailing Power* (Piscataway, NJ: Transaction Books, 1993).

12. *Port Huron Statement*, 168.

13. Peter B. Levy, *The New Left and Labor in The 1960s* (Champaign: University of Illinois Press, 1994).

Chapter 11: Lefts Old and New

1. Saul D. Alinsky, *Reveille for Radicals* (1946; repr., New York: Vintage, 1969), 184.

2. Wilhelm Reich, *Listen, Little Man* (1948; repr., Harmondsworth: Penguin, 1975), 38.

3. Henry F. May, "The End of American Radicalism," *American Quarterly* 2, no. 4 (Winter 1950): 291–302.

4. Staughton Lynd, *Living Inside Our Hope* (Ithaca, NY: ILR Press, 1997), 67.

Chapter 12: Of Little Rocks and Levittowns

1. *Port Huron Statement*, reprinted in Tom Hayden, *The Port Huron Statement: The Visionary Call of the 1960s Revolution* (New York: Thunder's Mouth Press, 2005), 45.

2. Kirkpatrick Sale, *SDS* (New York: Random House, 1973), 50.

3. Jo Freeman, *At Berkeley in the Sixties: The Making of an Activist* (Bloomington: Indiana University Press, 2003), 34.

4. *Port Huron Statement*, 114–15.

5. For two exceptions to this trend, see Wini Breines, *Young, White and Miserable: Growing Up Female in the Fifties* (Chicago: University of Chicago Press, 2001), and Mark D. Naison, *White Boy: A Memoir* (Philadelphia: Temple University Press, 2002).

6. Thomas J. Sugrue, *Sweet Land of Liberty: The Forgotten Struggle for Civil Rights in the North* (New York: Random House, 2008), 222–28.

7. Ibid., 200–212.

8. Matthew J. Countryman, *Up South: Civil Rights and Black Power in Philadelphia* (Philadelphia: University of Pennsylvania Press, 2006), 53.

9. Sugrue, *Sweet Land of Liberty*, 170–99; Mary Jo Frank, *A History of the Desegregation of the Ann Arbor Public Schools, 1954–76* (Ann Arbor: Program for Educational

Opportunity, School of Education, University of Michigan, 1976); Jim Schutze, "Race Story," in *When Race Becomes Real: Black and White Writers Confront their Personal Histories*, ed. Bernestine Singley (Chicago: Lawrence Hill Books, 2002), 3-20.

10. The Philadelphia Commission on Human Relations, "Annual Report, 1960," Commission on Human Relations papers, box 148, folder 1, Philadelphia Municipal Archives.

11. Sugrue, *Sweet Land of Liberty*, 130-62.

12. Peter Countryman, "Autobiographical Sketch," n.d., 27, in author's possession. Countryman is the author's father.

13. On CORE's campus chapters, see Freeman, *At Berkeley in the Sixties*, 87-107, and Naison, *White Boy*, 38-49. On the NSA Liberal Caucus, see Tom Hayden, *Reunion: A Memoir* (New York: Random House, 1988), 36-42, 50-52. On the Free Speech Movement, see W. J. Rorabaugh, *Berkeley at War: The 1960s* (New York: Oxford University Press, 1990), and Robert Cohen and Reginald E. Zelnick, eds., *The Free Speech Movement: Reflections on Berkeley in the 1960s* (Berkeley: University of California Press, 2002). On NSM, see D'Army Bailey with Roger Eason, *The Education of a Black Radical: A Southern Civil Rights Activist's Journey, 1959-1964* (Baton Rouge: Louisiana State University Press, 2009), 156-58, 179-208, and Wesley Hogan, *Many Minds, One Heart: SNCC's Dream for a New America* (Chapel Hill: University of North Carolina Press, 2009), 100, 111, 135-37.

14. Breines, *Young, White and Miserable*, 1-24.

15. Hayden, *Reunion*, 14.

16. David M. P. Freund, *Colored Property: State Policy and White Racial Politics in Suburban America* (Chicago: University of Chicago Press, 2010), 243.

17. Hayden, *Reunion*, 6-16; "Expert Report of James D. Anderson," Gratz, in *The Compelling Need for Diversity in Higher Education: Gratz, et al. vs. Bollinger, et al., no. 97-75231 (E.D. Mich.): Grutter, et al. v. Bollinger, et al., no. 97-75928 (E.D. Mich.)."

18. Freeman, *At Berkeley in the Sixties*, 2-6, 69.

19. Countryman, "Autobiographical Sketch," 26-27.

20. Ibid., 27-28.

21. Mario Savio, "Thirty Years Later: Reflections on the FSM," in Cohen and Zelnick, eds., *The Free Speech Movement*, 58.

22. Todd Gitlin, *The Sixties: Years of Hope, Days of Rage* (New York: Bantam Books, 1987), 1-77.

23. James Miller, "*Democracy is in the Streets*": *From Port Huron to the Siege of Chicago* (New York: Simon and Schuster, 1987), 31-33; Sharon Jeffrey Lehrer, "The Evolution of a Radical's Consciousness: Living an Authentic Life," in this volume.

24. Bettina F. Aptheker, *Intimate Politics: How I Grew Up Red, Fought for Free Speech, and Became a Feminist Rebel* (Berkeley: Seal Press, 2011), 33-86; Margot Adler, *Heretic's Heart: A Journey Through Spirit & Revolution* (Boston: Beacon Press, 1997), 1-67.

25. Marilyn Lowen, "I Knew I Wasn't White, but in America What Was I?," in *Hands on the Freedom Plow: Personal Accounts by Women in SNCC*, ed. Faith S. Holsaert et al. (Urbana: University of Illinois Press, 2010), 540-52.

26. Naison, *White Boy*, 31-32, 45-46.

27. Ibid.,14.

28. Ibid., 46-47.

29. Krystal D. Frazier, "Till They Come Back Home: Transregional Families and the Politicization of the Till Generation," in *Freedom Rights: New Perspectives on the Civil*

Rights Movement, ed. Danielle McGuire and John Dittmer (Lexington: The University of Kentucky Press, 2011), 137–62; David Halberstam, *The Children* (New York: Fawcett Books, 1999), 135–45; Cheryl Lynn Greenberg, *A Circle of Trust: Remembering SNCC* (New Brunswick: Rutgers University Press, 1998), 45; Stokely Carmichael with Ekwueme Michael Thelwell, *Ready for Revolution: The Life and Struggles of Stokely Carmichael (Kwame Ture)* (New York: Scribner, 2003); Prathia Hall, "Freedom-Faith," in Holsaert et al., 172–80; James Forman, *The Making of Black Revolutionaries* (Seattle: University of Washington Press, 1997); Robert P. Moses and Charles E. Cobb Jr., *Radical Equations: Civil Rights from Mississippi to the Algebra Project* (Boston: Beacon Press, 2002); Martha Prescod Noonan, "Captured by the Movement," in Holsaert et al., *Hands on the Freedom Plow*, 483–503.

30. Susan Sward, "Carolyn Craven, Reporter for KQED's Newsroom," *SFGate*, November 22, 2000, http://www.sfgate.com/news/article/Carolyn-Craven-Reporter-For-KQED-s-Newsroom-2695415.php; Phil Hutchings, interview by Joseph Mosnier, Library of Congress, September 1, 2011, http://www.loc.gov/item/afc2010039_crhp0042.

31. William L. Strickland, "Remembering Malcolm: A Personal Critique of Manning Marable's Non-Definitive Biography of Malcolm X," *Black Commentator*, October 13, 2011.

32. "About Representative Byron Rushing," Health Disparities Council, http://www.mass.gov/hdc/about-representative-byron-rushing.html; Joan Countryman, interview with Matthew Countryman, March 16, 1994; Joan Cannady Countryman is the author's mother; Charyn Sutton, interview with Matthew Countryman, March 5, 1994; John Churchville, interview with Matthew Countryman, February 16, 1994; Carl Wilmsen, "The Civil Rights Movement and Expanding the Boundaries of Environmental Justice in the San Francisco Bay Area, 1960–1999: Oral History Transcript," 2003, Regional Oral History Office, University of California, archive.org/stream/civilrightsmoveoocarlrich/civilrightsmoveoocarlrich_djvu.txt; Mike Heichman, "Chuck Turner's Story—Chapter 1: A Lifetime of Service," *Green Mass Group*, July 1, 2011, http://www.greenmassgroup.com/diary/599/chuck-turners-storychapter-1-a-lifetime-of-service.

33. Charyn Sutton, interview.

34. Joan Countryman, interview.

35. Carmichael, *Ready for Revolution*, 60–109.

36. Charyn Sutton, interview; Joan Countryman, interview; Phil Hutchings, interview.

37. Carmichael, *Ready for Revolution*, 100–101.

38. Countryman, *Up South*, 181, 188.

39. Freeman, *At Berkeley in the Sixties*, 63–102; Wilmsen "The Civil Rights Movement and Expanding the Boundaries"; Waldo Martin, "Holding One Another: Mario Savio and the Freedom Struggle in Mississippi and Berkeley," in *The Free Speech Movement: Reflections on Berkeley in the 1960s*, ed. Robert Cohen and Reginald E. Zelnick (Berkeley, CA: University of California Press, 2002), 83–103; Terry H. Anderson, *The Pursuit of Fairness: A History of Affirmative Action* (New York: Oxford University Press, 2004), 76.

40. Heichman, "Chuck Turner's Story—Chapter 1"; Paul Lyons, *The People of this Generation: The Rise and Fall of the New Left in Philadelphia* (Philadelphia: University of Pennsylvania Press, 2003).

41. Jennifer Frost, *"An Interracial Movement of the Poor": Community Organizing and the New Left in the 1960s* (New York: New York University Press, 2001), 71–173.

Chapter 13: The Lightning Bolt That Sparked the *Port Huron Statement*

1. James B. McKee, *Sociology and the Race Problem: The Failure of a Perspective* (Urbana: University of Illinois Press, 1993).

2. Gunnar Myrdal with the assistance of Richard Sterner and Arnold Rose, *An American Dilemma: The Negro Problem and Modern Democracy* (New York: Harper and Brothers, 1944), xxxiii.

3. Lawrence Bobo, "Reclaiming A Du Boisian Perspective On Racial Attitudes," *The Annals of the American Academy of Political and Social Science* 568, no. 1 (March 2000): 186–202.

4. See Martha Prescod Noonan's chapter, "Experiencing the Sixties at the Intersection of SDS and SNCC," in this volume.

5. W. E. B. Du Bois, *Black Reconstruction In America, 1860–1880* (New York: Harcourt, Brace and Company, 1935).

6. Ralph Ellison, *Invisible Man*, 2nd ed. (New York: Vintage International, 1995), 3.

7. C. Wright Mills, *The Sociological Imagination* (London: Oxford University Press, 1959), 5–6.

8. Stanley Aronowitz, "On Tom Hayden's Radical Nomad," in *Radical Nomad: C Wright Mills and His Times*, Tom Hayden (Boulder, CO: Paradigm Publishers, 2006), 25.

9. Dick Flacks, "C. Wright Mills, Tom Hayden, and the New Left," in Hayden, *Radical Nomad, 1–20*.

10. Aldon Morris, *Origins of the Civil Rights Movement: Black Communities Organizing for Change* (New York: Free Press, 1984); Belinda Robnett, *How Long? How Long?: African American Women in the Struggle for Civil Rights* (Oxford University Press, 1997).

11. Aldon Morris, "Black Southern Student Sit-In Movement: An Analysis of Internal Organization," *American Sociological Review* 46, no. 6 (1981): 744–67.

12. Tom Hayden, *Reunion* (New York: Random House, 1988), 39.

13. Ibid., 41.

14. Tom Hayden, "The Rise of White Power," *The Peace & Justice Resource Center* (blog), June 18, 2014, http://tomhayden.com/home/the-rise-of-white-power.html.

15. Ibid.

16. Hayden, *Reunion*, 35–36.

17. Ibid., 39–40.

18. Ibid., 62.

19. Ibid., 63.

20. Ibid., 55.

21. Sara Evans, *Personal Politics* (New York: Vintage Books, 1980); Jo Freeman, "On the Origins of the Women's Liberation Movement from a Strictly Personal Perspective," in *The Feminist Memoir Project*, ed. Rachel Blau DuPlessis and Ann Snitow (New York: Three Rivers Press, 1998).

22. Hayden, *Reunion*, 56.

23. Jo Freeman, "On the Origins of the Women's Liberation Movement from a Strictly Personal Perspective," 1995, http://www.jofreeman.com/aboutjo/persorg.htm (this is an extended version of the essay that appeared in *The Feminist Memoir Project*).

24. Evans, *Personal Politics*, 100.

25. Hayden, *Reunion*, 54.

26. "Statement of Purpose," Student Nonviolent Coordinating Committee, Spring 1960, wps.prenhall.com/wps/media/objects/173/177665/28_state.HTM.

27. Hayden, *Reunion*, 44.

28. *Port Huron Statement*, reprinted in Tom Hayden, *The Port Huron Statement: The Visionary Call of the 1960s Revolution* (New York: Thunder's Mouth Press, 2005), 45.

29. Ibid., 152.

30. "Student Nonviolent Coordinating Committee Founding Statement," *The Sixties Project*, 1993, http://www2.iath.virginia.edu/sixties/HTML_docs/Resources/Primary/Manifestos/SNCC_founding.html.

31. Martin Luther King Jr., "Loving Your Enemies" (sermon, Dexter Avenue Baptist Church, November 17, 1957), http://mlk-kpp01.stanford.edu/index.php/encyclopedia/documentsentry/doc_loving_your_enemies.

32. *Port Huron Statement*, 53.

33. Ibid., 53.

34. Ibid., 55.

35. Ibid., 53.

36. Carol Mueller, "*Ella Baker* and the Origins of 'Participatory Democracy,'" in *Women in the Civil Rights Movement: Trailblazers and Torchbearers, 1941–1965,* ed. Vicki L. Crawford, Anne Rouse, and Barbara Woods (Bloomington: Indiana University Press, 1990), 53.

37. Hayden, *Reunion*, 44.

38. *Port Huron Statement*, 45.

39. Ibid., 111.

40. Ibid.

41. Ibid.

42. W. E. B. Du Bois, *The Souls of Black Folk* (Chicago: A. C. McClurg and Company, 1903).

43. *Port Huron Statement*, 112.

44. Ibid.

Chapter 14: A New Left Philosophical Itinerary

1. Ronald Aronson, *After Marxism* (New York: Guilford Press, 1995), 12–13.

2. Ronald Aronson, "Dear Herbert: A Letter to Herbert Marcuse," *Radical America* 4, no. 3 (1970): 3–18.

3. Jean-Paul Sartre, *Being and Nothingness* (1956; repr., New York: Washington Square Press, 1992), 703.

4. Ronald Aronson, introduction to Jean-Paul Sartre, *We Have Only This Life to Live: The Selected Essays of Jean-Paul Sartre 1939–1975,* ed. Ronald Aronson and Adrian van den Hoven (New York: New York Review Editions, 2013), vii–xxiv.

5. Jean-Paul Sartre, *Sartre on Cuba* (New York: Ballantine, 1961), 7.

6. Sartre, "The Wretched of the Earth," in Sartre, *We Have Only This Life to Live,* 393.

7. Sartre, "The Wretched of the Earth," 397.

8. Albert Camus, *The Myth of Sisyphus* (New York: Vintage 1991), 121.

9. Ronald Aronson, *Camus and Sartre: The Story of a Friendship and the Quarrel That Ended It* (Chicago: University of Chicago Press, 2006), 52.

10. Albert Camus, *The Plague* (New York: Vintage, 1948), 232–33.

11. Albert Camus, "Neither Victims nor Executioners," originally published in *Combat* in 1946; English translation published in *Politics* 4 (July–August 1947): 141–45.

12. Jean-Paul Sartre, *What Is Literature?* (1965; repr., New York: Washington Square Press, 1960), 283–84.

13. Paul Berman, *Terror and Liberalism* (New York: Norton, 2003).

14. "Sartre and Terror," Terror Symposium, North American Sartre Society, Loyola University in New Orleans, March 2002; accessed February 2, 2015, http://www.is.wayne.edu/raronson/Articles/Terror%20Symposium.pdf.

Chapter 15: Participatory Art as Participatory Democracy

1. John Dewey, *Art as Experience*, ed. Jo Ann Boydston (Carbondale: Southern Illinois University Press, 1989), 352.

2. Ibid., 110.

3. Tom Hayden, *The Port Huron Statement: The Visionary Call of the 1960s Revolution* (New York: Thunder's Mouth Press, 2005), 53.

4. Todd Gitlin, *The Sixties: Years of Hope, Days of Rage* (New York: Bantam Books, 1993), 85.

5. Norman O. Brown, *Life Against Death: The Psychoanalytical Meaning of History*, 2nd ed. (Hanover: University Press of New England, 1985), 64.

6. Kathryn Mills and Pamela Mills, eds., *C. Wright Mills: Letters and Autobiographical Writings* (Berkeley: University of California Press, 2000), 112.

7. C. Wright Mills, *The Sociological Imagination* (New York: Oxford University Press, 1959), 214.

8. Ibid.

9. *Port Huron Statement*, 47.

10. Ibid., 9.

11. Jack Kerouac, *Good Blonde and Others* (San Francisco: Grey Fox Press, 1993), 81, 74.

12. Tom Hayden, *Rebel: A Personal History of the 1960s* (Los Angeles: Red Hen Press, 2003), 16.

13. Harold Rosenberg, *The Tradition of the New* (New York: McGraw-Hill, 1965), 33.

14. Ibid., 27.

15. On high modernism, see Robert Genter, *Late Modernism: Art, Culture, and Politics in Cold War America* (Philadelphia: University of Pennsylvania Press, 2010).

16. Kerouac, *Good Blonde*, 74.

17. *Port Huron Statement*, 59.

18. Ibid.

19. Gitlin, *The Sixties*, 134.

20. *Port Huron Statement*, 51.

21. Ibid., 52.

22. Ibid.

23. Ibid.

24. Ibid., 32.

25. James Miller, *"Democracy is in the Streets": From Port Huron to the Siege of Chicago* (New York: Simon and Schuster, 1987), 143–46.

26. Quoted in Kay Larson, *Where the Heart Beats: John Cage, Zen Buddhism, and the Inner Life of Artists* (New York: Penguin Press, 2012), 194.

27. John Cage, *For the Birds: John Cage in Conversation with Daniel Charles* (Boston: Marion Boyars, 1981), 80.

28. *Port Huron Statement*, 7.

29. Dewey, *Art as Experience*, 9.

30. Joseph Jacobs, "Crashing New York à la John Cage," in *Off Limits: Rutgers University and the Avant-Garde, 1957–1963*, ed. Joan Marter (New Brunswick: Rutgers University Press, 1999): 65–99.

31. Allan Kaprow, *Essays on the Blurring of Art and Life*, ed. Jeff Kelley (Berkeley: University of California Press, 1993), 6.

32. Ibid., 7.

33. Richard Kostelanetz, *The Theatre of Mixed-Means* (New York: RK Editions, 1980), 3.

34. Kaprow, *Essays*, 21.

35. Owen F. Smith, *Fluxus: The History of an Attitude* (San Diego: San Diego State University Press, 1998).

36. Quoted in Thomas Kellein, *The Dream of Fluxus* (London: Edition Hansjörg Mayer, 2007), 72.

37. Ibid.

38. Quoted in Smith, *Fluxus*, 165.

39. *Port Huron Statement*, 8.

40. Quoted in Kostelanetz, *Theatre of Mixed-Means*, 130.

41. *Port Huron Statement*, 5.

42. Gitlin, *The Sixties*, 123.

43. Ibid., 213.

44. Miller, *"Democracy is in the Streets,"* 253.

45. Bradford D. Martin, *The Theater Is in the Streets: Politics and Performance in Sixties America* (Amherst: University of Massachusetts Press, 2004).

46. Hannah Higgins, *Fluxus Experience* (Berkeley: University of California Press, 2002).

47. Claire Bishop, *Artificial Hells: Participatory Art and the Politics of Spectatorship* (New York: Verso, 2012); Carla Blumenkranz et al., eds., *Occupy!: Scenes from Occupied America* (New York: Verso, 2011).

48. *Port Huron Statement*, 48.

Chapter 16: Facing the Abyss

1. *Port Huron Statement*, reprinted in Tom Hayden, *The Port Huron Statement: The Visionary Call of the 1960s Revolution* (New York: Thunder's Mouth Press, 2005), 47.

2. Leon Festinger, Henry W. Riecken, and Stanley Schachter, *When Prophecy Fails: A Social and Psychological Study of a Modern Group that Predicted the Destruction of the World* (Minneapolis: University of Minnesota Press, 1956).

3. *Port Huron Statement*, 63.

4. Walter Sullivan, "Babies Surveyed for Strontium 90," *New York Times*, November 25, 1961. The second paragraph consisted of an on-the-other-hand qualification: "However, the radioactive material that is absorbed becomes a lifelong component of the teeth and skeleton."

5. The information in this paragraph is derived from a PBS documentary, *The Man Who Saved the World*, MPEG video, 53:10, from *Secrets of the Dead* television series, Bedlam Productions, October 23, 2012, http://www.pbs.org/wnet/secrets/episodes/the-man-who-saved-the-world-watch-the-full-episode/905, and Martin Sherwin, "The Cuban Missile Crisis Revisited: Nuclear Deterrence? Good Luck!" *Cornerstone*, July 16, 2012, http://cornerstone.gmu.edu/articles/4198.

6. Jean-Paul Sartre, foreword to *Aden, Arabie*, by Paul Nizan, trans. Joan Pinkham (1960; repr., New York: Monthly Review Press, 1968), 28.

7. John F. Kennedy, "American University Commencement Address," American Rhetoric Top 100 Speeches, June 10, 1963, http://www.americanrhetoric.com/speeches/jfkamericanuniversityaddress.html.

8. Ron Rosenbaum, *How the End Begins: The Road to a Nuclear World War III* (New York: Simon and Schuster, 2012), 53.

9. Todd Gitlin, "How to Reverse a Slow-Motion Apocalypse," *TomDispatch*, November 21, 2013, http://www.tomdispatch.com/post/175775.

10. C. Wright Mills, *The Causes of World War III* (New York: Ballantine, 1959), 89ff.

11. Albert Camus, *The Myth of Sisyphus and Other Essays*, trans. Justin O'Brien (New York: Vintage, 1955), 119ff.

Chapter 17: Beyond Port Huron

1. This chapter is dedicated to Ralph Levitt, who taught me how to think politically and historically. Some of the aspects of the events of October 24, 1962, and subsequent defense case are in dispute. A somewhat different version of this chapter was published as "The Audacity of American Trotskyism: The Indiana 'Subversion' Case Fifty Years Later," *Against the Current* no. 165 (July–August 2013): 27–31. It contains several footnotes of details and documentation cut by the editors of this volume for reasons of space. We are grateful for permission to reprint.

2. "Thousands of Students Smash Cuba Sympathizers' Protest at I. U.," *Indianapolis Star*, October 25, 1962, 1, 17.

3. Francesca Poletta, *Freedom Is an Endless Meeting: Democracy in American Social Movements* (Chicago: University of Chicago Press, 2004), 123–24.

4. The Young Socialist Alliance (1960–92), was a revolutionary socialist youth organization in solidarity with the Trotskyist SWP. The Fair Play for Cuba Committee (1960–63), was established by members of the SWP and others to mobilize support for Cuba in the face of US efforts to suppress the revolution.

5. To my knowledge, only two books have substantially discussed the case in recent decades: Mary Ann Wynkoop, *Dissent in the Heartland* (Bloomington: Indiana University Press, 2002), 13–18; Barry Sheppard, *The Party: A Political Memoir*, vol. 1 (Chippendale, Australia: Resistance Books, 2005), 86–92. Both are accurate about the events, with Wynkoop focusing principally on the impact on the university and Sheppard providing excellent firsthand details about the stages of the legal process and his own activities in the defense campaign.

6. This is a famous quotation from E. P. Thompson, *The Making of the English Working Class* (London: Gollancz, 1963), 12. Others who assisted in providing various information for this chapter, including all the Bloomington Three, are cited in various footnotes. I especially wish to acknowledge Jeff Mackler, National Secretary of Socialist Action; Michael

Tormey, a retired transit worker who was assigned to the Boston office of CABS; George Shriver, a translator; Barry Sheppard, author of several books about the SWP; the late Gerry Foley (a pseudonym for Gerry Paul), a Marxist journalist and member of Socialist Action at the time of his death; and the late Don Smith, a Chicago public school teacher who was a member of Workers World Party at the time of his death.

7. Ralph Levitt, personal communication, e-mail to author, May 28, 2000.

8. Little public information is available about McRae beyond his role in the Bloomington Case. He came from Pennsylvania and attended law school at Pennsylvania State University. In the fall of 1962 he ran on the SWP ticket for attorney general of New York, when he listed his occupation as a compositor. While National Organizational Secretary of the YSA, he participated in civil rights and Fair Play for Cuba Committee activities. Although he was widely admired for talent and leadership skills, his name disappeared from all available records of the SWP a year or so after the case was launched. Paulann Sheets (formerly Paulann Groninger) believes that attorney Louis Boudin subsequently uncovered evidence that McRae was an FBI informer, but this has not been confirmed by actual documentation and such allegations, spread sometimes by the FBI itself, must be treated cautiously. Paulann Sheets, personal communication, e-mail to author, June 12, 2013.

9. References to the sexual orientation of individuals in the pre-Stonewall era can be a tricky and often thankless task, but the historian who remains silent on such matters only contributes to an erasure of the gay and lesbian presence in the far left, which is much more significant than has been acknowledged. One of the two individuals, Gerry Paul, was not present at the demonstration, having transferred to the University of Wisconsin, but is credited with creating the fighting spirit of the Bloomington YSA. What is known about his intimate life is only a long-term partnership in his later years with a male companion named Pete who described the relation as a gay one. Jeff Mackler, personal communication, e-mail to author, June 21, 2012. The other, Leonard Boudin, head of the defense team for the Bloomington Three, was a legendary womanizer who had a passionate sexual relationship with anarchist Paul Goodman, according to the research in Susan Braudy, *Family Circle: The Boudins and the Aristocracy of the Left* (New York: Knopf, 2003). Therefore, the description "gay or bisexual" seems apt, although several former Bloomington YSA members object to this. Details about the personal lives of many of the other actors are simply not known.

10. Some of the information comes from George Shriver, "On Gerry Foley's Death Today" (personal communication, e-mail to SA-News at yahoogroups.com, April 12, 2012). See also the excellent obituary by Jeff Mackler, "Gerry Foley: A Life Dedicated to the Socialist Revolution," *International Viewpoint*, May 2, 2102, http://internationalviewpoint.org/spip.php?article2597.

11. Gerry Foley, personal communication, e-mail to author, June 4, 2000.

12. Ralph Levitt, personal communication, e-mail to author, May 26, 2000.

13. Ibid.

14. George Shriver, personal communication, e-mail to author, April 22, 2013.

15. These reminiscences, along with many additional (and fascinating) details, appear as a commentary in an early version of this chapter, Alan Wald, "The Indiana 'Subversion' Case 50 Years Later," solidarity-us.org/site/node/3936.

16. Ralph Levit, personal communication, e-mail to author, May 26, 2000.

17. Ibid.

18. This is from Frost's 1915 poem, "A Servant to Servants," although the exact meaning has been disputed.

19. This claim was based on information that during the winter of 1962, YSA and YPSL members brought canned goods and groceries to striking coal miners in Harland County, Kentucky; on one occasion, shots were fired at Jack Marsh, Jim Bingham, and Charlie Leinenweber. Tom Morgan, personal communication, e-mail to author, April 12, 2013.

20. Gregory Hildebrand, personal communication, e-mail to author, September 19, 2013.

21. Ibid.

22. John Crowley, personal communication, e-mail to author, December 7, 2013. The footage of the demonstration may exist in an archive of Bird.

23. Tom Morgan, personal communication, e-mail to author, April 13, 2013.

24. Todd Gitlin, personal communication, e-mail to author, September 13, 2013.

25. Tom Hayden, personal communication, e-mail to author, December 14, 2013.

26. Richard Flacks, personal communication, e-mail to author, December 13, 2013.

27. James Bingham, personal communication, e-mail to author, April 13, 2013; Barry Sheppard, personal communication, e-mail to author, May 23, 2002.

28. Ralph Levitt, personal communication, e-mail to author, May 26, 2000.

29. This is based on a recollection of Don Smith, telephone interview by author, July 22, 2000. In addition, Levitt stated in an e-mail to the author on May 23, 2013, "I recall that we were warned against holding the demonstration. This would probably have been a phone call since the matter was urgent and pressing." However, in an email to the author on May 23, 2013, Sheppard states that he has no recollection of any such warnings.

Part III

1. Naomi Klein, "Reclaiming the Commons," in *A Movement of Movements: Is Another World Really Possible?*, ed. Tom Mertes (London: Verso, 2004), 220.

Chapter 18: Refugees from the Fifties

1. Quoted in Ruth Rosen, *The World Split Open: How the Modern Women's Movement Changed America* (New York: Viking Penguin, 2000), vi.

2. Sheryl Burt Ruzek, *The Women's Health Movement: Feminist Alternatives to Medical Control* (New York: Praeger, 1978), 52–57.

3. Elaine Brown, *A Taste of Power* (New York: Pantheon Books, 1992), 367.

Chapter 19: The Empire at Home

1. *Port Huron Statement*, reprinted in Tom Hayden, *The Port Huron Statement: The Visionary Call of the 1960s Revolution* (New York: Thunder's Mouth Press, 2005), 46.

2. Vincenzo Petrullo, *Puerto Rican Paradox* (Philadelphia: University of Pennsylvania Press, 1947), offered the first use of this term. For an excellent orientation to the legal and constitutional framing of this contradiction, see Christina Duffy Burnett and Burke Marshall, eds., *Foreign in a Domestic Sense: Puerto Rico, American Expansion, and the Constitution* (Durham: Duke University Press, 2001).

3. Margaret Power, "The Puerto Rican Nationalist Party, Transnational Latin American Solidarity, and the United States during the Cold War," in *Human Rights and Transnational Solidarity in Cold War America*, ed. Jessica Stites Mor (Madison: University of Wisconsin Press, 2013): 21–47; Miñi Seijo Bruno, *La Insurrección Nacionalista en Puerto Rico, 1950* (San Juan: Editorial Edil, 1989); David Helfeld, "Discrimination for Political Beliefs and Associations," *Revista del Colegio de Abogados de Puerto Rico* 25, no. 1 (1964): 5; Stephen Hunter and John Bainbridge, *American Gunfight: The Plot to Kill Harry Truman—and the Shoot-Out That Stopped It* (New York: Simon and Schuster, 2005); Irene Vilar, *A Message from God in the Atomic Age: A Memoir* (New York: Pantheon Books, 1996); Federico Ribes Tovar, *Lolita Lebrón: La Prisionera* (New York: Plus Ultra Educational, 1974). The argument in this chapter rests on the expanded analysis of Cold War era debates about Puerto Rico's status in Andrea Friedman, *Citizenship in Cold War America: The National Security State and the Possibilities of Dissent* (Amherst: University of Massachusetts Press, 2014).

4. Ramón Bosque-Pérez and José Javier Colón Morera, eds., *Puerto Rico Under Colonial Rule: Political Persecution and the Quest for Human Rights* (Albany: State University of New York Press, 2006); Helfeld, "Discrimination"; Carlos Rodríguez Fraticelli, "US Solidarity with Puerto Rico: Rockwell Kent, 1937," in *Colonial Dilemma: Critical Perspectives on Contemporary Puerto Rico*, ed. Edwin Meléndez and Edgardo Meléndez (Boston: South End Press, 1993), 189–98.

5. Paul R. Dekar, *Creating the Beloved Community: A Journey with the Fellowship of Reconciliation* (Telford, PA: Cascadia Publishing, 2005), 97–100; Richard G. Fox, "Passage from India," in *Between Resistance and Revolution: Cultural Politics and Social Protest*, ed. Richard G. Fox and Orin Starn (New Brunswick: Rutgers University Press, 1997), 65–82; Joseph Kip Kosek, *Acts of Conscience: Christian Nonviolence and Modern American Democracy* (New York: Columbia University Press, 2009), 183–86; James Farmer, *Lay Bare the Heart: An Autobiography of the Civil Rights Movement* (Fort Worth: Texas Christian University Press, 2013), 149–52; Conrad Lynn, *There Is a Fountain: The Autobiography of a Civil Rights Lawyer* (Westport, CT: Lawrence Hill and Company, 1979), 85–91.

6. Reynolds Oral History, folders 1 and 2, box 45, Ruth M. Reynolds Papers, Archives of the Puerto Rican Diaspora, Centro de Estudios Puertorriqueños, Hunter College, City University of New York; [illeg.] to The Socialist Party of New York, January 23, 1944, folder 7, box 22, Reynold Papers.

7. Reynolds Oral History, folder 3, box 45, Reynolds Papers.

8. Pearl S. Buck to Dear Friend, March 22, 1945, folder 5, box 18, Reynolds Papers; "Statement of Position of The American League for Puerto Rico's Independence," folder 4, ibid.; "For Immediate Release," July 21, 1945, ibid.; Jay Holmes Smith and Ruth M. Reynolds to President Truman, September 5, 1945, Government-Status-Independence-For-General Folder, box 863, RG 126, National Archives and Records Administration, College Park (NARAII).

9. Ruth M. Reynolds, *Campus in Bondage: A 1948 Microcosm of Puerto Rico in Bondage*, Carlos Rodríguez Fraticelli and Blanca Vázquez Erazo, eds. (New York: Centro de Estudios Puertorriqueños, 1989), 286–87.

10. James L. Dietz, *Economic History of Puerto Rico: Institutional Change and Capitalist Development* (Princeton: Princeton University Press, 1986); César J. Ayala and Rafael Bernabe, *Puerto Rico in the American Century* (Chapel Hill: University of North Carolina Press, 2009), esp. 179–200.

11. Since 1917, Puerto Ricans had been empowered to elect a bicameral legislature, but its actions were subject to approval by federal authorities. They also had (and still have) a nonvoting Resident Commissioner intended to represent their interests to the US House of Representatives. Of course, they have never had any rights to vote in national elections.

12. "Statement by Dr. Fernos-Isern," *Department of State Bulletin*, December 7, 1953, 802; Kathleen McLaughlin, "India Disputes US over Puerto Rico," *New York Times*, September 2, 1953. On mid-century reforms in Puerto Rico, see Surendra Bhana, *The United States and the Development of the Puerto Rican Status Question, 1936–1968* (Lawrence: University Press of Kansas, 1975); José Trías Monge, *Puerto Rico: The Trials of the Oldest Colony in the World* (New Haven: Yale University Press, 1997).

13. Carl Colodne to Ruth Reynolds, October 12, 1951, folder 8, box 2, Reynolds Papers; Colodne to Reynolds, October 20, 1951, ibid.; Conrad Lynn to Ruth Reynolds, October 24, 1951, ibid.; "The Case of Ruth M. Reynolds," folder 3, box 24, ibid.; Reynolds to George P. Rawick, January 11, 1953, folder 7, box 23, ibid.; "Visit to Puerto Rico," October 6, 1951, folder 8, ibid.; "Peacemakers' Manifesto to the People of Puerto Rico," ibid. On the gag law, see Ivonne Acosta-Lespier, "The Smith Act Goes to San Juan: La Mordaza, 1948–1957," in Bosque-Pérez and Morera, *Puerto Rico under Colonial Rule*, 59–66.

14. Julius Eichel to President Truman, October 31, 1950, folder 7, box 18, Reynolds Papers; Ruth Reynolds to Marc [Vito Marcantonio], 1950, folder 2, box 9, ibid; "A Call to Protest Political Imprisonment of Puerto Ricans," folder 6, box 23, ibid; "Peacemakers Manifesto to the People of Puerto Rico," folder 8, ibid. On Puerto Rico's militarization, see Humberto García Muñiz, "US Military Installations in Puerto Rico: Controlling the Caribbean," in *Colonial Dilemma: Critical Perspectives on Contemporary Puerto Rico*, ed. Edwin Melendez and Edgardo Melendez (Boston: South End Press, 1993), 53–65; César J. Ayala and Viviana Carro-Figueroa, "Expropriation and Displacement of Civilians in Vieques, 1940–1950" in Bosque-Pérez and Morera, *Puerto Rico under Colonial Rule*, 173–205.

15. J. Edgar Hoover to James P. Davis, July 10, 1950, Withdrawn Item Tab 2A, box 355, Classified Files, 1951–71, RG 126, NARAII; Pedro Albizu Campos FBI file, vol. XII, frames 85–86, 91, in "The FBI Files on Puerto Ricans," The Center for Puerto Rican Studies at Hunter College, City University of New York.

16. Scott Bennett, *Radical Pacifism: The War Resisters League and Gandhian Nonviolence in America, 1915–1963* (Syracuse, NY: Syracuse University Press, 2003), 188–91; n.d. "Statement of Ralph Templin," folder 6, box 23, Reynolds Papers; Ruth M. Reynolds, "Puerto Rico and the Bomb" (reprint from the magazine *Liberation*), folder 1, box 12, ibid.

17. J. Edgar Hoover to U. E. Baughman, June 7, 1951, Campos FBI file, vol. VIII, frames 46–52; October 8, 1953, memo re Pedro Albizu Campos, ibid., vol. XI, frames 20–25; "Petition and Brief," folder 7, box 27, Reynolds Papers; Thelma Mielke, "Report of a Visit to Pedro Albizu-Campos," folder 2, box 31, ibid.; February 12, 1954, Memorandum, ibid.; "Doris Torresola on Prison Conditions Surrounding the Trial in July–August 1952," August 29, 1954, folder 6, box 28, ibid.; "Memorandum on Experiences Phenomenal, Mostly in the Princesa Hotel," folder 1, box 16, ibid.; Reynolds Oral History, folders 5–6, box 46, ibid. On these women prisoners' experience, see Margaret Power, "Puerto Rican Women Nationalists vs US Colonialism: An Exploration of Their Conditions and Struggles in Jail and Court," *Chicago-Kent Law Review* 87, no 2 (2012): 1–17. On Puerto Rico as a medical laboratory, see Laura Briggs, *Reproducing Empire: Race, Sex, Science, and US Imperialism in Puerto Rico* (Berkeley: University of California

Press, 2002); Pedro Aponte Vázquez, *The Unsolved Case of Dr. Cornelius P. Rhoads: An Indictment* (San Juan: René Publications, 2005); Susan E. Lederer, "'Porto Ricochet': Joking About Germs, Cancer, and Race Extermination in the 1930s," *American Literary History* 14, no. 4 (2002): 720–46.

18. David Dellinger to Albert Einstein, February 24, 1954, folder 3, box 31, Reynolds Papers; February 1, 1954, Meeting minutes, folder 5, ibid.; January 30, 1954, Sworn Statement by Herminia Rijos, folder 3, box 28, ibid.; Dave [Dellinger] to Reynolds, February 15, 1954, folder 6, box 3, ibid.; Reynolds to Dr. Buttrick, February 15, 1954, folder 4, box 9, ibid.; Sidney Aberman, David Dellinger, Ruth Reynolds, and Harold Wurp to Dr. Franklin Miller, February 17, 1954, ibid.; Reynolds to Herbert Jehle, February 18, 1954, ibid.; Reynolds to Dr. Victor Patschkiss, February 18, 1954, ibid. On recent evidence of government-sanctioned experimentation on prisoners and others during the early Cold War, including the use of both irradiation and psychotropic drugs, see Susan E. Lederer, "The Cold War and Beyond: Covert and Deceptive American Medical Experimentation," in *Military Medical Ethics*, vol. 2, ed. Thomas E. Beam and Linette R. Sparacino (Washington, DC: Borden Institute, 2003): 507–31; Andrew Goliszek, *In the Name of Science: A History of Secret Programs, Medical Research, and Human Experimentation* (New York: St. Martin's Press, 2003); Stephen Foster, ed., *The Project MKULTRA Compendium: The CIA's Program of Research in Behavioral Modification* (privately printed, 2009).

19. Statement of Purpose, 1954, folder 4, box 20, Reynolds Papers; Waldo Frank and Norman Mailer to Dear Friend, 1954, ibid.; A. J. Muste to David Dellinger, March 23, 1954, folder 5, box 20, ibid.

20. For example, see Julius Eichel to Dave [Dellinger], April 6, 1951, folder 4, box 24, Reynolds Papers.

21. For examples of the civil liberties argument, see "Statement of Purpose," folder 4, box 20, Reynolds Papers; Waldo Frank and Norman Mailer to Dear Friend, 1954, ibid.

22. "Hear Ye! Hear Ye!" folder 1, box 24, Reynolds Papers; "Free Puerto Rico," ibid.; Julius Eichel to Jim Peck, July 25, 1954, folder 5, box 20, ibid.

23. Call to the Peacemaker Puerto Rican Project, September 15, 1958, folder 6, box 23, Reynolds Papers; "Peacemaker Peace and Good Will Walk Across Puerto Rico," November 25, 1958, ibid.; Personal Statement of Albert Uhrie, ibid.; press release, December 22, 1960, ibid.; "We cross Puerto Rico on foot," folder 7, ibid.; John Forbes to Peacemakers, September 18, 1958, folder 9, ibid.; Bob Pope to Peacemakers, November 29, 1958, ibid.; Annot Jacobi to Valerie Aldrich, November 26, 1958, ibid.

24. Reynolds Oral History, folder 5, box 46, Reynolds Papers.

25. Andrés Torres and José E. Velázquez, eds., *The Puerto Rican Movement: Voices from the Diaspora* (Philadelphia, Temple University Press, 1998); Darrel Enck-Wanzer, ed., *The Young Lords: A Reader* (New York: New York University Press, 2010); Margaret Power, "From Freedom Fighters to Patriots: The Successful Campaign to Release the FALN Political Prisoners, 1980–1999," *Centro Journal* 25, no. 1 (2013): 146–79.

Chapter 20: Radical Pacifism in the Long 1950s

1. Holley Cantine to Ernest Bromley, October 22, 1960, Ernest Bromley Papers (hereafter cited as Bromley), carton 4, "Correspondence-1960(1)," private collection;

quote from narrator, *Polaris Action* (New York: Hilary Harris Films, 1960), 16mm. For descriptions of Henry and Martin's protests, see also *Polaris Action Bulletin* 16, December 3, 1960, author's collection; Richard H. Parke, "Biggest Submarine in the Polaris Fleet Launched by U.S.," *New York Times*, November 23, 1960, 1, 3. Articles and photos also appeared in papers across the country, including the *New York Post*, the *Christian Science Monitor*, and the *Chicago Daily News*. See press clippings from October 20 and November 22, 1960, *Polaris Action Scrapbook* (Oct 1960–Jan 1961), box 23, The Papers of the Committee for Nonviolent Action (hereafter cited as CNVA), Swarthmore College Peace Collection, Swarthmore, PA. Fox Movietone purchased film footage of the event and aired it on television as well as in cinemas across the nation. See *Polaris Action Bulletin* 16, December 3, 1960, author's collection.

2. Brad Lyttle, interview by author (tape recording), April 25–26, 1997. See also Barbara Deming, "The Peacemakers," in *Revolution and Equilibrium*, ed. Barbara Deming (New York: Grossman, 1971), 25; Richard Ahles, "Pacifists at Work," *Hartford Courant*, September 25, 1960; Ed Sanders, telephone interview by author (tape recording), August 13, 1998.

3. On the impact of the Gandhian model of nonviolent action on American pacifists, see Marian Mollin, *Radical Pacifism in Modern America: Egalitarianism and Protest* (Philadelphia: University of Pennsylvania Press, 2006); Maurice Isserman, *If I Had a Hammer: The Death of the Old Left and the Birth of the New Left* (1987; repr., Urbana: University of Illinois Press, 1993), 127–69; Joseph Kip Kosek, *Acts of Conscience: Christian Nonviolence and Modern American Democracy* (New York: Columbia University Press, 2009); Scott Bennett, *Radical Pacifism: The War Resisters League and Gandhian Nonviolence in America, 1915–1963* (Syracuse, NY: Syracuse University Press, 2003); Lawrence Wittner, *Rebels Against War: The American Peace Movement, 1933–1983* (Philadelphia: Temple University Press, 1984), 257–75. The Committee for Nonviolent Action (CNVA) published extensive reports on their activities of the late 1950s and early 1960s in the *Omaha Action, Polaris Action*, and *CNVA* bulletins, most of which can be found in the CNVA papers at the Swarthmore College Peace Collection. The radical pacifist newspaper, *Peacemaker*, published in Ohio but distributed nationally, also chronicled these events in great detail.

4. "Atom-Lopers to Quit State After Prayer Vigil at Test Site Today: Guilty 11 Get Year Probation," *Las Vegas Sun*, August 7, 1957. See also, "Summary Information on Non-Violent Action Against Nuclear Weapons" (July 1957), box 2, Lawrence Scott Papers, Swarthmore College Peace Collection; "Hold Major Protest Demonstration at Mercury, Nevada Atomic Test Site," *The Peacemaker* 10, August 26, 1957; George and Lillian Willoughby, interview by author (tape recording), November 15, 1996.

5. Lawrence Scott to Ernest and Marion Bromley, December 22, 1957, carton 4, "Correspondence–1957," Bromley. For more on the protest voyage of *The Golden Rule*, see Mollin, *Radical Pacifism*, 82–87; Albert Bigelow, *The Voyage of the Golden Rule: An Experiment with Truth* (Garden City, NY: Doubleday, 1959); George and Lillian Willoughby, interview with author (tape recording), November 15, 1996. For information about the Omaha Action campaign, see Mollin, *Radical Pacifism*, 90–96.

6. On radical pacifists and Third Camp politics, see Bennett, *Radical Pacifism*, 173–212; David Dellinger, *From Yale to Jail: The Life Story of a Moral Dissenter* (New York: Pantheon Books, 1993), 155–69. In 1950, radical pacifists called for the release of Eu-

gene Dennis, General Secretary of the Communist Party USA, Harry Justiz, Miguel Magana, and Louis Miller, all accused Communist Party members and part of the Joint Anti-Fascist Spanish Refugee Committee. See "Protest Political Jailings," *The Peace-maker* 2, July 26, 1950.

7. Laura McEnaney, *Civil Defense Begins at Home: Militarization Meets Everyday Life in the Fifties* (Princeton, NJ: Princeton University Press, 2000), 152.

8. On the notion of prefigurative politics and the New Left, see Wini Breines, *Community and Organization in the New Left, 1962-1968: The Great Refusal* (New York: Praeger, 1982); Barbara Epstein, *Political Protest and Cultural Revolution: Nonviolent Direct Action in the 1970s and 1980s* (Berkeley: University of California Press, 1991).

9. Mollin, *Radical Pacifism*, 30-31, 49-59.

10. David Dellinger paraphrased in "Report from August Conference," *Bulletin of the CNVR,* September 1, 1947, 2, box 4, The Papers of Igal Roodenko, Swarthmore College Peace Collection. For more on these early pacifist communes, see Mollin, *Radical Pacifism*, 58-59, 66-72; Dellinger, *From Yale to Jail*, 145-52; Alice Lynd and Staughton Lynd, *Stepping Stones: Memoir of a Life Together* (Lanham, MD: Lexington Books, 2009), 45-59.

11. Mollin, *Radical Pacifism*, 62-66, 78-82, 87-96, 107-50.

12. Sara McDonough, "Breaking Boundaries: Battling Race and Gender in Twentieth-Century America" (essay, Brian Bertoti Innovative Perspectives in History Graduate Conference, Virginia Tech, Blacksburg, VA, April 2012), in author's possession; James Farmer to A. J. Muste, Memorandum On Provisional Plans for *Brotherhood Mobilization,* January 8, 1942, series A, box 7, The Papers of the Fellowship of Reconciliation, Swarthmore College Peace Collection. On efforts to link a kind of strenuous and muscular masculinity to the concept of pacifist resistance during World War II, see Mollin, *Radical Pacifism*, 8-21.

13. George Houser, "A Personal Retrospective on the 1947 Journey of Reconciliation," typescript (1992), 6, box 1, Papers of the Congress of Racial Equality, Swarthmore College Peace Collection; Marjorie Swann, interview by author (tape recording), March 4, 1995. On the gendered limitations of the 1947 Journey of Reconciliation, see Mollin, *Radical Pacifism*, 36-42.

14. Jhan and June Robbins, "You Are a Bad Mother," *Redbook,* August 1960, 98; text of letter from "A Participant in Omaha Action" to Marj Swann, reprinted in "Friends of Marj Swann" to "Friends of Marj Swann and Sympathizers with her Concerns" (Fall 1959), box 4, The Papers of Horace Champney, Swarthmore College Peace Collection. On the celebration of pacifist maternalism among nonviolent direct action activists in the late 1950s, see Mollin, *Radical Pacifism*, 87-96. On the power of this trope in the early 1960s, see Dee Garrison, "'Our Skirts Gave Them Courage': The Civil Defense Protest Movement in New York City, 1955-1961," in *Not June Cleaver: Women and Gender in Postwar America, 1945-1960,* ed. Joanne Meyerowitz (Philadelphia: Temple University Press, 1994); Amy Swerdlow, *Women Strike for Peace: Traditional Motherhood and Radical Politics in the 1960s* (Chicago: University of Chicago Press, 1993).

15. Beverly Kanegson, text of letter to Judge Anderson on the occasion of Bill Henry's sentencing, *Polaris Action Bulletin* 20 (March 1961), author's collection; Ed Sanders, "Jail," *Polaris Action Bulletin* 26 (August 30, 1961), author's collection; *Polaris Action Bulletin* 9B (August 16, 1960), author's collection; caption with label of "unidentified

women" under photograph of June 1960 Pioneer Polaris Peace Walk, *Polaris Action Bulletin* 4 (July 13, 1960), author's collection. On the opportunities and challenges that women experienced as part of the 1960–61 Polaris Action campaign, see Mollin, *Radical Pacifism*, 119–23.

16. Isserman, *If I Had a Hammer*, and James Tracy, *Direct Action: Radical Pacifism from the Union Eight to the Chicago Seven* (Chicago: University of Chicago Press, 1996), both suggest that the radical pacifist movement, or, at the least, its emphasis on moral absolutism, helped lay the groundwork for the violent militancy of the later 1960s. For other influential studies that pay less attention to radical pacifism but similarly emphasize the paradigm of radical declension, see James Miller, *"Democracy in the Streets": From Port Huron to the Siege of Chicago* (New York: Simon and Schuster, 1987); Todd Gitlin, *The Sixties: Years of Hope, Days of Rage* (New York: Bantam Books, 1987). Wini Breines challenged this framework of declension, and its characterization of both a "good" early sixties and a "bad" late sixties quite forcefully in her review article, "Whose New Left?" *The Journal of American History* 75, no. 2 (September 1988): 528–45.

Chapter 21: An Ending and a Beginning

1. C. L. R. James, "Black Power," in *The C. L. R. James Reader*, ed. Anna Grimshaw (Oxford: Blackwell, 1992), 62.

2. James, "Black Power," 367.

3. "Remarks by James Boggs on 'The Political Economy of Black Power,' by Ray Franklin, Socialist Scholars Conference, New York, September 10, 1967," James and Grace Lee Boggs Papers, box 3, folder 14, Archives of Labor and Urban Affairs, Walter P. Reuther Library, Wayne State University.

4. Stephen M. Ward, ed., *Pages from a Black Radical's Notebook: A James Boggs Reader* (Detroit: Wayne State University Press, 2011): 171–79. The quotation appears on page 174.

5. Ibid., 7–8.

6. Ibid., 8–18.

7. Letter dated November 5, 1956, no signature or addressee, Glabernman Papers, box 5, folder 6, Archives of Labor and Urban Affairs, Walter P. Reuther Library, Wayne State University (emphasis in original). James wrote, "I want to repeat, and I say so because it will you some time to understand; the Hungarian Revolution is the greatest political event since the October Revolution of 1917." C. L. R. James to Martin Glaberman, December 13, 1956, Glaberman Papers, box 5, folder 7.

8. J (C. L. R. James) to Friends, November 15, 1956, 3, Glaberman Papers, box 5, folder 6.

9. Jim to J (James Boggs to C. L. R. James), November 28, 1956, Glaberman Papers, box 5, folder 6.

10. Ibid.

11. C. L. R. James, *The Black Jacobins: Toussaint L'Ouverture and the San Domingo Revolution* (New York: Vintage, 1989).

12. C. L. R. James to Martin Glaberman, February 8, 1957, Glaberman Papers, box 5, folder 9.

13. J (C. L. R. James) to Friends, March 3, 1957, Glaberman Papers, box 5, folder 10.

14. C. L. R. James to Everybody, March 20, 1957, Glaberman Papers, box 5, folder 10. All quotations in this paragraph are from this letter (emphasis in original).

15. Ibid.

16. J (C. L. R. James) to Friends, March 21, 1957, Glaberman Papers, box 5, folder 10.

17. C. L. R. James to Friends, March 25, 1957, Glaberman Papers, box 5, folder 10, published in Grimshaw, *The C. L. R. James Reader*.

18. Ibid.

19. Ibid.

20. Ibid.

21. Ibid. All quotations in this paragraph are from this letter.

22. C. L. R. James, Grace C. Lee, and Pierre Chaulieu, *Facing Reality* (1958; repr., Detroit: Bewick Editions, 1974), 27.

23. "Tide of Afro-American Nationalism Is Rising in the United States," *Correspondence*, April 8, 1961.

24. Marty Glaberman to C. L. R. James, January 25, 1961, Glaberman Papers, box 6, folder 8.

25. James Boggs to Friends, December 30, 1961, Glaberman Papers, box 6, folder 12.

26. C. L. R. James to Secretary, Resident Editorial Board, January 15, 1962, Glaberman Papers, box 6, folder 13.

27. For more on the context out of which the book emerged, its place in Boggs's trajectory, and for the full text of the book, see Part II of Ward, *Pages From a Black Radical's Notebook*.

Chapter 22: The Religious Origins of Reies López Tijerina's Land Grant Activism

1. Winthrop Yinger, *Cesar Chavez: The Rhetoric of Nonviolence* (Hicksville, NY: Exposition Press, 1975). The more unsavory aspects of Chavez's personality can be read in Matt Garcia, *From the Jaws of Victory: The Triumph and Tragedy of Cesar Chavez and the Farm Worker Movement* (Berkeley: University of California Press, 2012).

2. Reies López Tijerina, *Mi lucha por la tierra* (México: Fondo de la Cultura Económica, 1978), 163; Rodolfo Acuña, *Occupied America: The Chicano's Struggle Toward Liberation* (San Francisco: Canfield Press, 1972), 222–46; George Mariscal, *Brown-Eyed Children of the Sun: Lessons from the Chicano Movement, 1965–1975* (Albuquerque: University of New Mexico Press, 2005).

3. F. Arturo Rosales, ed., *Testimonio: A Documentary History of the Mexican American Struggle for Civil Rights* (Houston: Arte Público Press, 2000), 272.

4. Felipe Cabeza de Vaca, *The Legend of the Town of San Joaquín del Río de Chama* (Santa Fe: Synergetic Press, 1983).

5. Reies López Tijerina, *They Called Me "King Tiger": My Struggle for the Land and Other Rights* (Houston: Arte Público Press, 2000), 77–91; Peter Nabokov, *Tijerina and the Courthouse Raid* (Berkeley: Ramparts Press, 1969).

6. Rose Tijerina, in Larry Calloway, "June 5, 1967: The Courthouse Raid Recalled 40 Years Later," *Crestone Conglomerate* (blog), June 5, 2007, http://larrycalloway.com/courthouse-raid.

7. See the articles Patricia Bell Blawis wrote for *The Daily World*, the newspaper of the Communist Party of the United States, and her book, *Tijerina and the Land Grants:*

Mexican Americans in Struggle for the Heritage (New York: International Publishers, 1971).

8. Michael Jenkinson, *Tijerina: Land Grant Conflict in New Mexico* (Albuquerque: Paisano Press, 1968), 12–13; Maulana Ron Karenga, "People of Color: We Shall Survive," box 34, folder 24, Reies López Tijerina Papers, University of New Mexico. I thank Brian Behnken for providing me with a copy of the "Treaty of Peace, Harmony, and Mutual Assistance between the Spanish-American Federal Alliance of Free City States and _____," which originally was published in *La Raza Magazine*, October 29, 1967.

9. Box II, folder 22, item 18, page 5, Peter Nabokov Papers, Zimmerman Library, University of New Mexico.

10. Nabakov, *Tijerina and the Courthouse Raid*, 198.

11. Maria Escobar Chávez, interview with author, September 23, 2006.

12. Ibid.

13. Tijerina, *They Called Me "King Tiger,"* 77–91.

14. Nabokov, *Tijerina and the Courthouse Raid*, 201.

15. The Albuquerque *News Chieftain*, a local community newspaper, gave Tijerina a weekly column in which he reported how the cause of the Alianza and the restoration of the *mercedes* advanced between 1963 and 1967.

16. Carrol W. Cagle and Harry P. Stumpf, "The Trial of Reies López Tijerina," in *Great Courtroom Battles*, ed. Richard E. Rubenstein (New York: Playboy Press, 1973), 193–221; Nabokov, *Tijerina and the Courthouse Raid*, 264.

17. Larry Calloway, "JUNE 5, 1967: The Courthouse Raid Recalled 40 Years Later," *Crestone Conglomerate* (blog), June 5, 2007, http://larrycalloway.com/courthouse-raid; Tony Hillerman, *The Great Taos Bank Robbery and other True Stories of the Southwest* (New York: Perennial, 2001), 128–53.

18. Reies Lopez, "Tijerina, 'Letter from the Santa Fe Jail, August 15, 1969,'" *El Grito del Norte*, September 26, 1969.

19. Rosales, *Testimonio*, 272, 361–63.

20. Ramón A. Gutiérrez, "Chicano Struggles for Racial Justice: The Movement's Contributions to Social Theory," in *Mexicans in California: Emergent Challenges and Transformations*, ed. Gutiérrez and Zavella (Urbana: University of Illinois Press, 2009), 94–110; "Internal Colonialism: The History of a Theory," *Du Bois Review: Social Science Research on Race* 1, no. 2 (Summer 2004): 281–96.

Chapter 23: Before the Birth of Asian America

1. I wish to thank Tamio Wakayama for sharing his unpublished memoir and oral history, Chizu Iiyama and Patti Iiyama for sharing their oral histories, Renee Roberts for her research assistance, interview preparation and transcription, and Anisah Ali for her interview transcription.

2. See Daryl Maeda, *Rethinking the Asian American Movement* (New York: Routledge, 2012) and *Chains of Babylon: The Rise of Asian America* (Minneapolis: University of Minnesota Press, 2009); Michael Liu, Kim Geron, and Tracy Lai, *The Snake Dance of Asian American Activism: Community, Vision, and Power* (Lanham, MD: Lexington Books, 2008); William Wei, *The Asian American Movement* (Philadelphia: Temple University Press, 1992).

3. James Miller, *Democracy Is in the Streets: From Port Huron to the Siege of Chicago* (1987; repr., Cambridge: Harvard University Press, 1994), 28.

4. Maurice Isserman, *The Other American: The Life Of Michael Harrington* (New York: Public Affairs, 2000), 146.

5. Sheila Muto, "Berkeley's History of Tolerance Not Forgotten by Japanese Americans," *Asianweek*, April 21, 1995.

6. "Yamada, T. Robert," *San Francisco Chronicle*, June 27, 2004, http://www.sfgate.com/news/article/YAMADA-T-Robert-2745914.php.

7. Tamio Wakayama, telephone interview by Daryl Maeda, September 14, 2012; Tamio Wakayama, "Soul on Rice: A Nikkei Narrative of the 60s" (unpublished manuscript).

8. Ken Adachi, *The Enemy That Never Was: A History of the Japanese Canadians* (Toronto: McClelland and Stewart, 1976); Greg Robinson, *Tragedy of Democracy: Japanese Confinement in North America* (New York: Columbia University Press, 2009).

9. Wakayama, "Soul on Rice," 5.

10. Ibid., 7–11.

11. Wakayama, interview; Wakayama, "Soul on Rice," 7.

12. Wakayama, interview; Wakayama, "Soul on Rice," 13.

13. Wakayama, interview.

14. Wakayama, "Soul on Rice," 12.

15. Wakayama, interview; Wakayama, "Soul on Rice," 14–15.

16. Wakayama, "Soul on Rice," 17.

17. Ibid., 18.

18. Helen Gym, "'A high moral enterprise': Philadelphian Ed Nakawatase reflects on SNCC and 50 years of progress," *Young Philly Politics*, accessed October 7, 2012, http://youngphillypolitics.com/quota_high_moral_enterprisequot_philadelphian_ed_nakawatase_reflects_sncc_and_50_years_progress. On Seabrook Farms, see Mitziko Sawada, "After the Camps: Seabrook Farms, New Jersey, and the Resettlement of Japanese Americans, 1944–47," *Amerasia Journal* 13, no. 2 (1986–87): 117–36.

19. Wakayama, "Soul on Rice," 23–27.

20. Clayborne Carson, *In Struggle: SNCC and the Black Awakening of the 1960s* (Cambridge: Harvard University Press, 1981), 133–52.

21. Wakayama, "Soul on Rice," 28–29.

22. Wakayama, interview.

23. Wakayama, "Soul on Rice," 44, 54.

24. Ibid., 57.

25. Wakayama, "Soul on Rice," 57–69; Wakayama, interview.

26. Wakayama, "Soul on Rice," 76.

27. Ibid., 73–80.

28. Ibid., 81–84.

29. Chizu Iiyama, telephone interview by Daryl Maeda and Renee Roberts, Part I, August 8, 2012, and Part II, August 9, 2012; Patti Iiyama, telephone interview by Daryl Maeda, October 12, 2012.

30. Jere Takahashi, *Nisei/Sansei* (Philadelphia: Temple University Press, 1998), 66–74; Chizu Iiyama, interview, Part I.

31. Patti Iiyama, interview.

32. Chizu Iiyama, interview, Part I; Glenn Omatsu, "Always a Rebel: An Interview with Kazu Iijima," *Amerasia Journal* 13, no. 2 (1986–87): 94.

33. Chizu Iiyama, interview, Part I.

34. Greg Robinson, "Nisei in Gotham," *Prospects* 30 (2005): 581–95; Chizu Iiyama, interview, Part II.

35. Patti Iiyama, interview.

36. Chizu Iiyama, interview, Part II. Dates of moves are approximate, based on the date of an Ernie Iiyama–authored article in *JACD Newsletter*, dated April 1944 (Robinson, "Nisei in Gotham," 595n33).

37. Patti Iiyama, interview.

38. Ibid.

39. Ibid.

40. Ibid.

41. Ibid.

42. Fred Halstead, *Out Now! A Participant's Account of the American Movement Against the Vietnam War* (New York: Monad Press, 1978), 162.

43. Ibid., 349.

44. Ibid.

45. Maeda, *Chains of Babylon*, 97–126.

46. Patti Iiyama, interview.

47. Tom Wells, *The War Within: America's Battle over Vietnam* (Berkeley: University of California Press, 1994), 193–94, 399.

48. Patti Iiyama, interview.

49. Ibid.

50. Ibid.

51. Harvey C. Dong, "The Origins and Trajectory of Asian American Political Activism in the San Francisco Bay Area, 1968–1978" (PhD diss., University of California, Berkeley, 2002).

52. Daryl J. Maeda, "Black Panthers, Red Guards, and Chinamen: Constructing Asian American Identity through Performing Blackness, 1969–1972," *American Quarterly* 57, no. 4 (December 2005): 1079–1103.

53. Max Elbaum, *Revolution in the Air: Sixties Radicals turn to Lenin, Mao and Che* (London: Verso, 2002).

54. Liz Highleyman, "Kiyoshi Kuromiya: Integrating the Issues," in *Smash the Church, Smash the State!: The Early Years of Gay Liberation*, ed. Tommi Avicolli Mecca (San Francisco: City Lights Books, 2009), 17–21; Daniel C. Tsang, "Slicing Silence: Asian Progressives Come Out," in *Asian Americans: The Movement and the Moment*, ed. Steve Louie and Glenn Omatsu (Los Angeles: UCLA Asian American Studies Center Press, 2001), 221–23.

Chapter 25: New Indians in the New Frontier

1. *Port Huron Statement*, reprinted in Tom Hayden, *The Port Huron Statement: The Visionary Call of the 1960s Revolution* (New York: Thunder's Mouth Press, 2005), 169.

Chapter 26: The German New Left and Participatory Democracy

1. The term "new left" was especially introduced in the Autumn 1958 edition of *The New Reasoner: A Quarterly Journal of Socialist Humanism*, a journal edited by E. P. Thompson and John Saville.

2. E. P. Thompson, "Country and City," in *Persons & Polemics: Historical Essays* (London: Merlin Press, 1994), 244.

3. E. P. Thompson, ed., *Out of Apathy* (London: New Left Books, 1960).

4. Ibid., 9.

5. Ibid., 19–55.

6. C. Wright Mills, "Letter to the New Left," *New Left Review* 5, nos. 3–4 (September–October 1960): 18–23.

7. Raymond Williams, *The Long Revolution* (London: Chatto and Windus, 1961).

8. "Für Freiheit Westberlins" [For West Berlin's freedom], *neue kritik* 8 (November 1961): 9–10.

9. *Port Huron Statement*, reprinted in Tom Hayden, *The Port Huron Statement: The Visionary Call of the 1960s Revolution* (New York: Thunder's Mouth Press, 2005), 121.

10. Ibid., 122.

11. Ibid., 124–25.

12. Belinda Davis et al., eds., *Changing the World, Changing Oneself: Political Protest and Collective Identities in West Germany and the U.S. in the 1960s and 1970s* (New York: Berghahn Books, 2010), 278, 281.

13. This is more fully described in Martin Klimke, *The Other Alliance: Student Protest in West Germany and the United States in the Global Sixties* (Princeton: Princeton University Press, 2010), 28–39.

14. Although *Mitbestimmung* is typically translated in English as "codetermination," its fuller meaning is "democratic participation in decision making."

15. Arnold Kaufman, "Human Nature and Participatory Democracy," in *The Bias of Pluralism*, ed. William E. Connolly (New York: Atherton Press, 1969).

16. Ibid., 272.

17. Ibid., 282.

18. Ibid.

19. Ibid.

20. Ibid., 281.

21. Heinrich Popitz et al., *Das Gesellschaftsbild des Arbeiters* (Tübingen: Mohr, 1957); Ludwig von Friedeburg, *Soziologie des Betriebsklimas* (Frankfurt: Europäische Verlagsanstalt, 1963).

22. Wilma Aden-Grossmann, *Monika Seifert. Pädagogin der antiautoritären Erziehung. Eine Biographie* (Frankfurt: Brandes and Apsel, 2014).

23. Michael Vester et al., *Soziale Milieus im gesellschaftlichen Strukturwandel* (Frankfurt: Suhrkamp, 2001). A short English outline is given in Michael Vester, "Class and Culture in Germany," in *Rethinking Class: Cultures, Identities and Life-Styles*, ed. Fiona Devine et al. (Basingstoke: Palgrave Macmillan, 2005), 69–94.

24. Michael Vester, "Schöne neue Welt?," *neue kritik* 15 (March 1963): 3–8; Michael Vester, "Die Linke in den USA," *neue kritik* 17 (July 1963): 6–14; Michael Vester, "Falsche Alternativen," *neue kritik* 18 (November 1963): 5–11.

25. Klimke, *The Other Alliance*, 35.

26. Gerhard Brandt, "Die Neue Linke in England," *neue kritik–informationen* 6 (June 1961): 22–30.

27. Michael Vester, "John Kenneth Galbraith und der 'Amerikanische Kapitalismus,'" *neue kritik–informationen* 7 (July 1961): 18–29; Michael Vester, "Schöne neue Welt?," *neue kritik* 14 (March 1963): 3–8; Michael Vester, "Falsche Alternativen," neue kritik 19/20 (December 1963): 5–11.

28. Tom Hayden and I each completed a study of Mills's work in 1964. Thomas Hayden, *Radical Nomad: Essays on C. Wright Mills and His Time* (Ann Arbor: Center for the Research on Conflict Resolution, University of Michigan, 1964); Michael Vester, "Die politische Soziologie von C. Wright Mills" (diploma thesis in sociology, University of Frankfurt, December 1964).

29. Vester, "Schöne neue Welt?," 8.

30. Michael Vester, "Die Strategie der direkten Aktion," *neue kritik* 30 (June 1965): 12–20.

31. Todd Gitlin, *The Sixties: Years of Hope, Days of Rage* (1987; repr., New York: Bantam, 1993); Richard Flacks, *Making History: The American Left and the American Mind* (New York: Columbia University Press, 1988); Thomas Hayden, *The Long Sixties: From 1960 to Barack Obama* (Boulder, CO: Paradigm, 2009).

Chapter 27: European New Lefts, Global Connections, and the Problem of Difference

1. Timothy S. Brown, *West Germany and the Global Sixties: The Antiauthoritarian Revolt, 1962–1978* (Cambridge: Cambridge University Press, 2013), 2. Here Brown offers a pointed critique of the "reductionist tendency" evinced by histories of the protest movements written by first-hand participants.

2. Students for a Democratic Society, *The Port Huron Statement* (New York: Student Department of the League for Industrial Democracy, 1964), 3, 4.

3. Jeremi Suri, *Power and Protest: Global Revolution and the Rise of Détente* (Cambridge: Harvard University Press, 2003), 105.

4. Carole Fink, Philipp Gassert, and Detlef Junker, eds., *1968: The World Transformed* (New York: Cambridge University Press, 1998).

5. George Katsiaficas, *The Imagination of the New Left: A Global Analysis of 1968* (Boston: South End Press, 1987), 4.

6. James Miller, *"Democracy Is In the Streets": From Port Huron to the Siege of Chicago* (Cambridge: Harvard University Press, 1987), 123. For a more recent and more thorough treatment of Vester's role in fostering exchange between the American and West German SDS, see Martin Klimke, *The Other Alliance: Student Protest in West Germany and the United States in the Global Sixties* (Princeton: Princeton University Press, 2010), chap. 1; Michael Vester, "The German New Left and Participatory Democracy: The Impact on Social, Cultural, and Political Change," in this volume.

7. For more on the *Atelier populaire des Beaux-Arts*, see Kristin Ross, *May '68 and Its Afterlives* (Chicago: University of Chicago Press, 2002), 15–17; Rick Poynor, "Utopian Image: Politics and Posters," *The Design Observer Group*, March 10, 2013, http://observatory.designobserver.com/feature/utopian-image-politics-and-posters/37739.

8. Brown, *West Germany and the Global Sixties*, 3.

9. Arthur Marwick, *The Sixties: Cultural Revolution in Britain, France, Italy, and the United States, c. 1958–c. 1974* (Oxford: Oxford University Press, 1998).

10. Dennis Dworkin, *Cultural Marxism in Postwar Britain: History, the New Left, and the Origins of Cultural Studies* (Durham: Duke University Press, 1997), 101.

11. Jeremy Varon, *Bringing the War Home: The Weather Underground, the Red Army Faction, and Revolutionary Violence in the Sixties and Seventies* (Berkeley: University of California Press, 2004).

12. Richard Wolin, *The Wind from the East: French Intellectuals, the Cultural Revolution, and the Legacy of the 1960s* (Princeton: Princeton University Press, 2010).

13. Katsiaficas, *Imagination of the New Left*, 3.

14. Klimke, *The Other Alliance*, 2.

15. Ibid., 21.

16. Ibid., 24.

17. Ibid., 27.

18. Maria Höhn, "The Black Panther Solidarity Committees and the *Voice of the Lumpen*," *German Studies Review* 31, no. 1 (2008): 133–54, here 138.

19. See Klimke, *The Other Alliance*, chap. 4.

20. In addition to the authors I mention in the text, see also Donatella Della Porta, *Social Movements, Political Violence, and the State: A Comparative Analysis of Italy and Germany* (Cambridge: Cambridge University Press, 1995); Michael Schmidtke, *Der Aufbruch der jungen Intelligenz: Die 68er Jahre in der Bundesrepublik und den USA* (Frankfurt: Campus Verlag, 2003); Jeremi Suri, *Power and Protest (Cambridge: Harvard University Press, 2005)*; Jeremy Varon, *Bringing the War Home* (Berkeley: University of California Press, 2004); Gerd-Rainer Horn, *The Spirit of '68: Rebellion in Western Europe and North America, 1956–1976* (Oxford: Oxford University Press, 2006); Holger Nehring, *Politics of Security: British and West German Protest Movements and the Early Cold War, 1945–1970* (Oxford: Oxford University Press, 2013).

21. Paul Kramer, "Is the World Our Campus? International Students and U.S. Global Power in the Long Twentieth Century," *Diplomatic History* 33, no. 5 (2009): 775–806; Penny M. Von Eschen, *Race against Empire: Black Americans and Anticolonialism, 1937–1957* (Ithaca: Cornell University Press, 1997); Robin D. G. Kelley, *Freedom Dreams: The Black Radical Imagination* (Boston, Beacon Press, 2002); Nikhil Pal Singh, *Black Is a Country: Race and the Unfinished Struggle for Democracy* (Cambridge: Harvard University Press, 2005); Van Gosse, *Where the Boys Are: Cuba, Cold War America, and the Making of the New Left* (New York: Verso, 1993); Cynthia A. Young, *Soul Power: Culture, Radicalism, and the Making of a U.S. Third World Left* (Durham: Duke University Press, 2006).

22. Quinn Slobodian, *Foreign Front: Third World Politics in Sixties West Germany* (Durham: Duke University Press, 2011), 8.

23. Slobodian, *Foreign Front*, 5–6.

24. Ibid., 11.

25. Wolin, *Wind from the East*, 3.

26. Slobodian, *Foreign Front*, 28–29.

27. For more on Ajala's support from the DAAD, see Brown, *West Germany and the Global Sixties*, 40.

28. Slobodian, *Foreign Front*, 53.

29. Ibid., 54.

30. Ibid., 54.

31. For a more paternalistic reading of the relationship between Dutschke and the Latin American students in the international study group, see Ulrich Chaussy, *Die drei Leben des Rudi Dutschke. Eine Biographie* (Darmstadt: Luchterhand, 1983).

32. Hagen, 164.

33. The Argument Club was led by Wolfgang Fritz Haug and worked closely with the SDS. See Slobodian, *Foreign Front*, 73.

34. Brown, *West Germany and the Global Sixties*, 39.

35. Rudi Dutschke, *Diaries*, undated entry, 23. Quoted in Brown, *West Germany and the Global Sixties*, 39.

36. Niels Seibert, *Vergessene Proteste. Internationalismus und Antirassismus, 1964–1983* (Münster: Unrast, 2008); Katrina Hagen, "Internationalism in Cold War Germany" (PhD diss., University of Washington, 2008); Slobodian, *Foreign Front*; Brown, *West Germany and the Global Sixties*.

37. Paul Deslandes, "The Foreign Element: Newcomers and the Rhetoric of Race, Nation, and Empire in 'Oxbridge' Undergraduate Culture, 1850–1920," *Journal of British Studies* 37, no. 1 (1998): 54–90, here 59–60.

38. Jordanna Bailkin, *The Afterlife of Empire* (Berkeley: University of California Press, 2012), 96.

39. Bailkin, *Afterlife of Empire*, 97.

40. Stuart Hall, "The 'First' New Left: Life and Times," in *Out of Apathy: Voices of the New Left 30 Years On*, ed. Robin Archer et al. (London: Verson, 1989), 16–20.

41. It's worth noting that the early editorial boards of the *New Left Review* included Norm Fruchter, a founding figure of the American New Left, as well as Perry Anderson, Robin Blackburn, and Gareth Stedman Jones, who were part of the "younger" British New Left. See Hall, "The 'First' New Left," 22. For more on Hall's stature as the father of British cultural studies, see David Morley and Bill Schwarz, "Stuart Hall Obituary," *Guardian*, February 10, 2014, A39; and William Yardley, "Stuart Hall, Trailblazing British Scholar of Multicultural Influences, Is Dead at 82," *New York Times*, February 18, 2014, A24.

42. Hall, "The 'First' New Left," 23. For an in-depth analysis of the "first" New Left in Britain, see Michael Kenny, *The First New Left: British Intellectuals after Stalin* (London: Lawrence and Wishart, 1995).

43. Tariq Ali, *Street Fighting Years: An Autobiography of the Sixties* (London: Verso, 2005), 113.

44. Ali, *Street Fighting Years*, 254–55.

45. Arthur J. Pais, "Rebel with a Cause," *India Abroad*, November 14, 2008, http://search.proquest.com.proxy.lib.umich.edu/docview/362822134?accountid=14667.

46. Ali, *Street Fighting Years*, 246.

47. The concept of the "Third World" was first formulated by Alfred Sauvy in his 1952 article in *L'Observateur* entitled "Three Worlds, One Planet." See Alfred Sauvy, "Trois Mondes, Une Planete," *L'Observateur*, August 14, 1952, 257–75.

48. James D. Le Sueur, *Uncivil War: Intellectuals and Identity Politics During the Decolonization of Algeria*, 2nd ed. (Lincoln: University of Nebraska Press, 2005), 230–38.

49. Ross, *May '68 and Its Afterlives*, 51; Wolin, *The Wind from the East*, 116.

50. Claus Leggewie, *Kofferträger: Das Algerien-Projekt der Linken im Adenauer-Deutschland* (Berlin: Rotbuch Verlag, 1984), 9.

51. Christoph Kalter, *Die Entwicklung der Dritten Welt* (Frankfurt: Campus, 2011).

52. On the Maoists at the Renault factory, see Wolin, *The Wind from the East*, 32–33, 137–38. On the K-groups, see Geronimo, *Fire and Flames: A History of the Autonomist Movement* (Oakland: PM Press, 2012), 59–61. On the participation of K-groups and Spontis in the Ford Cologne wildcat strike, see Manuela Bojadzijev, *Die windige Internationale: Rassismus und Kämpfe der Migration* (Münster: Westfälisches Dampfboot, 2008), 157–60.

Chapter 28: "Thought Is Action for Us"

1. I would like to thank Howard Brick and Gregory Parker for their valuable feedback on this chapter. Norman Girvan, "New World and Its Critics," in *Caribbean Reasonings: The Thought of New World, The Quest for Decolonisation*, ed. Brian Meeks and Norman Girvan (Kingston, Jamaica: Ian Randle Publishers, 2010), 8–9; Horace Campbell, *Rasta and Resistance: From Marcus Garvey to Walter Rodney* (Trenton, NJ: Africa World Press, 1987).

2. Denis Benn, *The Caribbean: An Intellectual History, 1774-2003* (Kingston: Ian Randle Publishers, 2004), 122.

3. Girvan, "New World and Its Critics," 3–4; David Scott, "Vocation of a Caribbean Intellectual: An Interview with Lloyd Best by David Scott," *Small Axe* no. 1 (February 1997): 122.

4. Brian Meeks, Norman Girvan, and Anthony Bogues, "A Caribbean Life—An Interview with Lloyd Best," in *Caribbean Reasonings: The Thought of New World, The Quest for Decolonisation*, ed. Brian Meeks and Norman Girvan (Kingston: Ian Randle Publishers, 2010), 223; Scott, "Vocation of a Caribbean Intellectual," 123.

5. "Editorial Statement," *New World Quarterly* 2, no. 1 (1965): 2; Girvan, "New World and Its Critics," 4; Norman Girvan, "Caribbean Dependency Thought Revisited," *Canadian Journal of Development Studies/Revue Canadienne d'études du Développement* 27, no. 3 (September 2006): 331.

6. Scott, "Vocation of a Caribbean Intellectual," 131; Meeks, Girvan, and Bogues, "A Caribbean Life," 234–36.

7. Scott, "Vocation of a Caribbean Intellectual," 128–29.

8. New World Group, *The Sugar Industry: Our Life or Death?* (New World Group, December 1967); New World Group, *Devaluation—Occasional Pamphlet No. 3* (New World Group, January 1968); New World Group, *Unemployment: What It Is, Why It Exists, What We Can Do About It* (New World Group, 1967); New World Group, *Freedom from Enquiry* (New World Group, 1967); New World Group, *The Withdrawal of Dr. Beckford's Passport* (New World Group, 1966).

9. Meeks, Girvan, and Bogues, "A Caribbean Life," 243; Girvan, "New World and Its Critics," 5; Benn, *The Caribbean*, 122; Kari Levitt, "The Montreal New World Group," in *Caribbean Reasonings: The Thought of New World, the Quest for Decolonisation*, ed. Brian Meeks and Norman Girvan (Kingston, Jamaica: Ian Randle Publishers, 2010), 71–80; David Austin, *Fear of a Black Nation: Race, Sex, and Security in Sixties Montreal* (Toronto: Between the Lines, 2013).

10. Scott, "Vocation of a Caribbean Intellectual," 119.

11. Lloyd Best, "Independent Thought and Caribbean Freedom," *New World Quarterly* 3, no. 4 (1967): 7.

12. Eric Williams, *Capitalism and Slavery* (Chapel Hill: University of North Carolina Press, 1994); C. L. R. James, *The Black Jacobins: Toussaint L'Ouverture and the San Domingo Revolution*, 2nd ed. (New York: Vintage, 1989).

13. "Editorial," *New World Quarterly* 2, no. 2 (1966).

14. Carleen O'Loughlin, *A Survey of Economic Potential and Capital Needs of the Leeward Islands, Windward Islands, and Barbados* (London: Her Majesty's Stationery Office, 1963); Tripartite Economic Survey of the Eastern Caribbean, *Report of the Tripartite Economic Survey of the Eastern Caribbean* (London: Her Majesty's Stationery Office, 1967).

15. Richard Bernal, Mark Figueroa, and Michael Witter, "Caribbean Economic Thought: The Critical Tradition," *Social and Economic Studies* 33, no. 2 (June 1984): 5–97; Andrew S. Downes, "Arthur Lewis and Industrial Development in the Caribbean: An Assessment" (essay, The Lewis Model after 50 Years: Assessing Sir Arthur Lewis' Contribution to Development Economics and Policy, University of Manchester, UK, July 6–7, 2004), www.sed.manchester.ac.uk/research/events/conferences/documents/Arthur%20Lewis%20Papers/Downes.pdf.

16. Lloyd Best, "On the Teaching of Economics," in *Essays on the Theory of Plantation Economy: A Historical and Institutional Approach to Caribbean Economic Development*, ed. Lloyd Best and Kari Polanyi Levitt (Kingston: University of the West Indies Press, 2009), 6; Lloyd Best, "Chaguaramas to Slavery?" *New World Quarterly* 2, no. 1 (1965): 58; Lloyd Best and Kari Levitt, "A Historical and Institutional Approach to Caribbean Economic Development," in *Essays on the Theory of Plantation Economy: A Historical and Institutional Approach to Caribbean Economic Development*, ed. Lloyd Best and Kari Polanyi Levitt (Kingston: University of the West Indies Press, 2009), 9–10; Bernal, Figueroa, and Witter, "Caribbean Economic Thought," 35.

17. New World Group, *Unemployment*.

18. George Beckford, "Agricultural Development in 'Traditional' and 'Peasant' Economies," *Social and Economic Studies* 15, no. 2 (June 1966): 151; George Beckford, "Why We Are Dispossessed," *Abeng*, February 8, 1969; George Beckford and Michael Witter, *Small Garden, Bitter Weed: Struggle and Change in Jamaica* (Morant Bay: Maroon Publishing House, 1980); George Beckford, *Persistent Poverty: Underdevelopment in Plantation Economies of the Third World* (New York: Oxford University Press, 1972).

19. Norman Girvan, "Why We Need to Nationalize Bauxite, and How," in *Readings in the Political Economy of the Caribbean*, ed. Norman Girvan and Owen Jefferson (Kingston: New World Group, 1974), 217–40.

20. Best, "Independent Thought and Caribbean Freedom," 31.

21. Marcus Garvey, "The Work That Has Been Done," in *The Marcus Garvey and Universal Negro Improvement Association Papers*, vol. 7, ed. Robert A. Hill (Berkeley: University of California Press, 1983), 791.

22. Best, "On the Teaching of Economics," 2–4.

23. Lloyd Best, *The Afro-American Condition*, no. 11 (Tunapuna: Tapia House, 1969).

24. Alister McIntyre, "Some Issues of Trade Policy in the West Indies," *New World Quarterly* 2, no. 2 (1966): 1–20.

25. Best, "On the Teaching of Economics."

26. Beckford, *Persistent Poverty*, 233.

27. On bricolage, see W. Knepper, "Colonization, Creolization, and Globalization: The Art and Ruses of Bricolage," *Small Axe*, no. 3 (January 1, 2006): 70–86.

28. Best and Levitt, "Approach to Caribbean Economic Development," 11–12; Girvan,

"New World and Its Critics," 5–8; Norman Girvan, "Plantation Economy in the Age of Globalization," in *Essays on the Theory of Plantation Economy: A Historical and Institutional Approach to Caribbean Economic Development,* ed. Lloyd Best and Kari Polanyi Levitt (Kingston: University of the West Indies Press, 2009), xviii–xix; Bert J. Thomas, "Caribbean Black Power: From Slogan to Practical Politics," *Journal of Black Studies* 22, no. 3 (1992): 393–94.

29. Lloyd Best and Kari Levitt, "Outline of a General Theory of Caribbean Economy," in *Essays on the Theory of Plantation Economy: A Historical and Institutional Approach to Caribbean Economic Development,* ed. Lloyd Best and Kari Polanyi Levitt (Kingston: University of the West Indies Press, 2009), 19–39; Best, "On the Teaching of Economics," 6.

30. Beckford, *Persistent Poverty.*

31. Scott, "Vocation of a Caribbean Intellectual," 130.

32. Best, "Independent Thought and Caribbean Freedom," 21–22; Lloyd Best, "Race, Class, and Ethnicity in a Caribbean Interpretation" (essay, Third Annual Jagan Lecture, York University, Toronto, March 3, 2001), 337–38, http://www.yorku.ca/cerlac/abstracts.htm#; Best; Meeks, Girvan, and Bogues, "A Caribbean Life," 283–86.

33. Scott, "Vocation of a Caribbean Intellectual," 134.

34. Girvan, "Caribbean Dependency Thought Revisited," 337.

35. Best, "Independent Thought and Caribbean Freedom," 21–22.

36. Best, *The Afro-American Condition,* 3.

37. Best, "Independent Thought and Caribbean Freedom," 2.

38. Meeks, Girvan, and Bogues, "A Caribbean Life," 304–6.

39. Girvan, "Caribbean Dependency Thought Revisited," 333.

40. Meeks, Girvan, and Bogues, "A Caribbean Life," 286.

41. Best, "On the Teaching of Economics," 2.

42. Alfie Roberts, "Why We Must Think for Ourselves," *Flambeau,* November 1966, 6–7.

43. "Editorial Statement," 1–2.

44. C. L. R. James, "The Making of the Caribbean People," in *You Don't Play With Revolution,* ed. David Austin (Oakland: AK Press, 2009), 29–49.

45. Quoted in Kari Levitt, *From Decolonization to Neo-Liberalism: What Have We Learned about Economic Development?* (George Beckford Lecture Series; George Beckford Foundation and the University of the West Indies, 1996), 9.

46. Lloyd Best, "Independence and Responsibility: Self-Knowledge as an Imperative," in *The Critical Tradition of Caribbean Political Economy: The Legacy of George Beckford,* ed. Kari Levitt and Michael Witter (Kingston: Ian Randle Publishers, 1996), 8.

47. Trevor A. Campbell, "The Making of an Organic Intellectual: Walter Rodney (1942–80)," *Latin American Perspectives* 8, no. 1 (1981): 51.

48. Frantz Fanon, *The Wretched of the Earth,* trans. Richard Philcox (New York: Grove Press, 2004), 97–101.

49. Ibid., 99.

50. Ibid., 167.

51. Thomas, "Caribbean Black Power," 393–94.

52. Brian Meeks, "Introduction: Remembering New World," in *Caribbean Reasonings: The Thought of New World, The Quest for Decolonisation,* ed. Brian Meeks and Norman Girvan (Kingston, Jamaica: Ian Randle Publishers, 2010), xii–xiii.

53. Ikael Tafari, *Rastafari In Transition* (Chicago: Research Associates School Times Publications/Frontline Distribution International, 2001), 28.

54. Meeks, Girvan, and Bogues, "A Caribbean Life," 278–79; *Alfie Roberts, A View for Freedom: Alfie Roberts Speaks on the Caribbean, Cricket, Montreal, and C. L. R. James*, ed. David Austin (Montreal: Alfie Roberts Institute, 2005); Paul Buhle, *Tim Hector: A Caribbean Radical's Story* (Jackson: University Press of Mississippi, 2006).

55. Best, "Independent Thought and Caribbean Freedom," 29–31. Best expanded on the tensions between intellectual activity and political activism and the role of New World in "Whither New World," *New World Quarterly* 4, no. 1 (1967): 1–6.

56. Scott, "Vocation of a Caribbean Intellectual," 138.

57. For an example of Marxist analysis of West Indian history with a strong commitment to maintaining a focus on Caribbean thought, see Ken Post, *Arise Ye Starvelings: The Jamaican Labour Rebellion of 1938 and Its Aftermath* (The Hague: Martinus Nijhoff, 1978). For examples of West Indian Black Power, see *Abeng*, a short-lived but influential Jamaican newspaper which featured the writing of several thinkers associated with New World, available at http://www.dloc.com/UF00100338/00001/allvolumes?search=abeng. See also Selwyn D. Ryan and Taimoon Stewart, eds., *The Black Power Revolution 1970: A Retrospective* (St. Augustine: Institute of Social and Economic Research, University of the West Indies, 1995).

58. Michael Witter and Louis Lindsay, introduction to *The Critical Tradition of Caribbean Political Economy*, ed. Kari Levitt and Michael Witter (Kingston: Ian Randle Publishers, 1996), xxii.

59. Meeks, "Introduction," xii–xiii.

60. James Millette, "The New World Group: A Historical Perspective," in *Caribbean Reasonings: The Thought of New World, The Quest for Decolonisation*, ed. Brian Meeks and Norman Girvan (Kingston, Jamaica: Ian Randle Publishers, 2010), 52–53; Levitt, "The Montreal New World Group," 79. See also Girvan, "Plantation Economy in the Age of Globalization."

61. Girvan, "New World and Its Critics," 21–24; Meeks, "Introduction," xii–xiv.

62. Best, "Race, Class, and Ethnicity," 2–3.

Chapter 29: On the Shores of Japan's Postwar Left

1. The epigraph—the title of one of Nakai Masakazu's lead essays in a Popular Front newspaper—is lovingly invoked by the key actors in this chapter. *Doyōbi*, July 17, 1936, 7:2.

2. Wesley Sasaki-Uemura, *Organizing the Spontaneous: Citizen Protest in Postwar Japan* (Honolulu: University of Hawaii, 2001); Simon Avenell, *Making Japanese Citizens: Civil Society and the Mythology of the Shimin in Postwar Japan* (Berkeley: University of California Press, 2010); Kenji Hasegawa, *Waging Cold War in 1950s Japan: Zengakuren's Postwar Protests* (PhD diss., Stanford University, 2007); Takemasa Ando, *Japan's New Left Movements: Legacies for Civil Society* (Abingdon: Routledge, 2013).

3. Tsurumi Kazuko, *Social Change and the Individual: Japan Before and After Defeat in World War II* (Princeton, NJ: Princeton University Press, 1960), 308–9.

4. Nihon Senbotsu Gakusei Shuki Henshū Iinkai, *Kike, wadatsumi no koe* (Tokyo: Tokyo University Seikyō, 1949).

5. Tokumura Akira, "In Circumstances without Precedent." *Kodomo no mura tsūshin* (Children's Village Dispatch), 25:61, June 1, 2011, 3.

6. Akira alludes to a JCP policy of dispatching groups of young party members and student activists abroad in "truck units." Tokumura Tokiko and Tokumura Akira, interview by the author, Takinishi, Hokkaido, September 8, 2002.

7. Ibid.

8. Ibid.

9. Sasaki-Uemura, "Tanigawa Gan's Politics of the Margins in Kyushu and Nagano" *Positions* 7, no. 1 (Spring 1999): 140.

10. Sasaki-Uemura, *Organizing the Spontaneous*, 5.

11. Tokumura and Tokumura, interview.

12. Ibid.

13. Ibid.

14. Fernando Coronil, "The Future in Question: History and Utopia in Latin America (1989–2010)" (lecture, Eisenberg Institute for Historical Studies, University of Michigan, April 7, 2011).

15. Ando, *Japan's New Left Movements*, 72.

16. John Dower, "Peace and Democracy in Two Systems: External Policy and Internal Conflict," in *Postwar Japan as History*, ed. Andrew Gordon (Berkeley: University of California Press, 1993), 22.

17. Kurihara Akira, "New Social Movements in Present-Day Japan" in *The Journal of Pacific Asia* 5 (1999): 6–10.

18. Sasaki-Uemura, *Organizing the Spontaneous*, 201; Avenell, *Making Japanese Citizens*, 210–13.

19. Tokumura Akira and Tokumura Tokiko, *Kodomo ga shujinkō* (Tokyo: Komichi shobo, 1982), 14; Nakai Masakazu, "Chōshū zero no kōenkai (A lecture with no audience)" and "Chihō bunka undō hōkoku (Report from a local Culture Movement)" in *Nakai Masakazu Zenshū* vol. 4 (Tokyo: Bijutsu shuppansha, 1981).

20. Ishii Momoko, *Kodomo no toshokan* (The Children's Library) (Tokyo: Iwanami shinsho, 1965), iv–v.

21. Tokumura and Tokumura, *Kodomo ga shujinkō*, 14–16.

22. Ibid.

23. Ibid., 16–17.

24. Ibid., 24.

25. Ibid., 24–25.

26. Steven Platzer, ed. and trans., *Educational Thought and Ideology in Modern Japan: State Authority and Intellectual Freedom* (Tokyo: University of Tokyo Press, 1988), 214–18.

27. Tokumura and Tokumura, *Kodomo ga shujinkō*, 25–26.

28. Ibid., 28–32.

29. Tokumura Akira and Tokumura Tokiko, *Himawari bunko no denshō tezukuri asobi 1* [Traditional hand-crafted games 1] (Tokyo: Sōdo bunka, 1983), 7.

30. Tokumura and Tokumura, *Kodomo ga shujinkō*, 92–93.

31. Ibid., 45.

32. Ibid., 119–20.

33. Tokumura Akira and Tokumura Tikoko, *Komodo no mura e* (Bound for Children's Village) (Tokyo: Komichi shobo, 1982), 10–11.

34. Ibid., 150. The term "protean" echoes the language used by eminent public intellectual Tsurumi Shunsuke to describe the circle movement. Quoted in Simon Avenell, *Making Japanese Citizens*, 58.

35. At the foundation of this new community, the Tokumuras envisioned a more inclusive and participatory democracy: "Here adults and children will have equal voting power; we'll have noisy, heated debates." Tokumura and Tokumura, *Kodomo no mura e*, 151–52.

36. Ibid., 217.

37. Tokumura Akira, *Mori ni manabu* (Learning from the Forest) (Tokyo: Kirara Shobo, 2003), 92–94.

38. Ibid. Akira has been known to count the number of different kinds of trees in his small swathe of forest—at least eighty, he says—or identify the varieties of grasses in a single square meter—about twenty-five.

39. Akira further developed this idea in a series of essays under the running title "Mori no shisō, mori no bunka," [The forest: thought and culture], originally published in *Children's Village Dispatch* and later collected in a self-published booklet, *Mori wa mandara* [The forest as mandala], 2009.

40. Donald Worster, *Nature's Economy: A History of Ecological Ideas* (Cambridge: Cambridge University Press, 1977), 78.

41. Tokumura Akira, *Mori wa mandara*, 52.

42. Ibid., 71.

Chapter 30: Ashamed of Being Middle Class

1. This chapter is excerpted from the introduction and chapter one of Louise E. Walker, *Waking from the Dream: Mexico's Middle Classes after 1968* (Stanford: Stanford University Press, 2013), 1–44. I am grateful for permission to republish.

2. The PRI governed for an uninterrupted period from 1946 to 2000, and was heir to a political dynasty that had ruled since 1929. Most scholars thus refer to the PRI's seventy-one-year rule from 1929 to 2000.

3. My analysis of this archive draws on Sergio Aguayo, *La charola: Una historia de los servicios de inteligencia en México* (Mexico City: Grijalbo, 2001). For a historical analysis of specific spy reports and the methodological challenges and historiographical impact of this archive, see Tanalís Padilla and Louise E. Walker, eds., "Spy Reports: Content, Methodology and Historiography in Mexico's Secret Police Archive," special dossier, *Journal of Iberian and Latin American Research* 19, no. 1 (2013): 1–103.

4. While the books, films, and essays that tell and retell the story of 1968 often fall outside the domain of scholarly history (defined as works that cite all references and sources and provide a full bibliography), the heroic narrative has also been reproduced in academic accounts, even by scholars who aim to nuance our understanding of the events. For example, although Elaine Carey advances an analysis of gender politics and chauvinism in the Mexican student movement, she largely replicates the heroic narrative by relying extensively on interviews with the official custodians of the movement. Diana Sorensen also studies gender politics in 1960s Latin America, but she focuses on the most prominent writers of the Boom generation, which produces a celebratory and

nostalgic interpretation. See Elaine Carey, *Plaza of Sacrifices: Gender, Power, and Terror in 1968 Mexico* (Albuquerque: University of New Mexico Press, 2005); Diana Sorensen, *A Turbulent Decade Remembered: Scenes from the Latin American Sixties* (Stanford: Stanford University Press, 2007).

5. Carey, *Plaza of Sacrifices*, 49–50; Ariel Rodríguez Kuri, "Los primeros días: Una explicación de los orígenes inmediatos del movimiento estudiantil de 1968," *Historia Mexicana* 53, no. 1 (2003): 179–228. The students came from a broad spectrum of middle-class families. Those at the IPN tended to come from the emerging and lower-middle classes, while students at the UNAM generally belonged to the higher echelons of the middle classes and the élite. Jaime Pensado, *Rebel Mexico: Student Unrest and Authoritarian Political Culture During the Long Sixties* (Stanford: Stanford University Press, 2013), 19–23.

6. Elena Poniatowska, *Massacre in Mexico* (Columbia: University of Missouri Press, 1975), 53; Eric Zolov, *Refried Elvis: The Rise of Mexican Counterculture* (Berkeley: University of California Press, 1999), 120–23.

7. Diane E. Davis, *Urban Leviathan: Mexico City in the Twentieth Century* (Philadelphia: Temple University Press, 1994), 193–94.

8. Javier Mendoza Rojas, *Los conflictos de la UNAM en el siglo XX* (Mexico City: Universidad Nacional Autónoma de México, 2001), 146–52.

9. "En el periódico 'Universidad' . . . ," June 25, 1971, Dirección General de Investigaciones Políticas y Sociales (hereafter DGIPS), c. 619, exp. 3, Archivo General de la Nación (hereafter AGN).

10. "Por medio de la circular . . . ," April 14, 1972, DGIPS, c. 660, exp. 1, AGN.

11. Herbert Braun, "Protests of Engagement: Dignity, False Love, and Self-Love in Mexico during 1968," *Comparative Studies in Society and History* 39, no. 3 (1997): 540.

12. Ignacio Salas Obregón, "Acerca del movimiento revolucionario del proletariado estudiantil," Liga Comunista 23 de Septiembre folder, digital archive (CD-ROM) compiled by José Luis Moreno Borbolla (Mexico City, Centro de Investigaciones Históricas de los Movimientos Sociales A. C., 1973). Document in possession of author; CD-ROM in possession of Alexander Aviña. I am grateful to Aviña for sharing this document.

13. "Inspección ocular . . . ," June 12, 1971, DGIPS, c. 625, exp. 2, AGN.

14. For a study of the positive aspects of student-resident collaboration in shantytowns, see Alejandra Massolo, *Por amor y coraje: Mujeres en movimientos urbanos de la Ciudad de México* (Mexico City: Colegio de México, 1992)

15. Patrick Chabal, *Amílcar Cabral: Revolutionary Leadership and People's War* (New York: Cambridge University Press, 1983), 174–82 (quote from 174).

16. "Al estar repartiendo ropa . . . ," November 7, 1971, DGIPS, c. 624, exp. 3, AGN; "Brigadas de ayuda estudiantil . . . ," October 31, 1971, DGIPS, c. 624, exp. 3, AGN; "El comité de lucha . . . ," October 28, 1971, DGIPS, c. 624, exp. 3, AGN; "Alumnos de las preparatorias . . . ," September 26, 1973, DGIPS, c. 707, exp. 1, AGN.

17. Andrew Hunter Whiteford, *Two Cities of Latin America: A Comparative Description of Social Classes* (Prospect Heights: Waveland Press, 1991), 98–106.

18. Numbers are rounded. Coordinación General del Plan Nacional de Zonas Deprimidas y Grupos Marginados, *Necesidades esenciales en México: Educación* (Mexico City: Siglo Veintiuno, 1982), 54–58, esp. table 3.22.

19. Pierre Bourdieu, *Distinction: A Social Critique of the Judgment of Taste* (Cam-

bridge: Harvard University Press, 1984); Pierre Bourdieu, *The State Nobility: Elite Schools in the Field of Power* (Oxford: Polity Press, 1996).

20. "Francisco de la Cruz Velazco . . . ," June 1, 1973, DGIPS, c. 705, exp. 3, AGN.

21. Ibid.

22. Members of this group debated the sincerity of Echeverría's democratic opening but decided to take advantage of it and, if it proved insufficient, to take it over (*conquistarla*). In the end, Paz and Fuentes abandoned the project and Heberto Castillo and Demetrio Vallejo formed the Mexican Workers Party (*Partido Mexicano de los Trabajadores*, or PMT). Echeverría directed some of his allies to form the Socialist Workers Party (*Partido Socialista de los Trabajadores*, or PST), which successfully confused many with its similar name. José Agustin, *Tragicomedia mexicana 2: La vida en México de 1970 a 1988* (Mexico City: Planeta Mexicana, 1992), 106.

23. "Se llevó a cabo el final . . . ," November 13, 1971, DGIPS, c. 625, exp. 3, AGN; "A las 10.45 horas . . . ," November 14, 1971, DGIPS, c. 625, exp. 3, AGN.

24. Alterto Ulloa Bornemann, *Surviving Mexico's Dirty War: A Political Prisoner's Memoir* (Philadelphia: Temple University Press, 2007), 113.

25. Ibid., 54.

26. Ibid., 49.

27. Ibid., 47–49.

28. Elena Poniatowska, *Fuerte es el silencio* (Mexico City: Ediciones Era, 1980), 201.

29. "Explosión de un artefacto . . . ," July 20, 1974, Dirección Federal de Seguridad (hereafter DFS), 38-0-74, legajo 2, h. 20–27, AGN; "Llamada anónima . . . ," October 11, 1974, DFS, 11-235-74, legajo 22, h. 268, AGN; "Asalto a una caseta . . . ," June 26, 1973, DFS, 34-9-73, legajo 2, h. 45, AGN; "Comandos armados 'Lacandones' . . . ," March 1, 1973, DFS, 28-15-1-73, legajo 4, h. 30, AGN; "Liga Comunista 23 de Septiembre . . . ," November 14, 1975, DFS, 11-235-75, legajo 34, h. 7, AGN; [no title], September 5, 1975, DFS, 11-235-75, legajo 32, h. 117, AGN.

30. Régis Debray, *Revolution in the Revolution? Armed Struggle and Political Struggle in Latin America* (New York: Grove Press, 1967).

31. Jean Franco describes how "the 'liberated territory' was a power fantasy of the period of the Cold War, a hope of liberation that would turn first Cuba, then Nicaragua, and finally Chile into political and cultural showcases that bore the burden of high expectations." *Decline and Fall of the Lettered City: Latin America in the Cold War* (Cambridge: Harvard University Press, 2002), 86.

32. The university-factory thesis is formulated, in extensive detail, in Salas Obregón, "Acerca del movimiento revolucionario del proletariado estudiantil." See also Laura Castellanos and Alejandro Jiménez, *México armado, 1943–1981* (Mexico City: Ediciones Era, 2007), 206; Alfredo Tecla Jiménez, *Universidad, burguesía y proletariado* (Mexico City: Ediciones de Cultura Popular, 1976).

33. Salas Obregón, "Acerca del movimiento revolucionario," 3–4.

34. Ibid., 22.

35. Ibid., 3.

36. This raises serious methodological questions. These reports may tell us more about the state than about the guerrilla movement. It is likely that agents either over- or underestimated the threat, depending on the political expediency. I am not advancing an argument regarding the size or threat of the movement; rather, I am analyzing these documents for the middle-class background of the guerrilla fighters. As with other stud-

ies using police, secret police, or inquisition records, the information gleaned from them is corroborated in a variety of ways. Published, unpublished, and Internet testimonies, along with scholarship on this subject, help round out the information in these intelligence reports.

37. "Grupo afín a Genaro Vázquez Rojas," April 21, 1971, DFS, 100–10–16–2, legajo 3, h. 35–55, AGN. I am grateful to Alexander Aviña for this citation and for his suggestions regarding the tensions between the urban and rural guerrillas.

38. Poniatowska, *Massacre in Mexico*, 34.

39. Ibid.

40. Ibid., 79.

41. Ibid., 81.

42. Ibid., 47.

43. A complete bibliography cannot be listed here, but early influential texts include: Gastón García Cantú and Javier Barros Sierra, *Javier Barros Sierra, 1968: Conversaciones con Gastón García Cantú* (Mexico City: Siglo Veintiuno, 1972); Luis González de Alba, *Los días y los años* (Mexico City: Ediciones Era, 1971); Octavio Paz, *Posdata* (Mexico City: Siglo Veintiuno, 1970); Poniatowska, *Massacre in Mexico* (originally published in 1971); José Revueltas, *México 68: Juventud y revolución* (Mexico City: Ediciones Era, 1978). For analyses of the 1968 canon, see Braun, "Protests of Engagement"; Leslie Jo Frazier and Deborah Cohen, "Defining the Space of Mexico '68: Heroic Masculinity in the Prison and 'Women' in the Streets," *Hispanic American Historical Review* 83, no. 4 (2003): 617–60; Vania Markarian, "El movimiento estudiantil mexicano del 1968: Treinta años de debates públicos," *Anuario de Espacios Urbanos* 46 (2001): 239–64.

44. Field notes and recordings in possession of author. I attended more than fifty commemoration events in Mexico City in the summer and fall of 2008. There were remarkably few exceptions to this trend, among them talks by Soledad Loaeza, Ariel Rodríguez Kuri, Ilán Semo, Sergio Zermeño, and Eric Zolov.

45. At "A 40 años del 68," a colloquium at the Centro Cultural Universitario UNAM, October 2, 2008. Field notes and recordings in possession of author.

46. This analysis comes out most clearly in Paul H. Lewis, *Guerrillas and Generals: The "Dirty War" in Argentina* (Westport: Praeger, 2002), 51–69. Lewis condemns the middle-class guerrillas for suffering existential angst and provoking the military coup in Argentina. In contrast, Alexander Aviña documents the process of political radicalization as a response to state-sponsored repression and the closing down of legal channels of reform: state-sponsored terrorism provoked some to take up arms, not vice versa. Aviña, *Specters of Revolution: Peasant Guerrillas in the Cold War Mexican Countryside* (New York: Oxford University Press, 2014).

Chapter 31: New Left Melancholia, or Paul Potter Swallows Television

1. Walter Benjamin, "Left-Wing Melancholy (On Erich Kästner's New Book of Poems)," *Screen* 15, no. 2 (1974): 30.

2. Walter Benjamin, "The Author as Producer," in *The Work of Art in the Age of its Technological Reproducibility*, ed. Michael W. Jennings, Brigid Doherty, and Thomas Y. Levin (Cambridge: Harvard University Press, 2008), 88.

3. Benjamin, "Left-Wing Melancholy," 30–31.

4. Wendy Brown, "Resisting Left Melancholy," *Boundary 2* 26, no. 3 (Fall 1999): 19, 20, 21, 25.

5. Jodi Dean, *The Communist Horizon* (New York: Verso, 2012), 171.

6. Ibid., 173–74, 175.

7. Paddy Chayefsky, *The Collected Work of Paddy Chayefsky: The Screenplays,* vol. 2 (New York: Applause Theater and Cinema Books, 2000), 195.

8. Todd Gitlin, *The Whole World is Watching* (Berkeley: University of California Press, 1980), 30.

9. Paul Potter, *A Name for Ourselves,* forward by Leni Wildflower (New York: Little, Brown, 1971), 165, 166, 214.

10. Paul Potter, "Speech to the March on Washington to End the War in Vietnam," in *Landmark Speeches on the Vietnam War,* ed. Gregory Allen Olsen (College Station: Texas A&M University Press, 2010), 60.

11. Howard Brick, *Transcending Capitalism* (Ithaca: Cornell University Press, 2006), 124.

12. Potter, "Speech to the March on Washington," 61.

13. Arundhati Roy, *The Cost of Living* (New York: Modern Library Paperbacks, 1999), 17; Joseph Campbell, *The Power of Myth* (New York: Random House, 2011), 178.

14. Aniko Bodroghkozy, *Groove Tube: Sixties Television and the Youth Rebellion* (Durham: Duke University Press, 2001), 210.

15. Gitlin, *The Whole World,* 56.

16. Potter, "Speech to the March on Washington," 60.

17. Leni Wildflower, telephone interview by Michael Szalay, September 29, 2012.

18. Potter, "Speech to the March on Washington," 62.

19. Potter, *A Name,* 120.

20. Ibid., 148.

21. Ibid., 147.

22. Ibid., 182.

23. Ibid., 42.

24. Cited in Jefferson R. Cowie, *Stayin' Alive: the 1970s and the Last Days of the Working Class* (New York: The New Press, 2010), 217, 218, 219.

25. Sean McCann and Michael Szalay, "Introduction: Paul Potter and the Cultural Turn," *Yale Journal of Criticism,* 18, no. 2 (Fall 2005).

26. Lewis Coser and Irving Howe, "Images of Socialism," in *Legacy of Dissent: Forty Years of Writing in* Dissent *Magazine,* ed. Nicholas Mills (New York: Simon and Schuster, 1994), 30.

27. Sigmund Freud, "Mourning and Melancholia," *The Standard Edition of the Complete Psychological Works of Sigmund Freud, Volume XIV (1914–1916),* trans. James Strachey, ed. James Strachey and Anna Freud (London: Hogarth Press, 1957), 244.

28. Potter, *A Name,* 237.

29. Freud, "Mourning and Melancholia," 246, 247.

30. Potter, *A Name,* 220.

31. Ibid., 227.

32. Ibid., 221.

33. Ibid., 89.

34. Ibid., 95, 148.

35. Ibid., 134.

36. Freud, "Mourning and Melancholia," 245.

37. Leni Wildflower, telephone interview by Michael Szalay, Septebmer 29, 2012.

38. Freud, "Mourning and Melancholia," 243.

39. Potter, *A Name*, 11.

40. Ibid., 220.

41. Ibid., 191.

42. Freud, "Mourning and Melancholia," 248, 247.

43. Richard Sennett and Jonathan Cobb, *The Hidden Injuries of Class* (New York: W. W. Norton, 1993), 98, 105, 173.

44. Cowie, *Stayin' Alive*, 215–16.

45. Wendy Brown, *Edgework: Critical Essays on Knowledge and Politics* (Princeton: Princeton University Press, 2009), 54–55.

46. Dean, *The Communist Horizon*, 174.

47. The phrase "political liberalism" cited in Gitlin, *The Whole World*, 62.

48. Gitlin, *The Whole World*, 62.

49. Ibid., 83, 156.

50. Ibid., 94, 129 (italics in original).

51. Ibid., 91, 166.

52. Ibid., 175.

53. Ibid., 171 (italics in original).

54. Ibid., 123 (italics in original).

55. Ibid., 30.

56. Ibid., 145.

57. Ibid., 86.

58. Ibid., 186; Potter, *A Name*, 41 (italics in original).

59. Ibid., 216–17.

60. Ibid., 57.

61. Ibid., 58.

62. Ibid., 165.

63. Ibid.

64. Ibid., 161.

65. Chayefsky, *Collected Works*, 207–8.

66. Potter, *A Name*, 166.

67. Nicolas Abraham and Maria Torok, *The Shell and the Kernal: Renewals of Psychoanalysis* (Chicago: University of Chicago Press, 1994), 126–27 (italics in original).

68. Ibid., 126.

69. Ibid., 127.

70. Ibid., 128.

Chapter 32: Shulamith Firestone, Social Defeat, and Sixties Radicalism

1. Ann Snitow, "On Shulamith Firestone," *n+1*, no. 15 (Winter 2013), https://nplusonemag.com/issue-15/in-memoriam/on-shulamith-firestone.

2. Shulamith Firestone, *The Dialectic of Sex: The Case for Feminist Revolution* (1970; repr., New York: Farrar, Straus and Giroux, 2003), 3.

3. Shulamith Firestone, letter to the editor, *Guardian*, February 1, 1969.

4. I have relied upon the version of events offered by Jo Freeman herself in Snitow, "On Shulamith Firestone."

5. This is noted by Dana Tortorici, "On Firestone: Preface," *n+1*, Winter 2013, https://nplusonemag.com/online-only/online-only/on-shulamith-firestone-preface.

6. Susan Faludi, "American Chronicles: Death of a Revolutionary," *New Yorker*, April 15, 2013.

7. Tax quoted in Alice Echols, *Daring to Be Bad: Radical Feminism in America, 1967–1975* (Minneapolis: University of Minnesota Press, 1989), 5.

8. Faludi, "American Chronicles: Death of a Revolutionary," 54.

9. Carol Hanisch, "On Shulamith Firestone," *n+1*, no. 15 (Winter 2013), https://nplusonemag.com/issue-15/in-memoriam/on-shulamith-firestone.

10. See Firestone, *The Dialectic of Sex*, 81; Felicia Lee, "An Artist Demands Civility on the Street with Grit and Buckets of Paste," *New York Times*, April 9, 2014.

11. Willis quoted in Echols, *Daring to Be Bad*, 150.

12. Faludi, "American Chronicles: Death of a Revolutionary," 58.

13. Anselma Dell'Olio quoted in ibid., 59.

14. Firestone, *The Dialectic of Sex*, 37.

15. Alice Echols, "'Totally Ready to Go': Shulamith Firestone and *The Dialectic of Sex*," in *Shaky Ground: The Sixties and Its Aftershocks* (New York: Columbia University Press, 2002).

16. Firestone, *The Dialectic of Sex*, 12.

17. Ibid., 197–98.

18. This was her sister Laya's characterization, quoted in Margalit Fox, "Shulamith Firestone, Feminist Writer, Dies at 67," *New York Times*, August 30, 2012.

19. John Leonard, "Books of The Times: Adam Takes a Ribbing; It Hurts," *New York Times*, October 29, 1970.

20. Faludi, "American Chronicles: Death of a Revolutionary," 59.

21. Ibid., 60.

22. Rosalyn Baxandall, "On Shulamith Firestone," *n+1*, no. 15 (Winter 2013), https://nplusonemag.com/issue-15/in-memoriam/on-shulamith-firestone.

23. David Hildago and Louie Pérez, "Revolution," recorded by Los Lobos March 19, 1996, on *Colossal Head,* Warner Brothers.

24. Faludi, "American Chronicles: Death of a Revolutionary," 59.

25. Eli Zaretsky, "Rethinking the Split Between Feminists and the Left," *History Workshop Online*, September 30, 2013, http://www.historyworkshop.org.uk/rethinking-the-split-between-feminists-and-the-left; Alice Echols, "'A Party Without Men': Shulamith Firestone, Women's Liberation and the New Left," *History Workshop Online*, September 30, 2013, http://www.historyworkshop.org.uk/a-party-without-men-shulamith-firestone-womens-liberation-and-the-new-left.

26. Ann M. Little, "Susan Brownmiller Comments on Faludi & Firestone: 'You Need Nerves of Steel to Stay in for the Long Haul in a Radical Political Movement,'" *Historiann* (blog), April 15, 2013, http://www.historiann.com/2013/04/15/susan-brownmiller-comments-on-faludi-firestone-you-need-nerves-of-steel-to-stay-in-for-the-long-haul-in-a-radical-political-movement.

27. Faludi, "American Chronicles: Death of a Revolutionary," 59.

28. *Port Huron Statement*, reprinted in Tom Hayden, *The Port Huron Statement: The Visionary Call of the 1960s Revolution* (New York: Thunder's Mouth Press, 2005), 167.

29. Janis Joplin quoted in Alice Echols, *Scars of Sweet Paradise: The Life and Times of Janis Joplin* (New York: Henry Holt, 1999), 11.

30. Peter Coyote quoted in Nicholas von Hoffman, *We Are the People Our Parents Warned Us Against* (Chicago: Quadrangle, 1968), 131.

31. Carl Gottlieb, quoted in Alice Echols, *Shaky Ground: The Sixties and Its Aftershocks* (New York: Columbia University Press, 2002), 49.

32. Elizabeth Subrin, "On Shulamith Firestone," *n+1*, no. 15 (Winter 2013), https://nplusonemag.com/issue-15/in-memoriam/on-shulamith-firestone.

33. Firestone, *The Dialectic of Sex*, 207.

34. Bob Seidemann, quoted in Echols, *Scars of Sweet Paradise*, 304.

35. Ibid., 187.

36. Hester Eisenstein, *Feminism Seduced: How Global Elites Use Women's Labor and Ideas to Exploit the World* (Boulder, CO: Paradigm Publishers, 2010).

37. Angela McRobbie, *The Aftermath of Feminism: Gender, Culture and Social Change* (London: Sage, 2009).

38. On the counterculture functioning, in part, as "seedbeds for growth industries to come," see Carol Brightman, *Sweet Chaos: The Grateful Dead's American Adventure* (New York: Pocket Books, 1998), 223.

Chapter 33: Envisioning Another World

1. I have retained the now archaic gendered language of the original. For the text, see *Port Huron Statement*, reprinted in Tom Hayden, *The Port Huron Statement: The Visionary Call of the 1960s Revolution* (New York: Thunder's Mouth Press, 2005), 53–55.

2. "America and the New Era" is long out of print. A PDF file containing a facsimile of the mimeograph document is available at http://archive.lib.msu.edu/DMC/AmRad/americanewera.pdf. Material quoted here appears on page 20.

3. "Maximum feasible participation" of community residents was a requirement of the community action programs created under the Economic Opportunity Act of 1964, the act that created the War on Poverty programs of the Johnson years.

4. See The Real Utopias Project (conference and program website), http://www.ssc.wisc.edu/~wright/RealUtopias.htm.

5. Gar Alperovitz, *What Then Must We Do? Straight Talk about the Next American Revolution* (White River Jct., VT: Chelsea Green Publishing, 2013).

Chapter 34: The Wisconsin Uprising and Women's Power

1. Amanda Harrington quoted in Andy Kroll, "Wisconsin Gov. Scott Walker's Abortion Crusade," *Mother Jones*, March 21, 2011, http://www.motherjones.com/mojo/2011/02/wisconsin-scott-walker-abortion.

2. Rachel Benson Gold and Elizabeth Nash, "Troubling Trend: More States Hostile to Abortion Rights as Middle Ground Shrinks," *Guttmacher Policy Review* 15, no. 1 (Winter 2012), http://www.guttmacher.org/pubs/gpr/15/1/gpr150114.html.

Chapter 35: Democracy and the Arab Upheavals of 2011 and After

1. What follows is an interpretive chapter. For the book-length account with the Arabic sources see Juan Cole, *The New Arabs: How the Millennial Generation is Changing the Middle East* (New York: Simon and Schuster, 2014).

2. Alfred Stepan and Juan J. Linz, "Democratization Theory and the 'Arab Spring,'" *Journal of Democracy* 24, no. 2: (2013): 15–30.

3. Matt Buehler, "Safety-Valve Elections and the Arab Spring: The Weakening (and Resurgence) of Morocco's Islamist Opposition Party," *Terrorism and Political Violence* 25, no. 1 (2013): 137–56.

4. Paul Silverstein, "Weighing Morocco's New Constitution," MERIP Online, July 5, 2011, http://www.merip.org/mero/mero070511.

5. Adria Lawrence, "Morocco's resilient protest movement," *Foreign Policy*, February 20, 2012, http://mideastafrica.foreignpolicy.com/posts/2012/02/20/moroccos_resilient_protest_movement.

6. "Morocco," Human Rights Watch World Report, 2014, http://www.hrw.org/world-report/2014/country-chapters/moroccowestern-sahara.

7. Michele Penner Angrist, "Understanding the Success of Mass Civic Protest in Tunisia," *The Middle East Journal* 67, no. 4 (2013): 547–64; Malika Zeghal, "Competing Ways of Life: Islamism, Secularism, and Public Order in the Tunisian Transition," *Constellations* 20, no. 2 (June 2013): 254–74.

8. Juan Cole, "Tunisia: Demos, Parliament Resignations and the Republic of Sidi Bouzid Secedes," *Informed Comment*, July 27, 2013, http://www.juancole.com/2013/07/parliament-resignations-republic.html.

9. Larry Diamond, "The Impact of the Economic Crisis: Why Democracies Survive," *Midan Masr*, July 20, 2013, http://www.midanmasr.com/en/article.aspx?ArticleID=85.

10. Cole, *The New Arabs*, 189–225; Mieczystaw P. Boduszyński and Duncan Pickard, "Libya Starts from Scratch," *Journal of Democracy* 24, no. 4 (2013): 86–96.

11. "Libya MPs 'Agree on Early Elections,'" *Daily Star* (Beirut), February 16, 2014, http://www.dailystar.com.lb/News/Middle-East/2014/Feb-16/247515-libya-mps-agree-on-early-elections.ashx.

12. Tomas Jivanda, "Fresh Gun Battles Erupt in Tripoli as Rival Libyan Militias Clash," *The Independent*, November 16, 2013, http://www.independent.co.uk/news/world/africa/fresh-gun-battles-erupt-in-tripoli-as-rival-libyan-militias-clash-8944431.html.

13. "Libya," Foundation for the Future, 2014, http://foundationforfuture.org/en/Portals/0/PDFs/semi-final-libya.pdf.

14. Sami Zaptia, "Zeidan Government Reveals It Received LD 50.48 Billion in 2013," *Libya Herald*, February 11, 2014, http://www.libyaherald.com/2014/02/11/zeidan-government-reveals-it-received-ld-50-48-billion-in-2013/#axzz3QeScgWVB.

15. April Longley Alley, "Yemen Changes Everything . . . And Nothing," *Journal of Democracy* 24, no. 4 (2013): 74–85.

16. Theodore Karasik, "Tough Times Ahead for Yemen's Federation," *Al-Arabiya*, February 16, 2014, http://english.alarabiya.net/en/views/news/middle-east/2014/02/16/Tough-times-ahead-for-Yemen-s-federation.html.

17. Stephen Zunes, "Bahrain's Arrested Revolution," *Arab Studies Quarterly* 35, no. 2 (Spring 2013): 149–64; Toby Matthiesen, *Sectarian Gulf: Bahrain, Saudi Arabia, and the Arab Spring That Wasn't* (Palo Alto, CA Stanford University Press, 2013).

18. Paolo Gerbaudo, "The Roots of the Coup," *Soundings* 54 (Summer 2013): 104–13.

Chapter 36: Post-Occupy

1. Guy Standing, *The Precariat: The New Dangerous Class* (London: Bloomsbury Academic, 2011).

2. Italian philosopher Giorgio Agamben (b. 1942) is best known in the United States for his books *Homo Sacer: Sovereign Power and Bare Life*, trans. Daniel Heller-Roazen (Stanford: Stanford University Press, 1998), and *State of Exception*, trans. Kevin Attell (Chicago: University of Chicago Press, 2005).

3. Thomas Frank, "To the Precinct Station," *The Baffler*, no. 21 (2012): 31.

4. David Graeber, *Debt: The First 5,000 Years* (Brooklyn: Melville House, 2011).

5. Doug Henwood, personal communication, e-mail to author, October 28, 2012.

6. Alexis Goldstien, "The Volcker Rule: Wins, Losses, and Toss-ups," *The Nation*, December 13, 2013, http://www.thenation.com/article/177592/volcker-rule-wins-losses-and-toss-ups.

7. Chris Maisano, "From Protest to Disruption: Frances Fox Piven on Occupy Wall Street," *Democratic Socialists of America*, October 2011, http://www.dsausa.org/from_protest_to_disruption_frances_fox_piven_on_occupy_wall_street.

Chapter 37: Movements for Real Democracy

1. Walter Benjamin, *Walter Benjamin: Selected Writings, 1938–1940*, ed. Marcus Bullock and Michael W. Jennings (Cambridge: Harvard University Press, 1996), 402.

2. All interviews cited in this chapter took place between 2011 and 2013, and many appear in Dario Azzellini and Marina Sitrin, *They Can't Represent Us! Reinventing Democracy from Greece to Occupy* (London: Verso, 2014).

3. Some sources fear increased repression (particularly in Greece and Spain) and prefer to not include their last names. Others have been omitted for consistency.

4. Cheryl K. Chumley, "America Is an Oligarchy, Not a Democracy or Republic, University Study Finds," April 21, 2014, *Washington Times*, http://www.washingtontimes.com/news/2014/apr/21/americas-oligarchy-not-democracy-or-republic-unive.

5. Martin Gilens and Benjamin I. Page, "Testing Theories of American Politics: Elites, Interest Groups, and Average Citizens," *Perspectives on Politics* 12, no. 3 (September 2014): 564–81.

6. "Auctioneer: Stop All the Sales Right Now!" YouTube video, 4:03, from Kings County Supreme Court, Brooklyn, NY, posted by "Organizing for Occupation," October 14, 2011, https://www.youtube.com/watch?v=u3X89iViAlw.

www.ingramcontent.com/pod-product-compliance
Lightning Source LLC
Chambersburg PA
CBHW071822270326
41929CB00013B/1878